# AMERICAN CONSTITUTIONAL LAW

## VOLUME I
## THE STRUCTURE OF GOVERNMENT

Fifth Edition

# AMERICAN CONSTITUTIONAL LAW

## VOLUME I
## THE STRUCTURE OF GOVERNMENT

Fifth Edition

**Ralph A. Rossum**
*Claremont McKenna College*

**G. Alan Tarr**
*Rutgers University, Camden*

**St. Martin's / WORTH**

**American Constitutional Law, Volume I:**
**The Structure of Government, Fifth Edition**


Manufactured in the United States of America.
Library of Congress Catalog Card Number: 98-84994
ISBN: 0-312-18451-4
Printing: 1 2 3 4 5
Year: 02 01 00 99

*Executive Editor:* James R. Headley
*Project Director:* Scott E. Hitchcock
*Editorial Assistant:* Brian Nobile
*Design Director:* Jennie R. Nichols
*Production Editor:* Douglas Bell
*Production Manager:* Barbara Anne Seixas
*Project Coordination:* Ruttle, Shaw & Wetherill, Inc.
*Cover Design:* Paul Lacy
*Cover Photo:* U.S. Supreme Court Building (detail):
Copyright © Tom Wachs/Washington Stock Photo, Inc.
*Cover Printer:* Phoenix Color Corporation
*Composition:* Ruttle, Shaw & Wetherill, Inc.
*Printing and Binding:* R. R. Donnelley & Sons Company

**Worth Publishers**
33 Irving Place
New York, NY 10003

**www.worthpublishers.com**

# ABOUT THE AUTHORS

**Ralph A. Rossum** received his doctorate from the University of Chicago. He is Henry Salvatori Professor of Political Philosophy and American Constitutionalism at Claremont McKenna College. His other publications include *Congressional Control of the Judiciary: The Article III Option* (1988), *Reverse Discrimination: The Constitutional Debate* (1979) and *The Politics of the Criminal Justice System: An Organizational Analysis* (1978). He is coauthor of *The American Founding: Politics, Statesmanship, and the Constitution* (1981) with Gary McDowell, and of *Police, Criminal Justice, and the Community* (1976), with Alan Bent.

**G. Alan Tarr** received his doctorate from the University of Chicago. He is professor of political science and director of the Center for State Constitutional Studies at Rutgers University, Camden. Professor Tarr is the author of several books, including *Understanding State Constitutions* (1998), *Judicial Process and Judicial Policymaking,* Second Edition (1998), and *State Supreme Courts in State and Nation* (1987). He has served as a constitutional consultant in Russia, South Africa, and Cyprus. Twice an NEH Fellow, he is currently editor of a fifty-two volume reference series on state constitutions.

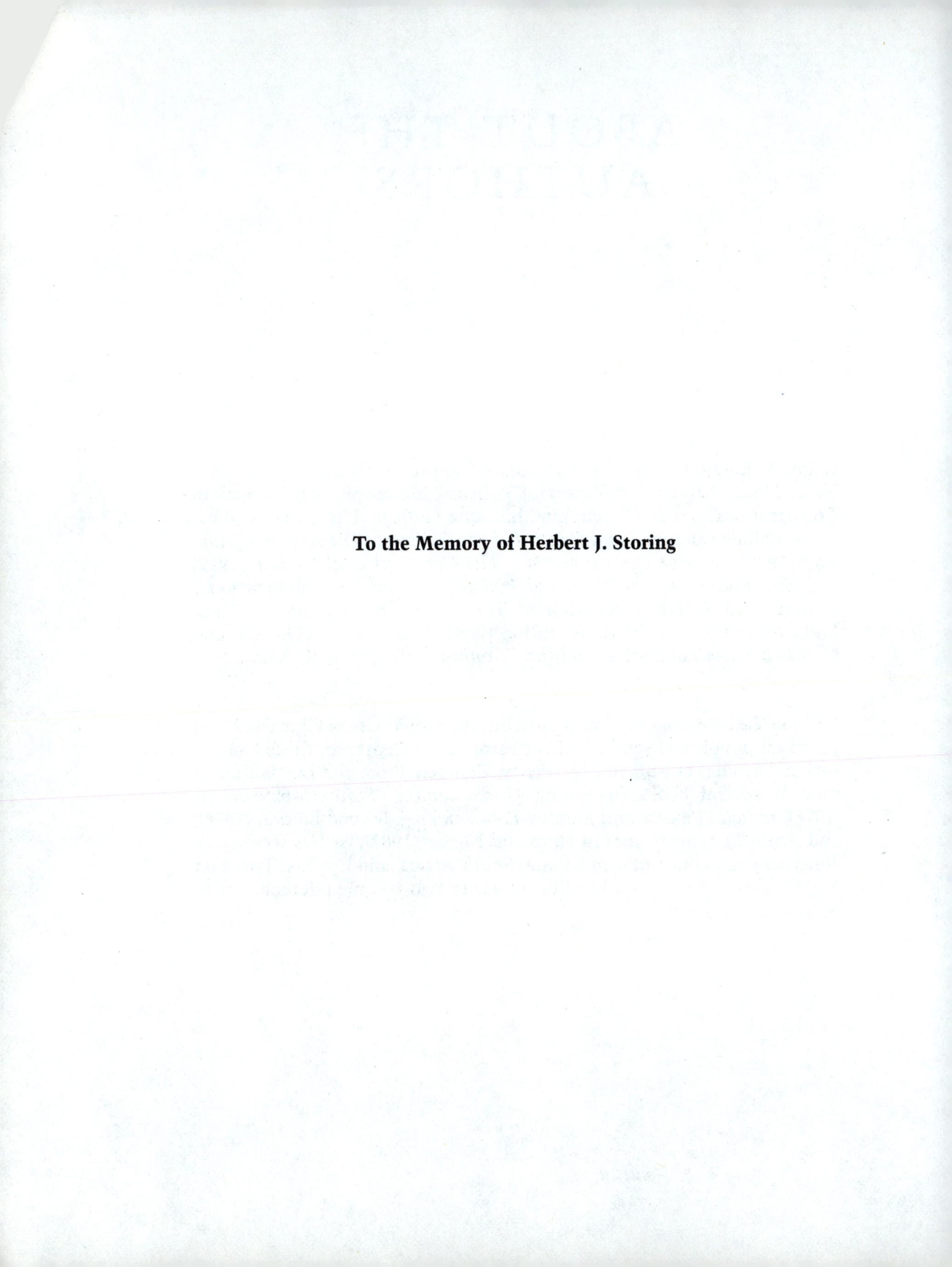

To the Memory of Herbert J. Storing

# CONTENTS

## 6. WAR AND FOREIGN AFFAIRS 211



## 7. FEDERALISM 241



## 8. THE EXERCISE OF NATIONAL POWER 321

**Note to Instructors**

If you plan to use both volumes (I and II) of *American Constitutional Law,* Fifth Edition, for a single semester or quarter course, please contact your local SASMP sales representative or call SASMP Faculty Services for information about special packages: 1-800-446-8923.

# PREFACE

*American Constitutional Law,* Fifth Edition, is designed as a basic text for courses in constitutional law and civil liberties. As with the previous editions, its approach to these subjects is based on three major premises.

First, the study of the Constitution and constitutional law is of fundamental importance to a full and coherent understanding of the principles, prospects, and problems of America's democratic republic. Cases should be examined not merely to foster an appreciation of what court majorities have thought of particular issues at certain points in time (although that is obviously important), but also to gain a deeper and fuller understanding of the principles that lie at the very heart of the American constitutional system. To that end, this text emphasizes precedent-setting cases and presents comprehensive expositions of alternative constitutional positions. Substantial excerpts from cases and other constitutionally significant pronouncements have been included so that students can grapple with the arguments and justifications for these alternative positions. To ensure that the best arguments on all sides of a constitutional question are presented, extensive extracts of both concurring and dissenting opinions have been included.

Second, no interpretation of the Constitution can be evaluated properly without an appreciation of what those who initially drafted and ratified the Constitution sought to accomplish. The text incorporates documentary evidence in seeking to identify and explain the original purposes of the Constitution and the means provided for the achievement of those purposes. This inquiry into the Framers' understanding of the Constitution, in turn, furnishes one of the criteria for evaluating judicial decisions and constitutionally significant pronouncements from the executive and legislative branches.

Third, the study of the Constitution involves much more than an examination of its judicial interpretation. The Constitution is not merely what the Supreme Court says it is; its words are not so many empty vessels into which justices can pour meaning. Accordingly, this volume examines the interpretations of a variety of sources. The original understanding of the founding generation is one source. Another, equally indispensable source is, of course, the Supreme Court, whose decisions have influenced so profoundly our understanding of the Constitution and its principles. And because other governmental bodies have contributed significantly to the overall interpretation of the Constitution, this text includes decisions of the lower federal courts and state judiciaries and also extrajudicial materials of constitutional significance such as certain congressional acts and resolutions.

As we approach constitutional questions throughout this text, we begin by turning to the Framers. We do so, however, not so much for specific answers as for general guidance concerning what the Constitution was designed to accomplish. Obviously no interpretation can be expected to conform strictly to the expectations of the Framers. Other legitimate approaches may also contribute to an understanding of the Constitution, relying variously on analysis of the text itself, judicial precedent, constitutional doctrine, logical reasoning, and adaptation of constitutional provisions to changing circumstances. All these approaches are described in Chapter 1.

The structure of the volumes might be seen as a reflection of James Madison's observation in *The Federalist,* No. 51, that "in framing a government which is to be administered by men over men, the great difficulty lies in this: you must first enable the government to control the governed; and in the next place, oblige it to control itself." Chapter 1 explores in general how the Constitution was designed to resolve this difficulty, and Chapter 2 introduces the reader to the actual process of constitutional adjudication. The remainder of this two-volume work systematically examines how the Constitution and its amendments not only grant the national and state governments sufficient power to control the governed, but also oblige these governments to control themselves. Chapters 3 through 6 (Volume I) consider the distribution of power in the national government. As a group, these chapters explore how the constitutional scheme of separation of powers and checks and balances both grants and controls power. Because of the importance of the distribution of power among the branches of the national government, we devote separate chapters to the Judiciary, the Congress, the Presidency, and war and foreign affairs. Chapters 7 through 10 (Volume I) consider the distribution of power between the national government and the states. These chapters focus on federalism, specifically how this institutional means carries out the ends of the Constitution. Chapters 11 and 12 of Volume I, which are repeated as Chapters 3 and 4 in Volume II, consider the division of the protection of rights and economic due process between national and state governments. Finally, Chapters 5 through 11 (Volume II) continue the examination of the distribution of power between the government and the individual. The emphasis in these chapters is not so much on institutional contrivances that oblige the government to control itself as on the Bill of Rights and those subsequent amendments that guarantee specific rights and liberties, an emphasis that illuminates the way in which our most precious rights and liberties increasingly have become dependent for their vindication, not upon constitutional structure but upon what *The Federalist* called mere "parchment barriers."

With the exception of the first two chapters, each chapter opens with an introductory essay which is then followed by cases and, where appropriate, extrajudicial materials. Each essay includes extensive notes which provide valuable explanatory details and references to further materials, and ends with a list of suggested readings including *Federalist* essays, additional cases, and scholarly books and articles. Each case also has its own introductory headnote, which provides historical perspective, indicates where the case stands in relation to current law, and gives the final court vote. Some cases have end notes that elaborate on the short- and long-term consequences of the decision. The text includes four appendices: the Constitution of the United States, a list of Supreme Court justices, a glossary of legal terms, and a table of cases.

One noteworthy innovation that began in 1997 is the creation of a Web site for *American Constitutional Law,* which is found at <www.worthpublishers.com/policenter.html>. We have included three sets of cases at this site. First, we annually post edited versions of the major rulings of the Supreme Court during its just-completed term. Instructors can use these cases to supplement and update the materials presented in the text, and the cases listed at the Web site give a good indication of those cases likely to be included in subsequent editions of *American Constitutional Law.* Second, we have included several cases and other materials that appear in one volume of *American Constitutional Law* but may also be of interest to instructors using the other volume. Cases appearing in Volume I and reproduced at the Web site include *Marbury* v. *Madison, Korematsu* v. *United States, The Civil Rights Cases, Patterson* v. *McLean Credit Union,* and *Jones* v. *Mayer.* Cases and materials appearing in Volume II and reproduced at the Web site include *Scott* v. *Sandford, Rostker* v. *Goldberg, Griswold* v. *Connecticut, Roe* v. *Wade,* and the Civil Rights Act of 1991. Finally, to accommodate the varying needs of instructors while keeping the casebook a manageable length, we have included several cases that appeared in earlier editions of *American Constitutional Law* but do not appear in the fifth edition.

The editorial staff at St. Martin's/Worth, especialy James Headley, executive editor, was cooperative, encouraging, and truly professional. We are also grateful to those scholars who reviewed drafts of the manuscript and contributed valuable comments and suggestions to the five editions. Any errors of fact or interpretation, of course, are solely our responsibility. Finally, we wish to express our gratitude to our wives, Constance and Susan, and to our children, Kristin, Brent, and Pierce Rossum, and Robert and Andrew Tarr, for their patience, understanding, and loving support throughout this project.

Ralph A. Rossum
G. Alan Tarr

★

APPROACHES TO CONSTITUTIONAL INTERPRETATION

THE APPROACHES IN PERSPECTIVE

THE ENDS OF THE CONSTITUTION

THE MEANS TO THE ENDS

NOTES

SELECTED READING

★

# 1
# INTERPRETATION OF THE CONSTITUTION

"We are under a Constitution, but the Constitution is what the Court says it is."[1] In the more than half-century since Charles Evans Hughes, then governor of New York and later Chief Justice of the Supreme Court, uttered these now-famous words, they have been repeated so often and in so many contexts that they have assumed a prescriptive as well as a descriptive character. But exactly how valid is this prescription for understanding the Constitution?

Hughes's observation certainly contains a degree of truth. Many of the provisions of the Constitution are not self-defining and hence have been the objects of considerable judicial interpretation and construction. Various criminal procedural protections found in Amendments Four through Eight immediately spring to mind. What, after all, makes a particular search or seizure "unreasonable"? What is sufficient to establish "probable cause"? What constitutes "due process of law"? What is a "speedy" trial? What is an "excessive" fine or bail? What is "cruel and unusual punishment"? These constitutional provisions resemble empty vessels into which the United States Supreme Court has had to pour meaning.

Hughes's claim also portrays accurately the perspective taken by lower-court judges and practicing attorneys. However erroneous they may believe the Supreme Court's understanding of a particular constitutional provision to be, they generally shy away from breaking with the previous decisions of the High Bench and offering contrary interpretations. Rather, they usually attempt to accomplish their objectives within the framework of the prevailing Court view.

Although valid to some extent, Hughes's assertion is also misleading (and therefore harmful) in several ways. Above all, it fails to recognize that governmental bodies other than the Supreme Court also contribute to an overall interpretation of the Constitution. By passing the War Powers Resolution of 1973, for example, Congress undertook to define the constitutional limits of the president's powers to initiate and conduct undeclared war, an issue the Supreme Court refused to consider. Likewise, in the Speedy Trial Act of 1984, Congress took upon itself constitutional interpretation in the sphere of criminal procedure, declaring that a defendant not brought to trial within one hundred days of arrest may move for a dismissal of the charges. By so doing, it gave meaning to a constitutional provision that the Supreme Court itself has acknowledged to be more vague than any other procedural right. To cite still another example, in the Voting Rights Act of 1982, Congress held that the Fifteenth Amendment (barring states from denying citizens the right to vote "on account of race, color, or previous condition of servitude") bans not only intentional discrimination against the voting rights of minorities (what the Supreme Court had held) but any electoral scheme that has the effect of preventing minority voters from electing "representatives of their choice." Constitutionally significant pronouncements have also emanated from the executive branch and from the lower federal and state courts. (Statements made by President Abraham Lincoln have had more to do with defining the outer bounds of presidential prerogative than have any statements of the Court, just as actions taken by President Franklin Roosevelt altered the balance of power between the national government and the state far more than any judicial opinion.)

Another problem with Hughes's assertion is that it obscures the extent to which the meaning of the Constitution is agreed on by all concerned parties. Most constitutional provisions are settled; what questions are raised about them pertain not to fundamental meaning, but rather to specific application. Relatively few constitutional provisions have sparked protracted debate and controversy: the Commerce Clause of Article I, Section 8, authorizing Congress to regulate commerce among the several states; the First Amendment guarantees of freedom of speech and of the press; the guarantees of the Fifth and Fourteenth Amendments that no person shall be deprived of life, liberty, or property without due process of law; the Fourteenth Amendment's guarantee that no person shall be denied the equal protection of the laws. Although these provisions are extremely important, the intense debate over them tends to obscure how ably the Constitution has governed our political actions for the past two centuries. By focusing exclusively on them and arguing, implicitly or explicitly, that they are fundamentally without meaning until construed by the Court, some jurists and legal scholars have reinforced the view that the Constitution is deficient in decisive respects and therefore unworthy of vital public support. As a result, the Constitution is deprived of what James Madison in *The Federalist*, No. 49, called "that veneration which time bestows on everything, and without which perhaps the wisest and freest governments would not possess the requisite stability." This is of no minor concern, for, as Madison continues, "the most rational government will not find it a superfluous advantage, to have the prejudices of the community on its side."[2]

Still another problem with the view that the Constitution means only what the Court says it means is that it denies the truth that the Constitution is a public document capable of being understood not only by those who made and ratified it, but also by those who continue to live under it. Justice Joseph Story put the matter succinctly in his *Commentaries on the Constitution of the United States*[3]:

> [E]very word employed in the Constitution is to be expounded in its plain, obvious, and common sense, unless the context provides some ground to control, quality, or enlarge it. Constitutions are not designed for metaphysical or logical subleties, for niceties of expression, for critical propriety, for elaborate shades of meaning, or for the exercise of philosophical acuteness or judicial research. They are instruments of a practical nature, founded on the common business of human life, adapted to common wants, designed for common use, and fitted for common understandings. The people make them; the people adopt them; the people must be supposed to read them, with the help of common sense, and cannot be presumed to admit in them any recondite meaning or extraordinary gloss.

In a popular government, the people should take an active interest in the Constitution that gives form to their politics and protection to their liberties; they should not be discouraged from doing so by talk that the Constitution is some obscure document capable of being understood only by august justices on the Supreme Court.

A related problem: the view that the Constitution is whatever the Court says it is further misleads by suggesting that the Constitution has no meaning in and of itself. If all meaning must be poured into it by the Court, we are unlikely to turn to it for basic instruction on the principles, problems, and prospects of the American regime. The proudest claim of those responsible for framing and ratifying the Constitution was that it provided "a Republican remedy for the diseases most incident to Republican Government."[4] If we strip the Constitution of all independent meaning, we are unlikely to remember the Founders' answers to the basic questions and dilemmas of democratic government—and what is even more regrettable, we are likely to forget the questions themselves.

Yet another negative by-product of presenting the Constitution as devoid of any independent meaning is the encouragement of uncritical public acceptance of Supreme Court decisions. If the Constitution has only that meaning that the Supreme Court gives it, on what basis, other than subjective preference, can anyone object to the Court's interpretations? To illustrate with concrete examples, if the Constitution has no meaning apart from its judicial gloss, on what constitutional basis can anyone object to the Supreme Court's decisions in *Dred Scott* (1857), declaring that blacks could not be citizens, and *Plessy* v. *Ferguson* (1896), upholding racial segregation? Students of the Court implicitly acknowledge this problem by routinely paying lip service to Hughes's assertion and then, as the scholarly journals attest, criticizing at length judicial interpretations that they find wanting infidelity to the language of the Constitution, in scholarship, in craftsmanship, or in deference to the popularly elected branches.

Finally, Hughes's claim ignores the influence that political institutions may have on political behavior. The Court is seen as influencing the Constitution; rarely is the influence the Constitution may have on the Court, or on politics more generally, even considered.

## APPROACHES TO CONSTITUTIONAL INTERPRETATION

To avoid the unpalatable ramifications of Hughes's aphorism, we will argue, along with Justice Felix Frankfurter, that the "ultimate touchstone of constitutionality is the Constitution itself and not what the [judges] have said about it."[5] But what, in fact, does the Constitution mean? How are we to understand its provisions and give them effect? In searching for satisfactory answers to these questions, students of the Constitution have come to employ several approaches to constitutional interpretation, each of which has its own strengths and weaknesses.[6]

### Textual Analysis

One approach to constitutional interpretation involves explicating the constitutional text simply on the basis of the words found there. The basic claim of this approach seems unarguable: If the Constitution is to control the outcome of a case, and its unadorned text is plain, then constitutional interpretation should stop right there. As Justice Noah Swayne observed in *United States* v. *Hartwell* (1868): "If the language be clear, it is conclusive. There cannot be construction where there is nothing to construe." Justice Scalia applied this approach in *Coy* v. *Iowa* (1988), a case involving the Sixth Amendment's Confrontation Clause. He insisted that its words guaranteed defendants "a right to meet face to face all those who appear and give evidence at trial." He turned to the Latin roots of the word, confront, for guidance: It "ultimately derives from the prefix 'con-' (from 'contra' meaning 'against' or 'opposed') and the noun 'frons' (forehead). Shakespeare was thus describing the root meaning of confrontation when he had Richard the Second say: 'Then call them to our presence—face to face, and frowning brow to brow, ourselves will hear the accuser and the accused freely speak.' "

On the other hand, this approach often is difficult to apply. Although many provisions of the Constitution are perfectly clear, many require extensive construction. Moreover, even if the meanings of all relevant words are perfectly plain, problems of emphasis remain. In many cases, two or more constitutional provisions come into play, and the justices must decide which is to be given priority. To cite just one example of this problem: Does the First Amendment guarantee of freedom of speech and the press supersede the Sixth Amendment guarantee of a trial "by an impartial jury"? As this example indicates, the constitutional text in and of itself cannot resolve all the questions that the Constitution raises.

## Precedent

When textual analysis alone is inadequate, many students of the Constitution turn to previously decided cases, searching for answers on the basis of precedent, or *stare decisis* ("to stand by decided matters"). Reliance on precedent, the primary method of legal reasoning in Anglo-American law, adds stability, continuity, and predictability to the entire legal enterprise.

For a variety of reasons, however, reliance on precedent has been applied only sporadically in constitutional law. Many jurists and scholars believe strongly that the Constitution itself, rather than previous decisions of the Court, should supply the standard for decision. Then, too, constitutional cases deal with momentous social and political issues that only temporarily take the form of litigation, and there is wide recognition that these issues cannot be resolved satisfactorily on the same basis as other legal problems. To the minds of some experts in the field, relying on precedent for constitutional interpretation is rather like driving an automobile down a busy street while looking only through the rear-view mirror: We get a good notion of where we have been but not where we should be going. As Thomas Hobbes observed in *A Dialogue between a Philosopher and a Student of the Common Laws of England*, "precedents prove only what was done, but not what was well done."[7] If this difficulty confronts the use of precedent in any legal matter, it seems especially troublesome and unnecessary in constitutional law. Most areas of law lack clearly defined ends or purposes and so must evolve via precedent. The common law, for example, is based mainly on longstanding usage or judicial precedent. Constitutional law, on the other hand, has before it (to borrow the language of Judge J. Skelly Wright) certain "directions, goals, and ideals" that are easily discernible in the Constitution. Once discerned, these guideposts make it possible for the Court to decide matters of political and social import not in terms of what previous Courts have held, but in light of what is most conducive to achieving the goals or purposes of the Constitution.[8]

## Constitutional Doctrine

When neither the constitutional text nor precedent can provide an adequate account of the meaning of the Constitution, arguments from "constitutional doctrine" may be raised. Constitutional doctrines are formulas—sometimes nothing more than slogans—extracted from a combination of the constitutional text and a series of related cases. The

Equal Protection Clause of the Fourteenth Amendment provides several examples of the development and use of constitutional doctrines. When considered as it applies to questions of race, this clause typically is understood to prohibit discrimination (although the word *discrimination* is nowhere to be found in the amendment); when considered as it applies to questions of legislative apportionment, it typically is understood to require "one person, one vote" (another phrase not found in the text). Similarly, the First Amendment's Establishment Clause, which charges Congress to "make no law respecting an establishment of religion," has been interpreted by many as erecting a "high wall of separatism" between church and state. In these illustrations, the constitutional doctrines enunciated serve as mediating principles that stand between specific controversies and the Constitution, giving meaning and content to ideals embodied in the text.

Although these examples suggest that constitutional doctrines broaden the scope of the constitutional text they reference, this is not invariably the case. The protection against "self-incrimination" provides an excellent illustration. The Fifth Amendment does not use the term, "self-incrimination"; rather, it says: "No person . . . shall be compelled in any criminal case to be a witness against himself." Unlike certain other reformulations of constitutional provisions, such as "separation of church and state" for the Establishment Clause and "freedom of expression" for "the freedom of speech, or of the press," this reformulation is narrower than the constitutional guarantee itself. Individuals can be witnesses against themselves in ways that do not incriminate them; they can, in criminal cases, injure their civil interests or disgrace themselves in the public mind. Thus, unlike the constitutional doctrine limiting the Fifth Amendment to "self-incrimination," the words of the amendment would seem to apply as well to any disclosures that would expose either criminal defendants or witnesses to civil liability or public obloquy.

Over time, many of these doctrines have come to give the constitutional provision in question its only meaning as a guide for decision. This usurption of the original texts has profound and disturbing implications. As such doctrines become increasingly important, public debate tends to center on the meaning of the doctrines and not on the meaning of the Constitution itself. In reference to the Equal Protection Clause, for example, the contemporary debate over affirmative action/reverse discrimination has focused almost exclusively on such questions as whether this policy is discriminatory against whites and whether the majority should be free to discriminate against itself and on behalf of minority groups if it so wishes; the question of what "equal protection of the law" truly means has been all but forgotten. Equally disturbing is the fact that reducing constitutional provisions to doctrines or slogans often interferes with thoughtful consideration of the constitutional issues. The "one person, one vote" rule provides a case in point. On only the most elemental level does this rule have meaning; when examined outside a very narrow context, it becomes a simplistic and confusing slogan.

After all, the question of permitting certain voters the opportunity to vote two, five, or ten times has never been raised by any of the legislative reapportionment cases. In *Baker* v. *Carr* (1962), for example, the central issue was how much the voter's one vote was to be worth—a question that moved Justice Frankfurter to ask:

> What is this question of legislative apportionment? Appellants invoke the right to vote and have their votes counted. But they are permitted to vote and their votes are counted. They go to the polls, they cast their ballots, they send their representatives to the state councils. Their complaint is simply that the representatives are not sufficiently numerous or powerful—in short, that Tennessee has adopted a basis of representation with which they are not satisfied. Talk of "debasement" or "dilution" is circular talk. One cannot speak of "debasement" or "dilution" of the value of a vote until there is first defined a standard of reference as to what a vote should be worth.

Emphasis on the slogan "one person, one vote" merely obscured these questions and added to doctrinal confusion. Because of this problem, Justice Abe Fortas broke from the Court majority in the legislative reapportionment cases, declaring that such "admittedly complex and subtle" matters must be governed by "substance, not shibboleth." Discussing simplistic formulas such as "one person, one vote," he complained that they "are not surgical instruments"; rather, "they have a tendency to hack deeply—to amputate."[9] Their bluntness often makes them brutally efficient, but such efficiency comes at the price of clarity in constitutional understanding. To a greater or lesser degree, the same criticism can be directed toward many other constitutional doctrines.

## Logical Reasoning

Another approach to constitutional interpretation emphasizes the use of logical reasoning as exemplified in the syllogism, a formal argument consisting of a major premise, a minor premise, and a conclusion. The major premise sets forth a proposition, such as "A law repugnant to the Constitution is void." The minor premise contains an assertion related to the major premise: "This particular law is repugnant to the Constitution." From these premises the conclusion logically follows: "This particular law is void." The foregoing example represents the essence of Chief Justice John Marshall's reasoning in *Marbury* v. *Madison* (1803), which formally established the Court's power of judicial review (that is, the power to void legislative or executive acts that it finds to be unconstitutional.)

Marshall himself was well aware, however, that logical analysis is an insufficient method of interpreting the Constitution. Assuming the validity of the major premise, the soundness of the conclusion depends on whether the minor premise is true. However, logic cannot determine whether a particular law is repugnant to the Constitution. Justice

Roberts made things too simple in *United States* v. *Butler* (1936) by arguing that "When an act of Congress is appropriately challenged in the courts as not conforming to the constitutional mandate the judicial branch of the Government has only one duty—to lay the article of the Constitution which is invoked beside the statute which is challenged and to decide whether the latter squares with the former." Whether an act in fact squares with the Constitution is a question that must be left to informed opinion and judgment—informed opinion about the purposes for which the Constitution was established, and judgment of whether the law in question is consistent with those ends or purposes. Logical analysis, therefore, must be supplemented with a clear understanding of what *The Federalist,* No. 10, calls the "great objects" of the Constitution. Even Marshall, the justice most commonly identified with the use of logical analysis, ultimately based his constitutional interpretations on his understanding of the ends the Constitution was intended to serve. Marshall believed that the Constitution points beyond itself to the purposes and policies that it serves, and that in the difficult (and most interesting) cases, constitutional interpretation must turn upon an understanding of the Constitution's proper ends. He confidently observed in *McCulloch* v. *Maryland* (1819) that the nature of the Constitution demands "that only its great outlines should be marked, its important objects designated." As for the "minor ingredients" that comprise these objects, he was convinced that they could be "deduced from the nature of the objects themselves."

## The Living Constitution

Based on changing conditions and the lessons of experience, the adaptive, or "living Constitution," approach treats the Constitution more as a political than as a legal document and holds that constitutional interpretation can and must be influenced by present-day values and the sum total of the American experience. Although they insist that each generation has the right to adapt the Constitution to its own needs, proponents of this approach acknowledge that these adaptations must be reconcilable with the language of the Constitution. They would concede, for example, that the provision that each state should have equal representation in the Senate cannot be interpreted to allow for proportional representation, no matter what the dictates of changing conditions. They argue, nevertheless, that the meaning of the Commerce Clause, what is protected by the Fourth Amendment, or the reach of the Eighth Amendment's prohibition of "cruel and unusual punishments" may legitimately change over time.

Defenders of the adaptive approach often cite Marshall's observation in *McCulloch* that "We must never forget that it is a Constitution we are expounding," one that is "intended to endure for ages to come, and consequently, to be adapted to the various crises of human affairs."[10] It should be noted, however, that Marshall was not asserting that the Court should adapt the Constitution, but was arguing instead that the powers of the Constitution should be understood as broad enough to provide Congress with latitude sufficient to confront various crises in the future. Also cited is the argument Justice Oliver Wendell Holmes put forward in *Missouri* v. *Holland* (1920):

> When we are dealing with words that also are a constituent act, like the Constitution of the United States, we must realize that they have called into life a being the development of which could not have been foreseen completely by the most gifted of its begetters. It was enough for them to realize or to hope that they had created an organism; it has taken a century and cost their successors much sweat and blood to prove that they created a nation. The case before us must be considered in the light of our whole experience and not merely in that of what was said a hundred years ago.[11]

Like the other approaches to constitutional interpretation considered thus far, the adaptive approach has its problems. Most importantly, too much adaptation can render the Constitution and its various provisions so pliant that the original document is no longer able to provide guidance concerning what is to be done. Those who embrace the adaptive approach too often misuse Marshall's statements in *McCulloch* and seek not merely an adaptation *within* the Constitution but rather an adaptation *of* the Constitution; they want not only to devise new means to the ends of the Constitution, but also to adopt entirely new ends as well. Justice White's frustration in *New York* v. *United States* (1992) with the Court's insistence that Congress act in conformity with federalism and the Tenth Amendment is a case in point:

> The Court rejects this . . . argument by resorting to generalities and platitudes about the purpose of federalism being to protect individual rights. Ultimately, I suppose, the entire structure of our federal constitutional government can be traced to an interest in establishing checks and balances to prevent the exercise of tyranny against individuals. But these fears seem extremely far distant to me in a situation such as this. We face a crisis of national proportions in the disposal of low-level radioactive waste . . . For me, the Court's civics lecture has a decidedly hollow ring at a time when action, rather than rhetoric, is needed to solve a national problem.

Justice Brennan's objections to capital punishment also illustrate the problems of the adaptive approach. He continually argued that the objective of the "cruel and unusual punishment" clause of the Eighth Amendment is the promotion of "human dignity" and, by insisting that capital punishment is a denial of human dignity, concluded that capital punishment is unconstitutional,[12] despite the fact that the Constitution permits capital trials when preceded by a "presentment or indictment of a

Grand Jury"; permits a person to be "put in jeopardy of life" provided it is not done twice "for the same offense"; and permits both the national government and the states to deprive persons of their lives provided it is not done "without due process of law." The consequences of such a course of action were recognized by James Madison: "If the sense in which the Constitution was accepted and ratified by the Nation . . . be not the guide in expounding it, there can be no security for a consistent and stable [government], more than for a faithful exercise of its powers."[13]

## Original Understanding

This approach is based on the premise that constitutional interpretation must proceed from an understanding of what those who initially drafted and ratified the Constitution intended for it to accomplish. As a consequence, it relies heavily on documentary evidence of the original understanding of the Constitution—especially on the notes taken by James Madison at the Federal Convention of 1787 and on *The Federalist*—to identify what ends the Framers intended the Constitution to achieve, what evils they sought to avoid, and what means they used to achieve these ends and avert these evils. Such reliance on the original understanding of the Framers has often been subjected to harsh criticism, and none harsher than by Justice Brennan who dismissed this approach as "little more than arrogance cloaked as humility. It is arrogant to pretend that from our vantage we can gauge accurately the intent of the Framers on application of principle to specific, contemporary questions."[14] As other critics have pointed out, the Framers' exact intentions are very difficult to determine in many cases. Of the fifty-five delegates present at one or more sessions of the 1787 Convention, for example, some took little or no part in the proceedings. Furthermore, what was said and the reasons given for votes cast are known largely through the remarkable yet necessarily incomplete notes of James Madison.[15] On only a few issues did a majority of the delegates speak, and on no issue did they all speak. Many decisions were compromises that completely satisfied no one, and others carried by the slimmest of majorities. And even if the intentions of the fifty-five delegates could somehow be divined, critics continue, how could we possibly know the intentions of the delegates to the states' ratifying conventions, whose votes put the Constitution into operation, or of the people who elected those delegates? As Justice Robert H. Jackson observed in *Youngstown Sheet & Tube Company* v. *Sawyer* (1952), "Just what our forefathers did envision, or would have envisioned had they foreseen modern conditions, must be divined from materials almost as enigmatic as the dreams Joseph was called to interpret for Pharoah."

Critics also raise a second and more fundamental objection—even if we could know the Framers' intention, why should we be bound by it? As Walton H. Hamilton has noted, "It is a little presumptuous for one generation, through a Constitution, to impose its will on posterity. Posterity has its own problems, and to deal with them adequately, it needs freedom of action, unhampered by the dead hand of the past."[16]

Although these criticisms seem forceful and cogent, they reflect a far too narrow understanding of the approach under discussion. To answer the most fundamental objection first, there should be no question of the founding generation "imposing its will on posterity." This approach seeks to understand the intentions of the Framers not because they were demigods whose judgments must be embraced unreservedly, but because they wrote the very Constitution we are called on to interpret and therefore are and will remain the best possible guides to discovering the ends and means of the constitutional order under which we live. As long as that order remains in force, we need to know as much about the Constitution as possible, including the purposes it was designed to achieve and the evils it was intended to avert. When constitutional questions are raised, therefore, this approach turns to the Founders not for specific answers, but rather for general guidance as to what the Constitution was intended to accomplish and how constitutional questions can be resolved in a manner consistent with these overall intentions. In examining Congress's power under the Commerce Clause to legislate on a particular issue, for example, followers of this approach turn to the founding documents not to ascertain whether the Framers would have favored the specific legislation in question—in all probability, they would never have taken up this question; and even if they had, their specific answers are unlikely to have any contemporary bearing—but to identify the intentions of the Framers to determine whether the objectives of the legislation in question are consistent with the ends for which the Commerce Clause and the Constitution were created. The Framers' intentions are not always clear or definitive, of course. However, protestations that it is very difficult to discover or verify these intentions miss the point. Any evidence pertaining to what the Framers sought to accomplish can only enhance our appreciation of what the Constitution means and what purposes it was designed to achieve, and therefore ought to weigh heavily in our overall understanding of the Constitution.

## THE APPROACHES IN PERSPECTIVE

Textual analysis, precedent, constitutional doctrine, logical analysis, adaption, and identification of original understanding have all been used by justices of the Supreme Court as they have engaged in constitutional interpretation and have all therefore contributed to the contemporary understanding of the Constitution. In this book, we are especially guided in our approach to constitutional interpretation by original understanding, following the prudent counsel given by Justice Joseph Story in his *Commentaries on the Constitution of the United States*:

> In construing the Constitution of the United States, we are, in the first instance, to consider, what are its nature and objects, its scope and design, as apparent from the structure of the instrument, viewed as a whole and also viewed in its component parts. Where its words

> are plain, clear and determinate, they require no interpretation . . . Where the words admit of two senses, each of which is conformable to general usage, that sense is to be adopted, which without departing from the literal import of the words, best harmonizes with the nature and objects, the scope and design of the instrument . . . In examining the Constitution, the antecedent situation of the country and its institutions, the existence and operations of the state governments, the powers and operations of the Confederation, in short all the circumstances, which had a tendency to produce, or to obstruct its formation and ratification, deserve careful attention.[17]

The original understanding approach explores what Story calls the Constitution's "nature and objects, its scope and design." It begins by identifying the ends the Framers intended for the Constitution to achieve and the means they used to achieve these ends, and based on that understanding, it proceeds to evaluate the decisions of the Supreme Court and the lower federal and state judiciaries and the constitutionally significant pronouncements of the executive and legislative branches. What are these ends and means? The remainder of this chapter is a brief introduction to this important question.

## THE ENDS OF THE CONSTITUTION

Justice Jackson's sentiments notwithstanding, the documentary evidence is far from hopelessly "enigmatic" in spelling out the ends of the Constitution. We can begin with the Preamble and by quoting Justice Joseph Story: "It is an admitted maxim in the ordinary course of the administration of justice, that the preamble of a statute is a key to open the mind of the makers, as to the mischiefs, which are to be remedied, and the objects, which are to be accomplished by the provisions of the statue . . . There does not seem any reason why, in a fundamental law or constitution of government, an equal attention should not be given to the intention of the framers, as stated in the preamble."[18] The Preamble is clear as to the ends of the Constitution: it was ordained and established by "We the People of the United States" in order "to form a more perfect Union, establish Justice, insure domestic Tranquility, provide for the common defense, promote the general Welfare, and secure the Blessings of Liberty to ourselves and our Posterity." The Preamble, when read in conjunction with the rest of the Constitution and the documentary history concerning its drafting and ratification, makes clear that the Founders set out to establish an efficient and powerful guarantor of rights and liberties based on the principle of qualitative majority rule, the principle that the majority not only should rule but should rule well. In *The Federalist,* No. 10, James Madison explicitly stated this goal:

> To secure the public good and private rights against the danger of [an overbearing majority], and at the same time to preserve the spirit and form of popular government is then the great object to which our in-

> quiries are directed. Let me add that it is the desideratum by which alone this form of government can be rescued from the opprobrium under which it has so long labored and be recommended to the esteem and adoption of mankind.[19]

As Madison and his colleagues were well aware, the "great object" of their inquiries presented daunting difficulties. They were irrevocably committed to popular or republican government, but historically, popular governments led inevitably to majority tyranny. In such governments, measures were decided "not according to the rules of justice, and the rights of the minor party; but by the superior force of an interested and over-bearing majority." Minority rights were disregarded—as were the "permanent and aggregate interests of the community." Because popular governments too easily allowed for "unjust combinations of the majority as a whole," they typically had proved to be "incompatible with personal security, or the rights of property" and "as short in their lives, as they have been violent in their deaths."[20] Such, according to Madison, was the great "opprobrium" under which "this form of government" had "so long labored."

The most commonly prescribed palliative for the problems of majority tyranny was to render the government powerless. However eager a majority might be to "concert and carry into effect its schemes of oppression," if its governmental vehicle were sufficiently impotent, it would pose no real threat. As William Symmes commented in the Massachusetts State Constitutional Ratifying Convention, "Power was never given . . . but it was exercised, nor ever exercised but it was finally abused."[21] The implication was clear: To prevent abuses, power must be consciously and jealously withheld.

This prescription was not without its shortcomings, however. Carried to an extreme, it rendered government not only powerless but also altogether unworkable. To this view, the leading Framers justifiably and appropriately responded that although the spirit of jealousy was extremely valuable, when carried too far it impinged on another equally important principle of government—that of "strength and stability in the organization of our government, and vigor in its operations."[22] They understood that a strong and stable government was necessary not only to cope with the problems that society faces, but also to render liberty fully secure. In order that popular government "be recommended to the esteem and adoption of mankind," they realized they would have to solve the twofold problem raised by majority rule: to establish a constitution capable of avoiding democratic tyranny on one hand and democratic ineptitude on the other. This problem had overwhelmed the government under the Articles of Confederation and led to the calling of the Federal Convention. Under the Articles, the member states were so powerful and their legislative assemblies so dominant and unchecked that the tyrannical impulses of the majority continually placed in jeopardy the life, liberty, and property of the citizenry; and the central federal government was so infirm and its responsibilities so few and limited that its situation often "bordered on anarchy." The Framers fully appreciated the challenge they faced. As Madison noted, "In framing a government which is to be administered by men over men, the great difficulty lies in this: You must first enable the government to controul the governed; and in the next place, oblige it to controul itself."[23] As we shall see, the Framers rose to this challenge by so arranging the various articles and provisions of the Constitution that they not only granted the federal and state governments sufficient power to control the governed but also obliged them to control themselves through such institutional arrangements and contrivances as the extended republic, separation of powers and checks and balances, and federalism.

## THE MEANS TO THE ENDS

The Framers' solution to the problems of republican government was altogether consistent with republican principle. *The Federalist* is replete with references to this matter. Recognizing that "a dependence on the people is no doubt the primary controul on the government," the Framers also understood that experience had "taught mankind the necessity of auxiliary precautions."[24] This understanding was fundamentally shaped by their assessment of human nature. They believed mankind to be driven by self-interest and consumed by the desire for distinction. Men were seen as "ambitious, rapacious, and vindictive" creatures whose passions for "power and advantage" are so powerful and basic that it is folly to expect that they can be controlled adequately by traditional republican reliance on pure patriotism, respect for character, conscience, or religion, or even the not very lofty maxim that "honesty is the best policy." Inevitably, human avarice and lust for power divide men into parties, inflame them with mutual animosity, and render them much more disposed to oppress one another than to cooperate for the common good. Men are predictable in such matters. They will form factions, whether or not there are readily apparent reasons to do so. As their passions lead them in directions contrary to the "dictates of reason and justice," their reason is subverted into providing arguments for self-indulgence rather than incentives to virtue.[25]

Given these sentiments, it is hardly surprising that the Framers placed little faith in improving human nature through moral reformation or in the activities of "enlightened statesmen." The only hope for republican government, they concluded, was the establishment of institutions that would depend on "the ordinary depravity of human nature."[26] Appreciating that human passion and pride were elemental forces that could never be stifled or contained by "parchment barriers,"[27] they sought to harness and direct these forces through the process of mutual checking. Consequently, they included in the Constitution checks and controls that might "make it the interest, even of bad men, to act for the public good."[28] Self-interest, the Framers contended, was one check that nothing could overcome and the principal hope for security and stability in a republican government. The rather ignoble but always reliable inclination of people to follow their own "sober second thoughts of self-interest" would serve to minimize the likelihood of majority tyranny.[29] As the observant Alexis de Tocqueville would later describe it, the Framers relied on institutional mechanisms to check one personal interest with another and to direct the passions with the very same instruments that excite them.

What kinds of institutional mechanisms—what constitutional means—could incorporate and redirect human self-interest in such a way as to enable the federal and state governments to control the governed and, at the same time, oblige those governments to control themselves? The answer to that question can be found in the three principal concepts underpinning the Constitution: the extended republic, separation of powers and checks and balances, and federalism.

## The Extended Republic

The multiplicity of interests present in the extended commercial republic established by the Constitution represents one of the principal mechanisms by which the Framers sought to establish an energetic government based on the principle of qualitative majority rule. The advantages of an extended republic can be best seen by examining the defects of a small republic. As Madison noted in *The Federalist,* No. 10, the smaller the republic, "the fewer probably will be the distinct parties and interests composing it; the fewer the distinct parties and interests, the more frequently will a majority be found of the same party; and the smaller the compass within which they are placed, the more easily will they concert and execute their plans of oppression." Thus arises democratic tyranny, which can be prevented only by rendering the government impotent and thereby fostering democratic ineptitude. In contrast, the larger the republic, the greater the variety of interests, parties, and sects present within it and the more moderate and diffused the conflict. In the words of *The Federalist,* No. 10, "Extend the sphere, and you take in a greater variety of parties and interests; you make it less probable that a majority of the whole will have a common motive to invade the rights of other citizens; or if such a common motive exists, it will be more difficult for all who feel it to discover their own strength, and to act in unison with each other."[30]

Because of the "greater variety" of economic, geographic, religious, political, cultural, and ethnic interests that an extended republic takes in, rule by a majority is effectively replaced by rule by ever-changing coalitions of minorities that come together on one particular issue to act as a majority but break up on the next. The coalition of minorities that acts as a majority on the issue of import duties is not likely to remain intact on such issues as national defense or governmental aid to private schools. The very real possibility that allies in one coalition may be opponents in the next encourages a certain moderation in politics, in terms of both the political objectives sought and the political tactics employed.

Political interests become reluctant to raise the political stakes too high: By scoring too decisive a political victory on one issue, an interest may find that it has only weakened itself by devastating a potential ally and thus rendering itself vulnerable to similar treatment in the future. Accordingly, politics is moderated not through idle appeals to conscience and beneficence, but rather through the reliance on the inclination of individuals to look after their own self-interest. As Madison observed in *The Federalist,* No. 51, this diversity of interests assures that "a coalition of a majority of the whole society" will seldom take place "on any other principles than those of justice and the common good."[31] The extended republic thus helped to make it possible for the Framers to give the national government sufficient power to prevent democratic ineptitude without raising the spectre of democratic tyranny.

The Framers' recognition of and reliance on the moderating effects brought about by an extended republic is apparent in such constitutional provisions as the Contract Clause in Article I, Section 10, which prohibits any state from passing laws "impairing the obligation of contracts." Note that only the states are restrained, but the federal government is not—and for good reasons. It was thought that no state, however large, was or would be extensive enough to contain a variety of interests wide enough to prevent majorities from acting oppressively and using their legislative power to nullify contracts for their own advantage. Consequently they had to have their power to do so limited by the Constitution. The federal government, by contrast, was large enough and contained the multiplicity of interests necessary to prevent oppression of this sort and so had no need of constitutional constraint. Thus could majority tyranny be avoided simply by relying on the popular principle to operate naturally in an extended republic. The elegant simplicity of this mechanism was pointed out by Madison: "In the extent and proper structure of the Union, therefore, we behold a Republican remedy for the disease most incident to Republican Government."[32]

## Separation of Powers and Checks and Balances

For the Framers, the "great desideratum of politics" was the formation of a "government that will, at the same time, deserve the seemingly opposite epithets—efficient and free."[33] The extended republic was one means by which they sought to realize this objective; a "government of separated institutions sharing powers"[34] was another. They were aware that "the accumulation of all powers legislative, executive, and judiciary in the same hands, whether of one, a few, or many, and whether hereditary, self-appointed, or elective may justly be pronounced the very definition of tyranny," and therefore that "the preservation of liberty requires that the three great departments of power should be separate and distinct."[35] Thus, they sought to construct a government consisting of three coordinate and equal branches, with each performing a blend of functions, thereby balancing governmental powers. Their goal was to structure the government so that the three branches would "by their mutual relations, be the means of keeping each other in their proper places."[36] This the Framers succeeded in doing. They began by giving most legislative power to the Congress, most executive power to the president, and most judicial power to the Supreme Court and to such inferior federal courts as Congress might establish. They then set out to "divide and arrange" the remaining powers in such a manner that each branch could be "a check on the others." Principally, they introduced the principle of bicameralism, under which Congress was divided into the House of Representatives and the Senate, and arranged for the president to exercise certain important legislative powers by requiring yearly addresses on the State of the Union and by providing him with a conditional veto power. They also assumed that the Congress would be restrained by the Supreme Court's power of judicial review and sought to keep the president in check by requiring senatorial confirmation of executive appointees and judicial nominees, mandating that the Senate advise on and consent to treaties, and allowing for impeachment by the Congress. Finally, they supplied the means for keeping the Supreme Court in its "proper place" by giving the Congress budgetary control over the judiciary, the power of impeachment, and the power to regulate the Court's appellate jurisdiction. On top of these specific arrangements, they provided for staggered terms of office (two years for the House, six years for the Senate, four years for the President, and tenure "for good behavior" for the judiciary) to give each branch a further "constitutional check over the others."[37] Knowing that the various branches of the government, even though popularly elected, might from time to time be activated by "an official sentiment opposed to that of the General Government and perhaps to that of the people themselves,"[38] they felt that separation of powers was needed to ensure the fidelity of these popular agents. Separation of powers would provide for a "balance of the parts" that would consist "in the independent exercise of their separate powers and, when their powers are separately exercised, then in their mutual influence and operation on one another. Each part acts and is acted upon, supports and is supported, regulates and is regulated by the rest." This balance would assure that even if these separate parts were to become activated by separate interests, they would nonetheless move "in a line of direction somewhat different from that, which each acting by itself, would have taken; but, at the same time, in a line partaking of the natural direction of each, and formed out of the natural direction of the whole—the true line of publick liberty and happiness."[39]

Not only would such a separation and balancing of powers prevent any branch of government from tyrannizing the people, it would also thwart the majority from tyrannizing the minority. In creating an independent executive and judiciary, the Framers provided a means of temporarily blocking the will of tyrannical majorities as expressed through a compliant or demagogic legislature. Although separation of powers cannot permanently frustrate the wishes of the people, on those occasions when "the interests of the people are at variance with their inclinations" it so structures these institutions that they are able to "withstand the temporary delusions" of people, in order to give them "time and opportunity for more cool and sedate reflection."[40] The prospects for democratic tyranny are dimmed accordingly.

In addition to keeping society free, separation of powers was seen by the Framers as helping to render the government efficient—as minimizing the prospects for democratic ineptitude. Realizing that the democratic process of mutual deliberation and consent can paralyze the government when swift and decisive action is necessary, the Framers reasoned that government would be more efficient if its various functions were performed by separate and distinct agencies. According to James Wilson, a leading member of the Constitutional Convention,

> In planning, forming, and arranging laws, deliberation is always becoming, and always useful. But in the active scenes of government, there are emergencies, in which the man . . . who deliberates is lost. Secrecy may be equally necessary as dispatch. But can either secrecy or dispatch be expected, when, to every enterprise, mutual communication, mutual consultation, and mutual agreement among men, perhaps of discordant views, of discordant tempers, and discordant interests, are indispensably necessary? How much time will be consumed! and when it is consumed, how little business will be done! . . . If, on the other hand, the executive power of government is placed in the hands of one person, who is to direct all the subordinate officers of that department; is there not reason to expect, in his plans and conduct, promptitude, activity, firmness, consistency, and energy.[41]

For the Framers, then, separation of powers not only forestalled democratic tyranny but also provided for an independent and energetic executive able to assure "that prompt and salutory execution of the laws, which enter into the very definition of good Government."[42]

## Federalism

The American constitutional system rests on a federal arrangement in which power is shared by the national government and the states. The primary purpose of this arrangement was to provide for a strong central government; however, it has also had the effect of promoting qualitative majority rule. The federalism created by the Framers can best be understood when contrasted to the confederalism that existed under the Articles of Confederation. Confederalism was characterized by three principles:

1. The central government exercised authority only over the individual governments (i.e., states) of which it was composed, never over the individual citizens of whom those governments were composed. Even this authority was limited, the resolutions of the federal authority amounting to little more than recommendations that the states could (and did) disregard.
2. The central government had no authority over the internal affairs of the individual states; its rule was limited mainly to certain external tasks of mutual interest to the member states.

3. Each individual state had an "exact equality of suffrage" derived from the equality of sovereignty shared by all states.[43]

The consequences of these three principles on the operation of the federal government were disastrous. They rendered the Articles of Confederation so weak that it was reduced, in Alexander Hamilton's words, "to the last stage of national humiliation."[44] There was obviously a need for a "more perfect union" and for new arrangements capable of rendering the political structure "adequate to the exigencies of Government and the preservation of the Union."[45]

The new federal structure erected by the Framers corrected each of the difficulties inherent in confederalism. To begin with, the power of the new federal government was enhanced considerably. Not only could it now operate directly on the individual citizen, just as the state governments could, but it could also deal with internal matters: for example, it now could regulate commerce among the several states, establish uniform rules of bankruptcy, coin money, establish a postal system, tax, and borrow money. Moreover, the federal government was made supreme over the states. As Article VI spelled out: "This Constitution, and the laws of the United States which shall be made in pursuance thereof . . . shall be the supreme law of the land."

If the federalism the Framers created strengthened the central government, it also contributed to qualitative majority rule by preserving the presence of powerful states capable of checking and controlling not only the central government but each other as well. Federalism granted the new central government only those powers expressly or implicitly delegated to it in the Constitution and allowed the states to retain all powers not prohibited to them. The states were permitted to regulate intrastate commerce and the health, safety, and welfare of the citizenry (i.e., the police power) and even were authorized to exercise certain powers concurrently with the central government—for example, the power of taxation and the power to regulate interstate commerce—so long as these powers were not exercised in a manner inconsistent with constitutional limitations or federal regulations. Finally, the Framers' federalism also contributed to qualitative majority rule by blending federal elements into the structure and procedures of the central government itself.[46] To take only the most obvious example, it mixed into the Senate the federal principle of equal representation of all states. When joined with bicameralism and separation of powers, this principle directly contributed to qualitative majority rule. For a measure to become law, it would have to pass the Senate, where because of the federal principle of equal representation of all states, the presence of a nationally distributed majority (with the moderating tendencies that provides) virtually would be guaranteed.

This division of power between the federal and state governments also provided another remedy for the ills of democratic ineptitude. As James Wilson emphasized, with two levels of government at their disposal, the people are in a position to assign their sovereign power to whichever level they believed to be more productive in promoting the common good. Moreover, efficiency is gained in still another way. The federal system permits the states to serve as, in the words of Justice John Marshall Harlan, "experimental social laboratories"[47] in which new policies and procedures can be implemented. If these experiments prove to be successful, they can be adopted elsewhere; if they fail, the damage is limited to the particular state in question. Because the risks are lessened, experimentation is encouraged, and the chances of positive reform and better governance are increased accordingly. In a wholly national or unitary system, on the other hand, experimentation can take place only on a national scale, and social inertia and a commitment to the status quo are encouraged.

The enhanced efficiency of the federal system, in turn, dims the prospect of democratic tyranny. As Madison observed in *The Federalist,* No. 20, "Tyranny has perhaps oftener grown out of the assumptions of power, called for, on pressing exigencies, by a defective constitution, than by the full exercise of the largest constitutional authorities."[48]

The Framers saw the multiplicity of interests present in an extended republic, separation of powers and checks and balances, and federalism as contributing to a government that is at once "efficient and free." These institutional mechanisms, operating in conjunction with each other, were designed to prevent the twin evils of democratic ineptitude and democratic tyranny. The Framers' intention was to institute an energetic and efficient government based on the principle of qualitative majority rule, and they systematically and consistently employed these means to achieve that end. This understanding is at the core of the approach to constitutional interpretation utilized in the discussion of the constitutional provisions that follows.

## NOTES

1 For Chief Justice Hughes's subsequent qualification of these remarks, see *The Autobiographical Notes of Charles Evans Hughes,* eds. David J. Danielski and J. S. Tulshin (Cambridge, Mass.: Harvard University Press, 1973), p. 143.

2 Alexander Hamilton, James Madison, and John Jay, *The Federalist,* ed. Jacob E. Cooke (New York: World, 1961), p. 340. All subsequent references to *The Federalist* are to this edition.

3 Joseph Story, *Commentaries on the Constitution of the United States.* Vol. I (Boston: Hilliard and Gray, 1833), pp. 436–437.

4 *The Federalist,* No. 10, p. 65.

5 *Graves* v. *O'Keefe* (1939). Justice Frankfurter concurring.

6 See Book III, Chapter V: "Rules of Interpretation," in Story, *Commentaries on the Constitution of the United States,* Vol. I, pp. 382–442. See also Francis Lieber, *Legal and Political Hermeneutics,* 2d ed. (Boston: Charles C. Little & James Brown, 1839), reprinted in *Cardozo Law Review* 16, no. 6 (April 1995): pp. 1879–2105; Christopher Wolfe, *How to Read the Constitution: Originalism, Constitutional Interpretation, and Judicial Power* (Lanham, Md.: Rowman & Littlefield, 1996); and Antonin Scalia, *A Matter of Interpretation* (Princeton, N.J.: Princeton University Press, 1997).

7 Thomas Hobbes, *A Dialogue between a Philosopher and a Student of the Common Laws of England,* ed. Joseph Cropsey (Chicago: University of Chicago Press, 1971), p. 129.

8 See J. Skelly Wright, "Professor Bickel, the Scholarly Tradition, and the Supreme Court," *Harvard Law Review* 84, no. 4 (February 1971):785.

9 *Avery* v. *Midland County* (1968). Mr. Justice Fortas dissenting.

10 See Christopher Wolfe, "A Theory of U.S. Constitutional History," *Journal of Politics* 43, no. 2 (May 1981):301.

11 The same Justice Holmes also wrote, however: "I have not yet adequately expressed the more than anxiety that I feel at the ever increasing scope given to the Fourteenth Amendment. . . . I cannot believe that the Amendment was intended to give us *carte blanche* to embody our economic or moral beliefs in its prohibitions." *Baldwin* v. *Missouri,* 281 U.S. 586, 595 (1930).

12 William J. Brennan, "The Constitution of the United States: Contemporary Ratification," presentation at the Text and Teaching Symposium, Georgetown University, Washington, D.C., October 12, 1985.

13 James Madison, *The Writings of James Madison,* ed. Gaillard Hunt (New York: Putnam, 1900–1910), vol. 9, p. 191.

14 See William J. Brennan, "The Constitution of the United States: Contemporary Ratification," presentation at the Text and Teaching Symposium, Georgetown University Law School, Washington, D.C., October 12, 1985.

15 For a defense of Madison's notes, see his "Preface to the Debates in the Convention of 1787," in *The Records of the Federal Convention of 1787,* ed. Max Farrand (New Haven: Yale University Press, 1937), vol. 3, pp. 539–551.

16 Walton H. Hamilton, "The Constitution—Apropos of Crosskey," *University of Chicago Law Review* 21, no. 1 (Fall 1953): 82. For more contemporary critiques of original intent, see William J. Brennan, "The Constitution of the United States: Contemporary Ratification," Text and Teaching Symposium, Georgetown University, October 12, 1985; Arthur S. Miller, *Toward Increased Judicial Activism: The Political Role of the Supreme Court* (Westport, Conn.: Greenwood Press, 1982); Leonard W. Levy, *Original Intent and the Framers' Constitution* (New York: Macmillan, 1988); and H. Jefferson Powell, "The Original Understanding of Original Intent," *Harvard Law Review* 98 (March 1985): 885–948. For responses to these critiques, see Raoul Berger, "Original Intent and Leonard Levy," *Rutgers Law Review* 42 (Fall 1989): 255–286; Raoul Berger, "The Founders' Views—According to Jefferson Powell," *Texas Law Review* 67 (April 1989): 1033–1096; James H. Hutson, "The Creation of the Constitution: The Integrity of the Documentary Record," *Texas Law Review* 65 (November 1986): 1–39; Charles A. Lofgren, "The Original Understanding of Original Intent?" *Constitutional Commentary* 5 (1988): 77–113; and Gary L. McDowell, *Curbing the Courts: The Constitution and the Limits of Judicial Power* (Baton Rouge: Louisiana State University Press, 1988).

17 Joseph Story, *Commentaries on the Constitution of the United States,* vol. 1, pp. 387–388. See also pp. 322, 404, 412, and 417.

18 Joseph Story, *Commentaries on the Constitution of the United States,* Vol. I, pp. 443–444.

19 *The Federalist,* No. 10, p. 61.

20 *The Federalist,* No. 10, pp. 57–61; No. 51, p. 351.

21 Jonathan Elliot (ed.), *The Debates in the Several State Conventions on the Adoption of the Federal Constitution,* 2d ed. (Philadelphia: Lippincott, 1863), vol. 2, p. 74.

22 Alexander Hamilton in the New York State Ratifying Convention: Elliot, *Debates,* vol. 2, p. 301.
23 *The Federalist,* No. 51, p. 349. See also No. 39, p. 233.
24 Ibid., No. 51, p. 349.
25 See *The Federalist,* No. 6, pp. 28–31; No. 10, pp. 59, 61; No. 15, pp. 96, 97; No. 30, p. 193; No. 42, p. 283; No. 48, p. 334; and No. 63, pp. 426–427. A qualification is necessary at this point. According to *The Federalist:* "As there is a degree of depravity in mankind which requires a certain degree of circumspection and distrust; so there are other qualities in human nature which justify a certain portion of esteem and confidence. Republican government presupposes the existence of these qualities in a higher degree than any other form." *The Federalist,* No. 55, p. 378.
26 *The Federalist,* No. 10, p. 60; No. 78, p. 530.
27 *The Federalist,* No. 25, p. 163; No. 41, pp. 41, 270; No. 48, pp. 333, 338.
28 David Hume, *Political Essays,* ed. Charles W. Handel (Indianapolis: Bobbs-Merrill, 1953), p. 13.
29 The phrase is Frederick Douglass's. See his "The Destiny of Colored Americans," in *The North Star* of November 16, 1849.
30 *The Federalist,* No. 10, pp. 63–64.
31 Ibid., No. 51, p. 353.
32 Ibid., No. 10, p. 65.
33 *The Works of James Wilson,* ed. Robert Green McCloskey (Cambridge, Mass.: Belknap Press of Harvard University Press, 1967), p. 791.
34 Richard E. Neustadt, *Presidential Power* (New York: John Wiley, 1960), p. 33.
35 *The Federalist,* No. 47, p. 324.
36 *The Federalist,* No. 51, pp. 348, 349.
37 Ibid., No. 48, p. 332.
38 James Wilson, in Farrand, *Records,* vol. 1, p. 359.
39 *The Works of James Wilson,* p. 300.
40 *The Federalist,* No. 71, pp. 482–483.
41 *The Works of James Wilson,* pp. 294, 296. See also *The Federalist,* No. 70.
42 *The Federalist,* No. 37, p. 233.
43 See Martin Diamond, "What the Framers Meant by Federalism," in *A Nation of States,* 2d ed., ed. Robert A. Goldwin (Chicago: Rand McNally, 1974), pp. 25–42.
44 See *The Federalist,* No. 9, p. 55; No. 15, p. 73; and No. 22, p. 138.
45 Resolution of the Congress calling for the Federal Convention of 1787, in Farrand, *Records,* vol. 3, p. 14.
46 See Martin Diamond, "*The Federalist* on Federalism: Neither a National Nor a Federal Constitution, But a Composition of Both," *Yale Law Journal* 86, no. 6 (May 1977): 1273–1285.
47 *Roth* v. *United States* (1957).
48 *The Federalist,* No. 20, p. 127.

## SELECTED READING

*The Federalist,* Nos. 1, 6, 9, 10, 15, 37, 39, 47–51, 63, 70–72, 78.

Agresto, John. *The Supreme Court and Constitutional Democracy* (Ithaca, N.Y.: Cornell University Press, 1984).

Anastaplo, George. *The Constitution of 1787: A Commentary* (Baltimore, Md.: Johns Hopkins University Press, 1989).

Baker, Thomas E. *"The Most Wonderful Work . . ." Our Constitution Interpreted* (St. Paul, Minn.: West Publishing Company, 1996).

Black, Charles L. *Decision According to Law* (New York: W. W. Norton, 1981).

Burt, Robert. *The Constitution in Conflict* (Cambridge, Mass.: Belknap Press, 1992).

Diamond, Martin. "Democracy and *The Federalist:* A Reconsideration of the Framers' Intent." *American Political Science Review* 53, no. 1 (March 1959): 52–68.

Douglas, William O. "Stare Decisis." *Columbia Law Review* 49 (1949): 725–758.

Eidelberg, Paul. *The Philosophy of the American Constitution* (New York: Free Press, 1968).

Elliot, Jonathan, ed. *The Debates in the Several State Conventions on the Adoption of the Federal Constitution as Recommended by the General Convention in Philadelphia in 1787.* 5 vols. (Philadelphia: Lippincott, 1963).

Farrand, Max, ed. *The Records of the Federal Convention of 1787.* 4 vols. (New Haven, Conn.: Yale University Press, 1937).

Faulkner, Robert K. *The Jurisprudence of John Marshall* (Princeton, N.J.: Princeton University Press, 1968).

Hickok, Eugene W., ed. *The Bill of Rights: Original Meaning and Current Understanding* (Charlottesville: University Press of Virginia, 1991).

Hickok, Eugene W., McDowell, Gary L., and Costopoulos, Philip J., eds. *Our Peculiar Security: The Written Constitution and Limited Government* (Lanham, Md.: Rowman & Littlefield Publishers, 1993).

Kesler, Charles R., ed. *Saving the Revolution: The Federalist Papers and the American Founding* (New York: Free Press, 1987).

Kurland, Philip B. and Lerner, Ralph, eds. *The Founders' Constitution.* 5 vols. (Chicago: University of Chicago Press, 1987).

Levy, Leonard W. and Mahoney, Dennis J., eds. *The Framing and Ratification of the Constitution* (New York: Macmillan Publishing, 1987).

McClellan, James. *Liberty, Order, and Justice: An Introduction to the Constitutional Principles of American Government,* 2d ed. (Indianapolis, Ind.: Liberty Fund, 1999).

Meese, Edwin. "Toward a Jurisprudence of Original Intention." *Benchmark* 2, no. 1 (1986): 1–10.

Rehnquist, William H. "The Notion of a Living Constitution." *Texas Law Review* 54 (May 1976): 693–707.

Rossum, Ralph A. and McDowell, Gary L., eds. *The American Founding: Politics, Statesmanship, and the Constitution* (Port Washington, N.Y.: Kennikat Press, 1981).

Scalia, Antonin. *A Matter of Interpretation* (Princeton, N.J.: Princeton University Press, 1997).

Storing, Herbert J., ed. *The Complete Anti-Federalist.* 7 vols. (Chicago: University of Chicago Press, 1981).

Wolfe, Christopher. *How to Read the Constitution: Originalism, Constitutional Interpretation, and Judicial Power* (Lantham, Md.: Rowman & Littlefield, 1996).

Wood, Gordon S. *The Creation of the American Republic* (Chapel Hill, N.C.: University of North Carolina Press, 1969).

★

THE JUSTICES OF THE SUPREME COURT

THE SUPREME COURT IN THE FEDERAL JUDICIAL SYSTEM

HOW CASES GET TO THE SUPREME COURT

HOW THE COURT DECIDES CASES

THE IMPACT OF SUPREME COURT DECISIONS

ANALYZING COURT DECISIONS

SOURCES IN CONSTITUTIONAL LAW

NOTES

SELECTED READING

★

# 2
# CONSTITUTIONAL ADJUDICATION

More than 150 years ago, Alexis de Tocqueville observed that "there is hardly a political question in the United States which does not sooner or later turn into a judicial one."[1] Today, as then, Americans tend to transform policy disputes into constitutional issues and to seek resolutions in the courts in general, and in the Supreme Court in particular. The Supreme Court's political and legal roles are inextricably intertwined. By deciding cases that raise important issues concerning the extent, distribution, and uses of governmental power, the Court necessarily participates in governing.

The Supreme Court's dual responsibilities as an interpreter of the Constitution and an agency of government provide the focus for this chapter. Five basic questions will be considered: Who are the justices serving on the U.S. Supreme Court? What is the Supreme Court's position in the American judicial system? How are political questions transformed into legal issues and brought before the justices for resolution? How do the justices go about deciding the cases involving those issues? What happens after the Supreme Court decides? The chapter's final section offers a framework for analyzing judicial decisions and surveys source materials in constitutional law.

## THE JUSTICES OF THE SUPREME COURT

### Appointment and Tenure

Supreme Court justices are appointed by the president with the advice and consent of the Senate. Once confirmed, a Supreme Court justice—like any other federal judge—serves during "good behavior." Only one justice, Samuel Chase, has ever been impeached by the House of Representatives, and the Senate failed to convict him. Usually, appointment to the Court represents the culmination of a career, and justices tend to remain on the bench until death or retirement. Justice William O. Douglas, for example, served 36 years on the Court, and Justice Oliver Wendell Holmes did not retire until he was older than 90. The average tenure for justices appointed during the twentieth century is more than 14 years.

### Choosing Justices

On average, vacancies on the Court occur roughly every two years, so a president serving two full terms can expect to have a considerable impact on the composition of the Court. President Ronald Reagan named four justices to the Court during his two terms, and President Bill Clinton named two justices during his first term. In making these appointments, presidents typically select persons with distinguished careers in public life. Among justices appointed up to 1998, 25 had served in Congress, and more than 20 had held Cabinet posts. Although prior judicial experience is not a requirement, all justices appointed since 1975 have served as appellate judges. Presidents also seek appointees who share their political affiliation (roughly 90 percent of appointees have been members of the president's party) and their constitutional views. Thus, President Reagan sought proponents of "judicial restraint," whereas President Clinton pledged to appoint justices sympathetic to the "right to privacy." Finally, presidents also consider demographic factors in their appointments. President Lyndon Johnson chose Thurgood Marshall as the first African American on the Supreme Court, and when Marshall retired, President George Bush replaced him with another African American, Clarence Thomas. President Reagan selected Sandra Day O'Connor as the first woman on the high court, and in 1993 President Clinton selected Ruth Bader Ginsburg as his first appointee.

### The Impact of Appointments

Through their power to appoint Supreme Court justices, presidents frequently can influence the orientation of the Supreme Court. For example, appointments by Presidents Reagan and Bush produced a substantially more conservative Court than existed in preceding decades. Nevertheless, these presidential efforts do not always succeed. The Senate may refuse to confirm a president's nominees—from 1968–1992, six nominees were rejected or withdrew when it became apparent they could not be confirmed. Even when the Senate does confirm nominees, the process has sometimes been arduous—for example, Justice Clarence Thomas received Senate approval by a close 52–48 vote after accusations of sexual harassment were leveled against him during confirmation hearings. Moreover, once on the Court, justices may not behave as the president expected. The president may have misjudged the prospective justice's views, those views may change after the justice is appointed, or new issues may arise that the president did not anticipate in choosing a justice. When a justice fails to meet the president's expectations, there is nothing the president can do about it.

## THE SUPREME COURT IN THE FEDERAL JUDICIAL SYSTEM

Article III of the Constitution established the United States Supreme Court and authorized "such inferior Courts as the Congress may from time to time ordain and establish." Acting under this authority, Congress has created a three-tiered system of federal courts, with the Supreme Court at the apex of the system and the federal courts of appeals and federal district courts below it. During the twentieth century, Congress has added to this system various specialized courts, such as the Court of Military Appeals and the Court of International Trade.

The district courts are the primary trial courts of the federal judicial system, with a single judge presiding over trials in civil or criminal cases. At present, there are ninety-four federal district courts, staffed by 649 judges, serving the fifty states, the District of Columbia, and various U.S. territories. Every state has at least one district court, with more populous states divided into multiple districts. California, New York, and Texas each have four district courts.

The twelve courts of appeals serve as the first-level appellate courts of the federal judicial system, hearing appeals from the district courts, from federal administrative agencies, and from various specialized courts. The courts of appeals typically hear cases as three-judge panels, which are randomly chosen for each case, and decide them by majority vote. Occasionally, however, a court of appeals may hear a case *en banc,* that is, with the court's entire membership participating in the decision of the case. Most courts of appeals are organized into regional "circuits" made up of three or more states. The Seventh Circuit, for example, includes Wisconsin, Illinois, and Indiana. The sole exception is the Court of Appeals for the District of Columbia, which hears large numbers of appeals from federal administrative agencies and serves as a sort of state supreme court for the District of Columbia.

The Supreme Court initially consisted of six justices, and the size of the Court fluctuated until 1869, when Congress established the number of justices at nine. Most cases come to the justices only after they have been tried and reviewed on appeal either by a federal district court and court of appeals or by state trial and appellate courts. The Court's rulings on federal law are binding on all lower courts—in that sense, it is truly a supreme court.

## HOW CASES GET TO THE SUPREME COURT

Each year over the past decade, the Supreme Court has received more than 5,000 petitions for review but has decided less than three percent of the cases appealed to it with full opinions. The cases the Court decides must fall within its jurisdiction, that is, it can only decide those cases it is empowered to hear by the Constitution or by statute. Once this requirement is fulfilled, the Court has broad discretion in determining what cases it will decide. The range of discretion available to the Court has increased over time, and with this expanded discretion have come significant shifts in its caseload.

## Jurisdiction of the Court

The Supreme Court has both an original jurisdiction (over those cases in which the Court functions as a trial court) and an appellate jurisdiction (over those cases in which the Court may review the decisions of other courts). Article III, Section 2 of the Constitution defines the Court's original jurisdiction but confers its appellate jurisdiction subject to "such Exceptions, and under such Regulations, as Congress shall make."

**Original Jurisdiction.** The Supreme Court's original jurisdiction extends to cases involving foreign diplomatic personnel and to cases in which a state is a party. Altogether, the Court has decided fewer than two hundred cases under its original jurisdiction. Two developments have minimized the number of cases initiated in the Supreme Court. The Eleventh Amendment, adopted in 1798, withdrew part of the Court's original jurisdiction by prohibiting those who were not citizens of a state from suing it in federal court.[2] More recently, Congress has deflected many potential original-jurisdiction cases to the federal district courts by giving those courts concurrent jurisdiction.

As a result of legislation, the Supreme Court currently retains exclusive original jurisdiction only over legal disputes between two states, which commonly deal with boundaries or with water or mineral rights. Because hearing testimony in even these few cases could prove a major drain on the time and energies of the Court, it typically appoints a Special Master—usually a retired judge—to conduct hearings and report back to it. In deciding these cases, the justices often endorse the findings of the Master.

**Appellate Jurisdiction.** The Supreme Court hears the vast majority of its cases on appeal from either one of the fifty state court systems or from federal courts, in which instances it operates as the court of last resort. The Court's decisions are final in the sense that there is no court to which one can appeal to reverse them. Its interpretation of statutes can be reversed only by congressional legislation, and its constitutional rulings overturned only by constitutional amendment; in the absence of these remedies, all courts are obliged to follow the Supreme Court's direction in matters of federal law. The Court's decisions also are final in the sense that the Court generally decides cases only after the litigants

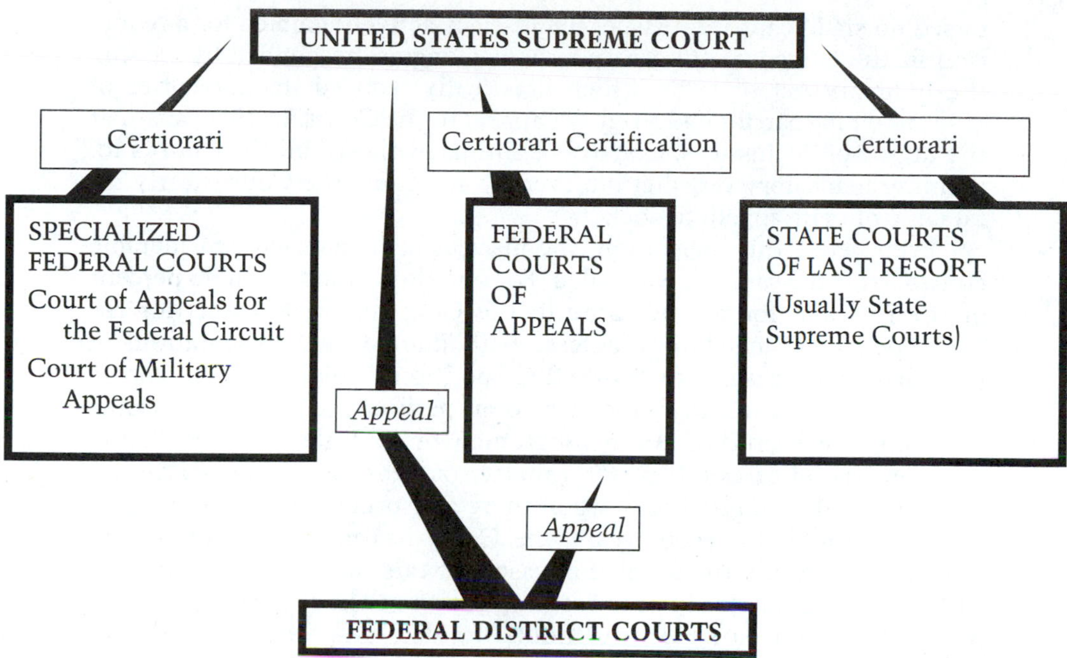


**FIGURE 2.1** How Cases Reach the Supreme Court

have exhausted their available appeals to other courts (Figure 2.1). As Justice Robert Jackson put it in *Brown* v. *Allen* (1953): "We are not final because we are infallible, but we are infallible only because we are final."

Cases initiated in state courts usually reach the U.S. Supreme Court on appeal from state supreme courts, although the Court occasionally hears a case on appeal from another state court when no further appeal is available in the state system. In *Thompson* v. *City of Louisville* (1960), for example, the justices accepted a case directly from the police court of Louisville, Kentucky, because under state law the defendant's fine was too low for appeal to any higher state court.[3] Cases initiated in federal district courts normally come to the Court following review by the appropriate court of appeals, but the Court can expedite consideration of cases. In *United States* v. *Nixon* (1974), which involved President Richard Nixon's refusal to surrender tapes of his conversations subpoenaed for use in a criminal prosecution, the importance of the dispute prompted the Court to hear the case immediately after the federal district court ruled.

Over the course of time, the Supreme Court has gained virtually total discretion in determining what cases it hears. Early in the twentieth century, cases on appeal (that is, cases in which the party appealing the case had a right to Supreme Court review) accounted for more than 80 percent of the Court's appellate docket. Because many of these cases raised no significant legal issue, the justices actively lobbied for a reduction in the burden of obligatory review. Congress responded by passing the Judiciary Act of 1925, which drastically reduced the categories of cases in which parties had a right of appeal to the Court. In 1988, again at the urging of the justices, Congress eliminated almost all the Court's remaining mandatory jurisdiction, thereby according the Court nearly total control of its appellate docket.

Even before this legislation, the justices had exercised considerable control over the cases they decided. For one thing, more than 90 percent of the petitions for review came to the Court on writs of certiorari.[4] These petitions ranged from professionally drafted legal presentations in so-called paid cases to lay-drafted petitions submitted *in forma pauperis.*[5] In determining which certiorari petitions to accept, the Court has complete discretion. As the Supreme Court's Rule 10 states, "A review on writ of certiorari is not a matter of right but of judicial discretion, and will be granted only when there are special and important reasons therefor."[6] In recent years, the Court has used its discretion to reduce dramatically the number of cases it hears each term.[7] During the early 1980s, the justices granted review in more than 180 cases per term. In its 1996 term, however, the Court decided only 90 cases with full opinion. Justice David Souter has suggested that this change did not reflect a conscious choice; rather, "it just happened. " Yet whatever the explanation, the Court's increasing selectivity underscores the importance of the process by which the justices select the cases they will hear.

## The Decision to Decide

Because the justices receive thousands of petitions for certiorari each year, they must establish criteria for determining which cases warrant review. It may be, as Chief Justice Earl Warren once suggested, that the standards that guide the justices' determinations "cannot be captured in any rule or guidelines that would be meaningful."[8] Nevertheless, this leaves unanswered the basic question of how the Court decides what to decide.

**The Case Selection Process.** The mechanics of case selection are relatively simple. Each justice has several law clerks (distinguished law school graduates selected annually by the justice after they have already served a year's clerkship), one of whose duties is to screen the petitions for review and prepare memos summarizing the materials. (Since 1972 the influx of cases has prompted several justices to pool their clerks for memo writing, so that the case memos each clerk prepares will be distributed to all participating justices.) Having evaluated the filings with the aid of the clerks' memos, the Chief Justice prepares a "discuss list" of the petitions he believes deserve collective consideration. Other justices can then add cases to the list. Unless a justice requests that a petition be discussed in conference, it is automatically denied. (More than 70 percent of all petitions are disposed of in this manner.)

Collective consideration of the petitions on the discuss list occurs during the three- or four-day conference before the beginning of the Court's term (in October) and at weekly conferences during the term. In the preterm conference, which is devoted exclusively to case selection, the justices dispose of the hundreds of petitions that have accumulated over the summer months. At the outset of its 1996 term, for example, the Court granted review in seven cases, disposed of six more without opinion, and denied review in 1,543 cases.[9] No case is accepted for review, at either the preterm or the regular weekly conference, unless four justices vote to hear it (the so-called rule of four).

**Criteria for Case Selection.** Because the justices do not publish or explain their votes, it is difficult to determine what factors influenced decisions to grant or deny review in particular cases.[10] The considerations affecting case selection may vary from justice to justice and from case to case. We can identify, however, the general considerations that affect the Court's decisions on petitions for certiorari.

One such consideration is the Court's acknowledged responsibility to promote uniformity and consistency in federal law. Supreme Court Rule 10, "Considerations Governing Review on Certiorari," reflects this responsibility in listing the factors that might prompt the Court to grant certiorari: (1) important questions of federal law on which the Court has not previously ruled; (2) conflicting interpretations of federal law by lower courts; (3) lower-court decisions that conflict with previous Supreme Court decisions; and (4) lower-court departures "from the accepted and usual course of judicial proceedings." This list is neither exhaustive nor binding: Reviews may be granted on the basis of other factors or denied when one or more of the cited factors is present. At times the Court may deny review even when lower courts have reached conflicting decisions on an issue. For example, for several years the justices refused to review challenges to states' use of roadblocks to detect drunk drivers, even though several state courts had disagreed about whether the roadblocks violated the constitutional prohibition on unreasonable searches and seizures. Only in 1990, after rejecting several earlier petitions for certiorari, did the Court address the issue.[11]

In denying certiorari despite disagreement among lower courts, the justices often rely on another case-selection criterion—the intrinsic importance of the issues raised in a case. Although occasionally the Court will reach out to correct gross miscarriages of justice, the justices recognize that they have important responsibilities in the governing of the nation, and they tend to be less concerned with correcting the errors of lower courts than with confronting "questions whose resolution will have immediate importance far beyond the particular facts and parties involved."[12] This criterion, of course, cannot be applied automatically. Some cases, because of the momentous political or legal issues they raise, clearly demand Supreme Court review. *United States* v. *Nixon,* which involved a confrontation over presidential claims of executive privilege, obviously fell into that category. Many other cases, including most *in forma pauperis* petitions, raise relatively minor issues that do not warrant the Court's attention. Whenever the choice is not so clear-cut, further considerations come into play.

Of paramount concern in some decisions to grant review is the effect the case might have on the long-run influence of the Court. Historically, the Court has sought to maintain its influence by avoiding unproductive involvement in political disputes, as when it refused to hear cases challenging the constitutionality of the Vietnam War. The justices also attempt to select cases in which the issues are clear and well-defined enough to facilitate wise and persuasive constitutional decisions.

Finally, the Court usually seeks to avoid unnecessarily inflaming public opinion by limiting the number of controversial issues it addresses at one time and by considering public reaction in choosing cases in which to announce important rulings. Thus, for thirteen years after *Brown* v. *Board of Education* (1954), which outlawed state-mandated school segregation, it refused to consider constitutional challenges to state laws prohibiting interracial marriage.[13] The Court chose *Gideon* v. *Wainright* (1963) to announce that indigent defendants had a right to counsel at trial in part because it involved a relatively minor offense rather than a violent crime.[14]

Perhaps even more important than the maintenance of the Court's influence are the justices' constitutional views—their notions of what constitutional issues are most important and how those issues should be resolved. Specifically, justices may vote to hear a case when they believe that review would further their conception of desirable constitutional policy. In some cases, certain justices might favor review if they believe that a majority of the Court will support their constitutional position, particularly if they disagree with the lower court's decision. Alternatively, if they expect to be in a minority on the Court, they might oppose review rather than risk creation of an unfavorable precedent.

**The Changing Agenda.** Our discussion of case selection has focused thus far on the factors underlying the selection of particular cases for review. However, the quotation from Tocqueville that opens the chapter suggests a broader perspective. If political questions tend to become judicial questions, then the cases from which the justices select presumably reflect the broad political issues confronting the nation. Put differently, if the Court seeks to decide cases of national concern, then the nation's political concerns necessarily furnish the Court's basic agenda.

The historical record confirms this point. Prior to the Civil War the paramount political issue was the distribution of political power between the national and state governments, and the constitutional cases considered by the Court characteristically required it to define the respective spheres of those governments. Following the Civil War the nation underwent rapid industrial development and the concurrent growth of large-scale economic enterprises, and governmental efforts to deal with these developments played a major role in the Court's constitutional decisions from the 1870s until the late 1930s. In the wake of the New Deal, an expansion in the scope of governmental concerns, facilitated by Court rulings permitting extensive regulation of economic activity, created new conflicts between government and the individual; accordingly, the contemporary Court's constitutional decisions have involved in large measure the delineation of individual rights.

## HOW THE COURT DECIDES CASES

In deciding cases, the justices first of all inform themselves about the facts and legal issues in the case and about the more general consequences that can be expected from a ruling. After oral argument, they discuss the case in closed conference and reach a tentative decision. Finally, through the process of opinion writing and continuing discussion, the justices confirm (or in rare instances, reconsider) the decision reached in conference, clarify and develop the basis for the ruling, and attempt to reconcile intracourt differences.

As this summary suggests, the Court's decisions inevitably have a dual aspect. The litigants in a case usually are most concerned with winning or losing: To a convicted felon challenging the constitutionality of a police search that uncovered incriminating evidence, avoiding prison is the primary goal. In announcing decisions, however, the Court justifies its rulings on the basis of principles and standards whose ramifications extend far beyond the confines of the individual case. Indeed, the justices consciously use their discretion to review only cases of broad societal importance. An appreciation of this combination of the specific and the general, of immediate results and broader implications, is crucial to understanding the decision-making of the Supreme Court.

### Informing and Persuading the Court

In weighing the merits of a particular case, the Court relies heavily on three sources of information: the briefs of the contending parties, *amicus curiae* (literally, "friend of the court") briefs, and oral argument. In all cases heard by the Court, the lawyers for both parties file legal briefs and then argue the case orally before the justices. In most cases other interested parties submit *amicus* briefs, which increase the range of information available to the justices. Because they resemble each other in basic purpose, the briefs of the parties and *amicus* briefs can be considered together.

**Legal Briefs.** A legal brief is first and foremost a partisan document—an attempt to persuade a court to rule in favor of one's client or position.

Persuasion takes the form of marshalling and then interpreting favorably the legal materials (precedents, statutes, constitutional provisions) and the facts involved in the case. For *amicus* briefs and for those submitted by the parties, the ultimate goal is to gain a favorable ruling.

*Amicus* briefs do differ from the briefs filed by the litigants. They ordinarily are filed by parties who are interested primarily in the general constitutional issue the case raises, rather than in the fate of the particular litigants. Some organizations file *amicus* briefs out of concern for the effects the Court's decision might have on them or on their members. In *Regents of the University of California* v. *Bakke* (1978), which involved an affirmative-action program for medical school admissions, several universities with similar programs filed *amicus* briefs, and so did the National Association for the Advancement of Colored People (NAACP) and several Jewish organizations. For other organizations, the principal concern is ideological: They wish to see the Constitution interpreted in a particular way. The American Civil Liberties Union (ACLU), for example, often files *amicus* briefs in First Amendment cases in an effort to gain or preserve a broad interpretation of the amendment's guarantees. Whatever the basis for their interest, those filing *amicus* briefs tend to be concerned largely with the constitutional standards that the Court announces and their implications.

Although legal briefs commonly focus on the interpretation of constitutional provisions, statutes, and precedents relevant to the case, they may also include nonlegal materials. In recent years lawyers have made extensive use of social science research to document conditions within the society, indicate the effects of governmental policies, or forecast the likely effects of a Court ruling. The prototype for such briefs was the famous "Brandeis brief" filed in *Muller* v. *Oregon* (1908). At issue in *Muller* was the constitutionality of an Oregon statute limiting female workers to a ten-hour workday, which the plaintiff challenged as an arbitrary interference with economic liberty. In response, Louis Brandeis, then counsel for the state of Oregon and later a Supreme Court justice, claimed that the law served important public purposes—a claim backed up by over one hundred pages of social and economic data demonstrating that long working hours were dangerous to the health, safety, and morals of working women. Brandeis's success in *Muller* prompted counsel in later cases to adopt a similar approach. In *Brown* v. *Board of Education,* for example, legal arguments for outlawing racial segregation in public education were supplemented by the results of psychological tests showing the adverse effects of segregation on black children. More recently, contending parties in cases involving the constitutionality of the death penalty have included in their briefs extensive data on the deterrent or nondeterrent effect of capital punishment and on the proportion of African Americans among those sentenced to death.

**Oral Argument.** In oral argument, the attorneys for each party have their last opportunity to influence the Court's decision. In the early nineteenth century, when the Court's docket was less crowded, the greatest lawyers in the country would spend several days arguing a case before the justices. Nowadays, oral presentations usually are limited to a half-hour for each party, although in particularly important cases more time may be allotted. In *Brown* v. *Board of Education II* (1955), which involved the question of how the Court's historic desegregation decision would be implemented, the Court permitted a total of fourteen hours of oral argument.

Despite severe time constraints, oral argument can provide an opportunity for influencing the justices, many of whom view it as vital for clarifying the written arguments presented in the briefs. Through their questions, the justices test the soundness of the opposing legal positions, and in this give-and-take, weaknesses in an argument or lack of preparation by attorneys soon becomes apparent. The justices' questions can also indicate issues on which they are undecided, and effective response to their inquiries can substantially improve a client's chances. As Justice John Marshall Harlan has observed, oral argument "may in many cases make the difference between winning and losing, no matter how good the briefs are."[15]

### The Decision-Making Process

On Wednesdays and Fridays during its annual term (October to late June), the Court meets in conference to consider the cases on which it has most recently heard oral argument. Because the confidentiality of these conferences is jealously guarded—only the justices themselves, without law clerks or other Court staff, attend them—our knowledge of them is necessarily fragmentary.

Deliberations begin only after the justices shake hands—a ritual instituted to symbolize that the inevitable disagreements are legal, not personal. The Chief Justice initiates discussion by indicating his views of the case at hand and his vote. The associate justices, in descending order of seniority, similarly present their views and votes, and the tallying of votes produces a tentative decision. Although the discussion at conference can on occasion be quite heated, Chief Justice Rehnquist has noted that, for the most part, justices merely announce their conclusions rather than seeking to persuade their fellow justices. If the Chief Justice has voted with the majority, he determines who will write the opinion of the Court (majority opinion). He may assign the opinion to another member of the majority or retain it for himself. If the Chief Justice finds himself in the minority, the senior justice aligned with the majority assigns the opinion of the Court. The other justices are free to express their views in concurring or dissenting opinions.

How do the justices decide how they will vote? Some scholars maintain that the justices' votes simply reflect their ideological orientations.[16] According to this account, Chief Justice Rehnquist votes as he does because he is a conservative, whereas Justice Thurgood Marshall voted as he did because he was a liberal. Other scholars insist that justices are not free to decide simply on the basis of their preferences, that law constrains the choices that justices make and directs their decisions.[17] Despite these disagreements, some points are clear. Accounts of the justices' deliberations indicate that in conference they rely extensively on legal arguments and precedent to buttress their positions and persuade their colleagues.[18] The emphasis on legal argument suggests that the justices acknowledge their duty to put aside their personal preferences and base their decisions on the Constitution. (Of course, whether they succeed in banishing their personal policy views from their deliberations may well be another matter.) The requirement that decisions be legally justifiable rarely promotes consensus, however. Conscientious justices can and often do disagree about the difficult constitutional issues facing them. In recent terms, dissenting opinions were filed in about two-thirds of the cases the Court decided. Yet although interaction among the justices may have some effect on their votes and a substantial effect on their opinions, the decision-making process is more individual than collective in nature. As Justice Lewis Powell put it, "For the most part, perhaps as much as 90 percent of our total time, we function as nine small, independent law firms."[19] This high degree of individuality, which helps to account for the remarkable consistency of any given justice's voting patterns over time, reflects both the well-developed constitutional views the members of the Court bring to their cases and the limited resources available to them for changing the views of their colleagues.

The vote in conference comprises only the initial phase of decision-making. Even after conference, discussion of cases continues, and during the extended period between the vote and announcement of the decision, the opinion of the Court and any concurring or dissenting opinions are prepared and circulated among the justices for their comments. Reviewing these opinions gives the justices an opportunity to reconsider their initial positions, and a particularly persuasive opinion may lead to a change of vote. On a closely divided Court, defection by a single justice can produce a new majority and, therefore, a different decision.

The likelihood of a postconference vote shift should not be exaggerated. A study of one ten-year period found that the justices' final votes differed from their votes in conference only about 9 percent of the time.[20] Even if no votes are changed, the period between the conference and the announcement of the Court's decision still represents a crucial stage in the decisional process. During this time, the justices who comprise the majority carefully review the opinion of the Court; frequently, they require changes in its language or argument before they will endorse it. Justices Lewis Powell and William Brennan have acknowledged circulating as many as ten drafts of an opinion before one was accepted by the majority.[21] Even after prolonged discussions, deep-seated differences may prevent a Court majority from coalescing behind a single opinion. In *Furman* v. *Georgia* (1971), all five members of the Court majority wrote separate opinions that presented quite disparate grounds for invalidating Georgia's death penalty statute.

Such close scrutiny of the opinion of the Court reflects in part a concern for the soundness of the legal arguments it presents, because public and congressional acceptance of a decision may depend on the persuasiveness of the arguments supporting it. The justices also realize that the justifications for their decision may play a large role in future decisions. The importance of this consideration was highlighted in the decision handed down in *United States* v. *Nixon,* in which the Court unanimously rejected the President's claim of executive privilege and voted to compel him to release the Watergate tapes. Before that decision was announced, several justices refused to join Chief Justice Warren Burger's opinion for the Court, because they felt that it provided too much support for future claims of executive power. Only after the Chief Justice agreed to extensive revisions of the original opinion did all the justices join it.

## THE IMPACT OF SUPREME COURT DECISIONS

Most Supreme Court decisions not only resolve disputes between particular litigants, but also have consequences for the nation as a whole. In ruling on the constitutionality of a particular program or practice, the Court also indicates the likely validity of similar programs or practices. In interpreting a constitutional provision, the Court announces standards that may guide future decisions involving that provision. In elaborating constitutional principles, the Court may educate the public about what our basic principles of government require.

Court decisions, like other governmental policies, do not always achieve their intended effects. Decisions may be misunderstood, misrepresented, or ignored; those responsible for carrying out the Court's mandates may seek to evade their responsibilities or may find ways to negate the effectiveness of the mandates; and opposition to Court rulings may lead to attempts to overturn them or to limit their effects. Rather than resolving conflicts, then, Court decisions sometimes merely aggravate them. Only if we understand what happens *after* the Court rules can we fully appreciate the role that the Court plays in governing.

### Legal Obligation

A Supreme Court decision invalidating a governmental program imposes legal obligations on three distinct sets of actors. Most immediately, the losing party in the case must either abandon the invalidated program or remedy its constitutional defects. In a case such as *Regents of the University of California* v. *Bakke,* in which it was held that the goal of the affirmative-action plan in question (increased minority-group representation in the medical profession) was within the law but the means employed to achieve this goal were unconstitutional, the university had merely to revise its program such that the goal could be achieved constitutionally. When, however, the aim of an invalidated program is itself unconstitutional, alternative programs designed to accomplish that goal cannot legally be instituted.

In addition, because of the Court's hierarchical position in the American judicial system, its decisions on matters of federal law constitute binding precedent for all other courts, both federal and state. This means that should a litigant challenge a program similar to one invalidated by the Court, lower-court judges are obliged to invalidate it. Moreover, in deciding other cases in which a federal law or constitutional provision comes into play, judges must treat the Court's interpretation as authoritative. As Judge Learned Hand of the Second Circuit Court of Appeals put it, "I have always felt that it was the duty of an inferior court to suppress its own opinions . . . and to try to prophesy what the appellate court would do. God knows, I have often been wrong in that too; but I have at least been obedient, which is as I conceive it a judge's prime duty."[22]

Finally, by striking down a program as unconstitutional, the Court may also oblige other governmental units to discontinue programs similar to the one invalidated. This consequence underlines the crucial importance of the opinion of the Court: The broader the basis for the ruling, the broader the range of affected programs. The progress of school-desegregation decisions illustrates this point. In a series of decisions handed down from 1938 to 1954, the Court ruled that certain segregated school systems had violated the Equal Protection Clause of the Fourteenth Amendment by failing to provide equal educational facilities for black students; but because these rulings were tied to the conditions in specific districts, their effects were not felt outside those districts. Then, in 1954 the Court ruled in *Brown* v. *Board of Education* that separate school systems for blacks and whites were *inherently* unequal and thereby obliged all states operating such systems to dismantle them. By choosing the broader basis for its decision in *Brown,* the Court assured that its ruling would have nationwide effects.

Yet there is considerable controversy over what obligations a Court ruling imposes on government officials. Although they may not legitimately defy the Court's decision in a specific case, they are not obliged in every instance to endorse the Court's interpretation of the Constitution. For such a requirement would imply that the Constitution is what the Court says it is or that the Court can never err in its reading of the Constitution. In the wake of the Court's infamous decision in *Dred Scott* v. *Sandford* (1857), for example, Abraham Lincoln, while professing respect for the Court and acknowledging the authority of its ruling in the case, denied that the Court had correctly interpreted the Constitution and indicated his intention to seek a reversal of the Court's position. More recently, critics of the Supreme Court's ruling in *Roe* v. *Wade* (1973) legalizing abortion adopted various restrictions on abortion that were susceptible to legal challenge, expecting that the resulting litigation would provide an opportunity for the Court to reconsider its position. Eventually, this strategy succeeded, when the Court retreated from *Roe* in *Webster* v. *Reproductive Health Services* (1989) and *Planned Parenthood of Southeastern Pennsylvania* v. *Casey* (1992).

### Response to Court Mandates

In invalidating a program or practice, the Supreme Court imposes an obligation to cease the unconstitutional activity or take steps to remedy the constitutional violation. In most cases those affected by the Court's rulings comply with the legal requirements. The mere existence of legal obligations does not guarantee compliance, however, and the cases in which Court mandates have not been carried out have had an importance far greater than their numbers might suggest.

**Communication of Court Mandates.** If its decisions are to achieve their intended effects, the Court must identify clearly what actions are to be undertaken or what practices eliminated and communicate that mandate to the appropriate officials. Rulings that are unclear or that fail to reach their intended audience are unlikely to have much effect.

Confusion over the exact scope or meaning of Court mandates may stem from disagreement on the Court. Not once during the 1960s, for example, did a majority of the justices agree on standards defining what kinds of sexually explicit materials were protected by the First Amendment. As a result, the Court handed down decisions marked by a multiplicity of opinions, each offering a different standard for determining whether movies or publications were obscene. State and local officials who tried to respect constitutional limitations while enforcing obscenity legislation consequently received little guidance from the Court.

Even when the justices agree among themselves, ambiguities in the opinion of the Court can create uncertainty about the scope of the ruling, as happened in *Escobedo* v. *Illinois* (1964). In *Escobedo,* the Court for the first time recognized that suspects had a right to counsel during police interrogations; but because the opinion of the Court did not clearly define that right, lower courts developed widely divergent interpretations of the ruling. Over an eighteen-month period, 150 cases raising *Escobedo*-type issues were appealed to the Supreme Court. Only after the Court clarified its position in *Miranda* v. *Arizona* (1966) did lower courts consistently enforce the right to counsel.[23]

Finally, the clarity of a Court ruling may disappear as that ruling is transmitted to its intended audience. The transmission to police officers of the Supreme Court's landmark criminal-justice decisions of the 1960s illustrates how confusion can occur at this stage. In determining what the Court required, police officers typically relied for information on nonjudicial sources such as police training sessions, local officials, and the mass media. Often, the Court's message was simplified and distorted in the course of transmission. A study of the initial response to *Miranda* in four Wisconsin police departments, for example, found that despite the clarity of the Court's guidelines, more than half the officers in three departments incorrectly identified what the decision required.[24] However, this is likely to be a problem only in the short run.

**Noncompliance.** A more serious concern is noncompliance, the refusal to undertake or refrain from actions as required by Supreme Court rulings. State and federal courts at times have failed to follow or enforce Court decisions, and state supreme courts, in particular, have displayed a penchant for ignoring Court precedents. More frequently, however, noncompliance crops up among state or local officials who resist Court directions to implement unpopular decisions or to observe new and potentially burdensome limitations on the exercise of their powers. Southern school boards, for instance, long sought to evade the Court's school desegregation requirements; in more recent years, Northern school boards did the same. School districts often ignored Court decisions requiring the elimination of prayer and Bible-reading from their schools. When police officers believed that Court decisions hampered their efforts to control crime, they sought to evade limitations on their power to conduct searches and interrogate suspects.

That individuals evade, or seek to evade, their legal responsibilities is nothing new: the very existence of courts testifies to the need to enforce legal norms. Yet noncompliance—particularly if it is widespread—poses a grave threat to the Court's effectiveness, because its capacity to enforce its decisions is limited. As Alexander Hamilton noted in T*he Federalist,* No. 78, the judiciary lacks control over "either the sword or the purse" and must "ultimately depend upon the aid of the executive arm even for the efficacy of its judgments." Should the executive prove reluctant to enforce its decisions vigorously, as happened initially after *Brown,* the Court can only depend on the willingness of litigants to initiate cases challenging instances of noncompliance. Even then, as previously noted, it cannot always rely on the lower courts to enforce its rulings. In sum, the Court's effectiveness ultimately depends less on its ability to punish noncompliance than on its ability to persuade the targets of its decisions to comply voluntarily.

### Political Impact

In addition to imposing legal obligations, Supreme Court decisions influence public opinion, political activity, and the development of public policies. By upholding a challenged governmental enactment, the justices authoritatively dispose of constitutional objections to its validity and may thereby promote public acceptance of the law's legitimacy. The Court's decision in *Heart of Atlanta Motel* v. *United States* (1964), which upheld a controversial section of the Civil Rights Act of 1964, resolved constitutional questions about the national government's power to ban racial discrimination in public accommodations. Its decisions in

*National Labor Relations Board* v. *Jones & Laughlin Steel Corporation* (1937) and in subsequent cases validated New Deal efforts to regulate the national economy. As these examples indicate, Supreme Court decisions have played a crucial role in legitimating the federal government's expanding exercise of power.[25] In addition, Court legitimation of one state's law may dispose other states to adopt similar measures. The full development of so-called Jim Crow laws, for example, did not occur until after the Court, in *Plessy* v. *Ferguson* (1896), upheld a Louisiana statute establishing racial segregation in public transportation.[26]

Even when the justices do not invalidate governmental policies, their rulings may still have political repercussions. The justices' interpretation of federal statutes have at times prompted campaigns for congressional action to overturn those interpretations. Thus, after a series of rulings during the late 1980s narrowly construed federal civil-rights statutes, civil-rights groups prevailed on Congress to pass the Civil Rights Act of 1991, reversing several of those decisions. Even rulings upholding governmental action against constitutional challenge may, by focusing attention on the issue, produce a political response. For example, after the Court in *Goldman* v. *Weinberger* (1986) rejected the claim of an Orthodox Jewish psychologist that he had a constitutional right to wear a yarmulke while on active duty in a military hospital, Congress enacted legislation establishing a statutory right to do so.

Decisions invalidating state or federal policies have also produced varied effects. An adverse Court ruling frequently activates the political forces supporting a program to seek alternative means of accomplishing their objectives. Thus five constitutional amendments have been adopted, in whole or in part, to overturn Supreme Court decisions.[27] During recent decades, opponents of Court decisions have sought, unsuccessfully, to strip the Court of its power to hear cases involving school prayer, busing, and abortion.

The response to the Supreme Court's abortion decisions illustrates the potential political consequences of judicial rulings. The Supreme Court's decision in *Roe* v. *Wade* striking down state restrictions on abortion prompted the formation of the pro-life movement, which supported legislation discouraging abortions or making them more difficult to obtain and a constitutional amendment outlawing abortion. More recently, the Court's validation of state laws limiting abortion activated pro-choice forces, which attempted to blunt the effects of the decisions by supporting candidates sympathetic to their cause and by pushing for adoption of state and federal laws protecting abortion rights.

Controversial decisions often generate support and opposition. For example, *Brown* v. *Board of Education* produced not only intransigent resistance by segregationists but also efforts by civil rights groups to solidify and extend the gains they had made. Such decisions have the added effect of subtly changing the political context in which conflicts between such forces occur, by giving proponents of the Court's view the potent political advantage of being able to claim that the Constitution supports their position. Finally, the public support for the Court that promotes voluntary compliance also enables it to influence public opinion. According to public-opinion polls, public attitudes toward desegregation changed markedly after *Brown*.[28] This change may not have resulted solely from the Court's ruling, but it does suggest that the authority of the Court enables it to influence public opinion even on controversial matters.

In sum, Supreme Court decisions establish government policy, just as decisions made by the executive or legislative branches do, and thereby help shape American society. Indeed, if the Court is to fulfill its constitutional functions, it cannot avoid making policy. The important question to ask is whether its policies can be constitutionally justified.

## ANALYZING COURT DECISIONS

Because judicial opinions provide justifications for constitutional positions, in reading cases one should bear in mind the modes of constitutional interpretation outlined in Chapter 1. Often it is helpful to "brief," or outline, a case to analyze its major elements (see Box 2.1 for an example). In general, one should look for the following elements that are common to all court cases.

**Title and Citation.** Case titles usually derive from the names of the parties to the controversy. The party listed first is seeking reversal of an unfavorable lower-court decision, whereas the party listed second typically wants that decision affirmed. If the case comes to the Court on appeal, the parties are referred to as the appellant and the appellee. If the case comes on a writ of certiorari, they are referred to as the petitioner and the respondent.

**Facts of the Case.** Because all Supreme Court cases arise as disputes between particular litigants, Court decisions represent attempts to apply constitutional principles to unique situations. Full understanding of a Court decision therefore requires an appreciation of the facts underlying the case, which have been established by testimony at trials. Supreme Court justices may differ in interpreting the facts, however; disagreement about the facts, as well as about the proper interpretation of the Constitution, may produce divisions on the Court. Frequently, the opinion of the Court, or majority opinion, summarizes the relevant facts before elaborating the Court's justification for its decision. In other cases, the facts must be pieced together from comments in several opinions. Preceding most cases presented in this volume are summaries of the facts, which indicate the factors one should look for in reading cases.

**BOX 2.1 A SAMPLE CASE BRIEF**

***Texas* v. *Johnson***
**491 U.S. 397 (1989)**

**Facts of the Case.** Gregory Johnson burned an American flag as a form of political protest. He was arrested and convicted of violating a Texas statute that forbade desecration of the American flag. He appealed his conviction, claiming that his action was protected by the First Amendment. The Texas Court of Criminal Appeals overturned his conviction, and the Supreme Court granted certiorari.

**The Law.** The Free Speech Clause of the First Amendment, made applicable to states by the Due Process Clause of the Fourteenth Amendment.

**Legal Questions.**

1. Does Johnson's conduct constitute expressive conduct, thus implicating the 1st Amendment? *Yes.*
2. Did Johnson's burning of the flag disturb the peace? *No.*
3. Is the state's interest in preserving the flag as a national symbol related to the suppression of free expression? *Yes.*
4. Does the Supreme Court's test for expressive conduct enunciated by *United States* v. *O'Brien* apply here? *No.*
5. Does the state have a valid interest in promoting respect for the flag as a symbol of the nation? *Yes.*
6. Can government prohibit flag desecration as a means of promoting that interest? *No.*
7. Is the Texas law constitutional? *No.*

**Opinion of the Court (Brennan).** Johnson's burning of the American flag was an attempt to convey a political message. When Texas banned flag desecration to promote respect for the flag, it prevented the use of the flag to communicate messages, such as Johnson's, that are critical of the government and of the nation. However, the First Amendment forbids government from prohibiting the expression of ideas and communication of messages merely because they are offensive or disagreeable, and therefore the Texas statute is unconstitutional.

**Concurring Opinion (Kennedy).** Commitment to the Constitution requires overturning Johnson's conviction, however distasteful it may be to do so.

**Dissenting Opinion (Rehnquist).** The American flag's unique position as a symbol of the nation justifies special protections against its desecration.

Texas's flag desecration statute does not prevent Johnson from communicating his criticism of the government, because his speech and other actions expressing that criticism were not prohibited or interfered with. The statute only prohibits one means of conveying his message, and it does so in response to the profound regard that Americans have for their flag.

**Dissenting Opinion (Stevens).** The rules developed for other forms of symbolic expression do not apply here, because of the flag's status as a special symbol of the nation.

**Evaluation.** The Court's ruling extended the range of expressive actions entitled to First Amendment protection. Forty-eight states and the national government had statutes banning flag desecration, so the effects of the Court's ruling were felt nationwide. Efforts to amend the Constitution to overturn the Court's ruling failed, and a congressional flag-desecration statute passed in the wake of this decision was subsequently invalidated by the Court.

**The Law.** Supreme Court decisions usually involve the interpretation of three elements of law: constitutional provisions, statutes and/or administrative regulations, and Supreme Court precedents. Large bodies of law have sprung from most constitutional provisions, so it is important to note precisely which provision the Court is interpreting. For example, if a constitutional challenge is raised under the Fourteenth Amendment, the first thing to determine is whether the challenge is based on the Due Process Clause or the Equal Protection Clause.

**Legal Questions.** A Court decision can be viewed as a response to a particular legal question or series of questions, a clear understanding of which is vital to any proper analysis of the opinions in a case and of the effects of the decision. One way of ensuring such clarity is to frame the questions involved in a yes-or-no format (see Box 2.1 for an example). Usually the Court's answers to the legal questions in a case can be determined from a close reading of the opinion of the Court. However, in cases in which five justices are unable to agree on a single opinion, one must search all opinions in the case for points of majority agreement.

**Opinion of the Court.** This opinion announces the Court's decision and supplies the justifications for that ruling. Because the decision may serve as a precedent in future cases, close attention should be paid to the chain of reasoning supporting the decision and to its possible implications. Frequently, the best approach is to trace how the Court arrived at its answers to each of the legal questions previously identified.

**Concurring Opinions.** Members of the Court majority may write concurring opinions either because they agree with the Court's decision but disagree with its justification, in which instance the concurring opinion will offer an alternative justification, or because they agree with both the decision and its justification but wish either to clarify their own view of the case or to respond to arguments made in a dissenting opinion. Determining the basis for the concurrence should be the initial step in analyzing a concurring opinion.

**Dissenting Opinions.** Dissenting opinions attempt to demonstrate why the Court's decision is wrong. They may point to alleged errors in reasoning, misinterpretation of precedents or constitutional provisions, or misunderstanding of the facts in a case. Analysis of dissenting opinions should focus on the bases of disagreement with the opinion of the Court.

**Evaluation.** No analysis of a case is complete without an evaluation of the decision. Is the opinion of the Court convincing? Is the decision consistent with previous Court decisions? If not, does the Court provide persuasive reasons for departing from precedent? What are the likely effects of the Court's decision?

## SOURCES IN CONSTITUTIONAL LAW

**Court Decisions.** The official edition of United States Supreme Court decisions, titled *United States Reports,* contains the text of all Supreme Court decisions handed down since 1790. For almost one hundred years, the volumes were issued under the names of individual court reporters. Thus, citations to cases in those volumes generally include the name of the particular reporter: *Marbury* v. *Madison,* 1 Cranch 137 (1803). After Volume 90 (1874), cases are cited only by the volume number of *U.S. Reports.* Thus *Adamson v. California,* 322 U.S. 46, can be found on page 46 of Volume 322.

Two other editions of the Supreme Court's decisions contain supplementary material not found in the official edition. The *Supreme Court Reporter* prefaces the Court's decisions with summaries of the legal issues in the case. Citations are again by volume and page; for example, the citation for *Adamson* is 67 Sup. Ct. 1672. The *Lawyers' Edition of the United States Supreme Court Reports* includes legal analyses of the more important rulings and summarizes the oral arguments of counsel in each case. Citations are by volume and number: for *Adamson,* the citation is 91 L.Ed. 1903.

Prior to publication in bound volumes, Supreme Court decisions are available in loose-leaf format in *U.S. Law Week* and on the Internet. The most accessible online site for Court decisions is the Cornell Law School Server. This server provides the full text of all Supreme Court decisions since 1990, which can be accessed at <www.law.cornell.edu/supct>, with current decisions posted the same day that they are released by the Court. A number of historic Supreme Court decisions are available as well at <www.law.cornell.edu/supct/cases/historic.html>. For oral arguments from historic Supreme Court cases, the Northwestern University site known as Oyez Oyez Oyez provides recordings digitized from tapes in the National Archives. The site can be accessed at <oyez.at.nwu.edu/oyez.html>. To listen to the arguments, one needs RealAudio software installed on a computer, but Oyez offers a link to another Internet site where this software can be downloaded for free. Finally, edited versions of some Supreme Court cases are available at the website for this text at <www.worthpublishers.com/policenter.html>.

Decisions by lower federal courts and state courts may also be important in studying constitutional law. The *Federal Reporter* series publishes most decisions of the United States Courts of Appeals, and the *Federal Supplement* series publishes selected United States District Court decisions. Important state decisions are published in official versions by the various states. In addition, the privately published *National Reporter* series groups most decisions of state appellate courts in regional reporters. The *Southeastern Reporter,* for example, contains state appellate decisions from West Virginia, Virginia, North Carolina, South Carolina, and Georgia.

**Statutes.** Statutes (laws) comprise another important source material in constitutional law. The U.S. Government Printing Office initially publishes each federal law separately as so-called slip laws, which are numbered chronologically: The Freedom of Information Act (1974) is cited as Pub. L 93-502, the *93* indicating the Congress and the *502* the numerical order in which the law appears. At the end of each session of Congress, the slip laws are collected and published in chronological order in *Statutes at Large.* Citations to *Statutes at Large* are by volume and page: The Freedom of Information Act is cited as 88 Stat. 1561, the *88* indicating the volume and the *1561* the initial page.

The single most useful official source for researching statutes is the *United States Code*. The *U.S. Code* arranges the law by subject into fifty titles, thus directing the researcher to all the federal laws pertaining to a topic. Each of the fifty titles is subdivided further into chapters, sections, and subsections. Accordingly, the citation for the Freedom of Information Act is 5 U.S.C. §552, the *5* indicating the title and the *552* the section of the code.

**Executive-Branch Materials.** Among the executive-branch materials that may be of interest in constitutional law are presidential documents, such as executive orders and presidential proclamations, and administrative agency rules and regulations. The most comprehensive source for presidential materials is the *Weekly Compilation of Presidential Documents,* published by the U.S. Government Printing Office. Orders and proclamations of general applicability and legal effect also can be found in the *Federal Register,* the daily official publication of executive branch actions.

The *Federal Register* also contains all rules, regulations, and orders issued by federal administrative agencies. Because the *Register* is published daily, it presents executive-branch materials chronologically. This mass of materials is organized topically in the *Code of Federal Regulations,* which divides the general and permanent rules published in the *Federal Register* into fifty titles representing broad areas subject to federal regulations. Each title is subdivided further into chapters, which usually bear the name of the issuing agency, and into parts, which pertain to specific regulatory areas. For example, the Department of Justice regulations pertaining to production or disclosure of information under the Freedom of Information Act are found at 28 CFR § 16.

## NOTES

1 Alexis de Tocqueville, *Democracy in America,* ed. J. P. Mayer (Garden City, N.Y.: Doubleday, 1969), p. 270.

2 Underlying the adoption of the Eleventh Amendment was widespread disenchantment with the Court's decision in *Chisholm* v. *Georgia* (1793), in which it was held that Chisholm, a citizen of South Carolina, could sue the state of Georgia in the federal courts.

3 "Shufflin' Sam" Thompson had been arrested for loitering while waiting in a bar for his bus and shuffling his feet in time to music from a jukebox. When he protested against his arrest, he was also charged with disorderly conduct. He was convicted on both charges and fined $10 for each. Because Kentucky law provided no opportunity to appeal fines of less than $20, Thompson petitioned for Supreme Court review. The Court accepted the case and ruled unanimously that the convictions were not supported by evidence and therefore amounted to a denial of due process of law.

4 Cases may also come to the Supreme Court by *certification.* Under this rarely used procedure, a lower federal court requests instruction from the Supreme Court on a point of law.

5 "Paid" cases are those in which the petitioners have paid the $200 filing fee and supplied the prescribed copies of briefs and other legal materials. An *in forma pauperis* case is one in which an impoverished petitioner requests review of a lower-court decision. These cases generally involve criminal appeals filed by prisoners who cannot afford expert legal assistance. In such cases the Court waives the filing fee and the other requirements it enforces in "paid" cases. For an excellent study of how one *in forma pauperis* petition led to a landmark Supreme Court decision guaranteeing indigent defendants a right to counsel at trial, see Anthony Lewis, *Gideon's Trumpet* (New York: Random House, 1964).

6 The Supreme Court established the procedural rules governing appeals to and the operations of the Court. These rules were revised most recently in 1980.

7 The discussion in this paragraph relies primarily on David M. O'Brien, "The Rehnquist Court's Shrinking Plenary Docket," *Judicature* 81 (1997): 58–65.

8 "Retired Chief Justice Warren Attacks . . . Freund Study Group's Composition and Proposal," *American Bar Association Journal* 59 (July 1973): 728.

9 65 U.S. Law Week 3217 (October 8, 1996).

10 During his tenure on the Supreme Court (1947–58), Justice Harold Burton kept systematic records of the conference votes on whether to hear cases. Studies based on his papers include Doris Marie Provine, *Case Selection in the United States Supreme Court* (Chicago: University of Chicago Press, 1980); S. Sidney Ulmer, "The Decision to Grant Certiorari as an Indicator to Decision 'On the Merits,' " *Polity* 4 (1972); and Ulmer, "Selecting Cases for Supreme Court Review: An Underdog Model," *American Political Science Review* 72 (1978).

11 Lawrence Baum, *The Supreme Court of the United States,* 5th ed. (Washington, D.C.: CQ Press, 1992), p. 116. The case upholding use of such roadblocks is *Michigan Department of State Police* v. *Sitz,* 110 L.Ed.2d 412 (1990).

12 Chief Justice Fred Vinson in "Work of the U.S. Supreme Court," *Texas Bar Journal* 12 (1949): 551.

13 It eventually struck down such laws in the aptly named *Loving* v. *Virginia,* 388 U.S. 1 (1967).

14 Baum, *The Supreme Court,* p. 115.

15 Harlan's statement is reported in Anthony Lewis, *Gideon's Trumpet,* p. 162, n. 23.

16 The leading exposition of this viewpoint is Jeffrey A. Segal and Harold J. Spaeth, *The Supreme Court and the Attitudinal Model* (New York: Cambridge University Press, 1993).

17 See, for example, Lee Epstein and Joseph F. Kobylka, *The Supreme Court and Legal Change: Abortion and the Death Penalty* (Chapel Hill: University of North Carolina Press, 1992).

18 See, for example, Lee Epstein and Jack Knight. *The Choices Justices Make* (Washington, D.C.: CQ Press, 1998); Walter F. Murphy, *Elements of Judicial Strategy* (Chicago: University of Chicago Press, 1964); Alexander M. Bickel, *The Unpublished Opinions of Mr. Justice Brandeis: The Supreme Court at Work* (Cambridge, Mass.: Harvard University Press, 1957); and David O'Brien, *Storm Center: The Supreme Court in American Politics* (New York: W. W. Norton, 1986).

19 Lewis F. Powell, Jr., "What the Justices are Saying . . . ," *American Bar Association Journal* 62 (1976): 1454.

20 Saul Brenner, "Fluidity on the United States Supreme Court: A Reexamination," *American Journal of Political Science* 24 (1980).

21 Henry J. Abraham, *The Judicial Process,* 5th ed. (New York: Oxford University Press, 1986), p. 223.

22 Hand's comment is contained in an intracourt memorandum quoted in Marvin Schick, *Learned Hand's Court* (Baltimore, Md.: Johns Hopkins Press, 1970), p. 167.

23 For a discussion of initial state-court responses to *Escobedo* v. *Illinois* and *Miranda* v. *Arizona,* see Neil T. Romans, "The Role of State Supreme Courts in Judicial Policy Making: *Escobedo, Miranda* and the Use of Impact Analysis," *Western Political Quarterly* 27 (1974): 526–535.

24 Neil A. Milner, *The Court and Local Enforcement: The Impact of Miranda* (Beverly Hills, Cal.: Sage Publications, 1971), p. 225, Table 11-2.

25 For a discussion of the Court's legitimating role, see Charles L. Black, Jr., *The People and the Court* (New York: Macmillan, 1960).

26 See C. Vann Woodward, *The Strange Career of Jim Crow,* rev. ed. (New York: Oxford University Press, 1966).

27 The Eleventh Amendment overruled *Chisholm* v. *Georgia* (1793); the Fourteenth Amendment, *Dred Scott* v. *Sandford* (1857); the Sixteenth Amendment, *Pollock* v. *Farmers' Loan & Trust Co.* (1895); the Twenty-fourth

Amendment, which overruled *Breedlove* v. *Suttles* (1937); and the Twenty-sixth Amendment, *Oregon* v. *Mitchell* (1970).

28 Data on changes in attitudes toward desegregation are summarized in Robert Weissberg, *Public Opinion and Popular Government* (Englewood Cliffs, N.J.: Prentice-Hall, 1976), pp. 110–111; and Gerald N. Rosenberg, *The Hollow Hope* (Chicago: University of Chicago Press, 1991), pp. 125–131.

## SELECTED READING


Abraham, Henry J. *Justices and Presidents: A Political History of Appointments to the Supreme Court,* 3d ed. (New York: Oxford University Press, 1992).

Baum, Lawrence. *The Supreme Court,* 5th ed. (Washington, D.C.: CQ Press, 1995).

Biskupic, Joan and Elder Witt. *Guide to the U.S. Supreme Court,* 3d ed. (Washington, D.C.: CQ Press, 1997).

Epstein, Lee and Jack Knight. *The Choices Justices Make* (Washington, D.C.: CQ Press, 1998).

———, Jeffery A. Segal, Harold J. Spaeth, and Thomas G. Walker. *The Supreme Court Compendium: Decisions and Developments* (Washington, D.C.: CQ Press, 1993).

Fisher, Louis. *Constitutional Dialogues* (Princeton, N.J.: Princeton University Press, 1988).

Fried, Charles. *Order and Law: Arguing the Reagan Revolution—A Firsthand Account* (New York: Simon & Schuster, 1991).

Gates, John B. and Charles A. Johnson, eds. *The American Courts: A Critical Assessment* (Washington, D.C.: CQ Press, 1991).

Hall, Kermit, ed. *The Oxford Companion to the Supreme Court of the United States* (New York: Oxford University Press, 1992).

Johnson, Charles A. and Bradley C. Canon. *Judicial Policies: Implementation and Impact* (Washington, D.C.: CQ Press, 1984).

Murphy, Walter F. *Elements of Judicial Strategy* (Chicago: University of Chicago Press, 1964).

O'Brien, David M. *Storm Center: The Supreme Court in American Politics,* 3d ed. (New York: W. W. Norton, 1993).

Perry, H. W., Jr. *Deciding to Decide: Agenda Setting in the United States Supreme Court* (Cambridge, Mass.: Harvard University Press, 1991).

Rehnquist, William H. *The Supreme Court: How It Was, How It Is* (New York: William Morrow and Co., 1987).

Rosenberg, Gerald N. *The Hollow Hope: Can Courts Bring About Social Change?* (Chicago: University of Chicago Press, 1991).

Segal, Jeffrey A. and Harold J. Spaeth. *The Supreme Court and the Attitudinal Model.* (Cambridge, Mass.: Cambridge University Press, 1993).

Silverstein, Mark. *Judicious Choices: The New Politics of Supreme Court Confirmations.* (New York: W. W. Norton & Co., 1994).

Stern, Robert L. and Eugene Gressman. *Supreme Court Practice,* 5th ed. (Washington, D.C.: Bureau of National Affairs, 1978).

Tarr, G. Alan. *Judicial Process and Judicial Policymaking,* 2d ed. (Belmont, Calif.: Wadsworth Publishing Co., 1998).

Witt, Elder. *Congressional Quarterly's Guide to the U. S. Supreme Court,* 2d ed. (Washington, D.C.: Congressional Quarterly, 1990).

★

THE POWER OF JUDICIAL REVIEW

*Marbury* v. *Madison* (1803)
*Eakin* v. *Raub* (1825)
*Cooper* v. *Aaron* (1958)
*Plaut* v. *Spendthrift Farm, Inc.* (1995)

EXTERNALLY IMPOSED RESTRAINTS ON JUDICIAL REVIEW

*Ex Parte McCardle* (1869)

COURT-IMPOSED RESTRAINTS ON JUDICIAL REVIEW

*Frothingham* v. *Mellon* (1923)
*Flast* v. *Cohen* (1968)
*Lujan* v. *Defenders of Wildlife* (1992)
*Luther* v. *Borden* (1849)
*Baker* v. *Carr* (1962)
*Nixon* v. *United States* (1993)

THE EXPANDING ROLE OF THE COURTS

*DeShaney* v. *Winnebago County Department of Social Services* (1989)

THE COURTS, JUDICIAL REVIEW, AND
THE PROBLEM OF LEGITMACY

NOTES

SELECTED READING

CASES

★

# 3
# THE JUDICIAL POWER

The significance the Framers attached to the courts and the judicial power can be surmised by noting the placement, brevity, and generality of the judicial article. To begin with, Article III, establishing the federal judiciary, follows Article I, establishing the legislative branch, and Article II, establishing the executive branch. By so arranging the articles, the Framers addressed each branch, in the words of James Wilson, a member of the Constitutional Convention and an original justice on the Supreme Court, "as its greatness deserves to be considered."[1] Further, Article III is only about a sixth as long as the legislative article and only about a third as long as the executive article. Article I specifies in great detail the qualifications of Representatives and Senators (including age and citizenship requirements), the size of the two houses of Congress, the procedures they must follow, and the powers they are authorized or prohibited to exercise. Article II is likewise quite detailed in its discussion of the president's qualifications, mode of appointment, powers, and responsibilities. By contrast, Article III merely vests the judicial power of the United States in one Supreme Court (its size is unspecified) and in "such inferior Courts as the Congress may from time to time ordain and establish." Article III imposes no qualifications on the judges—not even the requirement of citizenship—and outlines no procedures the courts are obliged to follow.

The Framers left the judicial article as brief and incomplete as they did because they believed what Alexander Hamilton would later declare in *The Federalist,* No. 78: "The judiciary is beyond comparison the weakest of the three departments of power." With him, they understood the judiciary to be "the least dangerous to the political rights of the constitution; because it will be least in a capacity to annoy or injure them."

They recognized that in any republican government the greatest threat of tyranny would come from the legislative branch, which, as James Madison declared in the Constitutional Convention, "had evinced a powerful tendency . . . to absorb all power into its vortex." Consequently, they devoted much of their time and energies during the Constitutional Convention to designing institutional arrangements and drafting specific delegations of power that would obviate the threat of legislative tyranny. Most of their discussions and decisions concerning the judiciary—its powers and functions—were influenced by that objective. The judicial branch was one more means by which they sought to check legislative oppression. They did not perceive the judiciary itself to be a potential source of oppression; to the extent that it might pose any danger, they believed it could be adequately checked by the very same Congress that the judiciary helped to curb.

While the judiciary is "the weakest of the three departments" of government, the courts are not entirely without power. Article III of the Constitution assigns to them the "judicial power" of the United States—a mandate never delineated clearly in the Constitution but usually understood to confer the power to decide conflicts between litigants and to issue writs and orders to carry them into effect. Also included under the umbrella of "judicial power" are the punishment of criminal contempts (to maintain the dignity of the court itself) and of civil contempts (to secure the rights of one party in a suit by forcing the other party to obey the court's ruling) and the issuance of writs of mandamus (ordering people or officials to do particular things), injunctions (ordering them to refrain from doing particular things), and habeas corpus (protecting citizens from illegal imprisonment).

Over and above these universally accepted powers, the federal courts have come to exercise the far more important power of judicial review, that is, the power to invalidate those actions of Congress, the executive, and the states that are, in the view of courts, contrary to the Constitution. Although this authority to determine the meaning and application of the Constitution is nowhere defined or even mentioned in the Constitution itself, the federal judiciary in general, and especially the Supreme Court, have come to wield it to such an extent as to have raised in the minds of some observers the specter of judicial supremacy or even of an emerging imperial judiciary. In this chapter, we examine the establishment and general justification of the power of judicial review and discuss the various restraints on its exercise imposed externally by the legislative and executive branches and internally by the courts themselves.

## THE POWER OF JUDICIAL REVIEW

Because the power of judicial review is not explicitly spelled out in the Constitution, it cannot be defended by mere reference to the relevant constitutional text, and its defenders have had to engage in other forms of constitutional interpretation. Two of the earliest and most influential of these interpretations were made by Alexander Hamilton in *The Federalist*, No. 78, and Chief Justice John Marshall in *Marbury* v. *Madison* (1803).

In *The Federalist*, Hamilton argued syllogistically that because "the interpretation of the law is the proper and peculiar province of the courts" and because the Constitution is a law (albeit a "fundamental" one), the courts must interpret the Constitution. He continued:

> It therefore belongs to them to ascertain its meaning as well as the meaning of any particular act proceeding from the legislative body. If there should happen to be an irreconcilable variance between the two, that which has the superior obligation and validity ought of course to be preferred; or in other words, the constitution ought to be preferred to the statute, the intention of the people to the intention of their agents.

In addition to justifying judicial review on the basis of logical reasoning, Hamilton also justified it based on the "natural feebleness of the judiciary." This feebleness arises from the judiciary's inherent incapacity, in comparison with the popularly elected branches, to injure the political rights of the Constitution.

> Whoever attentively considers the different departments of power must perceive, that, in a government in which they are separated from each other, the judiciary, from the nature of its functions, will always be the least in a capacity to annoy or injure them. The executive not only dispenses the honors, but holds the sword of the community. The legislature not only commands the purse, but prescribes the rules by which the duties and rights of every citizen are to be regulated. The judiciary, on the contrary, has no influence over either the sword or the purse; no direction either of the strength or of the wealth of the society; and can take no active resolution whatever. It may truly be said to have neither FORCE nor WILL, but merely judgment; and must ultimately depend upon the aid of the executive arm even for the efficacy of its judgments.

Hamilton also defended judicial review as the means by which the Constitution created by the Framers will remain "limited" in nature. "By a limited constitution, I understand one which contains certain specific exceptions to the legislative authority; such for instance as that it shall pass no bills of attainder, no *ex post facto* laws, and the like." According to Hamilton, "limitations of this kind can be preserved in practice no other way than through the medium of the courts of justice; whose duty it must be to declare all acts contrary to the manifest tenor of the constitution void." Without judicial review, all the reservations of particular rights and privileges would amount to nothing.

Hamilton's argument in *The Federalist*, No. 78, however, must be understood in historical context. His arguments there were primarily in response to a series of Anti-Federalist essays written by Brutus. Brutus sought to discredit the Constitution by, among other things, magnifying the power of the federal judiciary and presenting it as an instrument for consolidating national powers at the expense of the states.[2] In his response in *The Federalist,* No. 78, Hamilton was not so much advocating judicial review as attempting to turn Brutus's arguments against him when he suggested that the Court's power was intended to hold Congress in check and thereby safeguard the states against national aggrandizement by a Congress seeking consolidation. If the Congress were to act "contrary to the manifest tenor of the Constitution" and were to attempt to scuttle the federal structure that the Framers had established, Hamilton argued, the Court could be trusted to invalidate those congressional efforts.

Hamilton's argument in *The Federalist,* No. 78 concerning how the Congress's tendencies toward national aggrandizement would be checked was completely contrary to the argument he made on the same subject in *The Federalist,* No. 33. In No. 78, written after Brutus's essays, he relied exclusively on the Court; in No. 33, written before Brutus, Hamilton never even mentioned the Court. In No. 33, Hamilton discussed the necessary and proper clause, regarded by many Anti-Federalists as a source of unlimited power for Congress, and asked: "[W]ho is to judge the necessity and propriety of the laws to be passed for executing the powers of the Union?" His answer: Congress is to judge "in the first instance the proper exercise of its powers; and its constituents in the last." If the Congress were to use the necessary and proper clause "to overpass the just bounds of its authority and make a tyrannical use of its powers," Hamilton argued that "the people whose creature it is must appeal to the standard they have formed, and take such measures to redress the injury done to the constitution, as the exigency may suggest and prudence justify." He made no reference to the Supreme Court exercising judicial review to negative such congressional actions. All this has prompted the constitutional historian Leonard W. Levy to characterize Hamilton's remarks in No. 78 "as evidence of shrewd political tactics, not of the framers' intention to vest judicial review in the Supreme Court over acts of Congress."[3]

Chief Justice Marshall's defense of judicial review in *Marbury* begins in much the same way as Hamilton's defense in No. 78. In Marshall's own words, "It is emphatically the province and duty of the judicial department to say what the law is. Those who apply the rule to particular cases, must, of necessity, expound and interpret that rule." This argument led him to the conclusion that "a law repugnant to the Constitution is void." Applying that rule in *Marbury,* he found Section 13 of the Judiciary Act of 1789 to be unconstitutional because, he argued, it attempted to expand the original jurisdiction of the Supreme Court in violation of Article III, Section 2 of the Constitution.

The Judiciary Act of 1789 put "flesh on the bare bones" of the judicial article; with it, the First Congress created the entire federal judiciary. (The text of the Act is found in Chapter 7.) Section 13, *inter alia,* expressly gave the Supreme Court power, in cases of appellate jurisdiction, to issue "writs of mandamus, in cases warranted by the principles and usages of law, to any courts appointed, or persons holding office under the authority of the United States." Marshall, however, construed Section 13 as giving the Supreme Court power to issue writs of mandamus in original jurisdiction, thereby expanding the original jurisdiction of the Supreme Court. Marshall's statutory construction of Section 13 is highly questionable, as Section 13 made no reference whatsoever to original jurisdiction.[4] Marshall then engaged in equally questionable constitutional construction by arguing that Article III, Section 2 prohibits Congress from expanding the Court's original jurisdiction. This is questionable, for although Article III, Section 2 bars Congress from reducing the Court's original jurisdiction, it does not prohibit Congress from expanding that jurisdiction by "excepting" into original jurisdiction cases otherwise within the Court's appellate jurisdiction.[5]

George Anastaplo has pointed out the "serious consequences" of Marshall's argument in *Marbury*: "Once the Court insisted that 'excepting' a case from the appellate jurisdiction of the Supreme Court could never mean adding it to the original jurisdiction of the Supreme Court, then it tacitly conceded that it must mean that cases may be altogether removed by Congress from the jurisdiction of the Supreme Court." He continues: "It is revealing that in the very case in which the Supreme Court insisted upon its power of judicial review, it also tacitly recognized a power in Congress to remove cases altogether from the Court's jurisdiction, which means that Congress could routinely remove from review by the Court any cases within its appellate jurisdiction which might result in declarations of the unconstitutionality of acts of Congress. This, alone, should make one wonder about how much sense judicial review makes in our system."[6]

Hamilton's argument on behalf of judicial review in *The Federalist,* No. 78 and Marshall's argument in *Marbury* are reinforced by those who defend judicial review on separation of power grounds: they argue that it was the intention of the Framers that the Court should have the power of judicial review to check and balance the other branches, just as the Congress and the President have other powers at their disposal to check the Court. This line of reasoning suffers from one principal difficulty: The Constitution simply does not make explicit provisions for judicial review but does explicitly provide for impeachment; congressional control of the Court's appellate jurisdiction; congressional determination of the size, shape, and composition of the entire federal judiciary; presidential appointment of judges subject to Senate confirmation; congressional appropriations for the courts; etc. Separation of powers, from which judicial review is inferred, is itself never explicitly mentioned in the Constitution, rather it is inferred from the specific powers that the Constitution assigns to the branches. Judicial review is no more than an inference drawn from an inference.

Agreement with Hamilton and Marshall that it is the province of the Court to say what the law is and acceptance of the argument that judicial review is appropriately inferred from separation of powers does not ensure that differences will not arise over the reach of judicial review. In his opinion in *Eakin* v. *Raub* (1825), Justice Gibson of the Pennsylvania Supreme Court insisted that "[t]he ordinary and essential powers of the judiciary do not extend to the annulling of an act of the legislature." Rather,

> it is the business of the judiciary, to interpret the laws, not scan the authority of the lawgiver; and without the latter, it cannot take cognizance of a collision between a law and the constitution. . .
>
> But it has been said to be emphatically the business of the judiciary to ascertain and pronounce what the law is; and that this necessarily involves a consideration of the constitution. It does so: but how far? If the judiciary will inquire into anything beside the form of enactment, where shall it stop?

In its sharp opposition to the position of Hamilton and Marshall, Gibson's approach to judicial review indicates how differing understandings of "separation of powers" can shape contrasting views on the proper powers and responsibilities of the judiciary.[7]

Federalism, as well as separation of powers, played a role in the evolution of judicial review. In *Fletcher* v. *Peck* (1810), *Martin* v. *Hunter's Lessee* (1816), and *Cohens* v. *Virginia* (1821), the Marshall Court expanded its authority beyond that staked out in *Marbury* by asserting its powers to review the constitutionality of actions taken not only by the other branches of the national government, but also by the states. In *Fletcher,* it invalidated for the first time an act of a state legislature. Then, in *Martin* and *Cohens,* it defended the legitimacy of Supreme Court review of state court judgments in (respectively) civil and criminal cases that presented federal constitutional questions. These decisions rested primarily on the Marshall Court's interpretations of two constitutional provisions: Article III, Section 2, which provides that "the judicial Power shall extend to *all* Cases in Law and Equity, arising under this Constitution, the Laws of the United States, and Treaties made, or which shall be made, under their Authority"; and Article VI, Section 2, which declares that "this Constitution and the Laws of the United States which shall be made in Pursuance thereof; and all Treaties made, or which shall be made, under the Authority of the United States, shall be the supreme Law of the land; and the Judges in every State shall be bound thereby, any Thing in the Constitution or Laws of any State to the Contrary notwithstanding." The Court's contemporary reliance on and understanding of the supremacy clause is apparent in *Cooper* v. *Aaron* (1958); in this remarkable opinion, the Court held that its interpretations of the Constitution are as much "the supreme Law of the Land" as the Constitution itself.

Interestingly, judicial review has not only been justified as consistent with the principles of separation of powers and federalism but has, in turn, become a principal means of defending these principles. For example, in *Plaut* v. *Spendthrift Farms* (1995), the Supreme Court struck down a congressional measure that retroactively allowed for the reopening of final judgments in federal courts. The Court held that "[T]he doctrine of separation of powers is a *structural safeguard* rather than a remedy to be applied only when specific harm, or risk of specific harm, can be identified. In its major features (of which the conclusiveness of judicial judgments is assuredly one) it is a prophylactic device, establishing high walls and clear distinctions because low walls and vague distinctions will not be judicially defensible in the heat of interbranch conflict. . . ." It continued: "Separation of powers, a distinctively American political doctrine, profits from the advice authored by a distinctively American poet: Good fences make good neighbors." Similarly, in *Printz* v. *United States* (1997), the Supreme Court invalidated those provisions of the Brady Handgun Violence Prevention Act which commanded state and local law enforcement officers to conduct background checks on handgun purchasers. Relying on *New York* v. *United States* (1992) that held that Congress cannot compel the States to enact or enforce a federal regulatory program, the Court majority declared that "Congress cannot circumvent that prohibition by conscripting the State's officers directly. The Federal Government may neither issue directives requiring the States to address particular problems, nor command the States' officers, or those of their political subdivisions, to administer or enforce a federal regulatory program. It matters not whether policymaking is involved, and no case-by-case weighing of the burdens of benefits is necessary; such commands are fundamentally incompatible with our constitutional system of dual sovereignty."

Justifying its exercise of judicial review on the grounds of separation of powers or federalism, the Court through the end of its 1997 term has struck down a total of 141 different federal laws and voided 1,116 different state statutes and 128 municipal ordinances.[8] These statistics, however, do not reflect what defenders of judicial review consider the most significant effect of the Court's power of judicial review. In giving the Court the power to strike down an unconstitutional legislative action, judicial review *ipso facto* empowers the Court to validate a legislative action as being within constitutionally granted powers and not violating constitutional limitations.[9] The significance of this legitimating function was pointed out by Chief Justice Hughes: "[F]ar more important to the development of the country than the decisions holding acts of Congress to be invalid, have been those in which the authority of Congress has been sustained and adequate national power to meet the necessities of a growing country has been found to exist within constitutional limitations."[10] Together, the validating function and the checking function of judicial review have contributed mightily to the power of the Court—and to its vulnerability.

## EXTERNALLY IMPOSED RESTRAINTS ON JUDICIAL REVIEW

The Court's power of judicial review has often brought it into conflict with those whose measures it has invalidated. Given the necessarily problematic nature of the Court's power to review the acts of the coequal branches of the national government, it should come as no surprise that most such controversies have involved Congress and the executive. Individually or together, these branches have imposed or threatened to impose on the Court such sanctions as impeachment, court packing, congressional review of judicial decisions, remedial constitutional amendments, the requirement of an extraordinary majority of the Court to invalidate legislation, and presidential refusal to enforce a decision.[11] (At the state level, nullification and even resort to force have greeted Court decisions.) Historically more important than any of those measures, however, have been sporadic congressional attempts to reduce the Court's appellate jurisdiction. Article III, Section 2 of the Constitution grants to the Supreme Court "appellate Jurisdiction, both as to Law and Fact, with such Exceptions, and under such Regulations, as the Congress shall make." In the post-Civil War period, for example, Congress invoked this constitutional authority in withdrawing from the Court's appellate jurisdiction a politically embarrassing case on which the justices had already heard argument. In *Ex Parte McCardle* (1869), the Court agreed unanimously that such drastic action lay within Congress's power and dismissed the case for want of jurisdiction.

The unanimous *McCardle* decision reflects the prevailing view that the Congress's power over the appellate jurisdiction of the Supreme Court is plenary, or absolute. Some scholars have argued, however, that Congress's power to make exceptions is constitutionally limited to such exceptions as will not interfere with the essential role of the Court.[12] According to Leonard Ratner, a leading proponent of this position, "Reasonably interpreted, the clause means 'with such exceptions and under such regulations as Congress may make, not inconsistent with the essential functions of the Supreme Court under this Constitution.' "

Ratner's argument is fraught with difficulties. To begin with, it is contrary to the clear words of the Constitution. There is absolutely nothing in the unqualified letter of the Exceptions Clause that either expressly or implicitly suggests that congressional authority under Article III, Section 2, is limited to making "inessential exceptions." In addition, along with raising the problem of determining the Court's essential role, any circumscription of Congress's power makes the Court the final arbiter in any controversy over the extent of its own powers. In other words, despite the express grant of power to Congress given in the Constitution, Ratner and others of like mind maintain that no statute can constitutionally deprive the Court of its essential role *and* that that role is to be whatever the Court says it is. As Charles Rice points out in rebuttal, "It is hardly in keeping with the spirit of checks and balances to read such a virtually unlimited power into the Constitution. If the Framers intended so to permit the Supreme Court to define its own jurisdiction even against the will of Congress, it is fair to say that they would have made that intention explicit."[13] In fact, such an intention clearly contradicts the thinking of the Framers. Nothing in the records of the Federal Convention of 1787 or of the various state ratifying conventions contravenes the position set forth in *The Federalist*, No. 80, in which, in reviewing in detail the powers of the federal judiciary, Hamilton observed that "if some partial inconveniences should appear to be connected with the incorporation of any of them into the plan, it ought to be recollected that the national legislature will have ample authority to make such exceptions and to prescribe such regulations as will be calculated to obviate or remove these inconveniences."

Finally, the assertion that Congress's power under the Exceptions Clause is limited contradicts the firm, consistent, and unwavering understanding of the Supreme Court. No justice has ever denied Congress's broad power under Article III. As one scholar has observed, "the government body most ready to assert the power of Congress to deprive the Court of its appellate jurisdiction has been the Court itself."[14] In his dissent in *Glidden Co.* v. *Zdanok* (1962), Justice Douglas did declare that "[t]here is a serious question whether the *McCardle* case could command a majority today," and this passage is frequently cited to suggest that the contemporary Supreme Court would not accept congressional restrictions of its appellate jurisdiction equivalent to those upheld in *McCardle*. The context of Justice Douglas's dictum, however, suggests something quite different: namely, that if Congress were to attempt to deprive the Supreme Court of jurisdiction over a case that is already before the Court, it is questionable whether *McCardle* would be followed today. Douglas subsequently expressed his understanding of the broader question of Congress's power over the appellate jurisdiction of the Supreme Court in his concurrence in *Flast* v. *Cohen* (1968): "As respects our appellate jurisdiction, Congress may largely fashion it as Congress desires by reason of the express provisions of Section 2, Article III. See *Ex Parte McCardle*. . . ."

In the face of these formidable objections, those who would deny Congress's plenary power under the Exceptions Clause have failed to gain acceptance for their point of view.[15] Both the Warren and the Burger courts have been the targets of court-curbing initiatives. In 1957 the Jenner-Butler bill, prohibiting the Supreme Court from hearing appeal cases that dealt with national security issues, failed by the narrowest of margins in the Senate.[16] Two decades later, Senator Jesse Helms's amendment to S. 210 (the bill creating the Department of Education), which would have forbade the Supreme Court to hear cases challenging state-sanctioned voluntary school prayers, passed the Senate but ultimately died in the House when the Ninety-sixth Congress adjourned. During the early 1980s, scores of bills were introduced in the Congress that would deprive the Supreme Court of appellate jurisdiction either to hear cases involving such issues as abortion rights and voluntary prayer in the public schools or to order school busing to achieve racial integration.[17]

## COURT-IMPOSED RESTRAINTS ON JUDICIAL REVIEW

To minimize the likelihood of Congress or the executive seeking to impose restraints on its exercise of judicial review, the Court has developed a set of policies (Alexander Bickel calls them "passive virtues"[18]) restricting the general circumstances under which it and the lower courts will engage in constitutional adjudication. The part these restraints (at once both constitutionally based yet self-imposed) play in the exercise of judicial power is no less important than the part played by judicial review itself. As Professor John Roche observed,

> Judicial self-restraint and judicial power seem to be the opposite sides of the same coin: it has been by judicious application of the former that the latter has been maintained. A tradition beginning with Marshall's coup in *Marbury* v. *Madison* . . . suggests that the Court's power has been maintained by a wise refusal to employ it in unequal combat.[19]

The Court's self-declared limitations on its power of judicial review fall into the following categories.

### Cases and Controversies

Article III, Section 2 declares that the judicial power of the federal courts shall extend to "Cases" and "Controversies," that is, to litigation involving a real conflict of interests or rights between contending parties. According to its interpretation of this mandate, the federal judiciary generally will not entertain hypothetical, feigned, or collusive suits or render advisory opinions.[20] In recent years, though, this self-imposed barrier to litigation has been lowered by the Supreme Court itself. Whereas in 1955 Justice Robert Jackson could call this restriction "perhaps the most significant . . . limitation upon judicial power," by 1976 Archibald Cox felt compelled to acknowledge that the Court has moved "away from the view that constitutional adjudication is only collateral to the essential judicial task of deciding lawsuits and towards the notion that the primary function of the Supreme Court of the United States is to ensure that other organs of government observe constitutional limitations."[21]

### Standing to Sue

Closely related to the need for the presence of a case or controversy is the requirement that the party bringing suit must have standing to sue. To have standing, the party invoking judicial power must show "not only that the statute is invalid, but that he has sustained or is immediately in danger of sustaining some direct injury as the result of its enforcement, and not merely that he suffers in some indefinite way in common with people generally."[22] Standing is required because, as the Court noted in *Baker* v. *Carr,* "a personal stake in the outcome of the controversy . . . assures that concrete adverseness which sharpens the presentation of issues upon which the court so largely depends for illumination of difficult constitutional questions."

One of the most interesting questions involving standing faced by the Court over the years has been whether the mere payment of taxes provides the taxpayer with sufficient standing to challenge governmental action involving the expenditure of funds. The Court's original answer to this question was given in *Frothingham* v. *Mellon* (1923), in which it rejected unequivocally the contention that taxpayers *qua* taxpayers have standing. In the unanimous opinion of the justices, a taxpayer's interest in the monies of the Treasury "is shared by millions of others; is comparatively minute and indeterminable; and the effect upon future taxation, of any payment out of the funds, so remote, fluctuating and uncertain, that no basis is afforded for an appeal to the preventive powers of a court of equity." Standing, the Court concluded, requires the demonstration of a personal interest that is sharp and distinct from the interests of taxpayers in general. In *Flast* v. *Cohen,* however, the Court qualified *Frothingham* by easing somewhat the requirements for standing. Under the revised guidelines, federal taxpayers would be allowed to challenge congressional spending if the legislation in question emanated from the Taxing and Spending Clause of Article I, Section 8, and if the taxpayers could show a nexus, or link, between their status as taxpayers and a specific constitutional limitation on the exercise of the spending power.[23]

The relatively loose criteria for standing outlined in *Flast* made it easier for litigants to bring policy disputes before the judiciary, and they were soon tightened. In *United States* v. *Richardson* (1974) the Court held that a taxpayer as such has no standing to challenge the constitutionality of that provision of the Central Intelligence Agency Act which permits the CIA, unlike other federal agencies, to keep its budget secret. Five justices ruled that taxpayers are barred from using the courts as forums to air "general grievances" about governmental policies and procedures. Thus in *Richardson* (as well as in *Schlesinger* v. *Reservists' Committee to Stop the War,* announced the same day), the Court denied that *Flast* could be interpreted to allow a taxpayer's suit in the absence of a demonstrable and concrete injury suffered by the plaintiff.

An insistence that plaintiffs show something more than a generalized grievance to gain standing runs through the Court's rulings on the question of standing.[24] In *Valley Forge Christian College* v. *Americans United for Separation of Church and State* (1982), the Court rejected the respondents' assertion that they had standing by virtue of an " 'injury in fact' to their shared individuated right to a government that 'shall make no law respecting an establishment of religion.' " As Justice Rehnquist observed for the Court majority, "although they claim that the Constitution has been violated, they claim nothing else. They fail to identify any personal injury suffered by the plaintiffs as a consequence of the alleged constitutional error, other than the psychological consequence presumably produced by observation of conduct with which one disagrees. That is not sufficient to confer standing under Article III, even though the disagreement is phrased in constitutional terms." Moreover, he continued, "Their claim that the government has violated the Establishment Clause does not provide a special license to roam the country in search of governmental wrongdoing and to reveal their discoveries in federal court. The federal courts were simply not constituted as ombudsmen of the general welfare." Likewise, in *Allen* v. *Wright* (1984), the Court denied standing to black parents who sought to challenge the failure of the Internal Revenue Service to deny tax-exempt status to private schools that they alleged were practicing racial discrimination. The parents claimed that the tax exemptions harmed them directly and interfered with their children's opportunity to receive an education in desegregated public schools. Justice O'Connor dismissed the parents' claims as "speculative." She spoke for a six-member majority when she declared:

> The links in the chain of causation between the challenged Government conduct and the asserted injury are far too weak for the chain as a whole to sustain respondents' standing. . . . The idea of separation of powers that underlies standing doctrine explains why our cases preclude the conclusion that respondents' alleged injury "fairly can be traced to the challenged action" of the IRS. . . . Carried to its logical end, [respondents'] approach would have the federal courts as virtually continuing monitors of the wisdom and soundness of Executive action; such a role is appropriate for the Congress acting through its committees and the "power of the purse"; it is not the role of the judiciary, absent actual present or immediately threatened injury resulting from unlawful governmental action. The Constitution, after all, assigns to the Executive Branch, and not to the Judicial Branch, the duty to "take Care that the Laws be faithfully executed." We could not recognize respondents' standing in this case without running afoul of that structural principle.

Finally, in *Lujan* v. *Defenders of Wildlife* (1992), the Court denied standing to wildlife conservationists who argued unsuccessfully that they were injured by the Secretary of the Interior because he did not require the Agency for International Development (AID) to consult with him under the provisions of the Endangered Species Act of 1973 before the agency helped to fund the rehabilitation of the Aswan High Dam on the Nile, thereby threatening the traditional habitat of the endangered Nile crocodile that the respondent conservationists hoped someday to observe.

### Mootness

Another barrier to judicial review is mootness, a doctrine closely related to the Court's insistence on standing and its refusal to render advisory opinions. When plaintiffs who clearly have standing to sue at the outset of litigation confront a change either in the facts or in the law that deprives them of a necessary stake in the outcome, the issue involved in the suit is rendered moot. The mootness doctrine requires that the case or controversy exist at all stages of review, not merely at the time the complaint was filed.

Although the Court in the main adheres to the mootness doctrine, fidelity to this technical barrier to adjudication is by no means absolute, as the contrasting holdings in *Roe* v. *Wade* (1973) and *DeFunis* v. *Odegaard* (1974) illustrate. In *Roe,* the plaintiff was an (initially) pregnant woman who challenged the constitutionality of abortion laws; her suit was initiated in 1970, but the Court's decision was not handed down until January of 1973. Even though the plaintiff was no longer pregnant, the Court refused to dismiss the case as moot. Justice Blackmun spoke for the Court: "Pregnancy provides a classic justification for a conclusion of nonmootness. It truly could be 'capable of repetition, yet evading review.' "

In *DeFunis,* on the other hand, the Court invoked the mootness doctrine to avoid ruling on the emotionally charged issue of affirmative action/reverse discrimination. Under a lower court order Marco DeFunis, Jr. was admitted to law school at the University of Washington, and by a Supreme Court stay he was able to remain in law school while he litigated his claim that the law school had practiced reverse discrimination and violated the Equal Protection Clause when it denied him admission while accepting minority applicants with less qualifications. He was in his final term when the Supreme Court handed down its decision, and the Court in its per curiam opinion found that fact sufficient to render the case moot: "Since he was now registered for his final term, it is evident that he will be given an opportunity to complete all academic and other requirements for graduation, and, if he does so, will receive his diploma regardless of any decision this Court might reach on the merits of this case."

The Court majority did not find persuasive Justice Brennan's objection that "any number of unexpected events—illness, economic necessity, even academic failure—might prevent his graduation at the end of the term. Were that misfortune to befall, and were petitioner required to register for yet another term, the prospect that he would again face the hurdle of the admissions policy is real, not fanciful."

### Ripeness

Another technical barrier to adjudication of constitutional claims is the requirement that a suit not be brought to the courts prematurely, while the relationships between the parties are still developing or in flux. Unless a dispute is sufficiently real, well developed, and specific—in a word, *ripe*—any decision reached by the court necessarily will hinge on a series of predictions about the probable conduct of the parties, and those predictions will in turn depend on contingencies and guesses about the future. Because no principled judgment is possible in such circumstances, the courts have developed the ripeness requirement to avoid having to speculate about contingencies and uncertainties.[25]

### Nonjusticiable Political Questions

The presence of a case or controversy, standing to sue, the absence of mootness, and ripeness are characteristics that make a jurisdictional issue a justiciable one, that is, a case that the Supreme Court will decide. A different kind of restraint on judicial review comes into play when the Court considers a case to be nonjusticiable despite clear jurisdictional authority. The most common and controversial nonjusticiable cases are those in which the plaintiffs seek adjudication of questions that, in the view of the courts, can better be solved via the political process.

The first explicit application of the political-questions doctrine occured in *Luther* v. *Borden* (1849), in which the Court held that enforcement of Article IV, Section 4 of the Constitution, guaranteeing a republican form of government for all states, was the exclusive responsibility of the popularly elected branches. Until the Court's decision in *Baker* in 1962, questions involving legislative and congressional reapportionment were also deemed to be political. Specifically, in the crucial case of *Colegrove* v. *Green* (1946), Justice Frankfurter held for a plurality of the Court that districting was a political question beyond the reach of the Court, warning that "courts ought not to enter this political thicket." Sixteen years later, however, the justices did exactly that in *Baker* v. *Carr,* in which the Court directed a federal court in Tennessee to hear a case challenging legislative malapportionment as unconstitutional under the Equal Protection Clause. Justice William Brennan's opinion for the Court in *Baker* is generally considered to be the authoritative statement by the Court on the political-questions doctrine.[26]

In it, he declared that a political question is present if there is "a textually demonstrable constitutional commitment of the issue to a coordinate political department; or a lack of judicially discoverable and manageable standards for resolving it; or the impossibility of deciding without an initial policy determination of a kind clearly for nonjudicial discretion; or the impossibility of a court's undertaking independent resolution without expressing lack of the respect due coordinate branches of government; or an unusual need for unquestioning adherence to a political decision already made; or the potentiality of embarrassment from multifarious pronouncements by various departments on one question." Applying these *Baker* factors in *United States Department of Commerce v. Montana* (1992), the Court concluded that Montana's constitutional challenge to a congressional statute that authorized the allocation to that state of one (and not two) Representatives in Congress after the 1990 census did not raise a political question unamenable to judicial resolution. Justice

Stevens wrote for a unanimous Court when he declared: "The controversy between Montana and the Government turns on the proper interpretation of the relevant constitutional provisions. As our previous rejection of the political question doctrine in this context should make clear, the interpretation of the apportionment provisions of the Constitution is well within the competence of the Judiciary." A year later in *Nixon* v. *United States* (1993), however, it held a legal controversy over the Senate's conduct in the impeachment and removal of a federal judge to be a political question because of the "textually demonstrable commitment" to the Senate of the power to try impeachments and because of the lack of "manageable judicial standards" to review the Senate's actions.

### Avoiding the Constitutional Issue

In his concurrence in *Ashwander* v. *Tennessee Valley Authority* (1936), Justice Louis Brandeis spelled out yet another policy that the Court generally has followed to avoid antagonizing its coequal branches through too-frequent review of their actions:

> The Court will not pass on a constitutional question, although properly presented by the record, if there is also present some other ground on which the case may be disposed of. This rule has found some varied application. Thus, if a case can be decided on either of two grounds, one involving a constitutional question, the other a question of statutory construction or general law, the Court will decide only the latter. . . Appeals from the highest court of a state challenging its decision of a question under the federal Constitution are frequently dismissed because the judgment can be sustained on an independent state ground.

### Presumption of Constitutionality

In general, the Court presumes that a statute is constitutional unless the opposite is clearly demonstrated. Justice Bushrod Washington provided the rationale for this policy in his opinion for the Court in *Ogden* v. *Saunders* (1827): "It is but a decent respect due to the wisdom, integrity, and patriotism of the legislative body, by which any law is passed, to presume in favor of its validity. . . ." It must be emphasized, however, that today this presumption of constitutionality is confined almost exclusively to economic and social legislation. In the contemporary era, the Court usually has regarded as presumptively unconstitutional legislation that burdens "insular and discrete minorities" or that infringes upon First Amendment freedoms.[27]

## THE EXPANDING ROLE OF THE COURTS

Although the set of policies described above is not exhaustive, it does indicate the range and variety of techniques and devices available to the judiciary when it wishes to avoid adjudicating constitutional claims.

These techniques are not always employed. As Henry J. Abraham notes, they are little more than "maxims of judicial self-restraint." Different Courts and different justices have cleaved to them with varying degrees of fidelity.[28] Generally speaking, in recent decades, the Supreme Court has displayed less fidelity to these "passive virtues" than earlier Courts. Perceiving that its role includes representing those interests in society that failed to receive representation elsewhere in the government, it no longer embraces Justice Brandeis's observation that "The most important thing that we do is not doing."[29] Rather, it has felt compelled to lower the technical barriers to adjudication and, by reaching the constitutional merits of a case, to vindicate the rights of its clientele groups. Because the Burger and Rehnquist Courts have not raised these barriers appreciably, the federal judiciary as a whole has been faced with an expanded range of issues on which it must render final judgment.

Along with this lowering of barriers to constitutional adjudication, two other factors have contributed to an increased level of judicial activity in recent decades. The enormous expansion in the scope of government itself inevitably has raised the level of legal regulation, and thereby provided new opportunities for litigation. At the same time, special-interest groups have displayed an increasing willingness to use the courts to pursue political objectives. With the technical restrictions on constitutional adjudication eased, myriad organizations and lobbies—including civil rights groups, consumer groups, public interest groups, and environmental groups—have concluded that they may fare better in the courts than in the legislative and executive branches, and thus have sought to achieve their public policy objectives through litigation.[30]

Not only has the range of issues that the judiciary adjudicates expanded considerably, but the kind of response demanded from the courts by these new issues also is entirely different from past judicial responses. Previously, in the constitutional realm, the courts were called upon simply to protect the public from what the other branches of government may have wished to impose on it. Increasingly, however, they are now expected to participate more actively in the policy-making process and to expand what the popular branches must do, even when they do not wish, or know how, to act. Put another way, they are expected to be prescriptive as well as proscriptive and to address themselves not only to the government's "sins of commission" but also to its "sins of omission." This expectation that the judiciary engage in policy-making has set off a lively debate between those who argue that the judiciary lacks the institutional capacity necessary to make effective policy (they stress that the very attributes of the adjudicative process that render courts so well-suited for specific grievance resolution also render them most ill-suited for general policy making) and those who insist that it is capable of dealing with policy issues and that, compared to the popularly elected branches and the bureaucracy, it does so quite well.[31] *DeShaney* v. *Winnebago County Department of Social Services* shows the Court debating an invitation to expand the Due Process Clause of the Fourteenth Amendment (and therewith its own power) in an emotionally laden case. Chief Justice

Rehnquist for the majority relies on the actual words of the Constitution and on precedent to argue against further judicial control of the popular branches, while Justice Blackmun in his dissent invokes "Compassion" as his "only guide and comfort" to press for an expanded judicial role.

## THE COURTS, JUDICIAL REVIEW, AND THE PROBLEM OF LEGITIMACY

Ever since *Marbury* v. *Madison,* the Supreme Court's first exercise of judicial review, the federal judiciary has had to grapple with the problem of legitimacy. How large a role should a nonmajoritarian institution play in shaping American public policy? How often and to what extent should federal judges substitute their judgment for that of the people's representatives? Judge Gibson's apprehensions in *Eakin* v. *Raub* have never been allayed completely, and debate over the appropriate role, function, or purpose of the federal judiciary has continued to this day among judges and students of public law. At the heart of this debate has been the question of judicial activism versus judicial self-restraint, with advocates for both positions finding support in *The Federalist,* No. 78.

Those who favor judicial activism stress that the judiciary "was designed to be an intermediate body between the people and the legislature, in order among other things to keep the latter within the limits assigned to their authority."[32] They see the judiciary as a "noble guard,"[33] protecting the people from the tyrannical excesses which might otherwise be visited upon them by their more immediate representatives and justify an activist judiciary on the grounds that it helps to promote qualitative, not simply quantitative, majority rule.

Those who favor judicial self-restraint or passivity also begin with *The Federalist,* No. 78. Reminding the judiciary that it is by far the weakest of the three branches of government, having neither the power of the purse nor the power of the sword but only that of judgment, they caution the Court to avoid placing itself in "continuous jeopardy of being over-powered, awed, or influenced by its coordinate branches." In the seminal words of James Bradley Thayer, the judiciary

> can only disregard [a legislative] act when those who have the right to make laws have not merely made a mistake, but have made a very clear one—so clear that it is not open to rational question. That is the standard of duty to which the Courts bring legislative acts; that is the test which they apply—not merely their own judgment as to constitutionality, but their conclusion as to what judgment is permissible to another department which the Constitution has charged with the duty of making it. This rule recognizes that, having regard to the great, complex, ever-unfolding exigencies of government, much which will seem unconstitutional to one man, or body of men, may reasonably not seem so to another; that the Constitution often admits of different interpretations; that the Constitution does not impose upon the legislature any one specific opinion, but leaves

> open this range of choice; and that whatever choice is rational is constitutional.[34]

Unless the federal judiciary employs this "reasonable doubt" test in exercising judicial review, the argument goes, the people will lose that "political experience and moral education and stimulus that comes from fighting the question out in the ordinary way and correcting their own errors."[35]

The federal judiciary periodically has swung between activism and self-restraint, alternately attracted to and repelled by the implications of these two basic positions.[36] Whatever its stand of the moment, it historically has sought to reassure the popularly elected branches by emphasizing its inherent weakness and by deliberately avoiding unnecessary conflicts with these branches, principally through the erection of technical barriers to adjudication. In recent years, however, the judiciary increasingly has embraced the arguments of judicial activism, eased restrictions on adjudication, and become an active participant in policy-making.

The judiciary's embrace of judicial activism has been applauded and encouraged by many of the nation's most prominent legal scholars, who conceive the Supreme Court to be "the ultimate arbiter of social ethics in the nation," whose responsibility it is to "articulate the public good as . . . [the Justices] understand it."[37] In the name of "ethical norms" and "moral growth and evolution," they admonish the Court to "invent" new constitutional rights and to acknowledge openly "that the source of those rights is not the constitutional text but the enhanced seriousness of certain values in American society."[38] These scholars argue that the vast majority of those rights that the Court has come to protect are not constitutionally based (i.e., are not "applications of the value judgments constitutionalized by the Framers") but rather are wholly "extraconstitutional" (i.e., are newly invented rights that are the product of "our evolving, deepening moral understanding"[39]). They argue that "most political practices banned by the Supreme Court in human rights cases, including freedom of expression and equal protection cases, cannot plausibly be characterized as simply modern analogues of past, constitutionally-banned practices."[40] These practices are banned, not because they violate value judgments constitutionalized by the Framers but because they violate the value judgments of the judges, articulating, as they do, "the public good as they understand it."[41] Legal scholars who operate from this perspective argue that the Court must assume a "prophetic stance" and oppose itself to established conventions by submitting governmental actions to a moral critique and striking down such actions if they violate any human rights that the Court believes individuals ought to be deemed to have.[42] By institutionalizing prophecy in this manner, the Court provides the public with the occasion for "moral reevaluation and possible moral growth" in a way that the popular branches—guided by what these legal scholars consider to be "a stagnant or even repressive morality"—cannot.[43]

The Court, however, has been reluctant to admit candidly that it is performing this prophetic function and has displayed instead the "tendency to resort to bad legislative history and strained reading of constitutional language to support results that would be better justified by explication of contemporary moral and political ideals not drawn from the constitutional text." As Thomas Grey notes, this tendency undermines the Court's credibility for "if judges resort to bad interpretation in preference to honest exposition of deeply held but unwritten ideals, it must be because they perceive th[is] mode of decisionmaking to be . . . suspect."[44] Therefore, these legal scholars chide the Court for its lack of candor and admonish it to acknowledge openly that it is protecting human rights and dignity and fulfilling its prophetic mission. They urge the entire Court to follow the lead of Chief Justice Warren, who, in a peroration by Anthony Lewis, is described as "the closest thing the United States has had to a Platonic Guardian, dispensing law from a throne without any sensed limits of power except what was seen as the good of society."[45] As G. Edward White notes, "Most of Warren's energy on the Court was directed toward achieving the 'right' results. He did not often agonize, as did Frankfurter, over an outcome in a case, nor did he despair of finding an adequate constitutional basis for justifying his intuitions, nor did he worry about being overly activist. He spent his time on discerning results that seemed just and on marshalling support for those results by attempting to convince others of their inherent justice."[46] If the entire Court were to adopt this activist posture, these scholars insist, it would be more "effective" in its protection of human rights and better situated to foster "moral growth" among the citizenry;[47] it would lead the way to a "fuller realization of human dignity."[48]

The contention that constitutional rights can be identified and defended apart from the constitutional text is fraught with difficulties, the most serious of which is the way in which it undermines the legitimacy of the judiciary and its exercise of judicial review. Judicial activism has traditionally defended judicial review and voided acts of the popular branches in the name of the Constitution. It has drawn its strength from *The Federalist*, No. 78, and Hamilton's contention that judicial review does not suppose a superiority of the judiciary to the popular branches but "only supposes that the power of the people is superior to both; and that where the will of the legislature declared in its statutes, stands in opposition to that of the people declared in the constitution, the judges ought to be governed by the latter, rather than the former." However, the contention that the judiciary is justified in exercising judicial review in order to vindicate not the constitutional expression of the people's will but the "ethical premises" of the judges deprives the Courts of this defense and, therewith, of their fundamental legitimacy. As the federal judiciary expands both the reach and vulnerability of its judicial powers (and by so doing, reveals the limitations of their capacity to make policy), its legitimacy in the eyes of the public will depend as never before on the qualities of the judges themselves. As Tocqueville reminded us a century and a half ago, "They [the judges] are all-powerful so long as people respect the law; but they . . . [are] impotent against popular neglect or contempt of the law." Because of the intractability of public opinion, Tocqueville pointed out, judges must be more than "good citizens and men of the information and integrity which are indispensable to all magistrates"; they must also be "statesmen, wise to discern the signs of the time, not afraid to brave the obstacles that can be subdued, nor slow to turn away from the current when it threatens to sweep them off, and the supremacy of the Union and obedience due to the laws along with them."[49] Whether the judicial power will continue to serve as a means to the ends of the Constitution will in large measure depend on the presence of these qualities in the members of the federal judiciary.

## NOTES

1 Robert Green McCloskey, ed., *The Works of James Wilson* (Cambridge, Mass.: Belknap Press of Harvard University Press, 1967), p. 290.

2 "The Essays of Brutus," in *The Complete Anti-Federalist,* 7 vols., ed. Herbert J. Storing (Chicago: University of Chicago Press, 1981), Essay 11, II: 421.

3 Leonard W. Levy, "Judicial Review, History, and Democracy," in *Judicial Review and the Supreme Court,* ed. Leonard W. Levy (New York: Harper & Row, 1967), p. 6.

4 William W. Van Alstyne, "A Critical Guide to *Marbury* v. *Madison,*" *Duke Law Journal,* (January 1969), p. 15.

5 Ibid., p. 33.

6 George Anastaplo, *The Constitution of 1787: A Commentary* (Baltimore, Md.: Johns Hopkins University Press, 1989), p. 141.

7 Whatever the understanding of separation of powers, it is significant to note that the Supreme Court did not wield the power of judicial review again until the *Dred Scott* decision in 1857. While several constitutional law scholars have recently begun to write of a second Marshall Court decision that held a provision of a congressional act unconstitutional—the obscure case of *Hodgson* v. *Bowerbank* (1809), this revisionist interpretation has been convincingly rebutted by Dennis J. Mahoney, "A Historical Note on *Hodgson* v. *Bowerbank,*" *University of Chicago Law Review* 49 (1982): 725-740.

8 Congressional Research Service, *The Constitution of the United States: Analysis and Interpretation, 1996 Supplement.* Senate Document no. 104–14. Updated through July 1998.

9 Charles L. Black, Jr., *The People and the Court* (New York: Macmillan, 1960).

10 Charles Evans Hughes, *The Supreme Court of the United States* (New York: Columbia University Press, 1928), pp. 96–97.

11 Walter F. Murphy, *Congress and the Court* (Chicago: University of Chicago Press, 1962), p. 63.

12 See Henry M. Hart, Jr., "The Power of Congress to Limit the Jurisdiction of Federal Courts; An Exercise in Dialectic," *Harvard Law Review* 66 (June 1953): 1362; and Leonard G. Ratner, "Congressional Power Over the Appellate Jurisdiction of the Supreme Court," *University of Pennsylvania Law Review* 109 (December 1960): 157.

13 Charles Rice, "Limiting Federal Court Jurisdiction: The Constitutional Basis for the Proposals in Congress Today," *Judicature* 65, no. 4 (October 1981), p. 195. See also Ralph A. Rossum, "Congress, the Constitution, and the Appellate Jurisdiction of the Supreme Court: The Letter and Spirit of the Exceptions Clause," *William and Mary Law Review* 24 (April 1983): 385–428.

14 Comment, "Removal of Supreme Court Appellate Jurisdiction: A Weapon Against Obscenity?" *Duke Law Journal* (1969): 297.

15 For citations to congressional attempts to limit the Supreme Court's appellate jurisdiction, see Gerald Gunther, "Congressional Power to Curtail Federal Court Jurisdiction: An Opinionated Guide to the Ongoing Debate," *Stanford Law Review* 36 (1984): 895–898.
16 See Murphy, *Congress and the Court.*
17 See Rossum, *Congressional Control of the Judiciary: The Article III Option* (Washington, D.C.: The Center for Judical Studies, 1988).
18 Alexander M. Bickel, *The Least Dangerous Branch: The Supreme Court at the Bar of Politics* (New York: Bobbs-Merrill, 1962), pp. 111–198.
19 John P. Roche, "Judicial Self-Restraint," *American Political Science Review* 49 (September 1955): 722.
20 See *Muskrat* v. *United States,* (1911). Although the federal courts do not render advisory opinions, they do render declaratory judgments. An advisory opinion is advice on a hypothetical question given by the judiciary to the executive or to the legislature. A declaratory judgment, by way of contrast, grows out of an adjudication of an actual controversy between adverse parties and differs from an ordinary judgment principally in that it involves no compulsory process.
21 Robert H. Jackson, *The Supreme Court in the American System of Government* (Cambridge, Mass.: Harvard University Press, 1955), p. 11; and Archibald Cox, *The Role of the Supreme Court in American Government* (New York: Oxford University Press, 1976), p. 101.
22 *Frothingham* v. *Mellon* (1923).
23 See *Valley Forge Christian College* v. *Americans United for Separation of Church and State* (1982), in which the Supreme Court refused to expand *Flast* and allow taxpayer suits challenging congressional action under the Property Clause of Article IV, section 3, clause 2.
24 Although see *United States* v. *Students Challenging Regulatory Agency Procedures (SCRAP),* 412 U.S. 669 (1973), in which the Court held that a group of law students at George Washington University had standing to challenge the failure of the Interstate Commerce Commission to prepare an environmental impact statement before it permitted a railroad freight surcharge to take effect. The students' claimed standing to sue based on their assertions that they used parks and forests, that these areas would be less desirable if littered, that litter would increase if there were a reduction in the use of recycled goods, that a reduction in their use would result if the cost of these goods increased, and that the cost of these goods would increase if the freight surcharge went into effect. They further claimed standing by asserting that they breathed the air within the Washington metropolitan area and that this air would suffer from increased pollution caused by the modified rate structure.
25 See *United Public Workers* v. *Mitchell* (1947), and *Poe* v. *Ullman* (1961).
26 See also *Coleman* v. *Miller* (1939), in which the Court held that questions relating to the amending process of the United States Constitution are political.
27 See, for example, *United States* v. *Carolene Products Co.* (1938), fn. 4; and *New York Times* v. *United States* (1971).
28 Henry J. Abraham, *The Judicial Process,* 6th ed. (New York: Oxford University Press, 1993). See also Wallace Mendelson, "Mr. Justice Douglas and Government by Judiciary," *Journal of Politics* 38, no. 4 (November 1976): 918–937.
29 Alexander M. Bickel, ed., *The Unpublished Opinions of Mr. Justice Brandeis: The Supreme Court at Work* (Cambridge, Mass.: Harvard University Press, 1957), p. 17.
30 Nathan Glazer, "Towards an Imperial Judiciary?" *The Public Interest,* no. 41 (Fall 1975): 119–121.

31 The critique is presented in Donald L. Horowitz, *The Courts and Social Policy* (Washington, D.C.: Brookings Institution Press, 1977), pp. 33–56. See also Gerald N. Rosenberg, *The Hollow Hope: Can Courts Bring About Social Change?* (Chicago: University of Chicago Press, 1991), p. 343: "American courts are not all-powerful institutions. They were designed with severe limitations and placed in a political system of divided powers. To ask them to produce significant social reform is to forget their history and ignore their constraints. It is to cloud our vision with a naive and romantic belief in the triumph of rights over politics. And while romance and even naivete have their charms, they are not best exhibited in courtrooms." For a contrasting point of view, see R. Cavanaugh and A. Sarat, "Thinking About Courts: Towards and Beyond a Jurisprudence of Judicial Competence," *Law and Society Review* 14, no. 2 (Winter 1980): 371–420; and Stephen L. Wasby, "Arrogation of Power or Accountability: "Judicial Imperialism' Revisited," *Judicature* 65, no. 4 (October 1981): 208–219.

32 *The Federalist,* No. 78, p. 525.

33 *The Works of James Wilson,* ed. Robert Green McCloskey (Cambridge, Mass.: Harvard University Press, 1967), p. 330.

34 James Bradley Thayer, "The Origin and Scope of the American Doctrine of Constitutional Law," *Harvard Law Review* 7 (October 1893): 144. See also Philip Kurland, *Mr. Justice Frankfurter and the Supreme Court* (Chicago: University of Chicago Press, 1971), p. 5, who identifies six basic assumptions of the doctrine of self-restraint: "One is history and the obligation that constitutionalism imposes to adhere to the essential meaning put in the document by its framers. A second is the intrinsically undemocratic nature of the Supreme Court. A third is a corollary of the second, an abiding respect for the judgments of those branches of the government that are elected representatives of their constituents. A fourth is the recognition that judicial error at this level is more difficult of correction than other forms of judicial action. A fifth is respect for the judgments of earlier courts. But (sixth), the essential feature of judicial restraint that has gained most attention and aroused the greatest doubts—probably because few men are themselves big enough to abide by its command—is the notion of rejection of personal preference."

35 James Bradley Thayer, *John Marshall* (Boston: Houghton Mifflin, 1901), pp. 106–107. See also Sanford Gabin, *Judicial Review and the Reasonable Doubt Test* (New York: Kennikat Press, 1980), and Raoul Berger, *Government by Judiciary* (Cambridge, Mass.: Harvard University Press, 1977).

36 See Wallace Mendelson, "The Politics of Judicial Activism," *Emory Law Journal* 24 (1975): 43–66, who argues that periods of judicial activism coincide with periods of party decline: "judicial pretension appears to have thrived only in periods of unusual weakness in our political processes; at other times it has been effectively rebuffed. In short, 'government by judges' seems no more than flaws in the party system permit it to be." (p. 44)

37 See Arthur S. Miller, *Toward Increased Judicial Activism: The Political Role of the Supreme Court* (Westport, Conn.: Greenwood Press, 1982), pp. 28, 275.

38 G. Edward White, "Reflections on the Role of the Supreme Court: The Contemporary Debate and the 'Lessons' of History," *Judicature* 63, no. 4 (October 1979), p. 168.

39 Michael Perry, *The Constitution, the Courts, and Human Rights* (New Haven: Yale University Press, 1982), p. 41.

40 Ibid., p. 75.

41 Arthur S. Miller, *Toward Increased Judicial Activism,* p. 274.

42 Ibid., p. 20, and Michael Perry, *The Constitution, the Courts, and Human Rights*, pp. 97, 98, 101, 102, 112, 146, 162.
43 Michael Perry, *The Constitution, the Courts, and Human Rights*, pp. 100, 113.
44 Thomas C. Grey, "Do We Have an Unwritten Constitution?" *Stanford Law Review* 27 (1975): 706. For alternative justifications of judicial activism, see Ronald Dworkin, *Taking Rights Seriously* (Cambridge, Mass.: Harvard University Press, 1977), and Sotorios A. Barber, *On What the Constitution Means* (Baltimore, Md.: Johns Hopkins University Press, 1984).
45 Anthony Lewis, "Earl Warren," in *The Justices of the United States Supreme Court*, 4 vols., eds. L. Friedman and F. Israel (New York: Chelsea, 1969), vol. 4, pp. 2726.
46 G. Edward White, *Earl Warren: A Public Life* (New York: Oxford University Press, 1982), p. 190. See also p. 359: "Warren . . . equated judicial lawmaking with neither the dictates of reason, as embodied in established precedent or doctrine, nor the demands imposed by an institutional theory of the judge's role, nor the alleged 'command' of the constitutional text, but rather with his own reconstruction of the ethical structure of the Constitution."
47 Michael Perry, *The Constitution, the Courts, and Human Rights*, pp. 141–143.
48 Arthur S. Miller, *Toward Increased Judicial Activism*, p. 317.
49 Alexis de Tocqueville, *Democracy in America*, vol. 1 (New York: Random House, 1945), p. 157.

## SELECTED READING

*The Federalist*, Nos. 78, 80.

*Allen* v. *Wright*, 468 U.S. 737 (1984).
*Arizonans for Official English* v. *Arizona*, 117 S. Ct. 1055 (1997)
*Ashwander* v. *Tennessee Valley Authority*, 297 U.S. 288 (1936).
*Colegrove* v. *Green*, 328 U.S. 549 (1946).
*Coleman* v. *Miller*, 307 U.S. 433 (1939).
*Poe* v. *Ullman*, 367 U.S. 497 (1961).
*Powell* v. *McCormack*, 395 U.S. 486 (1969).
*United States* v. *Nixon*, 418 U.S. 683 (1974).
*Valley Forge Christian College* v. *Americans United for Separation of Church and State*, 454 U.S. 464 (1982).

Agresto, John. *The Supreme Court and Constitutional Democracy* (Ithaca, N.Y.: Cornell University Press, 1984).
Berger, Raoul. *Congress versus the Supreme Court* (Cambridge, Mass.: Harvard University Press, 1969).
Bickel, Alexander M. *The Least Dangerous Branch: The Supreme Court at the Bar of Politics* (New York: Bobbs-Merrill, 1962).
Bork, Robert H. *The Tempting of America: The Political Seduction of the Law* (New York: Free Press, 1990).
Chayes, Abram. "The Role of the Judge in Public Law Litigation." *Harvard Law Review* 89 (1976): 1281–1316.
Choper, Jesse H. *Judicial Review and the National Political Process* (Chicago: University of Chicago Press, 1980).
Clinton, Robert Lowry. *Marbury* v. *Madison and Judicial Review* (Lawrence, Kansas: University Press of Kansas, 1989).

Dorn, James A. and Manne, Henry G., eds. *Economic Liberties and the Judiciary* (Fairfax, Va.: George Mason University Press, 1987).

Dworkin, Ronald. *Taking Rights Seriously* (Cambridge, Mass.: Harvard University Press, 1980).

Ely, John Hart. *Democracy and Distrust: A Theory of Judicial Review* (Cambridge, Mass.: Harvard University Press, 1980).

Franck, Matthew J. *Against the Imperial Judiciary: The Supreme Court* v. *The Sovereignty of the People* (Lawrence: University Press of Kansas, 1996).

Glendon, Mary Ann. *Rights Talk* (New York: Free Press, 1991).

Hickok, Eugene W. and McDowell, Gary L. *Justice* vs. *Law: Courts and Politics in American Society* (New York: Free Press, 1993).

Horowitz, Donald L. *The Courts and Social Policy* (Washington, D.C.: Brookings Institution Press, 1977).

Jacobsohn, Gary L. *The Supreme Court and the Decline of Constitutional Aspiration* (Totowa, N.J.: Rowman & Littlefield, 1986).

Levinson, Sanford. *Constitutional Faith* (Princeton, N.J.: Princeton University Press, 1988).

Levy, Leonard, ed. *Judicial Review and the Supreme Court* (New York: Harper & Row, 1967).

McDowell, Gary L. "Coke, Corwin, and the Constitution: The 'Higher Law Background' Reconsidered." *The Review of Politics* 55 (Summer 1993): 393–420.

McDowell, Gary L. *Curbing the Courts: The Constitution and the Limits of Judicial Power* (Baton Rouge: Louisiana State University Press, 1988).

Nagel, Robert F. *Judicial Power and American Character: Censoring Ourselves in an Anxious Age* (New York: Oxford University Press, 1994).

Perry, Michael J. *The Constitution, the Courts, and Human Rights* (New Haven, Conn.: Yale University Press, 1982).

Perry, Michael J. *The Constitution in the Courts: Law or Politics?* (New York: Oxford University Press, 1994).

Rosenberg, Gerald N. *The Hollow Hope: Can Courts Bring About Social Change?* (Chicago: University of Chicago Press, 1991).

Rossum, Ralph A. *Congressional Control of the Judiciary: The Article III Option* (Washington, D.C.: Center for Judicial Studies, 1988).

Scalia, Antonin. "The Doctrine of Standing as an Essential Element of the Separation of Powers." *Suffolk University Law Review* 17 (1983): 881–899.

Strumm, Philippa. *The Supreme Court and "Political Questions": A Study in Judicial Evasion* (University, Ala.: University of Alabama Press, 1974).

Sunderland, Lane V. *Popular Government and the Supreme Court: Securing the Public Good and Private Rights* (Lawrence: University Press of Kansas, 1996).

Sunstein, Cass R. *The Partial Constitution* (Cambridge, Mass.: Harvard University Press, 1993).

Thayer, James Bradley. "The Origin and Scope of the American Doctrine of Constitutional Law." *Harvard Law Review* 7 (1893): 129–156.

Van Alstyne, William W. "A Critical Guide to *Marbury* v. *Madison*," *Duke Law Journal*, (1969), pp. 1–47.

Wilson, Bradford P. and Masugi, Ken (eds.). *The Supreme Court and American Constitutionalism* (Lanham, Md.: Rowman & Littlefield, 1998).

Wolfe, Christopher. *The Rise of Modern Judicial Review: From Constitutional Interpretation to Judge-Made Law* (rev. ed.; Lanham, Md.: Rowman & Littlefield, 1994).

# *Marbury* v. *Madison*

**5 U.S. (1 Cranch) 137; 2 L. Ed. 60 (1803)**

Before yielding control of the government to the Jeffersonians in 1801, the Federalist-controlled "lame duck" Congress created a number of new judicial posts. To fill the 42 justice-of-the-peace posts mandated for the District of Columbia, President John Adams nominated members of the Federalist Party, including one William Marbury. His commission, which had been confirmed by the Senate and signed by the president, was sealed by John Marshall, who, although appointed by President Adams as Chief Justice, was also serving as secretary of state. In the rush of the closing hours of the Adams administration, Marshall was unable to deliver Marbury's commission. When James Madison took over as Thomas Jefferson's secretary of state on March 4, he found Marbury's commission (and three others) and refused to deliver them. Marbury then brought suit in the Supreme Court to compel delivery of his commission, relying on Section 13 of the Judiciary Act of 1789, which, he claimed, gave the Supreme Court original jurisdiction in such a case. Despite his involvement in this matter, and with a bare quorum of four of the six justices participating, Chief Justice Marshall used this occasion to establish for the Court the power of judicial review. *Opinion of the Court: Marshall, Chase, Paterson, Washington. Not participating: Cushing, Moore.*

MR. JUSTICE MARSHALL delivered the opinion of the Court.

In the order in which the court has viewed this subject, the following questions have been considered and decided.

1. Has the applicant a right to the commission he demands?

2. If he has a right, and that right has been violated, do the laws of his country afford him a remedy?

3. If they do afford him a remedy, is it a *mandamus* issuing from this court?

... It is ... the opinion of the court,

1. That, by signing the commission of Mr. Marbury, the President of the United States appointed him a justice of peace, for the county of Washington in the District of Columbia; and that the seal of the United States, affixed thereto by the Secretary of State, is conclusive testimony of the verity of the signature, and of the completion of the appointment; and that the appointment conferred on him a legal right to the office for the space of five years.

2. That, having this legal title to the office, he has a consequent right to the commission; a refusal to deliver which, is a plain violation of that right, for which the laws of this country afford him a remedy.

It remains to be enquired whether,

3. He is entitled to the remedy for which he applies. This depends on,

1. The nature of the writ applied for and
2. The power of this court.

... This, then, is a plain case for mandamus, either to deliver the commission, or a copy of it from the record; and it only remains to be enquired, whether it can issue from this court.

The act to establish the judicial courts of the United States authorizes the Supreme Court "to issue writs of mandamus in cases warranted by the principles and usages of law, to any courts appointed, or persons holding office, under the authority of the United States."

---

Here and throughout the text, the authors of court opinions are underscored.

The Secretary of State, being a person holding an office under the authority of the United States, is precisely within the letter of the description, and if this court is not authorized to issue a writ of mandamus to such an officer, it must be because the law is unconstitutional, and therefore absolutely incapable of conferring the authority, and assigning the duties which its words purport to confer and assign.

The Constitution vests the whole judicial power of the United States in one supreme court, and such inferior courts as Congress shall, from time to time, ordain and establish. This power is expressly extended to all cases arising under the laws of the United States; and, consequently, in some form, may be exercised over the present case; because the right claimed is given by a law of the United States.

In the distribution of this power it is declared that "the Supreme Court shall have original jurisdiction in all cases affecting ambassadors, other public ministers and consuls, and those in which a state shall be a party. In all other cases, the Supreme Court shall have appellate jurisdiction."

It has been insisted at the bar, that, as the original grant of jurisdiction to the Supreme and inferior courts, is general, and the clause assigning original jurisdiction to the Supreme Court contains no negative or restrictive words, the power remains to the legislature to assign original jurisdiction to that court in other cases than those specified in the article which has been recited; provided those cases belong to the judicial power of the United States.

If it had been intended to leave it in the discretion of the legislature to apportion the judicial power between the Supreme and inferior courts according to the will of that body, it would certainly have been useless to have proceeded further than to have defined the judicial power, and the tribunals in which it should be vested. The subsequent part of the section is mere surplusage, is entirely without meaning. If Congress remains at liberty to give this court appellate jurisdiction, where the Constitution has declared their jurisdiction shall be original; and original jurisdiction where the Constitution has declared it shall be appellate, the distribution of jurisdiction made in the Constitution is form without substance.

Affirmative words are often, in their operation, negative of other objects than those affirmed; and in this case, a negative or exclusive sense must be given to them, or they have no operation at all.

It cannot be presumed that any clause in the Constitution is intended to be without effect; and, therefore, such a construction is inadmissible unless the words require it.

. . . To enable this court, then to issue a mandamus, it must be shown to be an exercise of appellate jurisdiction, or to be necessary to enable them to exercise appellate jurisdiction.

It has been stated at the bar that the appellate jurisdiction may be exercised in a variety of forms, and that, if it be the will of the legislature that a mandamus should be used for that purpose, that will must be obeyed. This is true, yet the jurisdiction must be appellate, not original.

It is the essential criterion of appellate jurisdiction that it revises and corrects the proceedings in a cause already instituted, and does not create that cause. Although, therefore, a mandamus may be directed to courts, yet to issue such a writ to an officer for the delivery of a paper is in effect the same as to sustain an original action for that paper, and, therefore, seems not to belong to appellate, but to original jurisdiction. Neither is it necessary, in such a case as this, to enable the court to exercise its appellate jurisdiction.

The authority, therefore, given to the Supreme Court by the act establishing the judicial courts of the United States, to issue writs of mandamus to public officers, appears not to be warranted by the Constitution; and it becomes necessary to inquire whether a jurisdiction so conferred can be exercised.

The question, whether an act repugnant to the Constitution can become the law of the land, is a question deeply interesting to the United States; but, happily, not of an intricacy proportioned to its interest. It seems only necessary to recognize certain principles, supposed to have been long and well established, to decide it.

That the people have an original right to establish, for their future government, such principles as, in their opinion, shall most conduce to their own happiness is the basis on which the whole American fabric had been erected. The exercise of this original right is a very great exertion; nor can it, nor ought it, to be frequently repeated. The principles, therefore, so established, are deemed fundamental. And as the authority from which they proceed is supreme, and can seldom act, they are designed to be permanent.

This original and supreme will organizes the government, and assigns to different departments their respective powers. It may either stop here, or establish certain limits not to be transcended by those departments.

The government of the United States is of the latter description. The powers of the legislature are defined and limited; and that those limits may not be mistaken, or forgotten, the Constitution is written. To what purpose are powers limited, and to what purpose is that limitation committed to writing, if these limits may, at any time, be passed by those intended to be restrained? The distinction between a government with limited and unlimited powers is abolished if those limits do not confine the persons on whom they are imposed, and if acts prohibited and acts allowed are of equal obligation. It is a proposition too plain to be contested, that the Constitution controls any legislative act repugnant to it; or, that the legislature may alter the Constitution by an ordinary act.

Between these alternatives there is no middle ground. The Constitution is either a superior paramount law, unchangeable by ordinary means, or it is on a level with ordinary legislative acts, and, like other acts, is alterable when the legislature shall please to alter it.

If the former part of the alternative be true, then a legislative act contrary to the Constitution is not law: if the latter part be true, then written constitutions are absurd attempts on the part of the people to limit a power in its own nature illimitable.

Certainly all those who have framed written constitutions contemplate them as forming the fundamental and paramount law of the nation, and consequently, the theory of every such government must be, that an act of the legislature, repugnant to the constitution, is void.

This theory is essentially attached to a written constitution, and is, consequently, to be considered by this court as one of the fundamental principles of our society. It is not therefore to be lost sight of in the further consideration of this subject.

If an act of the legislature, repugnant to the Constitution, is void, does it, notwithstanding its invalidity, bind the courts, and oblige them to give it effect? Or, in other words, though it be not law, does it constitute a rule as operative as if it was a law? This would be to overthrow in fact what was established in theory; and would seem, at first view, an absurdity too gross to be insisted on. It shall, however, receive a more attentive consideration.

It is emphatically the province and duty of the judicial department to say what the law is. Those who apply the rule to particular cases must, of necessity, expound and interpret that rule. If two laws conflict with each other, the courts must decide on the operation of each.

So if a law be in opposition to the Constitution; if both the law and the Constitution apply to a particular case, so that the court must either decide that case conformably to the law, disregarding the Constitution; or conformably to the Constitution, disregarding the law; the court must determine which of these conflicting rules governs the case. This is of the very essence of judicial duty.

If, then, the courts are to regard the Constitution, and the Constitution is superior to any ordinary act of the legislature, the Constitution, and not such ordinary act, must govern the case to which they both apply.

Those, then, who controvert the principle that the Constitution is to be considered, in court, as a paramount law, are reduced to the necessity of maintaining that courts must close their eyes on the Constitution, and see only the law.

This doctrine would subvert the very foundation of all written constitutions. It would declare that an act which, according to the principles and theory of our government, is entirely void, is yet, in practice, completely obligatory. It would declare that if the legislature shall do what is expressly forbidden, such act, notwithstanding the express prohibition, is in reality effectual. It would be giving to the legislature a practical and real omnipotence, with the same breath which professes to restrict their powers within narrow limits. It is prescribing limits and declaring that those limits may be passed at pleasure.

That it thus reduces to nothing what we have deemed the greatest improvement on political institutions—a written constitution—would of itself be sufficient, in America, where written constitutions have been viewed with so much reverence, for rejecting the construction. But the peculiar expressions of the Constitution of the United States furnish additional arguments in favor of its rejection.

The judicial power of the United States is extended to all cases arising under the Constitution.

Could it be the intention of those who gave this power to say that, in using it, the Constitution should not be looked into? That a case arising under the Constitution should be decided without examining the instrument under which it rises?

This is too extravagant to be maintained.

In some cases then, the Constitution must be looked into by the judges. And if they can open it at all, what part of it are they forbidden to read or to obey?

There are many other parts of the Constitution which serve to illustrate this subject.

It is declared that "no tax or duty shall be laid on articles exported from any state." Suppose a duty on the export of cotton, of tobacco, or of flour; and a suit instituted to recover it. Ought judgment to be rendered in such a case? Ought the judges to close their eyes on the Constitution, and see only the law?

The Constitution declares that "no bill of attainder or ex post facto law shall be passed."

If, however, such a bill should be passed and a person should be prosecuted under it; must the court condemn to death those victims who the Constitution endeavours to preserve?

"No person," says the Constitution, "shall be convicted of treason unless on the testimony of two witnesses to the same overt act, or on confession in open court."

Here the language of the Constitution is addressed especially to the courts. It prescribes, directly for them, a rule of evidence not to be departed from. If the legislature should change that rule, and declare *one* witness, or a confession *out* of court, sufficient for conviction, must the constitutional principle yield to the legislative act?

From these, and many other selections which might be made, it is apparent that the framers of the Constitution contemplated that instrument as a rule for the government of *courts,* as well as of the legislature.

Why otherwise does it direct the judges to take an oath to support it? This oath certainly applies in an especial manner to their conduct in their official character. How immoral to impose it on them, if they were to be used as the instruments, and the knowing instruments, for violating what they swear to support?

The oath of office, too, imposed by the legislature, is completely demonstrative of the legislative opinion on this subject. It is in these words: "I do solemnly swear that I will administer justice without respect to persons, and do equal right to the poor and to the rich; and that I will faithfully and impartially discharge all the duties incumbent on me as—, according to the best of my abilities and understanding agreeably to the *Constitution* and laws of the United States."

Why does a judge swear to discharge his duties agreeably to the Constitution of the United States, if that Constitution forms no rule for his government? If it is closed upon him, and cannot be inspected by him?

If such be the real state of things, this is worse than solemn mockery. To prescribe, or take this oath, becomes equally a crime.

It is also not entirely unworthy of observation that, in declaring what shall be the *supreme* law of the land, the *Constitution* itself is first mentioned; and not the laws of the United States generally, but those only which shall be made in *pursuance* of the Constitution, have that rank.

Thus, the particular phraseology of the Constitution of the United States confirms and strengthens the principle, supposed to be essential to all written constitutions, that a law repugnant to the Constitution is void; and that *courts,* as well as other departments, are bound by that instrument.

The rule must be

*Discharged.*

## *Eakin* v. *Raub*

**12 Sergeant & Rawle (Pennsylvania Supreme Court) 330 (1825)**

In this otherwise unimportant case, Judge Gibson of the Pennsylvania Supreme Court effectively presents, in a dissenting opinion, the opposite side of the argument made by Chief Justice Marshall in *Marbury* v. *Madison.* Since the facts of the case and the opinion of the Court do not contribute to an understanding of Judge Gibson's argument, they have been omitted.

MR. JUSTICE GIBSON, dissenting . . .

I am aware, that a right to declare all unconstitutional acts void . . . is generally held as a professional dogma; but I apprehend, rather as a matter of faith than of reason. I admit, that I once embraced the same doctrine, but without examination, and I shall, therefore, state the arguments that impelled me to abandon it, with great respect for those by whom it is still maintained. . . .

. . . The constitution is said to be a law of superior obligation; and consequently, that if it were to come into collision with an act of the legislature, the latter would have to give way; this is conceded. But it is a fallacy, to suppose, that they can come into collision *before the judiciary*. . . . The ordinary and essential powers of the judiciary do not extend to the annulling of an act of the legislature.

The constitution and the *right* of the legislature to pass the act, may be in collision; but is that a legitimate subject for judicial determination? If it be, the judiciary must be a peculiar organ, to revise the proceedings of the legislature, and to correct its mistakes; and in what part of the constitution are we to look for this proud preeminence? Viewing the matter in the opposite direction, what would be thought of an act of assembly in which it should be declared that the supreme court had, in a particular case, put a wrong construction on the constitution of the *United States*, and that the judgment should therefore be reversed? It would, doubtless, be thought a usurpation of judicial power. But it is by no means clear, that to declare a law void, which has been enacted according to the forms prescribed in the constitution, is not a usurpation of legislative power. . . . It is the business of the judiciary, to interpret the laws, not scan the authority of the lawgiver; and without the latter, it cannot take cognizance of a collision between a law and the constitution. So that to affirm that the judiciary has a right to judge of the existence of such collision, is to take for granted the very thing to be proved; and that a very cogent argument may be made in this way, I am not disposed to deny. . . . and pronounce what the law is; and that this necessarily involves a consideration of the constitution. It does so: but how far? If the judiciary will inquire into anything beside the form of enactment, where shall it stop? There must be some point of limitation to such an inquiry; for no one will pretend, that a judge would be justifiable in calling for the election returns, or scrutinizing the qualifications of those who composed the legislature. . . .

Every one knows how seldom men think exactly alike on ordinary subjects; and a government constructed on the principle of assent by all its parts, would be inadequate to the most simple operations. The notion of a complication of counter-checks has been carried to an extent in theory, of which the framers of the constitution never dreamt. When the entire sovereignty was separated into its elementary parts, and distributed to the appropriate branches, all things incident to the exercise of its powers were committed to each branch exclusively. The negative which each part of the legislature may exercise, in regard to the acts of the other, was thought sufficient to prevent material infractions of the restraints which were put on the power of the whole; for, had it been intended to interpose the judiciary as an additional barrier, the matter would surely not have been left in doubt. The judges would not have been left to stand on the insecure and ever-shifting ground of public opinion, as to constructive power; they would have been placed on the impregnable ground of an express grant; they would not have been compelled to resort to the debates in the convention, or the opinion that was generally entertained at the time. . . .

But the judges are sworn to support the constitution, and are they not bound by it as the law of the land? In some respects they are. In the very few cases in which the judiciary, and not the legislature, is the immediate organ to execute its provisions, they are bound by it, in preference to any act of assembly to the contrary; in such cases, the constitution is a rule to the courts. But what I have in view in this inquiry is, the supposed right of the judiciary, to interfere, in cases where the constitution is to be carried into effect through the instrumentality of the legislature, and where that organ must necessarily first decide on the constitutionality of its own act. The oath to support the constitution is not peculiar to the judges, but is taken indiscriminately by every officer of the government, and is designed rather as a test of the political principles of the man, than to bind the officer in the discharge of his duty: otherwise, it were difficult to determine, what operation it is to have in the case of a recorder of deeds, for instance, who, in the execution of his office, has nothing to do with the constitution. But granting it to relate to the official conduct of the judge, as well as every other officer, and not to his political principles, still, it must be understood in reference to supporting the constitution, *only as far as that may be involved in his official duty*; and consequently, if his official duty does not comprehend an inquiry into the authority of the legislature, neither does his oath. . . .

But do not the judges do a *positive* act in violation of the constitution, when they give effect to an unconstitutional law? Not if the law has been passed according to the forms established in the constitution. The fallacy of the question is, in supposing that the judiciary adopts the acts of the legislature as its own; whereas, the enactment of a law and the interpretation of it are not concurrent acts, and as the judiciary is not required to concur in the enactment, neither is it in the breach of the constitution which may be the consequence of the enactment; the fault is imputable to the legislature, and on it the responsibility exclusively rests. . . .

But it has been said, that this construction would deprive the citizen of the advantages which are peculiar to a written constitution, by at once declaring the power of the legislature, in practice, to be illimitable. . .But there is no magic or inherent power in parchment and ink, to command respect, and protect principles from violation. In the business of government, a recurrence to first principles answers the end of an observation at sea, with a view to correct the dead-reckoning; and for this purpose, a written constitution is an instrument of inestimable value. It is of inestimable value also, in rendering its principles familiar to the mass of the people; for, after all, there is no effectual guard against legislative usurpation, but public opinion, the force of which, in this country, is inconceivably great. . . . Once let public opinion be so corrupt, as to sanction every misconstruction of the constitution, and abuse of power, which the temptation of the moment may dictate, and the party which may happen to be predominant, will laugh at the puny efforts of a dependent power to arrest it in its course.

For these reasons, I am of opinion that it rests with the people, in whom full and absolute sovereign power resides, to correct abuses in legislation, by instructing their representatives to repeal the obnoxious act. What is wanting to plenary power in the government, is reserved by the people, for their own immediate use; and to redress an infringement of their rights in this respect, would seem to be an accessory of the power thus reserved. It might, perhaps, have been better to vest the power in the judiciary; as it might be expected, that its habits of deliberation, and the aid derived from the arguments of counsel, would more frequently lead to accurate conclusions. On the other hand, the judiciary is not infallible; and an error by it would admit of no remedy but a more distinct expression of the public will, through the extraordinary medium of a convention; whereas, an error by the legislature admits of a remedy by an exertion of the same will, in the ordinary exercise of the right of suffrage—a mode better calculated to attain the end, without popular excitement. It may be said, the people would probably not notice an error of their representatives. But they would as probably do so, as notice an error of the judiciary; and beside, it is a *postulate* in the theory of our government, and the very basis of the superstructure, that the people are wise, virtuous, and competent to manage their own affairs: and if they are not so, in fact, still, every question of this sort must be determined according to the principles of the constitution, as it came from the hands of its framers, and the existence of a defect which was not foreseen, would not justify those who administer the government, in applying a corrective in practice, which can be provided only by a convention. . . .

## *Cooper* v. *Aaron*

**358 U.S. 1, 78 S.Ct 1401, 3 L.Ed.2d 5 (1958)**

After the Arkansas governor, Orval Faubus, and state legislature openly resisted the Supreme Court's school desegregation decision of 1954 (Brown v. Board of Education), the Little Rock school board petitioned the United States District Court for the Eastern District of Arkansas to suspend for two and one-half years the implementation of the school board's plan for desegregation of a previously all-white high school. It feared continuation of the racial tensions and turmoil that had made it impossible for respondents to attend the high school until federal troops were sent there by President Eisenhower. The District Court granted petitioners' request. The Court of Appeals for the Eighth Circuit reversed, however, and the Supreme Court granted certiorari. In reasserting its supremacy to determine constitutional law, every justice signed the opinion, thereby underscoring their unanimity. Justice Frankfurter also prepared a concurring opinion, which he released one week after the Court handed down its decision. *Opinion of the Court: Warren, Black, Brennan, Burton, Clark, Douglas, Frankfurter, Harlan, Whittaker. Concurring opinion: Frankfurter.*

THE CHIEF JUSTICE, MR. JUSTICE BLACK, MR. JUSTICE FRANKFURTER, MR. JUSTICE DOUGLAS, MR. JUSTICE BURTON, MR. JUSTICE CLARK, MR. JUSTICE HARLAN, MR. JUSTICE BRENNAN, AND MR. JUSTICE WHITTAKER delivered the opinion of the Court.

As this case reaches us it raises questions of the highest importance to the maintenance of our federal system of government. It necessarily involves a claim by the Governor and Legislature of a State that there is no duty on state officials to obey federal court orders resting on this Court's considered interpretation of the United States Constitution. Specifically it involves actions by the Governor and Legislature of Arkansas upon the premise that they are not bound by our holding in *Brown* v. *Board of Education* [1954]. That holding was that the Fourteenth Amendment forbids States to use their governmental powers to bar children on racial grounds from attending schools where there is state participation through any arrangement, management, funds or property. We are urged to uphold a suspension of the Little Rock School Board's plan to do away with segregated public schools in Little Rock until state laws and efforts to upset and nullify our holding in *Brown* v. *Board of Education* have been further challenged and tested in the courts. We reject these contentions. . . .

In affirming the judgment of the Court of Appeals which reversed the District Court we have accepted without reservation the position of the School Board, the Superintendent of Schools, and their counsel that they displayed entire good faith in the conduct of these proceedings and in dealing with the unfortunate and distressing sequence of events which has been outlined. We likewise have accepted the findings of the District Court as to the conditions at Central High School during the 1957–1958 school year, and also the findings that the educational progress of all the students, white and colored, of that school has suffered and will continue to suffer if the conditions which prevailed last year are permitted to continue.

The significance of these findings, however, is to be considered in light of the fact, indisputably revealed by the record before us, that the conditions they depict are directly traceable to the actions of legislators and executive officials of the State of Arkansas, taken in their official capacities, which reflect their own determination to resist this Court's decision in the *Brown* case and which have brought about violent resistance to that decision in Arkansas. In its petition for certiorari filed in this Court, the School Board itself describes the situation in this language: "The legislative, executive, and judicial departments of the state government opposed the desegregation of Little Rock schools by enacting laws, calling out troops, making statements vilifying federal law and federal courts, and failing to utilize state law enforcement agencies and judicial processes to maintain public peace."

One may well sympathize with the position of the Board in the face of the frustrating conditions which have confronted it, but, regardless of the Board's good faith, the actions of the other state agencies responsible for those conditions compel us to reject the Board's legal position. Had Central High School been under the direct management of the State itself, it could hardly be suggested that those immediately in charge of the school should be heard to assert their own good faith as a legal excuse for delay in implementing the constitutional rights of these respondents, when vindication of those rights was rendered difficult or impossible by the actions of other state officials. The situation here is in no different posture because the members of the School Board and the Superintendent of Schools are local officials; from the point of view of the Fourteenth Amendment, they stand in this litigation as the agents of the State. . . .

The controlling legal principles are plain. The command of the Fourteenth Amendment is that no "State" shall deny to any person within its jurisdiction the equal protection of the laws. "A State acts by its legislative, its executive, or its judicial authorities. It can act in no other way. The constitutional provision, therefore, must mean that no agency of the State, or of the officers or agents by whom its powers are exerted, shall deny to any person within its jurisdiction the equal protection of the laws. Whoever, by virtue of public position under a State government . . . denies or takes away the equal protection of the laws, violates the constitutional inhibition; and as he acts in the name and for the State, and is clothed with the State's power, his act is that of the State. This must be so, or the constitutional prohibition has no meaning." *Ex parte Virginia,* 100 U.S. 339 [1880]. Thus the prohibitions of the Fourteenth Amendment extend to all action of the State denying equal protection of the laws; whatever the agency of the State taking the action, or whatever the guise in which it is taken. In short, the constitutional rights of children not to be discriminated against in school admission on grounds of race or color declared by this Court in the *Brown* case can neither be nullified openly and directly by state legislators or state executive or judicial officers, nor nullified indirectly by them through evasive schemes for segregation whether attempted "ingeniously or ingenuously." *Smith* v. *Texas* [1940]. . . .

What has been said, in the light of the facts developed, is enough to dispose of the case. However, we should answer the premise of the actions of the Governor and Legislature that they are not bound by our holding in the *Brown* case. It is necessary only to recall some basic constitutional propositions which are settled doctrine.

Article VI of the Constitution makes the Constitution the "supreme Law of the Land." In 1803, Chief Justice MARSHALL, speaking for a unanimous Court, referring to the Constitution as "the fundamental and paramount law of the nation," declared in the notable case of *Marbury* v. *Madison* that "It is emphatically the province and duty of the judicial department to say what the law is." This decision declared the basic principle that the federal judiciary is supreme in the exposition of the law of the Constitution, and that principle has ever since been respected by this Court and the Country as a permanent and indispensable feature of our constitutional system. It follows that the interpretation of the Fourteenth Amendment enunciated by this Court in the *Brown* case is the supreme law of the land, and Art. VI of the Constitution makes it of binding effect on the States "any Thing in the Constitution or Laws of any State to the Contrary notwithstanding." Every state legislator and executive and judicial officer is solemnly committed by oath taken pursuant to Art. VI, § 3 "to support this Constitution." . . .

No state legislator or executive or judicial officer can war against the Constitution without violating his undertaking to support it. Chief Justice MARSHALL spoke for a unanimous Court in saying that: "If the legislatures of the several states may, at will, annul the judgments of the courts of the United States, and destroy the rights acquired under those judgments, the constitution itself becomes a solemn mockery. . . ." *United States* v. *Peters* [1809].

It is, of course, quite true that the responsibility for public education is primarily the concern of the States, but it is equally true that such responsibilities, like all other state activity, must be exercised consistently with federal constitutional requirements as they apply to state action. The Constitution created a government dedicated to equal justice under law. The Fourteenth Amendment embodied and emphasized that ideal. State support of segregated schools through any arrangement, management, funds, or property cannot be squared with the Amendment's command that no State shall deny to any person within its jurisdiction the equal protection of the laws. The right of a student not to be segregated on racial grounds in schools so maintained is indeed so fundamental and pervasive that it is embraced in the concept of due process of law. *Bolling* v. *Sharpe* [1954]. The basic decision in *Brown* was unanimously reached by this Court only after the case had been briefed and twice argued and the issues had been given the most serious consideration. Since the first *Brown* opinion three new Justices have come to the Court. They are at one with the Justices still on the Court who participated in that basic decision as to its correctness, and that decision is now unanimously reaffirmed. The principles announced in that decision and the obedience of the States to them, according to the command of the Constitution, are indispensable for the protection of the freedoms guaranteed by our fundamental charter for all of us. Our constitutional ideal of equal justice under law is thus made a living truth.

MR. JUSTICE FRANKFURTER, concurring.

While unreservedly participating with my brethren in our joint opinion, I deem it appropriate also to deal individually with the great issue here at stake. . . .

We are now asked to hold that the illegal, forcible interference by the State of Arkansas with the continuance of what the Constitution commands, and the consequences in disorder that it entrained, should be recognized as justification for undoing what the School Board had formulated, what the District Court in 1955 had directed to be carried out, and what was in process of obedience. No explanation that may be offered in support of such a request can obscure the inescapable meaning that law should bow to force. To yield to such a claim would be to enthrone official lawlessness, and lawlessness if not checked is the precursor of anarchy. Violent resistance to law cannot be made a legal reason for its suspension without loosening the fabric of our society. What could this mean but to acknowledge that disorder under the aegis of a State has moral superiority over the law of the Constitution? For those in authority thus to defy the law of the land is profoundly subversive not only of our constitutional system but of the presuppositions of a democratic society.

The duty to abstain from resistance to "the supreme Law of the Land," U.S. Const., Art. VI, ¶ 2, as declared by the organ of our Government for ascertaining it, does not require immediate approval of it nor does it deny the right of dissent. Criticism need not be stilled. Active obstruction or defiance is barred. Our kind of society cannot endure if the controlling authority of the Law as derived from the Constitution is not to be the tribunal specially charged with the duty of ascertaining and declaring what is "the supreme Law of the Land." Particularly is this so where the declaration of what "the supreme Law" commands on an underlying moral issue is not the dubious pronouncement of a gravely divided Court but is the unanimous conclusion of a long-matured deliberative process. . . .

That the responsibility of those who exercise power in a democratic government is not to reflect inflamed public feeling but to help form its understanding, is especially true when they are confronted with a problem like a racially discriminating public school system. This is the lesson to be drawn from the heartening experience in ending enforced racial segregation in the public schools in cities with Negro populations of large proportions. Compliance with decisions of this Court, as the constitutional organ of the supreme Law of the Land, has often, throughout our history, depended on active support by state and local authorities. It presupposes such support. To withhold it, and indeed to use political power to try to paralyze the supreme Law, precludes the maintenance of our federal system as we have known and cherished it for one hundred and seventy years. . . .

## *Plaut* v. *Spendthrift Farm, Inc.*

**514 U.S. 211, 115 S. Ct. 1447, 131 L.Ed.2d 238 (1995)**

In 1987, petitioners alleged in a civil action that respondents committed fraud and deceit in 1983 and 1984 in the sale of stock in violation of the Securities Exchange Act of 1934. The District Court for the Eastern District of Kentucky dismissed petitioners' action with prejudice following the Supreme Court's 1991 decision in *Lampf, Pleva, Lipkind, Prupis & Petigrow* v. *Gilbertson*, 501 U.S. 350, that required suits such as the petitioners' be commenced within one year after the discovery of the facts constituting the violation and within three years after such violation.

Once the District Court's judgment had become final, Congress enacted § 27A(b) of the Securities Exchange Act, which provided for reinstatement on motion of any action commenced before Lampf but dismissed thereafter as time barred, if the action would have been timely filed under applicable pre-Lampf state law. Although finding the statute's terms required that petitioners' ensuing § 27A(b) motion be granted, the District Court denied the motion on the ground that § 27A(b) was unconstitutional. The Court of Appeals for the Six Circuit affirmed. The Supreme Court granted certiorari. *Opinion of the Court: Scalia, Kennedy, O'Connor, Rehnquist, Souter, Thomas. Concurring in the judgment: Breyer. Dissenting Opinions: Stevens, Ginsburg.*

JUSTICE SCALIA delivered the opinion of the Court.

Respondents submit that § 27A(b) violates both the separation of powers and the Due Process Clause of the Fifth Amendment. Because the latter submission, if correct, might dictate a similar result in a challenge to state legislation under the Fourteenth Amendment, the former is the narrower ground for adjudication of the constitutional questions in the case, and we therefore consider it first. *Ashwander* v. *TVA*, 297 U.S. 288, 347 (1936) (Brandeis, J., concurring). We conclude that in § 27A(b) Congress has exceeded its authority by requiring the federal courts to exercise "the judicial Power of the United States," U.S. Const., Art. III, § 1, in a manner repugnant to the text, structure and traditions of Article III. . . .

Article III establishes a "judicial department" with the "province and duty . . . to say what the law is" in particular cases and controversies. *Marbury* v. *Madison* (1803). The record of history shows that the Framers crafted this charter of the judicial department with an expressed understanding that it gives the Federal Judiciary the power, not merely to rule on cases, but to *decide* them, subject to review only by superior courts in the Article III hierarchy—with an understanding, in short, that "a judgment conclusively resolves the case" because "a 'judicial Power' is one to render dispositive judgments." By retroactively commanding the federal courts to reopen final judgments, Congress has violated this fundamental principle.

. . . The Framers of our Constitution lived among the ruins of a system of intermingled legislative and judicial powers, which had been prevalent in the colonies long before the Revolution, and which after the Revolution had produced factional strife and partisan oppression. In the 17th and 18th centuries colonial assemblies and legislatures functioned as courts of equity of last resort, hearing original actions or providing appellate review of judicial judgments. Often, however, they chose to correct the judicial process through special bills or other enacted legislation. It was common for such legislation not to prescribe a resolution of the dispute, but rather simply to set aside the judgment and order a new trial or appeal.

. . . The sense of a sharp necessity to separate the legislative from the judicial power, prompted by the crescendo of legislative interference with private judgments of the courts, triumphed among the Framers of the new Federal Constitution. The Convention made the critical decision to establish a judicial department independent of the Legislative Branch by providing that "the judicial Power of the United States shall be vested in one supreme Court, and in such inferior Courts as the Congress may from time to time ordain and establish." Before and during the debates on ratification, Madison, Jefferson, and Hamilton each wrote of the factional disorders and disarray that the system of legislative equity had produced in the years before the framing; and each thought that the separation of the legislative from the judicial power in the new Constitution would cure them. Madison's *Federalist* No. 48, the famous description of the process by which "[t]he legislative department is every where extending the sphere of its activity, and drawing all power into its impetuous vortex," referred to the report of the Pennsylvania Council of Censors to show that in that State "cases belonging to the judiciary department [had been] frequently drawn within legislative cognizance and determination." Madison relied as well on Jefferson's Notes on the State of Virginia, which mentioned, as one example of the dangerous concentration of governmental powers into the hands of the legislature, that "the Legislature . . . in many instances decided rights which should have been left to judiciary controversy."

If the need for separation of legislative from judicial power was plain, the principal effect to be accomplished by that separation was even plainer. As Hamilton wrote in his exegesis of Article III, § 1, in *Federalist* No. 81:

> It is not true . . . that the parliament of Great Britain, or the legislatures of the particular states, can rectify the exceptionable decisions of their respective courts, in any other sense that might be done by a future legislature of the United States. The theory neither of the British, nor the state constitutions, authorises the revisal of a judicial sentence, by a legislative act. . . . A legislature without exceeding its province cannot reverse a determination once made, in a particular case; though it may prescribe a new rule for future cases.

The essential balance created by this allocation of authority was a simple one. The Legislature would be possessed of power to "prescribe[e] the rules by which the duties and rights of every citizen are to be regulated," but the power of "[t]he interpretation of the laws" would be "the proper and peculiar province of the courts." *The Federalist* No. 78. The Judiciary would be, "from the nature of its functions, . . . the [department] least dangerous to the political rights of the constitution," not because its acts were subject to legislative correction, but because the binding effect of its acts was limited to particular cases and controversies. Thus, "though individual oppression may now and then proceed from the courts of justice, the general liberty of the people can never be endangered from that quarter: . . . so long as the judiciary remains truly distinct from both the legislative and executive." *The Federalist* No. 78.

Judicial decisions in the period immediately after ratification of the Constitution confirm the understanding that it forbade interference with the final judgments of courts. . . .

Section 27A(b) effects a clear violation of the separation-of-powers principle we have just discussed. It is, of course, retroactive legislation, that is, legislation that prescribes what the law *was* at an earlier time, when the act whose effect is controlled by the legislation occurred—in this case, the filing of the initial Rule 10b-5 action in the District Court. When retroactive legislation requires its own application in a case already finally adjudicated, it does no more and no less than "reverse a determination once made, in a particular case." *The Federalist* No. 81. . . .

It is true, as petitioners contend, that Congress can always revise the judgments of Article III courts in one sense: When a new law makes clear that it is retroactive, and appellate court must apply that law in reviewing judgments still on appeal that were rendered before the law was enacted, and must alter the outcome accordingly. . . . But a distinction between judgments from which all appeals have been forgone or completed, and judgments that remain on appeal (or subject to being appealed), is implicit in what Article III creates: not a batch of unconnected courts, but a judicial *department* composed of "inferior Courts" and "one supreme Court." Within that hierarchy, the decision of an inferior court is not (unless the time for appeal has expired) the final word of the department as a whole. It is the obligation of the last court in the hierarchy that rules on the case to give effect to Congress's latest enactment, even when that has the effect of overturning the judgment of an inferior court, since each court, at every level, must "decide according to existing laws." Having achieved finality, however, a judicial decision becomes the last word of the judicial department with regard to a particular case or controversy, and Congress may not declare by retroactive legislation that the law applicable *to that very case* was something other than what the courts said it was. Finality of a legal judgment is determined by statute, just as entitlement to a government benefit is a statutory creation; but that no more deprives the former of its constitutional significance for separation-of-powers analysis than it deprives the latter of its significance for due process purposes.

To be sure, § 27A(b) reopens (or directs the reopening of) final judgments in a whole class of cases rather than in a particular suit. We do not see how that makes any difference. The separation-of-powers violation here, if there is any, consists of depriving judicial judgments of the conclusive effect that they had when they were announced, not of acting in a manner—viz., with particular rather than general effect—that is unusual (though, we must note, not impossible) for a legislature. To be sure, a general statute such as this one may reduce the perception that legislative interference with judicial judgments were prompted by individual favoritism; but it is legislative interference with judicial judgments nonetheless. Not favoritism, nor even corruption, but *power* is the object of the separation-of-powers prohibition. The prohibition is violated when an individual final judgment is legislatively rescinded for even the *very best* of reasons, such as the legislature's genuine conviction (supported by all the law professors in the land) that the judgment was wrong; and it is violated 40 times over when 40 final judgments are legislatively dissolved.

It is irrelevant as well that the final judgments reopened by § 27A(b) rested on the bar of a statute of limitations. The rules of finality, both statutory and judge-made, treat a dismissal on statute-of-limitations grounds the same way they treat a dismissal for failure to state a claim, for failure to prove substantive liability, or for failure to prosecute: as a judgment on the merits.

. . . Apart from the statute we review today, we know of no instance in which Congress has attempted to set aside the final judgment of an Article III court by retroactive legislation. That prolonged reticence would be amazing if such interference were not understood to be constitutionally proscribed.

. . . [T]he doctrine of separation of powers is a *structural safeguard* rather than a remedy to be applied only when specific harm, or risk of specific harm, can be identified. In its major feature (of which the conclusiveness of judicial judgments is assuredly one) it is a prophylactic device, establishing high walls and clear distinctions because low walls and vague distinctions will not be judicially defensible in the heat of interbranch conflict. . . . We think legislated invalidation of judicial judgments deserves the same categorical treatment accorded by *Chadha* to congressional invalidation of executive action. The delphic alternative suggested by the concurrence (the setting aside of judgments is all right so long as Congress does not "impermissibly tr[y] to *apply*, as well as *make*, the law," simply prolongs doubt and multiplies confrontation. Separation of powers, a distinctively American political doctrine, profits from the advice authored by a distinctively American poet: "Good fences make good neighbors."

We know of no previous instance in which Congress has enacted retroactive legislation requiring an Article III court to set aside a final judgment, and for good reason. The Constitution's separation of legislative and judicial powers denies it the authority to do so. Section 27A(b) is unconstitutional to the extent that it requires federal courts to reopen final judgments entered before its enactment. The judgment of the Court of Appeals is affirmed.

*It is so ordered.*

JUSTICE BREYER, concurring in the judgment.

I agree with the majority that § 27A(b) of the Securities Exchange Act of 1934 is unconstitutional. In my view, the separation of powers inherent in our Constitution means that at least *sometimes* Congress lacks the power under Article I to reopen an otherwise closed court judgment. And the statutory provision here at issue, § 27A(b), violates a basic "separation of powers" principle—one intended to protect individual liberty. Three features of this law—its exclusively retroactive effect, its application to a limited number of individuals, and its reopening of closed judgments—taken together, show that Congress here impermissibly tried to *apply*, as well as *make*, the law. Hence, § 27A(b) falls outside the scope of Article I. But, it is far less clear, and unnecessary for the purposes of this case to decide, that separation of powers "is violated" *whenever* an "individual" final judgment is legislatively rescinded" or that it is "violated 40 times over when 40 final judgments are legislatively dissolved." I therefore write separately.

[B]ecause the law before us *both* reopens final judgments *and* lacks the liberty-protecting assurances that prospectivity and greater generality would have provided, we need not, and we should not, go further—to make of the reopening itself, an absolute, always determinative distinction, a "prophylactic device," or a foundation for the building of a new "high wal[l]" between the branches. Indeed, the unnecessary building of such walls is, in itself, dangerous, because the Constitution blends, as well as separates, powers in its effort to create a government that will work for, as well as protect the liberties of, its citizens. That doctrine does not "divide the branches into watertight compartments," nor "establish and divide fields of black and white." And, important separation of powers decisions of this Court have sometimes turned, not upon absolute distinctions, but upon degree. As the majority invokes the advice of an American poet, one might consider as well that poet's caution, for he not only notes that "Something there is that doesn't love a wall," but also writes, "Before I built a wall I'd ask to know/ What I was walling in or walling out."

JUSTICE STEVENS, with whom JUSTICE GINSBURG joins, dissenting.

The majority's rigid holding unnecessarily hinders the Government from addressing difficult issues that inevitably arise in a complex society. This Court, for example, lacks power to enlarge the time for filing petitions for certiorari in a civil case after 90 days from the entry of final judgment, no matter how strong the equities. If an Act of God, such as a flood or an earthquake, sufficiently disrupted communications in a particular area to preclude filing for several days, the majority's reasoning would appear to bar Congress from addressing the resulting inequity. If Congress passed remedial legislation that retroactively granted movants from the disaster area extra time to file petitions or motions for extensions of time to file, today's holding presumably would compel us to strike down the legislation as an attack on the finality of judgments. Such a ruling, like today's holding, would gravely undermine federal courts' traditional power "to set aside a judgment whose enforcement would work inequity."

. . . The Court has drawn the wrong lesson from the Framers' disapproval of colonial legislatures' appellate review of judicial decisions. The Framers rejected that practice, not out of a mechanistic solicitude for "final judgments," but because they believed the impartial application of rules of law, rather than the will of the majority, must govern the disposition of individual cases and controversies. Any legislative interference in the adjudication of the merits of a particular case carries the risk that political power will supplant even handed justice, whether the interference occurs before or after the entry of final judgment. Section 27A(b) neither commands the reinstatement of any particular case nor directs any result on the merits. Congress recently granted a special benefit to a single litigant in a pending civil rights case, but the Court saw no need even to grant certiorari to review that disturbing legislative favor. In an ironic counterpoint, the Court today places a higher priority on protecting the Republic from the restoration to a large class of litigants of the opportunity to have Article III courts resolve the merits of their claims.

"We must remember that the machinery of government would not work if it were not allowed a little play in its joints." *Bain Peanut Co. of Texas* v. *Pinson,* 282 U.S. 499, 501 (1931) (Holmes, J.). The three Branches must cooperate in order to govern. We should regard favorably, rather than with suspicious hostility, legislation that enables the judiciary to overcome impediments to the performance of its mission of administering justice impartially, even when, as here, this Court had created the impediment. Rigid rules often make good law, but judgments in areas such as the review of potential conflicts among the three coequal Branches of the Federal Government partake of art as well as science. That is why we have so often reiterated the insight of Justice Jackson:

> The actual art of governing under our Constitution does not and cannot conform to judicial definitions of the power of any of its branches based on isolated clauses or even single Articles torn from context. While the Constitution diffuses power the better to secure liberty, it also contemplates that practice will integrate the dispersed powers into a workable government. It enjoins upon its branches separateness but interdependence, autonomy but reciprocity. *Youngstown Sheet & Tube Co.* v. *Sawyer,* 343 U.S. 579, 635 (1952) (concurring opinion).

We have the authority to hold that Congress has usurped a judicial prerogative, but even if this case were doubtful I would heed Justice Iredell's admonition in *Calder* v. *Bull,* 3 Dall., at 309, that "the Court will never resort to that authority, but in a clear and urgent case." An appropriate regard for the interdependence of Congress and the judiciary amply supports the conclusion that § 27A(b) reflects constructive legislative cooperation rather than a usurpation of judicial prerogatives.

Accordingly, I respectfully dissent.

## *Ex Parte McCardle*

**74 U.S. (7 Wallace) 506; 19 L. Ed. 264 (1869)**

During the post–Civil War period, Radical Republicans in the Congress imposed upon the southern states a Reconstruction program. William McCardle, a Mississippi newspaper editor and opponent of Reconstruction, was held for trial before a military commission on charges that he had allowed to be published articles alleged to be "incendiary and libelous." As a civilian, McCardle asserted that he was being unlawfully restrained and sought a writ of habeas corpus before the Supreme Court under an 1867 statute. The Radical Republican leaders in the Congress feared that the Supreme Court—already hostile to Reconstruction—would use the occasion provided by *McCardle* to declare much of the Reconstruction program unconstitutional. Consequently, Congress, over President Andrew Johnson's veto, repealed the 1867 act on which McCardle's appeal was based. By this time, the Court had already heard full arguments in the case, but it had not yet announced its decision. *Opinion of the Court: Chase, Clifford, Davis, Field, Grier, Miller, Nelson, Swayne.*

MR. CHIEF JUSTICE CHASE delivered the opinion of the Court. . .

The first question necessarily is that of jurisdiction; for, if the act of March, 1868, takes away the jurisdiction defined by the act of February, 1867, it is useless, if not improper, to enter into any discussion of other questions.

It is quite true, as was argued by the counsel for the petitioner, that the appellate jurisdiction of this court is not derived from acts of Congress. It is, strictly speaking, conferred by the Constitution. But it is conferred "with such exceptions and under such regulations as Congress shall make."

It is unnecessary to consider whether, if Congress had made no exceptions and no regulations, this court might not have exercised general appellate jurisdiction under rules prescribed by itself. For among the earliest acts of the first Congress, at its first session, was the act of September 24th, 1789, to establish the judicial courts of the United States. That act provided for the organization of this court, and prescribed regulations for the exercise of its jurisdiction.

The source of that jurisdiction, and the limitations of it by the Constitution and by statute, have been on several occasions subjects of consideration here. In the case of *Durousseau* v. *The United States* [1810]. . . particularly, the whole matter was carefully examined, and the court held, that while "the appellate powers of this court are not given by the judicial act, but are given by the Constitution," they are, nevertheless, "limited and regulated by that act, and by such other acts as have been passed on the subject." The court said, further, that the judicial act was an exercise of the power given by the Constitution to Congress "of making exceptions to the appellate jurisdiction of the Supreme Court." "They have described affirmatively," said the court, "its jurisdiction, and this affirmative description has been understood to imply a negation of the exercise of such appellate power as is not comprehended within it."

The principle that the affirmation of appellate jurisdication implies that negation of all such jurisdiction not affirmed having been thus established, it was an almost necessary consequence that acts of Congress, providing for the exercise of jurisdiction, should come to be spoken of as acts granting jurisdiction, and not as acts making exceptions to the constitutional grant of it.

The exception to appellate jurisdiction in the case before us, however, is not an inference from the affirmation of other appellate jurisdiction. It is made in terms. The provision of the act of 1867, affirming the appellate jurisdiction of this court in cases of *habeas corpus* is expressly repealed. It is hardly possible to imagine a plainer instance of positive exception.

We are not at liberty to inquire into the motives of the legislature. We can only examine into its power under the Constitution; and the power to make exceptions to the appellate jurisdiction of this court is given by express words.

What, then, is the effect of the repealing act upon the case before us? We cannot doubt as to this. Without jurisdiction the court cannot proceed at all in any cause. Jurisdiction is power to declare the law, and when it ceases to exist, the only function remaining to the court is that of announcing the fact and dismissing the cause. And this is not less clear upon authority than upon principle.

Several cases were cited by the counsel for the petitioner in support of the position that jurisdiction of this case is not affected by the repealing act. But none of them, in our judgment, afford any support to it. They are all cases of the exercise of judicial power by the legislature, or of legislative interference with courts in the exercising of continuing jurisdiction.

On the other hand, the general rule, supported by the best elementary writers, is, that "when an act of the legislature is repealed, it must be considered, except as to transactions past and closed, as if it never existed." . . .

It is quite clear, therefore, that this court cannot proceed to pronounce judgment in this case, for it has no longer jurisdiction of the appeal; and judicial duty is not less fitly performed by declining ungranted jurisdiction than in exercising firmly that which the Constitution and the laws confer.

## *Frothingham* v. *Mellon*

**262 U.S. 447; 43 S. Ct. 597; 67 L. Ed. 1078 (1923)**

The Maternity Act of 1921 provided for grants from the United States Treasury to states that agreed to establish, under federal supervision, programs designed to reduce maternal and infant mortality and to protect the health of mothers and infants. Frothingham, a private citizen, brought suit as a taxpayer against Andrew Mellon, secretary of the treasury, alleging that this expenditure of federal funds violated the Due Process Clause of the Fifth Amendment. When the federal district court dismissed Frothingham's suit for want of jurisdiction and the court of appeals affirmed the lower court's decree, she appealed to the Supreme Court. *Opinion of the Court: Sutherland, Brandeis, Butler, Holmes, McKenna, McReynolds, Sanford, Taft, VanDevanter.*

MR. JUSTICE SUTHERLAND delivered the opinion of the Court. . . .

This . . . plaintiff alleges . . . that she is a taxpayer of the United States; and her contention, though not clear, seems to be that the effect of the appropriations complained of will be to increase the burden of future taxation and thereby take her property without due process of law. The right of a taxpayer to enjoin the execution of a federal appropriation act, on the ground that it is invalid and will result in taxation for illegal purposes, has never been passed upon by this Court. In cases where it was presented, the question has either been allowed to pass sub silentio or the determination of it expressly withheld. . . . The interest of a taxpayer of a municipality in the application of its moneys is direct and immediate and the remedy by injunction to prevent their misuse is not inappropriate. It is upheld by a large number of state cases and is the rule of this Court. . . . But the relation of a taxpayer of the United States to the Federal Government is very different. His interest in the moneys of the Treasury—partly realized from taxation and partly from other sources—is shared with millions of others; is comparatively minute and indeterminable; and the effect upon future taxation, of any payment out of the funds, so remote, fluctuating and uncertain, that no basis is afforded for an appeal to the preventive powers of a court of equity.

The administration of any statute, likely to produce additional taxation to be imposed upon a vast number of taxpayers, the extent of whose several liability is indefinite and constantly changing, is essentially a matter of public and not of individual concern. If one taxpayer may champion and litigate such a cause, then every other taxpayer may do the same, not only in respect of the statute here under review but also in respect of every other appropriation act and statute whose administration requires the outlay of public money, and whose validity may be questioned. The bare suggestion of such a result, with its attendant inconveniences, goes far to sustain the conclusion which we have reached, that a suit of this character cannot be maintained. It is of much significance that no precedent sustaining the right to maintain suits like this has been called to our attention, although, since the formation of the government, as an examination of the acts of Congress will disclose, a large number of statutes appropriating or involving the expenditure of moneys for non-federal purposes have been enacted and carried into effect.

The functions of government under our system are apportioned. To the legislative department has been committed the duty of making laws; to the executive the duty of executing them; and to the judiciary the duty of interpreting and applying them in cases properly brought before the courts. The general rule is that neither department may invade the province of the other and neither may control, direct or restrain the action of the other. We are not now speaking of the merely ministerial duties of officials. . . . We have no power per se to review and annul acts of Congress on the ground that they are unconstitutional. That question may be considered only when the justification for some direct injury suffered or threatened, presenting a justiciable issue, is made to rest upon such an act. Then the power exercised is that of ascertaining and declaring the law applicable to the controversy. It amounts to little more than the negative power to disregard an unconstitutional enactment, which otherwise would stand in the way of the enforcement of a legal right. The party who invokes the power must be able to show not only that the statute is invalid but that he has sustained or is immediately in danger of sustaining some direct injury as the result of its enforcement, and not merely that he suffers in some indefinite way in common with people generally. If a case for preventive relief be presented the court enjoins, in effect, not the execution of the statute, but the acts of the official, the statute notwithstanding. Here the . . . plaintiff [has] no such case. Looking through forms of words to the substance of [the] complaint, it is merely that officials of the executive department of the government are executing and will execute an act of Congress asserted to be unconstitutional; and this we are asked to prevent. To do so would be not to decide a judicial controversy, but to assume a position of authority over the governmental acts of another and coequal department, an authority which plainly we do not possess.

## *Flast* v. *Cohen*

**392 U.S. 83; 88 S. Ct. 1942; 20 L. Ed. 2d 947 (1968)**

Florence Flast and other federal taxpayers filed suit in federal district court to enjoin Wilbur Cohen, secretary of health, education and welfare, from expending funds authorized by Congress under the Elementary and Secondary Education Act of 1965. The act provided funds to finance the instruction of and the purchase of textbooks in reading, arithmetic, and other subjects in religious schools. Flast and the other plaintiffs contended that these expenditures promoted religious programs in violation of the Establishment Clause of the First Amendment. The district court, on the authority of *Frothingham,* held that they lacked standing and dismissed the suit. They appealed to the Supreme Court. *Opinion of the Court: Warren, Black, Brennan, Marshall, White. Concurring opinions: Douglas; Fortas; Stewart. Dissenting opinion: Harlan.*

MR. CHIEF JUSTICE WARREN delivered the opinion of the Court. . . .

This Court first faced squarely the question whether a litigant asserting only his status as a taxpayer has standing to maintain a suit in a federal court in *Frothingham* v. *Mellon* . . . and that decision must be the starting point for analysis in this case. . . .

Although the barrier *Frothingham* erected against federal taxpayer suits has never been breached, the decision has been the source of some confusion and the object of considerable criticism. The confusion has developed as commentators have tried to determine whether *Frothingham* establishes a constitutional bar to taxpayer suits or whether the Court was simply imposing a rule of self-restraint which was not constitutionally compelled. The conflicting viewpoints are reflected in the arguments made to this Court by the parties in this case. The Government has pressed upon us the view that *Frothingham* announced a constitutional rule, compelled by the Article III limitations on federal court jurisdiction and grounded in considerations of the doctrine of separation of powers. Appellants, however, insist that *Frothingham* expressed no more than a policy of judicial self-restraint which can be disregarded when compelling reasons for assuming jurisdiction over a taxpayer's suit exist. The opinion delivered in *Frothingham* can be read to support either position. . . .

The jurisdiction of federal courts is defined and limited by Article III of the Constitution. In terms relevant to the question for decision in this case, the judicial power of federal courts is constitutionally restricted to "cases" and "controversies." As is so often the situation in constitutional adjudication, those two words have an iceberg quality, containing beneath their surface simplicity submerged complexities which go to the very heart of our constitutional form of government. Embodied in the words "cases" and "controversies" are two complementary but somewhat different limitations. In part those words limit the business of federal courts to questions presented in an adversary context and in a form historically viewed as capable of resolution through the judicial process. And in part those words define the role assigned to the judiciary in a tripartite allocation of power to assure that the federal courts will not intrude into areas committed to the other branches of government. Justiciability is the term of art employed to give expression to this dual limitation placed upon federal courts by the case-and-controversy doctrine.

. . . As we understand it, the Government's position is that the constitutional scheme of separation of powers, and the deference owed by the federal judiciary to the other two branches of government within that scheme, presents an absolute bar to taxpayer suits challenging the validity of federal spending programs. The Government views such suits as involving no more than the mere disagreement by the taxpayer "with the uses to which tax money is put." According to the Government, the resolution of such disagreements is committed to other branches of Federal Government and not to the judiciary. Consequently, the Government contends that, under no circumstances, should standing be conferred on federal taxpayers to challenge a federal taxing or spending program. An analysis of the function served by standing limitations compels a rejection of the Government's position.

Standing is an aspect of justiciability and as such, the problem of standing is surrounded by the same complexities and vagaries that inhere in justiciability. . . . The "gist of the question of standing" is whether the party seeking relief has "alleged such a personal stake in the outcome of the controversy as to assure that concrete adverseness which sharpens the presentation of issues upon which the court so largely depends for illumination of difficult constitutional questions." *Baker* v. *Carr* 1962. . . . In other words, when standing is placed in issue in a case, the question is whether the person whose standing is challenged is a proper party to request an adjudication of a particular issue and not whether the issue itself is justiciable.

. . . A taxpayer may or may not have the requisite personal stake in the outcome, depending upon the circumstances of the particular case. Therefore, we find no absolute bar in Article III to suits by federal taxpayers challenging allegedly unconstitutional federal taxing and spending programs. There remains, however, the problem of determining the circumstances under which a federal taxpayer will be deemed to have the personal stake and interest that imparts the necessary concrete adverseness to such litigation so that standing can be conferred on the taxpayer *qua* taxpayer consistent with the constitutional limitations of Article III. . . . Whether such individuals have standing to maintain that form of action turns on whether they can demonstrate the necessary stake as taxpayers in the outcome of the litigation to satisfy Article III requirements.

The nexus demanded of federal taxpayers has two aspects to it. First, the taxpayer must establish a logical link between that status and the type of legislative enactment attacked. Thus, a taxpayer will be a proper party to allege the unconstitutionality only of exercises of congressional power under the taxing and spending clause of Art. I, § 8, of the Constitution. It will not be sufficient to allege an incidental expenditure of tax funds in the administration of an essentially regulatory statute. Secondly the taxpayer must establish a nexus between that status and the precise nature of the constitutional infringement alleged. Under this requirement, the taxpayer must show that the challenged enactment exceeds specific constitutional limitations imposed upon the exercise of the congressional taxing and spending power and not simply that the enactment is generally beyond the powers delegated to Congress by Art. I, § 8. When both nexuses are established, the litigant will have shown a taxpayer's stake in the outcome of the controversy and will be a proper and appropriate party to invoke a federal court's jurisdiction. . .

The taxpayer-appellants in this case have satisfied both nexuses to support their claim of standing under the test we announce today. Their constitutional challenge is made to an exercise by Congress of its power under Art. I, § 8, to spend for the general welfare, and the challenged program involves a substantial expenditure of federal tax funds. In addition, appellants have alleged that the challenged expenditures violate the Establishment and Free Exercise Clauses of the First Amendment. . . .

*Reversed.*

MR. JUSTICE HARLAN, dissenting.

The problems presented by this case are narrow and relatively abstract, but the principles by which they must be resolved involve nothing less than the proper functioning of the federal courts, and so run to the roots of our constitutional system. . . .

It is desirable first to restate the basic issues in this case. The lawsuits here and in *Frothingham.* They present the question whether federal taxpayers *qua* taxpayers may, in suits in which they do not contest the validity of their previous or existing tax obligations, challenge the constitutionality of the uses for which Congress has authorized the expenditure of public funds.

This Court has previously held that individual litigants have standing to represent the public interest, despite their lack of economic or other personal interests, if Congress has appropriately authorized such suits. . . . I would adhere to that principle. Any hazards to the proper allocation of authority among the three branches of the Government would be substantially diminished if public actions had been pertinently authorized by Congress and the President. I appreciate that this Court does not ordinarily await the mandate of other branches of the Government, but it seems to me that the extraordinary character of public actions, and of the mischievous, if not dangerous, consequences they involve for the proper functioning of our constitutional system, and in particular of the federal courts, makes such judicial forbearance the part of wisdom. It must be emphasized that the implications of these questions of judicial policy are of fundamental significance for the other branches of the Federal Government.

The question here is not, despite the Court's unarticulated premise, whether the religious clauses of the First Amendment are hereafter to be enforced by the federal courts; the issue is simply whether plaintiffs of an *additional* category, heretofore excluded from those courts, are to be permitted to maintain suits. The recent history of this Court is replete with illustrations, including even one announced today . . . that questions involving the religious clauses will not, if federal taxpayers are prevented from contesting federal expenditures, be left "unacknowledged, unresolved, and undecided."

Accordingly, for the reasons contained in this opinion, I would affirm the judgment of the District Court.

## *Lujan* v. *Defenders of Wildlife*

**112 S.Ct. 2130 119 L.Ed. 2d 351 (1992)**

The respondent and other wildlife conservation and environmental groups brought an action in U.S. District Court for the District of Minnesota against the Secretary of the Interior, challenging a regulation promulgated by his department implementing Section 7 of the Endangered Species Act (ESA) of 1973 and arguing that it failed to follow Congress's intentions. In Section 7 of the ESA, Congress sought to protect endangered species by requiring that all federal agencies consult with the Secretary of the Interior to ensure that any action funded by the agency not jeopardize the continued existence or habitat of any endangered or threatened species. The Interior Department's regulation implementing Section 7 extended the ESA's coverage to federally funded projects only in the United States and on the high seas but did not apply it to actions funded in foreign countries. The District Court dimissed the case for lack of standing, and the Court of Appeals for the Eighth Circuit reversed and remanded. On cross-motions for summary judgment, the District Court then rejected the Secretary's renewed objection to standing, granted the respondents' motion, and ordered the Secretary to publish a new regulation extending coverage to foreign countries. The Supreme Court granted certiorari. *Opinion of the Court: Scalia, Kennedy, Rehnquist, Souter, Thomas, White. Concurring in part and concurring in the judgment: Kennedy, Souter. Concurring in the judgment: Stevens. Dissenting opinion: Blackmun, O'Connor.*

JUSTICE SCALIA delivered the opinion of the Court.

This case involves a challenge to a rule promulgated by the Secretary of the Interior interpreting § 7 of the Endangered Species Act of 1973 (ESA), in such fashion as to render it applicable only to actions within the United States or on the high seas. The preliminary issue, and the only one we reach, is whether the respondents here, plaintiffs below, have standing to seek judicial review of the rule. . . .

While the Constitution of the United States divides all power conferred upon the Federal Government into "legislative Powers," "[t]he executive Power," and "[t]he judicial Power," it does not attempt to define those terms. To be sure, it limits the jurisdiction of federal courts to "Cases" and "Controversies," but an executive inquiry can bear the name "case" and a legislative dispute can bear the name "controversy." Obviously, then, the Constitution's central mechanism of separation of powers depends largely upon common understanding of what activities are appropriate to legislatures, to executives, and to courts. In *The Federalist,* No. 48, Madison expressed the view that "[i]t is not infrequently a question of real nicety in legislative bodies whether the operation of a particular measure will, or will not, extend beyond the legislative sphere," whereas "the executive power [is] restrained within a narrower compass and . . . more simple in its nature," and "the judiciary [is] described by landmarks still less uncertain." One of those landmarks, setting apart the "Cases" and "Controversies" that are of the justiciable sort referred to in Article III—"serv[ing] to identify those disputes which are appropriately resolved through the judicial process,"—is the doctrine of standing. Though some of its elements express merely prudential considerations that are part of judicial self-government, the core component of standing is an essential and unchanging part of the case-or-controversy requirement of Article III.

Over the years, our cases have established

that the irreducible constitutional minimum of standing contains three elements: First, the plaintiff must have suffered an "injury in fact"—an invasion of a legally protected interest which is (a) concrete and particularized, and (b) "actual or imminent, not 'conjectural' or 'hypothetical.'" Second, there must be a causal connection between the injury and the conduct complained of—the injury has to be "fairly . . . trace[able] to the challenged action of the defendant, and not . . . th[e] result [of] the independent action of some third party not before the court." Third, it must be "likely," as opposed to merely "speculative," that the injury will be "redressed by a favorable decision."

The party invoking federal jurisdiction bears the burden of establishing these elements. . . .

When the suit is one challenging the legality of government action or inaction, the nature and extent of facts that must be averred (at the summary judgment stage) or proved (at the trial stage) in order to establish standing depends considerably upon whether the plaintiff is himself an object of the action (or forgone action) at issue. If he is, there is ordinarily little question that the action or inaction has caused him injury, and that a judgment preventing or requiring the action will redress it. When, however, as in this case, a plaintiff's asserted injury arises from the government's allegedly unlawful regulation (or lack of regulation) of *someone else,* much more is needed. In that circumstance, . . . it becomes the burden of the plaintiff to adduce facts showing that those choices have been or will be made in such manner as to produce causation and permit redressability of injury. Thus, when the plaintiff is not himself the object of the government action or inaction he challenges, standing is not precluded, but it is ordinarily "substantially more difficult" to establish.

We think the Court of Appeals failed to apply the foregoing principles in denying the Secretary's motion for summary judgment. Respondents had not made the requisite demonstration of (at least) injury and redressability.

Respondents' claim to injury is that the lack of consultation with respect to certain funded activities abroad "increas[es] the rate of extinction of endangered and threatened species." Of course, the desire to use or observe an animal species, even for purely aesthetic purposes, is undeniably a cognizable interest for purpose of standing. "But the 'injury in fact' test requires more than an injury to a cognizable interest. It requires that the party seeking review be himself among the injured." . . .

With respect to this aspect of the case, the Court of Appeals focused on the affidavits of two Defenders' members—Joyce Kelly and Amy Skilbred. Ms. Kelly stated that she traveled to Egypt in 1986 and "observed the traditional habitat of the endangered Nile crocodile there and intend[s] to do so again, and hope[s] to observe the crocodile directly," and that she "will suffer harm in fact as a result of [the] American . . . role . . . in overseeing the rehabilitation of the Aswan High Dam on the Nile . . . and [in] develop[ing] . . . Egypt's . . . Master Water Plan." Ms. Skilbred averred that she traveled to Sri Lanka in 1981 and "observed th[e] habitat" of "endangered species such as the Asian elephant and the leopard" at what is now the site of the Mahaweli Project funded by the Agency for International Development (AID), although she "was unable to see any of the endangered species"; "this development project," she continued, "will seriously reduce endangered, threatened, and endemic species habitat including areas that I visited . . . [which] may severely shorten the future of these species;" that threat, she concluded, harmed her because she "intend[s] to return to Sri Lanka in the future and hope[s] to be more fortunate in spotting at least the endangered elephant and leopard." When Ms. Skilbred was asked at a subsequent deposition if and when she had any plans to return to Sri Lanka, she reiterated that "I intend to go back to Sri Lanka," but confessed that she had no current plans: "I don't know [when]. There is a civil war going on right now. I don't know. Not next year, I will say. In the future."

We shall assume for the sake of argument that these affidavits contain facts showing that certain agency-funded projects threaten listed species—though that is questionable. They plainly contain no facts, however, showing how damage to the species will produce "imminent" injury to Mss. Kelly and Skilbred. That the women "had visited" the areas of the projects before the projects commenced proves nothing. And the affiants' profession of an "inten[t]" to return to the places they had visited before—where they will presumably, this time, be deprived of the opportunity to observe animals of the endangered species—is simply not enough. Such "some day" intentions—without any description of concrete plans, or indeed even any specification of *when* the some day will be—do not support a finding of the "actual or imminent" injury that our cases require.

Besides relying upon the Kelly and Skilbred affidavits, respondents propose a series of novel standing theories. The first, inelegantly styled "ecosystem nexus," proposes that any person who uses *any part* of a "contiguous ecosystem" adversely affected by a funded activity has standing even if the activity is located a great distance away. . . .

To say that the Act protects ecosystems is not to say that the Act creates (if it were possible) rights of action in persons who have not been injured in fact, that is, persons who use portions of an ecosystem not perceptibly affected by the unlawful action in question.

Respondents' other theories are called, alas, the "animal nexus" approach, whereby anyone who has an interest in studying or seeing the endangered animals anywhere on the globe has standing; and the "vocational nexus" approach, under which anyone with a professional interest in such animals can sue. Under these theories, anyone who goes to see Asian elephants in the Bronx Zoo, and anyone who is a keeper of Asian elephants in the Bronx Zoo, has standing to sue because the Director of AID did not consult with the Secretary regarding the AID-funded project in Sri Lanka. This is beyond all reason. Standing is not "an ingenious academic exercise in the conceivable," but as we have said requires, at the summary judgment stage, a factual showing of perceptible harm. It is clear that the person who observes or works with a particular animal threatened by a federal decision is facing perceptible harm, since the very subject of his interest will no longer exist. It is even plausible—though it goes to the outermost limit of plausibility—to think that a person who observes or works with animals of a particular species in the very area of the world where the species is threatened by a federal decision is facing such harm, since some animals that might have been the subject of his interest will no longer exist. It goes beyond the limit, however, and into pure speculation and fantasy, to say that anyone who observes or works with an endangered species, anywhere in the world, is appreciably harmed by a single project affecting some portion of that species with which he has no more specific connection.

The Court of Appeals found that respondents had standing for an additional reason: because they had suffered a "procedural injury." . . .

The court held that the citizen-suit provision creates a "procedural righ[t]" to consultation in all "persons"—so that *anyone* can file suit in federal court to challenge the Secretary's (or presumably any other official's) failure to follow the assertedly correct consultative procedure, notwithstanding their inability to allege any discrete injury flowing from that failure. We reject this view.

We have consistently held that a plaintiff raising only a generally available grievance about government—claiming only harm to his and every citizen's interest in proper application of the Constitution and laws, and seeking relief that no more directly and tangibly benefits him than it does the public at large—does not state an Article III case or controversy. For example, in *Frothingham* v. *Mellon* (1923), we dismissed for lack of Article III standing a taxpayer suit challenging the propriety of certain federal expenditures. We said:

> The party who invokes the power [of judicial review] must be able to show not only that the statute is invalid but that he has sustained or is immediately in danger of sustaining some direct injury as the result of its enforcement, and not merely that he suffers in some indefinite way in common with people generally. . . .

More recent cases are to the same effect.

To be sure, our generalized-grievance cases have typically involved Government violation of procedures assertedly ordained by the Constitution rather than the Congress. But there is absolutely no basis for making the Article III inquiry turn on the source of the asserted right. Whether the courts were to act on their own, or at the invitation of Congress, in ignoring the concrete injury requirement described in our cases, they would be discarding a principle fundamental to the separate and distinct constitutional role of the Third Branch—one of the essential elements that identifies those "Cases" and "Controversies" that are the business of the courts rather than of the political branches. Vindicating the *public* interest (including the public interest in government observance of the Constitution and laws) is the function of Congress and the Chief Executive. The question presented here is whether the public interest in proper administration of the laws (specifically, in agencies' observance of a particular, statutorily prescribed procedure) can be converted into an individual right by a statute that denominates it as such, and that permits all citizens (or, for that matter, a subclass of citizens who suffer no distinctive concrete harm) to sue. If the concrete injury requirement has the separation-of-powers significance we have always said, the answer must be obvious: To permit Congress to convert the undifferentiated public interest in executive officers' compliance with the law into an "individual right" vindicable in the courts is to permit Congress to transfer from the President to the courts the Chief Executive's most important constitutional duty, to "take Care that the Laws be faithfully executed." It would enable the courts, with the permission of Congress, "to assume a position of authority over the governmental acts of another and co-equal department," and to become " 'virtually continuing monitors of the wisdom and soundness of Executive action.' " We have always rejected that vision of our role. . . .

We hold that respondents lack standing to bring this action and that the Court of Appeals erred in denying the summary judgment motion filed by the United States. The opinion of the Court of Appeals is hereby reversed, and the cause remanded for proceedings consistent with this opinion.

JUSTICE BLACKMUN, with JUSTICE O'CONNOR, dissenting.

I part company with the Court in this case in two respects. First, I believe that respondents have raised genuine issues of fact—sufficient to survive summary judgment—both as to injury and as to redressability. Second, I question the Court's breadth of language in rejecting standing for "procedural" injuries. I fear the Court seeks to impose fresh limitations on the constitutional authority of Congress to allow citizen-suits in the federal courts for injuries deemed "procedural" in nature. I dissent.

The Court expresses concern that allowing judicial enforcement of "agencies' observance of a particular statutorily prescribed procedure" would "transfer from the President to the courts the Chief Executive's most important constitutional duty, to "take Care that the Laws be faithfully executed,' Art. II, sec 3." *Ante,* at 2145. In fact, the principal effect of foreclosing judicial enforcement of such procedures is to transfer power into the hands of the Executive at the expense—not of the courts—but of Congress, from which that power originates and emanates.

Under the Court's anachronistically formal view of the separation of powers, Congress legislates pure, substantive mandates and has no business structuring the procedural manner in which the Executive implements these mandates. To be sure, in the ordinary course, Congress does legislate in black-and-white terms of affirmative commands or negative prohibitions on the conduct of officers of the Executive Branch. In complex regulatory areas, however, Congress often legislates, as it were, in procedural shades of gray. That is, it sets forth substantive policy goals and provides for their attainment by requiring Executive Branch officials to follow certain procedures, for example, in the form of reporting, consultation, and certification requirements.

In conclusion, I cannot join the Court on what amounts to a slash-and-burn expedition through the law of environmental standing.

## *Luther* v. *Borden*

**48 U.S. (7 Howard) 1; 12 L. Ed. 581 (1849)**

In 1841, Rhode Island was still operating under a system of government established in 1663 under a colonial charter, granted by Charles II, that made no provision for amendment and strictly limited the right to vote.

Dissident groups, protesting especially the limits on suffrage, combined that year to form a popular convention and draft a new constitution. In elections held in 1842, Thomas Dorr was elected governor. The old charter government continued to operate, however, and when it responded to the insurgent government by declaring martial law, the charter governor appealed to President John Tyler for military support. Although no federal troops were ever sent, the Dorr Rebellion was soon crushed, and the insurgent government collapsed.

On instructions from the charter government to gather up the dispersed and defeated insurgents, Luther Borden and other state militiamen set out to arrest Martin Luther, a Dorr supporter. In the process, they broke into and searched his home, whereupon Luther sued for illegal trespass, alleging that under Article IV, Section 4, which guarantees to each state a republican form of government, the charter government had been supplanted by the more representative insurgent government, and that as a consequence it was not the lawful government of the state. Because the charter government was not the lawful government, Luther continued, Borden and his men could not defend their actions by claiming to be agents of the state. Borden responded that the charter government was the lawful government and that his search was legitimate. Luther moved to Massachusetts in order to bring the case before the federal courts on the basis of diversity of citizenship. The federal courts were thus invited to determine which of the two governments was the lawful government of Rhode Island. After a federal circuit court ruled in Borden's favor, Luther brought the case to the Supreme Court on a writ of error. *Opinion of the Court: Taney, Grier, McLean, Nelson, Wayne. Dissenting opinion: Woodbury, Catron, Daniel. McKinley did not participate.*

Mr. Chief Justice Taney delivered the opinion of the Court. . . .

The fourth section of the fourth article of the Constitution of the United States provides that the United States shall guarantee to every State in the Union a republican form of government, and shall protect each of them against invasion; and on the application of the legislature or of the executive (when the legislature cannot be convened) against domestic violence.

Under this article of the Constitution it rests with Congress to decide what government is the established one in a State. For as the United States guarantee to each State a republican government, Congress must necessarily decide what government is established in the State before it can determine whether it is republican or not. And when the senators and representatives of a State are admitted into the councils of the Union, the authority of the government under which they are appointed, as well as its republican character, is recognized by the proper constitutional authority. And its decision is binding on every other department of the government, and could not be questioned in a judicial tribunal. It is true that the contest in this case did not last long enough to bring the matter to this issue; and as no senators or representatives were elected under the authority of the government of which Mr. Dorr was the head, Congress was not called upon to decide the controversy. Yet the right to decide is placed there, and not in the courts.

So, too, as relates to the clause in the above-mentioned article of the Constitution, providing for cases of domestic violence. It rested with Congress, too, to determine upon the means proper to be adopted to fulfill this guarantee. They might, if they had deemed it most advisable to do so, have placed it in the power of a court to decide when the contingency had happened which required the federal government to interfere. But Congress thought otherwise, and no doubt wisely; and by the act of February 28, 1795, provided, that "in case of an insurrection in any State against the government thereof, it shall be lawful for the President of the United States, on application of the legislature of such State or of the executive (when the legislature cannot be convened), to call forth such number of the militia of any other State or States, as may be applied for, as he may judge sufficient to suppress such insurrection."

By this act, the power of deciding whether the exigency had arisen upon which the government of the United States is bound to interfere, is given to the President. He is to act upon the application of the legislature or of the executive, and consequently he must determine what body of men constitute the legislature, and who is the governor, before he can act. The fact that both parties claim the right to the government cannot alter the case, for both cannot be entitled to it. If there is an armed conflict, like the one of which we are speaking, it is a case of domestic violence, and one of the parties must be in insurrection against the lawful government. And the President must, of necessity, decide which is the government, and which party is unlawfully arrayed against it, before he can perform the duty imposed upon him by the act of Congress.

After the President has acted and called out the militia, is a Circuit Court of the United States authorized to inquire whether his decision was right? Could the court, while the parties were actually contending in arms for the possession of the government, call witnesses before it and inquire which party represented a majority of the people? If it could, then it would become the duty of the court (provided it came to the conclusion that the President had decided incorrectly) to discharge those who were arrested or detained by the troops in the service of the United States or the government which the President was endeavoring to maintain. If the judicial power extends so far, the guarantee contained in the Constitution of the United States is a guarantee of anarchy, and not of order. Yet if this right does not reside in the courts when the conflict is raging, if the judicial power is at that time bound to follow the decision of the political, it must be equally bound when the contest is over. It cannot, when peace is restored, punish as offenses and crimes the acts which it before recognized, and was bound to recognize, as lawful.

It is true that in this case the militia were not called out by the President. But upon the application of the governor under the charter government, the President recognized him as the executive power of the State, and took measures to call out the militia to support his authority if it should be found necessary for the general government to interfere; and it is admitted in the argument, that it was the knowledge of this decision that put an end to the armed opposition to the charter government, and prevented any further efforts to establish by force the proposed constitution. The interference of the President, therefore, by announcing his determination, was as effectual as if the militia had been assembled under his orders. And it should be equally authoritative. For certainly no court of the United States, with a knowledge of this decision, would have been justified in recognizing the opposing party as the lawful government, or in treating as wrongdoers or insurgents the officers of the government which the President had recognized, and was prepared to support by an armed force. In the case of foreign nations, the government acknowledged by the President is always recognized by the courts of justice. And this principle has been applied by the act of Congress to the sovereign States of the Union.

It is said that this power in the President is dangerous to liberty, and may be abused. All power may be abused if placed in unworthy hands. But it would be difficult, we think, to point out any other hands in which this power would be more safe, and at the same time equally effectual. When citizens of the same State are in arms against each other, and the constituted authorities unable to execute the laws, the interposition of the United States must be prompt, or it is of little value. The ordinary course of proceedings in courts of justice would be utterly unfit for the crisis. And the elevated office of the President, chosen as he is by the people of the United States, and the high responsibility he could not fail to feel when acting in a case of so much moment, appear to furnish as strong safeguards against a wilful abuse of power as human prudence and foresight could well provide. At all events, it is conferred upon him by the Constitution and laws of the United States, and must therefore be respected and enforced in its judicial tribunals. . .

Undoubtedly, if the President in exercising this power shall fall into error, or invade the rights of the people of the State, it would be in the power of Congress to apply the proper remedy. But the courts must administer the law as they find it . . .

Much of the argument on the part of the plaintiff turned upon political rights and political questions, upon which the court has been urged to express an opinion. We decline doing so. The high power has been conferred on this court of passing judgment upon the acts of the State sovereignties, and of the legislative and executive branches of the federal government, and of determining whether they are beyond the limits of power marked out for them respectively by the Constitution of the United States. This tribunal, therefore, should be the last to overstep the boundaries which limit its own jurisdiction. And while it should always be ready to meet any question confided to it by the Constitution, it is equally its duty not to pass beyond its appropriate sphere of action, and to take care not to involve itself in discussions which properly belong to other forums. No one we believe, has ever doubted the proposition, that, according to the institutions of this country, the sovereignty in every State resides in the people of the State, and that they may alter and change their form of government at their own pleasure. But whether they have changed it or not by abolishing an old government, and establishing a new one in its place, is a question to be settled by the political power. And when that power has decided, the courts are bound to take notice of its decision, and to follow it.

The judgment of the circuit court must therefore be

*Affirmed*

## *Baker* v. *Carr*

**369 U.S. 186; 82 S. Ct. 691; 7 L. Ed. 2d 663 (1962)**

The Tennessee Constitution provides that representation in both houses of the state legislature shall be based on population and that legislators shall be apportioned every ten years on the basis of the federal census. Despite the constitutional requirement, the legislature had not reapportioned since 1901 when, in 1959, Charles Baker and other qualified voters in Tennessee brought suit in federal court against Joe Carr, Tennessee secretary of state, and other public officials, alleging deprivation of federal constitutional rights. The plaintiffs argued that the State's system of apportionment was "utterly arbitrary" and thereby deprived them of equal protection of the laws under the Fourteenth Amendment "by virtue of debasement of their votes." A three-member district court, relying on *Colegrove* v. *Green* (1946), dismissed their suit, whereupon the case went to the Supreme Court on appeal. *Opinion of the Court: Brennan, Black, Clark, Douglas, Stewart, Warren. Concurring opinions: Clark; Douglas; Stewart. Dissenting opinions: Frankfurter, Harlan; Harlan, Frankfurter. Not participating: Whittaker.*

MR. JUSTICE BRENNAN delivered the opinion of the Court. . . .

We hold today only (a) that the District Court possessed jurisdiction of the subject matter; (b) that a justiciable cause of action is stated upon which appellants would be entitled to appropriate relief; and (c) because appellees raise the issue before this Court, that the appellants have standing to challenge the Tennessee apportionment statutes. Beyond noting that we have no cause at this stage to doubt the District Court will be able to fashion relief if violations of constitutional rights are found, it is improper now to consider what remedy would be most appropriate if appellants prevail at the trial.

### Jurisdiction of the Subject Matter

The District Court was uncertain whether our cases withholding federal judicial relief rested upon a lack of federal jurisdiction or upon the inappropriateness of the subject matter for judicial consideration—what we have designated "nonjusticiability." The distinction between the two grounds is significant. In the instance of nonjusticiability, consideration of the cause is not wholly and immediately foreclosed; rather, the Court's inquiry necessarily proceeds to the point of deciding whether the duty asserted can be judicially identified and its breach judicially determined, and whether protection for the right asserted can be judicially molded. In the instance of lack of jurisdiction the cause either does not "arise under" the Federal Constitution, laws or treaties (or fall within one of the other enumerated categories of Art. III, § 2), or is not a "case or controversy" within the meaning of that section; or the cause is not one described by any jurisdictional statute. Our conclusion . . . that this cause presents no nonjusticiable "political question" settles the only possible doubt that it is a case or controversy. Under the present heading of "Jurisdiction of the Subject Matter" we hold only that the matter set forth in the complaint does arise under the Constitution. . . .

**Standing**

A federal court cannot "pronounce any statute, either of a state or of the United States, void, because irreconcilable with the constitution, except as it is called upon to adjudge the legal rights of litigants in actual controversies." *Liverpool, N.Y. & P. Steamship Co.* v. *Commissioners of Emigration*. . . . Have the appellants alleged such a personal stake in the outcome of the controversy as to assure that concrete adverseness which sharpens the presentation of issues upon which the court so largely depends for illumination of difficult constitutional questions? This is the gist of the question of standing. It is, of course, a question of federal law. . . .

We hold that the appellants do have standing to maintain this suit. Our decisions plainly support this conclusion. Many of the cases have assumed rather than articulated the premise in deciding the merits of similar claims. . . .

These appellants seek relief in order to protect or vindicate an interest of their own, and of those similarly situated. Their constitutional claim is, in substance, that the 1901 statute constitutes arbitrary and capricious state action, offensive to the Fourteenth Amendment in its irrational disregard of the standard of apportionment prescribed by the State's Constitution or of any standard, effecting a gross disproportion of representation to voting population. The injury which appellants assert is that this classification disfavors the voters in the counties in which they reside, placing them in a position of constitutionally unjustifiable inequality *vis-à-vis* voters in irrationally favored counties. . . .

It would not be necessary to decide whether appellants' allegations of impairment of their votes by the 1901 apportionment will, ultimately, entitle them to any relief, in order to hold that they have standing to seek it. If such impairment does produce a legally cognizable injury, they are among those who have sustained it. They are asserting "a plain, direct and adequate interest in maintaining the effectiveness of their votes," . . . not merely a claim of "the right possessed by every citizen "to require that the government be administered according to law.' " . . .

**Justiciability**

In holding that the subject matter of this suit was not justiciable, the District Court relied on *Colegrove* v. *Green* (1946) . . . and subsequent *per curiam* cases. . .We understand the District Court to have read the cited cases as compelling the conclusion that since the appellants sought to have a legislative apportionment held unconstitutional, their suit presented a "political question" and was therefore nonjusticiable. We hold that this challenge to an apportionment presents no nonjusticiable "political questions." The cited cases do not hold the contrary.

Of course the mere fact that the suit seeks protection of a political right does not mean it presents a political question. Such an objection "is little more than a play upon words." . . . Rather, it is argued that apportionment cases, whatever the actual wording of the complaint, can involve no federal constitutional right except one resting on the guaranty of a republican form of government, and that complaints based on that clause have been held to present political questions which are nonjusticiable.

We hold that the claim pleaded here neither rests upon nor implicates the Guaranty Clause and that its justiciability is therefore not foreclosed by our decisions of cases involving that clause. The District Court misinterpreted *Colegrove* v. *Green* and other decisions of this Court on which it relied. Appellants' claim that they are being denied equal protection is justiciable, and if "discrimination is sufficiently shown, the right to relief under the equal protection clause is not diminished by the fact that the discrimination relates to political rights." *Snowden* v. *Hughes* (1944). . . To show why we reject the argument based on the Guaranty Clause, we deem it necessary first to consider the contours of the "political question" doctrine.

Our discussion requires review of a number of political question cases, in order to expose the attributes of the doctrine. . . . That review reveals that in the Guaranty Clause cases and in the other "political question" cases, it is the relationship between the judiciary and the coordinate branches of the Federal Government, and not the federal judiciary's relationship to the States, which gives rise to the "political question." . . .

The nonjusticiability of a political question is primarily a function of the separation of powers. Much confusion results from the capacity of the "political question" label to obscure the need for case-by-case inquiry. Deciding whether a matter has in any measure been committed by the Constitution to another branch of government, or whether the action of that branch exceeds whatever authority has been committed, is itself a delicate exercise in constitutional interpretation, and is a responsibility of this Court as ultimate interpreter of the Constitution. . . .

. . . Prominent on the surface of any case held to involve a political question is found a textually demonstrable constitutional commitment of the issue to a coordinate political department; or a lack of judicially discoverable and manageable standards for resolving it; or the impossibility of deciding without an initial policy determination of a kind clearly for nonjudicial discretion; or the impossibility of a court's undertaking independent resolution without expressing lack of the respect due coordinate branches of government; or an unusual need for unquestioning adherence to a political decision already made; or the potentiality of embarrassment from multifarious pronouncements by various departments on one question.

Unless one of these formulations is inextricable from the case at bar, there should be no dismissal for nonjusticiability on the ground of a political question's presence. The doctrine of which we treat is one of "political questions," not one of "political cases." The courts cannot reject as "no law suit" a bona fide controversy as to whether some action denominated "political" exceeds constitutional authority. . . .

But it is argued that this case shares the characteristics of decisions that constitute a category not yet considered, cases concerning the Constitution's guaranty, in Art. IV, § 4, of a republican form of government. . . .

. . . A natural beginning is to note whether any of the common characteristics which we have been able to identify and label descriptively are present. We find none: The question here is the consistency of state action with the Federal Constitution. We have no question decided, or to be decided, by a political branch of government coequal with this Court. Nor do we risk embarrassment of our government abroad, or grave disturbance at home if we take issue with Tennessee as to the constitutionality of her action here challenged. Nor need the appellants, in order to succeed in this action, ask the Court to enter upon policy determinations for which judicially manageable standards are lacking. Judicial standards under the Equal Protection Clause are well developed and familiar, and it has been open to courts since the enactment of the Fourteenth Amendment to determine, if on the particular facts they must, that a discrimination reflects *no* policy, but simply arbitrary and capricious action.

This case does, in one sense, involve the allocation of political power within a State, and the appellants might conceivably have added a claim under the Guaranty Clause. Of course, as we have seen, any reliance on that clause would be futile. But because any reliance on the Guaranty Clause could not have succeeded it does not follow that appellants may not be heard on the equal protection claim which in fact they tender. True, it must be clear that the Fourteenth Amendment claim is not so enmeshed with those political question elements which render Guaranty Clause claims nonjusticiable as actually to present a political question itself. But we have found that not to be the case here. . . .

We conclude then that the nonjusticiability of claims resting on the Guaranty Clause which arises from their embodiment of questions that were thought "political," can have no bearing upon the justiciability of the equal protection claim presented in this case. Finally, we emphasize that it is the involvement in Guaranty Clause claims of the elements thought to define "political questions," and no other feature, which could render them nonjusticiable. Specifically, we have said that such claims are not held nonjusticiable because they touch matters of state governmental organization. . . .

We conclude that the complaint's allegations of a denial of equal protection present a justiciable constitutional cause of action upon which appellants are entitled to a trial and a decision. The right asserted is within the reach of judicial protection under the Fourteenth Amendment.

The judgment of the District Court is reversed and the cause is remanded for further proceedings consistent with this opinion.

*Reversed and remanded.*

MR. JUSTICE CLARK, concurring. . . .

Although I find the Tennessee apportionment statute offends the Equal Protection Clause, I would not consider intervention by this Court into so delicate a field if there were any other relief available to the people of Tennessee. But the majority of the people of Tennessee have no "practical opportunities for exerting their political weight at the polls" to correct the existing "invidious discrimination." Tennessee has no initiative and referendum. I have searched diligently for other "practical opportunities" present under the law. I find none other than through the federal courts. The majority of the voters have been caught up in a legislative strait jacket. Tennessee has an "informed, civically militant electorate" and "an aroused popular conscience," but it does not sear "the conscience of the people's representatives." This is because the legislative policy has riveted the present seats in the Assembly to their respective constituencies, and by the votes of their incumbents a reapportionment of any kind is prevented. The people have been rebuffed at the hands of the Assembly; they have tried the constitutional convention route, but since the call must originate in the Assembly it, too, has been fruitless. They have tried Tennessee courts with the same result and Governors have fought the tide only to flounder. It is said that there is recourse in Congress and perhaps that may be, but from a practical standpoint this is without substance. To date Congress has never undertaken such a task in any State. We therefore must conclude that the people of Tennessee are stymied and without judicial intervention will be saddled with the present discrimination in the affairs of their state government. . . .

MR. JUSTICE FRANKFURTER, whom MR. JUSTICE HARLAN joins, dissenting.

We were soothingly told at the bar of this Court that we need not worry about the kind of remedy a court could effectively fashion once the abstract constitutional right to have courts pass on a state-wide system of electoral districting is recognized as a matter of judicial rhetoric, because legislatures would heed the Court's admonition. This is not only an euphoric hope. It implies a sorry confession of judicial impotence in place of a frank acknowledgment that there is not under the Constitution a judicial remedy for every political mischief, for every undesirable exercise of legislative power. The Framers carefully and with deliberate forethought refused so to enthrone the judiciary. In this situation, as in others of like nature, appeal for relief does not belong here. Appeal must be to an informed, civically militant electorate. In a democratic society like ours, relief must come through an aroused popular conscience that sears the conscience of the people's representatives. In any event there is nothing judicially more unseemly nor more self-defeating than for this Court to make in terrorem pronouncements, to indulge in merely empty rhetoric, sounding a word of promise to the ear, sure to be disappointing to the hope. . . .

In sustaining appellants' claim, based on the Fourteenth Amendment, that the District Court may entertain this suit, this Court's uniform course of decision over the years is overruled or disregarded. Explicitly it begins with *Colegrove* v. *Green* . . . but its roots run deep in the Court's historic adjudicatory process. . . .

The *Colegrove* doctrine, in the form in which repeated decisions have settled it, was not an innovation. It represents long judicial thought and experience. From its earliest opinions this Court has consistently recognized a class of controversies which do not lend themselves to judicial standards and judicial remedies. . . .

The influence of . . . converging considerations—the caution not to undertake decision where standards meet for judicial judgment are lacking, the reluctance to interfere with matters of state government in the absence of an unquestionable and effectively enforceable mandate, the unwillingness to make courts arbiters of the broad issues of political organization historically committed to other institutions and for whose adjustment the judicial process is ill-adapted—has been decisive of the settled line of cases, reaching back more than a century, which holds that Article IV, Section 4, of the Constitution, guaranteeing to the States "a Republican Form of Government," is not enforceable through the courts. . . .

The present case involves all of the elements that have made the Guarantee Clause cases nonjusticiable. It is, in effect, a Guarantee Clause claim masquerading under a different label. But it cannot make the case more fit for judicial action that appellants invoke the Fourteenth Amendment rather then Article IV, Section 4, where, in fact, the gist of their complaint is the same—unless it can be found that the Fourteenth Amendment speaks with greater particularity to their situation. . . .

What, then, is this question of legislative apportionment? Appellants invoke the right to vote and to have their votes counted. But they are permitted to vote and their votes are counted. They go to the polls, they cast their ballots, they send their representatives to the state councils. Their complaint is simply that the representatives are not sufficiently numerous or powerful—in short, that Tennessee has adopted a basis of representation with which they are dissatisfied. Talk of "debasement" or "dilution" is circular talk. One cannot speak of "debasement" or "dilution" of the value of a vote until there is first defined a standard of reference as to what a vote should be worth. What is actually asked of the Court in this case is to choose among competing bases of representation—ultimately, really among competing theories of political philosophy—in order to establish an appropriate frame of government for the State of Tennessee and thereby for all the states of the Union.

What Tennessee illustrates is an old and still widespread method of representation—representation by local geographical division, only in part respective of population—in preference to others, others, forsooth, more appealing. Appellants contest this choice and seek to make this Court the arbiter of the disagreement. They would make the Equal Protection Clause the character of adjudication, asserting that the equality which it guarantees comports, if not the assurance of equal weight to every voter's vote, at least the basic conception that representation ought to be proportionate to the population, a standard by reference to which the reasonableness of apportionment plans may be judged.

To find such a political conception legally enforceable in the broad and unspecific guarantee of equal protection is to rewrite the Constitution. . . . Certainly, "equal protection" is no more secure a foundation for judicial judgment of the permissibility of varying forms of representative governments than is "Republican Form." Indeed since "equal protection of the laws" can only mean an equality of persons standing in the same relation to whatever governmental action is challenged, the determination whether treatment is equal presupposes a determination concerning the nature of the relationship. This, with respect to apportionment, means an inquiry into the theoretic base of representation in an acceptably republican state. For a court could not determine the equal-protection issue without in fact first determining the Republican-Form issue, simply because what is reasonable for equal protection purposes will depend upon what frame of government, basically, is allowed. To divorce "equal protection" from "Republican Form" is to talk about half a question.

The notion that representation proportioned to the geographic spread of population is so universally accepted as a necessary element of equality between man and man that it must be taken to be the standard of a political equality preserved by the Fourteenth Amendment—that it is, in appellants' words "the basic principle of representative government"—is, to put it bluntly, not true. However desirable and however desired by some among the great political thinkers and framers of our government, it has never been generally practiced, today or in the past. It was not the English system, it was not the colonial system, it was not the system chosen for the national government by the Constitution, it was not the system exclusively or even predominantly practiced by the States today. Unless judges, the judges of this Court, are to make their private views of political wisdom the measure of the Constitution—views which in all honesty cannot but give the appearance, if not reflect the reality, of involvement with the business of partisan politics so inescapably a part of apportionment controversies—the Fourteenth Amendment, "itself a historical product," . . . provides no guide for judicial oversight of the representation problem. . . .

Manifestly, the Equal Protection Clause supplies no clearer guide for judicial examination of apportionment methods than would the Guarantee Clause itself. Apportionment, by its character, is a subject of extraordinary complexity, involving—even after the fundamental theoretical issues concerning what is to be represented in a representative legislature have been fought out or compromised—considerations of geography, demography, electoral convenience, economic and social cohesions or divergencies among particular local groups, communications, the practical effects of political institutions like the lobby and the city machine, ancient traditions and ties of settled usage, respect for proven incumbents of long experience and senior status, mathematical mechanics, censuses compiling relevant data, and a host of others. Legislative responses throughout the country to the apportionment demands of the 1960 Census have glaringly confirmed that these are not factors that lend themselves to evaluations of a nature that are the staple of judicial determinations or for which judges are equipped to adjudicate by legal training or experience or native wit. And this is the more so true because in every strand of this complicated, intricate web of values meet the contending forces of partisan politics. The practical significance of apportionment is that the next election results may differ because of it. Apportionment battles are overwhelmingly party or intraparty contests. It will add a virulent source of friction and tension in federal-state relations to embroil the federal judiciary in them.

# *Nixon* v. *United States*

**113 S.Ct. 732, 122 L.Ed. 2d 1 (1993)**

Walter Nixon, a federal district court judge, was convicted of two counts of lying to a grand jury and sentenced to prison. However, he refused to resign from the federal bench and, therefore, continued to receive his judicial salary while in prison. In May, 1989, the House of Representatives adopted articles of impeachment, charging him with lying to a grand jury and with bringing disrepute on the federal judiciary. The Senate invoked its own Impeachment Rule XI, under which the presiding officer appoints a committee of senators to receive evidence and take testimony. The committee that was appointed held four days of hearings, during which it heard ten witnesses, including Nixon. Pursuant to Senate rules, it then submitted a report and a transcript of the proceeding to the full Senate. After receiving briefs from the parties and after three hours of oral argument, the Senate voted to convict Nixon of lying to a grand jury, and he was removed from office.

Nixon subsequently sued, claiming that the Senate's use of a committee to hear evidence violated the constitutional requirement that the Senate "try" all impeachments. After the district court and the court of appeals dismissed his suit as nonjusticiable, as a political question, the Supreme Court granted certiorari. *Opinion of the Court: Rehnquist, Stevens, O'Connor, Scalia, Kennedy, Thomas. Concurring opinion: Stevens. Concurring in the Judgment: White, Blackmun; Souter.*

CHIEF JUSTICE REHNQUIST delivered the opinion of the Court.

A controversy is nonjusticiable—i.e., involves a political question—where there is "a textually demonstrable constitutional commitment of the issue to a coordinate political department; or a lack of judicially discoverable and manageable standards for resolving it. . . . *Baker* v. *Carr* (1962). But the courts must, in the first instance, interpret the text in question and determine whether and to what extent the issue is textually committed.

As the discussion that follows makes clear, the concept of a textual commitment to a coordinate political department is not completely separate from the concept of a lack of judicially discoverable and manageable standards for resolving it; the lack of judicially manageable standards may strengthen the conclusion that there is a textually demonstrable commitment to a coordinate branch.

In this case, we must examine Art I, § 3, cl 6, to determine the scope of authority conferred upon the Senate by the Framers regarding impeachment. It provides:

> The Senate shall have the sole Power to try all Impeachments. When sitting for that Purpose, they shall be on Oath or Affirmation. When the President of the United States is tried, the Chief Justice shall preside: And no Person shall be convicted without the Concurrence of two thirds of the Members present.

The language and structure of this Clause are revealing. The first sentence is a grant of authority to the Senate, and the word "sole" indicates that this authority is reposed in the Senate and nowhere else. The next two sentences specify requirements to which the Senate proceedings shall conform: the Senate shall be on oath or affirmation, a two-thirds vote is required to convict, and when the President is tried the Chief Justice shall preside.

Petitioner argues that the word "try" in the first sentence imposes by implication an additional requirement on the Senate in that the proceedings must be in the nature of a judicial trial. From there petitioner goes on to argue that this limitation precludes the Senate from delegating to a select committee the task of hearing the testimony of witnesses, as was done pursuant to Senate Rule XI.

There are several difficulties with this position which lead us ultimately to reject it. The word "try," both in 1787 and later, has considerably broader meanings than those to which petitioner would limit it. Based on the variety of definitions, however, we cannot say that the Framers used the word "try" as an implied limitation on the method by which the Senate might proceed in trying impeachments.

The conclusion that the use of the word "try" in the first sentence of the Impeachment Trial Clause lacks sufficient precision to afford any judicially manageable standard of review of the Senate's actions is fortified by the existence of the three very specific requirements that the Constitution does impose on the Senate when trying impeachments: the members must be under oath, a two-thirds vote is required to convict, and the Chief Justice presides when the President is tried. These limitations are quite precise, and their nature suggests that the Framers did not intend to impose additional limitations on the form of the Senate proceedings by the use of the word "try" in the first sentence.

Petitioner devotes only two pages in his brief to negating the significance of the word "sole" in the first sentence of Clause 6. As noted above, that sentence provides that "[t]he Senate shall have the sole Power to try all Impeachments." We think that the word "sole" is of considerable significance. Indeed, the word "sole" appears only one other time in the Constitution—with respect to the House of Representatives' "*sole* Power of Impeachment." Art I, § 2, cl 5. The common sense meaning of the word "sole" is that the Senate alone shall have authority to determine whether an individual should be acquitted or convicted. The dictionary definition bears this out. "Sole" is defined as "having no companion," "solitary," "being the only one," and "functioning . . . independently and without assistance or interference." If the courts may review the actions of the Senate in order to determine whether that body "tried" an impeached official, it is difficult to see how the Senate would be "functioning . . . independently and without assistance or interference."

Petitioner also contends that the word "sole" should not bear on the question of justiciability because Art II, § 2, cl 1, of the Constitution grants the President pardon authority "except in Cases of Impeachment." He argues that such a limitation on the President's pardon power would not have been necessary if the Framers thought that the Senate alone had authority to deal with such questions. But the granting of a pardon is in no sense an overturning of a judgment of conviction by some other tribunal; it is "[a]n executive action that mitigates or sets aside *punishment* for a crime." Authority in the Senate to determine procedures for trying an impeached official, unreviewable by the courts, is therefore not at all inconsistent with authority in the President to grant a pardon to the convicted official.

Petitioner finally argues that even if significance be attributed to the word "sole" in the first sentence of the clause, the authority granted is to the Senate, and this means that "the Senate—not the courts, not a lay jury, not a Senate Committee—shall try impeachments." It would be possible to read the first sentence of the Clause this way, but it is not a natural reading. Petitioner's interpretation would bring into judicial purview not merely the sort of claim made by petitioner, but other similar claims based on the conclusion that the word "Senate" has imposed by implication limitations on procedures which the Senate might adopt. Such limitations would be inconsistent with the construction of the Clause as a whole, which, as we have noted, sets out three express limitations in separate sentences.

The history and contemporary understanding of the impeachment provisions support our reading of the constitutional language. The parties do not offer evidence of a single word in the history of the Constitutional Convention or in contemporary commentary that even alludes to the possibility of judicial review in the context of the impeachment powers. This silence is quite meaningful in light of the several explicit references to the availability of judicial review as a check on the Legislature's power with respect to bills of attainder, ex post facto laws, and statutes.

The Framers labored over the question of where the impeachment power should lie. Significantly, in at least two considered scenarios the power was placed with the Federal Judiciary. Despite these proposals, the Convention ultimately decided that the Senate would have "the sole Power to Try all Impeachments." According to Alexander Hamilton, the Supreme Court was not the proper body because the Framers "doubted whether the members of that tribunal would, at all times, be endowed with so eminent a portion of fortitude as would be called for in the execution of so difficult a task" or whether the Court "would possess the degree of credit and authority" to carry out its judgment if it conflicted with the accusation brought by the Legislature—the people's representative. In addition, the Framers believed the Court was too small in number. "The awful discretion, which a court of impeachments must necessarily have, to doom to honor or to infamy the most confidential and the most distinguished characters of the community, forbids the commitment of the trust to a small number of persons.

There are two additional reasons why the Judiciary, and the Supreme Court in particular, were not chosen to have any role in impeachments. First, the Framers recognized that most likely there would be two sets of proceedings for individuals who commit impeachable offenses—the impeachment trial and a separate criminal trial. In fact, the Constitution explicitly provides for two separate proceedings. The Framers deliberately separated the two forums to avoid raising the specter of bias and to ensure independent judgments.

Certainly judicial review of the Senate's "trial" would introduce the same risk of bias as would participation in the trial itself.

Second, judicial review would be inconsistent with the Framers' insistence that our system be one of checks and balances. In our constitutional system, impeachment was designed to be the *only* check on the Judicial Branch by the Legislature.

Judicial involvement in impeachment proceedings, even if only for purposes of judicial review, is counterintuitive because it would eviscerate the "important constitutional check" placed on the Judiciary by the Framers. Nixon's argument would place final reviewing authority with respect to impeachments in the hands of the same body that the impeachment process is meant to regulate.

Nevertheless, Nixon argues that judicial review is necessary in order to place a check on the Legislature. The Framers anticipated this objection and created two constitutional safeguards to keep the Senate in check. The first safeguard is that the whole of the impeachment power is divided between the two legislative bodies, with the House given the right to accuse and the Senate given the right to judge. This split of authority "avoids the inconvenience of making the same persons both accusers and judges; and guards against the danger of persecution from the prevalency of a factious spirit in either of those branches." The second safeguard is the two-thirds supermajority vote requirement. Hamilton explained that "[a]s the concurrence of two-thirds of the senate will be requisite to a condemnation, the security to innocence, from this additional circumstance, will be as complete as itself can desire."

In addition to the textual commitment argument, we are persuaded that the lack of finality and the difficulty of fashioning relief counsel against justiciability. We agree with the Court of Appeals that opening the door of judicial review to the procedures used by the Senate in trying impeachments would "expose the political life of the country to months, or perhaps years, of chaos." This lack of finality would manifest itself most dramatically if the President were impeached. The legitimacy of any successor, and hence his effectiveness, would be impaired severely, not merely while the judicial process was running its course, but during any retrial that a differently constituted Senate might conduct if its first judgment of conviction were invalidated. Equally uncertain is the question of what relief a court may give other than simply setting aside the judgment of conviction. Could it order the reinstatement of a convicted federal judge, or order Congress to create an additional judgeship if the seat had been filled in the interim?

For the foregoing reasons, the judgment of the Court of Appeals is affirmed.

JUSTICE WHITE, with JUSTICE BLACKMUN concurring in the judgment.

Petitioner contends that the method by which the Senate convicted him on two articles of impeachment violates Art I, § 3, cl 6 of the Constitution, which mandates that the Senate "try" impeachments. The Court is of the view that the Constitution forbids us even to consider his contention. I find no such prohibition and would therefore reach the merits of the claim. I concur in the judgment because the Senate fulfilled its constitutional obligation to "try" petitioner.

The majority states that the question raised in this case meets two of the criteria for political questions set out in *Baker* v. *Carr* (1962). It concludes first that there is " 'a textually demonstrable constitutional commitment of the issue to a coordinate political department.' "It also finds that the question cannot be resolved for "a lack of judicially discoverable and manageable standards.' "

The majority finds a clear textual commitment in the Constitution's use of the word "sole" in the phrase "the Senate shall have the sole Power to try all Impeachments."

The significance of the Constitution's use of the term "sole" lies in the fact that it appears exactly twice, in parallel provisions concerning impeachment. That the word "sole" is found only in the House and Senate Impeachment Clauses demonstrates that its purpose is to emphasize the distinct role of each in the impeachment process. As the majority notes the Framers, following English practice, were very much concerned to separate the prosecutorial from the adjudicative aspects of impeachment. While the majority is thus right to interpret the term "sole" to indicate that the Senate ought to " 'functio[n] independently and without assistance or interference,' " it wrongly identifies the judiciary, rather than the House, as the source of potential interference with which the Framers were concerned when they employed the term "sole."

The majority also claims support in the history and early interpretations of the Impeachment Clauses, noting the various arguments in support of the current system made at the Constitutional Convention and expressed powerfully by Hamilton in *The Federalist*, Nos. 65 and 66.

The majority's review of the historical record thus explains why the power to try impeachments properly resides with the Senate. It does not explain, however, the sweeping statement that the judiciary was "not chosen to have any role in impeachments." Not a single word in the historical materials cited by the majority addresses judicial review of the Impeachment Trial Clause. And a glance at the arguments surrounding the Impeachment Clauses negates the majority's attempt to infer nonjusticiability from the Framers' arguments in support of the Senate's power to try impeachments.

The historical evidence reveals above all else that the Framers were deeply concerned about placing in any branch the "awful discretion, which a court of impeachments must necessarily have." *The Federalist*, No. 65. Viewed against this history, the discord between the majority's position and the basic principles of checks and balances underlying the Constitution's separation of powers is clear. In essence, the majority suggests that the Framers conferred upon Congress a potential tool of legislative dominance yet at the same time rendered Congress' exercise of that power one of the very few areas of legislative authority immune from any judicial review. While the majority rejects petitioner's justiciability argument as espousing a view "inconsistent with the Framers' insistence that our system be one of checks and balances," it is the Court's finding of nonjusticiability that truly upsets the Framers' careful design. In a truly balanced system, impeachments tried by the Senate would serve as a means of controlling the largely unaccountable judiciary, even as judicial review would ensure that the Senate adhered to a minimal set of procedural standards in conducting impeachment trials.

The majority also contends that the term "try" does not present a judicially manageable standard.

This argument comes in two variants. The first, which asserts that one simply cannot ascertain the sense of "try" which the Framers employed and hence cannot undertake judicial review, is clearly untenable. To begin with, one would intuitively expect that, in defining the power of a political body to conduct an inquiry into official wrongdoing, the Framers used "try" in its legal sense. That intuition is borne out by reflection on the alternatives. The third clause of Art I, § 3 cannot seriously be read to mean that the Senate shall "attempt" or "experiment with" impeachments. It is equally implausible to say that the Senate is charged with "investigating" impeachments given that this description would substantially overlap with the House of Representatives' "sole" power to draw up articles of impeachment. Art I, § 2, cl 5.

The other variant of the majority position focuses not on which sense of "try" is employed in the Impeachment Trial Clause, but on whether the legal sense of that term creates a judicially manageable standard. The majority concludes that the term provides no "identifiable textual limit." Yet, as the Government itself conceded at oral argument, the term "try" is hardly so elusive as the majority would have it. Were the Senate, for example, to adopt the practice of automatically entering a judgment of conviction whenever articles of impeachment were delivered from the House, it is quite clear that the Senate will have failed to "try" impeachments. Indeed in this respect, "try" presents no greater, and perhaps fewer, interpretive difficulties than some other constitutional standards that have been found amenable to familiar techniques of judicial construction, including, for example, "Commerce . . . among the several States," and "due process of law."

The majority's conclusion that "try" is incapable of meaningful judicial construction is not without irony. One might think that if any class of concepts would fall within the definitional abilities of the judiciary, it would be that class having to do with procedural justice. Examination of the remaining question—whether proceedings in accordance with Senate Rule XI are compatible with the Impeachment Trial Clause—confirms this intuition.

Petitioner bears the rather substantial burden of demonstrating that simply by employing the word "try," the Constitution prohibits the Senate from relying on a fact-finding committee. It is clear that the Framers were familiar with English impeachment practice and with that of the States employing a variant of the English model at the time of the Constitutional Convention. Hence there is little doubt that the term "try" as used in Art I, § 3, cl 6 meant that the Senate should conduct its proceedings in a manner somewhat resembling a judicial proceeding. Indeed, it is safe to assume that Senate trials were to follow the practice in England and the States, which contemplated a formal hearing on the charges, at which the accused would be represented by counsel, evidence would be presented, and the accused would have the opportunity to be heard.

Petitioner argues, however, that because committees were not used in state impeachment trials prior to the Convention, the word "try" cannot be interpreted to permit their use. It is, however, a substantial leap to infer from the absence of a particular device of parliamentary procedure that its use has been forever barred by the Constitution.

It is also noteworthy that the delegation of fact-finding by judicial and quasi-judicial bodies was hardly unknown to the Framers. Jefferson, at least, was aware that the House of Lords sometimes delegated fact-finding in impeachment trials to committees and recommended use of the same to the Senate (T. Jefferson, *A Manual of Parliamentary Practice for the Use of the Senate of the United States*). The States also had on occasion employed legislative committees to investigate whether to draw up articles of impeachment.

Particularly in light of the Constitution's grant to each House of the power to "determine the Rules of its Proceedings," the existence of legislative and judicial delegation strongly suggests that the Impeachment Trial Clause was not designed to prevent employment of a fact-finding committee.

In short, textual and historical evidence reveals that the impeachment Trial Clause was not meant to bind the hands of the Senate beyond establishing a set of minimal procedures. Without identifying the exact contours of these procedures, it is sufficient to say that the Senate's use of a fact-finding committee under Rule XI is entirely compatible with the Constitution's command that the Senate "try all impeachments." Petitioner's challenge to his conviction must therefore fail.

JUSTICE SOUTER, concurring in the judgment.

I agree with the Court that this case presents a nonjusticiable political question. Because my analysis differs somewhat from the Court's, however, I concur in its judgment by this separate opinion.

Whatever considerations feature most prominently in a particular case, the political question doctrine is "essentially a function of the separation of powers," existing to restrain courts "from inappropriate interference in the business of the other branches of Government," *United States* v. *Munoz-Flores* (1990), and deriving in large part from prudential concerns about the respect we owe the political departments. Not all interference is inappropriate or disrespectful, however, and application of the doctrine ultimately turns, as Learned Hand put it, on "how importunately the occasion demands an answer."

This occasion does not demand an answer. The impeachment Trial Clause commits to the Senate "the sole Power to try all Impeachments," subject to three procedural requirements: the Senate shall be on oath or affirmation; the Chief Justice shall preside when the President is tried; and conviction shall be upon the concurrence of two-thirds of the Members present. It seems fair to conclude that the Clause contemplates that the Senate may determine, within broad boundaries, such subsidiary issues as the procedures for receipt and consideration of evidence necessary to satisfy its duty to "try" impeachments. Other significant considerations confirm a conclusion that this case presents a nonjusticiable political question: the "unusual need for unquestioning adherence to a political decision already made," as well as "the potentiality of embarrassment from multifarious pronouncements by various departments on one question."

One can, nevertheless, envision different and unusual circumstances that might justify a more searching review of impeachment proceedings. If the Senate were to act in a manner seriously threatening the integrity of its results, convicting, say, upon a coin-toss, or upon a summary determination that an officer of the United States was simply " 'a bad guy,' " judicial interference might well be appropriate. In such circumstances, the Senate's action might be so far beyond the scope of its constitutional authority, and the consequent impact on the Republic so great, as to merit a judicial response despite the prudential concerns that would ordinarily counsel silence.

## *DeShaney* v. *Winnebago County Department of Social Services*

**489 U.S. 189, 109 S.Ct. 998, 103 L.Ed 2d 249 (1989)**

The petitioner in this case, Joshua DeShaney, was subjected to a series of beatings by his father, Randy DeShaney, with whom he lived. The respondents, a county department of social services and several of its social workers, received complaints that Joshua was being abused by his father and took various steps to protect him; they did not, however, remove him from his father's custody. Joshua's father finally beat him so severely that he suffered massive and permanent brain damage and was rendered profoundly retarded. While Joshua's father was subsequently tried and convicted of child abuse, Joshua and his mother sued the respondents under 42 U.S.C. Section 1983, alleging that they had deprived Joshua of his "liberty interest in bodily integrity," in violation of his rights under the substantive component of the Fourteenth Amendment's Due Process Clause, by failing to intervene to protect him from his father's violence. The U.S. District Court for the Eastern District of Wisconsin granted summary judgment for the respondents; the Court of Appeals for the Seventh Circuit affirmed; and the Supreme Court granted certiorari. *Opinion of the Court: Rehnquist, Kennedy, O'Connor, Scalia, Stevens, White. Dissenting opinions: Brennan, Blackmun, Marshall; Blackmun.*

CHIEF JUSTICE REHNQUIST delivered the opinion of the Court. . . .

Petitioner is a boy who was beaten and permanently injured by his father, with whom he lived. The respondents are social workers and other local officials who received complaints that petitioner was being abused by his father and had reason to believe that this was the case, but nonetheless did not act to remove petitioner from his father's custody. Petitioner sued respondents claiming that their failure to act deprived him of his liberty in violation of the Due Process Clause of the Fourteenth Amendment to the United States Constitution. We hold that it did not. . . .

The Due Process Clause of the Fourteenth Amendment provides that "[n]o State shall . . . deprive any person of life, liberty, or property, without due process of law." Petitioners contend that the State deprived Joshua of his liberty interest in "free[dom] from . . . unjustified intrusions on personal security," . . . by failing to provide him with adequate protection against his father's violence. The claim is one invoking the substantive rather than procedural component of the Due Process Clause; petitioners do not claim that the State denied Joshua protection without according him appropriate procedural safeguards, . . . but that it was categorically obligated to protect him in these circumstances. . . .

But nothing in the language of the Due Process Clause itself requires the State to protect the life, liberty, and property of its citizens against invasion by private actors. The Clause is phrased as a limitation on the State's power to act, not as a guarantee of certain minimal levels of safety and security. It forbids the State itself to deprive individuals of life, liberty, or property without "due process of law," but its language cannot fairly be extended to impose an affirmative obligation on the State to ensure that those interests do not come to harm through other means. Nor does history support such an expansive reading of the constitutional text. Like its counterpart in the Fifth Amendment, the Due Process Clause of the Fourteenth Amendment was intended to prevent government "from abusing [its] power, or employing it as an instrument of oppression.". . . Its purpose was to protect the people from the State, not to ensure that the State protected them from each other. The Framers were content to leave the extent of governmental obligation in the latter area to the democratic political processes.

Consistent with these principles, our cases have recognized that the Due Process Clauses generally confer no affirmative right to governmental aid, even where such aid may be necessary to secure life, liberty, or property interests of which the government itself may not deprive the individual. . . . As we said in *Harris* v. *McRae* [1980], "[a]though the liberty protected by the Due Process Clause affords protection against unwarranted *government* interference . . . , it does not confer an entitlement to such [governmental aid] as may be necessary to realize all the advantages of that freedom." . . . If the Due Process Clause does not require the State to provide its citizens with particular protective services, it follows that the State cannot be held liable under the Clause for injuries that could have been averted had it chosen to provide them. As a general matter, then, we conclude that a State's failure to protect an individual against private violence simply does not constitute a violation of the Due Process Clause.

Petitioners contend, however, that even if the Due Process Clause imposes no affirmative obligation on the State to provide the general public with adequate protective services, such a duty may arise out of certain "special relationships" created or assumed by the State with respect to particular individuals. . . . Petitioners argue that such a "special relationship" existed here because the State knew that Joshua faced a special danger of abuse at his father's hands, and specifically proclaimed, by word and by deed, its intention to protect him against that danger. . . . Having actually undertaken to protect Joshua from this danger—which petitioners concede the State played no part in creating—the State acquired an affirmative "duty," enforceable through the Due Process Clause, to do so in a reasonably competent fashion. . . .

We reject this argument. It is true that in certain limited circumstances the Constitution imposes upon the State affirmative duties of care and protection with respect to particular individuals. In *Estelle* v. *Gamble* . . . (1976) we recognized that the Eighth Amendment's prohibition against cruel and unusual punishment . . . requires the State to provide adequate medical care to incarcerated prisoners. . . .

In *Youngberg* v. *Romeo* . . . (1982) we extended this analysis beyond the Eighth Amendment setting, holding that the substantive component of the Fourteenth Amendment's Due Process Clause requires the State to provide involuntarily committed mental patients with such services as are necessary to ensure their "reasonable safety" from themselves and others. . . .

But these cases afford petitioners no help. Taken together, they stand only for the proposition that when the State takes a person into its custody and holds him there against his will, the Constitution imposes upon it a corresponding duty to assume some responsibility for his safety and general well-being. . . . The rationale for this principle is simple enough: when the State by the affirmative exercise of its power so restrains an individual's liberty that it renders him unable to care for himself, and at the same time fails to provide for his basic human needs—*e.g.*, food, clothing, shelter, medical care, and reasonable safety—it transgresses the substantive limits on state action set by the Eighth Amendment and the Due Process Clause. . . . The affirmative duty to protect arises not from the State's knowledge of the individual's predicament or from its expressions of intent to help him, but from the limitation which it has imposed on his freedom to act on his own behalf. . . . In the substantive due process analysis, it is the State's affirmative act of restraining the individual's freedom to act on his own behalf—through incarceration, institutionalization, or other similar restraint of personal liberty—which is the "deprivation of liberty" triggering the protections of the Due Process Clause, not its failure to act to protect his liberty interests against harms inflicted by other means.

The *Estelle-Youngberg* analysis simply has no applicability in the present case. Petitioners concede that the harms Joshua suffered did not occur while he was in the State's custody, but while he was in the custody of his natural father, who was in no sense a state actor. While the State may have been aware of the dangers that Joshua faced in the free world, it played no part in their creation, nor did it do anything to render him any more vulnerable to them. That the State once took temporary custody of Joshua does not alter the analysis, for when it returned him to his father's custody, it placed him in no worse position than that in which he would have been had it not acted at all; the State does not become the permanent guarantor of an individual's safety by having once offered him shelter. Under these circumstances, the State had no constitutional duty to protect Joshua.

It may well be that, by voluntarily undertaking to protect Joshua against a danger it concededly played no part in creating, the State acquired a duty under state tort law to provide him with adequate protection against that danger. . . . But the claim here is based on the Due Process Clause of the Fourteenth Amendment, which, as we have said many times, does not transform every tort committed by a state actor into a constitutional violation. . . . Because . . . the State had no constitutional duty to protect Joshua against his father's violence, its failure to do so—though calamitous in hindsight—simply does not constitute a violation of the Due Process Clause.

Judges and lawyers, like other humans, are moved by natural sympathy in a case like this to find a way for Joshua and his mother to receive adequate compensation for the grievous harm inflicted upon them. But before yielding to that impulse, it is well to remember once again that the harm was inflicted not by the State of Wisconsin, but by Joshua's father. The most that can be said of the state functionaries in this case is that they stood by and did nothing when suspicious circumstances dictated a more active role for them. In defense of them it must also be said that had they moved too soon to take custody of the son away from the father, they would likely have been met with charges of improperly intruding into the parent-child relationship, charges based on the same Due Process Clause that forms the basis for the present charge of failure to provide adequate protection.

The people of Wisconsin may well prefer a system of liability which would place upon the State and its officials the responsibility for failure to act in situations such as the present one. They may create such a system, if they do not have it already, by changing the tort law of the State in accordance with the regular law-making process. But they should not have it thrust upon them by this Court's expansion of the Due Process Clause of the Fourteenth Amendment.

JUSTICE BRENNAN, with whom JUSTICE MARSHALL and JUSTICE BLACKMUN join, dissenting. . . .

To the Court, the only fact that seems to count as an "affirmative act of restraining the individual's freedom to act on his own behalf" is direct physical control. . . . I would not, however, give *Youngberg* and *Estelle* such a stingy scope. I would recognize, as the Court apparently cannot, that "the State's knowledge of [an] individual's predicament [and] its expressions of intent to help him" can amount to a "limitation of his freedom to act on his own behalf" or to obtain help from others. . . . Thus, I would read *Youngberg* and *Estelle* to stand for the much more generous proposition that, if a State cuts off private sources of aid and then refuses aid itself, it cannot wash its hands of the harm that results from its inaction.

Wisconsin has established a child-welfare system specifically designed to help children like Joshua. Wisconsin law places upon the local departments of social services such as respondent (DSS or Department) a duty to investigate reported instances of child abuse. . . . While other governmental bodies and private persons are largely responsible for the reporting of possible cases of child abuse, . . . Wisconsin law channels all such reports to the local departments of social services for evaluation and, if necessary, further action. . . . Even when it is the sheriff's office or police department that receives a report of suspected child abuse, that report is referred to local social services departments for action . . . the only exception to this occurs when the reporter fears for the child's *immediate* safety. . . . In this way, Wisconsin law invites—indeed, directs—citizens and other governmental entities to depend on local departments of social services such as respondent to protect children from abuse. . . .

In these circumstances, a private citizen, or even a person working in a government agency other than DSS, would doubtless feel that her job was done as soon as she had reported her suspicions of child abuse to DSS. Through its child-welfare program, in other words, the State of Wisconsin has relieved ordinary citizens and governmental bodies other than the Department of any sense of obligation to do anything more than report their suspicions of child abuse to DSS. If DSS ignores or dismisses these suspicions, no one will step in to fill the gap. Wisconsin's child-protection program thus effectively confined Joshua DeShaney within the walls of Randy DeShaney's violent home until such time as DSS took action to remove him. Conceivably, then, children like Joshua are made worse off by the existence of this program when the persons and entities charged with carrying it out fail to do their jobs. . . .

As the Court today reminds us, "the Due Process Clause of the Fourteenth Amendment was intended to prevent government 'from abusing [its] power, or employing it as an instrument of oppression.' " . . . My Disagreement with the Court arises from its failure to see that inaction can be every bit as abusive of power as action, that oppression can result when a State undertakes a vital duty and then ignores it. Today's opinion construes the Due Process Clause to permit a State to displace private sources of protection and then, at the critical moment, to shrug its shoulders and turn away from the harm that it has promised to try to prevent. Because I cannot agree that our Constitution is indifferent to such indifference, I respectfully dissent.

JUSTICE BLACKMUN, dissenting.

Today, the Court purports to be the dispassionate oracle of the law, unmoved by "natural sympathy." . . . But, in this pretense, the Court itself retreats into a sterile formalism which prevents it from recognizing either the facts of the case before it or the legal norms that should apply to those facts. As JUSTICE BRENNAN demonstrates, the facts here involve not mere passivity, but active state intervention in the life of Joshua DeShaney—intervention that triggered a fundamental duty to aid the boy once the State learned of the severe danger to which he was exposed. . . . The Court today claims that its decision, however harsh, is compelled by existing legal doctrine. On the contrary, the question presented by this case is an open one, and our Fourteenth Amendment precedents may be read more broadly or narrowly depending upon how one chooses to read them. Faced with the choice, I would adopt a "sympathetic" reading, one which comports with dictates of fundamental justice and recognizes that compassion need not be exiled from the province of judging. Cf. A. Stone, Law, Psychiatry, and Morality 262 (1984) ("We will make mistakes if we go forward, but doing nothing can be the worst mistake. What is required of us is moral ambition. Until our composite sketch becomes a true portrait of humanity we must live with our uncertainty; we will grope, we will struggle, and our compassion may be our only guide and comfort").

★

THE SCOPE OF CONGRESSIONAL POWER

*McCulloch* v. *Maryland* (1819)

POWERS THAT FACILITATE LEGISLATIVE ACTIVITY

*Powell* v. *McCormack* (1969)
*U.S. Term Limits, Inc.* v. *Thornton* (1995)
*Gravel* v. *United States* (1972)
*McGrain* v. *Daugherty* (1927)
*Watkins* v. *United States* (1957)

NONLEGISLATIVE POWERS

SAFEGUARDING LEGISLATIVE POWER

*Schechter Poultry Corporation* v. *United States* (1935)
*Mistretta* v. *United States* (1989)
*Immigration and Naturalization Service* v. *Chadha* (1983)

SOME CONCLUSIONS

NOTES

SELECTED READING

CASES

★

# 4
# THE LEGISLATIVE BRANCH

Aware of the inadequacies of the Articles of Confederation, the Framers of the Constitution set out to create a national government powerful enough to rule a large and diverse nation. Broad powers were conferred on the legislative branch of government, which the Framers expected to be the most powerful of the three branches. Before examining in detail the important legislative powers vested in Congress, however, we must address four important preliminary questions:

1. What principles underlie the interpretation of the extent of the national legislative power?
2. What powers and privileges does the Constitution grant to Congress to facilitate its legislative activity?
3. What nonlegislative powers does the Constitution confer on Congress?
4. Given the growth of the federal bureaucracy, what constitutional means are available for ensuring that Congress continues to make basic policy decisions?

## THE SCOPE OF CONGRESSIONAL POWER

Article I of the Constitution grants Congress a broad range of legislative powers, including taxing and spending powers (which enable it to control the government's purse strings), the power to declare war, and the power to regulate commerce. Various constitutional amendments—in particular, the Thirteenth, Fourteenth, and Fifteenth—confer important additional powers. Finally, the Necessary and Proper Clause (Article I, Section 8) gives Congress the authority to "make all laws which shall be necessary and proper for carrying into Execution the foregoing Powers, and all other Powers vested by this Constitution in the Government of the United States, or in any Department or Officer thereof."

Although the Constitution vests broad powers in Congress, it also imposes various restrictions on congressional power. Some of these restrictions, such as the ban on *ex post facto* laws (those having a retroactive effect), were incorporated into the original Constitution. Others were added with the ratification of the Bill of Rights, the first ten amendments to the Constitution. Most important, Congress can exercise only the powers explicitly or implicitly conferred on it by the Constitution.

This mandate distinguishes Congress from the British Parliament, which (at least in theory) can pass any law it wishes. It also means that Congress, unlike the legislature under the Articles of Confederation, is not limited to those powers expressly granted to it. How broad are Congress's implied powers? The answer to this question depends on the interpretation of the Necessary and Proper Clause. By inserting such a clause, the Framers sought to give Congress the flexibility necessary for dealing with complex and changing conditions. Yet some political figures—most notably, Thomas Jefferson—charged that if Congress were allowed too much discretion in determining how it would achieve its objectives, this "sweeping clause" could transform a government of limited powers into one of unlimited powers. They therefore maintained that the phrase "necessary and proper" should be interpreted as limiting, rather than expanding, congressional power. According to this view, Congress could exercise implied powers only insofar as such powers were necessary for carrying out its enumerated powers. For example, if Congress's enumerated powers could be implemented without chartering a national bank, then the power to charter a bank was not necessary and hence not authorized.

This restrictive interpretation of congressional power was rejected in *McCulloch* v. *Maryland* (1819), in which the Supreme Court recognized Congress's power to charter the Bank of the United States and invalidated a Maryland tax on that bank. Speaking for a unanimous Court, Chief Justice John Marshall persuasively argued for a broad construction of congressional powers. Acknowledging that the Constitution did not specifically authorize Congress to charter a bank, Marshall reasoned that this omission was not in itself determinative. In establishing "a constitution intended to endure for ages to come," Marshall argued, the Framers deliberately avoided cluttering it with excessive detail, choosing instead merely to sketch the "great outlines" of congressional power. To determine whether Congress possessed a particular power, therefore, it was necessary to read the Constitution in light of the ends it was created to achieve.

Because the Constitution confers on Congress considerable responsibility for the economic prosperity of the nation, Marshall went on, it must be interpreted as furnishing Congress with sufficient power for securing that end; any other interpretation would be contradictory and self-defeating. In addition, because effective congressional action is so essential, the Constitution must provide Congress with "that discretion, with respect to the means by which the powers it confers are to be carried into execution, which will enable that body to perform the high duties assigned to it, in the manner most beneficial to the people." To confine Congress to only those means necessary for carrying out its enumerated powers would be to jeopardize the ends for which the Constitution was established. Therefore, Marshall concluded, "Let the end be legitimate, let it be within the scope of the constitution, and all means which are appropriate, which are plainly adapted to that end, which are not prohibited, but consist with the letter and spirit of the constitution, are constitutional."

Marshall's opinion in *McCulloch* can serve as a model for interpreting the constitutional grants of power. By focusing on the ends the Framers sought to achieve, Marshall ensured that Congress neither overstepped its bounds nor was denied powers commensurate with its responsibilities. In allowing Congress to choose how best to achieve those ends, Marshall recognized (as did the Framers) that flexibility of response was essential for effective government. Although bitterly attacked at the time, his opinion was never successfully refuted and has remained the primary rationale for the broad exercise of congressional power.[1]

## POWERS THAT FACILITATE LEGISLATIVE ACTIVITY

The broad scope of Marshall's interpretation of congressional power leads inescapably to the conclusion that, having vested Congress with important responsibilities, the Constitution provided lawmakers with the powers and privileges necessary to fulfill those duties. To promote the efficient transaction of legislative business, the Framers gave each house of Congress a limited control over its membership and the power to discipline members who engage in improper conduct. To secure legislative independence, they inserted into Article I the Speech and Debate Clause, which protects members of Congress from legal inquiry into their legislative activities, and other provisions guaranteeing Congress control over its proceedings.[2] Implicitly, they promoted well-informed deliberations through the Necessary and Proper Clause, under whose authority Congress has undertaken investigations, subpoenaed witnesses to testify, and punished refusals to supply pertinent information. Although the existence of these powers and privileges has long been recognized, their scope has remained the subject of controversy and litigation.

### Membership, Qualifications, and Discipline

The Connecticut Compromise at the Constitutional Convention guaranteed each state equal representation in the Senate but apportioned representation in the House of Representatives on the basis of population. Initially, states had one representative in the House for every 30,000 residents.[3] When population increases threatened to make the House too large, impeding the transaction of legislative business, Congress by statute capped the size of the House at 435. Each state was guaranteed one representative, and the remaining representatives were allocated among the states on the basis of population. This system, however, posed the problem of how to deal with fractional remainders—that is, the remainders left when a state's total population was divided by the population of the ideal district. To solve this problem, Congress in 1941 adopted the method of "equal proportions" proposed by the National Academy of Sciences.[4] In *U.S. Department of Commerce* v. *Montana* (1929), the Supreme Court upheld Congress's choice, ruling that it had broad leeway in choosing among alternative approaches for dealing with fractional remainders.

Although the various states determine the electoral districts for House seats, they do so within severe constraints. As the Supreme Court ruled in *Wesberry* v. *Sanders* (1964), the districts within a state must meet the standard of "one person, one vote." Even minor deviations from equal-population districts may lead to invalidation. For example, in *Karcher* v. *Daggett* (1983) the Court struck down a New Jersey apportionment scheme even though the variation between the most and least populous districts was less than 1 percent. In *Wisconsin* v. *City of New York* (1996), however, the Court refused to require the Secretary of Commerce to use a statistical adjustment of census data to remedy the possible undercounting of population, even though undercounting could affect the apportionment of members of Congress among the states. (Issues relating to apportionment and representation are discussed in greater detail in Chapter 10 of Volume II.)

Article I, Section 5 of the Constitution gives each house of Congress control over the admission of members and authorizes it to impose sanctions (including expulsion) on them for improper conduct. The Constitution does not specify grounds for expelling or otherwise disciplining members of Congress; that lies within the discretion of each house. In fact, neither the Senate nor the House has been eager to sanction its members—as of 1993, only fifteen senators and four representatives had been expelled, all but two for disloyalty during the Civil War. Yet these figures do not reveal the full impact of congressional disciplinary powers, for members of Congress often prefer to resign rather than suffer condemnation by their colleagues. For example, Speaker of the House Jim Wright of Texas resigned in 1989 in the face of disclosures about financial dealings likely to lead to expulsion or censure by the House of Representatives.

Whereas the Constitution does not specify the grounds for disciplining or expelling members, it does prescribe qualifications of age, citizenship, and residency for serving as a Senator or a Representative. During the Constitutional Convention, some delegates proposed that the House and Senate be permitted to establish additional qualifications to maintain the integrity and reputation of their chambers. However, a majority of the delegates, fearful that such a power might be abused to deny constituents their choice of representatives, rejected this proposal. For more than seventy years thereafter, no person possessing the constitutional qualifications for office was denied his seat in Congress. After the Civil War, however, both houses departed from the original understanding, refusing to seat unregenerate Confederates. In 1900 the House denied admission to a Mormon who had allegedly violated the law outlawing polygamy, and in 1920 it refused to seat a socialist accused of publishing disloyal articles during World War I. In *Powell* v. *McCormack* (1969), the Supreme Court decisively rejected such practices and reaffirmed the original understanding of the constitutional qualifications as maximum requirements to which the House and Senate could not add.

However, *Powell* did not resolve whether the states could add eligibility requirements for their members of Congress. This issue arose in *United States Term Limits, Inc.* v. *Thornton* (1995), in which the Court considered the constitutionality of an Arkansas law limiting the number of terms that its members of Congress could serve.[5] The justices in *Thornton* invalidated the Arkansas law by a five-to-four vote. The majority and dissenters in *Thornton* both consulted the same historical records: the debates at the Constitutional Convention, the debates during ratification, postratification practices in the states, and congressional resolution of controversies over seating members. However, they repeatedly clashed over the conclusions to be drawn from this historical research. Their differences appear to reflect a more fundamental disagreement about the character of the Union created by the Constitution. According to the dissenters in *Thornton,* the states retain the power to regulate the national electoral process unless the Constitution has withdrawn that power, because the Tenth Amendment guarantees that all "powers not delegated to the United States by the Constitution, nor prohibited by it to the States, are reserved to the States respectively, or to the people." Congress may override the states' imposition of term limits, because Article I, Section 4 gives it the power to alter state regulations regarding the "Times, Places, and Manner of holding elections." In the absence of such action by Congress, states remain free to establish qualifications for their members of Congress beyond those enunciated in Article I, Section 5.

The Court majority in *Thornton* argued that although members of Congress are elected from separate constituencies, they become, once elected, "a uniform national body representing the interests of a single people" rather than "delegates appointed by separate, sovereign states." This explains why the Constitution provides for a uniform salary to be paid by the national treasury, limits the state role in federal elections, and allows the representatives of all states to judge disputes about the qualifications of representatives of a single state. In addition, the majority rejected the dissenters' interpretation of the Tenth Amendment, contending that it reserves to the states only those powers they possessed at the time the Constitution was adopted. Because no national electoral process existed before the ratification of the Constitution, no power to regulate that process existed in the states. Thus, insofar as states seek, to regulate the national electoral process, they must be authorized to do so by Congress, and Congress had given them no such authority.

The Court's ruling in *Thornton* had nationwide implications. By the time it was announced, twenty-two states had instituted term limits on their members of Congress, usually in conjunction with similar limits on their state legislators, and these congressional term limits could no longer be enforced. Proponents of term limits have sought a constitutional amendment limiting congressional terms, but as of 1998, no such amendment had ever been endorsed by Congress.

### The Speech and Debate Clause

In Article I, Section 6 of the Constitution, members of Congress are guaranteed that "for any Speech or Debate in either House, they shall not be questioned in any other Place." This safeguard against executive harassment or intimidation of legislators, which originated during the British Parliament's struggle for legislative supremacy, excited little controversy for most of the nation's history. Since 1966, however, the Supreme Court has decided several cases involving the Speech and Debate Clause, and the deep divisions on the Court in these cases have revealed basic disagreements about the purposes the clause was designed to serve.

The justices have disagreed, first of all, over who is and who is not protected by the Speech and Debate Clause. Even though the clause expressly protects only senators and representatives, the Court has recognized that its protection cannot be so limited. Some congressional employees perform tasks so essential to the legislative process that denying them protection would defeat the basic purpose of the provision. Thus in *Gravel* v. *United States* (1972), which involved a grand jury investigation into how Senator Mike Gravel obtained and arranged to publish top-secret government documents, all the justices recognized that Gravel's legislative aide was entitled to the same immunity from legal inquiry as the senator. Most justices, however, have been unwilling to extend such protection to other congressional employees. In *Dombrowski* v. *Eastland* (1967), the Court decided that the counsel for a Senate committee could be sued for conspiring to violate the civil rights of various activists, even though the committee chairman could not. In *Doe* v. *McMillan* (1973), it permitted parents to sue the Public Printer and Superintendent of Documents, who—with the authority of Congress—had publicly distributed a committee report that allegedly defamed and invaded the privacy of their children.

A more fundamental disagreement has developed over the range of activities protected by the Speech and Debate Clause. The Court recognized in *Kilbourn* v. *Thompson* (1881) that the clause covers not only debate within Congress but also all things "generally done in a session of the House by one of its members in relation to the business before it."[6] However, the justices have disagreed sharply over what activities comprise "legislative acts" and are immune from inquiry or prosecution. In *Gravel* the Court held that the clause did not foreclose inquiry into how Gravel obtained and arranged for the publication of the Pentagon Papers. Noting that the Constitution specified "Speech or Debate," the *Gravel* majority argued that it protected only those activities directly related to such "internal" legislative functions as deliberation and voting. This distinction between internal and external functions also underlay the Court's rulings in *Doe* and in *Hutchinson* v. *Proxmire* (1979). The majority opinion in *Doe* argued that whereas the Speech and Debate Clause protected the committee hearings and the circulation of the committee's report to other members of Congress, it did not cover public dissemination of the committee report. Similarly, the justices held in *Hutchinson* that although the clause protected speeches on the Senate floor in which Senator William Proxmire attacked a government agency's funding of allegedly worthless research, he could be sued for libel for reproducing those speeches in a newsletter sent to his constituents. The dissenters in these cases rejected this interpretation of the legislative function as unduly narrow. According to these justices, legislators in a representative government have a responsibility to inform the electorate about governmental operations, and publication of material introduced in congressional hearings and of speeches dealing with the expenditure of public funds is a legitimate and appropriate means of fulfilling this responsibility. Such activity, they argued, thus came under the protection of the Speech and Debate Clause.

Bribery prosecutions of members of Congress have also raised Speech and Debate Clause issues. Because the clause protects both speeches delivered in Congress and the motivations for making them, the Court has held that such speeches and motivations could not be used in establishing criminal violations. However, a prosecutor could introduce evidence at trial that a member of Congress had taken a bribe, because the clause "does not prohibit inquiry into activities that are casually or incidentally related to legislative affairs but not part of the process itself."[7] This position has facilitated prosecutions, and the three members of Congress who relied on the Speech and Debate Clause in conducting their defenses were all convicted after their cases were remanded to the lower courts.

### Congressional Investigations

Since 1792, when the House of Representatives appointed a committee to inquire into General St. Clair's defeat in battle by an Indian tribe, congressional committees have conducted investigations to gather information for legislation, to oversee the implementation of laws, or to pursue various other ends. The House of Representatives and the Senate grant most of their committees the power to hold hearings, subpoena witnesses and materials, and cite for contempt witnesses who refuse to cooperate. The vast majority of these investigations proceed without fanfare or dispute, furnishing Congress with the information it needs to discharge its constitutional responsibilities. Some congressional investigations, such as the Iran-Contra hearings, however, have excited great controversy and prompted allegations of constitutional violations.

The most controversial and contentious of modern-day investigations were the inquiries into Communist subversion conducted by the House Un-American Activities Committee (HUAC) during the late 1940s and the 1950s. Empowered by the House to investigate subversive and un-American activities and propaganda, HUAC in this period called over three thousand witnesses, many for questioning about their own or their acquaintances' political beliefs and affiliations. Some witnesses, invoking the protection of the Fifth Amendment's privilege against self-incrimination, refused to testify. Others claimed that the committee's inquiries exceeded its legitimate authority and declined to appear before the committee or to answer its questions, and 144 of these uncooperative witnesses were cited by HUAC for contempt of Congress.[8]

In appealing subsequent contempt convictions, witnesses attacked the constitutionality of HUAC's proceedings on two grounds. They asserted, first of all, that the committee's inquiries were unconstitutional because they did not serve any valid legislative purpose. In making this claim, witnesses did not challenge Congress's power to investigate—the Supreme Court had recognized in *McGrain* v. *Daugherty* (1927) that the Necessary and Proper Clause authorized Congress to conduct investigations to secure the information it needed for wise legislation. They did insist, however, that the Court's position in *McGrain* implied a limitation on congressional committees: namely, that if the power to investigate derives from the power to legislate, then investigations that do not further the processes of legislation have no constitutional warrant. Such was the case, they charged, with HUAC's inquiries. Because the committee sought to expose individuals' political beliefs rather than to obtain information for legislation, its investigations served no valid legislative purpose and were thus unconstitutional.

This argument enjoyed some initial success in *Watkins* v. *United States* (1957), in which the Court reversed the contempt conviction of a labor union official who refused to answer committee questions. Although the decision in *Watkins* rested on narrow grounds, Chief Justice Earl Warren expressly reaffirmed the *McGrain* limitation and pointedly noted that congressional committees had no power "to expose for the sake of exposure." Two years later, however, the Supreme Court in *Barenblatt* v. *United States* (1959) rejected the claim that HUAC's inquiries served no valid legislative purpose. The decisive consideration, the Court suggested, was not the motivation of individual committee members but the scope of Congress's legislative authority; as long as the subject under investigation was one on which Congress could legislate, the Court would assume that the investigation was designed to secure information for possible legislation. This willingness to infer a valid legislative purpose from the subject under investigation virtually eliminated the *McGrain* requirement as a check on congressional investigations.[9]

Some witnesses also protested that the committee's inquiries into political beliefs and affiliations violated their First Amendment rights of freedom of speech and freedom of association. In *Barenblatt,* however, the Court noted that these rights were not absolute and must be balanced against the interest of the congressional committee in obtaining the information it needed to carry out its responsibilities. Applying this balancing test, the Court consistently upheld congressional inquiries against First Amendment challenge. But in *Gibson* v. *Florida Legislative Investigating Committee* (1963) the justices ruled that the First Amendment protected a witness who refused to divulge membership information to a state committee purportedly investigating Communist infiltration into the Miami NAACP.

Although the Court has rejected direct constitutional challenges to congressional investigations, it has developed various safeguards that protect witnesses against arbitrary committee actions. Among these are the requirements, enunciated in *McGrain,* that the scope of a committee's inquiry cannot exceed the authority granted to it by the House or Senate and that committee questions must be pertinent to the topic under investigation. Relying on these requirements of authorization and pertinency, the Supreme Court overturned contempt convictions in *Rumely* v. *United States* (1953) and in *Watkins,* noting in the latter case that neither HUAC's vague authorizing resolution nor the committee members' statements furnished any basis for determining whether the questions Watkins refused to answer were pertinent to the committee's legislative purpose.

In sum, the Court's decisions in cases involving congressional investigations manifest a combination of deference and intervention. On the one hand, the justices have avoided directly confronting Congress by curtailing the scope of its power to investigate. On the other hand, the rulings in *McGrain, Rumely, Watkins,* and other cases reflect an underlying concern for the rights of witnesses, and the Court has not been reluctant to police the activities of congressional committees.

## NONLEGISLATIVE POWERS

Along with lawmaking responsibilities, the Constitution assigns to Congress the power of impeachment and important powers pertaining to the proposal and ratification of constitutional amendments.

### Impeachment

Members of the executive and judicial branches can be removed from office upon impeachment by a majority vote in the House of Representatives and conviction by a two-thirds vote in the Senate. For most of the nation's history, the full membership of the Senate participated in impeachment trials. During the 1980s, however, the Senate introduced a new procedure in conducting the impeachment trial of federal judges. A special bipartisan committee of twelve senators heard testimony and gathered evidence, with the full Senate convened only to hear final arguments, review the trial record, and vote on the articles of impeachment. The Supreme Court refused to rule on a challenge to the new procedure in *Nixon* v. *United States* (1993), maintaining that it involved a "political question" not appropriate for judicial resolution. Some concurring justices, while denying that the case raised a political question, endorsed the Senate's new procedure as constitutional.

In assigning the impeachment power to Congress, the Framers generally followed English parliamentary practice but departed from it in two important respects. Whereas under the Constitution impeachment and conviction carry purely political penalties—removal from office and ineligibility for future office—conviction by the House of Lords typically had led to the imposition of criminal penalties, including death. By eliminating such sanctions, the Framers sought to overcome legislative reluctance to use impeachment to punish official misconduct and to ensure impeached officials a trial by jury in subsequent prosecutions for any criminal offenses. The Constitution also departed from English practice in limiting impeachable offenses to "Treason, Bribery, or other high Crimes and Misdemeanors." Parliament had used impeachment as a political weapon in its struggles for power with the Crown, but the Framers did not intend that Congress should use the impeachment power to intimidate the executive. By specifying the grounds for impeachment and by defining treason in the Constitution (Article III, Section 3), they sought instead to create a check on executive misconduct that would not be subject to abuse.

Nevertheless, during both President Andrew Johnson's impeachment trial and President Richard Nixon's last year in office, considerable controversy arose over the constitutional grounds for impeachment, and in particular over the definition of "high Crimes and Misdemeanors." To some extent, purely partisan considerations dictated the positions taken—for example, Nixon's assertion that impeachment required a criminal violation. Yet these controversies reflected as well a genuine uncertainty about the Framers' intent. On the one hand, the Constitutional Convention's rejection of impeachment for "maladministration" bespeaks the Framers' determination to prevent impeachments motivated merely by political disagreements. On the other hand, the emphasis on "abuse or violation of some public trust" in *The Federalist,* No. 65, suggests that a criminal act is not necessary for impeachment. (This was the position taken by the House committee which recommended impeachment of President Nixon.) Most likely, no precise definition of "high Crimes or Misdemeanors" is possible. The Framers' concern about the proper forum for trying impeachments, as voiced both in the Constitutional Convention and *The Federalist,* suggests a recognition that ultimately these terms would be defined in the judgment of specific cases.

### Constitutional Amendment

The Framers' experience with the Articles of Confederation, under which constitutional amendments required the approval of all thirteen states, revealed that making constitutional change too difficult could block needed reforms. Nevertheless, their experience with the "mutability" of state laws also cautioned against making it too easy. The Constitution permits either Congress or specially elected representatives of the states to propose constitutional amendments (Figure 4.1). For although the Framers expected that the national government would be more aware of defects in the constitutional system and thus more likely to propose remedies, they sought to ensure that it could not block popular demands for constitutional change.[10] The ratification process reflects the federal character of the American political system in requiring that amendments be supported not merely by a numerical majority but also by a geographically dispersed majority. As a final guarantee that any constitutional change would coincide with state public opinion, the Framers required ratification by state legislatures or specially elected conventions in each state.[11]

Thus far, all constitutional amendments have been adopted by the less-cumbersome national mode, under which Congress proposes amendments for adoption and determines the mode of ratification. In addition, because Article V leaves numerous procedural questions unresolved, Congress, acting under the Necessary and Proper Clause, has assumed a supervisory authority over the ratification process, recording state ratifications; determining when amendments have been adopted;

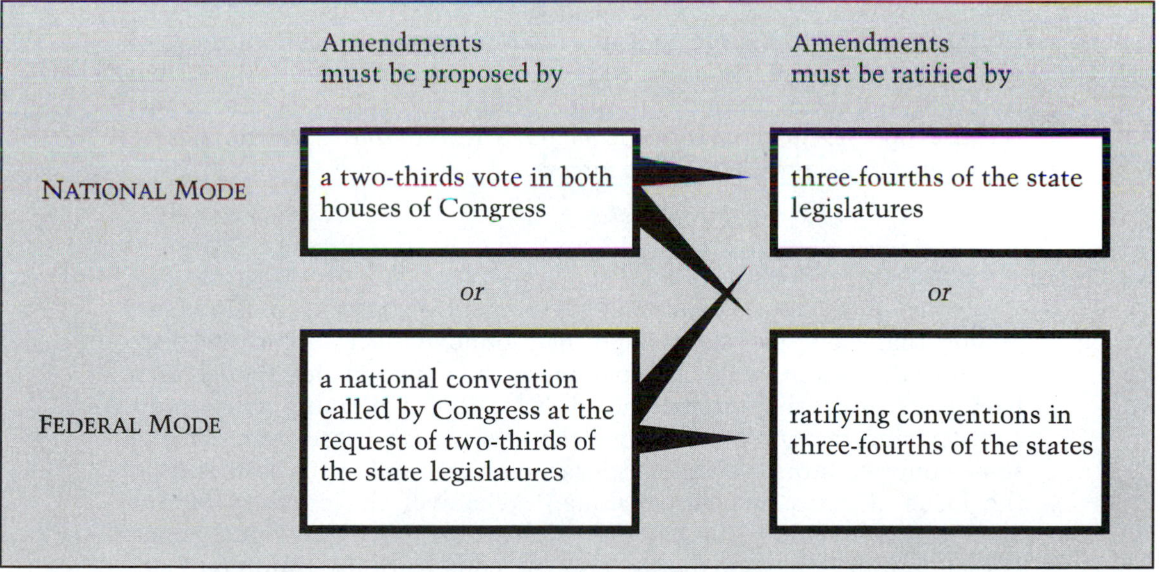


**FIGURE 4.1** Methods of Amending the Constitution

and in this century, establishing time limits for ratification. In *Dillon* v. *Gloss* (1921) the Supreme Court upheld Congress's power to establish a "reasonable" timespan for ratification. Later, in *Coleman* v. *Miller* (1939), the justices refused to define the term *reasonable* in this context, asserting that the political-questions doctrine substantially limits judicial review of Congress's actions.

Nevertheless, Congress's exercise of its supervisory power over the amendment process can be controversial. When Congress proposed the Equal Rights Amendment, which would have outlawed gender discrimination, it established a time limit of seven years for ratification. As the deadline for ratification neared without three-quarters of the state legislatures having ratified the amendment, Congress in 1978 extended the deadline for another thirty months. Furthermore, noting that five state legislatures had voted to rescind their earlier ratifications, it also prohibited such action. Both of these steps raised serious constitutional issues, but because the extended deadline also passed without the amendment being ratified, they ultimately had no effect on the Constitution.[12] More recently, Congress has apparently recognized some limits on its supervisory power. In 1992 it accepted as valid the ratification of an amendment proposed by the First Congress, despite a two-century gap between the first and last states' ratification.

During the 1980s, attention focused on the federal mode of constitutional amendment, as proponents of a balanced-budget amendment campaigned for a constitutional convention that could propose such an amendment. If this movement had succeeded, the convention would have been the first under Article V.[13] Before the convention could have met, however, Congress, acting under the Necessary and Proper Clause, would have had to restore thorny questions about the appointment of the delegates among the states and the convention's mode of operation. Congress has never enacted legislation dealing with these issues, in part because opponents of a convention have feared that such legislation might encourage pro-convention forces.

## SAFEGUARDING LEGISLATIVE POWER

Given the broad scope of national governmental concerns, it is not surprising that Congress increasingly has found it necessary to delegate power to the executive branch. In doing so, however, the legislators often have given executive officials broad discretion in defining policy aims and devising measures to achieve those aims—so broad, according to some commentators, that such delegations have produced a basic shift in the locus of national policy-making.[14] Whatever the accuracy of this assessment, it is clear that extensive delegations of congressional power raise important questions about possible constitutional limits on Congress's power to delegate this authority and about the extent to which Congress can retain control over the direction of national policy.

### Delegation of Power

Although particularly extensive during the twentieth century, congressional delegations of power have occurred throughout our history. As early as 1813 the Supreme Court, in *Brig Aurora* v. *United States,* upheld a statute authorizing the president to lift restrictions on trade with France and Great Britain if those nations ceased interfering with American shipping. Twelve years later, in *Wayman* v. *Southard* (1825), the justices upheld a provision of the Judiciary Act of 1789 that directed the courts "to make and establish all necessary rules" for the transaction of judicial business.

In upholding these laws, however, the Court recognized that the Constitution imposes a limitation on congressional delegations: whatever powers are surrendered, the determination of basic policy must remain with Congress. The laws challenged in *Brig Aurora* and *Wayman* met this requirement by providing clear standards governing the use of the delegated powers. In *Brig Aurora* the justices emphasized that Congress had specified the conditions under which the president was to act and the acts to be performed; in *Wayman* they noted that the legislators had decided the most important matters and merely authorized those operating under the law to "fill up the details." In contrast, a congressional delegation without adequate standards—one that allowed executive officials to make basic policy—would constitute a transfer of legislative power to the executive branch and would thus be unconstitutional.

Despite continued judicial invocation, the requirement that Congress furnish standards has not impeded broad congressional delegations of power. Not until 1935 did the Court invalidate a congressional delegation. Although in *Panama Refining Company* v. *Ryan* (1935) and *Schecter Poultry Corporation* v. *United States* (1935) it did strike down provisions of the National Industrial Recovery Act, those cases marked both the zenith and the end of effective judicial supervision of congressional delegations. Since 1935 the Supreme Court has not invalidated a single delegation of congressional power.

*Mistretta* v. *United States* (1989), a constitutional challenge to the Sentencing Reform Act of 1984, exemplifies the Court's current approach in delegation cases. The Act authorized the United States Sentencing Commission, made up of three federal judges and four lay members, to establish mandatory sentencing guidelines for all persons convicted in federal courts. Despite this broad grant of power, the Court upheld the legislation, concluding that this complicated task was precisely the sort appropriate for delegation and that Congress had furnished adequate standards to guide the Commission in its work. In solitary dissent, Justice Antonin Scalia insisted that the Act involved a dangerous innovation. Previously, the realization that delegations aggrandized the executive branch, "its primary competitor for political power," had served as a check on Congress. By permitting Congress to delegate power outside the three branches of government, Scalia asserted, the Court in

*Mistretta* removed the primary structural impediment to excessive congressional delegations.

## The Legislative Veto

Rather than limiting administrative policy-making by means of precisely drawn statutes, Congress in recent years typically has sought to safeguard its constitutional position by supervising the exercise of delegated power. One weapon Congress relied on for this purpose, particularly during the 1970s, was the legislative veto, under which it delegated power to the president or an administrative agency with the proviso that it could veto the exercise of that power. These conditional grants of power took various forms. The Budget and Impoundment Control Act of 1974 provided for a veto by congressional inaction: The president had to spend appropriated funds unless Congress affirmatively endorsed his failure to do so within forty-five days. The War Powers Resolution, in contrast, permitted Congress to terminate presidential commitments of troops by a concurrent resolution (one passed by both houses of Congress) not subject to presidential veto. Other statutes granted a single house of Congress—or even congressional committees—a veto over administrative regulations or actions of executive branch officials.

Such a one-house veto figured in *Immigration and Naturalization Service* v. *Chadha* (1983), the first Supreme Court ruling on the constitutionality of the legislative veto. Under the Immigration and Nationality Act, the Attorney General was authorized to allow deportable aliens to remain in the country, but a single house of Congress could invalidate the Attorney General's decision by majority vote. This procedure, the Court ruled in *Chadha,* violated the Constitution. Although Chief Justice Warren Burger acknowledged in the opinion of the Court that the legislative veto might at times promote efficiency, he insisted that it contravened "explicit and unambiguous provisions of the Constitution" defining the respective roles of Congress and the president in legislation. Whereas Article I directs that laws be enacted by majority vote in each house, the legislative veto in *Chadha* allowed action that was legislative in character and effect by majority vote in only one house, thus contravening the constitutional requirement of bicameralism. Whereas the Presentment Clause required that all legislation be submitted to the president before becoming law, the legislative veto enabled Congress to take legislative action without the threat of a presidential veto. Thus the legislative veto circumvented the procedures prescribed by the Constitution to ensure due deliberation, check ill-advised legislation, and maintain the separation of powers.

As Justice Byron White noted in his dissent, the Court's interpretation of the Presentment Clause doomed not only the one-house veto in *Chadha* but also "nearly 200 other statutory provisions in which Congress has reserved a 'legislative veto.' " Yet congressional efforts to exert control over the broad powers it delegates to the executive branch did not end with *Chadha*. Rather, in the wake of that ruling, Congress has devised various ingenious mechanisms for maintaining control. For example, if an executive-branch agency uses the broad power delegated to it to adopt a regulation that offends Congress, legislators attach language to an appropriations bill denying the use of the funds to implement the regulation, confident that the President would not veto the bill because of this provision. Congress has also by statute required executive agencies to notify congressional committees before implementing a program, in the expectation that the agency would not proceed if the committee that oversaw it expressed disapproval. Finally, Congress has developed a variation on the legislative veto that is arguably consistent with *Chadha*. Under this procedure, Congress grants broad discertion to executive officials with the proviso that a congressional committee retain the power to veto exercises of that discretion. Given the Court's ruling in *Chadha*, this veto is not legally binding. Nevertheless, executive officials typically agree to abide by the veto, lest Congress reduce their flexibility of action by a less-generous delegation of power. Thus, despite the Court's ruling, the legislative veto—and congressional efforts to continue broad delegations of power without losing control over policymaking—are far from dead.

## SOME CONCLUSIONS

Several conclusions emerge from our review of the constitutional provisions defining Congress's powers and regulating their exercise. First, Congress's constitutional powers are exceedingly broad. Along with conferring on Congress important enumerated powers the Constitution, through the Necessary and Proper Clause, provides extensive additional powers that allow Congress necessary flexibility in fulfilling its constitutional responsibilities. In addition, the Supreme Court, by foreclosing review through the "political-questions doctrine," has acknowledged Congress's broad discretion in the exercise of such nonlegislative powers as supervising the amendment process and hearing impeachments.

Second, the Constitution has provided Congress with important auxiliary powers and privileges that enable it to fulfill its constitutional responsibilities more effectively. Not only does the Constitution expressly confer on members of Congress various immunities that safeguard the independence of the legislative branch, but the Supreme Court also has recognized that the Constitution permits Congress to obtain necessary information for legislation by conducting investigations and punishing witnesses who refuse to supply pertinent information. Yet the Court's interpretation of these auxiliary powers and privileges offers considerable contrast. On the one hand, the justices have attempted to regulate congressional investigations without imposing requirements that would curtail the scope of congressional investigatory authority. On the other hand, in construing the Speech and Debate Clause, they have been much more willing to define the privilege narrowly and to rule against members of Congress.

Finally, the Constitution's generous grants of power have not ensured that Congress will play the decisive role in defining government policy. In recent decades the executive branch has increasingly dominated policy development. The Supreme Court's permissive interpretation of the nondelegation doctrine has facilitated the transfer of responsibility to the executive branch. In recent decades, Congress has attempted to maintain control not by curtailing the scope of its delegations of power but by regulating the use of delegated power. The Supreme Court's invalidation of the legislative veto in *Chadha* deprived Congress of one weapon on which it had relied for overseeing the executive branch. However, Congress has shown considerable ingenuity in developing other mechanisms for asserting its control over public policy.

## NOTES

1 For the most forceful attacks on *McCulloch* and Marshall's responses, see Gerald Gunther, ed., *John Marshall's Defense of McCulloch* v. *Maryland* (Stanford: Stanford University Press, 1969).

2 Several constitutional provisions safeguard legislative independence. Each house of Congress can choose its own officers (Article I, Section 2, Paragraph 5, and Section 3, Paragraph 5) and determine the "Elections, Returns, and Qualifications of its own Members" (Article I, Section 5, Paragraph 1). Each house can also determine the rules of its proceedings and discipline or expel members (Article I, Section 5, Paragraph 2). Finally, members of Congress generally are immune from arrest during their attendance in Congress.

3 In actuality, as a result of a compromise at the Constitutional Convention, the population base for determining representation in the House of Representatives included all free inhabitants and three-fifths of all slaves but excluded "all Indians not taxed."

4 The "method of equal proportions" was chosen because it minimizes the discrepancy between the size of the districts in any pair of states.

5 The Arkansas law in fact imposed term limits indirectly, denying a place on the ballot to Representatives who had served three or more terms and Senators who had served two or more terms. In theory, these legislators could seek reelection as write-in candidates, but the Court in *Thornton* concluded that, given the unlikelihood of success of write-in candidacies, the Arkansas law operated as a term limit.

6 *Kilbourn* v. *Thompson*, 103 U.S. 168, 204 (1881).

7 *United States* v. *Brewster*, 408 U.S. 501, 528 (1972).

8 The figures in this paragraph are drawn from Carl Beck's *Contempt of Congress* (New Orleans: Hauser Press, 1959), Appendix B, pp. 217–241. For other accounts of HUAC's activities, see Alan Barth, *Government by Investigation* (New York: Viking, 1955); William F. Buckley, Jr., ed., *The Committee and Its Critics* (Chicago: Henry Regnery, 1962); and Walter Goodman, *The Committee: The Extraordinary Career of the House Committee on Un-American Activities* (New York: Farrar, Straus, & Giroux, 1968).

9 For a perceptive discussion of this point and a proposal for an alternative approach, see Martin Shapiro, *Law and Politics in the Supreme Court* (New York: The Free Press of Glencoe, 1964), Chapter 2

10 Thus Alexander Hamilton emphasizes in *The Federalist*, No. 85, that when two-thirds of the states apply to Congress to call a convention for proposing amendments, Congress has no discretion and must do so.

11 The Twenty-First Amendment, which repealed Prohibition, was ratified by specially elected conventions. All other amendments have been ratified by the state legislatures.

12 A federal district court judge ruled in *Idaho* v. *Freeman*, 529 F. Supp. 1107 (1981), that the ERA deadline extension and prohibition on rescission were unconstitutional. However, the Supreme Court stayed the district court's ruling and granted certiorari, but the deadline for ratification passed before the Court ruled in the case, thereby rendering it moot.

13 However, there have been more than 230 state constitutional conventions under state constitutions.

14 See, for example, Theodore J. Lowi, *The End of Liberalism*, 2d ed. (New York: W. W. Norton, 1979), especially Chapter 5.

## SELECTED READING

*The Federalist*, Nos. 33, 44, 52–66, 85.

*Barenblatt* v. *United States*, Volume 2, Chapter 5, and website.
*Bowsher* v. *Synar*, 478 U.S. 714 (1986).
*Coleman* v. *Miller*, 307 U.S. 433 (1939).
*Gibson* v. *Florida Legislative Investigating Committee*, 372 U.S. 539 (1963).
*Hutchinson* v. *Proxmire*, 443 U.S. 111 (1979).
*Nixon* v. *United States*, 506 U.S. 224 (1993).
*U.S. Department of Commerce* v. *Montana*, 503 U.S. 442 (1992).

Ackerman, Bruce A. *We the People* (Cambridge, Mass.: Belknap Press, 1991).

Barber, Sotirios. *The Constitution and the Delegation of Congressional Power* (Chicago: University of Chicago Press, 1975).

Cella, Alexander J. "The Doctrine of Legislative Privilege of Speech or Debate: The New Interpretation as a Threat to Legislative Coequality." *Suffolk University Law Review* 8 (1974): 1019–1095.

*Congressional Quarterly's Guide to Congress*, 4th ed. (Washington, D.C.: CQ Press, 1991).

Craig, Barbara H. *Chadha: The Story of an Epic Constitutional Struggle* (New York: Oxford University Press, 1988).

Fisher, Louis. *Constitutional Conflicts Between Congress and the President*, 4th ed. (Lawrence: University Press of Kansas, 1997).

Hamilton, James. *The Power to Probe: A Study in Congressional Investigations* (New York: Random House, 1976).

Korn, Jessica. *The Power of Separation: American Constitutionalism and the Myth of the Legislative Veto.* (Princeton, N.J.: Princeton University Press, 1996).

Kyvig, David E. *Explicit and Authentic Acts: Amending the U.S. Constitution, 1776–1995* (Lawrence: University Press of Kansas, 1996).

Labovitz, John R. *Presidential Impeachments* (New Haven: Yale University Press, 1978).

Levinson, Sanford, ed. *Responding to Imperfection: The Theory and Practice of Constitutional Amendment* (Princeton, N.J.: Princeton University Press, 1995).

Schoenbrod, David. *Power Without Responsibility: How Congress Abuses the People Through Delegation.* New Haven: Yale University Press, 1993.

Shapiro, Martin. *Law and Politics in the Supreme Court* (New York: Free Press, 1964). Chapter 2.

Vile, John R. *Contemporary Questions Surrounding the Constitutional Amending Process* (New York: Praeger, 1992).

Weber, Paul J. and Barbara A. Perry. *Unfounded Fears: Myths and Realities of a Constitutional Convention* (New York: Praeger, 1989).

## *McCulloch* v. *Maryland*

**17 U.S. (Wheat.) 316; 4 L. Ed. 579 (1819)**

In 1816, Congress chartered the Second Bank of the United States, one branch of which was established in Baltimore the next year. In 1818 the Maryland legislature passed a statute taxing "all banks or branches thereof" operating in Maryland but not chartered by the state. The act levied a tax of approximately 2 percent of the value of all notes issued or, alternatively, an annual fee of $15,000; it also provided for a $500 penalty for every violation. When James McCulloch, cashier of the Baltimore branch, issued notes and refused to pay the tax, suit was brought on behalf of the state of Maryland to recover the penalties. A judgment was rendered against McCulloch in lower court and affirmed by the Maryland court of appeals, the state's highest court. From there, the case was brought to the United States Supreme Court by a writ of error. *Opinion of the Court: Marshall, Washington, Johnson, Livingston, Todd, Duval, Story.*

MR. CHIEF JUSTICE MARSHALL delivered the opinion of the Court.

In the case now to be determined, the defendant, a sovereign State, denies the obligation of a law enacted by the legislature of the Union, and the plaintiff, on his part, contests the validity of an act which has been passed by the legislature of that State. The constitution of our country, in its most interesting and vital parts, is to be considered; the conflicting powers of the government of the Union and of its members, as marked in that constitution, are to be discussed; and an opinion given, which may essentially influence the great operations of the government. . . .

The first question made in the cause is, has Congress power to incorporate a bank? . . .

The government of the Union is acknowledged by all to be one of enumerated powers. . . . That principle is now universally admitted. But the question respecting the extent of the powers actually granted, is perpetually arising, and will probably continue to arise, as long as our system shall exist.

In discussing these questions, the conflicting powers of the general and State governments must be brought into view, and the supremacy of their respective laws, when they are in opposition, must be settled.

If any one proposition could command the universal assent of mankind, we might expect it would be this—that the government of the Union, though limited in its powers, is supreme within its sphere of action. This would seem to result necessarily from its nature. It is the government of all; its powers are delegated by all; it represents all, and acts for all. . . . The nation, on those subjects on which it can act, must necessarily bind its component parts. But this question is not left to mere reason: The people have, in express terms, decided it, by saying, "this constitution, and the laws of the United States, which shall be made in pursuance thereof," "shall be the supreme law of the land," and by requiring that the members of the State legislatures, and the officers of the executive and judicial departments of the States, shall take the oath of fidelity to it.

The government of the United States, then, though limited in its powers, is supreme; and its laws, when made in pursuance of the constitution, form the supreme law of the land, "any thing in the constitution or laws of any State to the contrary notwithstanding."

Among the enumerated powers, we do not find that of establishing a bank or creating a corporation. But there is no phrase in the instrument which, like the articles of confederation, excludes incidental or implied powers; and which requires that every thing granted shall be expressly and minutely described. Even the 10th amendment, which was framed for the purpose of quieting the excessive jealousies which had been excited, omits the word "expressly," and declares only that the powers "not delegated to the United States, nor prohibited to the States, are reserved to the States or to the people;" thus leaving the question, whether the particular power which may become the subject of contest has been delegated to the one government, or prohibited to the other, to depend on a fair construction of the whole instrument. The men who drew and adopted this amendment had experienced the embarrassments resulting from the insertion of this word in the articles of confederation, and probably omitted it to avoid those embarrassments. A constitution, to contain an accurate detail of all the subdivisions of which its great powers will admit, and of all the means by which they may be carried into execution, would partake of the prolixity of a legal code, and could scarcely be embraced by the human mind. It would probably never be understood by the public. Its nature, therefore, requires, that only its great outlines should be marked, its important objects designated, and the minor ingredients which compose those objects be deduced from the nature of the objects themselves. That this idea was entertained by the framers of the American constitution, is not only to be inferred from the nature of the instrument, but from the language. Why else were some of the limitations, found in the ninth section of the 1st article, introduced? It is also, in some degree, warranted by their having omitted to use any restrictive term which might prevent its receiving a fair and just interpretation. In considering this question, then, we must never forget, that it is *a constitution* we are expounding.

Although, among the enumerated powers of government, we do not find the word "bank" or "incorporation," we find the great powers to lay and collect taxes; to borrow money; to regulate commerce; to declare and conduct a war; and to raise and support armies and navies. The sword and the purse, all the external relations, and no inconsiderable portion of the industry of the nation, are entrusted to its government. It can never be pretended that these vast powers draw after them others of inferior importance, merely because they are inferiors. Such an idea can never be advanced. But it may with great reason be contended, that a government, entrusted with such ample powers, on the due execution of which the happiness and prosperity of the nation so vitally depends, must also be entrusted with ample means for their execution. The power being given, it is the interest of the nation to facilitate its execution. It can never be their interest, and cannot be presumed to have been their intention, to clog and embarrass its execution by withholding the most appropriate means. Throughout this vast republic . . . revenue is to be collected and expended, armies are to be marched and supported. The exigencies of the nation may require that the treasure raised in the north should be transported to the south, *that* raised in the east conveyed to the west, or that this order should be reversed. Is that construction of the constitution to be preferred which would render these operations difficult, hazardous, and expensive? Can we adopt that construction, (unless the words imperiously require it), which would impute to the framers of that instrument, when granting these powers for the public good, the intention of impeding their exercise by withholding a choice of means? If, indeed, such be the mandate of the constitution, we have only to obey; but that instrument does not profess to enumerate the means by which the powers it confers may be executed; nor does it prohibit the creation of a corporation, if the existence of such a being be essential to the beneficial exercise of those powers. It is, then, the subject of fair inquiry, how far such means may be employed.

It is not denied, that the powers given to the government imply the ordinary means of execution. That, for example, of raising revenue, and applying it to national purposes, is admitted to imply the power of conveying money from place to place, as the exigencies of the nation may require, and of employing the usual means of conveyance. But it is denied that the government has its choice of means; or, that it may employ the most convenient means, if, to employ them, it be necessary to erect a corporation.

But the constitution of the United States has not left the right of Congress to employ the necessary means, for the execution of the powers conferred on the government, to general reasoning. To its enumeration of powers is added that of making "all laws which shall be necessary and proper, for carrying into execution the foregoing powers, and all other powers vested by this constitution, in the government of the United States, or in any department thereof."

The counsel for the State of Maryland have urged various arguments, to prove that this clause, though in terms a grant of power, is not so in effect; but is really restrictive of the general right, which might otherwise be implied, of selecting means for executing the enumerated powers. . . .

The argument on which most reliance is placed, is drawn from the peculiar language of this clause. Congress is not empowered by it to make all laws, which may have relation to the powers conferred on the government, but such only as may be *"necessary and proper"* for carrying them into execution. The word *"necessary,"* is considered as controlling the whole sentence, and as limiting the right to pass laws for the execution of the granted powers, to such as are indispensable, and without which the power would be nugatory. That it excludes the choice of means, and leaves to Congress, in each case, that only which is most direct and simple.

Is it true, that this is the sense in which the word "necessary" is always used? Does it always import an absolute physical necessity, so strong, that one thing, to which another may be termed necessary, cannot exist without that other? We think it does not. . . . To employ the means necessary to an end, is generally understood as employing any means calculated to produce the end, and not as being confined to those single means, without which the end would be entirely unattainable. . . . Almost all compositions contain words, which, taken in their rigorous sense, would convey a meaning different from that which is obviously intended. It is essential to just construction, that many words which import something excessive, should be understood in a more mitigated sense—in that sense which common usage justifies. The word "necessary" is of this description. . . . It admits of all degrees of comparison; and is often connected with other words, which increase or diminish the impression the mind receives of the urgency it imports. A thing may be necessary, very necessary, absolutely or indispensably necessary. To no mind would the same idea be conveyed, by these several phrases. This comment on the word is well illustrated by the passage cited at the bar, from the 10th section of the 1st article of the constitution. It is, we think, impossible to compare the sentence which prohibits a State from laying "imposts, or duties on imports or exports, except what may be *absolutely* necessary for executing its inspection laws," with that which authorizes Congress "to make all laws which shall be necessary and proper for carrying into execution" the powers of the general government, without feeling a conviction that the convention understood itself to change materially the meaning of the word "necessary," by prefixing the word "absolutely." . . . This provision is made in a constitution intended to endure for ages to come, and, consequently, to be adapted to the various *crises* of human affairs. To have prescribed the means by which government should, in all future time; execute its powers, would have been to change, entirely, the character of the instrument, and give it the properties of a legal code. . . . To have declared that the best means shall not be used, but those alone without which the power given would be nugatory, would have been to deprive the legislature of the capacity to avail itself of experience, to exercise its reason, and to accommodate its legislation to circumstances. If we apply this principle of construction to any of the powers of the government, we shall find it so pernicious in its operation that we shall be compelled to discard it. . . .

Take, for example, the power "to establish post offices and post roads." This power is executed by the single act of making the establishment. But, from this has been inferred the power and duty of carrying the mail along the post road, from one post office to another. And, from this implied power, has again been inferred the right to punish those who steal letters from the post office, or rob the mail. It may be said, with some plausibility, that the right to carry the mail, and to punish those who rob it, is not indispensably necessary to the establishment of a post office and post road. This right is indeed essential to the beneficial exercise of the power, but not indispensably necessary to its existence. So, of the punishment of the crimes of stealing or falsifying a record or process of a Court of the United States, or of perjury in such Court. To punish these offences is certainly conducive to the due administration of justice. But courts may exist, and may decide the causes brought before them, though such crimes escape punishment. . . .

If this limited construction of the word "necessary" must be abandoned in order to punish, whence is derived the rule which would reinstate it, when the government would carry its powers into execution by means not vindictive in their nature? If the word "necessary" means "needful," "requisite," "essential," "conducive to," in order to let in the power of punishment for the infraction of law; why is it not equally comprehensive when required to authorize the use of means which facilitate the execution of the powers of government without the infliction of punishment?" . . .

But the argument which most conclusively demonstrates the error of the construction contended for by the counsel for the State of Maryland, is founded on the intention of the Convention, as manifested in the whole clause. . . . This clause, as construed by the State of Maryland, would abridge, and almost annihilate this useful and necessary right of the legislature to select its means. That this could not be intended, is, we should think, had it not been already controverted, too apparent for controversy. We think so for the following reasons.

1st. The clause is placed among the powers of Congress, not among the limitations on those powers.

2nd. Its terms purport to enlarge, not to diminish the powers vested in the government. It purports to be an additional power, not a restriction on those already granted. No reason has been, or can be assigned for thus concealing an intention to narrow the discretion of the national legislature under words which purport to enlarge it. The framers of the constitution wished its adoption, and well knew that it would be endangered by its strength, not by its weakness. Had they been capable of using language which would convey to the eye one idea, and, after deep reflection, impress on the mind another, they would rather have disguised the grant of power, than its limitation. If, then, their intention had been, by this clause, to restrain the free use of means which might otherwise have been implied, that intention would have been inserted in another place, and would have been expressed in terms resembling these. "In carrying into execution the foregoing powers, and all others," &c. "no laws shall be passed but such as are necessary and proper." Had the intention been to make this clause restrictive, it would unquestionably have been so in form as well as in effect. . . .

We admit, as all must admit, that the powers of the government are limited, and that its limits are not to be transcended. But we think the sound construction of the constitution must allow to the national legislature that discretion, with respect to the means by which the powers it confers are to be carried into execution, which will enable that body to perform the high duties assigned to it, in the manner most beneficial to the people. Let the end be legitimate, let it be within the scope of the constitution, and all means which are appropriate, which are plainly adapted to that end, which are not prohibited, but consist with the letter and spirit of the constitution, are constitutional. . . .

Should Congress, in the execution of its powers, adopt measures which are prohibited by the constitution; or should Congress, under the pretext of executing its powers, pass laws for the accomplishment of objects not entrusted to the government; it would become the painful duty of this tribunal, should a case requiring such a decision come before it, to say that such an act was not the law of the land. But where the law is not prohibited, and is really calculated to effect any of the objects entrusted to the government, to undertake here to inquire into the degree of its necessity, would be to pass the line which circumscribes the judicial department, and to tread on legislative ground. This court disclaims all pretensions to such a power. . . .

After the most deliberate consideration, it is the unanimous and decided opinion of this Court, that the act to incorporate the Bank of the United States is a law made in pursuance of the constitution and is a part of the supreme law of the land. . . .

It being the opinion of the Court, that the act incorporating the bank is constitutional . . . we proceed to inquire— . . . Whether the State of Maryland may, without violating the constitution, tax that branch?

The argument on the part of the State of Maryland, is, not that the States may directly resist a law of Congress, but that they may exercise their acknowledged powers upon it, and that the constitution leaves them this right in the confidence that they will not abuse it. . . .

That the power to tax involves the power to destroy; that the power to destroy may defeat and render useless the power to create; that there is a plain repugnance, in conferring on one government a power to control the constitutional measures of another, which other, with respect to those very measures, is declared to be supreme over that which exerts the control, are propositions not to be denied. But all inconsistencies are to be reconciled by the magic of the word CONFIDENCE. Taxation, it is said, does not necessarily and unavoidably destroy. To carry it to the excess of destruction would be an abuse, to presume which, would banish that confidence which is essential to all government.

But is this a case of confidence? Would the people of any one State trust those of another with a power to control the most insignificant operations of their State government? We know they would not. Why, then, should we suppose that the people of any one State should be willing to trust those of another with a power to control the operations of a government to which they have confided their most important and most valuable interests? In the legislature of the Union alone, are all represented. The legislature of the Union alone, therefore, can be trusted by the people with the power of controlling measures which concern all, in the confidence that it will not be abused. This, then, is not a case of confidence, and we must consider it as it really is.

If we apply the principle for which the State of Maryland contends, to the constitution generally, we shall find it capable of changing totally the character of that instrument. We shall find it capable of arresting all the measures of the government, and of prostrating it at the foot of the States. The American people have declared their constitution, and the laws made in pursuance thereof, to be supreme; but this principle would transfer the supremacy, in fact, to the States.

It has also been insisted, that, as the power of taxation in the general and State governments is acknowledged to be concurrent, every argument which would sustain the right of the general government to tax banks chartered by the States, will equally sustain the right of the States to tax banks chartered by the general government.

But the two cases are not on the same reason. The people of all the States have created the general government, and have conferred upon it the general power of taxation. The people of all the States, and the States themselves, are represented in Congress, and, by their representatives, exercise this power. When they tax the chartered institutions of the States, they tax their constituents; and these taxes must be uniform. But, when a State taxes the operations of the government of the United States, it acts upon institutions created, not by their own constituents, but by people over whom they claim no control. It acts upon the measures of a government created by others as well as themselves, for the benefit of others in common with themselves. The difference is that which always exists, and always must exist, between the action of the whole on a part, and the action of a part on the whole—between the laws of a government declared to be supreme, and those of a government which, when in opposition to those laws, is not supreme. . . .

The Court has bestowed on this subject its most deliberate consideration. The result is a conviction that the States have no power, by taxation or otherwise, to retard, impede, burden, or in any manner control, the operations of the constitutional laws enacted by Congress to carry into execution the powers vested in the general government. This is, we think, the unavoidable consequence of that supremacy which the constitution has declared.

We are unanimously of opinion, that the law passed by the legislature of Maryland, imposing a tax on the Bank of the United States, is unconstitutional and void. . . .

## *Powell* v. *McCormack*

**395 U.S. 486, 23 L. Ed. 2d 491, 89 S. Ct. (1969)**

During the 89th Congress, a special subcommittee reported that Adam Clayton Powell, a representative from the 18th Congressional District in New York, had deceived House authorities regarding travel expenses. It also presented evidence that Powell had ordered illegal salary payments to his wife. No action was taken prior to adjournment, but after Powell was re-elected to serve in the 90th Congress, the Democratic members voted to remove him from his chairmanship of the Committee on Education and Labor.

When other representatives were sworn in, Powell was not given the oath of office. Instead, the House authorized the Speaker of the House to appoint a select committee to determine Powell's eligibility to serve. When the committee reported that Powell had engaged in various improprieties, the House voted by 307–116 to exclude Powell and declared his seat vacant. Powell, together with 13 voters from his congressional district, then sued the Speaker of the House and various House employees who had participated in his exclusion. He sought a declaratory judgment that his exclusion was unconstitutional and back pay for the period during which he was excluded. While the case was pending, the 90th Congress ended, and Powell was elected to, and seated by, the 91st Congress.

After the District Court dismissed the case "for want of jurisdiction of the subject matter," and the Court of Appeals affirmed, the Supreme Court granted certiorari. *Opinion of the Court: Warren, Black, Douglas, Harlan, Brennan, White, Fortas, Marshall. Concurring opinion: Douglas. Dissenting opinion: Stewart.*

MR. CHIEF JUSTICE WARREN delivered the opinion of the Court.

**Speech or Debate Clause**

Respondents assert that the Speech or Debate Clause of the Constitution, Art. I, § 6, is an absolute bar to petitioners' action. The Court first articulated in *Kilbourn* [v. *Thompson*] and followed in *Dombrowski* v. *Eastland* the doctrine that, although an action against a Congressman may be barred by the Speech or Debate Clause, legislative employees who participated in the unconstitutional activity are responsible for their acts. That House employees are acting pursuant to express orders of the House does not bar judicial review of the constitutionality of the underlying legislative decision. *Kilbourn* decisively settles this question, since the Sergeant at Arms was held liable for false imprisonment even though he did nothing more than execute the House Resolution that Kilbourn be arrested and imprisoned. Respondents' suggestions thus ask us to distinguish between affirmative acts of House employees and situations in which the House orders its employees not to act or between actions for damages and claims for salary. We can find no basis in either the history of the Speech or Debate Clause or our cases for either distinction. The purpose of the protection afforded legislators is not to forestall judicial review of legislative action but to insure that legislators are not distracted from or hindered in the performance of their legislative tasks by being called into court to defend their actions. Freedom of legislative activity and the purposes of the Speech or Debate Clause are fully protected if legislators are relieved of the burden of defending themselves. [T]hough this action may be dismissed against the Congressmen petitioners are entitled to maintain their action against House employees and to judicial review of the propriety of the decision to exclude petitioner Powell.

**Justiciability**

Respondents maintain that even if this case is otherwise justiciable, it presents only a political question. It is well established that the federal courts will not adjudicate political questions.

Respondents' first contention is that this case presents a political question because under Art. I, § 5, there has been a "textually demonstrable constitutional commitment" to the House of the "adjudicatory power" to determine Powell's qualifications. Thus it is argued that the House, and the House alone, has power to determine who is qualified to be a member.

In order to determine whether there has been a textual commitment to a co-ordinate department of the Government, we must interpret the Constitution. In other words, we must first determine what power the Constitution confers upon the House through Art. I, § 5, before we can determine to what extent, if any, the exercise of that power is subject to judicial review. Respondents maintain that the House has broad power under § 5, and, they argue, the House may determine which are the qualifications necessary for membership. On the other hand, petitioners allege that the Constitution provides that an elected representative may be denied his seat only if the House finds he does not meet one of the standing qualifications expressly prescribed by the Constitution.

In order to determine the scope of any "textual commitment" under Art. I, § 5, we necessarily must determine the meaning of the phrase to "be the Judge of the Qualifications of its own Members." Petitioners argue that the records of the debates during the Constitutional Convention; available commentary from the post-Convention, pre-ratification period; and early congressional applications of Art. I, § 5, support their construction of the section. Respondents insist, however, that a careful examination of the pre-Convention practices of the English Parliament and American colonial assemblies demonstrates that by 1787, a legislature's power to judge the qualifications of its members was generally understood to encompass exclusion or expulsion on the ground that an individual's character or past conduct rendered him unfit to serve. When the Constitution and the debates over its adoption are thus viewed in historical perspective, argue respondents, it becomes clear that the "qualifications" expressly set forth in the Constitution were not meant to limit the long-recognized legislative power to exclude or expel at will, but merely to establish "standing incapacities," which could be altered only by a constitutional amendment. Our examination of the relevant historical materials leads us to the conclusion that petitioners are correct and that the Constitution leaves the House without authority to *exclude* any person, duly elected by his constituents, who meets all the requirements for membership expressly prescribed in the Constitution.

**Convention Debates**

On August 10, the Convention considered the Committee of Detail's proposal that the "Legislature of the United States shall have authority to establish such uniform qualifications of the members of each House, with regard to property, as to the said Legislature shall seem expedient." The debate on this proposal discloses much about the views of the Framers on the issue of qualifications. For example, James Madison urged its rejection, stating that the proposal would vest

> an improper & dangerous power in the Legislature. The qualifications of electors and elected were fundamental articles in a Republican Govt. and ought to be fixed by the Constitution. If the Legislature could regulate those of either, it can by degrees subvert the Constitution. A Republic may be converted into an aristocracy or oligarchy as well by limiting the number capable of being elected, as the number authorized to elect. . . . It was a power also, which might be made subservient to the views of one faction agst. another. Qualifications founded on artificial distinctions may be devised, by the stronger in order to keep out partisans of [a weaker] faction.

Oliver Ellsworth, of Connecticut, noted that a legislative power to establish property qualifications was exceptional and "dangerous because it would be much more liable to abuse." Gouverneur Morris then moved to strike "with regard to property" from the Committee's proposal. His intention was "to leave the Legislature entirely at large." Hugh Williamson, of North Carolina, expressed concern that if a majority of the legislature should happen to be "composed of any particular description of men, of lawyers for example, . . . the future elections might be secured to their own body." [T]he Convention rejected both Gouverneur Morris' motion and the Committee's proposal. Later the same day, the Convention adopted without debate the provision authorizing each House to be "the judge of the . . . qualifications of its own members."

One other decision made the same day is very important to determining the meaning of Art. I, § 5. When the delegates reached the Committee of Detail's proposal to empower each House to expel its members, Madison "observed that the right of expulsion . . . was too important to be exercised by a bare majority of a quorum: and in emergencies [one] faction might be dangerously abused." He therefore moved that "with the concurrence of two-thirds" be inserted. With the exception of one State, whose delegation was divided, the motion was unanimously approved without debate, although Gouverneur Morris noted his opposition. The importance of this decision cannot be over-emphasized. None of the parties to this suit disputes that prior to 1787 the legislative powers to judge qualifications and to expel were exercised by a majority vote. Indeed, without exception, the English and colonial antecedents to Art. I, § 5, cls. 1 and 2, support this conclusion. Thus, the Convention's decision to increase the vote required to expel, because that power was "too important to be exercised by a bare majority," while at the same time not similarly restricting the power to judge qualifications, is compelling evidence that they considered the latter already limited by the standing qualifications previously adopted.

Petitioners also argue that the post-Convention debates over the Constitution's ratification support their interpretation of § 5. For example, they emphasize Hamilton's reply to the antifederalist charge that the new Constitution favored the wealthy and well-born:

> The truth is that there is no method of securing to the rich the preference apprehended but by prescribing qualifications of property either for those who may elect or be elected. But this forms no part of the power to be conferred upon the national government. Its authority would be expressly restricted to the regulation of the *times*, the *places*, the *manner* of elections. *The qualifications of the persons who may choose or be chosen, as has been remarked upon other occasions, are defined and fixed in the Constitution, and are unalterable by the legislature. The Federalist Papers* (Emphasis in last sentence added.)

### Post-Ratification

As clear as these statements appear, respondents dismiss them as "general statements . . . directed to other issues." They suggest that far more relevant is Congress' own understanding of its power to judge qualifications as manifested in post-ratification exclusion cases. Unquestionably, both the House and the Senate have excluded members-elect for reasons other than their failure to meet the Constitution's standing qualifications. For almost the first 100 years of its existence, however, Congress strictly limited its power to judge the qualifications of its members to those enumerated in the Constitution.

The abandonment of such restraint, however, was among the casualties of the general upheaval produced in [the Civil] war's wake. In 1868, the House voted for the first time in its history to exclude a member-elect. It refused to seat two duly elected representatives for giving aid and comfort to the Confederacy. From that time until the present, congressional practice has been erratic, and on the few occasions when a member-elect was excluded although he met all the qualifications set forth in the Constitution, there were frequently vigorous dissents.

Had these congressional exclusion precedents been more consistent, their precedential value still would be quite limited. That an unconstitutional action has been taken before surely does not render that same action any less unconstitutional at a later date. Particularly in view of the Congress' own doubts in those few cases where it did exclude members-elect, we are not inclined to give its precedents controlling weight. The relevancy of prior exclusion cases is limited largely to the insight they afford in correctly ascertaining the draftsmen's intent. Obviously, therefore, the precedential value of these cases tends to increase in proportion to their proximity to the Convention in 1787. And, what evidence we have of Congress' early understanding confirms our conclusion that the House is without power to exclude any member-elect who meets the Constitution's requirements for membership.

For these reasons, we have concluded that Art. I, § 5, is at most a "textually demonstrable commitment" to Congress to judge only the qualifications expressly set forth in the Constitution. Therefore, the "textual commitment" formulation of the political question doctrine does not bar federal courts from adjudicating petitioners' claims.

Respondents concede that Powell met these. Thus, there is no need to remand this case to determine whether he was entitled to be seated in the 90th Congress. Therefore, we hold that, since Adam Clayton Powell, Jr., was duly elected by the voters of the 18th Congressional District of New York and was not ineligible to serve under any provision of the Constitution, the House was without power to exclude him from its membership.

## *U.S. Term Limits, Inc.* v. *Thornton*

**514 U.S. 779, 115 S. Ct. 1842, 131 L. Ed. 2d 881 (1995)**

In November 1992, voters in Arkansas adopted Amendment 73 to their state constitution. Sections 1 and 2 of the amendment directly limited the reeligibility of state legislators and elected officials of Arkansas' executive branch. Section 3 sought through more indirect means to combat what the amendment's preamble referred to as "entrenched incumbency," leading to "an electoral system that is less free, less competitive and less representative than the system established by the Founding Fathers." More specifically, Section 3 provided: (a) Any person having been elected to three or more terms as a member of the United States House of Representatives from Arkansas shall not be certified as a candidate and shall not be eligible to have his/her name placed on the ballot for election to the United States House of Representatives from Arkansas, and (b) Any person having been elected to two or more terms as a member of the United States Senate from Arkansas shall not be certified as a candidate and shall not be eligible to have his/her name placed on the ballot for election to the United States Senate from Arkansas.

Section 3 was challenged in state court, with petitioners asserting that a state could not limit the number of terms that members of its congressional delegation could serve. After the trial court ruled that Section 3 violated Article I of the United States Constitution and the Arkansas Supreme Court affirmed the trial court's ruling, the U.S. Supreme Court granted certiorari. *Opinion of the Court: Stevens, Kennedy, Souter, Ginsburg, Breyer. Concurring opinion: Kennedy. Dissenting opinion: Thomas, Rehnquist, O'Connor, Scalia.*

JUSTICE STEVENS delivered the opinion of the Court.

Today's cases present a challenge to an amendment to the Arkansas State Constitution that prohibits the name of an otherwise-eligible candidate for Congress from appearing on the general election ballot if that candidate has already served three terms in the House of Representatives or two terms in the Senate. The Arkansas Supreme Court held that the amendment violates the Federal Constitution. We agree with that holding. Such a state-imposed restriction is contrary to the "fundamental principle of our representative democracy," embodied in the Constitution, that "the people should choose whom they please to govern them." *Powell* v. *McCormack* (1969).

Allowing individual States to adopt their own qualifications for congressional service would be inconsistent with the Farmers' vision of a uniform National Legislature representing the people of the United States. If the qualifications set forth in the text of the Constitution are to be changed, that text must be amended.

As the opinions of the Arkansas Supreme Court suggest, the constitutionality of Amendment 73 depends critically on the resolution of two distinct issues. The first is whether the Constitution forbids States from adding to or altering the qualifications specifically enumerated in the Constitution. The second is, if the Constitution does so forbid, whether the fact that Amendment 73 is formulated as a ballot access restriction rather than as an outright disqualification is of constitutional significance.

Petitioners argue that whatever the constitutionality of additional qualifications for membership imposed by Congress, the historical and textual materials discussed in *Powell* do not support the conclusion that the Constitution prohibits additional qualifications imposed by States. In the absence of such a constitutional prohibition, petitioners argue, the Tenth Amendment and the principle of reserved powers require that States be allowed to add such qualifications.

We disagree for two independent reasons. First, we conclude that the power to add qualifications is not within the "original powers" of the States, and thus is not reserved to the States by the Tenth Amendment. Second, even if States possessed some original power in this area, we conclude that the Framers intended the Constitution to be the exclusive source of qualifications for members of Congress, and that the Framers thereby "divested" States of any power to add qualifications.

Contrary to petitioners' assertions, the power to add qualifications is not part of the original powers of sovereignty that the Tenth Amendment reserved to the States. Petitioners' Tenth Amendment argument misconceives the nature of the right at issue because that Amendment could only "reserve" that which existed before. As Justice Story recognized, "the states can exercise no powers whatsoever, which exclusively spring out of the existence of the national government, which the constitution does not delegate to them. . . . No state can say, that it has reserved, what it never possessed."

Each Member of Congress is "an officer of the union, deriving his powers and qualifications from the constitution, and neither created by, dependent upon, nor controllable by, the states. . . . Those officers owe their existence and functions to the united voice of the whole, not of a portion, of the people." Representatives and Senators are as much officers of the entire union as is the President. States thus "have just as much right, and no more, to prescribe new qualifications for a representative, as they have for a president. . . . It is no original prerogative of state power to appoint a representative, a senator, or president for the union."

We believe that the Constitution reflects the Framers' general agreement with the approach later articulated by Justice Story. For example, Art. I, § 5, cl. 1 provides: "Each House shall be the Judge of the Elections, Returns and Qualifications of its own Members." The text of the Constitution thus gives the representatives of all the people the final say in judging the qualifications of the representatives of any one State. For this reason, the dissent falters when it states that "the people of Georgia have no say over whom the people of Massachusetts select to represent them in Congress."

Two other sections of the Constitution further support our view of the Framers' vision. First, consistent with Story's view, the Constitution provides that the salaries of representatives should "be ascertained by Law, and paid out of the Treasury of the United States," Art. I, § 6, rather than by individual States. The salary provisions reflect the view that representatives owe their allegiance to the people, and not to States. Second, the provisions governing elections reveal the Farmers' understanding that powers over the election of federal officers had to be delegated to, rather than reserved by, the States. It is surely no coincidence that the context of federal elections provides one of the few areas in which the Constitution expressly requires action by the States, namely that "[t]he Times, Places and Manner of holding Elections for Senators and Representatives, shall be prescribed in each State by the legislature thereof." This duty parallels the duty under Article II that "Each State shall appoint, in such Manner as the Legislature thereof may direct, a Number of Electors." Art II., § 1, cl. 2.

These Clauses are express delegations of power to the States to act with respect to federal elections.

In short, as the Framers recognized, electing representatives to the National Legislature was a new right, arising from the Constitution itself. The Tenth Amendment thus provides no basis for concluding that the States possess reserved power to add qualifications to those that are fixed in the Constitution. Instead, any state power to set the qualifications for membership in Congress must derive not from the reserved powers of state sovereignty, but rather from the delegated powers of national sovereignty. In the absence of any constitutional delegation to the States of power to add qualifications to those enumerated in the Constitution, such a power does not exist.

## THE PRECLUSION OF STATE POWER

Even if we believed that States possessed as part of their original powers some control over congressional qualifications, the text and structure of the Constitution, the relevant historical materials, and, most importantly, the "basic principles of our democratic system" all demonstrate that the Qualifications Clauses were intended to preclude the States from exercising any such power and to fix as exclusive the qualifications in the Constitution.

### The Convention and Ratification Debates

The available affirmative evidence indicates the Framers' intent that States have no role in the setting of qualifications. In Federalist Paper No. 52, dealing with the House of Representatives, Madison addressed the "qualifications of the electors and the elected." Madison first noted the difficulty in achieving uniformity in the qualifications for electors, which resulted in the Framers' decision to require only that the qualifications for federal electors be the same as those for state electors. Madison argued that such a decision "must be satisfactory to every State, because it is comfortable to the standard already established, or which may be established, by the State itself." Madison then explicitly contrasted the state control over the qualifications of electors with the lack of state control over the qualifications of the elected.

> The qualifications of the elected, being less carefully and properly defined by the State constitutions, and being at the same time more susceptible of uniformity, have been very properly considered and regulated by the convention. A representative of the United States must be of the age of twenty-five years; must have been seven years a citizen of the United States; must, at the time of his election be an inhabitant of the State he is to represent; and, during the time of his service must be in no office under the United States. Under these reasonable limitations, the door of this part of the federal government is open to merit of every description, whether native or adoptive, whether young or old, and without regard to poverty or wealth, or to any particular profession of religious faith.

The provisions in the Constitution governing federal elections confirm the Framers' intent that States lack power to add qualifications. The Framers feared that the diverse interests of the States would undermine the National Legislature, and thus they adopted provisions intended to minimize the possibility of state interference with federal elections. For example, to prevent discrimination against federal electors, the Framers required in Art. I, § 2, cl. 1, that the qualifications for federal electors be the same as those for state electors. As Madison noted, allowing States to differentiate between the qualifications for state and federal electors "would have rendered too dependent on the State governments that branch of the federal government which ought to be dependent on the people alone." *The Federalist,* No. 52. Similarly, in Art. I, § 4, cl. 1, though giving the States the freedom to regulate the "Times, Places and Manner of holding Elections," the Framers created a safeguard against state abuse by giving Congress the power to "by Law make or alter such Regulations." The Convention debates make clear that the Framers' overriding concern was the potential for State' abuse of the power to set the "Times, Places and Manner" of elections. Madison noted that "[ i]t was impossible to foresee all the abuses that might be made of the discretionary power."

In light of the Framers' evident concern that States would try to undermine the National

Government, they could not have intended States to have the power to set qualifications. Indeed, one of the more anomalous consequences of petitioners' argument is that it accepts federal supremacy over the procedural aspects of determining the times, places, and manner of elections while allowing the states *carte blanche* with respect to the substantive qualifications for membership in Congress.

We also find compelling the complete absence in the ratification debates of any assertion that States had the power to add qualifications. In those debates, the question whether to require term limits, or "rotation," was a major source of controversy. The draft of the Constitution that was submitted for ratification contained no provision for rotation. In arguments that echo in the preamble to Arkansas' Amendment 73, opponents of ratification condemned the absence of a rotation requirement, noting that "there is no doubt that senators will hold their office perpetually; and in this situation, they must of necessity lose their dependence, and their attachments to the people. Even proponents of ratification expressed concern about the "abandonment in every instance of the necessity of rotation in office." At several ratification conventions, participants, proposed amendments that would have required rotation.

The Federalists' responses to those criticisms and proposals addressed the merits of the issue, arguing that rotation was incompatible with the people's right to choose. Regardless of which side has the better of the debate over rotation, it is most striking that nowhere in the extensive ratification debates have we found any statement by either a proponent or an opponent of rotation that the draft constitution would permit States to require rotation for the representatives of their own citizens. If the participants in the debate had believed that the States retained the authority to impose term limits, it is inconceivable that the Federalists would not have made this obvious response to the arguments of the pro-rotation forces. The absence in an otherwise freewheeling debate of any suggestion that States had the power to impose additional qualifications unquestionably reflects the Framers' common understanding that States lacked that power.

In short, if it had been assumed that States could add additional qualifications, that assumption would have provided the basis for a powerful rebuttal to the arguments being advanced. The failure of intelligent and experienced advocates to utilize this argument must reflect a general agreement that its premise was unsound, and that the power to add qualifications was one that the Constitution denied the States.

### Congressional Experience

Congress' subsequent experience with state-imposed qualifications provides further evidence of the general consensus on the lack of state power in this area.

Congress first confronted the issue in 1807 when it faced a challenge to the qualifications of William McCreery, a Representative from Maryland who allegedly did not satisfy a residency requirement imposed by that State. In recommending that McCreery be seated, the Report of the House Committee on Elections noted:

> The committee proceeded to examine the Constitution, with relation to the case submitted to them, and find that *qualifications of members are therein determined, without reserving any authority to the State Legislatures to change, add to, or diminish those qualifications;* and that, by that instrument, Congress is constituted the sole judge of the qualifications prescribed by it, and are obliged to decide agreeably to the Constitutional rules. . . .

The Senate experience with state-imposed qualifications further supports our conclusions. In 1887, for example, the Senate seated Charles Faulkner of West Virginia, despite the fact that a provision of the West Virginia Constitution purported to render him ineligible to serve. The Senate Committee on Privileges and Elections unanimously concluded that "no State can prescribe any qualification to the office of United States Senator in addition to those declared in the Constitution of the United States."

### Democratic Principles

Our conclusion that States lack the power to impose qualifications vindicates that same "fundamental principle of our representative democracy" that we recognized in *Powell,* namely that "the people should choose whom they please to govern them." Additional qualifications pose the same obstacle to open elections whatever their source. The egalitarian ideal, so valued by the Framers, is thus compromised to the same degree by additional qualifications imposed by States as by those imposed by Congress.

Similarly, we believe that state-imposed qualifications, as much as congressionally imposed qualifications, would undermine the second critical idea recognized in *Powell*: that an aspect of sovereignty is the right of the people to vote for whom they wish. Again, the source of the qualification is of little moment in assessing the qualification's restrictive impact.

Finally, state-imposed restrictions, unlike the congressionally imposed restrictions at issue in *Powell*, violate a third idea central to this basic principle: that the right to choose representatives belongs not to the States, but to the people.

Consistent with these views, the constitutional structure provides for a uniform salary to be paid from the national treasury, allows the States but a limited role in federal elections, and maintains strict checks on state interference with the federal election process. The Constitution also provides that the qualifications of the representatives of each State will be judged by the representatives of the entire Nation. The Constitution thus creates a uniform national body representing the interests of a single people.

Permitting individual States to formulate diverse qualifications for their representatives would result in a patchwork of state qualifications, undermining the uniformity and the national character that the Framers envisioned and sought to ensure. Cf. *McCulloch* v. *Maryland* (1819) ("Those means are not given by the people of a particular State, not given by the constituents of the legislature, . . . but by the people of all the States. They are given by all, for the benefit of all—and upon theory should be subjected to that government only which belongs to all"). Such a patchwork would also sever the direct link that the Framers found so critical between the National Government and the people of the United States.

### State Practice

Petitioners attempt to overcome this formidable array of evidence against the States' power to impose qualifications by arguing that the practice of the States immediately after the adoption of the Constitution demonstrates their understanding that they possessed such power. One may properly question the extent to which the States' own practice is a reliable indicator of the contours of restrictions that the Constitution imposed on States, especially when no court has ever upheld a state-imposed qualification of any sort. But petitioners' argument is unpersuasive even on its own terms.

At the time of the Convention, States widely supported term limits in at least some circumstances. The Articles of Confederation contained a provision for term limits. As we have noted, some members of the Convention had sought to impose term limits for Members of Congress. In addition, many States imposed term limits on state officers, four placed limits on delegates to the Continental Congress, and several States voiced support for term limits for Members of Congress. Despite this widespread support, no State sought to impose any term limits on its own federal representatives. Thus, a proper assessment of contemporaneous state practice provides further persuasive evidence of a general understanding that the qualifications in the Constitution were unalterable by the States.

In sum, the available historical and textual evidence, read in light of the basic principles of democracy underlying the Constitution and recognized by this Court in *Powell*, reveal the Framers' intent that neither Congress nor the States should possess the power to supplement the exclusive qualifications set forth in the text of the Constitution.

Petitioners argue that, even if States may not add qualifications, Amendment 73 is constitutional because it is not such a qualification, and because Amendment 73 is a permissible exercise of state power to regulate the "Times, Places and Manner of Holding Elections." We reject these contentions.

In our view, Amendment 73 is an indirect attempt to accomplish what the Constitution prohibits Arkansas from accomplishing directly. As the plurality opinion of the Arkansas Supreme Court recognized, Amendment 73 is an "effort to dress eligibility to stand for Congress in ballot access clothing," because the "intent and the effect of Amendment 73 are to disqualify congressional incumbents from further service."

We must, of course, accept the State Court's view of the purpose of its own law: we are thus authoritatively informed that the sole purpose of § 3 of Amendment 73 was to attempt to achieve a result that is forbidden by the Federal Constitution. Indeed, it cannot be seriously contended that the intent behind Amendment 73 is other than to prevent the election of incumbents.

Petitioners do, however, contest the Arkansas Supreme Court's conclusion that the Amendment has the same practical effect as an absolute bar. They argue that the possibility of a write-in campaign creates a real possibility for victory, especially for an entrenched incumbent.

But even if petitioners are correct that incumbents may occasionally win reelection as write-in candidates, there is no denying that the ballot restrictions will make it significantly more difficult for the barred candidate to win the election. In our view, an amendment with the avowed purpose and obvious effect of evading the requirements of the Qualifications Clauses by handicapping a class of candidates cannot stand.

The merits of term limits, or "rotation," have been the subject of debate since the formation of our Constitution, when the Framers unanimously rejected a proposal to add such limits to the Constitution. It is not our province to resolve this longstanding debate.

We are, however, firmly convinced that allowing the several States to adopt term limits for congressional service would effect a fundamental change in the constitutional framework. Any such change must come not by legislation adopted either by Congress or by an individual State, but rather—as have other important changes in the electoral process—through the Amendment procedures set forth in Article V. The Framers decided that the qualifications for service in the Congress of the United States be fixed in the Constitution and be uniform throughout the Nation. That decision reflects the Framers' understanding that Members of Congress are chosen by separate constituencies, but that they become, when elected, servants of the people of the United States. They are not merely delegates appointed by separate, sovereign States; they occupy offices that are integral and essential components of a single National Government. In the absence of a properly passed constitutional amendment, allowing individual States to craft their own qualifications for Congress would thus erode the structure envisioned by the Framers, a structure that was designed, in the words of the Preamble to our Constitution, to form a "more perfect Union."

The judgment is affirmed.

JUSTICE THOMAS, with whom THE CHIEF JUSTICE, JUSTICE O'CONNOR, and JUSTICE SCALIA join, dissenting.

It is ironic that the Court bases today's decision on the right of the people to "choose whom they please to govern them." Under our Constitution, there is only one State whose people have the right to "choose whom they please" to represent Arkansas in Congress. The Court holds, however, that neither the elected legislature of that State nor the people themselves (acting by ballot initiative) may prescribe any qualifications for those representatives. The majority therefore defends the right of the people of Arkansas to "choose whom they please to govern them" by invalidating a provision that won nearly 60% of the votes cast in a direct election and that carried every congressional district in the State.

I dissent. Nothing in the Constitution deprives the people of each State of the power to prescribe eligibility requirements for the candidates who seek to represent them in Congress. The Constitution is simply silent on this question. And where the Constitution is silent, it raises no bar to action by the States or the people.

## I

Because the majority fundamentally misunderstands the notion of "reserved" powers, I start with some first principles. Contrary to the majority's suggestion, the people of the States need not point to any affirmative grant of power in the Constitution in order to prescribe qualifications for their representatives in Congress, or to authorize their elected state legislators to do so. When they adopted the Federal Constitution, of course, the people of each State surrendered some of their authority to the United States (and hence to entities accountable to the people of other States as well as to themselves). In each State, the remainder of the people's powers—[t]he powers not delegated to the United States by the Constitution, nor prohibited by it to the States," Amdt. 10—are either delegated to the state government or retained by the people. The Federal Government and the States thus face different default rules: where the Constitution is silent about the exercise of a particular power—that is, where the Constitution does not speak either expressly or by necessary implication—the Federal Government lacks that power and the States enjoy it.

These basic principles are enshrined in the Tenth Amendment, which declares that all powers neither delegated to the Federal Government nor prohibited to the States "are reserved to the States respectively, or to the people." Any ambiguity in the Tenth Amendment's use of the phrase "the people" is cleared up by the body of the Constitution itself. Article I begins by providing that the Congress of the United States enjoys "[a]ll legislative Powers herein granted." § 1, and goes on to give a careful enumeration of Congress' powers, § 8. It then concludes by enumerating certain powers that are *prohibited* to the States. The import of this structure is the same as the import of the Tenth Amendment: if we are to invalidate Arkansas' Amendment 73, we must point to something in the Federal Constitution that deprives the people of Arkansas of the power to enact such measures.

The majority begins by announcing an enormous and untenable limitation on the principle expressed by the Tenth Amendment. According to the majority, the States possess only those powers that the Constitution affirmatively grants to them or that they enjoyed before the Constitution was adopted; the Tenth Amendment "could only 'reserve' that which existed before." The majority's essential logic is that the state governments could not "reserve" any powers that they did not control at the time the Constitution was drafted. But it was not the state governments that were doing the reserving. The Constitution derives its authority instead from the consent of *the people* of the States. Given the fundamental principle that all governmental powers stem from the people of the States, it would simply be incoherent to assert that the people of the States could not reserve any powers that they had not previously controlled.

The majority also sketches out what may be an alternative (and narrower) argument. Again citing Story, the majority suggests that it would be inconsistent with the notion of "national sovereignty" for the States or the people of the States to have any reserved powers over the selection of Members of Congress.

The majority apparently reaches this conclusion in two steps. First, it asserts that because Congress as a whole is an institution of the National Government, the individual Members of Congress "owe primary allegiance not to the people of a State, but to the people of the Nation." Second, it concludes that because each Member of Congress has a nationwide constituency once he takes office, it would be inconsistent with the Framers' scheme to let a single State prescribe qualifications for him.

[W]hile the majority is correct that the Framers expected the selection process to create a "direct link" between members of the House of Representatives and the people, the link was between the Representatives from each State and the people of that State; the people of Georgia have no say over whom the people of Massachusetts select to represent them in Congress. This arrangement must baffle the majority, whose understanding of Congress would surely fit more comfortably within a system of nationwide elections. But the fact remains that when it comes to the selection of Members of Congress, the people of each State have retained their independent political identity. As a result, there is absolutely nothing strange about the notion that the people of the States or their state legislatures possess "reserved" powers in this area.

In a final effort to deny that the people of the States enjoy "reserved" powers over the selection of their representatives in Congress, the majority suggests that the Constitution expressly delegates to the States certain powers over congressional elections. Such delegations of power, the majority argues, would be superfluous if the people of the States enjoyed reserved powers in this area.

Only one constitutional provision—the Times, Places and Manner Clause of Article I, § 4—even arguably supports the majority's suggestion. Contrary to the majority's assumption, however, this Clause does not delegate any authority to the States. Instead, it simply imposes a duty upon them. The majority gets it exactly right: by specifying that the state legislatures "shall" prescribe the details necessary to hold congressional elections, the Clause "expressly requires action by the States." This command meshes with one of the principal purposes of Congress' "make or alter" power: to ensure that the States hold congressional elections in the first place, so that Congress continues to exist.

I take it to be established, then, that the people of Arkansas do enjoy "reserved" powers over the selection of their representatives in Congress. Purporting to exercise those reserved powers, they have agreed among themselves that the candidates covered by § 3 of Amendment 73—those whom they have already elected to three or more terms in the House of Representatives or to two or more terms in the Senate—should not be eligible to appear on the ballot for reelection, but should nonetheless be returned to Congress if enough voters are sufficiently enthusiastic about their candidacy to write in their names. Whatever one might think of the wisdom of this arrangement, we may not override the decision of the people of Arkansas unless something in the Federal Constitution deprives them of the powers to enact such measures.

The majority settles on "the Qualifications Clauses" as the constitutional provisions that Amendment 73 violates.

The Qualifications Clauses do prevent the individual States from abolishing all eligibility requirements for Congress. This restriction on state power reflects that fact that when the people of one State send immature, disloyal, or unknowledgeable representatives to Congress, they jeopardize not only their own interests but also the interests of the people of other States. Because Congress wields power over all the States, the people of each State need some guarantee that the legislators elected by the people of other States will meet minimum standards of competence. The Qualifications Clauses provide that guarantee: they list the requirements that the Framers considered essential to protect the competence of the National Legislature.

If the people of a State decide that they would like their representatives to possess additional qualifications, however, they have done nothing to frustrate the policy behind the Qualifications Clauses. Anyone who possesses all the constitutional qualifications, plus some qualifications required by state law, still has all of the federal qualifications. Accordingly, the fact that the Constitution specifies certain qualifications that the Framers deemed necessary to protect the competence of the National Legislature does not imply that it strips the people of the individual States of the power to protect their own interests by adding other requirements for their own representatives.

The majority responds that "a patchwork of state qualifications" would "undermin[e] the uniformity and the national character that the Framers envisioned and sought to ensure." Yet the Framers thought it perfectly consistent with the "national character" of Congress for the Senators and Representatives from each State to be chosen by the legislature or the people of that State. The majority never explains why Congress' fundamental character permits this state-centered system, but nonetheless prohibits the people of the States and their state legislatures from setting any eligibility requirements for the candidates who seek to represent them.

In discussing the ratification period, the majority stresses two principal data. One of these pieces of evidence is no evidence at all—literally. The majority devotes considerable space to the fact that the recorded ratification debates do not contain any affirmative statement that the States can supplement the constitutional qualifications. For the majority, this void is "compelling" evidence that "unquestionably reflects the Framers' common understanding that States lacked that power." The majority reasons that delegates at several of the ratifying conventions attacked the Constitution for failing to require Members of Congress to rotate out of office. If supporters of ratification had believed that the individual States could supplement the constitutional qualifications, the majority argues, they would have blunted these attacks by pointing out that rotation requirements could still be added State by State.

But the majority's argument cuts both ways. The recorded ratification debates also contain no affirmative statement that the States *cannot* supplement the constitutional qualifications. While ratification was being debated, the existing rule in America was that the States could prescribe eligibility requirements for their delegates to Congress, even though the Articles of Confederation gave Congress itself no power to impose such qualifications. If the Federal Constitution had been understood to deprive the States of this significant power, one might well have expected its opponents to seize on this point in arguing against ratification. The fact is that arguments based on the absence of recorded debate at the ratification conventions are suspect, because the surviving records of those debates are fragmentary.

If one concedes that the absence of relevant records from the ratification debates is not strong evidence for either side, then the majority's only significant piece of evidence from the ratification period is Federalist No. 52. Contrary to the majority's assertion, however, this essay simply does not talk about "the lack of state control over the qualifications of the elected," whether "explicitly" or otherwise.

It is true that Federalist No. 52 contrasts the Constitution's treatment of the qualifications of voters in elections for the House of Representatives with its treatment of the qualifications of the Representatives themselves. As Madison noted, the Framers did not specify any uniform qualifications for the franchise in the Constitution; instead, they simply incorporated each State's rules about eligibility to vote in elections for the most numerous branch of the state legislature. By contrast, Madison continued, the Framers chose to impose some particular qualifications that all members of the House had to satisfy. But while Madison did say that the qualifications of the elected were "more susceptible of uniformity" than the qualifications of electors, The Federalist No. 52, at 326, he did not say that the Constitution prescribes anything but uniform minimum qualifications for congressmen. That, after all, is more than it does for congressional electors.

It is radical enough for the majority to hold that the Constitution implicitly precludes the people of the States from prescribing any eligibility requirements for the congressional candidates who seek their votes. In order to invalidate § 3 of Amendment 73, however, the majority must go farther. The bulk of the majority's analysis addresses the issues that would be raised if Arkansas had prescribed "genuine, unadulterated, undiluted term limits."

But as the parties have agreed, Amendment 73 does not actually create this kind of disqualification.

It does not say that covered candidates may not serve any more terms in Congress if reelected, and it does not indirectly achieve the same result by barring those candidates from seeking reelection. It says only that if they are to win reelection, they must do so by write-in votes.

One might think that this is a distinction without a difference. As the majority notes, "[t]he uncontested data submitted to the Arkansas Supreme Court" show that write-in candidates have won only six congressional elections in this century. But while the data's accuracy is indeed "uncontested," petitioners filed an equally uncontested affidavit challenging the data's relevance. As political science professor James S. Fay swore to the Arkansas Supreme Court, "[m]ost write-in candidacies in the past have been waged by fringe candidates, with little public support and extremely low name identification." To the best of Professor Fay's knowledge, in modern times only two incumbent Congressmen have ever sought reelection as write-in candidates. One of them was Dale Alford of Arkansas, who had first entered the House of Representatives by winning 51% of the vote as a write-in candidate in 1958; Alford then waged a write-in campaign for reelection in 1960, winning a landslide 83% of the vote against an opponent who enjoyed a place on the ballot.

The other incumbent write-in candidate was Philip J. Philbin of Massachusetts, who—despite losing his party primary and thus his spot on the ballot—won 27% of the vote in his unsuccessful write-in candidacy. According to Professor Fay, these results—coupled with other examples of successful write-in campaigns, such as Ross Perot's victory in North Dakota's 1992 Democratic presidential primary—"demonstrate that when a write-in candidate is well-known and well-funded, it is quite possible for him or her to win an election."

[Today's] decision reads the Qualifications Clauses to impose substantial implicit prohibitions on the States and the people of the States. I would not draw such an expansive negative inference from the fact that the Constitution requires Members of Congress to be a certain age, to be inhabitants of the States that they represent, and to have been United States citizens for a specified period. Rather, I would read the Qualifications Clauses to do no more than what they say. I respectfully dissent.

## *Gravel* v. *United States*

**408 U.S. 606, 9 S. Ct. 614, 33 L. Ed. 2d 583 (1972)**

In 1971 Senator Mike Gravel received from Daniel Ellsberg, a consultant to the Defense Department, a copy of the so-called Pentagon Papers, a classified Defense Department study on how the United States became involved in the Vietnam War. Gravel then convened a meeting of the Senate Subcommittee on Public Buildings and Grounds (of which he was chairman), read excerpts from the papers, and introduced all forty-seven volumes of the study into the record as an exhibit. Press reports indicated that the senator had also arranged with Beacon Press for private publication of the Pentagon Papers. A federal grand jury, impaneled to investigate possible violations of federal law in the release of the papers, subpoenaed Leonard Rodberg, a Gravel aide, to testify about his role in obtaining and arranging for publication of the Pentagon Papers. Senator Gravel intervened, contending that requiring Rodberg to testify about activities he undertook in Gravel's service would violate the Speech or Debate Clause. *Opinion of the Court: White, Burger, Blackmun, Powell, Rehnquist. Dissenting opinions: Stewart (in part); Douglas; Brennan, Douglas, Marshall.*

MR. JUSTICE WHITE delivered the opinion of the Court. . . .

Because the claim is that a Member's aide shares the Member's constitutional privilege, we consider first whether and to what extent Senator Gravel himself is exempt from process or inquiry by a grand jury investigating the commission of a crime. . . .

. . . His insistence is that the Speech or Debate Clause at the very least protects him from criminal or civil liability and from questioning elsewhere than in the Senate, with respect to the events occurring at the subcommittee hearing at which the Pentagon Papers were introduced into the public record. To us this claim is incontrovertible. The Speech or Debate Clause was designed to assure a co-equal branch of the government wide freedom of speech, debate, and deliberation without intimidation or threats from the Executive Branch. It thus protects Members against prosecutions that directly impinge upon or threaten the legislative process. . . .

Even so, the United States strongly urges that because the Speech or Debate Clause confers a privilege only upon "Senators and Representatives," Rodberg himself has no valid claim to constitutional immunity from grand jury inquiry. In our view both courts below correctly rejected this position. . . . It is literally impossible, in view of the complexities of the modern legislative process, with Congress almost constantly in session and matters of legislative concern constantly proliferating, for Members of Congress to perform their legislative tasks without the help of aides and assistants; the day-to-day work of such aides is so critical to the Members' performance that they must be treated as the latter's alter egos; and if they are not so recognized, the central role of the Speech or Debate Clause—to prevent intimidation of legislators by the Executive and accountability before a possibly hostile judiciary—will inevitably be diminished and frustrated. . . .

The United States fears the abuses that history reveals have occurred when legislators are invested with the power to relieve others from the operation of otherwise valid civil and criminal laws. But these abuses, it seems to us, are for the most part obviated if the privilege applicable to the aide is viewed, as it must be, as the privilege of the Senator, and invocable only by the Senator or by the aide on the Senator's behalf* and if in all events the privilege available to the aide is confined to those services that would be immune legislative conduct if performed by the Senator himself. This view places beyond the Speech or Debate Clause a variety of services characteristically performed by aides for Members of Congress, even though within the scope of their employment. . . . Thus our refusal to distinguish between Senator and aide in applying the Speech or Debate Clause does not mean that Rodberg is for all purposes exempt from grand jury questioning.

We are convinced also that the Court of Appeals correctly determined that Senator Gravel's alleged arrangement with Beacon Press to publish the Pentagon Papers was not protected speech or debate within the meaning of Art. I, § 6, cl. 1, of the Constitution.

Historically, the English legislative privilege was not viewed as protecting republication of an otherwise immune libel on the floor of the House. . . .

Prior cases have read the Speech or Debate Clause "broadly to effectuate its purposes," . . . and have included within its reach anything "generally done in a session of the House by one of its members in relation to the business before it." . . . But the Clause has not been extended beyond the legislative sphere. That Senators generally perform certain acts in their official capacity as Senators does not necessarily make all such acts legislative in nature. Members of Congress are constantly in touch with the Executive Branch of the Government and with administrative agencies—they may cajole, and exhort with respect to the administration of a federal statute—but such conduct, though generally done, is not protected legislative activity. . . . The heart of the Clause is speech or debate in either House. Insofar as the Clause is construed to reach other matters, they must be an integral part of the deliberative and communicative processes by which Members participate in committee and House proceedings with respect to the consideration and passage or rejection of propsed legislation or with respect to other matters which the Constitution places within the jurisdiction of either House . . .

Here, private publication by Senator Gravel through the cooperation of Beacon Press was in no way essential to the deliberations of the Senate; nor does questioning as to private publication threaten the integrity or independence of the Senate by impermissibly exposing its deliberation to executive influence. . . . We cannot but conclude that the Senator's arrangements with Beacon Press were not part and parcel of the legislative process. . . .

MR. JUSTICE BRENNAN, with whom MR. JUSTICE DOUGLAS and MR. JUSTICE MARSHALL join, dissenting. . . .

In holding that Senator Gravel's alleged arrangement with Beacon Press to publish the Pentagon Papers is not shielded from extra-senatorial inquiry by the Speech or Debate Clause, the Court adopts what for me is a far too narrow view of the legislative function. . . . The Court excludes from the sphere of protected legislative activity a function that I had supposed lay at the heart of our democratic system. I speak, of course, of the legislator's duty to inform the public about matters affecting the administration of government. . . .

The informing function has been cited by numerous students of American politics, both within and without the Government, as among the most important responsibilities of legislative office. . . . Though I fully share these . . . views on the educational values served by the informing function, there is yet another, and perhaps more fundamental, interest at stake. It requires no citation of authority to state that public concern over current issues—the war, race relations, governmental invasions of privacy—has transformed itself in recent years into what many believe is a crisis of confidence, in our system of government and its capacity to meet the needs and reflect the

*It follows that an aide's claim of privilege can be repudiated and thus waived by the Senator.

wants of the American people. Communication between Congress and the electorate tends to alleviate that doubt by exposing and clarifying the workings of the political system, the policies underlying new laws and the role of the Executive in their administration. To the extent that the informing function succeeds in fostering public faith in the responsiveness of Government, it is not only an "ordinary" task of the legislator but one that is essential to the continued vitality of our democratic institutions.

Unlike the Court, therefore, I think that the activities of Congressmen in communicating with the public are legislative acts protected by the Speech or Debate Clause. I agree with the Court that not every task performed by a legislator is privileged; intervention before Executive departments is one that is not. But the informing function carries a far more persuasive claim to the protections of the Clause. It has been recognized by this Court as something "generally done" by Congressmen, the Congress itself has established special concessions designed to lower the cost of such communication, and, most important, the function furthers several well-recognized goals of representative government. To say in the face of these facts that the informing function is not privileged merely because it is not necessary to the internal deliberations of Congress is to give the Speech or Debate Clause an artificial and narrow reading unsupported by reason. . . .

Whether the Speech or Debate Clause extends to the informing function is an issue whose importance goes beyond the fate of a single Senator or Congressman. What is at stake is the right of an elected representative to inform, and the public to be informed, about matters relating directly to the workings of our Government. The dialogue between Congress and people has been recognized, from the days of our founding, as one of the necessary elements of a representative system. We should not retreat from that view merely because, in the course of that dialogue, information may be revealed that is embarrassing to the other branches of government or violates their notions of necessary secrecy. A Member of Congress who exceeds the bounds of propriety in performing this official task may be called to answer by the other Members of his chamber. We do violence to the fundamental concepts of privilege, however, when we subject that same conduct to judicial scrutiny at the instance of the Executive. . . .

Equally troubling in today's decision is the Court's refusal to bar grand jury inquiry into the source of documents received by the Senator and placed by him in the hearing record. The receipt of materials for use in a congressional hearing is an integral part of the preparation for that legislative act. . . . It would accomplish little toward the goal of legislative freedom to exempt an official act from intimidating scrutiny, if other conduct leading up to the act and intimately related to it could be deterred by a similar threat. . . . I would hold that Senator Gravel's receipt of the Pentagon Papers, including the name of the person from whom he received them, may not be the subject of inquiry by the grand jury.

I would go further, however, and also exclude from grand jury inquiry any knowledge that the Senator or his aides might have concerning how the source himself first came to possess the Papers. This immunity, it seems to me, is essential to the performance of the informing function. Corrupt and deceitful officers of the government do not often post for public examination the evidence of their own misdeeds. That evidence must be ferreted out, and often is, by fellow employees and subordinates. Their willingness to reveal that information and spark congressional inquiry may well depend on assurances from their contact in Congress that their identities and means of obtaining the evidence will be held in strictest confidence. To permit the grand jury to frustrate that expectation through an inquiry of the Congressman and his aides can only dampen the flow of information to the Congress and thus to the American people. There is a similar risk, of course, when the Member's own House requires him to break the confidence. But the danger, it seems to me, is far less if the Member's colleagues, and not an "unfriendly executive" or "hostile judiciary," are charged with evaluating the propriety of his conduct. In any event, assuming that a Congressman can be required to reveal the sources of his information and the methods used to obtain that information, that power of inquiry, as required by the Clause, is that of the Congressman's House, and of that House only.

I respectfully dissent.

## *McGrain* v. *Daugherty*

**273 U.S. 135, 47 S. Ct. 319, 71 L. Ed. 580 (1927)**

A Senate select committee investigating the Department of Justice's failure to prosecute key figures in the Teapot Dome scandal and other violators of federal statutes subpoenaed Mally Daugherty, a banker and the brother of the former attorney general, but Daugherty failed to appear. Acting on a warrant issued by the Senate, McGrain, the deputy sergeant at arms of the Senate, took Daugherty into custody so that the committee might question him. Daugherty successfully petitioned for a writ of habeas corpus from a federal district court, which ruled that the Senate had exceeded its constitutional powers in detaining him. The case was then appealed to the Supreme Court. *Opinion of the Court: Van Devanter, Taft, Holmes, McReynolds, Brandeis, Sutherland, Butler, Sanford. Not participating: Stone.*

MR. JUSTICE VAN DEVANTER delivered the opinion of the Court. . . .

. . . The principal questions involved are . . . (a) whether the Senate—or the House of Representatives, both being on the same plane in this regard—has power, through its own process, to compel a private individual to appear before it or one of its committees and give testimony needed to enable it efficiently to exercise a legislative function belonging to it under the Constitution, and (b) whether it sufficiently appears that the process was being employed in this instance to obtain testimony for that purpose. . . .

. . . We are not now concerned with the right of the Senate to propound or the duty of the witness to answer specific questions, for as yet no questions have been propounded to him. He is asserting . . . that the Senate is without power to interrogate him, even if the questions propounded be pertinent and otherwise legitimate—which for present purposes must be assumed. . . .

. . . There is no provision expressly investing either house with power to make investigations and exact testimony to the end that it may exercise its legislative function advisedly and effectively. So the question arises whether this power is so far incidental to the legislative function as to be implied.

We are of the opinion that the power of inquiry—with process to enforce it—is an essential and appropriate auxiliary to the legislative function. It was so regarded and employed in American legislatures before the Constitution was framed and ratified. Both houses of Congress took this view of it early in their history . . . and both houses have employed the power accordingly up to the present time. . . . So, when their practice in the matter is appraised according to the circumstances in which it was begun and to those in which it has been continued, it falls nothing short of a practical construction, long continued, of the constitutional provisions respecting their powers, and therefore should be taken as fixing the meaning of those provisions, if otherwise doubtful.

We are further of opinion that the provisions are not of doubtful meaning, but . . . are intended to be effectively exercised, and therfore to carry with them such auxiliary powers as are necessary and appropriate to that end. . . . A legislative body cannot legislate wisely or effectively in the absence of information respecting the conditions which the legislation is intended to affect or change; and where the legislative body does not itself possess the requisite information—which not infrequently is true—recourse must be had to others who do possess it. Experience has taught that mere requests for such information often are unavailing, and also that information which is volunteered is not always accurate or complete; so some means of compulsion are essential to obtain what is needed. . . .

We come now to the question whether it sufficiently appears that the purpose for which the witness's testimony was sought was to obtain information in aid of the legislative function. . . .

It is quite true that the resolution directing the investigation does not in terms avow that it is intended to be in aid of legislation; but it does show that the subject to be investigated was the administration of the Department of Justice—whether its functions were being properly discharged or were being neglected or misdirected, and particularly whether the Attorney General and his assistants were performing or neglecting their duties in respect of the institution and prosecution of proceedings to punish crimes and enforce appropriate remedies against the wrongdoers—specific instances of alleged neglect being recited. Plainly the subject was one on which legislation could be had and would be materially aided by the information which the investigation was calculated to elicit. . . .

The only legitimate object the Senate could have in ordering the investigation was to aid it in legislating; and we think the subject-matter was such that the presumption should be indulged that this was the real object. . . .

We conclude that the investigation was ordered for a legitimate object; that the witness wrongfully refused to appear and testify before the committee and was lawfully attached; that the Senate is entitled to have him give testimony pertinent to the inquiry, either at its bar or before the committee; and that the district court erred in discharging him from custody under the attachment. . . .

## *Watkins* v. *United States*

**354 U.S. 178, 77 S. Ct. 1173, 1 L. Ed. 2d 1273 (1957)**

As part of its investigation into communist influence in the labor movement, the House Un-American Activities Committee summoned John Watkins, an organizer for the United Auto Workers, to testify before it. Watkins willingly answered questions about his own personal involvement in Communist Party activities and about persons who he believed were still Communist Party members. He refused to respond, however, to questions about persons who had previously been active in the Communist Party but were no longer involved with it, maintaining that an inquiry into their activities was not pertinent to the committee's investigation. He was cited for contempt by the committee and subsequently convicted in federal district court. After the court of appeals upheld his conviction, the Supreme Court granted certiorari. *Opinion of the Court: Warren, Black, Douglas, Harlan, Brennan. Concurring opinion: Frankfurter. Dissenting opinion: Clark. Not participating: Burton, Whittaker.*

MR. CHIEF JUSTICE WARREN delivered the opinion of the Court.

We start with several basic premises on which there is general agreement. The power of the Congress to conduct investigations is inherent in the legislative process. That power is broad. It encompasses inquiries concerning the administration of existing laws as well as proposed or possibly needed statutes. It includes surveys of defects in our social, economic or political system for the purpose of enabling the Congress to remedy them. It comprehends probes into departments of the Federal Government to expose corruption, inefficiency or waste. But, broad as is this power of inquiry, it is not unlimited. There is no general authority to expose the private affairs of individuals without justification in terms of the functions of the Congress. . . . Nor is the Congress a law enforcement or trial agency. These are functions of the executive and judicial departments of government. No inquiry is an end in itself; it must be related to, and in furtherance of, a legitimate task of the Congress. Investigations conducted solely for the personal aggrandizement of the investigators or to "punish" those investigated are indefensible.

It is unquestionably the duty of all citizens to cooperate with Congress in its efforts to obtain the facts needed for intelligent legislative action. It is their unremitting obligation to respond to subpoenas, to respect the dignity of the Congress and its committees and to testify fully with respect to matters within the province of proper investigation. This, of course, assumes that the constitutional rights of witnesses will be respected by the Congress as they are in a court of justice. The Bill of Rights is applicable to investigations as to all forms of government action. . . .

Abuses of the investigative process may imperceptibly lead to abridgment of protected freedoms. The mere summoning of a witness and compelling him to testify, against his will, about his beliefs, expressions or associations is a measure of governmental interference. And when those forced revelations concern matters that are unorthodox, unpopular, or even hateful to the general public, the reaction in the life of the witness may be disastrous. This effect is even more harsh when it is past beliefs, expressions or associations that are disclosed and judged by current standards rather than those contemporary with the matters exposed. Nor does the witness alone suffer the consequences. Those who are identified by witnesses and thereby placed in the same glare of publicity are equally subject to public stigma, scorn and obloquy. Beyond that, there is the more subtle and immeasurable effect upon those who tend to adhere to the most orthodox and uncontroversial views and associations in order to avoid a similar fate at some future time. That this impact is partly the result of nongovernmental activity by private persons cannot relieve the investigators of their responsibility for initiating the reaction. . . .

Petitioner has earnestly suggested that the difficult questions of protecting these rights from infringement by legislative inquiries can be surmounted in this case because there was no public purpose served in his interrogation. . . . The sole purpose of the inquiry, he contends, was to bring down upon himself and others the violence of public reaction because of their past beliefs, expressions and associations. In support of this argument, petitioner has marshalled an impressive array of evidence that some Congressmen have believed that such was their duty, or part of it.

We have no doubt that there is no congressional power to expose for the sake of exposure. . . . But a solution to our problem is not to be found in testing the motives of committee members for this purpose. Such is not our function. Their motives alone would not vitiate an investigation which had been instituted by a House of Congress if that assembly's legislative purpose is being served.

Petitioner's contentions do point to a situation of particular significance from the standpoint of the constitutional limitations upon congressional investigations. The theory of a committee inquiry is that the committee members are serving as the representatives of the parent assembly in collecting information for a legislative purpose. . . . An essential premise in this situation is that the House or Senate shall have instructed the committee members on what they are to do with the power delegated to them. It is the responsibility of the Congress, in the first instance, to insure that compulsory process is used only in furtherance of a legislative purpose. That requires that the instructions to an investigating committee spell out that group's jurisdiction and purpose with sufficient particularity. Those instructions are embodied in the authorizing resolution. That document is the committee's charter . . . The more vague the committee's charter is, the greater becomes the possibility that the committee's specific actions are not in conformity with the will of the parent House of Congress.

The authorizing resolution of the Un-American Activities Committee . . . defines the Committee's authority as follows:

""The Committee on Un-American Activities, as a whole or by subcommittee, is authorized to make from time to time investigations of (1) the extent, character, and objects of un-American propaganda activities in the United States, (2) the diffusion within the United States of subversive and un-American propaganda that is instigated from foreign countries or of a domestic origin and attacks the principle of the form of government as guaranteed by our Constitution, and (3) all other questions in relation thereto that would aid Congress in any necessary remedial legislation."

It would be difficult to imagine a less explicit authorization resolution. . . .

Combining the language of the resolution with the construction it has been given, it is evident that the preliminary control of the Committee exercised by the House of Representatives is slight or non-existent. No one could reasonably deduce from the charter the kind of investigation that the Committee was directed to make. . . .

In fulfillment of their obligation under [the statute for contempt of Congress], the courts must accord to the defendants every right which is guaranteed to defendants in all other criminal cases. Among these is the right to have available, through a sufficiently precise statute, information revealing the standard of criminality before the commission of the alleged offense. Applied to persons prosecuted under § 192, this raises a special problem in that the statute defines the crimes as a refusal to answer "any question pertinent to the question under inquiry." Part of the standard of criminality, therefore, is the pertinency of the questions propounded to the witness. . . .

It is obvious that a person . . . is entitled to have knowledge of the subject to which the interrogation is deemed pertinent. That knowledge must be available with the same degree of explicitness and clarity that the Due Process Clause requires in the expression of any element of a criminal offense. The "vice of vagueness" must be avoided here as in all other crimes. There are several sources that can outline the "question under inquiry" in such a way that the rules against vagueness are satisfied. The authorizing resolution, the remarks of the chairman or members of the committee, or even the nature of the proceedings themselves, might sometimes make the topic clear. . . .

The first possibility is that the authorizing resolution itself will so clearly declare the "question under inquiry" that a witness can understand the pertinency of questions asked him. The Government does not contend that the authorizing resolution of the Un-American Activities Committee could serve such a purpose. . . .

No aid is given as to the "question under inquiry" in the action of the full Committee that authorized the creation of the Subcommittee before which petitioner appeared. The Committee adopted a formal resolution giving the Chairman the power to appoint subcommittees ". . . for the purpose of performing any and all acts which the Committee as a whole is authorized to do." . . .

The Government believes that the topic of inquiry before the Subcommittee concerned Communist infiltration in labor. In his introductory remarks, the Chairman made reference to a bill, then pending before the Committee, which would have penalized labor unions controlled or dominated by persons who were, or had been, members of a "Communist-action" organization, as defined in the Internal Security Act of 1950. The Subcommittee, it is contended, might have been endeavoring to determine the extent of such a problem.

This view is corroborated somewhat by the witnesses who preceded and followed petitioner before the Subcommittee. Looking at the entire hearings, however, there is strong reason to doubt that the subject revolved about labor matters. The published transcript is entitled: Investigation of Community Activities in the Chicago Area, and six of the nine witnesses had no connection with labor at all

The most serious doubts as to the Subcommittee's "question under inquiry," however, stem from the precise questions that petitioner has been charged with refusing to answer. Under the terms of the statute, after all, it is these which must be proved pertinent. Petitioner is charged with refusing to tell the Subcommittee whether or not he knew that certain named persons had been members of the Communist Party in the past. The Subcommittee's counsel read the list from the testimony of a previous witness who had identified them as Communists. Although this former witness was identified with labor, he had not stated that the persons he named were involved in union affairs. Of the thirty names propounded to petitioner, seven were completely unconnected with organized labor. . . .

The final source of evidence as to "the question under inquiry" is the Chairman's response when petitioner objected to the questions on the grounds of lack of pertinency. The Chairman then announced that the Subcommittee was investigating "subversion and subversive propaganda." This is a subject at least as broad and indefinite as the authorizing resolution of the Committee, if not more so.

Having exhausted the several possible indicia of the "question under inquiry," we remain unenlightened as to the subject to which the questions asked petitioner were pertinent. . . . Fundamental fairness demands that no witness be compelled to make such a determination with so little guidance. Unless the subject matter has been made to appear with undisputable clarity, it is the duty of the investigative body, upon objection of the witness on grounds of pertinency, to state for the record the subject under inquiry at that time and the manner in which the propounded questions are pertinent thereto. . . .

The statement of the Committee Chairman in this case, in response to petitioner's protest, was woefully inadequate to convey sufficient information as to the pertinency of the questions to the subject under inquiry. Petitioner was thus not accorded a fair opportunity to determine whether he was within his rights in refusing to answer, and his conviction is necessarily invalid under the Due Process Clause of the Fifth Amendment.

We are mindful of the complexities of modern government and the ample scope that must be left to the Congress as the sole constitutional depository of legislative power. Equally mindful are we of the indispensable function, in the exercise of that power, of congressional investigations. The conclusions we have reached in this case will not prevent the Congress, through its committees, from obtaining any information it needs for the proper fulfillment of its role in our scheme of government. The legislature is free to determine the kinds of data that should be collected. It is only those investigations that are conducted by use of compulsory process that give rise to a need to protect the rights of individuals against illegal encroachment. That protection can be readily achieved through procedures which prevent the separation of power from responsibility and which provide the constitutional requisites of fairness for witnesses. . . .

*The Watkins decision provoked an immediate reaction in Congress. Senator Albert Jenner of Indiana introduced legislation withdrawing the Supreme Court's jurisdiction over "any function or practice of, or the jurisdiction of, any committee or sub-committee of the United States Congress or any action or proceedings against a witness charged with contempt of Congress." Although favorably reported by a Senate Committee, Jenner's bill was tabled by the Senate. Prior to its reintroduction, several of its supporters were defeated in the congressional elections of 1958, and the Supreme Court allayed congressional fears in* Barenblatt *v.* United States. *As a result, the bill restricting the Court's jurisdiction was handily defeated in 1959.*

## *Schechter Poultry Corporation* v. *United States*

**295 U.S. 495, 55 S. Ct. 837, 79 L. Ed. 1570 (1935)**

The National Industrial Recovery Act of 1933 was a major element in the Roosevelt administration's program to stimulate the economy and reduce unemployment. Under the act, trade associations were to propose industrywide codes of fair competition governing wages, hours, and modes of competition; these codes would take legal effect when the president endorsed them by executive order. The act specified that the trade associations should be truly representative, that the codes should not tend to produce monopolies, and that the codes should promote economic recovery.

The Schechter brothers were convicted for violating the Live Poultry Code by filing false sales and price reports and selling diseased chickens. They challenged their convictions, contending that the National Industrial Recovery Act constituted an unconstitutional delegation of legislative power and that their business activities were not part of interstate commerce and thus could not be regulated by the federal government. After a court of appeals generally sustained the district court, the Supreme Court granted certiorari. *Opinion of the Court: Hughes, Van Devanter, McReynolds, Brandeis, Sutherland, Butler, Roberts. Concurring opinion: Cardozo, Stone.*

MR. CHIEF JUSTICE HUGHES delivered the opinion of the Court. . . .

We are told that the provision of the statute authorizing the adoption of codes must be viewed in the light of the grave national crisis with which Congress was confronted. Undoubtedly, the conditions to which power is addressed are always to be considered when the exercise of power is challenged. Extraordinary conditions may call for extraordinary remedies. But the argument necessarily stops short of an attempt to justify action which lies outside the sphere of constitutional authority. Extraordinary conditions do not create or enlarge constitutional power. . . . Such assertions of extra-constitutional authority were anticipated and precluded by the explicit terms of the Tenth Amendment,—"The powers not delegated to the United States by the Constitution, nor prohibited by it to the States, are reserved to the States respectively, or to the people." . . .

. . . *The question of the delegation of legislative power*. . . . The Congress is not permitted to abdicate or to transfer to others the essential legislative functions with which it is thus vested. We have repeatedly recognized the necessity of adapting legislation to complex conditions involving a host of details with which the national legislature cannot deal directly. We pointed out in the *Panama Company* case [*Panama Refining Company* v. *Ryan* (1935)] that the Constitution has never been regarded as denying to Congress the necessary resources of flexibility and practicality, which will enable it to perform its function in laying down policies and establishing standards, while leaving to selected instrumentalities the making of subordinate rules within prescribed limits and the determination of facts to which the policy as declared by the legislature is to apply. But we said that the constant recognition of the necessity and validity of such provisions, and the wide range of administrative authority which has been developed by means of them, cannot be allowed to obscure the limitations of the authority to delegate, if our constitutional system is to be maintained. . . .

Accordingly, we look to the statute to see whether Congress has overstepped these limitations,—whether Congress in authorizing "codes of fair competition" has itself established the standards of legal obligation, thus performing its essential legislative function, or, by the failure to enact such standards, has attempted to transfer that function to others. . . .

What is meant by "fair competition" as the term is used in the Act? Does it refer to a category established in the law, and is the authority to make codes limited accordingly? Or is it used as a convenient designation for whatever set of laws the formulators of a code for a particular trade or industry may propose and the President may approve (subject to certain restrictions), or the President may himself prescribe, as being wise and beneficent provisions for the government of the trade or industry in order to accomplish the broad purposes of rehabilitation, correction and expansion which are stated in the first section of Title I?

The Government urges that the codes will "consist of rules of competition deemed fair for each industry by representative members of that industry—by the persons most vitally concerned and most familiar with its problems." Instances are cited in which Congress has availed itself of such assistance. . . . But would it be seriously contended that Congress could delegate its legislative authority to trade or industrial associations or groups so as to empower them to enact the laws they deem to be wise and beneficent for the rehabilitation and expansion of their trade or industries? . . . The answer is obvious. Such a delegation of legislative power is unknown to our law and is utterly inconsistent with the constitutional prerogatives and duties of Congress.

The question, then, turns upon the authority which § 3 of the Recovery Act vests in the President to approve or prescribe. If the codes have standing as penal statutes, this must be due to the effect of the executive action. But Congress cannot delegate legislative power to the President to exercise an unfettered discretion to make whatever laws he thinks may be needed or advisable for the rehabilitation and expansion of trade or industry. . . .

Section 3 of the Recovery Act is without precedent. It supplies no standards for any trade, industry or activity. It does not undertake to prescribe rules of conduct to be applied to particular states of fact determined by appropriate administrative procedure. Instead of prescribing rules of conduct, it authorizes the making of codes to prescribe them. For that legislative undertaking, § 3 sets up no standards, aside from the statement of the general aims of rehabilitation, correction and expansion described in section one. In view of the scope of that broad declaration, and of the nature of the few restrictions that are imposed, the discretion of the President in approving or prescribing codes, and thus enacting laws for the government of trade and industry throughout the country, is virtually unfettered. We think that the code-making authority thus conferred is an unconstitutional delegation of legislative power. . . .

On both the grounds we have discussed, the attempted delegation of legislative power, and the attempted regulation of intrastate transactions which affect interstate commerce only indirectly, we hold the code provisions here in question to be invalid and that the judgment of conviction must be reversed.

Mr. Justice Cardozo, concurring.

The delegated power of legislation which has found expression in this code is not canalized within banks that keep it from overflowing. It is unconfined and vagrant. . . .

This court has held that delegation may be unlawful though the act to be performed is definite and single, if the necessity, time and occasion of performance have been left in the end to the discretion of the delegate. *Panama Refining Co.* v. *Ryan,* . . . I thought that ruling went too far. . . . Here, in the case before us, is an attempted delegation not confined to any single act nor to any class or group of acts identified or described by reference to a standard. Here in effect is a roving commission to inquire into evils and upon discovery correct them.

The code does not confine itself to the suppression of methods of competition that would be classified as unfair according to accepted business standards or accepted norms of ethics. It sets up a comprehensive body of rules to promote the welfare of the industry, if not the welfare of the nation, without reference to standards, ethical or commercial, that could be known or predicted in advance of its adoption. One of the new rules, the source of ten counts in the indictment, is aimed at an established practice, not unethical or oppressive, the practice of selective buying. Many others could be instanced as open to the same objection if the sections of the code were to be examined one by one. . . . Even if the statute itself has fixed the meaning of fair competition by way of contrast with practices that are oppressive or unfair, the code outruns the bounds of the authority conferred. What is excessive is not sporadic or superficial. It is deep-seated and pervasive.

. . . But there is another objection, far-reaching and incurable, aside from any defect of unlawful delegation.

If this code had been adopted by Congress itself, and not by the President on the advice of an industrial association, it would even then be void unless authority to adopt it is included in the grant of power "to regulate commerce with foreign nations and among the several states." . . .

I find no authority in that grant for the regulation of wages and hours of labor in the intrastate transactions that make up the defendants' business. As to this feature of the case little can be added to the opinion of the court. There is a view of causation that would obliterate the distinction between what is national and what is local in the activities of commerce. . . .

# *Mistretta* v. *United States*

**488 U.S. 109 S. Ct. 647, 102 L. Ed. 2d 714 (1989)**

The Sentencing Act of 1984 was designed to eliminate the wide disparity in sentences which resulted from the broad sentencing discretion available to federal judges. In place of such discretion, the Act proposed a system of determinate sentencing, with mandatory sentencing guidelines to ensure similar sentences for comparable offenders and offenses. To devise this system, the Act created the U.S. Sentencing Commission, an independent commission within the judicial branch, with seven voting members (three of them federal judges) appointed by the president. The Commission was charged with developing sentencing guidelines, on the basis of criteria outlined in the Act, that would prescribe the range of sentences for various categories of offenses and offenders. If a federal judge departs from the guidelines in a particular case because of an aggravating or mitigating factor not considered by the Commission, the judge must give reasons for the deviation, and the sentence is subject to appellate review.

After the Commission announced its guidelines, their constitutionality was widely challenged in federal district courts—prior to the Supreme Court's decision in this case, over 150 district judges had declared the guidelines unconstitutional, while over 100 had upheld them. This case involved a challenge to the guidelines by John Mistretta, who was charged in connection with a sale of cocaine. After the District Court rejected Mistretta's claim that the guidelines involved an excessive delegation of congressional power and violated the separation of powers, he pleaded guilty and was sentenced under the guidelines. When Mistretta filed a notice of appeal to the Court of Appeals, both he and the United States petitioned the Supreme Court for certiorari prior to judgment, and the Court granted the request. *Opinion of the Court: Blackmun, Rehnquist, Brennan (in part), White, Marshall, Stevens, O'Connor, Kennedy. Dissenting opinion: Scalia.*

JUSTICE BLACKMUN delivered the opinion of the Court.

### Delegation of Power

. . . Petitioner argues that in delegating the power to promulgate sentencing guidelines for every federal criminal offense to an independent Sentencing Commission, Congress has granted the Commission excessive legislative discretion in violation of the constitutionally based nondelegation doctrine. We do not agree. . . . The separation-of-powers principle, and the nondelegation doctrine in particular, do not prevent Congress from obtaining the assistance of its coordinate Branches. In a passage now enshrined in our jurisprudence, Chief Justice Taft, writing for the Court, explained our approach to such cooperative ventures: "In determining what [Congress] may do in seeking assistance from another branch, the extent and character of that assistance must be fixed according to common sense and the inherent necessities of the government co-ordination." *J. W. Hampton, Jr., & Co.* v. *United States* . . . (1928). So long as Congress "shall lay down by legislative act an intelligible principle to which the person or body authorized to [exercise the delegated authority] is directed to conform, such legislative action is not a forbidden delegation of legislative power." *Id.* . . . The Act sets forth more than merely an "intelligible principle" or minimal standards. One court has aptly put it: "The statute outlines the policies which prompted establishment of the Commission, explains what the Commission should do and how it should do it, and sets out specific directives to govern particular situations." *United States* v. *Chambless* . . . (1988).

Developing proportionate penalties for hundreds of different crimes by a virtually limitless array of offenders is precisely the sort of intricate, labor-intensive task for which delegation to an expert body is especially appropriate. Although Congress has delegated significant discretion to the Commission to draw judgments from its analysis of existing sentencing practice and alternative sentencing models, "Congress is not confined to that method of executing its policy which involves the least possible delegation of discretion to administrative officers." *Yakus* v. *United States* . . . (1944).

### Separation of Powers

Having determined that Congress has set forth sufficient standards for the exercise of the Commission's delegated authority, we turn to Mistretta's claim that the Act violates the constitutional principle of separation of powers.

This Court consistently has given voice to, and has reaffirmed, the central judgment of the Framers of the Constitution that, within our political scheme, the separation of governmental powers into three coordinate Branches is essential to the preservation of liberty. . . . Madison, in writing about the principle of separated powers, said: "No political truth is certainly of greater intrinsic value or is stamped with the authority of more enlightened patrons of liberty." The Federalist No. 47. . . .

In applying the principle of separated powers in our jurisprudence, we have sought to give life to Madison's view of the appropriate relationship among the three coequal Branches. Accordingly, we have recognized, as Madison admonished at the founding, that while our Constitution mandates that "each of the three general departments of government [must remain] entirely free from the control of coercive influence, direct or indirect, of either of the others," *Humphrey's Executor* v. *United States* . . . (1935), the Framers did not require—and indeed rejected—the notion that the three Branches must be entirely separate and distinct. . . .

In adopting this flexible understanding of separation of powers, we simply have recognized Madison's teaching that the greatest security against tyranny—the accumulation of excessive authority in a single branch—lies not in a hermetic division between the Branches, but in a carefully crafted system of checked and balanced power within each Branch. . . .

### Location of the Commission

The Sentencing Commission unquestionably is a peculiar institution within the framework of our Government. Although placed by the Act in the Judicial Branch, it is not a court and does not exercise judicial power. . . . Our constitutional principles of separated powers are not violated, however, by mere anomaly or innovation. . . . Congress' decision to create an independent rulemaking body to promulgate sentencing guidelines and to locate that body within the Judicial Branch is not unconstitutional unless Congress has vested in the Commission powers that are more appropriately performed by the other Branches or that undermine the integrity of the Judiciary. . . . Although the judicial power of the United States is limited by express provision of Article III to "Cases" and "Controversies," we have never held, and have clearly disavowed in practice, that the Constitution prohibits Congress from assigning to courts or auxiliary bodies within the Judicial Branch administrative or rulemaking duties that, in the words of Chief Justice Marshall, are "necessary and proper . . . for carrying into execution all the judgments which the judicial department has the power to pronounce." *Wayman* v. *Southard* (1825) . . . .

Given the consistent responsibility of federal judges to pronounce sentence within the statutory range established by Congress, we find that the role of the Commission in promulgating guidelines for the exercise of that judicial function bears considerable similarity to the role of this Court in establishing rules of procedure under the various enabling acts. Such guidelines, like the Federal Rules of Criminal and Civil Procedure, are court rules—rules, to paraphrase Chief Justice Marshall's language in *Wayman*, for carrying into execution judgments that the judiciary has the power to pronounce. Just as the rules of procedure bind judges and courts in the proper management of the cases before them, so the Guidelines bind judges and courts in the exercise of their uncontested responsibility to pass sentence in criminal cases. In other words, the Commission's functions, like this Court's function in promulgating procedural rules, are clearly attendant to a central element of the historically acknowledged mission of the Judicial Branch. . . . Although the Guidelines are intended to have substantive effects on public behavior (as do the rules of procedure), they do not bind or regulate the primary conduct of the public or vest in the Judicial Branch the legislative responsibility for establishing minimum and maximum penalties for every crime. They do no more than fetter the discretion of sentencing judges to do what they have done for generations—impose sentences within the broad limits established by Congress. Given their limited reach, the special role of the Judicial Branch in the field of sentencing, and the fact that the Guidelines are promulgated by an independent agency and not a court, it follows that as a matter of "practical consequence" the location of the Sentencing Commission within the Judicial Branch simply leaves with the Judiciary what long has belonged to it. . . .

### Composition of the Commission

. . . We now turn to petitioner's claim that Congress' decision to require at least three federal judges to serve on the Commission and to require those judges to share their authority with nonjudges undermines the integrity of the Judicial Branch. . . .

The text of the Constitution contains no prohibition against the service of active federal judges on independent commissions such as that established by the Act. The Constitution does include an Incompatibility Clause applicable to national legislators. . . . No comparable restriction applies to judges, and we find it at least inferentially meaningful that at the Constitutional Convention two prohibitions against plural officeholding by members of the judiciary were proposed, but did not reach the floor of the Convention for a vote.

. . . Our inferential reading that the Constitution does not prohibit Article III judges from undertaking extrajudicial duties finds support in the historical practice of the Founders after ratification. . . .

Subsequent history, moreover, reveals a frequent and continuing, albeit controversial, practice of extrajudicial service. . . .

. . . In light of the foregoing history and precedent, we conclude that the principle of separation of powers does not absolutely prohibit Article III judges from serving on commissions such as that created by the Act. The judges serve on the Sentencing Commission not pursuant to their status and authority as Article III judges, but solely because of their appointment by the President as the Act directs. Such power as these judges wield as Commissioners is not judicial power; it is administrative power derived from the enabling legislation. Just as the nonjudicial members of the Commission act as administrators, bringing their experience and wisdom to bear on the problems of sentencing disparity, so too the judges, uniquely qualified on the subject of sentencing, assume a wholly administrative role upon entering into the deliberations of the Commission. In other words, the Constitution, at least as a *per se* matter, does not forbid judges from wearing two hats; it merely forbids them from wearing both hats at the same time.

### Presidential Control

The Act empowers the President to appoint all seven members of the Commission with the advice and consent of the Senate. The Act further provides that the President shall make his choice of judicial appointees to the Commission after considering a list of six judges recommended by the Judicial Conference of the United States. The Act also grants the President authority to remove members of the Commission, although "only for neglect of duty or malfeasance in office or for other good cause shown." . . .

Mistretta argues that this power of Presidential appointment and removal prevents the Judicial Branch from performing its constitutionally assigned functions. . . .

. . . since the President has no power to affect the tenure or compensation of Article III judges, even if the Act authorized him to remove judges from the Commission at will, he would have no power to coerce the judges in the exercise of their judicial duties. In any case, Congress did not grant the President unfettered authority to remove Commission members. Instead, precisely to ensure that they would not be subject to coercion even in the exercise of their nonjudicial duties, Congress insulated the members from Presidential removal except for good cause. Under these circumstances, we see no risk that the President's limited removal power will compromise the impartiality of Article III judges serving on the Commission and, consequently, no risk that the Act's removal provision will prevent the Judicial Branch from performing its constitutionally assigned function of fairly adjudicating cases and controversies.

We conclude that in creating the Sentencing Commission—an unusual hybrid in structure and authority—Congress neither delegated excessive legislative power nor upset the constitutionally mandated balance of powers among the coordinate Branches. . . .

The judgment of United States District Court for the Western District of Missouri is affirmed.

*It is so ordered.*

JUSTICE SCALIA, dissenting.

While the products of the Sentencing Commission's labors have been given the modest name "Guidelines," . . . they have the force and effect of laws, prescribing the sentences criminal defendants are to receive. A judge who disregards them will be reversed. . . . I dissent from today's decision because I can find no place within our constitutional system for an agency created by Congress to exercise no governmental power other than the making of laws. . . .

Petitioner's most fundamental and far-reaching challenge to the Commission is that Congress' commitment of such broad policy responsibility to any institution is an unconstitutional delegation of legislative power. . . .

But while the doctrine of unconstitutional delegation is unquestionably a fundamental element of our constitutional system, it is not an element readily enforceable by the courts. Once it is conceded, as it must be, that no statute can be entirely precise, and that some judgments, even some judgments involving policy considerations, must be left to the officers executing the law and to the judges applying it, the debate over unconstitutional delegation becomes a debate not over a point of principle but over a question of degree. . . .

In short, I fully agree with the Court's rejection of petitioner's contention that the doctrine of unconstitutional delegation of legislative authority has been violated because of the lack of intelligible, congressionally prescribed standards to guide the Commission. . . .

Precisely because the scope of delegation is largely uncontrollable by the courts, we must be particularly rigorous in preserving the Constitution's structural restrictions that deter excessive delegation. The major one, it seems to me, is that the power to make law cannot be exercised by anyone other than Congress, except in conjunction with the lawful exercise of executive or judicial power.

The whole theory of *lawful* congressional "delegation" is not that Congress is sometimes too busy or too divided and can therefore assign its responsibility of making law to someone else; but rather that a certain degree of discretion, and thus of law-making, *inheres* in most executive or judicial action, and it is up to Congress, by the relative specificity or generality of its statutory commands, to determine—up to a point—how small or how large that degree shall be. . . . Strictly speaking, there is *no* acceptable delegation of legislative power. As John Locke put it almost three hundred years ago, "[t]he power of the *legislative* being derived from the people by a positive voluntary grant and institution, can be no other, than what the positive grant conveyed, which being only to make *laws*, and not to make *legislators*, the *legislative* can have no power to transfer their authority of making laws, and place it in other hands." . . . In the present case, however, a pure delegation of legislative power is precisely what we have before us. It is irrelevant whether the standards are adequate, because they are not standards related to the exercise of executive or judicial powers; they are, plainly and simply, standards for further legislation.

The lawmaking function of the Sentencing Commission is completely divorced from any responsibility for execution of the law or adjudication of private rights under the law. . . .

The delegation of lawmaking authority to the Commission is, in short, unsupported by any legitimating theory to explain why it is not a delegation of legislative power. To disregard structural legitimacy is wrong in itself—but since structure has purpose, the disregard also has adverse practical consequences. In this case, as suggested earlier, the consequence is to facilitate and encourage judicially uncontrollable delegation. Until our decision last Term in *Morrison* v. *Olson* . . . (1988), it could have been said that Congress could delegate lawmaking authority only at the expense of increasing the power of either the President or the courts. Most often, as a practical matter, it would be the President, since the judicial process is unable to conduct the investigations and make the political assessments essential for most policymaking. Thus, the need for delegation would have to be important enough to induce Congress to aggrandize its primary competitor for political power, and the recipient of the policymaking authority, while not Congress itself, would at least be politically accountable. . . .

By reason of today's decision, I anticipate that Congress will find delegation of its lawmaking powers much more attractive in the future. If rulemaking can be entirely unrelated to the exercise of judicial or executive powers, I foresee all manner of "expert" bodies, insulated from the political process, to which Congress will delegate various portions of its lawmaking responsibility. How tempting to create an expert Medical Commission (mostly MDs, with perhaps a few PhDs in moral philosophy) to dispose of such thorny, "no-win" political issues as the withholding of life-support systems in federally funded hospitals, or the use of fetal tissue for research. This is an undemocratic precedent that we set—not because of the scope of the delegated power, but because its recipient is not one of the three Branches of Government. The only governmental power the Commission possesses is the power to make law; and it is not the Congress.

## *Immigration and Naturalization Service* v. *Chadha*

**462 U.S. 919; 103 S. Ct. 2764; 77 L. Ed. 2d 317 (1983)**

Jagdish Rai Chadha, an East Indian born in Kenya, was admitted to the United States in 1966 on a nonimmigrant student visa. When he remained in America after the visa expired in 1972, he became susceptible to deportation under the Immigration and Nationality Act. The Act authorized the Attorney General to suspend deportation if the alien had resided continuously in the United States for seven years, was of good moral character, and would suffer "extreme hardship" if deported. However, the Act reserved to each house of Congress the power to overrule the Attorney General's determinations. When Chadha's deportation was suspended and a report of the suspension was transmitted to Congress, the House of Representatives vetoed the action. Chadha challenged the House's authority to order his deportation, and when the Court of Appeals ruled the legislative veto in the Act unconstitutional, the case was appealed to the Supreme Court. *Opinion of the Court: Burger, Brennan, Marshall, Blackmun, Stevens, O'Connor. Concurring opinion: Powell. Dissenting opinions: White; Rehnquist, White.*

CHIEF JUSTICE BURGER delivered the opinion of the Court.

We turn . . . to the question whether action of one House of Congress under § 244(c)(2) violates strictures of the Constitution. We begin, of course, with the presumption that the challenged statute is valid. Its wisdom is not the concern of the courts; if a challenged action does not violate the Constitution, it must be sustained. . . .

By the same token, the fact that a given law or procedure is efficient, convenient, and useful in facilitating functions of government, standing alone, will not save it if it is contrary to the Constitution. Convenience and efficiency are not the primary objectives—or the hallmarks—of democratic government and our inquiry is sharpened rather than blunted by the fact that Congressional veto provisions are appearing with increasing frequency in statutes which delegate authority to executive and independent agencies. . . .

Explicit and unambiguous provisions of the Constitution prescribe and define the respective functions of the Congress and of the Executive in the legislative process. . . . The very structure of the articles delegating and separating powers under Arts I, II, and III exemplify the concept of separation of powers and we now turn to Art I.

**The Presentment Clauses**

The records of the Constitutional Convention reveal that the requirement that all legislation be presented to the President before becoming law was uniformly accepted by the Framers. Presentment to the President and the Presidential veto were considered so imperative that the draftsmen took special pains to assure that these requirements could not be circumvented.

The decision to provide the President with a limited and qualified power to nullify proposed legislation by veto was based on the profound conviction of the Framers that the powers conferred on Congress were the powers to be most carefully circumscribed. . . .

The President's role in the lawmaking process also reflects the Framers' careful efforts to check whatever propensity a particular Congress might have to enact oppressive, improvident, or ill-considered measures. . . . The Court also has observed that the Presentment Clauses serve the important purpose of assuring that a "national" perspective is grafted on the legislative process.

**Bicameralism**

The bicameral requirement of Art I, §§ 1, 7 was of scarcely less concern to the Framers than was the Presidential veto and indeed the two concepts are interdependent. By providing that no law could take effect without the concurrence of the prescribed majority of the Members of both Houses, the Framers reemphasized their belief, already remarked upon in connection with the Presentment Clauses, that legislation should not be enacted unless it has been carefully and fully considered by the Nation's elected officials. . . .

. . . Apart from their fear that special interests could be favored at the expense of public needs, the Framers were also concerned, although not of one mind, over the apprehensions of the smaller states. Those states feared a commonality of interest among the larger states would work to their disadvantage; representatives of the larger states, on the other hand, were skeptical of a legislature that could pass laws favoring a minority of the people. It need hardly be repeated here that the Great Compromise, under which one House was viewed as representing the people and the other the states, allayed the fears of both the large and small states.

We see therefore that the Framers were acutely conscious that the bicameral requirement and the Presentment Clauses would serve essential constitutional functions. The President's participation in the legislative process was to protect the Executive Branch from Congress and to protect the whole people from improvident laws. The division of the Congress into two distinctive bodies assures that the legislative power would be exercised only after opportunity for full study and debate in separate settings. The President's unilateral veto power, in turn, was limited by the power of two thirds of both Houses of Congress to overrule a veto thereby precluding final arbitrary action of one person. It emerges clearly that the prescription for legislative action in Art I, §§ 1, 7 represents the Framers' decision that the legislative power of the Federal government be exercised in accord with a single, finely wrought and exhaustively considered, procedure.

The Constitution sought to divide the delegated powers of the new federal government into three defined categories, legislative, executive and judicial, to assure, as nearly as possible, that each Branch of government would confine itself to its assigned responsibility. The hydraulic pressure inherent within each of the separate Branches to exceed the outer limits of its power, even to accomplish desirable objectives, must be resisted.

Although not "hermetically" sealed from one another, the powers delegated to the three Branches are functionally identifiable. When any Branch acts, it is presumptively exercising the power the Constitution has delegated to it. When the Executive acts, it presumptively acts in an executive or administrative capacity as defined in Art II. And when, as here, one House of congress purports to act, it is presumptively acting within its assigned sphere.

Beginning with this presumption, we must nevertheless establish that the challenged action under § 244(c)(2) is of the kind to which the procedural requirements of Art I, § 7 apply. Not every action taken by either House is subject to the bicameralism and presentment requirements of Art I. Whether actions taken by either House are, in law and fact, an exercise of legislative power depends not on their form but upon "whether they contain matter which is properly to be regarded as legislative in its character and effect."

Examination of the action taken here by one House pursuant to § 244(c)(2) reveals that it was essentially legislative in purpose and effect. In purporting to exercise power defined in Art I, § 8, cl 4 to "establish an uniform Rule of Naturalization," the House took action that had the purpose and effect of altering the legal rights, duties and relations of persons, including the Attorney General, Executive Branch officials and Chadha, all outside the legislative branch. Section 244(c)(2) purports to authorize one House of Congress to require the Attorney General to deport an individual alien whose deportation otherwise would be cancelled under § 244. The one-House veto operated in this case to overrule the Attorney General and mandate Chadha's deportation; absent the House action, Chadha would remain in the United States. Congress has *acted* and its action has altered Chadha's status.

. . . Disagreement with the Attorney General's decision on Chadha's deportation—that is, Congress' decision to deport Chadha—no less than Congress' original choice to delegate to the Attorney General the authority to make that decision, involves determinations of policy that Congress can implement in only one way; bicameral passage followed by presentment to the President. Congress must abide by its delegation of authority until that delegation is legislatively altered or revoked.

Finally, we see that when the Framers intended to authorize either House of Congress to act alone and outside of its prescribed bicameral legislative role, they narrowly and precisely defined the procedure for such action. . . . These exceptions are narrow, explicit, and separately justified; none of them authorize the action challenged here. On the contrary, they provide further support for the conclusion that Congressional authority is not to be implied and for the conclusion that the veto provided for in § 244(c)(2) is not authorized by the constitutional design of the powers of the Legislative Branch.

The veto authorized by § 244(c)(2) doubtless has been in many respects a convenient shortcut; the "sharing" with the Executive by Congress of its authority over aliens in this manner is, on its face, an appealing compromise. In purely practical terms, it is obviously easier for action to be taken by one House without submission to the President; but it is crystal clear from the records of the Convention, contemporaneous writings, and debates, that the Framers ranked other values higher than efficiency. The records of the Convention and debates in the States preceding ratification underscore the common desire to define and limit the exercise of the newly created federal powers affecting the states and the people. There is unmistakable expression of a determination that legislation by the national Congress be a step-by-step, deliberate and deliberative process.

The choices we discern as having been made in the Constitutional Convention impose burdens on governmental processes that often seem clumsy, inefficient, even unworkable, but those hard choices were consciously made by men who had lived under a form of government that permitted arbitrary governmental acts to go unchecked. There is no support in the Constitution or decisions of this Court for the proposition that the cumbersomeness and delays often encountered in complying with explicitly Constitutional standards may be avoided, either by the Congress or by the President. . . .

We hold that the Congressional veto provision in § 244(c)(2) is severable from the Act and that it is unconstitutional.

JUSTICE WHITE, dissenting.

Today the Court not only invalidates § 244(c)(2) of the Immigration and Nationality Act, but also sounds the death knell for nearly 200 other statutory provisions in which Congress has reserved a "legislative veto." . . .

The prominence of the legislative veto mechanism in our contemporary political system and its importance to Congress can hardly be overstated. It has become a central means by which Congress secures the accountability of executive and independent agencies. Without the legislative veto, Congress is faced with a Hobson's choice: either to refrain from delegating the necessary authority, leaving itself with a hopeless task of writing laws with the requisite specificity to cover endless special circumstances across the entire policy landscape, or in the alternative, to abdicate its lawmaking function to the executive branch and independent agencies. To choose the former leaves major national problems unresolved; to opt for the latter risks unaccountable policymaking by those not elected to fill that role. Accordingly, over the past five decades, the legislative veto has been placed in nearly 200 statutes.

[Justice White then reviewed at length the history of the legislative veto.]

Even this brief review suffices to demonstrate that the legislative veto is more than "efficient, convenient, and useful." It is an important if not indispensable political invention that allows the President and Congress to resolve major constitutional and policy differences, assures the accountability of independent regulatory agencies, and preserves Congress' control over lawmaking. Perhaps there are other means of accommodation and accountability, but the increasing reliance of Congress upon the legislative veto suggests that the alternatives to which Congress must now turn are not entirely satisfactory.

The history of the legislative veto also makes clear that it has not been a sword with which Congress has struck out to aggrandize itself at the expense of the other branches—the concerns of Madison and Hamilton. Rather, the veto has been a means of defense, a reservation of ultimate authority necessary if Congress is to fulfill its designated role under Article I as the nation's lawmaker. While the President has often objected to particular legislative vetoes, generally those left in the hands of congressional committees, the Executive has more often agreed to legislative review as the price for a broad delegation of authority. To be sure, the President may have preferred unrestricted power, but that could be precisely why Congress thought it essential to retain a check on the exercise of delegated authority.

. . . The constitutional question posed today is one of immense difficulty over which the executive and legislative branches—as well as scholars and judges—have understandably disagreed. That disagreement stems from the silence of the Constitution on the precise question: The Constitution does not directly authorize or prohibit the legislative veto. Thus, our task should be to determine whether the legislative veto is consistent with the purposes of Art I and the principles of Separation of Powers which are reflected in that Article and throughout the Constitution. We should not find the lack of a specific constitutional authorization for the legislative veto surprising, and I would not infer disapproval of the mechanism from its absence. From the summer of 1787 to the present the government of the United States has become an endeavor far beyond the contemplation of the Framers. Only within the last half century has the complexity and size of the Federal Government's responsibilities grown so greatly that the Congress must rely on the legislative veto as the most effective if not the only means to insure their role as the nation's lawmakers. But the wisdom of the Framers was to anticipate that the nation would grow and new problems of governance would require different solutions. Accordingly, our Federal Government was intentionally chartered with the flexibility to respond to contemporary needs without losing sight of fundamental democratic principles. . . .

This is the perspective from which we should approach the novel constitutional questions presented by the legislative veto. In my view, neither Article I of the Constitution nor the doctrine of separation of powers is violated by this mechanism by which our elected representatives preserve their voice in the governance of the nation. . . .

The terms of the Presentment Clauses suggest only that bills and their equivalent are subject to the requirements of bicameral passage and presentment to the President. . . . This reading is consistent with the historical background of the Presentation Clause itself which reveals only that the Framers were concerned with limiting the methods for enacting new legislation. The Framers were aware of the experience in Pennsylvania where the legislature had evaded the requirements attached to the passing of legislation by the use of "resolves," and the criticisms directed at this practice by the Council of Censors. There is no record that the Convention contemplated, let alone intended, that these Article I requirements would someday be invoked to restrain the scope of Congressional authority pursuant to duly-enacted law. . . .

When the Convention did turn its attention to the scope of Congress' lawmaking power, the Framers were expansive. The Necessary and Proper Clause, Art I, § 8, cl 18, vests Congress with the power "to make all laws which shall be necessary and proper for carrying into Execution the foregoing Powers [the enumerated powers of § 8], and all other Powers vested by this Constitution in the government of the United States, or in any Department or Officer thereof." It is long-settled that Congress may "exercise its best judgment in the selection of measures, to carry into execution the constitutional powers of the government," and "avail itself of experience, to exercise its reason, and to accommodate its legislation to circumstances." *McCulloch* v. *Maryland*.

The Court heeded this counsel in approving the modern administrative state. The Court's holding today that all legislative-type action must be enacted through the lawmaking process ignores that legislative authority is routinely delegated to the Executive branch, to the independent regulatory agencies, and to private individuals and groups. . . .

This Court's decisions sanctioning such delegations make clear that Article I does not require all action with the effect of legislation to be passed as a law. . . .

If Congress may delegate lawmaking power to independent and executive agencies, it is most difficult to understand Article I as forbidding Congress from also reserving a check on legislative power for itself. Absent the veto, the agencies receiving delegations of legislative or quasi-legislative power may issue regulations having the force of law without bicameral approval and without the President's signature. It is thus not apparent why the reservation of a veto over the exercise of that legislative power must be subject to a more exacting test. In both cases, it is enough that the initial statutory authorizations comply with the Article I requirements.

. . . The Court concedes that certain administrative agency action, such as rulemaking, "may resemble lawmaking" and recognizes that" [t]his Court has referred to agency activity as being "quasi-legislative' in character. . . . Under the Court's analysis, the Executive Branch and the independent agencies may make rules with the effect of law while Congress, in whom the Framers confided the legislative power, Art I, § 1, may not exercise a veto which precludes such rules from having operative force. If the effective functioning of a complex modern government requires the delegation of vast authority which, by virtue of its breadth, is legislative or "quasi-legislative" in character, I cannot accept that Article I—which is, after all, the source of the non-delegation doctrine—should forbid Congress from qualifying that grant with a legislative veto

The central concern of the presentation and bicameralism requirements of Article I is that when a departure from the legal status quo is undertaken, it is done with the approval of the President and both Houses of Congress—or, in the event of a presidential veto, a two-thirds majority in both Houses. This interest is fully satisfied by the operation of § 244(c)(2). The President's approval is found in the Attorney General's action in recommending to Congress that the deportation order for a given alien be suspended. The House and the Senate indicate their approval of the Executive's action by not passing a resolution of disapproval within the statutory period. Thus, a change in the legal status quo—the deportability of the alien—is consummated only with the approval of each of the three relevant actors. The disagreement of any one of the three maintains the alien's pre-existing status: the Executive may choose not to recommend suspension; the House and Senate may each veto the recommendation. The effect on the rights and obligations of the affected individuals and upon the legislative system is precisely the same as if a private bill were introduced but failed to receive the necessary approval.

I do not suggest that all legislative vetoes are necessarily consistent with separation of powers principles. A legislative check on an inherently executive function, for example that of initiating prosecutions, poses an entirely different question. But the legislative veto device here—and in many other settings—is far from an instance of legislative tyranny over the Executive. It is a necessary check on the unavoidably expanding power of the agencies, both executive and independent, as they engage in exercising authority delegated by Congress.

# 5
# THE EXECUTIVE BRANCH

In *The Federalist,* No. 51, James Madison suggested that " In republican government, the legislative authority necessarily predominates." Many contemporary observers of American government would disagree: certainly the development of American political institutions during the twentieth century has promoted executive rather than legislative domination. The discrepancy between Madison's statement and current realities raises troubling constitutional questions. How has "an executive magistracy carefully limited . . . in the extent and duration of its power" become the most powerful branch of government?[1] If American political development has not coincided with Madison's expectations, has the presidency exceeded its constitutional bounds? Can the modern presidency, in other words, be squared with the Constitution?

Constitutional scholars have long debated these questions. Some experts maintain that the constitutional system of checks and balances continues to operate. Others assert that those checks no longer effectively constrain the president and that the contemporary American government is largely presidential government. Whereas some scholars contend that the expansion of presidential power has occurred within the constitutional framework, others insist that "the history of the presidency is a history of aggrandizement."[2] This debate cannot be resolved conclusively in these pages. However, careful analysis of the Framers' conception of the office, the powers constitutionally assigned to the president, and the means by which presidential power has expanded can provide the basis for an informed judgment on the legitimate scope of presidential power.

## THE AIMS OF THE FRAMERS

The events leading to the American Revolution created a profound distrust of executive power that was reflected in the constitutions ratified following independence. The Articles of Confederation, which created a national government of very limited powers, did not establish a separate executive branch. Every state had a separate executive, but the state governors were rendered politically impotent by short terms of office, restrictions on reeligibility, election by the legislature, and/or the division of executive responsibilities among various officials.[3] The results, predictably, were disastrous. At the national level, the absence of a separate executive frustrated effective administration. At the state level, the lack of any effective check on the state legislatures led to the adoption of ill-considered and unjust laws. By the outset of the Constitutional Convention, most of the Framers were convinced of the need for a vigorous and independent executive. Alexander Hamilton reflected this view when he observed in *The Federalist,* No. 70, that "energy in the executive is a leading character in the definition of good government."

The delegates took several steps to ensure an energetic executive.[4] To begin with, they lodged the executive power in a single individual. Only a unified executive, they reasoned, could act with the necessary decisiveness and dispatch; moreover, such a concentration of power would promote accountability, because a single person would be responsible for the results of executive action. Second, they established a lengthy term of office and made the president eligible for reelection. An extended tenure, in their view, would not only promote continuity in administration but also give the president both the opportunity and the incentive to undertake long-range projects. The prospect of reelection, meanwhile, would encourage faithful performance of presidential duties and provide a basis for accountability. Third, they secured presidential independence by granting to the president powers (e.g., the veto) designed to safeguard his constitutional position and by creating a system of election (the electoral college) that rendered him independent of Congress. The electoral college had the additional advantage, according to *The Federalist,* No. 68, of ensuring that only figures of national stature would be elected, thereby affording "a moral certainty that the office of President will seldom fall to the lot of any man who is not in an eminent degree endowed with the requisite qualifications."

Most significantly, the Framers granted to the president extensive powers. Primary among these powers are those enumerated in Article II of the Constitution:

In the legislative sphere the president

- Must inform Congress as to the State of the Union (Section 3)
- Can recommend legislation to Congress (Section 3)
- Can call Congress into special session and, if the two houses disagree on the time of adjournment, adjourn it (Section 3)[5]
- Can veto legislation (Section 7, Paragraphs 2 and 3)

As chief executive the president

- Can appoint executive officers and fill vacancies in such offices (Section 2, Paragraphs 2 and 3)
- Can require the heads of executive departments to furnish advice, in writing, on subjects relating to the duties of their offices (Section 2, Paragraph 1)
- Must take care that the laws are faithfully executed (Section 3)

As chief law enforcer the president

- Can grant pardons and reprieves (Section 2, Paragraph 1)
- Must take care that the laws are faithfully executed (Section 3)

More generally, presidents have claimed broad powers to

- Exercise "the executive Power" vested in the President (Section 1, Paragraph 1)
- "Preserve, protect, and defend the Constitution," as required in the presidential oath of office (Section 1, Paragraph 8)

Presidential powers are not limited to those expressly listed in the Constitution, however. Much of the debate about the presidency has involved how far beyond those enumerated powers presidential power extends. What emerges from the Framers' discussions is a desire to give the president powers adequate to the responsibilities of the office.

## GRANTS OF POWER AND THEIR USE

Surprisingly enough, presidential power has grown in large measure through the exercise of powers expressly granted in the Constitution. The executive branch has benefited greatly from historical developments that have increased the importance of particular governmental functions, and thereby the power of the branch assigned responsibility for those functions. For example, extensive American involvement in foreign affairs has augmented presidential power, because the Constitution assigns the president a major role in the conduct of foreign policy (see Chapter 6). In the domestic sphere, the vast expansion in the size of the federal government and the rise of administrative policy-making have enhanced the significance of the president's power to make appointments and to supervise administration.

Presidential power also has been expanded through the more vigorous exercise of powers granted by the Constitution. Presidential activity in the legislative sphere provides the clearest instance of this expansion. From the Founding through the nineteenth century, presidents generally did not exploit the potentialities of the legislative functions assigned to the executive in the Constitution. Because the chief executives of this era neither recommended detailed legislative programs to Congress nor consistently used the veto to enforce their legislative priorities, Congress tended to dominate the legislative process. Then, in the twentieth century, presidents began to assume a more active role in legislation. Woodrow Wilson and the two Roosevelts established the idea that presidents should submit extensive legislative programs and work for their enactment, and they transformed the State of the Union address and other messages to Congress into vehicles for the announcement of presidential programs. Subsequent presidents, Republicans and Democrats, have continued this practice, to the point where in one year President Lyndon Johnson sought congressional action on 469 separate proposals. In recent decades, Congress has usually allowed presidential initiatives to define its legislative agenda, but this is not always the case. When the Republican Party captured control of Congress in 1995, it drew its agenda not from President Clinton's proposals but from the Contract with America that it had proposed during the 1994 election campaign.

Presidential use of the veto presents a parallel case. During the first seventy-five years of the Republic, presidents were reluctant to veto legislation—no president before Andrew Johnson vetoed more than twelve bills—and even then the veto most frequently was used to prevent enactment of legislation the president believed unconstitutional. As presidents became more active participants in the legislative process, however, the veto emerged as a formidable weapon. It is extremely effective in preventing the enactment of legislation—only about 4 percent of all presidential vetoes have been overridden. Given its proven effectiveness, presidential willingness to use the veto inevitably increases the executive's influence on Congress. Just as the power to suggest legislation gives presidents considerable control over the issues Congress addresses, so the veto power ensures that their views will be taken into account in congressional deliberations, as members of Congress seek to avoid the threat of a veto.

Congressional legislation has also contributed to the growth of presidential power. By enacting broad legislation without clear standards for their exercise, Congress has allowed the executive branch to make important policy decisions, and congressional requirements that the president submit programs or reports have created additional opportunities for presidential leadership in the legislative process. The Budget and Accounting Act of 1921 exemplifies how assignment of responsibilities to the president can enhance presidential power. The act requires that the president submit a budget to Congress each year and thereby provide a basis for congressional action. Inevitably, however, the budget submitted represents not merely the aggregate requests of the various executive departments, but also the policy priorities of the president. Thus, simply by fulfilling their statutory responsibility, presidents necessarily set the agenda for public debate and congressional action. The success of President Ronald Reagan's budget initiatives in 1981–82 demonstrated the legislative leverage this process can give the executive.

The Line Item Veto Act represented another congressional attempt to delegate important power to the President. For years presidents had complained that they were regularly confronted with the disagreeable alternatives of signing legislation that included spending programs that they deemed wasteful or unwise or vetoing worthwhile legislation because of objections to one or a few provisions. During the twentieth century, most state constitutions had relieved governors of this dilemma by authorizing them to veto individual provisions of appropriations bills, and presidents argued that they too needed this item-veto power. In 1955, Congress—concerned about federal budget deficits—responded to these presidential complaints by enacting the Line Veto Act, which granted the president a limited item-veto authority. Four members of Congress immediately challenged the constitutionality of the act, claiming that a constitutional amendment was necessary to invest the president with such power; in *Raines* v. *Byrd* (1997), the Supreme Court dismissed their suit, ruling that they lacked standing to sue. After President Clinton used his item-veto authority to strike tax and spending provisions from congressional enactments, a new constitutional challenge to the Act was mounted by those who claimed to be affected by the item vetoes. In *Clinton* v. *City of New York* (1998), a six-member Court majority invalidated the Line Item Veto Act, ruling that it violated the constitutionally established procedure for the enactment of legislation.

## IMPLIED POWERS

Presidential power has also increased through the recognition of the implied powers of the office. Chief Justice (and ex-President) William Howard Taft summarized the basis for claims of implied powers: "The true view of the Executive function is . . . that the President can exercise no power which cannot be fairly and reasonably traced to some specific grant of power or justly implied and included within such express grant as necessary and proper for its exercise."[6] In taking this position, Taft actually was arguing against a more expansive view of presidential power enunciated by Theodore Roosevelt.[7] Yet Taft's view also supports a broad exercise of executive power, for it suggests that the president is not restricted to the powers enumerated in Article II. Because those grants relate to particular governmental functions and because the Framers intended that the executive fulfill those functions, it follows that they must have provided the executive with the means necessary to carry them out. Thus, the character of the powers assigned to the president logically points to the existence of implied powers.

Taft's position has been endorsed in court decisions and incorporated into governmental practice. Yet acceptance of the principle of implied powers does not prevent disagreements about the scope of those powers. Examination of the president's powers as chief executive and the disputes over executive privilege and presidential immunity illustrates both the bases for claims of implied powers and possible limits on those powers.

### The President as Chief Executive

Article II of the Constitution recognizes the president as head of the executive branch, assigning him "the Executive Power" and making him responsible for ensuring "that the laws be faithfully executed." To enable him to meet his responsibilities, it grants him the power to appoint major executive officers. This promotes presidential control over those who shall execute the laws—a necessary precondition for the effective supervision of administration. It also leads to accountability in the executive: a president who selects executive officials and has authority over them can be held responsible for their actions.

Yet the Constitution limits presidential control over the selection of executive-branch officials in several ways. To begin with, presidential nominees for most major offices must be confirmed by the Senate. Although usually they are—since 1789 only eight nominees for Cabinet posts have been voted down—on occasion presidents have been forced to withdraw nominations, and the necessity of securing senatorial confirmation also may affect presidential choices. In addition, Congress by statute defines the offices to be filled and can require Senate approval for appointment to them. Under legislation enacted in 1974, for example, the director of the Office of Management and the Budget must be confirmed by the Senate. Furthermore, Congress can establish qualifications for offices that restrict the president's range of choice in filling them.

Finally, the presidential appointment power extends only to principal officers. Article II authorizes Congress to vest the appointment of "inferior" officers in the president, the courts, or the heads of executive departments. Exactly what distinguishes principal from "inferior" officers is far from clear. In *Morrison* v. *Olson* (1988), for example, the Court ruled that an independent counsel with the power to investigate and prosecute violations of federal law largely free from executive-branch control was an inferior officer and upheld congressional legislation vesting her appointment in a federal court. Nevertheless, this congressional power is subject to an important separation-of-powers limitation: although Congress may designate who will appoint inferior officers, it cannot put that power in its own hands. When Congress attempted to vest in the president pro tem of the Senate and the speaker of the House the power to appoint a majority of the voting members of the Federal Election Commission, the Supreme Court in *Buckley* v. *Valeo* (1976) unanimously struck down the plan.

If the Constitution gives the president the power to appoint executive-branch officials to promote effective administration, does it also give him the power to remove them? This question is of vital concern, for the power to remove from office is in effect the power to control behavior in office. Aside from noting that "civil officers" are impeachable, however, the Constitution is silent on this point. Thus if the president has a constitutional power to remove officials, it must be an implied power.

The First Congress confronted this question in establishing a Department of Foreign Affairs. After prolonged debate, it concluded that the president acting alone could remove the secretary of state. Many members of Congress accepted the view, best presented by James Madison, that the removal power was implied in the grant of executive power to the president. Others insisted that Congress could determine who would exercise the removal power. The issue arose intermittently thereafter—most notably in the impeachment trial of President Andrew Johnson—but did not reach the Supreme Court until *Myers* v. *United States* [1926]. In *Myers* the Court upheld the president's removal of a postmaster in violation of legislation establishing a four-year term for postmasters and requiring senatorial consent for their removal. In support of this decision, Chief Justice Taft cited the actions of the First Congress, which he viewed as an authoritative recognition of an implied presidential power of removal. In addition, he noted, the president's responsibilities required that this implied power be recognized: "Made responsible under the Constitution for the effective enforcement of the law, the President needs as an indispensable aid to meet it the disciplinary influence upon those who act under him of a reserve power of removal."

The Court's ruling in *Myers* has not prevented disputes about the scope of the president's removal power. *Myers* seemed to imply that the president had the power to remove all those involved in the execution of the laws. If so, this raises questions about the constitutionality of independent regulatory commissions, such as the Federal Communications Commission, whose members can be removed by the president before the expiration of their terms only for dereliction of duty. However, the Court appears to have retreated from its position in *Myers*. It did recognize in *Bowsher* v. *Synar* (1986) that those exercising executive functions could not be under the control of Congress. However, it has rejected presidential efforts to remove members of independent regulatory commissions before expiration of their terms of office, contending that the powers they exercised were only partly executive in character.[8] More recently, in *Morrison* v. *Olson,* it upheld restrictions on the removal of an independent counsel, who was involved in investigating and prosecuting official wrong-doing. The Court argued that the restrictions did not substantially impede the president's ability to perform his constitutional duty or unduly interfere with the functioning of the executive branch. In dissent, Justice Antonin Scalia insisted that if prosecution of crimes is an executive function, then the president must have control over those exercising the function. Otherwise, the unity of the executive is compromised.

### Executive Privilege

Other recent controversies over implied powers and privileges have involved presidential claims of executive privilege and immunity from suit. Executive privilege is the power of the president to refuse to provide information requested by the other branches of government. Because the

Constitution does not explicitly grant this power to the executive, presidents generally have relied on three arguments to support claims of executive privilege. First, they have maintained that in order to fulfill their military, diplomatic, and national security responsibilities, they must at times withhold sensitive information from congressional and public scrutiny; otherwise, the argument runs, they could not successfully carry out the tasks assigned to the executive by the Framers. Another defense of executive privilege rests on the fact that presidents frequently depend on advice from associates and subordinates in implementing their policymaking responsibilities. Only by ensuring the confidentiality of these communications, they have argued, can they secure that candid interchange of views needed for wise decisions. Like the "national security" argument, this "candid interchange" argument suggests that the president's constitutional responsibilities by implication support claims of executive privilege. Some presidents have gone even further in claiming this privilege, asserting that the principle of separation of powers vests the president with control over the executive branch and, thereby, with the authority to control all communications emanating from that branch. This argument has been used to support the most extensive claims of executive privilege, because it implies that the provision of information to the other two branches is entirely a matter of presidential discretion.

Presidential invocation of executive privilege has become more frequent since World War II, in part because of increased American involvement in world affairs. Even so, conflicts between the president and Congress over the withholding of information were resolved by interbranch compromises, not by testing the legitimacy of executive privilege in the courts. This changed, however, when during the Watergate investigation President Richard Nixon relied on executive privilege to deny White House tapes and other records to congressional investigating committees, the Watergate special prosecutor, and the courts. When the president refused to turn over sixty-four tapes for use in the Watergate coverup trial, the issue of executive privilege came to the Supreme Court, in *United States* v. *Nixon* (1974). Rejecting the broad separation-of-powers argument for executive privilege, the Court ordered the president to turn over the tapes. Nevertheless, the justices did not reject the notion of implied powers. They acknowledged that presidential claims of executive privilege had a basis in the Constitution and that such claims had particular force when information pertaining to war and foreign affairs was involved. To determine the scope of this implied power, therefore, it was necessary in each instance to balance the interest in confidentiality against the need for disclosure of the specific information.

The Supreme Court's resolution of this case suggests one possible limitation on the president's implied powers: although presidents legitimately can claim the powers necessary to fulfill their constitutional responsibilities, so too can Congress and the courts. When these claims conflict, the executive will not always prevail. In *United States* v. *Nixon*, for example, the Court ruled that the interest in securing evidence necessary for a fair trial outweighed the president's "generalized assertion of privilege."

### Presidential Immunity

When presidential claims of implied powers or privileges do not collide with the claims of a coequal branch of government, the Supreme Court has been more receptive to them. Presidential immunity from civil suit is a case in point. In *Nixon* v. *Fitzgerald* (1982), the Court ruled that the Constitution implicitly grants the president an absolute immunity from private suit for all actions that fall "within the outer perimeter of his authority." Such an immunity, the Court argued, was necessary so that presidents could fulfill their constitutional responsibilities unimpeded by the threat of private suit. Even those justices who dissented from granting an absolute immunity for official conduct recognized that the Constitution implicitly provided the president with the immunities necessary to carry out the responsibilities of the office.

The issue of presidential immunity arose again in litigation stemming from the sexual harrassment suit filed by Paula Jones against President William Clinton for actions allegedly undertaken while he was governor of Arkansas. In *Clinton* v. *Jones* (1997) the Supreme Court ruled against the president. The Court reiterated that the president enjoys an absolute immunity from civil suits for damages arising out of his official acts. However, it refused to extend this immunity to suits arising out of the president's private conduct, because such suits would not deter the president from vigorous exercise of his constitutional powers. In addition, the Court rejected President Clinton's argument that the civil suit should be postponed until the completion of his term of office. The president argued that the burden of defending the suit would impose burdens on his time and energy that would impair the effective performance of his office. The Court pointed out that the narrow focus of the suit suggested that it would be unlikely to occupy a significant proportion of the president's time and that prior presidents had responded to court orders to testify or provide information without it interfering with the exercise of their responsibilities. Thus, the Court permitted the suit to proceed.

## PREROGATIVE POWERS

A third basis for the expansion of executive power has been presidential exercise of prerogative powers. The concept of prerogative powers derives from the writings of the English political philosopher John Locke, who defined *prerogative* as the power of the executive "to act according to discretion for the public good, without the prescription of law and sometimes even against it."[9] In the American context, prerogative justifies the use of powers beyond those granted or implied in Article II. According to this concept, presidential power varies with changes in circumstances, and under extraordinary conditions includes the power to go beyond or against the law. This absence of set limits on presidential power raises the question of whether prerogative is compatible with constitutional government.

There is some evidence that the Framers expected presidents to exercise prerogative powers. Whereas Article I restricts Congress to "all legislative powers herein granted," Article II vests the "executive power" in the president. The open-ended character of this provision suggests that the president can legitimately claim all powers, including prerogative powers, characteristically exercised by the executive in other governments. Certainly, the Framers were familiar with Locke's writings on the scope of executive power. In addition, Hamilton's emphasis in *The Federalist* on "energy in the executive"—the ability of the president to respond swiftly and decisively to emergency situations—seems to presuppose the availability of prerogative powers.

Nevertheless, the status of prerogative under the Constitution has remained uncertain. Some assertions of prerogative powers have been accepted as justified responses to extraordinary conditions. At the outset of the Civil War, President Abraham Lincoln, acting on his own initiative while Congress was adjourned, ordered several measures of questionable legality (see Chapter 6). He later justified his actions on the grounds that they had been necessary to preserve the Union:

> I did understand, however, that my oath to preserve the constitution to the best of my ability, imposed upon me the duty of preserving, by every indispensable means, that government—that nation—of which that constitution was the organic law. Was it possible to lose the nation, and yet preserve the constitution? . . . I felt that measures, otherwise unconstitutional, might become lawful, by becoming indispensable to the preservation of the constitution, through the preservation of the nation.[10]

Once convened, Congress ratified Lincoln's actions, and the verdict of history has supported his forceful assertion of prerogative powers.

At times the Supreme Court has also lent support to the idea of prerogative powers. In *In Re Neagle* (1890), it ruled that the president did not need legislative authorization to assign a U.S. marshal to protect a Supreme Court justice. Although there was no statutory basis for such action, the justices held that the president's responsibility to "ensure that the laws be faithfully executed" extends beyond acts of Congress and includes "the rights, duties, and obligations growing out of the Constitution itself, our international relations, and all the protection implied by the nature of the government under the Constitution." Put differently, because the responsibility for preserving the peace of the nation—a requirement common to all societies—is lodged in the president, so is the power necessary to fulfill that responsibility.

Other assertions of prerogative powers have been viewed less sympathetically. In *Youngstown Sheet & Tube Company* v. *Sawyer* (1952) the Supreme Court invalidated President Harry Truman's order, given during the Korean War, that the nation's steel mills be seized to prevent a strike. The Court held that because Congress had designated steps to be followed in such emergencies, its determination bound the president and foreclosed consideration of alternative responses. When President Richard Nixon attempted to justify actions taken during the Watergate scandal by invoking prerogative powers, the public reaction was overwhelmingly negative.

Yet the condemnation of presidential actions in these instances does not indicate a wholesale rejection of prerogative powers. Rather, it reflects a judgment that the situations involved did not warrant the exercise of such powers. The deeper issue remains: Are prerogative powers necessary in "a constitution intended to endure for ages to come, and consequently to be adapted to the various crises of human affairs"? And if they are, can they be entrusted to the executive without jeopardizing the system of republican government?

The problem raised by prerogative powers puts into clear focus the continuing problem of the presidency. When the proposed constitution was submitted for adoption, leading Anti-Federalists charged that, in the words of Patrick Henry, it "squints toward monarchy." The Framers sought to allay this concern by combining energy in the executive with "other ingredients which constitute safety in the republican sense." The debate over the modern presidency, with its greatly expanded powers, is largely a dispute over the success of their efforts.

## NOTES

1 *The Federalist,* No. 48, p. 309.

2 The quotation is from Edward S. Corwin, *The President: Office and Powers,* 4th ed. (New York: New York University Press, 1957), pp. 29–30.

3 The sole exception, which served as a model to the delegates, was the governorship in New York.

4 The discussion here follows Hamilton's delineation in *The Federalist,* No. 70: "The ingredients which constitute energy in the executive are unity; duration; an adequate provision for its support; and competent powers."

5 With the advent of year-round congressional sessions, this power has ceased to be important.

6 William Howard Taft, *Our Chief Magistrate and His Powers* (New York: Columbia University Press, 1916), p. 139.

7 Roosevelt's view was spelled out in his autobiography: "My view was that every officer, and above all every executive officer in high position, was a steward of the people. . . . I declined to adopt the view that what was imperatively necessary for the Nation could not be done by the President unless he could find some specific authorization to do it. My belief was that it was not only his right but his duty to do anything that the needs of the Nation demanded unless such action was forbidden by the Constitution or the laws." [Theodore Roosevelt, *An Autobiography* (New York: Charles Scribner's Sons, 1931), p. 388.]

8 See *Humphrey's Executor* v. *United States* (1935) and *Wiener* v. *United States* (1958).

9 Locke, *Second Treatise of Civil Government,* Chapter XIV, Section 160.
10 From the letter to A. G. Hodges, April 4, 1864, in *The Complete Works of Abraham Lincoln,* John Nicolay and John Hay, eds. (New York: Francis D. Tandy Co., 1894), vol. 10, pp. 65–68.

## SELECTED READING

*The Federalist,* Nos. 67–77.

*Bowsher* v. *Synar,* 478 U.S. 714 (1986).
*Humphrey's Executor* v. *United States,* 295 U.S. 602 (1935).
*Mississippi* v. *Johnson,* 4 Wall. 475 (1867).
*Nixon* v. *Administrator of General Services,* 433 U.S. 425 (1977).
*Nixon* v. *Fitzgerald,* 457 U.S. 731 (1982).
*Raines* v. *Byrd,* 138 L.Ed.2d 849 (1997) and Website.

Berger, Raoul. *Executive Privilege: A Constitutional Myth* (Cambridge, Mass.: Harvard University Press, 1974).

Bessette, Joseph and Jeffrey Tulis, eds. *The Presidency in the Constitutional Order* (Baton Rouge: Louisiana State University Press, 1981).

Corwin, Edward S. *The President: Office and Powers,* 4th rev. ed. (New York: New York University Press, 1957).

Cronin, Thomas E., ed. *Inventing the American Presidency* (Lawrence: University Press of Kansas, 1989).

Fisher, Louis. *Constitutional Conflicts Between Congress and the President,* 4th ed. (Lawrence: University Press of Kansas, 1997).

Pierce, Richard J. "Morrison v. Olson, Separation of Powers, and the Structure of Government." In Gerhard Casper and Dennis J. Hutchinson, eds. *The Supreme Court Review 1988* (Chicago: University of Chicago Press, 1989).

Pious, Richard M. *The American Presidency* (New York: Basic Books, 1970).

Rohr, John. *To Run a Constitution: The Legitimacy of the Administrative State* (Lawrence: University Press of Kansas, 1986).

Rozell, Mark J. *Executive Privilege: The Dilemma of Secrecy and Democratic Accountability.* Baltimore, Md.: Johns Hopkins Press, 1994.

Spitzer, Robert J. "The Constitutionality of the Presidential Line-Item Veto." *Political Science Quarterly* 112 (1997):261–283.

Thach, Charles C., Jr. *The Creation of the Presidency, 1775–1789* (Baltimore, Md.: Johns Hopkins Press, 1922).

Westin, Alan F. *Anatomy of a Constitutional Law Case* (New York: Macmillan, 1958).

# *Clinton* v. *City of New York*

**97–1374 (1998)**

The Line Item Veto Act authorizes the President to "cancel in whole" three types of provisions that have been signed into law: "(1) any dollar amount of discretionary budget authority; (2) any item of new direct spending; or (3) any limited tax benefit." In doing so, he must determine that the cancellation will "(i) reduce the Federal budget deficit; (ii) not impair any essential Government functions; and (iii) not harm the national interest." He must also transmit a special message to Congress notifying it of each cancellation within five calendar days after the enactment of the canceled provision. The effect of a cancellation, according to the Act, is to prevent the canceled item from having legal force or effect." Congress by majority vote of both houses can enact a "disapproval bill" rendering the cancellations "null and void." Although the President cannot cancel a disapproval bill, he retains his constitutional authority to veto such a bill.

The Line Item Veto Act became effective on January 1, 1997. On January 2, six Members of Congress who had opposed the Act brought suit, claiming that it violated the Presentment Clause (Article I, Section 7, clause 2 of the Constitution), which specifies the procedure for enactment of legislation. The District Court agreed, but the Supreme Court in *Raines* v. *Byrd* (1997) ruled that the Members of Congress did not have standing to sue because they had not "alleged a sufficiently concrete injury to have established Article III standing." Less than two months after this ruling, President Clinton exercised his authority under the Act. He canceled section 4722 (c) of the Balanced Budget Act of 1997, which waived the Federal Government's statutory right to recoup as much as $2.6 billion in taxes that the State of New York had levied against Medicaid providers, and section 968 of the Taxpayer Relief Act of 1997, which permitted the owners of certain food refiners and processors to defer recognition of capital gains if they sold their stock to eligible farmers' cooperatives. The City of New York filed suit, challenging the first cancellation, and the Snake River farmers' cooperative challenged the second. The District Court consolidated the cases, determined that the plaintiffs had standing under Article III, and ruled the Act's cancellation procedures unconstitutional. The Supreme Court then granted expedited review. *Opinion of the Court: Stevens, Rehnquist, Kennedy, Souter, Thomas, Ginsburg. Concurring in part and dissenting in part: Scalia, O'Connor, and (in part) Breyer. Dissenting opinion: Breyer and (in part) O'Connor, Scalia.*

JUSTICE STEVENS delivered the opinion of the Court.

We hold that these appellees have standing to challenge the constitutionality of the Act and, reaching the merits, we agree that the cancellation procedures set forth in the Act violate the Presentment Clause, Art. I, sec. 7, cl. 2, of the Constitution.

## III

As in the prior challenge to the Line Item Veto Act, we initially confront jurisdictional questions. The appellees invoked the jurisdiction of the District Court under the section of the Act entitled "Expedited Review." That section expressly authorizes "[a]ny Members of Congress or any individual adversely affected" by the Act to bring an action for declaratory judgment or injunctive relief on the ground that any provision of the Act is unconstitutional. [T]he Government . . . argues that, with the exception of Mike Cranney, the appellees are not "individuals" within the meaning of section 692 (a) (1). [I]n the context of the entire section, Congress undoubtedly intended the word "individual" to be construed as synonymous with the word "person." The special section authorizing expedited review evidences an unmistakable congressional interest in a prompt and authoritative judicial determination of the constitutionality of the Act. There is no plausible reason why Congress would have intended to provide for such special treatment of actions filed by natural persons and to have precluded entirely jurisdiction over comparable cases brought by corporate persons. Acceptance of the Government's newfound reading of section 692 "would produce an absurd and unjust result which Congress could not have intended."

We are also unpersuaded that appellees' challenge to the constitutionality of the Act is nonjusticiable. . . . In both the New York and the Snake River cases, the Government argues that the appellees are not actually injured because the claims are too speculative. . . . We find no merit in the suggestion that New York's injury is merely speculative because . . . the State now has a multibillion dollar contingent liability that had been eliminated by section 4722(c) of the Balanced Budget Act of 1997.

The Snake River farmers' cooperative also suffered an immediate injury when the President canceled the limited tax benefit that Congress had enacted to facilitate the acquisition of processing plants. Three critical facts identify the specificity and the importance of that injury. First, Congress enacted section 968 for the specific purpose of providing a benefit to a defined category of potential purchasers of a defined category of assets. The members of that statutorily defined class received the equivalent of a statutorily "bargaining chip" to use in carrying out the congressional plan to facilitate their purchase of such assets. Second, the President selected section 968 as one of only two tax benefits in the Taxpayer Relief Act of 1997 that should be canceled. The cancellation rested on his determination that the use of those bargaining chips would have a significant impact on the Federal budget deficit. Third, the Snake River cooperative was organized for the very purpose of acquiring processing facilities, it had concrete plans to utilize the benefits of section 968, and it was engaged in ongoing negotiations with the owner of a processing plant who had expressed an interest in structuring a tax-deferred sale when the President canceled section 968. Moreover, it is actively searching for other processing facilities for possible future purchase if the President's cancellation is reversed; and there are ample processing facilities in the State that Snake River may be able to purchase. By depriving them of their statutory bargaining chip, the cancellation inflicted a sufficient likelihood of economic injury to establish standing under our precedents. Appellees' injury in this regard is at least as concrete as the injury suffered by the respondents in *Bryant* v. *Yellen* (1980).

## IV

The Line Item Veto Act gives the President the power to "cancel in whole" three types of provisions that have been signed into law: "(1) any dollar amount of discretionary budget authority; (2) any item of new direct spending; or (3) any limited tax benefit." It is undisputed that the New York case involves an "item of new direct spending" and that the Snake River case involves a "limited tax benefit" as those terms are defined in the Act. It is also undisputed that each of those provisions had been signed into law pursuant to Article I, section 7, of the Constitution before it was canceled.

In both legal and practical effect, the President has amended two Acts of Congress by repealing a portion of each. "[R]epeal of statutes, no less than enactment, must conform with Art. I." *INS* v. *Chadha* (1983). There is no provision in the Constitution that authorizes the President to enact, to amend, or to repeal statutes. . . . There are important differences between the President's "return" [veto] of a bill pursuant to Article I, section 7, and the exercise of the President's cancellation authority pursuant to the Line Item Veto Act. The constitutional return takes place *before* the bill becomes law; the statutory cancellation occurs *after* the bill becomes law. The constitutional return is of the entire bill; the statutory cancellation is of only a part. Although the Constitution expressly authorizes the President to play a role in the process of enacting statutes, it is silent on the subject of unilateral Presidential action that either repeals or amends parts of duly enacted statutes.

There are powerful reasons for construing constitutional silence on this profoundly important issue as equivalent to an express prohibition. The procedures governing the enactment of statutes set forth in the text of Article I were the product of the great debates and compromises that produced the Constitution itself. Familiar historical materials provide abundant support for the conclusion that the power to enact statutes may only "be exercised in accord with a single, finely wrought and exhaustively considered, procedure." *Chadha.* Our first President understood the text of the Presentment Clause as requiring that he either "approve all the parts of a Bill, or reject it in toto."

What has emerged in these cases from the President's exercise of his statutory cancellation powers, however, are truncated versions of two bills that passed both Houses of Congress. They are not the product of the "finely wrought" procedure that the Framers designed. At oral argument, the Government suggested that the cancellations at issue in these cases do not effect a "repeal" of the canceled items because under the special "lockbox" provisions of the Act, a canceled item "retain[s] real, legal budgetary effect" insofar as it prevents Congress and the President from spending the savings that result from the cancellation. The text of the Act expressly provides, however, that a concellation prevents a direct spending or tax benefit provision "from having legal force or effect." That a canceled item may have "real, legal budgetary effect" as a result of the lockbox procedure does not change the fact that by canceling the items at issue in these cases, the President made them entirely inoperative as to appellees. Section 968 of the Taxpayer Relief Act no longer provides a tax benefit, and section 4722(c) of the Balanced Budget Act of 1997 no longer relieves New York of its contingent liability. Such significant changes do not lose their character simply because the canceled provisions may have some continuing financial effect on the Government. The cancellation of one section of a statute may be the functional equivalent of a partial repeal even if a portion of the section is not canceled.

## V

The Government advances two related arguments to support its position that despite the unambiguous provisions of the Act, cancellations do not amend or repeal properly enacted statutes in violation of the Presentment Clause. First, relying primarily on *Field* v. *Clark,* 143 U.S. 649 (1892), the Government contends that the cancellations were merely exercises of discretionary authority granted to the President by the Balanced Budget Act and the Taxpayer Relief Act read in light of the previously enacted Line Item Veto Act. Second, the Government submits that the substance of the authority to cancel tax and spending items "is, in practical effect, no more and no less than the power to 'decline to spend' specified sums of money, or to 'decline to implement' specified tax measures." Neither argument is persuasive.

In *Field* v. *Clark,* the Court upheld the constitutionality of the Tariff Act of 1890. That statute contained a "free list" of almost 300 specific articles that were exempted from import duties "unless otherwise specially provided for in this act." Section 3 was a special provision that directed the President to suspend that exemption for sugar, molasses, coffee, tea, and hides "whenever, and so often" as he should be satisfied that any country producing and exporting those products imposed duties on the agricultural products of the United States that he deemed to be "reciprocally unequal and unreasonable. . . ." The section then specified the duties to be imposed on those products during any such suspension.

The Court . . . identifies three critical differences between the power to suspend the exemption from import duties and the power to cancel portions of a duly enacted statute. First, the exercise of the suspension power was contingent upon a condition that did not exist when the Tariff Act was passed: the imposition of "reciprocally unequal and unreasonable" import duties by other countries. In contrast, the exercise of the cancellation power within five days after the enactment of the Balanced Budget and Tax Reform Acts necessarily was based on the same conditions that Congress evaluated when it passed those statutes. Second, under the Tariff Act, when the President determined that the contingency had arisen, he had a duty to suspend; in contrast, while it is true that the President was required by the Act to make three determinations before he canceled a provision, those determinations did not qualify his discretion to cancel or not to cancel. Finally, whenever the President suspended an exemption under the Tariff Act, he was executing the policy that Congress had embodied in the statute. In contrast, whenever the President cancels an item of new direct spending or a limited tax benefit he is rejecting the policy judgment made by Congress and relying on his own policy judgment.

Thus, the conclusion in *Field* v. *Clark* that the suspensions mandated by the Tariff Act were not exercises of legislative power does not undermine our opinion that cancellations pursuant to the Line Item Veto Act are the functional equivalent of partial repeals of Acts of Congress that fail to satisfy Article I, section 7.

The Government's reliance upon other tariff and import statutes . . . that contain provisions similar to the one challenged in *Field* is unavailing for the same reasons. . . . The cited statutes all relate to foreign trade, and this Court has recognized that in the foreign affairs arena, the President has "a degree of discretion and freedom from statutory restriction which would not be admissible were domestic affairs alone involved." *United States* v. *Curtiss Wright Export Corp.* (1936). More important, when enacting the statutes discussed in *Field,* Congress itself made the decision to suspend or repeal the particular provisions at issue upon the occurrence of particular events subsequent to enactment, and it left only the determination of whether such events occurred up to the President. The Line Item Veto Act authorizes the President himself to effect the repeal of laws, for his own policy reasons, without observing the procedures set out in Article I, section 7. The fact that Congress intended such a result is of no moment. Although Congress presumably anticipated that the President might cancel some of the items in the Balanced Budget Act and in the Taxpayer Relief Act, Congress cannot alter the procedures set out in Article I, section 7, without amending the Constitution.

Neither are we persuaded by the Government's contention that the President's authority to cancel new direct spending and tax benefit items is no greater than his traditional authority to decline to spend appropriated funds. . . . The critical difference between this statute and all of its predecessors . . . is that this Act gives the President the unilateral power to change the text of duly enacted statutes. None of the Act's predecessors could even arguably have been construed to authorize such a change.

## VI

[W]e express no opinion about the wisdom of the procedures authorized by the Line Item Veto Act. Many members of both major political parties who have served in the Legislative and the Executive Branches have long advocated the enactment of such procedures for the purpose of "ensur[ing] greater fiscal accountability in Washington." . . . [But] if there is to be a new procedure in which the President will play a different role in determining the final text of what may "become a law," such change must come not by legislation but through the amendment procedures set forth in Article V of the Constitution.

The judgment of the District Court is affirmed.

*It is so ordered.*

JUSTICE SCALIA, with whom JUSTICE O'CONNOR joins, and with whom JUSTICE BREYER joins as to Part III, concurring in part and dissenting in part.

Today the Court acknowledges the "overriding and time-honored concern about keeping the Judiciary's power within its proper constitutional sphere." It proceeds, however, to ignore the prescribed statutory limits of our jurisdiction by permitting the expedited-review provisions of the Line Item Veto Act to be invoked by persons who are not "individual[s]," and to ignore the constitutional limits of our jurisdiction by permitting one party to challenge the Government's denial to another party of favorable tax treatment from which the first party might, but just as likely might not, gain a concrete benefit. In my view, the Snake River appellees lack standing to challenge the President's cancellation of the "limited tax benefit," and the constitutionality of that action should not be addressed. I think the New York appellees have standing to challenge the President's cancellation of an "item of new direct spending"; I believe we have statutory authority (other than the expedited-review provision) to address that challenge; but unlike the Court I find the President's cancellation of spending items to be entirely in accord with the Constitution.

I

The Court's unrestrained zeal to reach the merits of this case is evident in its disregard of the statute's expedited review provision, which extends that special procedure to "[a]ny Member of Congress or any individual adversely affected by [the Act]." With the exception of Mike Cranney, a natural person, the appellees—corporations, cooperatives, and governmental entities—are not "individuals" under any accepted usage of that term. Worse still, the first provision of the United States Code confirms that insofar as this word is concerned, Congress speaks English like the rest of us: "In determining the meaning of any Act of Congress, unless the context indicates otherwise . . . the wor[d] 'person' . . . include[s] corporations, companies, associations, firms, partnerships, societies, and joint stock companies, as well as individuals." And doubly worse, one of the definitional provisions of this very Act expressly distinguishes "individuals" from "persons."

The Court majestically sweeps the plain language of the statute aside, declaring that "[t]here is no plausible reason why Congress would have intended to provide for such special treatment of actions filed by natural persons and to have precluded entirely jurisdiction over comparable cases brought by corporate persons." Indeed, the Court says, it would be "absurd" for Congress to have done so. But Congress treats individuals more favorably than corporations and other associations *all the time.* There is nothing whatever extraordinary—and surely nothing so bizarre as to permit this Court to declare a "scrivener's error"—in believing that individuals will suffer more seriously from delay in the receipt of "vetoed" benefits or tax savings than corporations will, and therefore according individuals (but not corporations) expedited review. It may be unlikely that this is what Congress actually had in mind; but it is what Congress said, it is not so absurd as to be an obvious mistake, and it is therefore the law.

II

Not only must we be satisfied that we have statutory jurisdiction to hear this case; we must be satisfied that we have jurisdiction under Article III. "To meet the standing requirements of Article III, '[a] plaintiff must allege *personal injury* fairly traceable to the defendant's allegedly unlawful conduct and likely to be redressed by the requested relief.' " *Raines,* 521 U.S., at ___, quoting *Allen* v. *Wright,* 468 U.S. 737, 751 (1984).

In the first action before us, appellees Snake River Potato Growers, Inc. (Snake River) and Mike Cranney, Snake River's Director and Vice-Chairman, challenge the constitutionality of the President's cancellation of section 968 of the Taxpayer Relief Act of 1997. The Snake River appellees have standing, in the Court's view, because section 968 gave them "the equivalent of a statutory 'bargaining chip,' " and "[b]y depriving them of their statutory bargaining chip, the cancellation inflicted a sufficient likelihood of economic injury to establish standing under our precedents." It is unclear whether the Court means that deprivation of a "bargaining chip" itself suffices for standing, or that such deprivation suffices in the present case because it creates a likelihood of economic injury. The former is wrong as a matter of law, and the latter is wrong as a matter of fact, on the facts alleged. . . .

[E]ven if harm to one's bargaining position *were* a legally cognizable injury, Snake River has not alleged, as it must, facts sufficient to demonstrate that *it personally* has suffered that injury. See *Warth* v. *Seldin,* 422 U.S. 490 (1975). Snake River has presented no evidence to show that it was engaged in bargaining, and that that bargaining was impaired by the President's cancellation of section 968. [A]ll we know from the record is that Snake River had two discussions with IPP concerning the sale of its processing facility on the tax deferred basis the Act would allow; that IPP was interested; and that Snake River ended the discussions after the President's action. On these facts—which never even bring things to the *point* of bargaining—it is pure conjecture to say that Snake River suffered an impaired bargaining position. As we have said many times, conjectural or hypothetical injuries do not suffice for Article III standing. See *Lujan* v. *Defenders of Wildlife,* 504 U.S. 555 (1992).

Nor has Snake River demonstrated, as the Court finds, that "the cancellation inflicted a sufficient likelihood of economic injury to establish standing under our precedents." Presumably the economic injury the Court has in mind in Snake River's loss of a bargain purchase of a processing plant. But there is no evidence, and indeed not even an allegation, that before the President's action such a purchase was *likely*. . . . All we know is that a potential seller was "interested" in talking about the subject before the President's action, and that after the President's action Snake River itself decided to proceed no further. If this establishes a "likelihood" that Snake River would have made a bargain purchase but for the President's action, or even a "likelihood" that the President's action rendered "more difficult" a purchase that was realistically within Snake River's grasp, then we must adopt for our standing jurisprudence a new definition of likely: "plausible."

The closest case the Court can appeal to as precedent for its finding of standing is *Bryant* v. *Yellen,* 447 U.S. 352 (1980). Even on its own terms, *Bryant* is distinguishable. . . . More fundamentally, however, the reasoning of *Bryant* should not govern the present case because it represents a crabbed view of the standing doctrine that has been superseded. *Bryant* was decided at the tail-end of "an era in which it was thought that the only function of the constitutional requirement of standing was 'to assure that concrete adverseness which sharpens the presentation of issues,' " *Spencer* v. *Kemma,* 523 U.S. ____, ____ (1998), quoting *Baker* v, *Carr,* 369 U.S. 186 (1962). Thus, the *Bryant* Court ultimately afforded the respondents standing simply because they "had a sufficient stake in the outcome of the controversy," not because they had demonstrated injury in fact, causation and redressability. "That parsimonious view of the function of Article III standing has since yielded to the acknowledgement that the constitutional requirement is a 'means of "defin[ing] the role assigned to the judiciary in a tripartite allocation of power," ' and 'a part of the basic charter . . . provid[ing] for the interaction between [the federal] government and the governments of the several States,' " *Spencer,* quoting *Valley Forge Christian College* v. *Americans United for Separation of Church and State,* 454 U.S. 464 (1982). While Snake River in the present case may indeed have enough of a "stake" to assure adverseness, the matter it brings before us is inappropriate for our resolution because its allegations do not establish an injury in fact, attributable to the Presidential action it challenges, and remediable by this Court's invalidation of that Presidential action.

Because, in my view, Snake River has no standing to bring this suit, we have no jurisdiction to resolve its challenge to the President's authority to cancel a "limited tax benefit."

## III

The Presentment Clause requires, in relevant part, that "[e]very Bill which shall have passed the House of Representatives and the Senate, shall, before it becomes a Law, be presented to the President of the United States; If he approves he shall sign it, but if not he shall return it." There is no question that enactment of the Balanced Budget Act complied with these requirements: the House and Senate passed the bill, and the President signed it into law. It was only *after* the requirements of the Presentment Clause had been satisfied that the President exercised his authority under the Line Item Veto Act to cancel the spending item. Thus, the Court's problem with the Act is not that it authorizes the President to veto parts of a bill and sign others into law, but rather that it authorizes him to "cancel"—prevent from "having legal force or effect"—certain parts of duly enacted statutes.

Article I, section 7 of the Constitution obviously prevents the President from cancelling a law that Congress has not authorized him to cancel. But that is not this case. It was certainly arguable, as an original matter, that Art. I, sec. 7 also prevents the President from cancelling a law which itself *authorizes* the President to cancel it. But as the Court acknowledges, that argument has long since been made and rejected. In 1809, Congress passed a law authorizing the

President to cancel trade restrictions against Great Britain and France if either revoked edicts directed at the United States. Joseph Story regarded the conferral of that authority as entirely unremarkable in *The Orono,* 18 F. Cas. 830 (No. 10,585) (CCD Mass. 1812). The Tariff Act of 1890 authorized the President to "suspend, by proclamation to that effect" certain of its provisions if he determined that other countries were imposing "reciprocally unequal and unreasonable" duties. This Court upheld the constitutionality of that Act in *Field* v. *Clark,* 143 U.S. 649 (1892), reciting the history since 1798 of statutes conferring upon the President the power to "discontinue the prohibitions and restraints hereby enacted and declared, suspend the operation of the aforesaid act," and "declare the provisions of this act to be inoperative."

As much as the Court goes on about Art. I, sec. 7, therefore, that provision does not demand the result the Court reaches. It no more categorically prohibits the Executive *reduction* of congressional dispositions in the course of implementing statutes that authorize such reduction, than it categorically prohibits the Executive *augmentation* of congressional dispositions in the course of implementing statutes that authorize such augmentation—generally known as substantive rulemaking. There are, to be sure, limits upon the former just as there are limits upon the latter—and I am prepared to acknowledge that the limits upon the former may be much more severe. Those limits are established, however, not by some categorical prohibition of Art. I, sec. 7, which our cases conclusively disprove, but by what has come to be known as the doctrine of unconstitutional delegation of legislative authority: When authorized Executive reduction or augmentation is allowed to go too far, it usurps the nondelegable function of Congress and violates the separation of powers.

It is this doctrine, and not the Presentment Clause, that was discussed in the *Field* opinion, and it is this doctrine, and not the Presentment Clause, that is the issue presented by the statute before us here. That is why the Court is correct to distinguish prior authorizations of Executive cancellation, such as the one involved in *Field,* on the ground that they were contingent upon an Executive finding of fact, and on the ground that they related to the field of foreign affairs, an area where the President has a special "degree of discretion and freedom." These distinctions have nothing to do with whether the details of Art. I, sec. 7 have been complied with, but everything to do with whether the authorizations went too far by transferring to the Executive a degree of political, law-making power that our traditions demand be retained by the Legislative Branch.

I turn, then, to the crux of the matter: whether Congress's authorizing the President to cancel an item of spending gives him a power that our history and traditions show must reside exclusively in the Legislative Branch. I may note, to begin with, that the Line Item Veto Act is not the first statute to authorize the President to "cancel" spending items. In *Bowsher* v. *Synar,* 478 U.S. 714 (1986), we addressed the constitutionality of the Balanced Budget and Emergency Deficit Control Act of 1985, which required the President, if the federal budget deficit exceeded a certain amount, to issue a "sequestration" order mandating spending reductions specified by the Comptroller General. The effect of sequestration was that "amounts sequestered . . . shall be *permanently cancelled.*" We held that the Act was unconstitutional, not because it impermissibly gave the Executive legislative power, but because it gave the Comptroller General, an officer of the Legislative Branch over whom Congress retained removal power, "the ultimate authority to determine the budget cuts to be made, functions . . . *plainly entailing execution of the law in constitutional terms.*" The President's discretion under the Line Item Veto Act is certainly broader than the Comptroller General's discretion was under the 1985 Act, but it is no broader than the discretion traditionally granted the President in his execution of spending laws.

Insofar as the degree of political, "lawmaking" power conferred upon the Executive is concerned, there is not a dime's worth of difference between Congress's authorizing the President to *cancel* a spending item, and Congress's authorizing money to be spent on a particular item at the President's discretion. And the latter has been done since the Founding of the Nation. . . . The constitutionality of such appropriations has never seriously been questioned. Rather, "[t]hat Congress has wide discretion in the matter of prescribing details of expenditures for which it appropriates must, of course, be plain. Appropriations and other acts of Congress are replete with instances of general appropriations of large amounts, to be allotted and expended as directed by designated government agencies." *Cincinnati Soap Co.* v. *United States,* 301 U.S. 308 (1937).

The short of the matter is this: Had the Line Item Veto Act authorized the President to "decline to spend" any item of spending contained in the Balanced Budget Act of 1997, there is not the slightest doubt that authorization would have been constitutional. What the Line Item Veto Act does instead—authorizing the President to "cancel" an item of spending—is technically different. But the technical difference does *not* relate to the technicalities of the Presentment Clause, which have been fully complied with; and the doctrine of unconstitutional delegation, which *is at issue here,* is *preeminently* not a doctrine of technicalities. The title of the Line Item Veto Act, which was perhaps designed to simplify for public comprehension, or perhaps merely to comply with the terms of a campaign pledge, has succeeded in faking out the Supreme Court. The President's action it authorizes in fact is not a line-item veto and thus does not offend Art. I, sec. 7; and insofar as the substance of that action is concerned, it is no different from what Congress has permitted the President to do since the formation of the Union.

For the foregoing reasons, I respectfully dissent.

# *Myers* v. *United States*

**272 U.S. 52, 47 S. Ct. 21, 71 L. Ed. 160 (1926)**

According to an act passed by Congress in 1876, "Postmasters of the first, second, and third classes shall be appointed and may be removed by the President by and with the advice and consent of the Senate, and shall hold their offices for four years unless sooner removed or suspended according to law." Myers was appointed to a first-class postmastership under this statute in 1917. The postmaster general, at the direction of President Woodrow Wilson, removed Myers from his post in 1920, prior to the expiration of Myers's term and without Senate approval. Myers protested his removal and sued to recover his lost salary in the U.S. Court of Claims. When the court of claims sustained the removal, the case was appealed to the Supreme Court. *Opinion of the Court: Taft, Sutherland, Butler, Sanford, Stone. Dissenting opinions: Holmes; Brandeis; McReynolds.*

MR. CHIEF JUSTICE TAFT delivered the opinion of the Court.

This case presents the question whether under the Constitution the President has the exclusive power of removing executive officers of the United States whom he has appointed by and with the advice and consent of the Senate. . . .

The question where the power of removal of executive officers appointed by the President by and with the advice and consent of the Senate was vested, was presented early in the first session of the First Congress. There is no express provision respecting removals in the Constitution, except as Section 4 of Article II, above quoted, provides for removal from office by impeachment. . . .

Mr. Madison and his associates in the discussion in the House dwelt at length upon the necessity there was for construing Article II to give the President the sole power of removal in his responsibility for the conduct of the executive branch, and enforced this by emphasizing his duty expressly declared in the third section of the Article to "take care that the laws be faithfully executed." . . .

The vesting of the executive power in the President was essentially a grant of the power to execute the laws. But the President alone and unaided could not execute the laws. He must execute them by the assistance of subordinates. This view has since been repeatedly affirmed by this Court. . . . As he is charged specifically to take care that they be faithfully executed, the reasonable implication, even in the absence of express words, was that as part of his executive power he should select those who were to act for him under his direction in the execution of the laws. The further implication must be, in the absence of any express limitation respecting removals, that as his selection of administrative officers is essential to the execution of the laws by him, so must be his power of removing those for whom he can not continue to be responsible. . . .

The power to prevent the removal of an officer who has served under the President is different from the authority to consent to or reject his appointment. When a nomination is made, it may be presumed that the Senate is, or may become, as well advised as to the fitness of the nominee as the President, but in the nature of things like defects in ability or intelligence or loyalty in the administration of the law of one who has served as an officer under the President, are facts as to which the President, or his trusted subordinates, must be better informed than the Senate, and the power to remove him may, therefore, be regarded as confined, for very sound and practical reasons, to the governmental authority which has administrative control. The power of removal is incident to the power of appointment, not to the power of advising and consenting to appointment, and when the grant of the executive power is enforced by the express mandate to take care that the laws be faithfully executed, it emphasizes the necessity for including within the executive power as conferred the exclusive power of removal. . . .

Made responsible under the Constitution for the effective enforcement of the law, the President needs as an indispensable aid to meet it the disciplinary influence upon those who act under him of a reserve power of removal. . . .

In all such cases, the discretion to be exercised is that of the President in determining the national public interest and in directing the action to be taken by his executive subordinates to protect it. In this field his cabinet officers must do his will. He must place in each member of his official family, and his chief executive subordinates, implicit faith. The moment that he loses confidence in the intelligence, ability, judgment or loyalty of any one of them, he must have the power to remove him without delay. To require him to file charges and submit them to the consideration of the Senate might make impossible that unity and co-ordination in executive administration essential to effective action.

The duties of the heads of departments and bureaus in which the discretion of the President is exercised and which we have described, are the most important in the whole field of executive action of the Government. There is nothing in the Constitution which permits a distinction between the removal of the head of a department or a bureau, when he discharges a political duty of the President or exercises his direction, and the removal of executive officers engaged in the discharge of their other normal duties. The imperative reasons requiring an unrestricted power to remove the most important of his subordinates in their most important duties must, therefore, control the interpretation of the Constitution as to all appointed by him.

But this is not to say that there are not strong reasons why the President should have a like power to remove his appointees charged with other duties than those above described. The ordinary duties of officers prescribed by statute come under the general administrative control of the President by virtue of the general grant to him of the executive power, and he may properly supervise and guide their construction of the statutes under which they act in order to secure that unitary and uniform execution of the laws which Article II of the Constitution evidently contemplated in vesting general executive power in the President alone. Laws are often passed with specific provision for the adoption of regulations by a department or bureau head to make the law workable and effective. The ability and judgment manifested by the official thus empowered, as well as his energy and stimulation of his subordinates, are subjects which the President must consider and supervise in his administrative control. Finding such officers to be negligent and inefficient, the President should have the power to remove them. Of course there may be duties so peculiarly and specifically committed to the discretion of a particular officer as to raise a question whether the President may overrule or revise the officer's interpretation of his statutory duty in a particular instance. Then there may be duties of a quasi-judicial character imposed on executive officers and members of executive tribunals whose decisions after hearing affect interests of individuals, the discharge of which the President can not in a particular case properly influence or control. But even in such a case he may consider the decision after its rendition as a reason for removing the officer, on the ground that the discretion regularly entrusted to that officer by statute has not been on the whole intelligently or wisely exercised. Otherwise he does not discharge his own constitutional duty of seeing that the laws be faithfully executed. . . .

We have devoted much space to this discussion and decision of the question of the Presidential power of removal in the First Congress, not because a Congressional conclusion on a constitutional issue is conclusive, but, first, because of our agreement with the reasons upon which it was avowedly based; second, because this was the decision of the First Congress, on a question of primary importance in the organization of the Government, made within two years after the Constitutional Convention and within a much shorter time after its ratification: and, third, because that Congress numbered among its leaders those who had been members of the Convention. It must necessarily constitute a precedent upon which many future laws supplying the machinery of the new Government would be based, and, if erroneous, it would be likely to evoke dissent and departure in future Congresses. It would come at once before the executive branch of the Government for compliance, and might well be brought before the judicial branch for a test of its validity. As we shall see, it was soon accepted as a final decision of the question by all branches of the Government.

An argument *ab inconvenienti* has been made against our conclusion in favor of the executive power of removal by the President, without the consent of the Senate—that it will open the door to a reintroduction of the spoils system. . . . Reform in the federal civil service was begun by the Civil Service Act of 1883. It has been developed from that time, so that the classified service now includes a vast majority of all the civil officers. It may still be enlarged by further legislation. The independent power of removal by the President alone, under present conditions, works no practical interference with the merit system. Political appointments of inferior officers are still maintained in one important class, that of the first, second and third class postmasters, collecters of internal revenue, marshals, collectors of customs and other officers of that kind, distributed through the country. They are appointed by the President with the consent of the Senate. It is the intervention of the Senate in their appointment, and not in their removal, which prevents their classification into the merit system. If such appointments were vested in the heads of departments to which they belong, they could be entirely removed from politics, and that is what a number of Presidents have recommended. . . .

For the reasons given, we must therefore hold that the provision of the law of 1876, by which the unrestricted power of removal of first class postmasters is denied to the President, is in violation of the Constitution, and invalid.

*Judgment affirmed.*

MR. JUSTICE HOLMES, dissenting. . . .

The arguments drawn from the executive power of the President, and from his duty to appoint officers of the United States (when Congress does not vest the appointment elsewhere), to take care that the laws be faithfully executed, and to commission all officers of the United States, seem to me spider's webs inadequate to control the dominant facts.

We have to deal with an office that owes its existence to Congress and that Congress may abolish tomorrow. Its duration and the pay attached to it while it lasts depend on Congress alone. Congress alone confers on the President the power to appoint to it and at any time may transfer the power to other hands. With such power over its own creation, I have no more trouble in believing that Congress has power to prescribe a term of life for it free from any interference than I have in accepting the undoubted power of Congress to decree its end. I have equally little trouble in accepting its power to prolong the tenure of an incumbent until Congress or the Senate shall have assented to his removal. The duty of the President to see that the laws be executed is a duty that does not go beyond the laws or require him to achieve more than Congress sees fit to leave within his power.

MR. JUSTICE BRANDEIS, dissenting. . . .

The ability to remove a subordinate executive officer, being an essential of effective government, will, in the absence of express constitutional provision to the contrary, be deemed to have been vested in some person or body. . . . But it is not a power inherent in a chief executive. The President's power of removal from statutory civil inferior offices, like the power of appointment to them, comes immediately from Congress. It is true that the exercise of the power of removal is said to be an executive act; and that when the Senate grants or withholds consent to a removal by the President, it participates in an executive act. But the Constitution has confessedly granted to Congress the legislative power to create offices, and to prescribe the tenure thereof; and it has not in terms denied to Congress the power to control removals. To prescribe the tenure involves prescribing the conditions under which incumbency shall cease. For the possibility of removal is a condition or qualification of the tenure. When Congress provides that the incumbent shall hold the office for four years unless sooner removed with the consent of the Senate, it prescribes the term of the tenure. . . .

To imply a grant to the President of the uncontrollable power of removal from statutory inferior executive offices involves an unnecessary and indefensible limitation upon the constitutional power of Congress to fix the tenure of inferior statutory offices. That such a limitation cannot be justified on the ground of necessity is demonstrated by the practice of our governments, state and national. . . .

The historical data submitted present a legislative practice, established by concurrent affirmative action of Congress and the President, to make consent of the Senate a condition of removal from statutory inferior, civil, executive offices to which the appointment is made for a fixed term by the President with such consent. They show that the practice has existed, without interruption, continuously for the last fifty-eight years; that, throughout this period, it has governed a great majority of all such offices; that the legislation applying the removal clause specifically to the office of postmaster was enacted more than half a century ago; and that recently the practice has, with the President's approval, been extended to several newly created offices. The data show further, that the insertion of the removal clause in acts creating inferior civil offices with fixed tenures is part of the broader legislative practice, which has prevailed since the formation of our Government, to restrict or regulate in many ways both removal from and nomination to such offices. A persistent legislative practice which involves a delimitation of the respective powers of Congress and the President, and which has been so established and maintained, should be deemed tantamount to judicial construction, in the absence of any decision by any court to the contrary. . . .

The persuasive effect of this legislative practice is strengthened by the fact that no instance has been found, even in the earlier period of our history, of concurrent affirmative action of Congress and the President which is inconsistent with the legislative practice of the last fifty-eight years to impose the removal clause. . . .

The separation of the powers of government did not make each branch completely autonomous. It left each, in some measure, dependent upon the others, as it left to each power to exercise, in some respects, functions in their nature executive, legislative and judicial. Obviously the President cannot secure full execution of the laws if Congress denies to him adequate means of doing so. . . . The President performs his full constitutional duty, if, with the means and instruments provided by Congress and within the limitations prescribed by it, he uses his best endeavors to secure the faithful execution of the laws enacted. . . .

The doctrine of the separation of powers was adopted by the Convention of 1787, not to promote efficiency but to preclude the exercise of arbitrary power. The purpose was, not to avoid friction, but, by means of the inevitable friction incident to the distribution of the governmental powers among three departments, to save the people from autocracy. . . . Nothing in support of the claim of uncontrollable power can be inferred from the silence of the Convention of 1787 on the subject of removal. For the outstanding fact remains that every specific proposal to confer such uncontrollable power upon the President was rejected. In America, as in England, the conviction prevailed then that the people must look to representative assemblies for the protection of their liberties. And protection of the individual, even if he be an official, from the arbitrary or capricious exercise of power was then believed to be an essential of free government.

## *Morrison* v. *Olson*

**487 U.S. 654, 108 S. Ct. 2597, 101 L. Ed. 2d 569 (1988)**

The Ethics in Government Act of 1978 (Act) provides for the appointment of an independent counsel to investigate and prosecute violations of federal criminal laws by high-ranking officials of the executive branch. The executive branch's control over the independent counsel is quite limited: the counsel is appointed by a Special Division of the Court of Appeals (District of Columbia Circuit) and can be removed by the attorney general only for "good cause."

The constitutional challenge to the Act arose out of a congressional investigation of the Environmental Protection Agency (EPA). In 1982 two subcommittees of the House of Representatives issued subpoenas directing the EPA to produce documents relating to its implementation of the "Superfund Law." At that time Theodore Olson was assistant attorney general for the Office of Legal Counsel, Edward Schmults deputy attorney general, and Carol Dinkins assistant attorney general for the Land and Resources Division. President Reagan ordered the administrator of EPA to invoke executive privilege to withhold certain documents, but after the House voted to hold the administrator in contempt, a compromise was reached whereby the House obtained limited access to the documents. In 1984 the House Judiciary Committee began an investigation into the controversy over the withheld documents, at which Olson testified. Following the investigation, the committee issued a report which suggested that Olson had given false and misleading testimony and that Schmults and Dinkins had wrongfully withheld documents, thereby obstructing the investigation. The chairman of the Judiciary Committee sent the report to Attorney General Edwin Meese, requesting that he seek the appointment of an independent counsel to investigate the allegations.

Under the Act, the attorney general is obliged to request appointment of an independent counsel if there are "reasonable grounds" to believe further investigation or prosecution is warranted. When Meese did so, the Special Division designated Alexia Morrison as independent counsel. Morrison caused a grand jury to issue subpoenas to Olson, Schmults, and Dinkins, who moved to quash the subpoenas, claiming that the independent counsel provisions of the Act were unconstitutional and that Morrison therefore had no authority to proceed. The District Court rejected their motion, but the Court of Appeals reversed, ruling the Act unconstitutional, and Morrison appealed that decision to the Supreme Court. *Opinion of the Court: Rehnquist, Brennan, White, Marshall, Blackmun, Stevens, O'Connor. Dissenting opinion: Scalia.*

CHIEF JUSTICE REHNQUIST delivered the opinion of the Court. . . .

This case presents us with a challenge to the independent counsel provisions of the Ethics in Government Act of 1978. . . . We hold today that these provisions of the Act do not violate the Appointments Clause of the Constitution, Art II, § 2, cl 2, or the limitations of Article III, nor do they impermissibly interfere with the President's authority under Article II in violation of the constitutional principle of separation of powers. . . .

The Appointments Clause of Article II reads as follows:

[The President] shall nominate, and by and with the Advice and Consent of the Senate, shall appoint Ambassadors, other public Ministers and Consuls, Judges of the supreme Court, and all other Officers of the United States, whose Appointments are not herein otherwise provided for, and which shall be established by Law: but the Congress may by Law vest the Appointment of such inferior Officers, as they think proper, in the President alone, in the Courts of Law, or in the Heads of Departments." . . .

. . . The initial question is, accordingly, whether appellant is an "inferior" or a "principal" officer. . . .

The line between "inferior" and "principal" officers is one that is far from clear, and the Framers provided little guidance into where it should be drawn. . . . We need not attempt here to decide exactly where the line falls between the two types of officers, because in our view appellant clearly falls on the "inferior officer" side of that line. Several factors lead to this conclusion.

First, appellant is subject to removal by a higher Executive Branch official. Although appellant may not be "subordinate" to the Attorney General (and the President) insofar as she possesses a degree of independent discretion to exercise the powers delegated to her under the Act, the fact that she can be removed by the Attorney General indicates that she is to some degree "inferior" in rank and authority. Second, appellant is empowered by the Act to perform only certain, limited duties. An independent counsel's role is restricted primarily to investigation and, if appropriate, prosecution for certain federal crimes. Admittedly, the Act delegates to appellant "full power and independent authority to exercise all investigative and prosecutorial functions and powers of the Department of Justice," but this grant of authority does not include any authority to formulate policy for the Government or the Executive Branch, nor does it give appellant any administrative duties outside of those necessary to operate her office. The Act specifically provides that in policy matters appellant is to comply to the extent possible with the policies of the Department. . . .

Third, appellant's office is limited in jurisdiction. Not only is the Act itself restricted in applicability to certain federal officials suspected of certain serious federal crimes, but an independent counsel can only act within the scope of the jurisdiction that has been granted by the Special Division pursuant to a request by the Attorney General. Finally, appellant's office is limited in tenure. There is concededly no time limit on the appointment of a particular counsel. Nonetheless, the office of independent counsel is "temporary" in the sense that an independent counsel is appointed essentially to accomplish a single task, and when that task is over the office is terminated, either by the counsel herself or by action of the Special Division. Unlike other prosecutors, appellant has no ongoing responsibilities that extend beyond the accomplishment of the mission that she was appointed for and authorized by the Special Division to undertake. In our view, these factors relating to the "ideas of tenure, duration . . . and duties" of the independent counsel, . . . are sufficient to establish that appellant is an "inferior" officer in the constitutional sense. . . . Appellees argue that even if appellant is an "inferior" officer, the Clause does not empower Congress to place the power to appoint such an office outside the Executive Branch. They contend that the Clause does not contemplate congressional authorization of "interbranch appointments," in which an officer of one branch is appointed by officers of another branch. The relevant language of the Appointments Clause is worth repeating. It reads: ". . . but the Congress may by Law vest the Appointment of such inferior Officers, as they think proper, in the President alone, in the courts of Law, or in the Heads of Departments." On its face, the language of this "excepting clause" admits of no limitation on interbranch appointments. Indeed, the inclusion of "as they think proper" seems clearly to give Congress significant discretion to determine whether it is "proper" to vest the appointment of, for example, executive officials in the "courts of Law." . . .

We do not mean to say that Congress' power to provide for interbranch appointments of "inferior officers" is unlimited. In addition to separation of powers concerns, which would arise if such provisions for appointment had the potential to impair the constitutional functions assigned to one of the branches, [*Ex Parte*] Siebold [1880] itself suggested that Congress' decision to vest the appointment power in the courts would be improper if there was some "incongruity" between the functions normally performed by the courts and the performance of their duty to appoint. . . . In this case, however, we do not think it impermissible for Congress to vest the power to appoint independent counsels in a specially created federal court. . . . Congress of course was concerned when it created the office of independent counsel with the conflicts of interest that could arise in situations when the Executive Branch is called upon to investigate its own high-ranking officers. If it were to remove the appointing authority from the Executive Branch, the most logical place to put it was in the Judicial Branch. In the light of the Act's provision making the judges of the Special Division ineligible to participate in any matters relating to an independent counsel they have appointed . . . we do not think that appointment of the independent counsels by the court runs afoul of the constitutional limitation on "incongruous" interbranch appointments. . . .

We now turn to consider whether the Act is invalid under the constitutional principle of separation of powers. . . .

Two Terms ago we had occasion to consider whether it was consistent with the separation of powers for Congress to pass a statute that authorized a government official who is removable only by Congress to participate in what we found to be "executive powers." *Bowsher* v. *Synar*, . . . (1986). We held in *Bowsher* that "Congress cannot reserve for itself the power of removal of an officer charged with the execution of the laws except by impeachment." . . . A primary antecedent for this ruling was our 1926 decision in *Myers* v. *United States* . . . .

Unlike both *Bowsher* and *Myers*, this case does not involve an attempt by Congress itself to gain a role in the removal of executive officials other than its established powers of impeachment and conviction. The Act instead puts the removal power squarely in the hands of the Executive Branch; an independent counsel may be removed from office, "only by the personal action of the Attorney General, and only for good cause." . . . There is no requirement of congressional approval of the Attorney General's removal decision, though the decision is subject to judicial review. . . . In our view, the removal provisions of the Act make this case more analogous to *Humphrey's Executor* v. *United States* . . . (1935), and *Wiener* v. *United States* . . . (1958) [rulings denying presidential power to remove members of independent commissions before their terms expired], than to *Myers* or *Bowsher*. . . .

We undoubtedly did rely on the terms "quasi-legislative" and "quasi-judicial" to distinguish the officials involved in *Humphrey's Executor* and *Wiener* from those in *Myers*, but our present considered view is that the determination of whether the Constitution allows Congress to impose a "good cause"-type restriction on the President's power to remove an official cannot be made to turn on whether or not that official is classified as "purely executive." . . . But the real question is whether the removal restrictions are of such a nature that they impede the President's ability to perform his constitutional duty, and the functions of the officials in question must be analyzed in that light. . . . It is undeniable that the Act reduces the amount of control or supervision that the Attorney General and, through him, the President exercises over the investigation and prosecution of a certain class of alleged criminal activity. The Attorney General is not allowed to appoint the individual of his choice; he does not determine the counsel's jurisdiction; and his power to remove a counsel is limited. Nonetheless, the Act does give the Attorney General several means of supervising or controlling the prosecutorial powers that may be wielded by an independent counsel. Most importantly, the Attorney General retains the power to remove the counsel for "good cause," a power that we have already concluded provides the Executive with substantial ability to ensure that the laws are "faithfully executed" by an independent counsel. . . .

JUSTICE SCALIA, dissenting.

That is what this suit is about. Power. The allocation of power among Congress, the President and the courts in such fashion as to preserve the equilibrium the Constitution sought to establish—so that "a gradual concentration of the several powers in the same department," Federalist No. 51, p 321 (J. Madison), can effectively be resisted. Frequently an issue of this sort will come before the Court clad, so to speak, in sheep's clothing: the potential of the asserted principle to effect important change in the equilibrium of power is not immediately evident, and must be discerned by a careful and perceptive analysis. But this wolf comes as a wolf. . . .

. . . by the application of this statute in the present case, Congress has effectively compelled a criminal investigation of a high-level appointee of the President in connection with his actions arising out of a bitter power dispute between the President and the Legislative Branch. Mr. Olson may or may not be guilty of a crime; we do not know. But we do know that the investigation of him has been commenced, not necessarily because the President or his authorized subordinates believe it is the interest of the United States, in the sense that it warrants the diversion of resources from other efforts, and is worth the cost in money and in possible damage to other governmental interests; and not even, leaving aside those normally considered factors, because the President or his authorized subordinates necessarily believe that an investigation is likely to unearth a violation worth prosecuting; but only because the Attorney General cannot affirm, as Congress demands, that there are *no reasonable grounds to believe* that further investigation is warranted. The decisions regarding the scope of that further investigation, its duration, and, finally, whether or not prosecution should ensue, are likewise beyond the control of the President and his subordinates. . . .

If to describe this case is not to decide it, the concept of a government of separate and coordinate powers no longer has meaning. . . .

. . . Art II, § 1, cl 1 of the Constitution provides:

> The executive Power shall be vested in a President of the United States.

. . . this does not mean *some of* the executive power, but *all of* the executive power. It seems to me, therefore, that the decision of the Court of Appeals invalidating the present statute must be upheld on fundamental separation-of-powers principles if the following two questions are answered affirmatively: (1) Is the conduct of a criminal prosecution (and of an investigation to decide whether to prosecute) the exercise of purely executive power? (2) Does the statute deprive the President of the United States of exclusive control over the exercise of that power? Surprising to say, the Court appears to concede an affirmative answer to both questions, but seeks to avoid the inevitable conclusion that since the statute vests some purely executive power in a person who is not the President of the United States it is void. . . .

The utter incompatibility of the Court's approach with our constitutional traditions can be made more clear, perhaps, by applying it to the powers of the other two Branches. Is it conceivable that if Congress passed a statute depriving itself of less than full and entire control over some insignificant area of legislation, we would inquire whether the matter was "*so central* to the functioning of the Legislative Branch" as really to require complete control, or whether the statute gives Congress "*sufficient* control over the surrogate legislator to ensure that Congress is able to perform its constitutionally assigned duties"? Of course we would have none of that. Once we determined that a purely legislative power was at issue we would require it to be exercised, wholly and entirely, by Congress. Or to bring the point closer to home, consider a statute giving to non-Article III judges just a tiny bit of purely judicial power in a relatively insignificant field, with substantial control, though not total control, in the courts—perhaps "clear error" review, which would be a fair judicial equivalent of the Attorney General's "for cause" removal power here. Is there any doubt that we would not pause to inquire whether the matter was *"so central* to the functioning of the Judicial Branch" as really to require complete control, or whether we retained *"sufficient* control over the matters to be decided that we are able to perform our constitutionally assigned duties"? We would say that our "constitutionally assigned duties" include *complete* control over all exercises of the judicial power—or, as the plurality opinion said in *Northern Pipeline Construction Co.* v. *Marathon Pipe Line Co.* . . . (1982), that "[t]he inexorable command of [Article III] is clear and definite: The judicial power of the United States must be exercised by courts having the attributes prescribed in Art III." We should say here that the President's constitutionally assigned duties include *complete* control over investigation and prosecution of violations of the law, and that the inexorable command of Article II is clear and definite: the executive power must be vested in the President of the United States.

The Court has, nonetheless, replaced the clear constitutional prescription that the executive power belongs to the President with a "balancing test." What are the standards to determine how the balance is to be struck, that is, how much removal of presidential power is too much? Many countries of the world get along with an Executive that is much weaker than ours—in fact, entirely dependent upon the continued support of the legislature. Once we depart from the text of the Constitution, just where short of that do we stop? The most amazing feature of the Court's opinion is that it does not even purport to give an answer. It simply *announces,* with no analysis, that the ability to control the decision whether to investigate and prosecute the President's closest advisors, and indeed the President himself, is not "so central to the functioning of the Executive Branch" as to be constitutionally required to be within the President's control. . . . Evidently, the governing standard is to be what might be called the unfettered wisdom of a majority of this Court, revealed to an obedient people on a case-by-case basis. This is not only not the government of laws that the Constitution established; it is not a government of laws at all.

## *United States* v. *Nixon*

**418 U.S. 683, 94 S. Ct. 3090, 41 L. Ed. 2d 1039 (1974)**

On March 1, 1974, a federal grand jury returned indictments against Attorney General John Mitchell, presidential assistants H. R. Haldeman and John Ehrlichman, and four other officials, charging them with conspiracy to defraud the government and obstruction of justice. The grand jury also named President Richard Nixon as an unindicted co-conspirator. Special Prosecutor Leon Jaworski obtained from the trial court a subpoena directing the president to produce as evidence certain tape recordings and memoranda of conversations held in the White House. Although he surrendered some of the subpoenaed materials, President Nixon refused to produce others, basing his right to refuse primarily on a claim of executive privilege. When the trial judge denied this claim, the president appealed the decision to the court of appeals. The special prosecutor petitioned the Supreme Court to expedite the matter by granting certiorari before the court of appeals reached a decision. The Supreme Court agreed to the prosecutor's request, heard oral argument in special session on July 8, and announced its decision on July 24. Six days later, the House Judiciary Committee voted articles of impeachment against the president. *Opinion of the Court: Burger, Douglas, Brennan, Stewart, White, Marshall, Blackmun, Powell. Not participating: Rehnquist.*

MR. CHIEF JUSTICE BURGER delivered the opinion of the Court. . . .

### Justiciability

In the District Court, the President's counsel argued that the court lacked jurisdiction to issue the subpoena because the matter was an intra-branch dispute between a subordinate and superior officer of the Executive Branch and hence not subject to judicial resolution. . . . Since the Executive Branch has exclusive authority and absolute discretion to decide whether to prosecute a case, it is contended that a President's decision is final in determining what evidence is to be used in a given criminal case. . . . The Special Prosecutor's demand for the items therefore presents, in the view of the President's counsel, a political question . . . . since it involves a "textually demonstrable" grant of power under Art. II. The mere assertion of a claim of an "intra-branch dispute," without more, has never operated to defeat federal jurisdiction. . . .

Our starting point is the nature of the proceeding for which the evidence is sought—here a pending criminal prosecution. . . . Under the authority of Art. II § 2, Congress has vested in the Attorney General the power to conduct the criminal litigation of the United States Government. . . . It has also vested in him the power to appoint subordinate officers to assist him in the discharge of his duties. . . . Acting pursuant to those statutes, the Attorney General has delegated the authority to represent the United States in these particular matters to a Special Prosecutor with unique authority and tenure. The regulation gives the Special Prosecutor explicit power to contest the invocation of executive privilege in the process of seeking evidence deemed relevant to the performance of these specially delegated duties. . . . So long as this regulation is extant it has the force of law. Here at issue is the production or nonproduction of specified evidence deemed by the Special Prosecutor to be relevant and admissible in a pending criminal case. It is sought by one official of the Executive Branch within the scope of his express authority; it is resisted by the Chief Executive on the ground of his duty to preserve the confidentiality of the communications of the President. Whatever the correct answer on the merits, these issues are "of a type which are traditionally justiciable."

### The Claim of Privilege

. . . we turn to the claim that the subpoena should be quashed because it demands "confidential conversations between a President and his close advisors that it would be inconsistent with the public interest to produce." . . . The first contention is a broad claim that the separation of powers doctrine precludes judicial review of a President's claim of privilege. The second contention is that if he does not prevail on the claim of absolute privilege, the court should hold as a matter of constitutional law that the privilege prevails over the subpoena *duces tecum.*

In the performance of assigned constitutional duties each branch of the Government must initially interpret the Constitution, and the interpretation of its powers by any branch is due great respect from the others. The President's counsel, as we have noted, reads the Constitution as providing an absolute privilege of confidentiality for all Presidential communications. Many decisions of this Court, however, have unequivocally reaffirmed the holding of *Marbury* v. *Madison* [1803] . . . that "it is emphatically the province and duty of the judicial department to say what the law is." . . .

In support of his claim of absolute privilege, the President's counsel urges two grounds, one of which is common to all governments and one of which is peculiar to our system of separation of powers. The first ground is the valid need for protection of communications between high Government officials and those who advise and assist them in the performance of their manifold duties; the importance of this confidentiality is too plain to require further discussion. Human experience teaches that those who expect public dissemination of their remarks may well temper candor with a concern for appearances and for their own interests to the detriment of the decisionmaking process. Whatever the nature of the privilege of confidentiality of Presidential communications in the exercise of Art. II powers, the privilege can be said to derive from the supremacy of each branch within its own assigned area of constitutional duties. Certain powers and privileges flow from the nature of enumerated powers; the protection of the confidentiality of Presidential communications has similar constitutional underpinnings and rests on the doctrine of separation of powers. Here it is argued that the independence of the Executive Branch within its own sphere . . . insulates a President from a judicial subpoena in an ongoing criminal prosecution, and thereby protects confidential Presidential communications.

However, neither the doctrine of separation of powers, nor the need for confidentiality of high-level communications, without more, can sustain an absolute, unqualified Presidential privilege of immunity from judicial process under all circumstances. The President's need for complete candor and objectivity from advisers calls for great deference from the courts. However, when the privilege depends solely on the broad, undifferentiated claim of public interest in the confidentiality of such conversations, a confrontation with other values arises. Absent a claim of need to protect military, diplomatic, or sensitive national security secrets, we find it difficult to accept the argument that even the very important interest in confidentiality of Presidential communications is significantly diminished by production of such material for *in camera* inspection with all the protection that a district court will be obliged to provide.

The impediment that an absolute, unqualified privilege would place in the way of the primary constitutional duty of the Judicial Branch to do justice in criminal prosecutions would plainly conflict with the function of the courts under Art. III. . .

Since we conclude that the legitimate needs of the judicial process may outweigh Presidential privilege, it is necessary to resolve those competing interests in a manner that preserves the essential functions of each branch.

The expectation of a President to the confidentiality of his conversations and correspondence, like the claim of confidentiality of judicial deliberations, for example, has all the values to which we accord deference for the privacy of all citizens and, added to those values, is the necessity for protection of the public interest in candid, objective, and even blunt or harsh opinions in Presidential decisionmaking. . . .

But this presumptive privilege must be considered in light of our historic commitment to the rule of law. . . . The ends of criminal justice would be defeated if judgments were to be founded on a partial or speculative presentation of the facts. The very integrity of the judicial system and public confidence in the system depend on full disclosure of all the facts, within the framework of the rules of evidence. To ensure that justice is done, it is imperative to the function of courts that compulsory process be available for the production of evidence needed either by the prosecution or by the defense. . . . In this case the President challenges a subpoena served on him as a third party requiring the production of materials for use in a criminal prosecution; he does so on the claim that he has a privilege against disclosure of confidential communications. He does not place his claim of privilege on the ground they are military or diplomatic secrets. As to these areas of Art. II duties the courts have traditionally shown the utmost deference to Presidential responsibilities. . . No case of the Court, however, has extended this high degree of deference to a President's generalized interest in confidentiality. . . .

On the other hand, the allowance of the privilege to withhold evidence that is demonstrably relevant in a criminal trial would cut deeply into the guarantee of due process of law and gravely impair the basic function of the courts. . . . Without access to specific facts a criminal prosecution may be totally frustrated. . . .

We conclude that when the ground for asserting privilege as to subpoenaed materials sought for use in a criminal trial is based only on the generalized interest in confidentiality, it cannot prevail over the fundamental demands of due process of law in the fair administration of criminal justice. The generalized assertion of privilege must yield to the demonstrated, specific need for evidence in a pending criminal trial.

# *Clinton* v. *Jones*

**520 U.S. 681, 137 L. Ed. 2d 945, 117 S. Ct. 1636 (1997)**

Paula Corbin Jones sued under 42 U. S. C. sections 1983 and 1985 and under Arkansas law to recover damages from President William Clinton, alleging that while Clinton was Governor of Arkansas, he made "abhorrent " sexual advances to her, and that her rejection of those advances led to punishment by her supervisors in the state job she held at the time. President Clinton filed a motion to dismiss the suit on Presidential immunity grounds, and requested that all other pleadings and motions be deferred until the immunity issue was resolved. The Federal district court granted that request but ultimately refused to dismiss the suit on immunity grounds and ruled that discovery—the pre-trial exchange of information between the parties—could go forward, but ordered any trial stayed until the conclusion of the Clinton presidency. The Eighth Circuit affirmed the dismissal denial, but reversed the trial postponement as the "functional equivalent" of a grant of temporary immunity to which petitioner was not constitutionally entitled. The Supreme Court then granted certiorari. *Opinion of the Court: Stevens, Rehnquist, O'Connor, Scalia, Kennedy, Souter, Thomas, Ginsburg. Concurring in the judgment: Breyer.*

JUSTICE STEVENS delivered the opinion of the Court.

The President submits that in all but the most exceptional cases the Constitution requires federal courts to defer civil suits against the president until his term ends and that, in any event, respect for the office warrants such a stay. Despite the force of the arguments supporting the President's submissions, we conclude that they must be rejected.

It is true that we have often stressed the importance of avoiding the premature adjudication of constitutional questions. That doctrine of avoidance . . . make[s] it appropriate to identify two important constitutional issues not encompassed within the questions presented by the petition for certiorari that we need not address today.

First, because the claim of immunity is asserted in a federal court and relies heavily on the doctrine of separation of powers that restrains each of the three branches of the Federal Government from encroaching on the domain of the other two, it is not necessary to consider or decide whether a comparable claim might succeed in a state tribunal. Second, our decision rejecting the immunity claim and allowing the case to proceed does not require us to confront the question whether a court may compel the attendance of the President at any specific time or place. Petitioner's principal submission—that "in all but the most exceptional cases," the Constitution affords the President temporary immunity from civil damages litigation arising out of events that occurred before he took office—cannot be sustained on the basis of precedent. Only three sitting Presidents have been defendants in civil litigation involving their actions prior to taking office. [N]one of those cases sheds any light on the constitutional issue before us.

The principal rationale for affording certain public servants immunity from suits for money damages arising out of their official acts is inapplicable to unofficial conduct. In cases involving prosecutors, legislators, and judges we have repeatedly explained that the immunity serves the public interest in enabling such officials to perform their designated functions effectively without fear that a particular decision may give rise to personal liability. That rationale provided the principal basis for our holding that a former President of the United States was "entitled to absolute immunity from damages liability predicated on his official acts," [Nixon v.] *Fitzgerald* (1982). Our central concern was to avoid rendering the President "unduly cautious in the discharge of his official duties." This reasoning provides no support for an immunity for unofficial conduct. [W]e have never suggested that the President, or any other official, has an immunity that extends beyond the scope of any action taken in an official capacity.

Petitioner's strongest argument supporting his immunity claim is based on the text and structure of the Constitution. He does not contend that the occupant of the Office of the President is "above the law," in the sense that his conduct is entirely immune from judicial scrutiny. The President argues merely for a postponement of the judicial proceedings that will determine whether he violated any law. His argument is grounded in the character of the office that was created by Article II of the Constitution, and relies on separation of powers principles that have structured our constitutional arrangement since the Founding.

As a starting premise, petitioner contends that he occupies a unique office with powers and responsibilities so vast and important that the public interest demands that he devote his undivided time and attention to his public duties. He submits that—given the nature of the office—the doctrine of separation of powers places limits on the authority of the Federal Judiciary to interfere with the Executive Branch that would be transgressed by allowing this action to proceed.

We have no dispute with the initial premise of the argument. It does not follow, however, that separation of powers principles would be violated by allowing this action to proceed. Of course the lines between the powers of the three branches are not always neatly defined. But in this case there is no suggestion that the Federal Judiciary is being asked to perform any function that might in some way be described as "executive." Respondent is merely asking the courts to exercise their core Article III jurisdiction to decide cases and controversies. Whatever the outcome of this case, there is no possibility that the decision will curtail the scope of the official powers of the Executive Branch. The litigation of questions that relate entirely to the unofficial conduct of the individual who happens to be the President poses no perceptible risk of misallocation of either judicial power or executive power.

Rather than arguing that the decision of the case will produce either an aggrandizement of judicial power or a narrowing of executive power, petitioner contends that—as a byproduct of an otherwise traditional exercise of judicial power—burdens will be placed on the President that will hamper the performance of his official duties. We have recognized that "[e]ven when a branch does not arrogate power to itself . . . the separation-of-powers doctrine requires that a branch not impair another in the performance of its constitutional duties." *Loving* v. *United States* (1996). As a factual matter, petitioner contends that this particular case—as well as the potential additional litigation that an affirmance of the Court of Appeals judgment might spawn—may impose an unacceptable burden on the President's time and energy, and thereby impair the effective performance of his office.

Petitioner's predictive judgment finds little support in either history or the relatively narrow compass of the issues raised in this particular case. [I]n the more than 200-year history of the Republic, only three sitting Presidents have been subjected to suits for their private actions. If the past is any indicator, it seems unlikely that a deluge of such litigation will ever engulf the Presidency. As for the case at hand, if properly managed by the District Court, it appears to us highly unlikely to occupy any substantial amount of petitioner's time.

Of greater significance, petitioner errs by presuming that interactions between the Judicial Branch and the Executive, even quite burdensome interactions, necessarily rise to the level of constitutionally forbidden impairment of the Executive's ability to perform its constitutionally mandated functions. The fact that a federal court's exercise of its traditional Article III jurisdiction may significantly burden the time and attention of the Chief Executive is not sufficient to establish a violation of the Constitution. Sitting Presidents have responded to court orders to provide testimony and other information with sufficient frequency that such interactions between the Judicial and Executive Branches can scarcely be thought a novelty. President Monroe responded to written interrogatories, President Nixon produced tapes in response to a *subpoena duces tecum,* President Ford complied with an order to give a deposition in a criminal trial, and President Clinton has twice given videotaped testimony in criminal proceedings. Moreover, sitting Presidents have also voluntarily complied with judicial requests for testimony.

In sum, "[i]t is settled law that the separation-of-powers doctrine does not bar every exercise of jurisdiction over the President of the United States." *Fitzgerald.* If the Judiciary may severely burden the Executive Branch by reviewing the legality of the President's official conduct, and if it may direct appropriate process to the President himself, it must follow that the federal courts have power to determine the legality of his unofficial conduct. The burden on the President's time and energy that is a mere by-product of such review surely cannot be considered as onerous as the direct burden imposed by judicial review and the occasional invalidation of his official actions. We therefore hold that the doctrine of separation of powers does not require federal courts to stay all private actions against the President until he leaves office.

If Congress deems it appropriate to afford the President stronger protection, it may respond with appropriate legislation. [O]ur holding today raises no barrier to a statutory response to these concerns.

The Federal District Court has jurisdiction to decide this case. Like every other citizen who properly invokes that jurisdiction, respondent has a right to an orderly disposition of her claims. Accordingly, the judgment of the Court of Appeals is affirmed.

*It is so ordered.*

JUSTICE BREYER, concurring in the judgment.

I agree with the majority that the Constitution does not automatically grant the President an immunity from civil lawsuits based upon his private conduct. [H]owever, once the President sets forth and explains a conflict between judicial proceeding and public duties, the matter changes. At that point, the Constitution permits a judge to schedule a trial in an ordinary civil damages action (where postponement normally is possible without overwhelming damage to a plaintiff) only within the constraints of a constitutional principle—a principle that forbids a federal judge in such a case to interfere with the President's discharge of his public duties. I have no doubt that the Constitution contains such a principle applicable to civil suits, based upon Article II's vesting of the entire "executive Power" in a single individual, implemented through the Constitution's structural separation of powers, and revealed both by history and case precedent.

I recognize that this case does not require us now to apply the principle specifically, thereby delineating its contours; nor need we now decide whether lower courts are to apply it directly or categorically through the use of presumptions or rules of administration. Yet I fear that to disregard it now may appear to deny it. I also fear that the majority's description of the relevant precedents deemphasizes the extent to which they support a principle of the President's independent authority to control his own time and energy. Further, if the majority is wrong in predicting the future infrequency of private civil litigation against sitting Presidents, acknowledgement and future delineation of the constitutional principle will prove a practically necessary institutional safeguard.

## *In Re Neagle*

### 135 U.S. 1, 10 S. Ct. 658, 34 L. Ed. 55 (1890)

U.S. Marshal David Neagle was appointed by the attorney general to protect Supreme Court Justice Field while he rode circuit in California. When David Terry, a disappointed litigant with a grudge against Field, appeared about to attack the justice, Neagle shot and killed him. After California authorities arrested Neagle and charged him with murder, the United States sought to secure Neagle's release on habeas corpus. In the absence of any law specifically authorizing the president or the attorney general to assign marshals as bodyguards to the justices, the United States relied on a federal statute that made the writ available to those "in custody for an act done or omitted in pursuance of a law of the United States." *Opinion of the Court: Miller, Bradley, Harlan, Gray, Blatchford, Brewer. Dissenting opinion: Lamar, Fuller. Not participating: Field.*

MR. JUSTICE MILLER delivered the opinion of the Court. . . .

. . . Without a more minute discussion of this testimony, it produces upon us the conviction of a settled purpose on the part of Terry and his wife, amounting to a conspiracy, to murder Justice Field. And we are quite sure that if Neagle had been merely a brother or a friend of Judge Field, travelling with him, and aware of all the previous relations of Terry to the Judge,—as he was,—of his bitter animosity, his declared purpose to have revenge even to the point of killing him, he would have been justified in what he did in defence of Mr. Justice Field's life, and possibly of his own.

But such a justification would be a proper subject for consideration on a trial of the case for murder in the courts of the State of California, and there exists no authority in the courts of the United States to discharge the prisoner while held in custody by the State authorities for this offence, unless there be found in aid of the defence of the prisoner some element of power and authority asserted under the government of the United States.

This element is said to be found in the facts that Mr. Justice Field, when attacked, was in the immediate discharge of his duty as judge of the Circuit Courts of the United States within California; that the assault upon him grew out of the animosity of Terry and wife, arising out of the previous discharge of his duty as circuit justice in the case for which they were committed for contempt of court; and that the deputy marshal of the United States, who killed Terry in defence of Field's life, was charged with a duty under the law of the United States to protect Field from the violence which Terry was inflicting, and which was intended to lead to Field's death. . . .

It is urged, however, that there exists no statute authorizing any such protection as that which Neagle was instructed to give Judge Field in the present case, and indeed no protection whatever against a vindictive or malicious assault growing out of the faithful discharge of his official duties; and that the language of section 753 of the Revised Statutes, that the party seeking the benefit of the writ of *habeas corpus* must in this connection show that he is "in custody for an act done or omitted in pursuance of a law of the United States," makes it necessary that upon this occasion it should be shown that the act for which Neagle is imprisoned was done by virtue of an act of Congress. It is not supposed that any special act of Congress exists which authorizes the marshals or deputy marshals of the United States in express terms to accompany the judges of the Supreme Court through their circuits, and act as a body-guard to them, to defend them against malicious assaults against their persons. But we are of opinion that this view of the statute is an unwarranted restriction of the meaning of a law designed to extend in a liberal manner the benefit of the writ of *habeas corpus* to persons imprisoned for the performance of their duty. And we are satisfied that if it was the duty of Neagle, under the circumstances, a duty which could only arise under the laws of the United States, to defend Mr. Justice Field from a murderous attack upon him, he brings himself within the meaning of the section we have recited. . . .

In the view we take of the Constitution of the United States, any obligation fairly and properly inferrible from that instrument, or any duty of the marshal to be derived from the general scope of his duties under the laws of the United States, is "a law" within the meaning of this phrase. It would be a great reproach to the system of government of the United States, declared to be within its sphere sovereign and supreme, if there is to be found within the domain of its powers no means of protecting the judges, in the conscientious and faithful discharge of their duties, from the malice and hatred of those upon whom their judgments may operate unfavorably. . . .

Where, then, are we to look for the protection which we have shown Judge Field was entitled to when engaged in the discharge of his official duties? . . . The Constitution, section 3, Article 2, declares that the President "shall take care that the laws be faithfully executed," and he is provided with the means of fulfilling this obligation by his authority to commission all the officers of the United States, and, by and with the advice and consent of the Senate, to appoint the most important of them and to fill vacancies. He is declared to be commander-in-chief of the army and navy of the United States. The duties which are thus imposed upon him he is further enabled to perform by the recognition in the Constitution, and the creation by acts of Congress, of executive departments, which have varied in number from four or five to seven or eight, the heads of which are familiarly called cabinet ministers. These aid him in the performance of the great duties of his office, and represent him in a thousand acts to which it can hardly be supposed his personal attention is called, and thus he is enabled to fulfil the duty of his great department, expressed in the phrase that "he shall take care that the laws be faithfully executed."

Is this duty limited to the enforcement of acts of Congress or of treaties of the United States according to their *express terms*, or does it include the rights, duties and obligations growing out of the Constitution itself, our international relations, and all the protection implied by the nature of the government under the Constitution? . . .

We cannot doubt the power of the President to take measures for the protection of a judge of one of the courts of the United States, who, while in the discharge of the duties of his office, is threatened with a personal attack which may probably result in his death. . . .

But there is positive law investing the marshals and their deputies with powers which not only justify what Marshal Neagle did in this matter, but which imposed it upon him as a duty. In chapter fourteen of the Revised Statutes of the United States, which is devoted to the appointment and duties of the district attorneys, marshals, and clerks of the courts of the United States, section 788 declares:

"The marshals and their deputies shall have, in each State, the same powers, in executing the laws of the United States, as the sheriffs and their deputies in such State may have, by law, in executing the laws thereof."

If, therefore, a sheriff of the State of California was authorized to do in regard to the laws of California what Neagle did, that is, if he was authorized to keep the peace, to protect a judge from assault and murder, then Neagle was authorized to do the same thing in reference to the laws of the United States.

That there is a peace of the United States; that a man assaulting a judge of the United States while in the discharge of his duties violates that peace; that in such case the marshal of the United States stands in the same relation to the peace of the United States which the sheriff of the county does to the peace of the State of California; are questions too clear to need argument to prove them. . . .

The result at which we have arrived upon this examination is, that in taking the life of Terry, under the circumstances, he was acting under the authority of the law of the United States, and was justified in so doing; and that he is not liable to answer in the courts of California on account of his part in that transaction.

*We therefore affirm the judgment of the Circuit Court authorizing his discharge from the custody of the sheriff of San Joaquin County.*

## *Youngstown Sheet & Tube Company* v. Sawyer

**343 U.S. 579, 72 S. Ct. 863, 96 L. Ed. 1153 (1952)**

In order to avert an apparently imminent nationwide steel strike during the Korean War, President Harry Truman issued an executive order directing the secretary of commerce to seize and operate the nation's steel mills. By taking such a step, he implicitly rejected the remedy offered by the Taft-Hartley Act: the seeking of an injunction against the strike. Reporting his action to Congress, the president justified the seizure by citing his aggregate powers as chief executive and commander in chief. He also noted that Congress could reverse or endorse the seizure. Congress took no action prior to the Supreme Court's consideration of the case, however.

Shortly after the seizure, the steel companies obtained from a federal district court an injunction restraining the secretary of commerce from "continuing the seizure and possession of the plants"; but on the same day the court of appeals stayed the injunction. The Supreme Court granted certiorari and expedited consideration of the case, announcing its decision less than two months after the seizure. *Opinion of the Court: Black, Frankfurter, Burton, Jackson. Concurring opinions: Frankfurter; Burton; Jackson; Clark; Douglas. Dissenting opinion: Vinson, Reed, Minton.*

MR. JUSTICE BLACK delivered the opinion of the Court.

We are asked to decide whether the President was acting within his constitutional power when he issued an order directing the Secretary of Commerce to take possession of and operate most of the Nation's steel mills. . . .

The President's power, if any, to issue the order must stem either from an act of Congress or from the Constitution itself. There is no statute that expressly authorizes the President to take possession of property as he did here. Nor is there any act of Congress to which our attention has been directed from which such a power can fairly be implied. Indeed, we do not understand the Government to rely on statutory authorization for this seizure. . . .

It is clear that if the President had authority to issue the order he did, it must be found in some provision of the Constitution. And it is not claimed that express constitutional language grants this power to the President. The contention is that presidential power should be implied from the aggregate of his powers under the Constitution. Particular reliance is placed on provisions in Article II which say that "The executive Power shall be vested in a President . . ."; that "he shall take Care that the Laws be faithfully executed"; and that he "shall be Commander in Chief of the Army and Navy of the United States."

The order cannot properly be sustained as an exercise of the President's military power as Commander in Chief of the Armed Forces. The Government attempts to do so by citing a number of cases upholding broad powers in military commanders engaged in day-to-day fighting in a theater of war. Such cases need not concern us here. Even though "theater of war" be an expanding concept, we cannot with faithfulness to our constitutional system hold that the Commander in Chief of the Armed Forces has the ultimate power as such to take possession of private property in order to keep labor disputes from stopping production. This is a job for the Nation's lawmakers, not for its military authorities.

Nor can the seizure order be sustained because of the several constitutional provisions that grant executive power to the President. In the framework of our Constitution, the President's power to see that the laws are faithfully executed refutes the idea that he is to be a lawmaker. The Constitution limits his functions in the lawmaking process to the recommending of laws he thinks wise and the vetoing of laws he thinks bad. And the Constitution is neither silent nor equivocal about who shall make laws which the President is to execute. The first section of the first article says that "All legislative Powers herein granted shall be vested in a Congress of the United States. . . ." After granting many powers to the Congress, Article I goes on to provide that Congress may "make all Laws which shall be necessary and proper for carrying into Execution the foregoing Powers, and all other Powers vested by this Constitution in the Government of the United States, or in any Department or Officer thereof." . . .

The Founders of this Nation entrusted the lawmaking power to the Congress alone in both good and bad times. It would do no good to recall the historical events, the fears of power and the hopes for freedom that lay behind their choice. Such a review would but confirm our holding that this seizure order cannot stand.

The judgment of the District Court is

*Affirmed.*

MR. JUSTICE FRANKFURTER, concurring in the judgment and opinion of the Court.

Congress has frequently—at least 16 times since 1916—specifically provided for executive seizure of production, transportation, communications, or storage facilities. In every case it has qualified this grant of power with limitations and safeguards. . . .

Congress in 1947 was again called upon to consider whether governmental seizure should be used to avoid serious industrial shutdowns. . . . A proposal that the President be given powers to seize plants to avert a shutdown where the "health or safety" of the Nation was endangered, was thoroughly canvassed by Congress and rejected. No room for doubt remains that the proponents as well as the opponents of the bill which became the Labor Management Relations Act of 1947 clearly understood that as a result of that legislation the only recourse for preventing a shutdown in any basic industry, after failure of mediation, was Congress. . . . Perhaps as much so as is true of any piece of modern legislation, Congress acted with full consciousness of what it was doing and in the light of much recent history. . . .

It cannot be contended that the President would have had power to issue this order had Congress explicitly negated such authority in formal legislation. Congress has expressed its will to withhold this power from the President as though it had said so in so many words. The authoritatively expressed purpose of Congress to disallow such power to the President and to require him, when in his mind the occasion arose for such a seizure, to put the matter to Congress and ask for specific authority from it, could not be more decisive if it had been written into §§206–210 of the Labor Management Relations Act of 1947. . . .

MR. JUSTICE JACKSON, concurring in the judgment and opinion of the Court.

A judge, like an executive adviser, may be surprised at the poverty of really useful and unambiguous authority applicable to concrete problems of executive power as they actually present themselves. Just what our forefathers did envision, or would have envisioned had they foreseen modern conditions, must be divined from materials almost as enigmatic as the dreams Joseph was called upon to interpret for Pharaoh. A century and a half of partisan debate and scholarly speculation yields no net result but only supplies more or less apt quotations from respected sources on each side of any question. They largely cancel each other. And court decisions are indecisive because of the judicial practice of dealing with the largest questions in the most narrow way.

The actual art of governing under our Constitution does not and cannot conform to judicial definitions of the power of any of its branches based on isolated clauses or even single Articles torn from context. While the Constitution diffuses power the better to secure liberty, it also contemplates that practice will integrate the dispersed powers into a workable government. It enjoins upon its branches separateness but interdependence, autonomy but reciprocity. Presidential powers are not fixed but fluctuate, depending upon their disjunction or conjunction with those of Congress. We may well begin by a somewhat over-simplified grouping of practical situations in which a President may doubt, or others may challenge, his powers, and by distinguishing roughly the legal consequences of this factor of relativity.

1. When the President acts pursuant to an express or implied authorization of Congress, his authority is at its maximum, for it includes all that he possesses in his own right plus all that Congress can delegate. In these circumstances, and in these only, may he be said (for what it may be worth) to personify the federal sovereignty. If his act is held unconstitutional under these circumstances, it usually means that the Federal Government as an undivided whole lacks power. A seizure executed by the President pursuant to an Act of Congress would be supported by the strongest of presumptions and the widest latitude of judicial interpretation, and the burden of persuasion would rest heavily upon any who might attack it.

2. When the President acts in absence of either a congressional grant or denial of authority, he can only rely upon his own independent powers, but there is a zone of twilight in which he and Congress may have concurrent authority, or in which its distribution is uncertain. Therefore, congressional inertia, indifference or quiescence may sometimes, at least as a practical matter, enable, if not invite, measures on independent presidential responsibility. In this area, any actual test of power is likely to depend on the imperatives of events and contemporary imponderables rather than on abstract theories of law.

3. When the President takes measures incompatible with the expressed or implied will of Congress, his power is at its lowest ebb, for then he can rely only upon his own constitutional

powers minus any constitutional powers of Congress over the matter. Courts can sustain exclusive presidential control in such a case only by disabling the Congress from acting upon the subject. Presidential claim to a power at once so conclusive and preclusive must be scrutinized with caution, for what is at stake is the equilibrium established by our constitutional system.

Into which of these classifications does this executive seizure of the steel industry fit? It is eliminated from the first by admission, for it is conceded that no congressional authorization exists for this seizure. . . .

Can it then be defended under flexible tests available to the second category? It seems clearly eliminated from that class because Congress has not left seizure of private property an open field but has covered it by three statutory policies inconsistent with this seizure. . . . In choosing a different and inconsistent way of his own, the President cannot claim that it is necessitated or invited by failure of Congress to legislate upon the occasions, grounds and methods for seizure of industrial properties.

This leaves the current seizure to be justified only by the severe tests under the third grouping, where it can be supported only by any remainder of executive power after subtraction of such powers as Congress may have over the subject. In short, we can sustain the President only by holding that seizure of such strike-bound industries is within his domain and beyond control by Congress. Thus, this Court's first review of such seizures occurs under circumstances which leave presidential power most vulnerable to attack and in the least favorable of possible constitutional postures. . . .

That seems to be the logic of an argument tendered at our bar—that the President having, on his own responsibility, sent American troops abroad derives from that act "affirmative power" to seize the means of producing a supply of steel for them. . . .

I cannot foresee all that it might entail if the Court should indorse this argument. Nothing in our Constitution is plainer than that declaration of a war is entrusted only to Congress. Of course, a state of war may in fact exist without a formal declaration. But no doctrine that the Court could promulgate would seem to me more sinister and alarming than that a President whose conduct of foreign affairs is so largely uncontrolled, and often even is unknown, can vastly enlarge his mastery over the internal affairs of the country by his own commitment of the Nation's armed forces to some foreign venture. . . .

That military powers of the Commander in Chief were not to supersede representative government of internal affairs seems obvious from the Constitution and from elementary American history. . . .

We should not use this occasion to circumscribe, much less to contract, the lawful role of the President as Commander in Chief. I should indulge the widest latitude of interpretation to sustain his exclusive function to command the instruments of national force, at least when turned against the outside world for the security of our society. But, when it is turned inward, not because of rebellion but because of a lawful economic struggle between industry and labor, it should have no such indulgence. . . .

In view of the ease, expedition and safety with which Congress can grant and has granted large emergency powers, certainly ample to embrace this crisis, I am quite unimpressed with the argument that we should affirm possession of them without statute. Such power either has no beginning or it has no end. If it exists, it need submit to no legal restraint. I am not alarmed that it would plunge us straightway into dictatorship, but it is at least a step in that wrong direction. . . .

But I have no illusion that any decision by this Court can keep power in the hands of Congress if it is not wise and timely in meeting its problems. A crisis that challenges the President equally, or perhaps primarily, challenges Congress. If not good law, there was worldly wisdom in the maxim attributed to Napoleon that "The tools belong to the man who can use them." We may say that power to legislate for emergencies belongs in the hands of Congress, but only Congress itself can prevent power from slipping through its fingers.

The essence of our free Government is "leave to live by no man's leave, underneath the law"—to be governed by those impersonal forces which we call law. Our Government is fashioned to fulfill this concept so far as humanly possible. The Executive, except for recommendation and veto, has no legislative power. The executive action we have here originates in the individual will of the President and represents an exercise of authority without law. No one, perhaps not even the President, knows the limits of the power he may seek to exert in this instance and the parties affected cannot learn the limit of their rights. We do not know today what powers over labor or property would be claimed to flow from Government possession if we should legalize it, what rights to compensation would be claimed or recognized, or on what contingency it would end. With all its defects, delays and inconveniences, men have discovered no technique for long preserving free government except that the Executive be under the law, and that the law be made by parliamentary deliberations.

Such institutions may be destined to pass away. But it is the duty of the Court to be last, not first, to give them up.

MR. CHIEF JUSTICE VINSON, with whom MR. JUSTICE REED and MR. JUSTICE MINTON join, dissenting. . .

In passing upon the question of Presidential powers in this case, we must first consider the context in which those powers were exercised. . . .

One is not here called upon even to consider the possibility of executive seizure of a farm, a corner grocery store or even a single industrial plant. Such considerations arise only when one ignores the central fact of this case—that the Nation's entire basic steel production would have shut down completely if there had been no Government seizure. Even ignoring for the moment whatever confidential information the President may possess as "the Nation's organ for foreign affairs," the uncontroverted affidavits in this record amply support the finding that "a work stoppage would immediately jeopardize and imperil our national defense."

Plaintiffs do not remotely suggest any basis for rejecting the President's finding that *any* stoppage of steel production would immediately place the Nation in peril. . . .

Focusing now on the situation confronting the President on the night of April 8, 1952, we cannot but conclude that the President was performing his duty under the Constitution to "take Care that the Laws be faithfully executed"—a duty described by President Benjamin Harrison as "the central idea of the office."

The President reported to Congress the morning after the seizure that he acted because a work stoppage in steel production would immediately imperil the safety of the Nation by preventing execution of the legislative programs for procurement of military equipment. And, while a shutdown could be averted by granting the price concessions requested by plaintiffs, granting such concessions would disrupt the price stabilization program also enacted by Congress. Rather than fail to execute either legislative program, the President acted to execute both.

Much of the argument in this case has been directed at straw men. We do not now have before us the case of a President acting solely on the basis of his own notions of the public welfare. Nor is there any question of unlimited executive power in this case. The President himself closed the door to any such claim when he sent his Message to Congress stating his purpose to abide by any action of Congress, whether approving or disapproving his seizure action. Here, the President immediately made sure that Congress was fully informed of the temporary action he had taken only to preserve the legislative programs from destruction until Congress could act.

The absence of a specific statute authorizing seizure of the steel mills as a mode of executing the laws—both the military procurement program and the anti-inflation program—has not until today been thought to prevent the President from executing the laws. Unlike an administrative commission confined to the enforcement of the statute under which it was created, or the head of a department when administering a particular statute, the President is a constitutional officer charged with taking care that a "mass of legislation" be executed. Flexibility as to mode of execution to meet critical situations is a matter of practical necessity. . . . Faced with the duty of executing the defense programs which Congress had enacted and the disastrous effects that any stoppage in steel production would have on those programs, the President acted to preserve those programs by seizing the steel mills. . . . The President immediately informed Congress of his action and clearly stated his intention to abide by the legislative will. No basis for claims of arbitrary action, unlimited powers or dictatorial usurpation of congressional power appears from the facts of this case. On the contrary, judicial, legislative and executive precedents throughout our history demonstrate that in this case the President acted in full conformity with his duties under the Constitution.

★

## THE INTERBRANCH DISTRIBUTION OF POWER

*The Prize Cases* (1863)
The Gulf of Tonkin Resolution (1964)
The War Powers Resolution (1973)

## THE FOUNDATION AND EXTENT OF THE FOREIGN AFFAIRS POWER

*United States* v. *Curtiss-Wright Export Corporation* (1936)
*Missouri* v. *Holland* (1920)

## WAR AND INDIVIDUAL RIGHTS

*Ex Parte Milligan* (1866)
*Korematsu* v. *United States* (1944)

## NOTES

## SELECTED READING

## CASES

★

# 6
# WAR AND FOREIGN AFFAIRS

Throughout the Vietnam War, congressional opponents of the conflict charged that it involved an executive usurpation of legislative war-making powers. During the 1980s, President Ronald Reagan protested that Congress had undermined his ability to conduct foreign policy by imposing restrictions on aid to guerillas seeking to overthrow the Nicaraguan government. There is nothing novel in these conflicts. Within five years of the ratification of the Constitution, James Madison and Alexander Hamilton—the principal authors of *The Federalist*—disagreed about whether President George Washington had the authority to issue a proclamation of American neutrality in the war between France and Great Britain.[1] Since then, clashes over the constitutional distribution of power for the direction of foreign affairs and for the commitment of American troops have been a recurring feature of American politics. The constitutional separation of powers, in fact, virtually guarantees periodic interbranch conflict in these areas: as Edward Corwin has noted, the division of powers "is an invitation to struggle for the privilege of directing American foreign policy."[2]

The extent of the national power over war and foreign affairs also has raised constitutional questions. The Framers clearly intended to lodge power over these subjects in the national government. As Madison observed in *The Federalist*, No. 42, "If we are to be one nation in any respect, it clearly ought to be in respect to other nations." But this grant of power, in the view of some observers, may pose a threat to the general division of power between the national and state governments and to constitutional protections of individual rights. The difficulty of delineating the limits of the foreign affairs power, for instance, has fueled suspicions that the national government might use that power as a pretext to invade state prerogatives. Similar problems attend the protection of individual rights. Indisputably, the Framers sought to create a constitution "intended to endure for ages to come, and, consequently, to be adapted to the various crises of human affairs."[3] Less clear is whether this aim is compatible with the protection of individual rights, or whether a successful response to extreme crises of war or foreign affairs may not require a temporary sacrifice of those rights.

Conflicts over the constitutional distribution of power regarding foreign affairs and war characteristically involve the distribution of power (1) among the branches of the national government, (2) between the levels of the federal system, or (3) between government and the people. The material in this chapter is organized around these three basic conflicts.

## THE INTERBRANCH DISTRIBUTION OF POWER

Table 6.1 summarizes the war and foreign affairs powers expressly granted in the Constitution to each department. Perhaps its most striking feature is the complete absence of the judiciary. Although the power of judicial review extends to the exercise of governmental power in war and foreign affairs, several interrelated factors have severely restricted the frequency and importance of judicial intervention in those areas.

Of prime importance is the nonjusticiability of most questions involving war and foreign affairs under the political questions doctrine (see Chapter 3). For example, although many people believed the Vietnam War to be unconstitutional, attempts to secure a judicial ruling consistently failed under the political questions doctrine (see Chapter 3) or because the plaintiffs lacked standing to sue.[4] The Supreme Court also invoked the political-questions doctrine in *Goldwater* v. *Carter* (1979) to avoid a ruling on whether President Jimmy Carter could unilaterally terminate the nation's mutual defense treaty with Taiwan. An additional barrier has been the Court's understandable reluctance even to consider such delicate questions. On five separate occasions, for instance, the Court used its discretionary jurisdiction to refuse to hear challenges to the constitutionality of the Vietnam War. This unwillingness to rule on foreign policy issues tends to discourage potential litigants from pursuing their goals through the courts. Moreover, when the Court does intervene, it characteristically defers—because of its limited expertise and the lack of clear constitutional standards—to the judgment of other branches. The Court's decisions upholding President Carter's settlement of the Iran hostage crisis, the all-male draft registration system, and President Ronald Reagan's restrictions on travel to Cuba all reflect this deferential posture.[5] Overall, then, although the judiciary has on occasion considered the constitutional division of powers in war and foreign affairs, the most important sources of constitutional law in these spheres have been the executive and legislative branches.

**TABLE 6.1 The Constitutional Distribution of Powers of War and Foreign Affairs**

| Presidential Powers | Congressional Powers | Senatorial Powers |
|---|---|---|
| | *Foreign Relations Powers* | |
| 1. To make treaties (Senate consent required)<br>2. To appoint envoys (Senate consent required)<br>3. To receive envoys | 1. To regulate foreign commerce<br>2. To lay duties<br>3. To define and punish piracies and felonies committed on the high seas and offenses against the law of nations | 1. To advise on and consent to treaties<br>2. To advise on and consent to appointment of envoys |
| | *Defense Powers* | |
| 1. Commander-in-Chief power<br>2. To repel sudden attacks on the United States or its armed forces (not mentioned in the constitutional text but indisputably granted) | 1. To raise and support armies<br>2. To provide and maintain a navy<br>3. To make rules for the government and regulation of the land and naval forces<br>4. To provide for calling forth the militia to repel invasions<br>5. To suspend the writ of habeas corpus in cases of rebellion or invasion or when the public safety may require such action<br>6. To declare war | |
| | *General Powers* | |
| 1. To inform the Congress about the state of the union and make recommendations<br>2. To convene both houses of Congress, or either one of them, on extraordinary occasions<br>3. To veto legislation<br>4. To execute the laws (which includes unmentioned, delegated rulemaking powers)<br>5. To appoint (Senate consent generally required) | 1. To lay taxes, etc., and provide for the common defense and general welfare<br>2. To make all laws necessary and proper for carrying into execution congressional powers, and all other powers vested in the government, or in any department or officer thereof<br>3. To make appropriations<br>4. To impeach | 1. To advise on and consent to appointments |

## Checks and Balances

Constitutional interpretations characteristically have emerged as a result of political interactions between the legislative and executive branches. Because both branches have long agreed that the president should serve as the "sole organ of the nation in its external relations," for example, this monopoly on communications with foreign governments has been recognized as constitutionally based.[6] On the other hand, dissatisfaction with the results of presidential control over commitment of troops led Congress to attempt to limit this control through the War Powers Resolution, which was passed over a presidential veto in 1973. Although these instances of interbranch cooperation and conflict mix policy and constitutional considerations, their outcomes do not represent merely "political" adjustments. For one thing, the participants in interbranch disputes generally have recognized the seriousness of constitutional questions and, rather than simply basing constitutional interpretations on their own policy positions, have sought correct solutions to them. More importantly, the Constitution itself regulates and in large measure determines the outcomes of such conflicts.

Under the system of checks and balances incorporated into the Constitution, powers are distributed to the various branches so that each branch can adequately defend its prerogatives and prevent domination of the government by any other single branch. These powers, in turn, represent political resources that can be brought to bear in interbranch conflicts. Should the dispute concern the regulation of foreign imports, both Congress and the president have constitutionally defined roles in the legislative process that prevent a single branch from acting alone. Should the president and the Senate conclude a treaty that the House of Representatives opposes, the House can refuse to pass legislation necessary to implement the treaty or to appropriate money for its implementation. The division of powers indicated in Table 6.1 suggests that these examples could be multiplied indefinitely. What is noteworthy is that the constitutional division of power provides each branch with the means to frustrate the achievement of foreign policy goals favored only by a single branch, and thereby places a premium on interbranch cooperation. This, of course, assumes that no branch would cooperate if it believed that its constitutional powers were being usurped in the process. Some critics have charged that Congress has been all too willing to cede power to the executive.

The Constitution also influences the nature and outcomes of interbranch conflicts by imparting a particular character to each branch. The unity of the executive, Hamilton noted in *The Federalist,* No. 70, is conducive to "decision, activity, secrecy, and dispatch." These qualities enable the president to seize the initiative in foreign affairs—as President Carter did in the Middle East peace negotiations of the late 1970s—and to provide effective leadership during the nation's war efforts. In addition, the unity of the executive frequently allows the president to portray himself as the nation's representative in its dealings with other countries. In contrast, the two houses of Congress are deliberative bodies that more adequately reflect the varying viewpoints and interests in the nation.

These differences in composition have had two important ramifications. First, as relations with other countries increasingly have demanded swift and decisive reactions to events, the power of the executive naturally has increased. Second, the success over time of presidential initiatives—that is, whether they will lead over time to interbranch cooperation or conflict—depends on the president's ability to convince the people and their representatives of the initiatives' wisdom. Woodrow Wilson's attempt to secure the participation of the United States in the League of Nations, for example, foundered when the Senate refused to ratify the treaty leading to membership. President Harry Truman, on the other hand, gained congressional backing for the Marshall Plan by involving influential members in the negotiations establishing the plan. So although the character of the branches affects the roles they assume in foreign affairs, the constitutional structure again encourages interbranch cooperation.

## War and Other Hostilities

The most severe test of the constitutional division of powers has been posed by the commitment of American troops in combat. As the Supreme Court ruled in *The Prize Cases* (1863), when the nation is attacked, the president may recognize that a state of war exists and, as Commander-in-Chief, respond accordingly. In all other circumstances the Constitution confers on Congress the choice between war and peace, by granting to the legislative branch the power to declare war. Does political practice reflect this constitutional assignment of power, or does the president in fact exercise decisive control?

Since World War II, American troops have been involved in hostilities ranging from short-term engagements for limited purposes (for example, safeguarding Americans in Grenada during the Reagan administration) to protracted conflicts in Korea and Vietnam. Many of these combat situations, like the invasion of Panama and the Gulf War against Iraq during the Bush administration, have fallen somewhere in between these two extremes. Yet only in the case of the Gulf War was the commitment of troops preceded by a formal congressional authorization. Actually, this sort of presidential commitment of forces has not been confined to recent years—during the debates on the War Powers Resolution, one source listed 161 such instances of unilateral presidential action.[7] What is new is the willingness of some presidents to claim this power as a presidential preserve that is beyond congressional control. In support of this claim, presidents have asserted that the commander-in-chief power permits them to deploy troops wherever they wish and to use the armed forces for various purposes short of war, such as protecting the lives and property of American citizens abroad, defending American troops from attack, and protecting American foreign policy interests.

Although the president can direct the movements of American troops, this power can lead—either inadvertently or by design—to the preemption of congressional decision-making. Once the forces committed are attacked, public opinion almost automatically supports retaliatory measures, and Congress is left with no choice but to endorse presidential requests for the continuation and expansion of hostilities. In the most blatant instance of presidential war-making, President James Polk in 1846 ordered troops to occupy disputed territory along the Rio Grande, thereby provoking a Mexican attack and in effect forcing Congress to declare war against Mexico.[8] Similarly, in 1964 President Lyndon Johnson used an alleged attack on American ships operating off North Vietnam to secure passage of the Gulf of Tonkin Resolution which provided the primary basis for the nation's involvement in Vietnam.

In an effort to clarify the limits of unilateral presidential action and reclaim lost powers, Congress in 1973 adopted the War Powers Resolution, which obliges the president to consult with Congress "in every possible instance" before committing troops "into hostilities or into situations where imminent involvement in hostilities is clearly indicated by the circumstances." If circumstances prevent prior consultation, the act requires the president to report his actions to Congress within forty-eight hours. Further, the president is required to terminate any use of military forces within sixty days after submitting such a report (with a possible extension of 30 days), unless Congress specifically authorizes their continued use. Finally, the act reserves to Congress a legislative veto over troop commitments, that is, the power to compel the withdrawal of troops by an unvetoable concurrent resolution.

In practice, the War Powers Resolution has failed to restore the constitutional division of powers. Some critics note that the law has neither prevented presidential commitment of troops nor promoted consultation beforehand—President Carter sent a rescue force to Iran without informing Congress, and President Reagan dispatched troops to Grenada on his own initiative.[9] At times, presidents have refused to acknowledge the applicability of the resolution to their commitment of troops—President Reagan's stationing of Marines in Lebanon is a prime example—thereby preventing the start of the sixty-day time limit for congressional authorization. Even when the presidents have notified Congress or its leadership, as President Bush did before dispatching troops to Panama, they have done so to announce a decision rather than to seek advice. In addition, congressional control after the commitment of troops has been limited. When the Grenada incursion succeeded, Congress was hard-pressed to object to the unilateral presidential action; when the Iran rescue failed, Congress was more concerned with the details of the failure than the lack of consultation. On the other hand, when a president seeks sustained American involvement in a conflict, the resolution's requirement that Congress specifically authorize prolonged troop commitments provides it with a weapon to ensure consultation.

Other critics have charged that the War Powers Resolution infringes on presidential authority and undermines the conduct of foreign policy.[10]

In 1995, congressional Republicans sought the repeal of the Resolution on that basis, although their effort ultimately failed. Certainly presidents have been reluctant to comply with its provisions, and some have raised doubts about its constitutionality.[11] This dispute will most likely be resolved through interbranch interaction rather than by a judicial decision.

## THE FOUNDATION AND EXTENT OF THE FOREIGN AFFAIRS POWER

The conduct of foreign affairs is preeminently a national, rather than a state, concern. The Constitution recognizes this not only by granting pertinent powers to the president and to Congress but also by expressly denying them to the states. Thus, Article I, Section 10 of the Constitution prohibits states from entering into alliances or other agreements with foreign nations and forbids them from engaging in war unless actually invaded or in imminent danger of invasion. Furthermore, as the Supreme Court recognized when in *Perpich* v. *Department of Defense* (1990) it upheld—over gubernatorial objections—a congressional authorization for training national guard troops outside the United States, the exercise of national powers in foreign affairs supersedes state prerogatives.

Nevertheless, the constitutional foundation for vesting control over foreign relations exclusively in the national government is somewhat sketchy. For one thing, the Constitution's assignment of particular powers to various branches does not exhaust the range of powers necessary for the conduct of foreign affairs. The power to terminate treaties, the legal status of executive agreements, the circumstances under which the president may commit American troops to hostilities—none of these matters are dealt with expressly in the Constitution. Moreover, although the Constitution in no way limits national authority over foreign affairs, neither does it explicitly grant a comprehensive foreign affairs power.

This problem of the "missing powers" has generated two radically different approaches to providing a basis for national control. The so-called extrapolation approach suggests that the particular powers assigned to the various branches or denied to the states necessarily imply the missing powers required for the conduct of foreign affairs. Thus the power to make treaties implies the power to break them; the power to make war implies the power to make peace; the power to receive ambassadors (thereby granting diplomatic recognition) implies the power to refuse recognition by not receiving ambassadors; and so on. According to this view, a complete picture of the extent and distribution of the powers over foreign affairs can be derived from the express grants of power in the Constitution. A contrasting approach, suggested by Justice George Sutherland in *United States* v. *Curtiss-Wright Export Corporation* (1936), bases national control over foreign affairs on an extraconstitutional foundation. The Constitution, Sutherland maintained, distributed only the "internal powers" of government, that is, those powers pertaining to domestic affairs. In Sutherland's view the powers pertaining to foreign affairs—external powers—had already been lodged in the national government as an inheritance from the British Crown at the time that the United States became a sovereign nation, and thus did not rest on a delegation from the people or the states. What is assumed to be an incomplete grant of powers under the extrapolation approach, therefore, becomes for Sutherland merely the assignment of those powers that do not belong naturally to either the legislative or the executive branch.

Neither approach is altogether without difficulties. The extrapolation approach requires an extraordinarily broad reading of specific constitutional provisions that is at variance with how grants of authority in domestic affairs are interpreted. Proponents of extrapolation argue, for example, that the power to appoint ambassadors includes the power to direct their activities and thus to define the ends, or policy objectives, to which those activities shall be directed. Nevertheless, this appointment power might as readily be interpreted as a narrow and specific grant of power that has nothing to do with the power to set foreign policy goals. In addition, this approach does not resolve conflicts about the distribution of powers: although the president may infer the power to set foreign policy objectives from the power to appoint ambassadors, Congress may conclude that its power to declare war carries with it a power to decide on policies that might propel the nation into war. The Sutherland approach, on the other hand, relies on a historical interpretation that is subject to challenge on two counts. Although Justice Sutherland contended that sovereignty—and therefore control over foreign affairs—passed directly from the Crown to a national government, the fact that several states during the post-Independence period acted independently in foreign affairs appears to belie Sutherland's assertion that a sense of nationhood was present. Although most people during the period were alarmed by the idea of a strong national government, there is no discussion of a preexisting foreign affairs power in the Constitution, in the records of the Constitutional Convention, or in other contemporary sources. It hardly seems credible that such a departure from the system of delegated powers would occur without discussion.

Whatever their differences, both approaches assign the foreign affairs power to the national government. The extent of this power remains a matter of controversy, however. In *Curtiss-Wright,* Justice Sutherland contended that national control over external affairs could be complete only if the line between external and internal affairs—and between external and internal powers—reflected changing world conditions. Sixteen years earlier, this argument had been advanced by Justice Oliver Wendell Holmes in *Missouri* v. *Holland* (1920), which upheld congressional legislation in pursuance of a treaty regulating the killing of migratory birds. To Holmes, neither the Framers' failure to anticipate treaties about migratory birds nor a lower court's invalidation of similar legislation before the treaty's ratification was decisive. As long as the treaty involved a matter of national concern that could be regulated through an international agreement, it constituted a valid exercise of the foreign affairs power. Holmes went on to point out that even if congressional legislation exceeded specific constitutional grants of power to Congress, it might nonetheless be valid if necessary and proper to implement a treaty or other exercise of the foreign affairs power.

Not surprisingly, the idea that the national government might expand its sphere of domestic control through the foreign affairs power has been disputed. Defenders of state prerogatives have argued that this interpretation threatens the division of power between nation and state, particularly because contemporary multilateral treaties (e.g., United Nations covenants on the elimination of racial discrimination) may involve matters of exclusively domestic concern. During the early 1950s, this concern led Senator John Bricker of Ohio to propose a constitutional amendment that would have required congressional legislation before any treaty became effective as internal law in the United States. Bricker's effort dramatized the concern that the states may lack constitutional protection against national foreign-policy decisions. However, the requirement that treaties be ratified by the Senate, in which the states are equally represented, probably affords the states adequate protection.

## WAR AND INDIVIDUAL RIGHTS

The Framers of the Constitution sought to design a system of government that could respond successfully to crises of war and foreign affairs. In *The Federalist,* No. 23, Hamilton acknowledged that the achievement of this aim required a broad grant of power to the national government:

> The circumstances that endanger the safety of nations are infinite, and for this reason no constitutional shackles can wisely be imposed on the power to which the care of it is committed. This power ought to be coextensive with all the possible combinations of such circumstances; and ought to be under the direction of the same councils which are appointed to preside over the common defense.

Because war places a premium on swift and decisive action, Congress in wartime has characteristically concentrated this broad governmental power in the executive. During World War I, Congress delegated to President Woodrow Wilson virtually standardless regulatory power over major sectors of the economy, private communications with foreign countries, and numerous other concerns. Even before the United States' entry into World War II, the Lend-Lease Act empowered the president to transfer "defense articles" to the "government of any country whose defense he deems vital to the defense of the United States" under any terms that he deemed satisfactory. During the war, President Franklin Roosevelt was authorized to direct war production, to control the prices of goods, to introduce rationing, and generally to regulate the economic life of the country.

At times, presidents have relied on their own authority rather than on congressional delegations of power in responding to crisis situations.

President Lincoln's actions during the ten weeks between the fall of Fort Sumter and the convening of Congress represent the prime example of unilateral executive action. During that period, Lincoln enlarged the army and navy, called up the state militias, spent unappropriated funds, and instituted a blockade of Southern ports. In defending his actions, he asserted that the "war power," a combination of the Commander-in-Chief Clause and of his responsibility to ensure that "the laws be faithfully executed," provided a sufficient constitutional justification. He also submitted his extraordinary exercise of power to Congress, which ratified the actions shortly after it convened.

Several times in this century, presidents have claimed the power to act in crisis situations even without a declaration of war. During the undeclared war in Korea, President Harry Truman seized the steel mills to prevent a strike that would have stopped steel production; during the Vietnam conflict, President Richard Nixon attempted to halt publication of the Pentagon Papers, a classified study of how the United States became involved in the war. Although the Supreme Court in both instances rejected the claims of executive power, the justices implicitly recognized that the national government as a whole has sufficient power to deal with such crises.

Both governmental practice and judicial decisions, then, confirm that the national government possesses broad powers to deal with crises in external affairs, and that the exercise of these powers may justify the temporary overriding of the constitutional separation of powers. Does it also permit the temporary suspension of constitutionally protected rights? The question is not merely hypothetical. During the Civil War, President Lincoln suspended the writ of habeas corpus to all persons "guilty of any disloyal practice" and authorized trial and punishment of such persons by courts-martial and military tribunals. Early in World War II, President Franklin Roosevelt issued an executive order, later supported by congressional action, that led to the forced evacuation from the West Coast of 112,000 residents of Japanese ancestry, many of whom were American citizens. Not surprisingly, those affected in both instances complained that the government's actions had violated their constitutional rights. In *Ex Parte Milligan* (1866) and *Korematsu* v. *United States* (1944), the Supreme Court ruled directly on these complaints.

Four alternative interpretations of the extent of governmental power during wartime emerged from *Korematsu* and *Milligan.* According to the broadest interpretation of governmental power, which was espoused by the Court majority in *Korematsu* and by the four concurring justices in *Milligan,* the fundamental consideration is that the government's power to wage war is the power to wage war successfully. From this it follows that the national government possesses all powers necessary and proper to the successful prosecution of the war. When an area of the country is an actual or potential theater of military operations, accordingly, the government may engage in actions that would be unconstitutional during peacetime. As long as the actions taken are "reasonably expedient military precautions" relating to the public safety, they are constitutionally permissible under the Necessary and Proper Clause.

The Court majority in *Milligan* took a more restrictive view of governmental power, asserting that all constitutional limitations on governmental action apply with equal force during wartime. According to the *Milligan* majority, the decisive factor is the Framers' decision not to insert exceptions for wartime in the constitutional protections of rights. Their judgment that the government did not need the power to suspend constitutionally protected rights, based as it was on a personal familiarity with war during the Revolution, is authoritative for future generations. Therefore, any action that infringes on rights during peacetime remains unconstitutional during wartime, because "the Constitution of the United States is a law for rulers and ruled, equally in war and in peace."

Justice Frank Murphy, dissenting in *Korematsu,* proposed a third constitutional standard. According to Murphy, military necessity can justify the deprivation of individual rights, but government assertions of necessity should not be accepted uncritically. When the government undertakes such a radical step, judges must scrutinize closely the bases for this action. Only when such deprivations can be "reasonably related to a public danger that is so immediate, imminent, and impending as not to admit of delay and not to permit the intervention of ordinary constitutional processes," Murphy concluded, should they be upheld. The judiciary thus would play a major role in enforcing constitutional limitations.

In his dissent in *Korematsu,* Justice Robert Jackson offered a distinctive interpretation of the extent of governmental power in wartime. Jackson maintained that what is expedient on military grounds may not be constitutionally permissible—a situation that obviously creates a dilemma for the Supreme Court. On the one hand, the judiciary cannot expect the national government to refrain from actions it deems essential to the public safety merely because of judicial disapproval. On the other hand, Court endorsement of unconstitutional actions on the basis of alleged military necessity would provide a precedent for similar abuses whenever "any authority . . . can bring forward a plausible claim of an urgent need." Because the Constitution does not provide sufficient power to deal with all the exigencies of war, necessity—self-preservation—and not constitutionality will inevitably (and properly) be the standard for governmental action during wartime. The Supreme Court, Jackson argued, should play no role in such situations.

## NOTES

1 Hamilton defended the president's power to issue the Neutrality Proclamation in the "Pacificus" letters. See Alexander Hamilton, *The Works of Alexander Hamilton,* ed. Henry Cabot Lodge (New York: Federal Edition, 1904) 4:76. Madison challenged this view, at times quoting Hamilton's statements in *The Federalist* in the "Helvidius" letters. See James Madison, *The Writings of James Madison,* ed. Gaillard Hunt (New York: 1900–1910) 4:148.

2 Edward S. Corwin, The President: *Office and Powers,* 4th rev. ed. (New York: New York University Press, 1957), p. 171.

3 *McCulloch* v. *Maryland,* 4 Wheat. 316, 415 (1819).
4 Representative cases include *Katz* v. *Tyler,* (1967), and *Sarnoff* v. *Schultz,* (1972).
5 The relevant cases are *Dames & Moore* v. *Regan,* (1981); *Rostker* v. *Goldberg,* (1981), excerpted in Chapter 16; and *Regan* v. *Wald,* (1984).
6 John Marshall applied this label to the president during a debate in the House of Representatives in 1800.
7 American Enterprise Institute, *The War Powers Bill, Legislative Analysis No. 19,* (April 17, 1972), pp. 47–55.
8 The House of Representatives subsequently amended a resolution of thanks to General Zachary Taylor to include a condemnation of President Polk for unconstitutionally involving the nation in war.
9 For discussions critical of the effectiveness of the War Powers Resolution, see Michael Glennon, "The War Powers Resolution: Sad Record, Dismal Promises," *Loyala of Los Angeles Law Review* 17 (1984): 657–670, and John Hart Ely, "Suppose Congress Wanted a War Powers Act That Worked," *Columbia Law Review* 88 (1988): 1379–1431.
10 See, for example, Robert F. Turner, "The War Powers Resolution: Unconstitutional, Unnecessary, and Unhelpful," *Loyola of Los Angeles Law Review* 17 (1984): 683–713.
11 In reporting his efforts to free the *Mayaguez,* President Gerald Ford stated that he did so "[i]n accordance with my desire that the Congress be informed on this matter and *taking note of sec. 4(a)(1)*" of the Resolution (emphasis added). Similarly, President Jimmy Carter's letter to Congress following the attempt to rescue the hostages in Iran stated that his report was *"consistent with"* the requirements of sec. 4(a)(1) (emphasis added). Thus in neither case did the president indicate that such a report was a legal responsibility.

## SELECTED READING

*The Federalist,* Nos. 23–26, 64, 70, 75.

*Dames & Moore* v. *Regan,* 453 U.S. 654 (1981).
*Ex Parte Endo,* 323 U.S. 283 (1944).
*Perpich* v. *Department of Defense,* 496 U.S. 334 (1990).
*United States* v. *Pink,* 315 U.S. 203 (1942).

Casper, Gerhard. "Constitutional Constraints on the Conduct of Foreign and Defense Policy: A Nonjudicial Model." *University of Chicago Law Review* 43 (1976): 463–498.

Ely, John Hart. *War and Responsibility: Constitutional Lessons of Vietnam and Its Aftermath* (Princeton, N.J.: Princeton University Press, 1993).

Fisher, Louis. *Constitutional Conflicts Between Congress and the President,* 4th ed. (Lawrence: University Press of Kansas, 1997).

Glennon, Michael J. *Constitutional Diplomacy* (Princeton, N.J.: Princeton University Press, 1990).

Irons, Peter H. *Justice at War* (New York: Oxford University Press, 1983).

Lofgren, Charles A. *"Government from Reflection and Choice": Constitutional Essays on War, Foreign Relations, and Federalism* (New York: Oxford University Press, 1986).

May, Christopher N. *In the Name of War: Judicial Review and the War Powers since 1918* (Cambridge, Mass.: Harvard University Press, 1989).

Scigliano, Robert. "The War Powers Resolution and the War Powers." In Joseph M. Bessette and Jeffrey Tulis, eds. *The Presidency in the Constitutional Order* (Baton Rouge: Louisiana State University Press, 1981).

Silverstein, Gordon. *Imbalance of Power: Constitutional Interpretation and the Making of American Foreign Policy* (New York: Oxford University Press, 1997).

"Symposium: The War Powers Resolution." *Loyola of Los Angeles Law Review* 17 (1984): 579–808.

Treanor, William M. "Fame, the Founding, and the Power to Declare War." *Cornell Law Review* 82 (1997): 695–772.

Yoo, John C. "The Continuation of Politics by Other Means." *California Law Review* 84 (1996): 167–235.

## *The Prize Cases*

**2 Black 635, 17 L. Ed. 459 (1863)**

In April 1861, after the initial outbreak of Civil War hostilities but prior to the convening of a special session of Congress, President Abraham Lincoln proclaimed a blockade of Confederate ports. During the period between the issuance of the president's proclamation and the passage of congressional legislation endorsing the blockade, several ships were seized as blockade runners and their cargoes confiscated. The owners of the ships challenged the legality of the blockade, and questions arising from the litigation were certified to the Supreme Court. *Opinion of the Court: Grier, Wayne, Swayne, Miller, Davis. Dissenting opinion: Nelson, Taney, Catron, Clifford.*

MR. JUSTICE GRIER delivered the opinion of the Court.

Let us inquire whether, at the time this blockade was instituted, a state of war existed which would justify a resort to these means of subduing the hostile force. . . .

If a war be made by invasion of a foreign nation, the President is not only authorized but bound to resist force by force. He does not initiate the war, but is bound to accept the challenge without waiting for any special legislative authority. And whether the hostile "party be a foreign invader, or States organized in rebellion, it is nonetheless a war, although the declaration of it be *"unilateral."* . . .

Whether the President in fulfilling his duties, as Commander in-chief, in suppressing an insurrection, has met with such armed hostile resistance, and a civil war of such alarming proportions as will compel him to accord to them the character of belligerents, is a question to be decided *by him,* and this Court must be governed by the decisions and acts of the political department of the Government to which this power was entrusted. "He must determine what degree of force the crisis demands." The proclamation of blockade is itself official and conclusive evidence to the Court that a state of war existed which demanded and authorized a recourse to such a measure, under the circumstances peculiar to the case. . . .

If it were necessary to the technical existence of a war, that it should have a legislative sanction, we find it in almost every act passed at the extraordinary session of the Legislature of 1861, which was wholly employed in enacting laws to enable the Government to prosecute the war with vigor and efficiency. And finally, in 1861, we find Congress . . . passing an act "approving, legalizing, and making valid all the acts, proclamations, and orders of the President, &c., as if they had been *issued and done under the previous express authority* and direction of the Congress of the United States."

Without admitting that such an act was necessary under the circumstances, it is plain that if the President had in any manner assumed powers which it was necessary should have the authority or sanction of Congress, . . . this ratification has operated to perfectly cure the defect. . . .

. . . we are of the opinion that the President had a right, *jure belli,* to institute a blockade of ports in possession of the States in rebellion, which neutrals are bound to regard.

MR. JUSTICE NELSON, dissenting.

. . . The right of making war belongs exclusively to the supreme or sovereign power of the State. This power in all civilized nations is regulated by the fundamental laws or municipal constitution of the country. By our Constitution this power is lodged in Congress. . . .

An idea seemed to be entertained that all that was necessary to constitute a war was organized hostility in the district of country in a state of rebellion. . . .

Now, in one sense, no doubt this is war, and may be a war of the most extensive and threatening dimensions and effects, but it is a statement simply of its existence in a material sense, and has no relevancy or weight when the question is what constitutes war in a legal sense, in the sense of the law of nations, and of the Constitution of the United States? . . .

. . . Ample provision has been made under the Constitution and laws against any sudden and unexpected disturbance of the public peace from insurrection at home or invasion from abroad. The whole military and naval power of the country is put under the control of the President to meet the emergency. . .But it is the exercise of a power under the municipal laws of the country and not under the law of nations. . . .

. . . I am compelled to the conclusion that no civil war existed between this Government and the States in insurrection till recognized by the Act of Congress 13th of July, 1861; that the President does not possess the power under the Constitution to declare war or recognize its existence within the meaning of the law of nations, which carries with it belligerent rights, and thus change the country and all its citizens from a state of peace to a state of war; that this power belongs exclusively to the Congress of the United States, and, consequently, that the President had no power to set on foot a blockade under the law of nations, and that the capture of the vessel and cargo in this case, and in all cases before us in which the capture occurred before the 13th of July, 1861 . . . are illegal and void, and that the decrees of condemnation should be reversed and the vessel and cargo restored.

## The Gulf of Tonkin Resolution

**78 Stat. 384 (1964)**

On August 2, 1964, North Vietnamese torpedo boats allegedly attacked two U.S. destroyers in the Gulf of Tonkin. President Lyndon Johnson quickly called for a resolution from Congress to support his determination to repel attacks on American forces and to prevent further aggression. On August 7, the House and the Senate passed the requested resolution by margins of 416–0 and 88–2, respectively. Until its repeal by Congress in 1970, this so-called Gulf of Tonkin Resolution was relied upon to justify escalation and expansion of the Vietnam War.

Whereas naval units of the Communist regime in Vietnam, in violation of the principles of the Charter of the United Nations and of international law, have deliberately and repeatedly attacked United States naval vessels lawfully present in international waters, and have thereby created a serious threat to international peace: and

Whereas these attacks are part of a deliberate and systematic campaign of aggression that the Communist regime in North Vietnam has been waging against its neighbors and the nations joined with them in the collective defense of their freedom: and

Whereas the United States is assisting the people of southeast Asia to protect their freedom and has no territorial, military or political ambitions in that area, but desires only that these peoples should be left in peace to work out their own destinies in their own way: Now, therefore, be it

*Resolved by the Senate, and House of Representatives of the United States of America in Congress assembled.* That the Congress approves and supports the determination of the President, as Commander in Chief, to take all necessary measures to repel any armed attack against the forces of the United States and to prevent further aggression. . . .

*Section 2.* The United States regards as vital to its national interest and to world peace the maintenance of international peace and security in southeast Asia. Consonant with the Constitution of the United States and the Charter of the United Nations and in accordance with its obligations under the Southeast Asia Collective Defense Treaty, the United States is, therefore, prepared, as the President determines, to take all necessary steps, including the use of armed force, to assist any member or protocol state of the Southeast Asia Collective Defense Treaty requesting assistance in defense of its freedom.

*Section 3.* This resolution shall expire when the President shall determine that the peace and security of the area is reasonably assured by international conditions created by action of the United Nations or otherwise, except that it may be terminated earlier by concurrent resolution of the Congress.

## The War Powers Resolution

**87 Stat. 555, 50 U.S.C. 1541 (1973)**

As criticism of the Vietnam War mounted during the early 1970s, members of Congress sought to reassert congressional control over the use of American troops. In 1972 the Senate passed a war powers bill that defined the circumstances under which the president could commit American troops to hostilities, but this bill was rejected by the House of Representatives. The following resolution, passed over President Richard Nixon's veto in 1973, does not specify when troops may be used, but it does require presidential consultation with Congress, when possible, and allows Congress to terminate American involvement in hostilities.

§1541 (a) It is the purpose of this joint resolution to fulfill the intent of the framers of the Constitution of the United States and insure that the collective judgment of both the Congress and the President will apply to the introduction of United States Armed Forces into hostilities, or into situations where imminent involvement in hostilities is clearly indicated by the circumstances, and to the continued use of such forces in hostilities or in such situations. . . .

(b) Under article I, section 8, of the Constitution, it is specifically provided that the Congress shall have the power to make all laws necessary and proper for carrying into execution, not only its own powers but also all other powers vested by the Constitution in the Government of the United States, or in any department or officer hereof.

(c) The constitutional powers of the President as Commander-in-Chief to introduce United States Armed Forces into hostilities, or into situations where imminent involvement in hostilities is clearly indicated by the circumstances, are exercised only pursuant to (1) a declaration of war (2) specific statutory authorization, or (3) a national emergency created by attack upon the United States, its territories or possessions, or its armed forces. . . .

§1542. . .The President in every possible instance shall consult with Congress before introducing United States Armed Forces into hostilities or into situations where imminent involvement in hostilities is clearly indicated by the circumstances, and after every such introduction shall consult regularly with the Congress until United States Armed Forces are no longer engaged in hostilities or have been removed from such situations. . . .

§1543. . . .

(a) In the absence of a declaration of war, in any case in which United States Armed Forces are introduced—(1) into hostilities or into situations where imminent involvement in hostilities is clearly indicated by the circumstances; (2) into the territory, airspace or waters of a foreign nation, while equipped for combat, except for deployments which relate solely to supply, replacement, repair, or training of such forces; or (3) in numbers which substantially enlarge United States Armed Forces equipped for combat already located in a foreign nation; the President shall submit within 48 hours to the Speaker of the House of Representatives and to the President pro tempore of the Senate a report, in writing, setting forth—(A) the circumstances necessitating the introduction of the United States Armed

Forces; (B) the constitutional and legislative authority under which such introduction took place; and (C) the estimated scope and duration of the hostilities or involvement.

(b) . . . The President shall provide such other information as the Congress may request in the fulfillment of its constitutional responsibilities with respect to committing the Nation to war and to the use of United States Armed Forces abroad. . . .

§1544. . . .

(b) . . . Within sixty calendar days after a report is submitted or is required to be submitted pursuant to section 1543(a)(1) of this title, whichever is earlier, the President shall terminate any use of United States Armed Forces with respect to which such report was submitted (or required to be submitted), unless the Congress (1) has declared war or has enacted a specific authorization for such use of United States Armed Forces, (2) has extended by law such sixty-day period, or (3) is physically unable to meet as a result of an armed attack upon the United States. Such sixty-day period shall be extended for not more than an additional thirty days if the President determines and certifies to the Congress in writing that unavoidable military necessity respecting the safety of United States Armed Forces requires the continued use of such armed forces in the course of bringing about a prompt removal of such forces.

(c) . . . Notwithstanding subsection (b) of this section, at any time that United States Armed Forces are engaged in hostilities outside the territory of the United States, its possessions and territories without a declaration of war or specific statutory authorization, such forces shall be removed by the President if the Congress so directs by concurrent resolution. . . .

§1547. . .Authority to introduce United States Armed Forces into hostilities or into situations wherein involvement in hostilities is clearly indicated by the circumstances shall not be inferred—(1) from any provision of law (whether or not in effect before November 7, 1973), including any provision contained in any appropriation Act, unless such provision specifically authorizes the introduction of United States Armed Forces into hostilities or into such situations and states that it is intended to constitute specific statutory authorization within the meaning of this joint resolution; or (2) from any treaty heretofore or hereafter ratified unless such treaty is implemented by legislation specifically authorizing the introduction of United States Armed Forces into hostilities or into such situations and stating that it is intended to constitute specific statutory authorization within the meaning of this joint resolution.

(d) . . . Nothing in this joint resolution—(1) is intended to alter the constitutional authority of the Congress or of the President, or the provisions of existing treaties; or (2) shall be construed as granting any authority to the President with respect to the introduction of United States Armed Forces into hostilities or into situations wherein involvement in hostilities is clearly indicated by the circumstances which authority he would not have had in the absence of this joint resolution. . . .

## *United States* v. *Curtiss-Wright Export Corporation*

**299 U.S. 304; 57 S. Ct. 216; 81 L. Ed. 255 (1936)**

On May 28, 1934, Congress passed a joint resolution authorizing the president to prohibit the sale of arms and munitions to the warring countries of Bolivia and Paraguay, should he determine that such a prohibition would "contribute to the reestablishment of peace between those countries." In pursuance of this authority, President Franklin D. Roosevelt immediately embargoed the sale of war materials to those countries. The defendants in this case, charged with conspiring to sell arms to Bolivia in violation of the embargo, contended that the presidential proclamation was invalid because Congress could not constitutionally delegate such broad power to the president. When a federal district court upheld this contention, the United States appealed directly to the Supreme Court. *Opinion of the Court: Sutherland, Hughes, Van Devanter, Brandeis, Butler, Roberts, Cardozo. Dissenting opinion: McReynolds. Not participating: Stone.*

MR. JUSTICE SUTHERLAND delivered the opinion of the Court. . . .

Whether, if the Joint Resolution had related solely to internal affairs it would be open to the challenge that it constituted an unlawful delegation of legislative power to the Executive, we find it unnecessary to determine. The whole aim of the resolution is to affect a situation entirely external to the United States, and falling within the category of foreign affairs. The determination which we are called to make, therefore, is whether the Joint Resolution, as applied to that situation, is vulnerable to attack under the rule that forbids a delegation of the law-making power. In other words, assuming (but not deciding) that the challenged delegation, if it were confirmed to internal affairs, would be invalid, may it nevertheless be sustained on the ground that its exclusive aim is to afford a remedy for a hurtful condition within foreign territory?

It will contribute to the elucidation of the question if we first consider the differences between the powers of the federal government in respect of foreign or external affairs and those in respect of domestic or internal affairs. That there are differences between them, and that these differences are fundamental, may not be doubted.

The two classes of powers are different, both in respect of their origin and their nature. The broad statement that the federal government can exercise no powers except those specifically enumerated in the Constitution, and such implied powers as are necessary and proper to carry into effect the enumerated powers, is categorically true only in respect of our internal affairs. In that field, the primary purpose of the Constitution was to carve from the general mass of legislative powers *then possessed by the states* such portions as it was thought desirable to vest in the federal government, leaving those not included in the enumeration still in the states. . . . Since the states severally never possessed international powers, such powers could not have been carved from the mass of state powers but obviously were transmitted to the United States from some other source. During the colonial period, those powers were possessed exclusively by and were entirely under the control of the Crown. By the Declaration of Independence, "the Representatives of the United States of America" declared the United (not the several) Colonies to be free and independent states, and as such to have "full Power to levy War, conclude Peace, contract Alliances, establish Commerce and to do all other Acts and Things which Independent States may of right do."

As a result of the separation from Great Britain by the colonies acting as a unit, the powers of external sovereignty passed from the Crown not to the colonies severally, but to the colonies in their collective and corporate capacity as the United States of America. Even before the Declaration, the colonies were a unit in foreign affairs, acting through a common agency—namely the Continental Congress, composed of delegates from the thirteen colonies. That agency exercised the powers of war and peace, raised an army, created a navy, and finally adopted the Declaration of Independence. Rulers come and go; governments end and forms of government change; but sovereignty survives. A political society cannot endure without a supreme will somewhere. Sovereignty is never held in suspense. When, therefore, the external sovereignty of Great Britain in respect of the colonies ceased, it immediately passed to the Union. . . .

The Union existed before the Constitution, which was ordained and established among other things to form "a more perfect Union." Prior to that event, it is clear that the Union, declared by the Articles of Confederation to be "perpetual," was the sole possessor of external sovereignty and in the Union it remained without change save in so far as the Constitution in express terms qualified its exercise. The Framers' Convention was called and exerted its powers upon the irrefutable postulate that though the states were several their people in respect of foreign affairs were one. . .

It results that the investment of the federal government with the powers of external sovereignty did not depend upon the affirmative grants of the Constitution. The powers to declare and wage war, to conclude peace, to make treaties, to maintain diplomatic relations with other sovereignties, if they had never been mentioned in the Constitution, would have vested in the federal government as necessary concomitants of nationality. . . . As a member of the family of nations, the right and power of the United States in that field are equal to the right and power of the other members of the international family. Otherwise, the United States is not completely sovereign. . . .

Not only, as we have shown, is the federal power over external affairs in origin and essential character different from that over internal affairs, but participation in the exercise of the power is significantly limited. In this vast external realm, with its important, complicated, delicate and manifold problems, the President alone has the power to speak or listen as a representative of the nation. . . . As Marshall said in his great argument of March 7, 1800, in the House of Representatives, "The President is the sole organ of the nation in its external relations, and its sole representative with foreign nations." . . . It is important to bear in mind that we are here dealing not alone with an authority vested in the President by an exertion of legislative power, but with such an authority plus the very delicate, plenary and exclusive power of the President as the sole organ of the federal government in the field of international relations—a power which does not require as a basis for its exercise an act of Congress, but which, of course, like every other governmental power, must be exercised in subordination to the applicable provisions of the Constitution. It is quite apparent that if, in the maintenance of our international relations, embarrassment—perhaps serious embarrassment—is to be avoided and success for our aims achieved, congressional legislation which is to be made effective through negotiation and inquiry within the international field must often accord to the President a degree of discretion and freedom from statutory restriction which would not be admissible were domestic affairs alone involved. Moreover, he, not Congress, has the better opportunity of knowing the conditions which prevail in foreign countries, and especially is this true in time of war. He has his confidential sources of information. He has his agents in the form of diplomatic, consular and other officials. Secrecy in respect of information gathered by them may be highly necessary, and the premature disclosure of it productive of harmful results. Indeed, so clearly is this true that the first President refused to accede to a request to lay before the House of Representatives the instructions, correspondence and documents relating to the negotiation of the Jay Treaty—a refusal the wisdom of which was recognized by the House itself and has never since been doubted. . . .

The marked difference between foreign affairs and domestic affairs in this respect is recognized by both houses of Congress in the very form of their requisitions for information from the executive departments. In the case of every department except the Department of State, the resolution *directs* the official to furnish the information. In the case of the State Department, dealing with foreign affairs, the President is *requested* to furnish the information "if not incompatible with the public interest." A statement that to furnish the information is not compatible with the public interest rarely, if ever, is questioned.

When the President is to be authorized by legislation to act in respect of a matter intended to affect a situation in foreign territory, the legislator properly bears in mind the important consideration that the form of the President's action—or, indeed, whether he shall act at all—may well depend, among other things, upon the nature of the confidential information which he has or may thereafter receive, or upon the effect which his action may have upon our foreign relations. This consideration, in connection with what we have already said on the subject, discloses the unwisdom of requiring Congress in this field of governmental power to lay down narrowly definite standards by which the President is to be governed. As this court said in *Mackenzie* v. *Hare* (1915), "As a government, the United States is invested with all the attributes of sovereignty. As it has the character of nationality it has the powers of nationality, especially those which concern its relations and intercourse with other countries. *We should hesitate long before limiting or embarrassing such powers.*"

In the light of the foregoing observations, it is evident that this court should not be in haste to apply a general rule which will have the effect of condemning legislation like that under review as constituting an unlawful delegation of legislative power. The principles which justify such legislation find overwhelming support in the unbroken legislative practice which has prevailed almost from the inception of the national government to the present day. . . .

The result of holding that the joint resolution here under attack is void and unenforceable as constituting an unlawful delegation of legislative power would be to stamp this multitude of comparable acts and resolutions as likewise invalid. And while this court may not, and should not, hesitate to declare acts of Congress, however many times repeated, to be unconstitutional if beyond all rational doubt it finds them to be so, an impressive array of legislation such as we have just set forth, enacted by nearly every Congress from the beginning of our national existence to the present day, must be given unusual weight in the process of reaching a correct determination of the problem. A legislative practice such as we have here, evidenced not by only occasional instances, but marked by the movement of a steady stream for a century and a half of time, goes a long way in the direction of proving the presence of unassailable ground for the constitutionality of the practice, to be found in the origin and history of the power involved, or in its nature, or in both combined.

The judgment of the court below must be reversed and the cause remanded for further proceedings in accordance with the foregoing opinion.

*Reversed.*

## *Missouri* v. *Holland*

**252 U.S. 346; 91 S. Ct. 382; 64 L. Ed. 641 (1920)**

In 1913, Congress passed legislation regulating the hunting of migratory birds. When two federal district courts ruled that the legislation was unconstitutional in that it lay beyond Congress's enumerated powers under the Constitution, the government accepted the decisions without appeal. In 1916, however, the United States entered into a treaty with Great Britain regulating the hunting of birds that migrated between the United States and Canada, and two years later, Congress passed the Migratory Bird Treaty Act in pursuance of that treaty. A lower federal court denied the state of Missouri's challenge to the legislation, and Missouri appealed. *Opinion of the Court: Holmes, McKenna, White, Day, McReynolds, Brandeis, Clarke. Dissenting (without opinion): VanDevanter, Pitney.*

MR. JUSTICE HOLMES delivered the opinion of the Court.

. . . The question raised is the general one whether the treaty and statute are void as an interference with the rights reserved to the States.

To answer this question it is not enough to refer to the Tenth Amendment, reserving the powers not delegated to the United States, because by Article II, § 2, the power to make treaties is delegated expressly, and by Article VI treaties made under the authority of the United States, along with the Constitution and laws of the United States made in pursuance thereof, are declared the supreme law of the land. If the treaty is valid there can be no dispute about the validity of the statute under Article I, § 8, as a necessary and proper means to execute the powers of the Government. The language of the Constitution as to the supremacy of treaties being general, the question before us is narrowed to an inquiry into the ground upon which the present supposed exception is placed.

It is said that a treaty cannot be valid if it infringes the Constitution, that there are limits, therefore, to the treaty-making power, and that one such limit is that what an act of Congress could not do unaided, in derogation of the powers reserved to the States, a treaty cannot do. An earlier act of Congress that attempted by itself and not in pursuance of a treaty to regulate the killing of migratory birds within the States had been held bad in the District Court. . . .

Whether the two cases were decided rightly or not they cannot be accepted as a test of the treaty power. Acts of Congress are the supreme law of the land only when made in pursuance of the Constitution, while treaties are declared to be so when made under the authority of the United States. It is open to question whether the authority of the United States means more than the formal acts prescribed to make the convention. We do not mean to imply that there are no qualifications to the treaty-making power; but they must be ascertained in a different way. It is obvious that there may be matters of the sharpest exigency for the national well being that an act of Congress could not deal with but that a treaty followed by such an act could, and it is not lightly to be assumed that, in matters requiring national action, "a power which must belong to and somewhere reside in every civilized government" is not to be found. . . . We are not yet discussing the particular case before us but only are considering the validity of the test proposed. With regard to that we may add that when we are dealing with words that also are a constituent act, like the Constitution of the United States, we must realize that they have called into life a being the development of which could not have been foreseen completely by the most gifted of its begetters. It was enough for them to realize or to hope that they had created an organism; it has taken a century and has cost their successors much sweat and blood to prove that they created a nation. The case before us must be considered in the light of our whole experience and not merely in that of what was said a hundred years ago. The treaty in question does not contravene any prohibitory words to be found in the Constitution. The only question is whether it is forbidden by some invisible radiation from the general terms of the Tenth Amendment. We must consider what this country has become in deciding what that Amendment has reserved.

The State as we have intimated founds its claim of exclusive authority upon an assertion of title to migratory birds, an assertion that is embodied in statute. . . . The whole foundation of the State's rights is the presence within their jurisdiction of birds that yesterday had not arrived, tomorrow may be in another State and in a week a thousand miles away. If we are to be accurate we cannot put the case of the State upon higher ground than that the treaty deals with creatures that for the moment are within the state borders, that it must be carried out by officers of the United States within the same territory, and that but for the treaty the State would be free to regulate this subject itself. . . .

Here a national interest of very nearly the first magnitude is involved. It can be protected only by national action in concert with that of another power. The subject-matter is only transitorily within the State and has no permanent habitat therein. But for the treaty and the statute there soon might be no birds for any powers to deal with. We see nothing in the Constitution that compels the Government to sit by while a food supply is cut off and the protectors of our forests and our crops are destroyed. It is not sufficient to rely upon the States. The reliance is vain, and were it otherwise, the question is whether the United States is forbidden to act. We are of opinion that the treaty and statute must be upheld. . . .

*Decree affirmed.*

## *Ex Parte Milligan*

**71 U.S. (4 Wall.) 2; 18 L. Ed. 281 (1866)**

In 1862, President Abraham Lincoln ordered that all persons "guilty of any disloyal practice affording aid and comfort to rebels" should be subject to trial and punishment by "courts-martial or military commissions." Two years later, a military commission acting under this authority tried and convicted Lambdin P. Milligan, a notorious Confederate sympathizer in Indiana, on charges of disloyalty. Since the civil courts were functioning and Indiana was not a battle zone, Milligan charged that the commission lacked jurisdiction over him and sought a writ of habeas corpus in circuit court. He also contended that trial before the military commission violated his constitutional right to trial by jury. After failing to reach agreement on the issues Milligan raised, the circuit court certified the questions to the Supreme Court. *Opinion of the Court: Davis, Nelson, Grier, Clifford, Field. Concurring opinion: Chase, Wayne, Swayne, Miller.*

MR. JUSTICE DAVIS delivered the opinion of the Court.

. . . Milligan, not a resident of one of the rebellious states, or a prisoner of war, but a citizen of Indiana for twenty years past, and never in the military or naval service, is, while at his home, arrested by the military power of the United States, imprisoned and, on certain criminal charges preferred against him, tried, convicted, and sentenced to be hanged by a military commission, organized under the direction of the military commander of the military district of Indiana. Had this tribunal the legal power and authority to try and punish this man?

No graver question was ever considered by this court, nor one which more nearly concerns the rights of the whole people; for it is the birthright of every American citizen when charged with crime, to be tried and punished according to law. . . . The provisions of that instrument on the administration of criminal justice are too plain and direct to leave room for misconstruction or doubt of their true meaning. Those applicable to this case are found in that clause of the original Constitution which says "that the trial of all crimes, except in case of impeachment, shall be by jury;" and in the fourth, fifth, and sixth articles of the amendments. . . .

. . . Even these provisions, expressed in such plain English words, that it would seem the ingenuity of man could not evade them, are now, after the lapse of more than seventy years, sought to be avoided. . . . The Constitution of the United States is a law for rulers and people, equally in war and in peace, and covers with the shield of its protection all classes of men, at all times and under all circumstances. No doctrine, involving more pernicious consequences, was ever invented by the wit of man than that any of its provisions can be suspended during any of the great exigencies of government. Such a doctrine leads directly to anarchy or despotism, but the theory of necessity on which it is based is false; for the government, within the Constitution, has all the powers granted to it which are necessary to preserve its existence, as has been happily proved by the result of the great effort to throw off its just authority.

Have any of the rights guaranteed by the Constitution been violated in the case of Milligan? and if so, what are they?

Every trial involves the exercise of judicial power; and from what source did the Military Commission that tried him derive their authority? Certainly no part of the judicial power of the country was conferred on them: because the Constitution expressly vests it "in one Supreme Court and such inferior courts as the Congress may from time to time ordain and establish," and it is not pretended that the commission was a court ordained and established by Congress. They cannot justify on the mandate of the President: because he is controlled by law, and has his appropriate sphere of duty, which is to execute, not to make, the laws. . . .

But it is said that the jurisdiction is complete under the "laws and usages of war." found, and on whom they operate; they can never be applied to citizens in states which have upheld the authority of the government, and where the courts are open and their process unobstructed. This court has judicial knowledge that in Indiana the Federal authority was always unopposed, and its courts always open to hear criminal accusations and redress grievances; and no usage of war could sanction a military trial there for any offense whatever of a citizen in civil life, in nowise connected with the military service. Congress could grant no such power; and to the honor of our national legislature be it said, it has never been provoked by the state of the country even to attempt its exercise. One of the plainest constitutional provisions was, therefore, infringed when Milligan was tried by a court not ordained and established by Congress, and not composed of judges appointed during good behavior. . . .

Another guarantee of freedom was broken when Milligan was denied a trial by jury. . . . This privilege is a vital principle, underlying the whole administration of criminal justice; it is not held by sufferance, and cannot be frittered away on any plea of state or political necessity. When peace prevails, and the authority of the government is undisputed, there is no difficulty in preserving the safeguards of liberty; for the ordinary modes of trial are never neglected, and no one wishes it otherwise; but if society is disturbed by civil commotion—if the passions of men are aroused and the restraints of law weakened, if not disregarded—these safeguards need, and should receive, the watchful care of those intrusted with the guardianship of the Constitution and laws. . . .

It is claimed that martial law covers with its broad mantle the proceedings of this Military Commission. The proposition is this: That in a time of war the commander of an armed force (if in his opinion the exigencies of the country demand it, and of which he is to judge), has the power, within the lines of his military district, to suspend all civil rights and their remedies, and subject citizens as well as soldiers to the rule of his will; and in the exercise of his lawful authority cannot be restrained, except by his superior officer or the President of the United States. . . .

This nation, as experience has proved, cannot always remain at peace, and has no right to expect that it will always have wise and humane rulers, sincerely attached to the principles of the Constitution. Wicked men, ambitious of power, with hatred of liberty and contempt of law, may fill the place once occupied by Washington and Lincoln; and if this right is conceded, and the calamities of war again befall us, the dangers to human liberty are frightful to contemplate. . . .

. . . it is insisted that the safety of the country in time of war demands that this broad claim for martial law shall be sustained. If this were true, it could be well said that a country, preserved at the sacrifice of all the cardinal principles of liberty, is not worth the cost of preservation. Happily, it is not so. . . .

. . . Martial rule can never exist where the courts are open, and in the proper and unobstructed exercise of their jurisdiction. It is also confined to the locality of actual war. Because, during the late Rebellion it could have been enforced in Virginia, where the national authority was overturned and the courts driven out, it does not follow that it should obtain in Indiana, where that authority was never disputed, and justice was always administered.

MR. CHIEF JUSTICE CHASE delivered the following opinion.

. . . The opinion which has just been read . . . asserts not only that the Military Commission held in Indiana was not authorized by Congress, but that it was not in the power of Congress to authorize it.

We cannot agree to this. . . .

We think that Congress had power, though not exercised, to authorize the Military Commission which was held in Indiana. . . .

Congress has power to raise and support armies; to provide and maintain a navy; to make rules for the government and regulation of the land and naval forces; and to provide for governing such part of the militia as may be in the service of the United States.

It is not denied that the power to make rules for the government of the army and navy is a power to provide for trial and punishment by military courts without a jury. It has been so understood and exercised from the adoption of the Constitution to the present time.

Nor, in our judgment, does the fifth or any other amendment, abridge that power. . . .

. . . It is not necessary to attempt any precise definition of the boundaries of this power. But may it not be said that government includes protection and defense as well as the regulation of internal administration? And is it impossible to imagine cases in which citizens conspiring or attempting the destruction of great injury of the national forces may be subjected by Congress to military trial and punishment in the just exercise of this undoubted constitutional power? . . .

But we do not put our opinion, that Congress might authorize such a military commission as was held in Indiana, upon the power to provide for the government of the national forces.

Congress has the power not only to raise and support and govern armies, but to declare war. It has, therefore, the power to provide by law for carrying on war. This power necessarily extends to all legislation essential to the prosecution of war with vigor and success, except such as interferes with the command of the force and conduct of campaigns. That power and duty belong to the President as Commander-in-Chief. Both these powers are derived from the Constitution, but neither is defined by that instrument. Their extent must be determined: by their nature, and by the principles of our institutions. . . .

Where peace exists the laws of peace must prevail. What we do maintain is that when the nation is involved in war, and some portions of the country are invaded, and all are exposed to invasion, it is within the power of Congress to determine to what states or districts such great and imminent public danger exists as justifies the authorization of military tribunals for the trial of crimes and offenses against the discipline or security of the army or against the public safety.

In Indiana, for example, at the time of the arrest of Milligan and his co-conspirators, it is established by the papers in the record, that the state was a military district, was the theater of military operations, had been actually invaded, and was constantly threatened with invasion. It appears, also, that a powerful secret association, composed of citizens and others, existed within the state, under military organization, conspiring against the draft, and plotting insurrection, the liberation of the prisoners of war at various depots, the seizure of the state and national arsenals, armed co-operation with the enemy, and war against the national government.

We cannot doubt that, in such a time or public danger, Congress had power, under the Constitution, to provide for the organization of a military commission, and for trial by that commission of persons engaged in this conspiracy. The fact that the Federal courts were open was regarded by Congress as a sufficient reason for not exercising the power; but that fact could not deprive Congress of the right to exercise it. Those courts might be open and undisturbed in the execution of their functions, and yet wholly incompetent to avert threatened danger, or to punish, with adequate promptitude and certainty, the guilty conspirators.

In Indiana, the judges and officers of the courts were loyal to the government. But it might have been otherwise. In times of rebellion and civil war it may often happen, indeed, that judges and marshals will be in active sympathy with the rebels, and courts their most efficient allies. . . .

We think that the power of Congress, in such times and in such localities, to authorize trials for crimes against the security and safety of the national forces, may be derived from its constitutional authority to raise and support armies and to declare war, if not from its constitutional authority to provide for governing the national forces.

We have no apprehension that this power, under our American system of government, in which all official authority is derived from the people and exercised under direct responsibility to the people, is more likely to be abused than the power to regulate commerce or the power to borrow money. And we are unwilling to give our assent by silence to expressions of opinion which seem to us calculated, though not intended, to cripple the constitutional powers of the government, and to augment the public dangers in times of invasion and rebellion. . . .

*Although Milligan dealt with presidential actions, the opinion of the Court also stated that Congress could not have authorized the trial of civilians by military tribunals. After the Civil War, many members of Congress believed that the* Milligan *decision cast doubt on the constitutionality of the Reconstruction program in the Southern states. Its suspicions of the Court thus fueled, Congress responded in part by withdrawing the Court's jurisdiction to decide* Ex Parte McCardle *(see Chapter 3), which called into question a validity of the Reconstruction Acts.*

## *Korematsu* v. *United States*

**323 U.S. 214; 65 S. Ct. 193; 89 L. Ed. 194 (1944)**

In February 1942, President Franklin D. Roosevelt issued Executive Order No. 9066, which authorized the creation of military areas from which individuals might be excluded to prevent espionage or sabotage. The order also permitted military commanders to regulate who might enter or remain in such areas. A month later, Congress passed legislation establishing criminal penalties for violations of these regulations. Acting pursuant to the authority delegated to him under the executive order, the commander of the Western Defense Command initially imposed a curfew on residents of Japanese ancestry and ultimately ordered that they be evacuated to inland detention centers. In *Hirabayashi* v. *United States* (1943), the Court upheld the curfew program in a narrow ruling that involved no consideration of the evacuation program. When Toyosaburo Korematsu, an American citizen of Japanese ancestry, refused to leave his home in California, he was convicted in federal district court of violating the exclusion order. After the conviction was upheld by the circuit court of appeals, the Supreme Court granted certiorari. *Opinion of the Court: Black, Stone, Reed, Frankfurter, Douglas, Rutledge. Concurring opinion: Frankfurter. Dissenting opinions: Roberts; Murphy; Jackson.*

MR. JUSTICE BLACK delivered the opinion of the Court.

. . . All legal restrictions which curtail the civil rights of a single racial group are immediately suspect. That is not to say that all such restrictions are unconstitutional. It is to say that courts must subject them to the most rigid scrutiny. Pressing public necessity may sometimes justify the existence of such restrictions; racial antagonism never can . . .

In the light of the principles we announced in the *Hirabayashi* case [*Hirabayashi* v. *United States* (1943)], we are unable to conclude that it was beyond the war power of Congress and the Executive to exclude those of Japanese ancestry from the West Coast war area at the time they did. . . . Nothing short of apprehension by the proper military authorities of the gravest imminent danger to the public safety can constitutionally justify either. But exclusion from a threatened area . . . has a definite and close relationship to the prevention of espionage and sabotage. . . .

. . . It was because we could not reject the finding of the military authorities that it was impossible to bring about an immediate segregation of the disloyal from the loyal that we sustained the validity of the curfew order as applying to the whole group. In the instant case, temporary exclusion of the entire group was rested by the military on the same ground. The judgment that exclusion of the whole group was for the same reason a military imperative answers the contention that the exclusion was in the nature of group punishment based on antagonism to those of Japanese origin.

We uphold the exclusion order as of the time it was made and when the petitioner violated it. . . . In doing so, we are not unmindful of the hardships imposed by it upon a large group of American citizens. . . . But hardships are part of war, and war is an aggregation of hardships. All citizens alike, both in and out of uniform, feel the impact of war in greater or lesser measure. Citizenship has its responsibilities as well as its privileges, and in time of war the burden is always heavier. Compulsory exclusion of large groups of citizens from their homes, except under circumstances of direst emergency and peril, is inconsistent with our basic governmental institutions. But when under conditions of modern warfare our shores are threatened by hostile forces, the power to protect must be commensurate with the threatened danger. . . .

It is said that we are dealing here with the case of imprisonment of a citizen in a concentration camp solely because of his ancestry, without evidence or inquiry concerning his loyalty and good disposition towards the United States. To cast this case into outlines of racial prejudice, without reference to the real military dangers which were presented, merely confuses the issue. Korematsu was not excluded from the Military Area because of hostility to him or his race. He was excluded because we are at war with the Japanese Empire, because the properly constituted military authorities feared an invasion of our West Coast and felt constrained to take proper security measures, because they decided that the military urgency of the situation demanded that all citizens of Japanese ancestry be segregated from the West Coast temporarily, and finally, because Congress, reposing its confidence in this time of war in our military leaders—as inevitably it must—determined that they should have the power to do just this. There was evidence of disloyalty on the part of some, the military authorities considered that the need for action was great, and time was short. We cannot—by availing ourselves of the calm perspective of hindsight—now say that at that time these actions were unjustified.

*Affirmed.*

MR. JUSTICE FRANKFURTER, concurring. . . .

The provisions of the Constitution which confer on the Congress and the President powers to enable this country to wage war are as much part of the Constitution as provisions looking to a nation at peace. And we have had recent occasion to quote approvingly the statement of former Chief Justice Hughes that the war power of the Government is "the power to wage war successfully." . . . Therefore, the validity of action under the war power must be judged wholly in the context of war. That action is not to be stigmatized as lawless because like action in times of peace would be lawless. To talk about a military order that expresses an allowable judgment of war needs by those entrusted with the duty of conducting war as "an unconstitutional order" is to suffuse a part of the Constitution with an atmosphere of unconstitutionality. . . . To recognize that military orders are "reasonably expedient military precautions" in time of war and yet to deny them constitutional legitimacy makes of the Constitution an instrument for dialectic subtleties not reasonably to be attributed to the hard-headed Framers, of whom a majority had had actual participation in war. If a military order such as that under review does not transcend the means appropriate for conducting war, such action by the military is as constitutional as would be any authorized action by the Interstate Commerce Commission within the limits of the constitutional power to regulate commerce. . . . To find that the Constitution does not forbid the military measures now complained of does not carry with it approval of that which Congress and the Executive did. That is their business, not ours.

MR. JUSTICE MURPHY, dissenting.

This exclusion of "all persons of Japanese ancestry, both alien and non-alien," from the Pacific Coast area on a plea of military necessity in the absence of martial law ought not to be approved. Such exclusion goes over "the very brink of constitutional power" and falls into the ugly abyss of racism.

In dealing with matters relating to the prosecution and progress of a war, we must accord great respect and consideration to the judgments of the military authorities who are on the scene and who have full knowledge of the military facts. The scope of their direction must, as a matter of necessity and common sense, be wide. And their judgments ought not to be overruled lightly by those whose training and duties ill-equip them to deal intelligently with matters so vital to the physical security of the nation.

At the same time, however, it is essential that there be definite limits to military discretion, especially where martial law has not been declared. Individuals must not be left impoverished of their constitutional rights on a plea of military necessity that has neither substance nor support.

The judicial test of whether the Government, on a plea of military necessity, can validly deprive an individual of any of his constitutional rights is whether the deprivation is reasonably related to a public danger that is so "immediate, imminent, and impending" as not to admit of delay and not to permit the intervention of ordinary constitutional processes to alleviate the danger. . . .

. . . In adjudging the military action taken in light of the then apparent dangers, we must not erect too high or too meticulous standards; it is necessary only that the action have some reasonable relation to the removal of the dangers of invasion, sabotage and espionage. But the exclusion, either temporarily or permanently, of all persons with Japanese blood in their veins has no such reasonable relation. And that relation is lacking because the exclusion order necessarily must rely for its reasonableness upon the assumption that *all* persons of Japanese ancestry may have a dangerous tendency to commit sabotage and espionage and to aid our Japanese enemy in other ways. . . . That this forced exclusion was the result in good measure of this erroneous assumption of racial guilt rather than bona fide military necessity is evidenced by the Commanding General's Final Report on the evacuation from the Pacific Coast area. In it he refers to all individuals of Japanese descent as "subversive," as belonging to "an enemy race" whose "racial strains are undiluted," and as constituting over 112,000 potential enemies . . . at large today" along the Pacific Coast*. In support of this blanket condemnation of all persons of Japanese descent, however, no reliable evidence is cited to show that such individuals were generally disloyal, or had generally so conducted themselves in this area as to constitute a special menace to defense installations or war industries, or had otherwise by their behavior furnished reasonable ground for their exclusion as a group.

Justification for the exclusion is sought, instead, mainly upon questionable racial and sociological grounds not ordinarily within the realm of expert military judgment, supplemented by certain semi-military conclusions drawn from an unwarranted use of circumstantial evidence.

No adequate reason is given for the failure to treat these Japanese Americans on an individual basis by holding investigations and hearings to separate the loyal from the disloyal, as was done in the case of persons of German and Italian ancestry. . . . It is asserted merely that the loyalties of this group "were unknown and time was of the essence." Yet nearly four months elapsed after Pearl Harbor before the first exclusion order was issued; nearly eight months went by until the last order was issued; and the last of these "subversive" persons was not actually removed until almost eleven months had elapsed. Leisure and deliberation seem to have been more of the essence than speed. And the fact that conditions were not such as to warrant a declaration of martial law adds strength to the belief that the factors of time and military necessity were not as urgent as they have been represented to be . . .

---

*Further evidence of the Commanding General's attitude toward individuals of Japanese ancestry is revealed in his voluntary testimony . . .
"I don't want any of them (persons of Japanese ancestry) here. They are a dangerous element. There is no way to determine their loyalty. The west coast contains too many vital installations essential to the defense of the country to allow any Japanese on this coast. . . . The danger of the Japanese was, and is now—if they are permitted to come back—espionage and sabotage. It makes no difference whether he is an American citizen, he is still a Japanese. American citizenship does not necessarily determine loyalty. . . . But we must worry about the Japanese all the time until he is wiped off the map. Sabotage and espionage will make problems as long as he is allowed in this area . . ."

I dissent, therefore, from this legalization of racism. . . . All residents of this nation are kin in some way by blood or culture to a foreign land. Yet they are primarily and necessarily a part of the new and distinct civilization of the United States. They must accordingly be treated at all times as the heirs of the American experiment and as entitled to all the rights and freedoms guaranteed by the Constitution.

MR. JUSTICE JACKSON, dissenting.

. . . It is said that if the military commander had reasonable military grounds for promulgating the orders, they are constitutional and become law, and the Court is required to enforce them. There are several reasons why I cannot subscribe to this doctrine.

It would be impracticable and dangerous idealism to expect or insist that each specific military command in an area of probable operations will conform to conventional tests of constitutionality. When an area is so beset that it must be put under military control at all, the paramount consideration is that its measures be successful, rather than legal. The armed services must protect a society, not merely its Constitution. The very essence of the military job is to marshal physical force, to remove every obstacle to its effectiveness, to give it every strategic advantage. Defense measures will not, and often should not, be held within the limits that bind civil authority in peace. No court can require such a commander in such circumstances to act as a reasonable man; he may be unreasonably cautious and exacting. Perhaps he should be. But a commander in temporarily focusing the life of a community on defense is carrying out a military program; he is not making law in the sense the courts know the term. He issues orders, and they may have a certain authority as military commands, although they may be very bad as constitutional law.

But if we cannot confine military expedients by the Constitution, neither would I distort the Constitution to approve all that the military may deem expedient. That is what the Court appears to be doing, whether consciously or not. I cannot say, from any evidence before me, that the orders of General DeWitt were not reasonably expedient military precautions, nor could I say that they were. But even if they were permissible military procedures, I deny that it follows that they are constitutional. If, as the Court holds, it does follow, then we may as well say that any military order will be constitutional and have done with it. . . .

In the very nature of things, military decisions are not susceptible of intelligent judicial appraisal. They do not pretend to rest on evidence, but are made on information that often would not be admissible and on assumptions that could not be proved. Information in support of an order could not be disclosed to courts without danger that it would reach the enemy. Neither can courts act on communications made in confidence. Hence courts can never have any real alternative to accepting the mere declaration of the authority that issued the order that it was reasonably necessary from a military viewpoint.

Much is said of the danger to liberty from the Army program for deporting and detaining these citizens of Japanese extraction. But a judicial construction of the due process clause that will sustain this order is a far more subtle blow to liberty than the promulgation of the order itself. A military order, however unconstitutional, is not apt to last longer than the military emergency. Even during that period a succeeding commander may revoke it all. But once a judicial opinion rationalizes such an order to show that it conforms to the Constitution, or rather rationalizes the Constitution to show that the Constitution sanctions such an order, the Court for all time has validated the principle of racial discrimination in criminal procedure and of transplanting American citizens. The principle then lies about like a loaded weapon ready for the hand of any authority that can bring forward a plausible claim of an urgent need. Every repetition imbeds that principle more deeply in our law and thinking and expands it to new purposes. . . .

I should hold that a civil court cannot be made to enforce an order which violates constitutional limitations even if it is a reasonable exercise of military authority. The courts can exercise only the judicial power, can apply only law, and must abide by the Constitution, or they cease to be civil courts and become instruments of military policy.

Of course the existence of a military power resting on force, so vagrant, so centralized, so necessarily heedless of the individual, is an inherent threat to liberty. But I would not lead people to rely on this Court for a review that seems to me wholly delusive. The military reasonableness of these orders can only be determined by military superiors. If the people ever let command of the war power fall into irresponsible and unscrupulous hands, the courts wield no power equal to its restraint. The chief restraint upon those who command the physical forces of the country, in the future as in the past, must be their responsibility to the political judgments of their contemporaries and to the moral judgments of history.

My duties as a justice as I see them do not require me to make a military judgment as to whether General DeWitt's evacuation and detention program was a reasonable military necessity. I do not suggest that the courts should have attempted to interfere with the Army in carrying out its task. But I do not think they may be asked to execute a military expedient that has no place in law under the Constitution. I would reverse the judgment and discharge the prisoner.

*In 1948, following condemnation by a presidential commission of the forced evacuation of Japanese-Americans, Congress passed the Evacuation Claims Act, under which claimants received over $37 million. In 1984 another governmental commission concluded that internment resulted from "race prejudice, wartime hysteria, and a failure of political leadership" and recommended a national apology and further monetary compensation. That same year a Federal District Court vacated Korematsu's conviction based on newly discovered evidence that the government had deliberately withheld and falsified relevant evidence in the materials it presented in court. In 1988 Congress formally apologized for the internment and established a fund to pay reparations.*

★

## FEDERALISM AND THE FOUNDING

## FEDERALISM AND THE FIRST CONGRESS

### The Judiciary Act of 1789

## FEDERALISM AND THE MARSHALL COURT

*Cohens* v. *Virginia* (1821)

## DUAL FEDERALISM

*Dred Scott* v. *Sandford* (1857)

## FEDERALISM AND INTERPRETATION BASED ON STRUCTURE AND RELATIONSHIP

*Coyle* v. *Smith* (1911)
*Younger* v. *Harris* (1971)
*Baldwin* v. *Montana Fish and Game Commission* (1978)
*Garcia* v. *San Antonio Metropolitan Transit Authority* (1985)
*New York* v. *United States* (1992)
*Printz* v. *United States* (1997)

## THE POST–CIVIL WAR AMENDMENTS AND THE SHIFTING OF THE FEDERAL BALANCE

*The Civil Rights Cases* (1883)
*Jones* v. *Alfred H. Mayer Company* (1968)
*Patterson* v. *McLean Credit Union* (1989)

## NOTES

## SELECTED READING

## CASES

★

# 7
# FEDERALISM

As a central feature of the American constitutional system, federalism is considered by many to be one of the most important contributions made by the Founders to the art of government and to represent the paradigm of what is called federal government. Most contemporary definitions of federalism amount to little more than generalized descriptions of the way governing power is divided in the United States between the states and the national government.[1] The Framers, however, did not consider the system they had designed to be federal. As their writings make clear, they thought that the Constitution was "in strictness, neither a national nor a federal Constitution, but a composition of both."[2] Further, James Madison argued, the "compound government" created by the Constitution must "be explained by itself, [and] not by similitudes or analogies."[3] In order to appreciate the difficulties facing the Supreme Court when it deals with questions of federalism and to evaluate its decisions in this area, we must attempt to comprehend the Framers' understanding of this "neither wholly federal, nor wholly national" political arrangement and how they thought that it contributed to the overall ends of the Constitution.

## FEDERALISM AND THE FOUNDING

It is essential to understand that the Framers recognized only two fundamental modes, or elements, of political organization, the federal and the national,[4] which they thought they had combined into a compound system. Today, in contrast, it is commonplace to speak of three elemental forms: confederal, federal, and national or unitary. This modern typology treats the confederal and national forms as the extremes, with a confederation preserving the primacy and autonomy of the states and a nation giving unimpeded primacy to the government of the whole society. Federalism, in this view, stands between these two poles and combines the best characteristics of each. Specifically, federalism is thought to combine states, which confederally retain sovereignty within a certain sphere, with a central body that nationally possesses sovereignty within another sphere.

The Framers, however, saw no more difference between the confederal and the federal than we see, for example, between the words *inflammable* and *flammable:* nothing more was involved than the accidental presence or absence of a nonsignifying prefix. For them, the confederal or federal was opposed to the unitary or national, and they viewed the Constitution as a composition of both elemental modes. Today, we regard as a third fundamental mode or element what they regarded as a mere compound, bestowing the simple word *federal* on what the Framers considered to be a composition of both federal and national elements.

The founding generation's idea of confederal or federal arrangements, as represented in the Articles of Confederation, was characterized by three operative principles, each of which drastically limited the power of the federal authority and preserved the primacy of the member states.[5] First, the central federal authority did not govern individual citizens: it dealt only with the individual states that composed the federal system and operated primarily by the voluntary consent of those states. Second, the central government had no authority to deal with the internal affairs of the member states; rather, its rule was narrowly confined to certain external tasks of mutual interest to all—for example, war and common defense. Third, each member state had an exact equality of sufferage—an equal vote derived from the equal sovereignty possessed by each state, regardless of size, strength, or wealth.

In the Founders' conception of a national government, in contrast, all power resided in the central authority and local units of government, if retained at all, were mere subdivisions that existed for administrative purposes only. Such powers as these localities possessed were delegated by the national government and could be overridden or withdrawn altogether at its will. The national authority, then, extended to all matters of internal administration and acted directly, through its own officials, not merely on the local governments but upon every citizen as well. Finally, since the national government was independent of the local units, it could continue in existence even if they were to disappear.

Given these two modes from which to choose, confederal or federal association traditionally had been preferred by those in favor of republican government, who regarded it as the only way in which the advantages of size could be combined with the blessings of republicanism. Proponents of this view argued that, first of all, only small countries with homogeneous populations could possess republican government, for only small countries could secure the public's voluntary attachment to the government and voluntary obedience to the laws; and that, second, when such small republics seek the advantages and safety of greater size, as inevitably they must, they can preserve their republican character only by uniting in a federal manner. Federalism would be, for them, the protective husk that preserved the kernels of free government.[6]

The leading Framers realized, however, that the traditional republican embrace of federalism, as incorporated in the Articles of Confederation, had reduced the people to "the last stage of national humiliation." As Alexander Hamilton complained, "There is scarcely anything that can wound the pride, or degrade the character of an independent nation, which we do not experience." The principles of federalism had rendered the Articles so weak that the situation "sometimes bordered on anarchy." Nor was the government's ineptitude limited to the realm of foreign affairs. Domestically, "the security of private rights" had been rendered precarious and the "steady dispensation of justice" interrupted by the practices of many states.[7] Convinced of the need for a more powerful government, many delegates to the Constitutional Convention supported the Virginia Plan. As amended, the plan declared that "a Union of the States merely federal will not accomplish the objects proposed by the Articles of Confederation, namely common defense, security of liberty, and general welfare" and proposed, therefore, that "a *national* Government ought to be established consisting of a *supreme* Legislative, Executive and Judiciary."[8]

At this juncture, a serious question arose: Could a national government be formed without jeopardizing republican liberty? Those who favored the establishment of such a government had to persuade their contemporaries that the proposed plan was also compatible with republican government—that federalism as it had been understood to that time was not indispensable to republicanism. To do so, they chose to undermine the prevailing notion that without federalism, only small countries could possess republican governments. Madison's arguments in this regard were decisive. Turning the small-republic view on its head, he contended that smallness, not largeness, was fatal to republican liberty. History demonstrated that small republics continuously were racked with faction and oppression; indeed, the Constitutional Convention itself had been instigated by the fear for liberty in the small American states. "Was it to be supposed that republican liberty could long exist under the abuses of it practiced in some of the States? . . . Were we not thence admonished to enlarge the sphere as far as the nature of the government would admit?" Because smallness had proven fatal to republicanism, "the only remedy is to enlarge the sphere, and thereby divide the community into so great a number of interests and parties, that in the first place a majority will not be likely at the same moment to have a common interest separate from that of the whole or of the minority; and in the second place, that in case they should have such an interest, they may not be apt to unite in the pursuit of it."[9] The multiplicity of interests present in a large republic thus was the true guardian of republican liberty—the republican remedy for the diseases most incident to republican government.[10]

Madison's arguments on behalf of a large extended republic effectively demolished the small-republic argument but failed to convince the convention to adopt a wholly national government. Most of the delegates, reluctant to abolish the states altogether, sought some means for preserving their existence and agency. Increasingly, they came to recognize that because, as William Johnson of Connecticut pointed out, the states were both distinct "political societies" and "districts of people composing one political society,"[11] neither a wholly federal nor a wholly national constitution was appropriate. Spurred on by, among others, George Mason of Virginia and James Wilson of Pennsylvania, they realized that it was possible for the people to create and assign power to more than "one set of immediate representatives."[12] The people could have their cake and eat it too: not only could they preserve the states while at the same time establishing a new national government, but they could also have a political structure in which both levels of government operated over the same geographic area. Power would be divided between these two levels according to a simple yet elegant formula: any object of government confined in operation and effect wholly within the bounds of a particular state would belong to the government of that state, and any object of government extended in its operation and effect beyond the bounds of the particular state would belong to the government of the United States.

Beyond this straightforward division of power between the central government and the states, federalism to the convention delegates also meant the presence of federal elements in the central government itself. They anticipated that the new constitution would "in some respects operate on the States, in others on the people."[13] Because the new central government would act upon both the states and the people, the delegates concluded that both ought to be represented in the new government. Accordingly, they mixed together varying proportions of federal and national elements to create a composition that was neither wholly federal nor wholly national. This blend of elements is apparent in such constitutional provisions as the mode by which the Constitution was to be ratified, the amending process, equal representation of the states in the Senate, election of the Senate by state legislatures, and the electoral college.

When Alexis de Tocqueville examined the American Constitution, he described it as "neither exactly national nor exactly federal; but the new word which ought to express this novel thing does not yet exist."[14] While he was correct in declaring that a new word had not been devised, a familiar term from the beginning had been pressed into service to express this novel thing: the term *federal.* Well aware that federalism was generally thought to be essential for a republican government, the Framers seized the word for themselves and called their new compound arrangement federalism. This stratagem proved to be of considerable value during the ratification campaign, as it enabled them to present themselves as defenders of federalism and to refer to the adherents of true federalism as Anti-Federalists. But the Framers' identification of their compound government as federal, although an effective ploy at the time, has been the source of much subsequent confusion over exactly what federalism means and what mode of government the American Constitution establishes. Such confusion can be avoided by reference to the Constitution's Preamble. The Constitution was intended neither to provide for a perfect union (i.e., a wholly national government), nor to preserve the radically imperfect union of the Articles of Confederation; rather, it was ordained and established "in order to form a more perfect Union." The phrase "a more perfect Union" is no grammatical solecism; to the contrary, it is an accurate description of the compound government, made up of both federal and national elements, that the convention had devised.

It was, in part, through the means of this "more perfect Union" that the overall ends of the Constitution were to be served. As Madison had observed in The *Federalist,* No. 51, in framing the Constitution the convention's great object was "first [to] enable the government to control the governed; and in the next place, [to] oblige it to control itself." Madison and the other leading Framers recognized that the federal arrangements they had devised could contribute to the realization of both goals. The division of power between the states and the national government allowed them to entrust to the entire federal structure more power than they would have been willing to grant to either the states or the national government alone, and thereby to assure that the government would have sufficient power to control the governed and to avoid the near-anarchy that had existed under the Articles of Confederation. They also appreciated, on the other hand, that the federalism they had devised helped to oblige the government to control itself. By creating two levels of government and dividing power between them, the Framers made each level less threatening to liberty. And by interjecting federal elements into the national government itself, they checked the threat of tyranny from regionally concentrated factious majorities. In short, the Framers' federalism helped to provide energetic government organized around the principle of qualitative majority rule.

## FEDERALISM AND THE FIRST CONGRESS

The Framers understood the new Constitution they were establishing to be neither wholly national nor wholly federal but a composition of both. The members of the First Congress acted in conformity with this statement as they drafted the Judiciary Act of 1789. With this act, Congress constituted the Supreme Court, consisting of a chief justice and five associate justices. Significantly, the Congress also exercised its constitutional option to establish a system of inferior federal courts. It did so principally because it believed that an effective maritime commerce (essential to the new nation) needed a dependable body of maritime law and that the most reliable method to ensure its development would be to entrust it to a new set of courts. Thus, it established thirteen federal district courts of one judge each—one district for each of the eleven states that had, by that time, ratified the Constitution and two additional districts, in Virginia and Massachusetts for Kentucky and Maine. It also provided for three circuit courts, each composed of two justices of the Supreme Court sitting in conjunction with one district court judge.

Parts of the Judiciary Act were unquestionably national in character. Thus in addition to establishing inferior federal tribunals rather than simply relying on state courts, the Congress also included Section 25, which brought the state courts directly under federal appellate jurisdiction by providing for appeals from state courts to the federal judiciary. Under Section 25, appeals could be taken to the U.S. Supreme Court whenever the highest state court having jurisdiction of the case ruled against the constitutionality of a federal law or treaty, ruled in favor of the validity of a state act that had been challenged as contrary to the Constitution or federal law, or ruled against a right or privilege claimed under the Constitution or federal law. (Interestingly, however, it withheld from the Supreme Court the power to review cases in which state courts invalidated state conduct on federal grounds, even in those cases in which state conduct was invalidated under an overly broad reading of federal laws that in turn defeated other federal rights.)

While the creation of inferior federal courts and Section 25 were national in character, other provisions of the Judiciary Act of 1789 were federal. Thus, it granted state courts concurrent original jurisdiction in all civil suits at common law and equity, conferring upon the federal courts exclusive jurisdiction only in admiralty and maritime cases and in cases involving the few crimes and offenses cognizable under the authority of the United States. It withheld from the federal trial courts jurisdiction over cases "arising under" the Constitution and laws of the United States, leaving these to be adjudicated in the state courts. (Congress did not provide the federal courts with federal question jurisdiction until the Judiciary Act of 1875.)

The Judiciary Act of 1789 also set a monetary minimum for Supreme Court review of civil cases, a requirement that Congress did not eliminate for all cases involving constitutional issues until 1891 and did not abolish with respect to Supreme Court review of all federal questions until 1925. It also withheld Supreme Court review of federal criminal cases, something Congress did not provide until 1891. Still another provision that was definitely federal in character was Section 34, called the Rules of Decision Act. It provided that "the laws of the several States, except where the Constitution, treaties, or statutes of the United States shall otherwise require or provide, shall be regarded as rules of decision in trials at common law in the court of the United States in cases where they apply."

## FEDERALISM AND THE MARSHALL COURT

As is true of many compounds, the government created by the Framers is potentially unstable. Under the pressure of events and with the proper catalytic agents present, it may break down into its elemental modes and become either wholly federal or wholly national. A principal responsibility of the Supreme Court, consistent with its claim in *Marbury* v. *Madison* (1803) that "it is emphatically the province and duty of the judicial department to say what the law is," has been to prevent such an occurrence and to preserve the "mixed nature" of the Constitution. In discharging this responsibility, the Court often has had to counteract whichever element is in danger of gaining ascendancy. For the most part, the justices have accomplished this task by the way in which they have drawn the line between the powers of the national government and those of the states. The line of demarcation cannot be fixed permanently or precisely. As Chief Justice John Marshall remarked in *McCulloch* v. *Maryland* (1819), "The question respecting the extent of the powers actually granted, is perpetually arising, and will probably continue to arise, as long as our system shall exist." The answers given by the Court to this "perpetually arising" question have helped to maintain a balance of power between the states and the national government, and thereby to preserve the compound nature of our constitutional system.[15]

Initially, under Marshall's leadership, the Court defined state and national powers in such a way as to benefit the national government. At that time, the people felt a "habitual attachment" to their state governments. As Hamilton pointed out in the Constitutional Convention, the state's "sovereignty is immediately before the eyes of the people: its protection is immediately enjoyed by them. From its hand distributive justice, and all those acts which familiarize and endear government to a people, are dispensed to them." Given that "the passions . . . of avarice, ambition, interest, which govern most individuals and all public bodies, fall into the current of the States and do not flow in the stream of the General Government," the states were likely to be "an overmatch for the General Government."[16] In the face of this imbalance in power, the compound government created by the Framers easily could be broken down into its elemental modes to such an extent that a simple confederation—with all its attendant evils, once again would emerge. To prevent such a calamity, the Marshall Court systematically interpreted the Constitution so as to render secure the power and authority of the general government, as its opinions in *McCulloch* (found in Chapter 4), *Martin* v. *Hunter's Lessee* (1816), and *Cohens* v. *Virginia* (1821) make clear.

In *McCulloch,* Chief Justice Marshall set forth three basic rules of constitutional interpretation that in general favored the national government and in particular supported his argument for upholding the constitutionality of the Bank of the United States and invalidating Maryland's tax on that bank. First, he argued that the enumerated powers of the national government ought to be seen as means to the accomplishment of certain ends. Because these powers helped designate the Constitution's "great outlines" and "important objects," Marshall contended, they should not be considered to be limitations on the national government. A broad and expansive construction of the powers of the national government was essential: "A constitution, to contain an accurate detail of all the subdivisions of which its great powers will admit, and of all the means by which they may be carried into execution, would partake of the prolixity of a legal code, and could scarcely be embraced by the human mind." The United States Constitution was not a statute, and it ought not to be read as one. Emphasizing that "we must never forget that it is *a constitution* we are expounding, . . . intended to endure for ages to come," Marshall advanced the following principle, which he felt would assure a "sound construction" of the Constitution: "Let the end be legitimate, let it be within the scope of the constitution, and all means which are appropriate, which are plainly adapted to that end, which are not prohibited, but consist with the letter and spirit of the constitution, are constitutional." To Marshall, this principle of constitutional construction was dictated not only by logic, but also by the presence of the Necessary and Proper Clause.

The second basic rule of constitutional interpretation advanced in *McCulloch* was related to the first: the Tenth Amendment, Marshall declared, constitutes no bar to a broad construction of even the incidental or implied powers of the national government. The Chief Justice drew attention to the fact that unlike the Articles of Confederation, which required "that everything granted shall be expressly and minutely described," the Tenth Amendment declares only that the powers "not delegated to the United States, nor prohibited to the States, are reserved to the States or to the people." Thus, the answer to the question of whether "the particular power which may become the subject of contest has been delegated to the one government or prohibited to the other, [is] to depend on a fair construction of the whole instrument."

Marshall's third and final rule arose out of his reading of the Supremacy Clause in Article VI. He contended that within its sphere the national government is supreme, and its policies must prevail, regardless of whatever state powers or functions it may touch: "It is of the very essence of supremacy to remove all obstacles to its action within its own sphere, and so to modify every power vested in subordinate governments, as to exempt its own operations from their own influence."

In *Martin* v. *Hunter's Lessee* and *Cohens* v. *Virginia,* the Marshall Court further sought to protect the compound nature of the American constitutional system from the excessive centrifugal forces generated by state loyalties, by establishing the authority of the Supreme Court to review state court decisions in the civil and criminal realms. In *Martin,* Justice Joseph Story spoke for his judicial brethren when he declared that Section 25 of the Judiciary Act of 1789, which extended federal jurisdiction over civil cases pending in state courts, was "supported by the letter and spirit of the Constitution." He stressed

> the importance, and even necessity of uniformity of decisions throughout the whole United States, upon all subjects within the purview of the constitution. Judges of equal learning and integrity, in different states, might differently interpret the statute, or a treaty of the United States, or even the Constitution itself: if there were no re-

> vising authority to control these jarring and discordant judgments, and harmonize them into uniformity, the laws, the treaties and the constitution of the United States would be different, in different states, and might, perhaps, never have precisely the same construction, obligation or efficiency, in any two states. The public mischiefs that would attend such a state of things would be truly deplorable; and it cannot be believed, that they could have escaped the enlightened convention which formed the constitution. What, indeed, might then have been only prophecy, has now become fact; and the appellate jurisdiction must continue to be the only adequate remedy for such evils.

And in *Cohens,* Chief Justice Marshall rejected the arguments of the State of Virginia that state judiciaries were totally separate from and independent of the federal judiciary. He pointed out, first of all, that the states have "chosen to be, in many respects, and to many purposes, a nation; and for all these purposes, her government is complete; to all these objects, it is competent. The people have declared, that in the exercise of all powers given for these objects, it is supreme." From these facts, Marshall went on, it followed inevitably that in a government that is acknowledged to be supreme with respect to objects of vital interest to the nation, "the exercise of the appellate power over those judgments of the State tribunals which may contravene the Constitution or laws of the United States, is, we believe, essential to the attainment of those objects."

## DUAL FEDERALISM

Marshall's efforts to protect the national elements of the Constitution proved so successful that most subsequent concern for the preservation of the government's compound nature has been directed toward retaining its federal elements and ensuring the independent existence and agency of the states. From the appointment of Chief Justice Roger Brooke Taney as Marshall's successor in 1835 until President Franklin D. Roosevelt's clash with the Supreme Court during the New Deal era, this concern most often was manifested in what usually is called dual federalism. This doctrine was clearly defined by Justice Peter V. Daniel in the *License Cases* (1847): "Every power delegated to the federal government must be expounded in coincidence with a perfect right in the states to all that they have not delegated; in coincidence, too, with the possession of every power and right necessary for their existence and preservation." Dual federalism assumes that the two levels of government are coequal sovereignties and that each is supreme within its own sphere. Accordingly, the national government may not undertake any action, even in the exercise of its enumerated powers, that touches upon those functions that the Constitution has reserved to the states. The notorious decision handed down in *Dred Scott* v. *Sandford* (1857), in which the Court held unconstitutional the Missouri Compromise of 1820 and declared that

Congress had no power to limit the spread of slavery in the territories, is based on these assumptions.

The proponents of dual federalism insist that the Constitution is a compact among the states, which have, on certain enumerated issues, ceded a portion of their sovereignty to the national government. All sovereignty not ceded, they argue, is retained. To prevent that retained sovereignty from slipping away, they interpret very narrowly the enumerated powers of the national government in general, and the Necessary and Proper Clause in particular. Also, they strongly emphasize the Tenth Amendment, which they consider to be an affirmative base of power from which the states may challenge the wide-ranging effects of national legislation.

All of these considerations are present in *Hammer* v. *Dagenhart* (1918), perhaps the Supreme Court's clearest statement of the theory of dual federalism. In *Hammer* the Court, by a 5–4 vote, invalidated a congressional statute that restricted the transportation in interstate commerce of goods produced by child labor. The majority held that despite the express delegation to the national government of the power "to regulate commerce among the several states," the national government was excluded from regulating any matter that was subject to state power. [17] In the words of Justice William R. Day, author of the majority opinion, "The grant of authority over a purely federal [i.e., national] matter was not intended to destroy the local power always existing and carefully reserved to the States in the Tenth Amendment." He admonished all those who would interpret the Constitution to recall that "the powers not expressly delegated to the national government" are reserved to the states and to the people by the Tenth Amendment.

C. Herman Pritchett has pointed out that in the *Hammer* ruling, Justice Day misquoted the Tenth Amendment (the term *expressly* does not appear in the text), ignored judicial precedent (in *McCulloch* v. *Maryland,* Chief Justice Marshall had held that because the word *expressly* had been intentionally omitted from the amendment, the question of whether a particular power had been delegated to the national government could only be answered by a "fair construction of the whole instrument"), and denied the historical record (in considering the Tenth Amendment, the First Congress rejected a proposal to insert the word *expressly*).[18] These problems did not go unnoticed at the time. Speaking for the four dissenters, Justice Oliver Wendell Holmes declared, "I should have thought that the most conspicuous decisions of this Court had made it clear that the power to regulate commerce and other constitutional powers could not be cut down or qualified by the fact that it might interfere with the carrying out of the domestic policy of any State." Justice Day's argument in effect accorded such primacy to the purely federal elements in the constitutional system that it jeopardized the Constitution's mixed nature and gravely restricted the national government's ability to respond to nationwide problems.

In contending that Congress could not use its admitted powers if they interfered in any way with the states' exercise of their admitted powers, the advocates of dual federalism not only denied the compound nature of the Constitution but also ignored practical necessity. In the end, they did themselves a decided disservice: by the mid 1930s, not surprisingly, the doctrine had fallen into disgrace.[19] Dual federalism soon was replaced by what is often referred to as cooperative federalism—a pragmatic sharing of governmental functions by federal, state, and local authorities that takes little account of whether or not federal or national elements are present and governing.[20]

## FEDERALISM AND INTERPRETATION BASED ON STRUCTURE AND RELATIONSHIP

By stubbornly insisting on the virtual supremacy of federal elements, the defenders of dual federalism ultimately succeeded only in rendering the defense of those elements more difficult.[21] Such a defense is necessary, however. Even Chief Justice Marshall, who often favored the claims of the national government over those of the states, emphasized in *Cohens* that although the states are subordinate for some purposes, for other purposes they are sovereign. Marshall argued that the question of whether a state is to be considered as sovereign or subordinate must be answered through a "fair construction" of the entire Constitution. As Charles L. Black, Jr., has described it, his method was one of "inference from the structure and relationships created by the Constitution in all its parts," not one of elaborate interpretation or exegesis of a particular constitutional provision.[22]

After Marshall, Courts that attempted to preserve the federal elements in the Constitution without relying on dual federalism followed for the most part his example and reasoned from the total structure that the Constitution created. In *Coyle* v. *Smith* (1911), for example, the Court denied Congress the power to specify in Oklahoma's Enabling Act the location of the state's capital, arguing that congressional power was limited to admitting states into "a union of States, equal in power, dignity and authority, each competent to exert that residuum of sovereignty not delegated to the United States by the Constitution itself." To allow Congress selectively to impose conditions on some states would destroy the equality of status that the states enjoy as an inherent attribute of the federal union; more, it would mean that the powers of Congress, rather than being defined by the Constitution alone, in this instance could be enlarged or restricted by the conditions imposed on new states by congressional legislation admitting them into the union. If such legislation were to be sanctioned, finally, new States might bargain away some of the powers reserved to them by the Constitution in an effort to gain admission into the Union.

The same emphasis on reasoning from the total structure of the Constitution is also apparent in *Younger* v. *Harris* (1971) and *Baldwin* v. *Montana Fish and Game Commission* (1978). In *Younger* the Court refused to enjoin, on First Amendment grounds, a pending state criminal prosecution because of its commitment to what Justice Hugo Black called "Our Federalism." Stressing that the Court must be sensitive to the legitimate interests of both the states and the national government, Black declared that this sensitivity requires "a proper respect for state functions, a recognition of the fact that the entire country is made up of a Union of separate state governments, and a continuance of the belief that the National Government will fare best if the States and their institutions are left free to perform their separate functions in their separate ways" and that therefore federal courts should not intervene to protect plaintiffs' rights, allegedly jeopardized by state laws, before the state courts themselves have had the opportunity to hear these challenges to their laws and to demonstrate their own fidelity to the U.S. Constitution. Over the years, the federal courts increasingly appeared to honor the *Younger* principle only in the breach. For example, when the voters of California passed Proposition 187 (banning state-sponsored health and education benefits for illegal aliens), a federal court immediately enjoined its enforcement and refused to allow California courts to offer authoritative constructions of the law that might have eliminated (or at least reduced the number) of constitutional objections to its implementation. Likewise, when the voters of California passed Proposition 209 (barring the state from discriminating against or granting preference to any individual or group on the basis of race, sex, color, ethnicity, or national origin), a federal judge quickly enjoined its implementation before California's own courts could construe its own law and address questions concerning its constitutionality. "Our Federalism," as defined by Justice Black, appeared to be dead. In *Arizonans for Official English* v. *Arizona* (1997), however, the Supreme Court made it clear that *Younger* remains good law. When the Arizona electorate approved by ballot initiative Article XXVIII of the Arizona Constitution, declaring English "the official language of the State" and requiring the State to "act in English and in no other language," a state employee working as an insurance claims manager, sued the State, its Governor, and its Attorney General in federal court, alleging that this constitutional provision violated the Free Speech Clause of the First Amendment. After rejecting the Attorney General's narrow interpretation of the Article and declining to allow the Arizona courts the initial opportunity to construe the Article, the federal district court declared the Article fatally overbroad after reading it to impose a sweeping ban on the use of any language other than English by all Arizona governmental employees. When the Ninth Circuit affirmed the decision of the district court, an angry Supreme Court vacated the judgment of the Court of Appeals on the ground of mootness (the state employee had subsequently resigned to take a job in the private sector) and directed the district court to dismiss the action. It read a stern lecture to the courts involved in this case for their failure to help build a "cooperative judicial federalism."

> In litigation generally, and in constitutional litigation most prominently, courts in the United States characteristically pause to ask: Is this conflict really necessary? When anticipatory relief is sought in federal court against a state statute, respect for the place of the States in our federal system calls for close consideration of that core question.
>
> Arizona's Attorney General, in addition to releasing his own opinion on the meaning of Article XXVIII, asked both the District Court and the Court of Appeals to pause before proceeding to judgment; specifically, he asked both federal courts to seek, through the State's certification process, an authoritative construction of the new measure from the Arizona Supreme Court.
>
> Both lower federal courts in this case refused to invite the aid of the Arizona Supreme Court because they found the language of Article XXVIII "plain," and the Attorney General's limiting construction unpersuasive. . . . A more cautious approach was in order. Through certification of novel or unsettled questions of state law for authoritative answers by a State's highest court, a federal court may save "time, energy, and resources and hel[p] build a cooperative judicial federalism."

In *Baldwin* v. *Montana Fish and Game Commission,* the Court relied on the same logic it employed in *Younger* and reasoned from the total structure of the Constitution to uphold a Montana law that mandated substantially higher hunting fees for nonresidents than for residents. Speaking for a six-member majority, Justice Harry Blackmun contended that this distinction between residents and nonresidents did not violate the Privileges and Immunities Clause of Article IV, Section 2:

> Some distinctions between residents and nonresidents merely reflect the fact that this is a Nation composed of individual States, and are permitted; other distinctions are prohibited because they hinder the formation, purpose, or development of a single Union of those States. Only with respect to those "privileges" and "immunities" bearing upon the vitality of the Nation as a single entity must the State treat all citizens, resident and nonresident, equally.

Blackmun rejected the contention of Justice William Brennan and other dissenters that the state must justify all distinctions, even those that neither trench upon the "basic rights" and "essential activities" of the citizenry nor "frustrate the purposes of the formation of the Union."[23]

Even when the entire Court reasons from the structure and relationship created by the Constitution, there is no guarantee that all of the justices will reach the same conclusions, as *National League of Cities* v.

*Usery* (1976) and *Garcia* v. *San Antonio Metropolitan Transit Authority* (1985) illustrate. In *National League of Cities,* the Court invalidated a congressional attempt to apply minimum-wage and maximum-hours legislation to state governments and their political subdivisions because of the threat it posed to federalism. Justice Rehnquist argued for a five-member majority that this congressional amendment to the Fair Labor Standards Act would "significantly alter or displace the States' abilities to structure employer-employee relationships in such areas as fire prevention, police protection, sanitation, public health, and parks and recreation." Yet those are the very functions and services that the state governments were created to provide, and "if Congress may withdraw from the States the authority to make those fundamental employment decisions upon which their systems for performance of these functions must rest, . . . there would be little left of the States' 'separate and independent existence.' " Rehnquist then noted that "the Constitution, in all its provisions, looks to an indestructible Union, composed of indestructible States." Reasoning from the total structure created by the Constitution, Justice Rehnquist concluded that Congress could no more use its commerce power to usurp the states' right to carry out their traditional functions than it could to deny the right to trial by jury contained in the Sixth Amendment or violate the Due Process Clause of the Fifth Amendment.

In his dissent, Justice William Brennan charged that Rehnquist in effect was embracing the discredited doctrine of dual federalism. He accused his fellow justice of finding in the Tenth Amendment an express limitation on the national government's delegated powers and quoted approvingly from Justice Harlan Stone's opinion in *United States* v. *Darby Lumber* (1941): "The amendment states but a truism that all is retained which has not been surrendered. There is nothing in the history of its adoption to suggest that it was more than declaratory of the relationship between the national and state governments as it had been established by the Constitution before the amendment. . . ." Justice Brennan also insisted that since the "Congress is constituted of representatives in both Senate and House elected from the States, . . . decision upon the extent of federal intervention under the Commerce Clause into the affairs of the States are in that sense decisions of the States themselves."

In *Garcia,* in another 5–4 decision, the Supreme Court overruled *National League of Cities,* arguing that any attempt to draw the boundaries of state regulatory immunity in terms of "traditional governmental functions" is not only unworkable but is also inconsistent with the established principles of federalism on which *National League of Cities* purported to rest. Justice Blackmun declared for the Court majority that there is nothing in the overtime and minimum-wage requirements of the Fair Labor Standards Act that is destructive of state sovereignty or violative of any constitutional provision. In his dissent, Justice Powell excoriated the Court for its belief that "the role of the States in the federal system may depend upon the grace of elected federal officials, rather than on the Constitution as interpreted by this Court." Justice O'Connor also objected to the Court's refusal to fulfill its constitutional role of judicial review: "If federalism so conceived and so carefully cultivated by the Framers of our Constitution is to remain meaningful, this Court cannot abdicate its constitutional responsibility to oversee the Federal Government's compliance with its duty to respect the legitimate interests of the States."

In her majority opinion in *New York* v. *United States* (1992), in which the Court struck down a key provision of the Low-level Radioactive Waste Policy Amendments Act of 1985 for "infringing upon the core of state sovereignty reserved by the Tenth Amendment," Justice O'Connor saw to it that this time the Court did not "abdicate its constitutional responsibility" to protect federalism. The Constitution does not authorize "Congress to command a state government to enact *state* regulation," she contended. "No matter how powerful the federal interest involved, the Constitution simply does not give Congress the authority to require the States to regulate. The Constitution instead gives Congress the authority to regulate matters directly and to pre-empt contrary state regulation." She insisted that "[w]here a federal interest is sufficiently strong to cause Congress to legislate, it must do so directly; it may not conscript state governments as its agents."

Justice Scalia built on Justice O'Connor's opinion in *Printz* v. *United States* (1997), when he held for the Court that those provisions of the Brady Handgun Violence Prevention Act that commanded state and local law enforcement officers to conduct background checks on prospective handgun purchasers were unconstitutional. "We held in *New York* that Congress cannot compel the State to enact or enforce a federal regulatory program. Today we hold that Congress cannot circumvent that prohibition by conscripting the State's officers directly." Scalia observed that conscripting state officers to carry out a federal program violated the states' "residuary and inviolable sovereignty." Scalia went further, however; not only did it violate federalism but it violated the principle of separation of powers as well.

> The Constitution does not leave to speculation who is to administer the laws enacted by Congress; the President, it says, "shall take Care that the Laws be faithfully executed," personally and through officers whom he appoints (save for such inferior officers as Congress may authorize to be appointed by the "Courts of Law" or by "the Heads of Departments" who are themselves presidential appointees). The Brady Act effectively transfers this responsibility to thousands of CLEOs (chief law enforcement officers, e.g., local sheriffs) in the 50 States, who are left to implement the program without meaningful Presidential control (if indeed meaningful Presidential control is possible without the power to appoint and remove). The insistence of the Framers upon unity in the Federal Executive—to insure both vigor and accountability—is well known. That unity would be shat-

> tered, and the power of the President would be subject to reduction, if Congress could act as effectively without the President as with him, by simply requiring state officers to execute its laws.

Interestingly, when Scalia made precisely the same separation-of-powers argument in *Morrison* v. *Olson* (see Chapter 5), he spoke in dissent and for himself alone. By contrast in *Printz,* by first sugar-coating this argument with a concern for federalism, Scalia was able to speak for the majority.

## THE POST–CIVIL WAR AMENDMENTS AND THE SHIFTING OF THE FEDERAL BALANCE

Thus far the discussion has been confined to the relationship between the national and state governments that originally was established by the Constitution, into which the Framers incorporated a balance of national and federal elements. Now we must consider the extent to which the mixed nature of the constitutional system has been altered by the Civil War amendments and the statutes flowing from them.

At a minimum, the Thirteenth, Fourteenth, and Fifteenth amendments were intended to safeguard the civil rights of the recently emancipated slaves. Although the protection of such civil rights previously had been among the broad mass of police powers reserved to the states, the last section of each of these amendments gave Congress the "power to enforce" them "by appropriate legislation." Pursuant to these grants of power, Congress passed the Civil Rights Acts of 1866 (which protected the right of blacks to make and enforce contracts and prohibited any person acting under color of state law from depriving any citizen of rights secured by the Constitution or federal law), 1870 (which protected voting rights), 1871 (which created a cause of civil action for deprivations, under color of state law, of secured rights), and 1875 (which secured for blacks the "full and equal enjoyment" of public accommodations). The pressures generated by the racial problems that these and subsequent civil rights acts were intended to address, together with the catalytic presence of the Civil War amendments themselves, have helped to break down the compound nature of the government and to give primacy to its national elements. However, the rate at which this process has taken place largely has been determined by Supreme Court decisions interpreting the Thirteenth, Fourteenth, and Fifteenth Amendments and the acts passed pursuant thereto.

Initially, the Court construed these constitutional and statutory provisions narrowly, in order to preserve the federal balance. In 1873, for example, it held in the *Slaughterhouse Cases*—found in Chapter 12—that the "privileges and immunities of citizens of the United States" protected from state abridgement by Section 1 of the Fourteenth Amendment were few in number and limited to such rights as access to the nation's seaports and the privilege of habeas corpus writs. That left the vast majority of legal rights and relations under the protection of the state governments. In reaching this decision, the Court majority pronounced itself reluctant to "fetter and degrade the State governments by subjecting them to the control of Congress, in the exercise of powers heretofore universally conceded to them of the most ordinary and fundamental character" and to change "the whole theory of the relations of the State and Federal governments to each other and of both these governments to the people . . . in the absence of language which expresses such a purpose too clearly to admit of doubt." This led Justice Stephen B. Field to file a furious dissent; he insisted that the purpose of the Fourteenth Amendment was exactly that—to shift decisively the federal-state balance by giving vast new powers to the national government at the expense of the states. The Fourteenth Amendment, he insisted:

> recognizes in express terms . . . citizens of the United States, and it makes their citizenship dependent upon the place of their birth, or the fact of their adoption, and not upon the constitution or laws of any State or the condition of their ancestry. A citizen of a State is now only a citizen of the United States residing in that State. The fundamental rights, privileges, and immunities which belong to him as a free man and a free citizen, now belong to him as a citizen of the United States, and are not dependent upon his citizenship of any State. . . . The amendment does not attempt to confer any new privileges or immunities upon citizens, or to enumerate or define those already existing. It assumes that there are such privileges and immunities which belong of right to citizens as such, and ordains that they shall not be abridged by State legislation. If this [Amendment] has no reference to privileges and immunities of this character, but only refers, as held by the majority of the court in their opinion, to such privileges and immunities as were before its adoption specially designated in the Constitution or necessarily implied as belonging to citizens of the United States, it was a vain and idle enactment, which accomplished nothing, and most unnecessarily excited Congress and the people on its passage. . . . But if the amendment refers to the natural and inalienable rights which belong to all citizens, the inhibition has a profound significance and consequence.

The Court repeated the narrow view expressed by the majority in the *Slaughterhouse Cases* in the *Civil Rights Cases* (1883), where it held that the public-accommodations provisions of the Civil Rights Act of 1875 were unconstitutional. Noting that the Fourteenth Amendment reads "no *state* shall . . .," it declared that the amendment prohibited only state actions of certain types, not "individual invasion of individual rights." Legislation that attempted to prohibit such purely private discrimination, therefore, was beyond the constitutional powers of Congress to enact. The first Justice Harlan strenuously dissented; he argued that Congress has power under Sections 1 and 5 of the Fourteenth

Amendment to protect the civil rights of citizens of the United States. Section 1 begins by declaring that "All persons born or naturalized in the United States, and subject to the jurisdiction thereof, are citizens of the United States, and of the State wherein they reside." These words, Harlan observed, made "the colored race . . . , instantly, citizens of the United States, and of their respective States." And that citizenship "may be protected" by Section 5. "Congress is not restricted to the enforcement of prohibitions upon State laws or State action." Rather, it is free to enforce "all of the provisions—affirmative and prohibitive—of the amendment." Harlan insisted it was "a grave misconception to suppose" Section 5 "has reference exclusively to express prohibitions upon State laws or State action." Quite the contrary, he argued, Section 5 "authorizes Congress, by means of legislation, operating throughout the entire Union, to guard, secure, and protect" any right created by the Fourteenth Amendment. He denied that his construction "in any degree intrench[es] upon the just rights of the States in the control of their domestic affairs. It simply recognizes the enlarged powers conferred by the recent amendments upon the general government."

While the state-action doctrine promulgated in the *Civil Rights Cases* (see Chapter 8 of Volume II for a detailed discussion) has sharply limited the ability of Congress to enter the domain of the states' police power and to use its Section 5 enforcement powers to protect the civil rights of American citizens, it has not, however, precluded the national government from intervening when the states themselves have violated constitutionally protected rights. To take perhaps the most famous example, the doctrine did not prevent the Supreme Court from declaring in *Brown* v. *Board of Education* (1954) that the defendant states were guilty of violating the Equal Protection Clause of the Fourteenth Amendment by requiring that schools be racially segregated. Nor has the theory of state action prevented federal prosecution of state officials and others who, while acting under color of state law, have deprived citizens of their constitutionally protected rights. Nonetheless, the state-action doctrine historically has sharply limited the ability of the national government to enter the domain of the states' police power and, to that extent, has helped to preserve the compound quality of the Constitution.

Moreover, the state-action doctrine is increasingly being sidestepped altogether by those who seek to expand the power of the national government to protect the civil rights of the citzenry. Of decisive importance in this respect is *Jones* v. *Alfred H. Mayer Company* (1968), in which the Court held that the national government has the power to regulate purely private property transactions where racial discrimination is present. In his majority opinion, Justice Potter Stewart exhumed the Civil Rights Act of 1866 and held that it "bars all racial discrimination, private as well as public, in the sale or rental of property, and that the statute, thus construed, is a valid exercise of the power of Congress to enforce the Thirteenth Amendment." Making many of the same arguments found in the first Justice Harlan's dissent in the *Civil Rights Cases,* Stewart insisted that the Thirteenth Amendment authorized Congress not only to dissolve the legal bonds by which slaves had been held to their masters, but also to determine rationally what the badges and the incidents of slavery are and to translate that determination into effective legislation.

*Jones* was followed by *Griffin* v. *Breckenridge* (1971) and *Runyon* v. *McCrary* (1976), in both of which the Court avoided the state-action doctrine and relied on the Thirteenth Amendment to justify congressional bars to wholly private discrimination. In *Griffin* a unanimous Court, reversing its decision in *Collins* v. *Handyman* (1951), held that those sections of the Civil Rights Acts of 1866 and 1871 that granted civil remedies against racially motivated conspiracies to deprive individuals of their civil rights were applicable even to wholly private conspiracies. Speaking for the Court, Justice Stewart concluded that "Congress was wholly within its power under Section 2 of the Thirteenth Amendment in creating a statutory cause of action for Negro citizens who have been the victims of conspiratorial, racially discriminatory private action aimed at depriving them of the basic rights that the law secures to all free men." Employing the same arguments, Stewart held in *Runyon* that the section of the Civil Rights Act of 1866 that forbids discrimination in the making and enforcing of contracts prohibits private schools from excluding qualified students solely on the basis of race. In this particular case, blacks had been denied the opportunity to enter into a contract for the provision of educational services in return for the payment of tuition. This, in Justice Stewart's estimation, constituted a "class violation" of the law in question.[24]

In seeking to rectify glaring injustices, the decisions reached in these cases contributed to a shifting of the federal balance. The shift has been so pronounced that the Court seriously entertained overturning *Runyon* in its 1989 case of *Patterson* v. *McLean Credit Union;* it ultimately declined to do so and left the federal government free to continue to reach wholly private discriminatory conduct. *Patterson* and the Court's earlier decisions make clear how profoundly the Framer's original understanding of federalism was altered by the post–Civil War Amendments—so, too, do other Supreme Court decisions, including those incorporating the Bill of Rights into the Fourteenth Amendment so that they apply to the states (see Chapter 11) and those holding that national law preempts state law if considerations of national policy so warrant and if these considerations are consistent with either enumerated powers or broader national security interests.[25] What Madison declared in *The Federalist,* No. 39—that the Constitution is "neither wholly federal, nor wholly national" but "a composition of both"—cannot be asserted in the same way after the ratification of the post–Civil War Amendments, for they simply have made the Constitution much more national in character. Subsequent amendments have done likewise; two deserve special mention. The ratification of the Sixteenth Amendment, authorizing a federal income tax, gave the Congress access to revenues it has used to influence states to behave in a manner consistent with its wishes (see *South*

*Dakota* v. *Dole* in Chapter 8). And the ratification of the Seventeenth Amendment, replacing the election of the Senate by state legislatures with direct election by the people, removed one of the principal structural devices the Framers employed to protect the interests of states as states[26] and made the "residuary and inviolable sovereignty" of the states dependent on congressional discretion and/or whether an occasional Court majority can be mustered on its behalf (as in *Printz*). By constitutional amendment and judicial construction of those amendments, one of the principal means employed by the Framers to achieve the ends of the Constitution has been enfeebled; the result is that we have become more reliant on the two remaining means of separation of powers and the multiplicity of interest in the extended republic.

## NOTES

1 See Martin Diamond, "*The Federalist* on Federalism: 'Neither a National nor a Federal Constitution, But a Composition of Both,' " *Yale Law Journal* 86, no. 6 (May 1977): 1273–1285.
2 *The Federalist,* No. 39.
3 James Madison, "Outline," in *The Writings of James Madison,* ed. Gaillard Hunt, 9 vols. (New York: G. P. Putnam's Sons, 1910), 9:351.
4 The discussion that follows relies heavily on Martin Diamond, "What the Framers Meant by Federalism," in *A Nation of States,* 2d ed., Robert A. Goldwin, ed. (Chicago: Rand McNally, 1974), pp. 25–42.
5 See Martin Diamond, "The Ends of Federalism," *Publius,* 3, no. 2 (Fall 1973):131–132.
6 Herbert J. Storing, "Foreword," in Paul Eidelberg, *The Philosophy of the American Constitution* (New York: Free Press, 1968).
7 See *The Federalist,* Nos. 15, 16, and 22.
8 Max Farrand, ed., *The Records of the Federal Convention of 1787,* 4 vols. (New Haven, Conn.: Yale University Press, 1937), 1:33. Emphasis in the original.
9 *Ibid.,* 1:134–136.
10 *The Federalist,* No. 10.
11 Farrand, *Records,* 1:461.
12 See *Ibid,* 1:339, 405–406.
13 *Ibid.,* 1:488.
14 Alexis de Tocqueville, *Democracy in America,* ed. Phillips Bradley, 2 vols. (New York: Random House, 1945), 1:165.
15 It should be noted that the Supreme Court's interest in federalism is limited almost exclusively to the balance between state power and the enumerated powers of the central government; the justices have not concerned themselves with the presence of federal elements in the design and the politics of the national government itself. This situation is understandable, as the former issue is far more amenable than the latter to legal disputation and judicial determination. Nevertheless, it should be recognized that the Court's treatment of federalism is not necessarily definitive or exhaustive and that in this matter, as in others, the Constitution is not merely what the Supreme Court has said it is.

16 Farrand, *Records*, 1:284–285.

17 In *Bailey* v. *Drexel Furniture Company*, 259 U.S. 20 (1922), the Court relied on *Hammer* to invalidate the Child Labor Tax Law of 1919, which imposed a 10 percent tax on the annual net profits of manufacturers that employed children under the age of sixteen. Chief Justice Taft wrote: "In the act before us, the presumption of validity cannot prevail, because the proof of the contrary is found on the very fact of its provisions. Grant the validity of this law, and all that Congress would need do thereafter, in seeking to take over to its control any one of the great number of subjects . . . the states have never parted with, and which are reserved to them by the Tenth Amendment, would be to enact a detailed measure of complete regulation of the subject and enforce it by a so-called tax upon departures from it."

18 C. Herman Pritchett, *The American Constitution*, 3d ed. (New York: McGraw-Hill, 1977), pp. 50–51.

19 See *United States* v. *Darby Lumber Company* (1941).

20 See Stephen Gardbaum, "New Deal Constitutionalism and the Unshackling of the States," *University of Chicago Law Review*, Vol. 64 (Spring 1997), pp. 483–567. Gardbaum challenges the "conventional wisdom" that holds that "the expanded powers of Congress under the Commerce Clause, which enabled it to reach 'local' activities for the first time, were transferred from the states, thereby ending (in effect if not in name) their previously exclusive power over intrastate matters." This view holds that "the consequence was that the states became constitutionally dependent on the will of Congress through the latter's power of preemption and the operation of the Supremacy Clause," and that "this not only radically changed the nature and balance of the federal system, but abolished federalism as a matter of constitutional law." Gardbaum argues that this view is "myopic" in that it "fails to appreciate that the states were the direct and sole beneficiaries of much . . . that the Court did in this period. While it certainly bestowed extensive new powers on the federal government under the Commerce Clause, the Court also granted many new powers to the states under various other clauses of the Constitution, especially as compared with the previous era of constitutional interpretation." As he continues, "If one isolates and analyzes the history of state power alone under the Constitution, the net effect of the New Deal era on the states was to reassert the traditional position that their powers are presumed to be significantly unconstrained by the Constitution absent express limitations, a position from which the federal courts in the previous, *Lochner* era had radically departed" (p. 386).

21 The defenders of economic due process suffered a similar fate. See Robert G. McCloskey, "Economic Due Process: An Exhumation and Reburial," 1962 *Supreme Court Review:* 42–43.

22 Charles L. Black, Jr., *Structure and Relationship in Constitutional Law* (Baton Rouge, La.: Louisiana State University Press, 1969), p. 7.

23 See *Lundinget ux.* v. *New York Tax Appeals Tribunal* (1998), in which the Supreme Court held that when a state is confronted with a challenge under the Privileges and Immunities Clause to a law distinguishing between residents and nonresidents, it may defend its position by demonstrating that "(i) there is a substantial reason for the difference in treatment; and (ii) the discrimination practiced against nonresidents bears a substantial relationship to the State's objective." In this particular case, the Court found that New York violated the Privileges and Immunities Clause of Article IV, Section 2 as it lacked

a substantial reason for denying only nonresidents an income tax deduction for alimony payments.

24 See also *Memphis* v. *Greene* (1981). In this case, black residents sued Memphis, Tennessee, because it had closed a street at the border between a white and a black neighborhood. The Supreme Court sustained the street closing, with Justice Stevens arguing for the majority that the City's interest in safety and tranquility was sufficient to "justify an adverse impact on motorists who are somewhat inconvenienced by the street closing. That inconvenience cannot be equated to an actual restraint on the liberty of black citizens that is in any sense comparable to the odious practice the Thirteenth Amendment was designed to eradicate."

25 See *Pennsylvania* v. *Nelson* (1956).

26 See *Federalist* No. 46, in which Madison remarked that if the House of Representatives were to sponsor legislation that advantaged the national government at the expense of the states, "a few representatives of the people would be opposed to the people themselves; or rather one set of representatives would be contending against thirteen sets of representatives, with the whole body of their common constituents on the side of the latter." Roger Sherman made the same argument in a July 1789 letter to John Adams: "The senators, being eligible by the legislatures of the several states, and dependent on them for reelection, will be vigilant in supporting their rights against infringement by the legislative or executive of the United States." Philip B. Kurland and Ralph Lerner (eds.), *Founders' Constitution,* 5 Vols. (Chicago: University of Chicago Press, 1987), II, p. 232.

## SELECTED READING

*The Federalist,* Nos. 15, 16, 17, 18, 21, 22, 39.

*Moore* v. *Sims,* 442 U.S. 415 (1979).
*Pennzoil* v. *Texaco,* 481 U.S. 95 (1987).
*Runyon* v. *McCrary,* 427 U.S. 160 (1976).
*United States* v. *Guest,* 383 U.S. 745 (1966).

Berger, Raoul. *Federalism: The Founders' Design* (Norman: University of Oklahoma Press, 1987).

Black, Charles L., Jr. *Structure and Relationship in Constitutional Law* (Baton Rouge: Lousiana State University Press, 1969).

Choper, Jesse H. *Judicial Review and the National Political Process: A Functional Reconsideration of the Role of the Supreme Court* (Chicago: University of Chicago Press, 1980).

Corwin, Edward S. "The Passing of Dual Federalism." *Virginia Law Review* 36 (February 1950): 1–24.

Diamond, Martin. "*The Federalist* on Federalism." *Yale Law Journal* 86 (May 1977): 1273–1285.

Frankfurter, Felix, and Landis, James M. *The Business of the Supreme Court: A Study of the Federal Judicial System* (New York: Macmillan, 1928).

Goebel, Julius. *History of the Supreme Court of the United States: Antecedents and Beginnings to 1801* (New York: Macmillan, 1971).

Goldwin, Robert A., ed. *A Nation of States,* 2d ed. (Chicago: Rand McNally, 1974).

Grodzins, Morton. *The American System: A New View of Government in the United States* (Chicago: Rand McNally, 1966).

Hobson, Charles F. "A Nation of States: Federalism in the Framing of the Constitution." In *Our Peculiar Security: The Written Constitution and Limited Government,* edited by Eugene W. Hickok, Jr., Gary L. McDowell, and Philip J. Costopoulos (Lanham, Md.: Rowman & Littlefield Publishers, 1993).

Hoebeke, C. H. *The Road to Mass Democracy: Original Intent and the Seventeenth Amendment* (New Brunswick, N.J.: Transaction Publishers, 1995).

McConnell, Michael W. "Federalism: Evaluating the Founders' Design." *University of Chicago Law Review* 54 (1987): 1484–1512.

Nagel, Robert F. "Federalism as a Fundamental Value." *1981 Supreme Court Review,* edited by Philip B. Kurland and Dennis J. Hutchinson (Chicago: University of Chicago Press, 1982).

Riker, William H. "Federalism." In *Handbook of Political Science,* Vol. 5, edited by Fred I. Greenstein and Nelson Polsby (Reading, Mass.: Addison-Wesley, 1975).

Vile, M. J. C. *The Structure of American Federalism* (Oxford: Oxford University Press, 1961).

Wechsler, Herbert. "The Political Safeguards of Federalism: The Role of the States in the Composition and Selection of the National Government." In *Federalism: Mature and Emergent,* edited by Arthur W. MacMahon (Garden City, N.Y.: Doubleday, 1955).

Zuckert, Michael P. "Federalism and the Founding: Toward a Reinterpretation of the Constitutional Convention." *Review of Politics* 41 (Spring 1986): 166–210.

# *The Judiciary Act of 1789*

**1 Statutes at Large 73**

On September 24, 1789, Congress passed the Judiciary Act of 1789. Its thirty-five sections took the sketchy provisions of the Constitution's judicial article (Article III) and transformed them into the federal judicial system.

Chap. XX.—*An act to establish the Judicial Courts of the United States.*

*Section 1. Be it enacted by the Senate and House of Representatives of the United States of America in Congress assembled,* That the supreme court of the United States shall consist of a chief justice and five associate justices, any four of whom shall be a quorum, and shall hold annually at the seat of government two sessions, the one commencing the first Monday of February, and the other the first Monday of August. That the associate justices shall have precedence according to the date of their commissions, or when the commission of two or more of them bear date on the same day, according to their respective ages.

*Sec. 2. And be it further enacted,* That the United States shall be, and they hereby are divided into thirteen districts, to be limited and called as follows, to wit: one to consist of that part of the State of Massachusetts which lies easterly of the State of New Hampshire, and to be called Maine District; one to consist of the State of New Hampshire, and to be called New Hampshire District; one to consist of the remaining part of the State of Massachusetts, and to be called Massachusetts District; one to consist of the State of Connecticut, and to be called Connecticut District; one to consist of the State of New York, and to be called New York District; one to consist of the State of New Jersey, and to be called New Jersey District; one to consist of the State of Pennsylvania, and to be called Pennsylvania District; one to consist of the State of Delaware, and to be called Delaware District; one to consist of the State of Maryland, and to be called Maryland District; one to consist of the State of Virginia, except that part called the District of Kentucky, and to be called Virginia District; one to consist of the remaining part of the State of Virginia, and to be called Kentucky District; one to consist of the State of South Carolina, and to be called South Carolina District; and one to consist of the State of Georgia, and to be called Georgia District.

*Sec. 3. And be it further enacted,* That there be a court called a District Court, in each of the aforementioned districts, to consist of one judge, who shall reside in the district for which he is appointed, and shall be called a District Judge, and shall hold annually four sessions. . . .

*Sec. 4. And be it further enacted,* That the before mentioned districts, except those of Maine and Kentucky, shall be divided into three circuits, and be called the eastern, the middle, and the southern circuit. That the eastern circuit shall consist of the districts of New Hampshire, Massachusetts, Connecticut and New York; that the middle circuit shall consist of the districts of New Jersey, Pennsylvania, Delaware, Maryland and Virginia; and that the southern circuit shall consist of the districts of South Carolina and Georgia, and that there shall be held annually in each district of said circuits, two courts, which shall be called Circuit Courts, and shall consist of any two justices of the Supreme Court, and the district judge of such districts, any two of whom shall constitute a quorum: *Provided,* That no district judge shall give a vote in any case of appeal or error from his own decision; but may assign the reasons of such his decision. . . .

*Sec. 7. And be it [further] enacted,* That the Supreme Court, and the district courts shall have power to appoint clerks for their respective courts, and that the clerk for each district court shall be clerk also of the circuit court in such district. . . .

*Sec. 8. And be it further enacted,* That the justices of the Supreme Court, and the district judges, before they proceed to execute the duties of their respective offices, shall take the following oath or affirmation, to wit: "I, A. B., do solemnly swear or affirm, that I will administer justice without respect to persons, and do equal right to the poor and to the rich, and that I will faithfully and impartially discharge and perform all the duties incumbent on me as ________ according to the best of my abilities and understanding, agreeably to the constitution and laws of the United States. So help me God."

*Sec. 9. And be it further enacted,* That the district courts shall have, exclusively of the courts of the several States, cognizance of all crimes and offences that shall be cognizable under the authority of the United States, committed within their respective districts, or upon the high seas; where no other punishment than whipping, not exceeding thirty stripes, a fine not exceeding one hundred dollars, or a term of imprisonment not exceeding six months, is to be inflicted; and shall also have exclusive original cognizance of all civil causes of admiralty and maritime jurisdiction, including all seizures under laws of impost, navigation or trade of the United States, where the seizures are made, on waters which are navigable from the sea by vessels of ten or more tons burthen, within their respective districts as well as upon the high seas; saving to suitors, in all cases, the right of a common law remedy, where the common law is competent to give it; and shall also have exclusive original cognizance of all seizures on land, or other waters than as aforesaid, made, and of all suits for penalties and forfeitures incurred, under the laws of the United States. And shall also have cognizance, concurrent with the courts of the several States, or the circuit courts, as the case may be, of all causes where an alien sues for a tort only in violation of the law of nations or a treaty of the United States. And shall also have cognizance, concurrent as last mentioned, of all suits at common law where the United States sue, and the matter in dispute amounts, exclusive of costs, to the sum or value of one hundred dollars. And shall also have jurisdiction exclusively of the courts of the several States, of all suits against consuls or vice-consuls, except for offences above the description aforesaid. And the trial of issues in fact, in the district courts, in all causes except civil causes of admiralty and maritime jurisdiction, shall be by jury.

*Sec. 11. And be it further enacted,* That the circuit courts shall have original cognizance, concurrent with the courts of the several States, of all suits of a civil nature at common law or in equity, where the matter in dispute exceeds, exclusive of costs, the sum or value of five hundred dollars, and the United States are plaintiffs, or petitioner; or an alien is a party, or the suit is between a citizen of the State where the suit is brought, and a citizen of another State. And shall have exclusive cognizance of all crimes and offences cognizable under the authority of the United States, except where this act otherwise provides, or the laws of the United States shall otherwise direct, and concurrent jurisdiction with the district courts of the crimes and offences cognizable therein. . . . And the circuit courts shall also have appellate jurisdiction from the district courts under the regulations and restrictions herein after provided.

*Sec. 12. And be it further enacted,* That if a suit be commenced in any state court against an alien, or by a citizen of the state in which the suit is brought against a citizen of another state, and the matter in dispute exceeds the aforesaid sum or value of five hundred dollars, exclusive of costs, to be made to appear to the satisfaction of the court; and the defendant shall, at the time of entering his appearance in such state court, file a petition for the removal of the cause for trial into the next circuit court, . . . the cause shall there proceed in the same manner as if it had been brought there by original process. . . .

*Sec. 13. And be it further enacted,* That the Supreme Court shall have exclusive jurisdiction of all controversies of a civil nature, where a state is a party, except between a state and its citizens; and except also between a state and citizens of other states, or aliens, in which latter case it shall have original but not exclusive jurisdiction. And shall have exclusively all such jurisdiction of suits or proceedings against ambassadors, or other public ministers, or their domestics, or domestic servants, as a court of law can have or exercise consistently with the law of nations; and original, but not exclusive jurisdiction of all suits brought by ambassadors or other public ministers, or in which a consul, or vice consul, shall be a party. And the trial of issues in fact in the Supreme Court, in all actions at law against citizens of the United States, shall be by jury. The Supreme Court shall also have appellate jurisdiction from the circuit courts and courts of the several states, in the cases herein after specially provided for; and shall have power to issue writs of prohibition to the district courts, when proceeding as courts of admiralty and maritime jurisdiction, and writs of *mandamus,* in cases warranted by the principles and usages of law, to any courts appointed, or persons holding office, under the authority of the United States.

*Sec. 14. And be it further enacted,* That all the before-mentioned courts of the United States, shall have power to writs of *scire facias, habeas corpus,* and all other writs not specially provided for by statute, which may be necessary for the exercise of their respective jurisdictions, and agreeable to the principles and usages of law. . . .

*Sec. 16. And be it further enacted,* That suits in equity shall not be sustained in either of the courts of the United States, in any case where plain, adequate and complete remedy may be had at law. . . .

*Sec. 22. And be it further enacted,* That final decrees and judgments in civil actions in a district court, where the matter in dispute exceeds the sum or value of fifty dollars, exclusive of costs, may be reexamined, and reversed or affirmed in a circuit court. . . . And upon a like process, may final judgments and decrees in civil actions, and suits in equity in a circuit court, brought there by original process, or removed there from courts of the several States, or removed there by appeal from a district court where the matter in dispute exceeds the sum or value of two thousand dollars, exclusive of costs, be re-examined and reversed or affirmed in the Supreme Court, the citation being in such case signed by a judge of such circuit court, or justice of the Supreme Court, and the adverse party having at least thirty days' notice. . . .

*Sec. 25. And be it further enacted,* That a final judgment or decree in any suit, in the highest court of law or equity of a State in which a decision in the suit could be had, where is drawn in question the validity of a treaty or statute of, or an authority exercised under the United States, and the decision is against their validity; or where is drawn in question the validity of a statute of, or an authority exercised under any State, on the ground of their being repugnant to the constitution, treaties or laws of the United States, and the decision is in favour of such their validity, or where is drawn in question the construction of any clause of the constitution or of a treaty, or statute of, or commission held under the United States, and the decision is against the title, right, privilege or exemption specially set up or claimed by either party, under such clause of the said Constitution, treaty, statute or commission, may be re-examined and reversed or affirmed in the Supreme Court of the United States upon a writ of error, the citation being signed by the chief justice, or judge or chancellor of the court rendering or passing the judgment or decree complained of, or by a justice of the Supreme Court of the United States, in the same manner and under the same regulations, and the writ shall have the same effect, as if the judgment or decree complained of had been rendered or passed in a circuit court, and the proceeding upon the reversal shall also be the same, except that the Supreme Court, instead of remanding the cause for a final decision as before provided, may at their discretion, if the cause shall have been once remanded before, proceed to a final decision of the same, and award execution. But no other error shall be assigned or regarded as a ground of reversal in any such case as aforesaid, than such as appears on the face of the record, and immediately respects the before mentioned questions of validity or construction of the said constitution, treaties, statutes, commissions, or authorities in dispute.

*Sec. 27. And be it further enacted,* That a marshal shall be appointed in and for each district for the term of four years, but shall be removable from office at pleasure, whose duty it shall be to attend the district and circuit courts when sitting therein, and also the Supreme Court in the district in which that court shall sit. . . .

*Sec. 29. And be it further enacted,* That in cases punishable with death, the trial shall be had in the county where the offence was committed, or where that cannot be done without great inconvenience, twelve petit jurors at least shall be summoned from thence. And jurors in all cases to serve in the courts of the United States shall be designated by lot or otherwise in each State respectively according to the mode of forming juries therein now practised, so far as the laws of the same shall render such designation practicable by the courts or marshals of the United States; and the jurors shall have the same qualifications as are requisite for jurors by the laws of the State of which they are citizens, to serve in the highest courts of law of such State, and shall be returned as there shall be occasion for them, from such parts of the district from time to time as the court shall direct, so as shall be most favourable to an impartial trial, and so as not to incur an unnecessary expense, or unduly to burthen the citizens of any part of the district with such services. . . .

*Sec. 34. And be it further enacted,* That the laws of the several states, except where the constitution, treaties or statutes of the United States shall otherwise require or provide, shall be regarded as rules of decision in trials at common law in the courts of the United States in cases where they apply.

# *Cohens* v. *Virginia*

**19 U.S. (6 Wheaton) 264; 5 L. Ed. 257 (1821)**

In 1802, Congress passed an act authorizing the District of Columbia to conduct lotteries to finance "any important improvements in the City, which the ordinary funds or revenue thereof will not accomplish." Pursuant to this act, the City of Washington passed an ordinance creating a lottery. The state of Virginia had a law that prohibited the sale of lottery tickets except for lotteries authorized by that state. P. J. and M. J. Cohen were arrested for selling the Washington lottery tickets at their office in Norfolk, Virginia. After the Cohens were found guilty in borough court and fined $100, the case went to the United States Supreme Court on a writ of error, and the justices unanimously upheld the Cohens' conviction on the grounds that Congress did not authorize the District of Columbia to "force the sale of these lottery tickets in States where such sales may be prohibited by law." *Opinion of the Court: Marshall, Duvall, Johnson, Livingston, Story, Todd. Washington did not participate.*

MR. CHIEF JUSTICE MARSHALL delivered the opinion of the Court . . .

The questions presented to the Court . . . are of great magnitude, and may be truly said vitally to affect the Union. They exclude the inquiry whether the constitution and laws of the United States have been violated by the judgment which the plaintiffs in error seek to review; and maintain that, admitting such violation, it is not in the power of the government to apply a corrective. They maintain that the nation does not possess a department capable of restraining peaceably, and by authority of law, any attempts which may be made, by a part, against the legitimate powers of the whole; and that the government is reduced to the alternative of submitting to such attempts, or of resisting them by force. They maintain that the constitution of the United States has provided no tribunal for the final construction of itself, or of the laws or treaties of the nation; but that this power may be exercised in the last resort by the Courts of every State in the Union. . .

If such be the constitution, it is the duty of the Court to bow with respectful submission to its provisions. If such be not the constitution, it is equally the duty of this Court to say so; and to perform that task which the American people have assigned to the judicial department.

1st. The first question to be considered is, whether the jurisdiction of this Court is excluded by the character of the parties, one of them being a State, and the other a citizen of that State?

The second section of the third article of the constitution defines the extent of the judicial power of the United States. Jurisdiction is given to the Courts of the Union in two classes of cases. In the first, their jurisdiction depends on the character of the cause, whoever may be the parties. This class comprehends "all cases in law and equity arising under this constitution, the laws of the United States, and treaties made, or which shall be made, under their authority." This clause extends the jurisdiction of the Court to all the cases described, without making in its terms any exception whatever, and without any regard to the condition of the party. If there be any exception, it is to be implied against the express words of the article.

In the second class, the jurisdiction depends entirely on the character of the parties. In this are comprehended "controversies between two or more States, between a State and citizens of another State," "and between a State and foreign States, citizens or subjects." If these be the parties, it is entirely unimportant what may be the subject of controversy. Be it what it may, these parties have a constitutional right to come into the Court of the Union. . .

The jurisdiction of the Court, then, being extended by the letter of the constitution to all cases arising under it, or under the laws of the United States, it follows that those who would withdraw any case of this description from that jurisdiction, must sustain the exemption they claim on the spirit and true meaning of the constitution, which spirit and true meaning must be so apparent as to overrule the words which its framers have employed.

The counsel for the defendant in error have undertaken to do this; and have laid down the general proposition, that a sovereign independent State is not suable, except by its own consent.

This general proposition will not be controverted. But its consent is not requisite in each particular case. It may be given in a general law. And if a State has surrendered any portion of its sovereignty, the question whether a liability to suit be a part of this portion, depends on the instrument by which the surrender is made. If, upon a just construction of that instrument, it shall appear that the State has submitted to be sued, then it has parted with this sovereign right of judging in every case on the justice of its own pretensions, and has entrusted that power to a tribunal in whose impartiality it confides.

The American States, as well as the American people, have believed a close and firm Union to be essential to their liberty and to their happiness. They have been taught by experience, that this Union cannot exist without a government for the whole; and they have been taught by the same experience that this government would be a mere shadow, that must disappoint all their hopes, unless invested with large portions of that sovereignty which belongs to independent States. Under the influence of this opinion, and thus instructed by experience, the American people, in the conventions of their respective States, adopted the present constitution.

If it could be doubted, whether from its nature, it were not supreme in all cases where it is empowered to act, that doubt would be removed by the declaration, that "this constitution, and the laws of the United States, which shall be made in pursuance thereof, and all treaties made, or which shall be made, under the authority of the United States, shall be the supreme law of the land; and the judges in every State shall be bound thereby; any thing in the constitution or laws of any State to the contrary notwithstanding."

This is the authoritative language of the American people; and, if gentlemen please, of the American States. It marks, with lines too strong to be mistaken, the characteristic distinction between the government of the Union, and those of the States. The general government, though limited as to its objects, is supreme with respect to those objects. This principle is a part of the constitution; and if there be any who deny its necessity, none can deny its authority.

To this supreme government ample powers are confided; and if it were possible to doubt the great purposes for which they were so confided, the people of the United States have declared, that they are given "in order to form a more perfect union, establish justice, ensure domestic tranquillity, provide for the common defence, promote the general welfare, and secure the blessings of liberty to themselves and their posterity."

With the ample powers confided to this supreme government, for these interesting purposes, are connected many express and important limitations on the sovereignty of the States, which are made for the same purposes. The powers of the Union, on the great subjects of war, peace, and commerce, and on many others, are in themselves limitations of the sovereignty of the States; but in addition to these, the sovereignty of the States is surrendered in many instances where the surrender can only operate to the benefit of the people and where, perhaps, no other power is conferred on Congress than a conservative power to maintain the principles established in the constitution. The maintenance of these principles in their purity, is certainly among the great duties of the government. One of the instruments by which this duty may be peaceably performed, is the judicial department. It is authorized to decide all cases of every description, arising under the constitution or laws of the United States. From this general grant of jurisdiction, no exception is made of those cases in which a State may be a party. When we consider the situation of the government of the Union and of a State, in relation to each other; the nature of our constitution; the subordination of the State governments to that constitution; the great purpose for which jurisdiction over all cases arising under the constitution and laws of the United States, is confided to the judicial department; are we at liberty to insert in this general grant, an exception of those cases in which a State may be a party? Will the spirit of the constitution justify this attempt to control its words? We think it will not. We think a case arising under the constitution or laws of the United States, is cognizable in the Courts of the Union, whoever may be the parties to that case. . .

The mischievous consequences of the construction contended for on the part of Virginia, are also entitled to great consideration. It would prostrate, it has been said, the government and its laws at the feet of every State in the Union. And would not this be its effect? What power of the government could be executed by its own means, in any State disposed to resist its execution by a course of legislation? The laws must be executed by individuals acting within the several States. If these individuals may be exposed to penalties, and if the Courts of the Union cannot correct the judgments by which these penalties may be enforced, the course of the government may be, at any time, arrested by the will of one of its members. Each member will possess a *veto* on the will of the whole.

The answer which has been given to this argument, does not deny its truth, but insists that confidence is reposed, and may be safely reposed, in the State institutions; and that, if they shall ever become so insane or so wicked as to seek the destruction of the government, they many accomplish their object by refusing to perform the functions assigned to them. . . .

. . . A constitution is framed for ages to come, and is designed to approach immortality as nearly as human institutions can approach it. Its course cannot always be tranquil. It is exposed to storms and tempests, and its framers must be unwise statesmen indeed, if they have not provided it, as far as its nature will permit, with the means of self-preservation from the perils it may be destined to encounter. No government ought to be so defective in its organization, as not to contain within itself the means of securing the execution of its own laws against other dangers than those which occur every day. Courts of justice are the means most usually employed; and it is reasonable to expect that a government should repose on its own Courts, rather than on others. There is certainly nothing in the circumstances under which our constitution was formed; nothing in the history of the times, which would justify the opinion that the confidence reposed in the States was so implicit as to leave in them and their tribunals the power of resisting or defeating in the form of law, the legitimate measures of the Union. . . .

It has been also urged, as an additional objection to the jurisdiction of the Court, that cases between a State and one of its own citizens, do not come within the general scope of the constitution; and were obviously never intended to be made cognizable in the federal Courts. . . .

If jurisdiction depended entirely on the character of the parties, and was not given where the parties have not an original right to come into Court, that part of the 2d section of the 3d article, which extends the judicial power to all cases arising under the constitution and laws of the United States, would be mere surplusage. It is to give jurisdiction where the character of the parties would not give it, that this very important part of the clause was inserted. It may be true, that the partiality of the State tribunals, in ordinary controversies between a State and its citizens, was not apprehended, and therefore the judicial power of the Union was not extended to such cases; but this was not the sole nor the greatest object for which this department was created. A more important, a much more interesting object, was the preservation of the constitution and laws of the United States, so far as they can be preserved by judicial authority; and therefore the jurisdiction of the Courts of the Union was expressly extended to all cases arising under that constitution and those laws. If the constitution or laws may be violated by proceedings instituted by a State against its own citizens, and if that violation may be such as essentially to affect the constitution and the laws, such as to arrest the progress of government in its constitutional course, why should these cases be excepted from that provision which expressly extends the judicial power of the Union to *all* cases arising under the constitution and laws? . . .

It is most true that this Court will not take jurisdiction if it should not: but it is equally true, that it must take jurisdiction if it should. The judiciary cannot, as the legislature may, avoid a measure because it approaches the confines of the constitution. We cannot pass it by because it is doubtful. With whatever doubts, with whatever difficulties, a case may be attended, we must decide it, if it be brought before us. We have no more right to decline the exercise of jurisdiction which is given, than to usurp that which is not given. The one or the other would be treason to the constitution. Questions may occur which we would gladly avoid; but we cannot avoid them. All we can do is, to exercise our best judgment, and conscientiously to perform our duty. In doing this, on the present occasion, we find this tribunal invested with appellate jurisdiction in *all* cases arising under the constitution and laws of the United States. We find no exception to this grant, and we cannot insert one. . .

2d. The second objection to the jurisdiction of the Court is, that its appellate power cannot be exercised, in any case, over the judgment of a State Court.

This objection is sustained chiefly by arguments drawn from the supposed total separation of the judiciary of a state from that of the Union, and their entire independence of each other. The argument considers the federal judiciary as completely foreign to that of a State; and as being no more connected with it in any respect whatever, than the Court of a foreign State. If this hypothesis be just, the argument founded on it is equally so; but if the hypothesis be not supported by the constitution, the argument fails with it.

This hypothesis is not founded on any words in the constitution, which might seem to countenance it, but on the unreasonableness of giving a contrary construction to words which seem to require it; and on the incompatibility of the application of the appellate jurisdiction to the judgments of State Courts, with that constitutional relation which subsists between the government of the Union and the governments of those States which compose it.

Let this unreasonableness, this total incompatibility, be examined.

That the United States form, for many, and for most important purposes, a single nation, has not yet been denied. In war, we are one people. In making peace, we are one people. In all commercial regulations, we are one and the same people. In many other respects, the American people are one; and the government which is alone capable of controling and managing their interests in all these respects, is the government of the Union. It is their government, and in that character they have no other. America has chosen to be, in many respects, and to many purposes, a nation, and for all these purposes, her government is complete; to all these objects, it is competent. The people have declared, that in the exercise of all powers given for these objects, it is supreme. It can, then, in effecting these objects, legitimately control all individuals or governments within the American territory. The constitution and laws of a State, so far as they are repugnant to the constitution and laws of the United States, are absolutely void. These States are constituent parts of the United States. They are members of one great empire—for some purposes sovereign, for some purposes subordinate.

In a government so constituted, is it unreasonable that the judicial power should be competent to give efficacy to the constitutional laws of the legislature? That department can decide on the validity of the constitution or law of a State, if it be repugnant to the constitution or to a law of the United States. Is it unreasonable that it should also be empowered to decide on the judgment of a State tribunal enforcing such unconstitutional law? Is it so very unreasonable as to furnish a justification for controling the words of the constitution?

We think it is not. We think in a government acknowledgedly supreme, with respect to objects of vital interest to the nation, there is nothing inconsistent with sound reason, nothing incompatible with the nature of government, in making all its departments supreme, so far as respects those objects, and so far as is necessary to their attainment. The exercise of the appellate power over those judgments of the State tribunals which may contravene the constitution or laws of the United States, is, we believe, essential to the attainment of those objects.

The propriety of entrusting the construction of the constitution, and laws made in pursuance thereof, to the judiciary of the Union, has not, we believe, as yet, been drawn into question. It seems to be a corollary from this political axiom, that the federal Courts should either possess exclusive jurisdiction in such cases, or a power to revise the judgment rendered in them, by the State tribunals. If the federal and State Courts have concurrent jurisdiction in all cases arising under the constitution, laws, and treaties of the

United States; and if a case of this description brought in a State Court cannot be removed before judgment, nor revised after judgment, then the construction of the constitution, laws, and treaties of the United States, is not confided particularly to their judicial department, but is confided equally to that department and to the State Courts, however they may be constituted. "Thirteen independent Courts," says a very celebrated statesman (and we have now more than twenty such Courts,) "of final jurisdiction over the same causes, arising upon the same laws, is a hydra in government, from which nothing but contradiction and confusion can proceed."

Dismissing the unpleasant suggestion, that any motives which may not be fairly avowed, or which ought not to exist, can ever influence a State or its Courts, the necessity of uniformity, as well as correctness in expounding the constitution and laws of the United States, would itself suggest the propriety of vesting in some single tribunal the power of deciding, in the last resort, all cases in which they are involved.

We are not restrained, then, by the political relations between the general and State governments, from construing the words of the constitution, defining the judicial power, in their true sense. We are not bound to construe them more restrictively than they naturally import.

They give to the Supreme Court appellate jurisdiction in all cases arising under the constitution, laws, and treaties of the United States. The words are broad enough to comprehend all cases of this description, in whatever Court they may be decided. In expounding them, we may be permitted to take into view those considerations to which Courts have always allowed great weight in the exposition of laws.

## *Dred Scott* v. *Sandford*

**60 U.S. (19 Howard) 393; 15 L. Ed. 691 (1857)**

Dred Scott was a Negro slave belonging to Dr. Emerson, a U.S. Army surgeon stationed in Missouri. In 1834, Dr. Emerson was transferred to a military post in Rock Island, Illinois, a state in which slavery was forbidden, and he took Dred Scott with him. Two years later, Dr. Emerson again took Scott with him when he moved to Fort Snelling, in the territory of Louisiana (now Minnesota), an area in which slavery was prohibited by the terms of the Missouri Compromise of 1820. In 1838, Dr. Emerson returned with his slave to Missouri. In 1846, Dred Scott brought suit in a Missouri state court to obtain his freedom on the claim that his residence in a free territory conferred freedom upon him. Scott won, but the judgment was reversed by the Missouri Supreme Court. Seeking further judicial review of his case, abolitionists and other friends of Dred Scott arranged for a fictitious sale of Scott to John Sandford, a citizen of New York and a brother of the widow of the late Dr. Emerson, so that jurisdiction could be taken by the federal circuit court in Missouri. The federal court held against Scott, and he appealed his case to the Supreme Court on a writ of error. *Opinion of the Court: Taney, Campbell, Catron, Grier, Nelson, Wayne. Concurring opinions: Campbell; Catron; Grier; Nelson; Wayne. Concurring in the result: Daniel. Dissenting opinions: Curtis; McLean.*

MR. CHIEF JUSTICE TANEY delivered the opinion of the Court.

. . . The question is simply this: can a negro whose ancestors were imported into this country and sold as slaves, become a member of the political community formed and brought into existence by the Constitution of the United States, and as such become entitled to all the rights, and privileges, and immunities, guaranteed by that instrument to the citizen. One of these rights is the privilege of suing in a court of the United States in the cases specified in the Constitution.

It will be observed, that the plea applies to that class of persons only whose ancestors were negroes of the African race, and imported into this country, and sold and held as slaves. The only matter in issue before the Court, therefore, is whether the descendants of such slaves, when they shall be emancipated, or who are born of parents who had become free before their birth, are citizens of a state, in the sense in which the word "citizen" is used in the Constitution of the United States. And this being the only matter in dispute on the pleadings, the Court must be understood as speaking in this opinion of that class only; that is, of those persons who are the descendants of Africans who were . . . imported into this country and sold as slaves.

In discussing this question, we must not confound the rights of citizenship which a State may confer within its own limits, and the rights of citizenship as a member of the Union. It does not by any means follow, because he has all the rights and privileges of a citizen of a State, that he must be a citizen of the United States. He may have all of the rights and privileges of the citizen of a State, and yet not be entitled to the rights and privileges of a citizen in any other State. For previous to the adoption of the Constitution of the United States, every State had the undoubted right to confer on whomsoever it pleased the character of citizen, and to endow him with all its rights. . . .

The question then arises, whether the provisions of the Constitution, in relation to the personal rights and privileges to which the citizen of a State should be entitled, embraced the negro African race, at that time in this country, or who might afterwards be imported, who had then or should afterwards be made free in any State; and to put it in the power of a single State to make him a citizen of the United States, and endue him with the full rights of citizenship in every other State without their consent? Does the Constitution of the United States act upon him whenever he shall be made free under the laws of a State, and raised there to the rank of a citizen, and immediately clothe him with all the privileges of a citizen in every other State, and in its own courts?

The court think the affirmative of these propositions cannot be maintained. And if it cannot, the plaintiff in error could not be a citizen of the State of Missouri, within the meaning of the Constitution of the United States, and, consequently, was not entitled to sue in its courts.

It becomes necessary, therefore, to determine who were citizens of the several States when the Constitution was adopted. And in order to do this, we must recur to the Governments and institutions of the thirteen colonies, when they separated from Great Britain and formed new sovereignties, and took their places in the family of independent nations. We must inquire who, at that time, were recognised as the people or citizens of a State, whose rights and liberties had been outraged by the English Government; and who declared their independence, and assumed the powers of Government to defend their rights by force of arms.

In the opinion of the court, the legislation and histories of the times, and the language used in the Declaration of Independence, show, that neither the class of persons who had been imported as slaves, nor their descendants, whether they had become free or not, were then acknowledged as a part of the people, nor intended to be included in the general words used in that memorable instrument.

It is difficult at this day to realize the state of public opinion in relation to that unfortunate race, which prevailed in the civilized and enlightened portions of the world at the time of the Declaration of Independence, and when the Constitution of the United States was framed and adopted. But the public history of every European nation displays it in a manner too plain to be mistaken.

They had for more than a century before been regarded as beings of an inferior order, and altogether unfit to associate with the white race, either in social or political relations; and so far inferior, that they had no rights which the white man was bound to respect; and that the negro might justly and lawfully be reduced to slavery for his benefit. He was bought and sold, and treated as an ordinary article of merchandise and traffic, whenever a profit could be made by it. This opinion was at that time fixed and universal in the civilized portion of the white race. It was regarded as an axiom in morals as well as in politics, which no one thought of disputing, or supposed to be open to dispute; and men in every grade and position in society daily and habitually acted upon it in their private pursuits, as well as in matters of public concern, without doubting for a moment the correctness of this opinion.

And in no nation was this opinion more firmly fixed or more uniformly acted upon than by the English Government and English people. They not only seized them on the coast of Africa, and sold them or held them in slavery for their own use; but they took them as ordinary articles of merchandise to every country where they could make a profit on them, and were far more extensively engaged in this commerce than any other nation in the world.

The legislation of the different Colonies furnishes positive and indisputable proof of this fact. . . .

[They] show that a perpetual and impassable barrier was intended to be erected between the white race and the one which they had reduced to slavery, and governed as subjects with absolute and despotic power, and which they then looked upon as so far below them in the scale of created beings, that intermarriages between white persons and negroes or mulattoes were regarded as unnatural and immoral, and punished as crimes, not only in the parties, but in the person who joined them in marriage. And no distinction in this respect was made between the free negro or mulatto and the slave, but this stigma, of the deepest degradation, was fixed upon the whole race.

The language of the Declaration of Independence is equally conclusive. It [says] "We hold these truths to be self-evident: that all men are created equal; that they are endowed by their Creator with certain unalienable rights; that among them is life, liberty, and the pursuit of happiness; that to secure these rights, Governments are instituted, deriving their just powers from the consent of the governed."

The general words above quoted would seem to embrace the whole human family, and if they were used in a similar instrument at this day would be so understood. But it is too clear for dispute that the enslaved African race were not intended to be included, and formed no part of the people who framed and adopted this declaration; for if the language, as understood in that day, would embrace them, the conduct of the distinguished men who framed the Declaration of Independence would have been utterly and flagrantly inconsistent with the principles they asserted; and instead of the sympathy of mankind, to which they so confidently appealed, they would have deserved and received universal rebuke and reprobation.

Yet the men who framed this declaration were great men—high in literary acquirements—high in their sense of honor, and incapable of asserting principles inconsistent with those on which they were acting. They perfectly understood the meaning of the language they used, and how it would be understood by others; and they knew that it would not in any part of the civilized world be supposed to embrace the negro race, which, by common consent, had been excluded from civilized Governments and the family of nations and doomed to slavery. They spoke and acted according to the then established doctrines and principles, and in the ordinary language of the day, and no one misunderstood them. The unhappy black race were separated from the white by indelible marks, and laws long before established, and were never thought of or spoken of except as property, and when the claims of the owner or the profit of the trader were supposed to need protection.

The legislation of the States . . . shows, in a manner not to be mistaken, the inferior and subject condition of . . . [the Negro] race at the time the Constitution was adopted, and long afterward, throughout the thirteen States by which that instrument was framed; and it is hardly consistent with the respect due to these States, to suppose that they regarded at that time as fellow-citizens and members of the sovereignty, a class of beings whom they had thus stigmatized; whom, as we are bound, out of respect to the State sovereignties, to assume they had deemed it just and necessary thus to stigmatize, and upon whom they had impressed such deep and enduring marks of inferiority and degradation; or, that when they met in convention to form the Constitution, they looked upon them as a portion of their constituents, or deigned to include them in the provisions so carefully inserted for the security and protection of the liberties and rights of their citizens. It cannot be supposed that they intended to secure to them rights, and privileges, and rank, in the new political body throughout the Union, which every one of them denied within the limits of its own dominion. More especially, it cannot be believed that the large slaveholding States regarded them as included in the word citizens, or would have consented to a Constitution which might compel them to receive them in that character from another State. For if they were so received, and entitled to the privileges and immunities of citizens, it would exempt them from the operation of the special laws and from the police regulations which they considered to be necessary for their own safety. It would give to persons of the Negro race, who were recognized as citizens in any one State of the Union, the right to enter every other State whenever they pleased, singly or in companies, without pass or passport, and without obstruction to sojourn there as long as they pleased, to go where they pleased at every hour of the day or night without molestation, unless they committed some violation of law for which a white man would be punished; and it would give them the full liberty of speech in public and in private upon all subjects upon which its own citizens might speak; to hold public meetings upon political affairs, and to keep and carry arms wherever they went. And all of this would be done in the face of the subject race of the same color, both free and slaves, and inevitably producing discontent and insubordination among them, and endangering the peace and safety of the State. . . .

Undoubtedly, a person may be a citizen, that is, a member of the community who form the sovereignty, although he exercises no share of the political power, and is incapacitated from holding particular offices. Women and minors, who form a part of the political family, cannot vote; and when a property qualification is required to vote or hold a particular office, those who have not the necessary qualification cannot vote or hold the office, yet they are citizens.

So, too, a person may be entitled to vote by the law of the State, who is not a citizen even of the State itself. And in some of the States of the Union foreigners not naturalized are allowed to vote. And the State may give the right to free negroes and mulattoes, but that does not make them citizens of the State, and still less of the United States. And the provisions in the Constitution giving privileges and immunities in other States does not apply to them.

Neither does it apply to a person who, being the citizen of a State, migrates to another State. For then he becomes subject to the laws of the State in which he lives, and he is no longer a citizen of the State from which he removed. And the State in which he resides may then, unquestionably, determine his status or condition, and place him among the class of persons who are not recognised as citizens, but belong to an inferior and subject race; and may deny him the privileges and immunities enjoyed by its citizens. . . .

No one, we presume, supposes that any change in public opinion or feeling, in relation to this unfortunate race, in the civilized nations of Europe or in this country, should induce the court to give to the words of the Constitution a more liberal construction in their favor than they were intended to bear when the instrument was framed and adopted. Such an argument would be altogether inadmissible in any tribunal called on to interpret it. If any of its provisions are deemed unjust, there is a mode prescribed in the instrument itself by which it may be amended; but while it remains unaltered, it must be construed now as it was understood at the time of its adoption. It is not only the same in words, but the same in meaning, and delegates the same powers to the Government, and reserves and secures the same rights and privileges to the citizen; and as long as it continues to exist in its present form, it speaks not only in the same words, but with the same meaning and intent with which it spoke when it came from the hands of its framers, and was voted on and adopted by the people of the United States. Any other rule of construction would abrogate the judicial character of this court, and make it the mere reflex of the popular opinion or passion of the day. This court was not created by the Constitution for such purposes. Higher and graver trusts have been confided to it, and it must not falter in the path of duty. . . .

. . . [T]he court is of opinion, that, . . . Dred Scott was not a citizen of Missouri within the meaning of the Constitution of the United States, and not entitled as such to sue in its courts: and, consequently, that the Circuit Court had no jurisdiction of the case. . . .

We proceed, therefore, to inquire whether the facts relied on by the plaintiff entitled him to his freedom. . . .

In considering this part of the controversy, two questions arise: (1.) Was he, together with his family, free in Missouri by reason of the stay in the territory of the United States . . . ? and (2.) If they were not, is Scott himself free by reason of his removal to Rock Island, in the State of Illinois. . . .

We proceed to examine the first question.

The act of Congress [Missouri Compromise] upon which the plaintiff relies, declares that slavery and involuntary servitude, except as a punishment for crime, shall be forever prohibited in all that part of the territory ceded by France, under the name of Louisiana, which lies north of 36°30′ north latitude, and not included within the limits of Missouri. And the difficulty which meets us at the threshold of this part of the inquiry is, whether Congress was authorized to pass this law under any of the powers granted to it by the Constitution; for if the authority is not given by that instrument, it is the duty of this court to declare it void and inoperative, and incapable of conferring freedom upon any one who is held as a slave under the laws of any one of the States.

The counsel for the plaintiff has laid much stress upon that article in the Constitution which confers on Congress the power "to dispose of and make all needful rules and regulations respecting the territory or other property belonging to the United States"; but, in the judgment of the court, that provision has no bearing on the present controversy, and the power there given, whatever it may be, is confined, and was intended to be confined, to the territory which at that time belonged to, or was claimed by, the United States, and was within their boundaries as settled by the treaty with Great Britain, and can have no influence upon a territory afterwards acquired from a foreign Government. It was a special provision for a known and particular territory, and to meet a present emergency, and nothing more. . . .

The language used in the clause, the arrangement and combination of the powers, and the somewhat unusual phraseology it uses, when it speaks of the political power to be exercised in the government of the territory, all indicate the design and meaning of the clause to be such as we have mentioned. It does not speak of *any* territory, nor of *Territories,* but uses language which, according to its legitimate meaning, points to a particular thing. The power is given in relation only to *the* territory of the United States—that is, to a territory then in existence, and then known or claimed as the territory of the United States. . . .

This brings us to examine by what provision of the Constitution the present Federal Government, under its delegated and restricted powers, is authorized to acquire territory outside of the original limits of the United States, and what powers it may exercise therein over the person or property of a citizen of the United States, while it remains a Territory, and until it shall be admitted as one of the States of the Union.

There is certainly no power given by the Constitution to the Federal Government to establish or maintain colonies bordering on the United States or at a distance, to be ruled and governed at its own pleasure; nor to enlarge its territorial limits in any way, except by the admission of new States. That power is plainly given; and if a new State is admitted, it needs no further legislation by Congress, because the Constitution itself defines the relative rights and powers, and duties of the State, and the citizens of the State, and the Federal Government. But no power is given to acquire a Territory to be held and governed permanently in that character. . . .

. . . It may be safely assumed that citizens of the United States who migrate to a Territory belonging to the people of the United States, cannot be ruled as mere colonists, dependent upon the will of the General Government, and to be governed by any laws it may think proper to impose. The principle upon which our Governments rest, and upon which alone they continue to exist, is the union of States, sovereign and independent within their own limits in their internal and domestic concerns, and bound together as one people by a General Government possessing certain enumerated and restricted powers, delegated to it by the people of the several States, and exercising supreme authority within the scope of the powers granted to it, throughout the dominion of the United States. A power, therefore, in the General Government to obtain and hold colonies and dependent territories, over which they might legislate without restriction, would be inconsistent with its own existence in its present form. Whatever it acquires it acquires for the benefit of the people of the several States who created it. It is their trustee acting for them, and charged with the duty of promoting the interests of the whole people of the Union in the exercise of the powers specifically granted. . . .

. . . The Territory being a part of the United States, the Government and the citizen both enter it under the authority of the Constitution, with their respective rights defined and marked out; and the Federal Government can exercise no power over his person or property, beyond what that instrument confers, nor lawfully deny any right which it has reserved. . . .

Now, as we have already said in an earlier part of this opinion, upon a different point, the right of property in a slave is distinctly and expressly affirmed in the Constitution. The right to traffic in it, like an ordinary article of merchandise and property, was guaranteed to the citizens of the United States, in every State that might desire it, for twenty years. And the Government in express terms is pledged to protect it in all future time, if the slave escapes from his owner. This is done in plain words—too plain to be misunderstood. And no word can be found in the Constitution which gives Congress a greater power over slave property, or which entitles property of that kind to less protection than property of any other description. The only power conferred is the power coupled with the duty of guarding and protecting the owner in his rights.

Upon these considerations, it is the opinion of the court that the act of Congress which prohibited a citizen from holding and owning property of this kind in the territory of the United States north of the line therein mentioned, is not warranted by the Constitution, and is therefore void; and that neither Dred Scott himself, nor any of his family, were made free by being carried into this territory; even if they had been carried there by the owner, with the intention of becoming a permanent resident. . . .

But there is another point in the case which depends on State power and State law. And it is contended, on the part of the plaintiff, that he is made free by being taken to Rock Island, in the State of Illinois, independently of his residence in the territory of the United States; and being so made free, he was not again reduced to a state of slavery by being brought back to Missouri.

Our notice of this part of the case will be very brief; for the principle on which it depends was decided in this court, upon much consideration, in the case of *Strader et al.* v. *Graham*, reported in 19th Howard, 82. In that case, the slaves had been taken from Kentucky to Ohio, with the consent of the owner, and afterwards brought back to Kentucky. And this court held that their status or condition, as free or slave, depended upon the laws of Kentucky, when they were brought back into the State, and not of Ohio; and that this court had no jurisdiction to revise the judgment of a State court upon its own laws. . . .

So in this case. As Scott was a slave when taken into the State of Illinois by his owner, and was there held as such, and brought back in that character, his status, as free or slave, depended on the laws of Missouri, and not of Illinois. . . .

Upon the whole, therefore, it is the judgment of this court, that it appears by the record before us that the plaintiff in error is not a citizen of Missouri, in the sense in which that word is used in the Constitution; and that the Circuit Court of the United States, for that reason, had no jurisdiction in the case, and could give no judgment in it. Its judgment for the defendant must, consequently, be reversed, and a mandate issued, directing the suit to be dismissed for want of jurisdiction. . . .

MR. JUSTICE MCLEAN, dissenting.

In the argument, it was said that a colored citizen would not be an agreeable member of society. This is more a matter of taste than of law. Several of the States have admitted persons of color to the right of suffrage, and in this view have recognised them as citizens; and this has been done in the slave as well as the free States. On the question of citizenship, it must be admitted that we have not been very fastidious. Under the late treaty with Mexico, we have made citizens of all grades, combinations, and colors. The same was done in the admission of Louisiana and Florida. No one ever doubted, and no court ever held, that the people of these Territories did not become citizens under the treaty. They have exercised all the rights of citizens, without being naturalized under the acts of Congress.

In the formation of the Federal Constitution, care was taken to confer no power on the Federal Government to interfere with this institution [*of slavery*] in the States. In the provision respecting the slave trade, in fixing the ratio of representation, and providing for the reclamation of fugitives from labor, slaves were referred to as persons, and in no other respect are they considered in the Constitution.

We need not refer to the mercenary spirit which introduced the infamous traffic in slaves, to show the degradation of negro slavery in our country. This system was imposed upon our colonial settlements by the mother country, and it is due to truth to say that the commercial colonies and States were chiefly engaged in the traffic. But we know as a historical fact, that James Madison, that great and good man, a leading member in the Federal Convention, was solicitous to guard the language of that instrument so as not to convey the idea that there could be property in man.

I prefer the lights of Madison, Hamilton, and Jay, as a means of construing the Constitution in all its bearings, rather than to look behind that period into a traffic which is now declared to be piracy, and punished with death by Christian nations. I do not like to draw the sources of our domestic relations from so dark a ground. Our independence was a great epoch in the history of freedom; and while I admit the Government was not made especially for the colored race, yet many of them were citizens of the New England States, and exercised the rights of suffrage when the Constitution was adopted, and it was not doubted by any intelligent person that its tendencies would greatly ameliorate their condition.

Many of the States, on the adoption of the Constitution, or shortly afterward, took measures to abolish slavery within their respective jurisdictions; and it is a well-known fact that a belief was cherished by the leading men, South as well as North, that the institution of slavery would gradually decline, until it would become extinct. The increased value of slave labor, in the culture of cotton and sugar, prevented the realization of this expectation. Like all other communities and States, the South were influenced by what they considered to be their own interests.

But if we are to turn our attention to the dark ages of the world, why confine our view to colored slavery? On the same principles, white men were made slaves. All slavery has its origin in power, and is against right.

The power of Congress to establish Territorial Governments, and to prohibit the introduction of slavery therein, is the next point to be considered.

The prohibition of slavery north of 36°30′, and of the State of Missouri, contained in the act admitting that State into the Union, was passed by a vote of 134, in the House of Representatives, to 42. Before Mr. Monroe signed the act, it was submitted by him to his Cabinet, and they held the restriction of slavery in a Territory to be within the constitutional powers of Congress. It would be singular, if in 1804 Congress had power to prohibit the introduction of slaves in Orleans Territory from any other part of the Union, under the penalty of freedom to the slave, if the same power, embodied in the Missouri Compromise, could not be exercised in 1820.

But this law of Congress, which prohibits slavery north of Missouri and of 36°30′ is declared to have been null and void by my brethren. And this opinion is founded mainly, as I understand, on the distinction drawn between the *[Northwest]* ordinance of 1787 and the Missouri Compromise line. In what does the distinction consist? The ordinance, it is said, was a compact entered into by the confederated States before the adoption of the Constitution; and that in the cession of territory authority was given to establish a Territorial Government.

It is clear that the ordinance did not go into operation by virtue of the authority of the Confederation, but by reason of its modification and adoption by Congress under the Constitution. It seems to be supposed, in the opinion of the court, that the articles of cession placed it on a different footing from territories subsequently acquired. I am unable to perceive the force of this distinction. That the ordinance was intended for the government of the Northwestern Territory, and was limited to such Territory, is admitted. It was extended to Southern Territories, with modifications, by acts of Congress, and to some Northern Territories. But the ordinance was made valid by the act of Congress, and without such act could have been of no force. It rested for its validity on the act of Congress, the same, in my opinion, as the Missouri Compromise line.

If Congress may establish a Territorial Government in the exercise of its discretion, it is a clear principle that a court cannot control that discretion. This being the case, I do not see on what ground the act is held to be void. It did not purport to forfeit property, or take it for public purposes. It only prohibited slavery; in doing which, it followed the ordinance of 1787.

MR. JUSTICE CURTIS, dissenting.

I dissent from the opinion pronounced by the Chief Justice, and from the judgment which the majority of the court think it proper to render in this case. . . .

To determine whether any free persons, descended from Africans held in slavery, were citizens of the United States under the Confederation, and consequently at the time of the adoption of the Constitution of the United States, it is only necessary to know whether any such persons were citizens of either of the States under the Confederation, at the time of the adoption of the Constitution.

Of this there can be no doubt. At the time of the ratification of the Articles of Confederation, all free native-born inhabitants of the States of New Hampshire, Massachusetts, New York, New Jersey, and North Carolina, though descended from African slaves, were not only citizens of those States, but such of them as had the other necessary qualifications possessed the franchise of electors, on equal terms with other citizens. . . .

I shall not enter into a examination of the existing opinions of that period respecting the African race, nor into any discussion concerning the meaning of those who asserted, in the Declaration of Independence, that all men are created equal; that they are endowed by their Creator with certain inalienable rights; that among these are life, liberty, and the pursuit of happiness. My own opinion is, that a calm comparison of these assertions of universal abstract truths, and of their own individual opinions and acts, would not leave these men under any reproach of inconsistency; that the great truths they asserted on that solemn occasion, they were ready and anxious to make effectual, wherever a necessary regard to circumstances, which no statesman can disregard without producing more evil than good, would allow; and that it would not be just to them, nor true in itself, to allege that they intended to say that the Creator of all men had endowed the white race, exclusively, with the great natural rights which the Declaration of Independence asserts. But this is not the place to vindicate their memory. As I conceive, we should deal here, not with such disputes, if there can be a dispute concerning this subject, but with those substantial facts evinced by the written constitutions of States, and by the notorious practice under them. And they show, in a manner which no argument can obscure, that in some of the original thirteen States, free colored persons, before and at the time of the formation of the Constitution, were citizens of those States.

Did the Constitution of the United States deprive them or their descendants of citizenship?

That Constitution was ordained and established by the people of the United States through the action, in each State, of those persons who were qualified by its laws to act thereon, in behalf of themselves and all other citizens of that State. In some of the States, as we have seen, colored persons were among those qualified by law to act on this subject. These colored persons were not only included in the body of "the people of the United States by whom the Constitution was ordained and established," but in at least five of the States they had the power to act, and doubtless did act, by their suffrages, upon the question of its adoption. It would be strange, if we were to find in that instrument anything which deprived of their citizenship any part of the people of the United States who were among those by whom it was established.

I can find nothing in the Constitution which deprives of their citizenship any class of persons who were citizens of the United States at the time of its adoption, or who should be native-born citizens of any State after its adoption; nor any power enabling Congress to disfranchise persons born on the soil of any State, and entitled to citizenship of such State by its constitution and laws. And my opinion is, that, under the Constitution of the United States, every free person born on the soil of a State, who is a citizen of that State by force of its Constitution or laws, is also a citizen of the United States. . . .

Confining our view to free persons born within the several States, we find that the Constitution has recognized the general principle of public law, that allegiance and citizenship depend on the place of birth; that it has not attempted practically to apply this principle by designating the particular classes of persons who should or should not come under it; that when we turn to the Constitution for an answer to the question, what free persons, born within the several States, are citizens of the United States, the only answer we can receive from any of its express provisions is, the citizens of the several States are to enjoy the privileges and immunities of citizens in every State, and their franchise as electors under the Constitution depends on their citizenship in the several States. Add to this, that the Constitution was ordained by the citizens of the several States; that they were "the people of the United States," for whom and whose posterity the government was declared in the preamble of the Constitution to be made; that each of them was "a citizen of the United States at the time of the adoption of the Constitution," within the meaning of those words in that instrument; that by them the government was to be and was in fact organized; and that no power is conferred on the Government of the Union to discriminate between them, or to disfranchise any of them—the necessary conclusion is, that those persons born within the several States, who, by force of their respective constitutions and laws, are citizens of the State, are thereby citizens of the United States.

It has been often asserted that the Constitution was made exclusively by and for the white race. It has already been shown that in five of the thirteen original States, colored persons then possessed the elective franchise, and were among those by whom the Constitution was ordained and established. If so, it is not true, in point of fact, that the Constitution was made exclusively by the white race? And that it was made exclusively for the white race is, in my opinion, not only an assumption not warranted by anything in the Constitution, but contradicted by its opening declaration, that it was ordained and established by the people of the United States, for themselves and their posterity. And as free colored persons were then citizens of at least five States, and so in every sense part of the people of the United States, they were among those for whom and whose posterity the Constitution was ordained and established.

I dissent, therefore, from that part of the opinion of the majority of the court, in which it is held that a person of African descent cannot be a citizen of the United States; and I regret I must go further, and dissent both from what I deem their assumption of authority to examine the constitutionality of the act of Congress commonly called the Missouri Compromise act, and the grounds and conclusions announced in their opinion.

Having first decided that they were bound to consider the sufficiency of the plea to the jurisdiction of the Circuit Court, and having decided that this plea showed that the Circuit Court had not jurisdiction, and consequently that this is a case to which the judicial power of the United States does not extend, they have gone on to examine the merits of the case as they appeared on the trial before the court and jury, on the issues joined on the pleas in bar, and so have reached the question of the power of Congress to pass the act of 1820. On so grave a subject as this, I feel obliged to say that, in my opinion, such an exertion of judicial power transcends the limits of the authority of the court, as described by its repeated decisions and, as I understand, acknowledged in this opinion of the majority of the court. . . .

The question here is whether . . . the court [is authorized] to insert into [Article 4, Section 2—concerning Territories] an exception of the exclusion or allowance of slavery, not found therein, nor in any other part of that instrument. To engraft on any instrument a substantive exception not found in it, must be admitted to be a matter attended with great difficulty. And the difficulty increases with the importance of the instrument, and the magnitude and complexity of the interests involved in its construction. To allow this to be done with the Constitution, upon reasons purely political, renders its judicial interpretation impossible—because judicial tribunals, as such, cannot decide upon political considerations. Political reasons have not the requisite certainty to afford rules of juridical interpretation. They are different in different men. They are different in the same men at different times. And when a strict interpretation of the Constitution, according to the fixed rules which govern the interpretation of laws, is abandoned, and the theoretical opinions of individuals are allowed to control its meaning, we have no longer a Constitution; we are under the government of individual men, who for the time being have power to declare what the Constitution is, according to their own views of what it ought to mean. When such a method of interpretation of the Constitution obtains, in place of a republican government, with limited and defined powers, we have a government which is merely an exponent of the will of Congress; or what, in my opinion, would not be preferable, an exponent of the individual political opinions of the members of this court.

If it can be shown by anything in the Constitution itself that when it confers on Congress the power to make all needful rules and regulations respecting the Territory belonging to the United States, the exclusion or the allowance of slavery was excepted; or if anything in the history of this provision tends to show that such an exception was intended by those who framed and adopted the Constitution to be introduced into it, I hold it to be my duty carefully to consider, and to allow just weight to such considerations in interpreting the positive text of the Constitution. But where the Constitution has said all needful rules and regulations, I must find something more than theoretical reasoning to induce me to say it did not mean all.

Looking at the power of Congress over the Territories as of the extent just described, what positive prohibition exists in the Constitution, which restrained Congress from enacting a law in 1820 to prohibit slavery north of 36°30′ north latitude?

The only one suggested is that clause in the 5th article of the Amendments of the Constitution which declares that no person shall be deprived of his life, liberty, or property, without due process of law. I will now proceed to examine the question, whether this clause is entitled to the effect thus contributed to it. It is necessary, first, to have a clear view of the nature and incidents of that particular species of property which is now in question.

Slavery being contrary to natural right, is created only by municipal law. This is not only plain in itself, and agreed by all writers on the subject, but is inferable from the Constitution, and has been explicitly declared by this court. The Constitution refers to slaves as "persons held to service in one State, under the laws thereof." Nothing can more clearly describe a status created by municipal law. In *Prigg* v. *Pennsylvania,* 16 Pet. 611, this court said: "The state of slavery is deemed to be a mere municipal regulation, founded on and limited to the range of territorial laws." In *Rankin* v. *Lydia,* 2 A. K. Marsh. 470, the Supreme Court of Appeals of Kentucky said: "Slavery is sanctioned by the laws of this State, and the right to hold them under our municipal regulations is unquestionable. But we view this as a right existing by positive law of a municipal character, without foundation in the law of nature or the unwritten common law." I am not acquainted with any case or writer questioning the correctness of this doctrine.

The status of slavery is not necessarily always attended with the same powers on the part of the master. The master is subject to the supreme power of the State, whose will controls his action towards his slave, and this control must be defined and regulated by the municipal law. In one State, as at one period of the Roman law, it may put the life of the slave into the hand of the master; others, as those of the United States, which tolerate slavery, may treat the slave as a person when the master takes his life; while in others, the law may recognize a right of the slave to be protected from cruel treatment. In other words, the status of slavery embraces every condition, from that in which the slave is known to the law simply as a chattel, with no civil rights, to that in which he is recognized as a person for all purposes, save the compulsory power of directing and receiving the fruits of his labor. Which of these conditions shall attend the status of slavery, must depend on the municipal law which creates and upholds it.

And not only must the status of slavery be created and measured by municipal law, but the rights, powers and obligations which grow out of that status, must be defined, protected and enforced by such laws. The liability of the master for the torts and crimes of his slave, and of third persons for assaulting or injuring or harboring or kidnapping him, the forms and modes of emancipation and sale, their subjection to the debts of the master, succession by the death of the master, suits for freedom, the capacity of the slave to be party to a suit, or to be a witness, with such police regulations as have existed in all civilized States where slavery has been tolerated, are among the subjects upon which municipal legislation becomes necessary when slavery is introduced.

Is it conceivable that the Constitution has conferred the right on every citizen to become a resident on the Territory of the United States with his slaves, and there to hold them as such, but has neither made nor provided for any municipal regulations which are essential to the existence of slavery?

Is it not more rational to conclude that they who framed and adopted the Constitution were aware that persons held to service under the laws of a State are property only to the extent and under the conditions fixed by those laws; that they must cease to be available as property, when their owners voluntarily place them permanently within another jurisdiction, where no municipal laws on the subject of slavery exist; and that, being aware of these principles, and having said nothing to interfere with or displace them, or compel Congress to legislate in any particular manner on the subject, and having empowered Congress to make all needful rules and regulations respecting the Territory of the United States, it was their intention to leave to the discretion of Congress what regulations, if any, should be made concerning slavery therein? . . .

. . . I am of opinion that so much of the several acts of Congress as prohibited slavery and involuntary servitude within that part of the Territory of Wisconsin lying north of 36°30′ north latitude, and west of the river Mississippi, were constitutional and valid laws.

## *Coyle* v. *Smith*

**221 U. S. 559; 31 S. Ct. 688; 55 L. Ed. 853 (1911)**

Under the 1906 enabling act admitting Oklahoma as a state, Congress specified that the capital should be located in Guthrie until at least 1913. This arrangement was agreed to by the voters of the state at the time of the adoption of the state's constitution. In 1910, however, the Oklahoma legislature passed an act that provided for the removal of the capital to Oklahoma City. W. H. Coyle, a property owner in Guthrie, brought suit against Thomas P. Smith, secretary of state of Oklahoma, to test the legality of the removal. The Oklahoma Supreme Court upheld the legislative act, and the case went to the United States Supreme Court on a writ of error. *Opinion of the Court: Lurton, Day, Harlan, Hughes, Lamar, Van Devanter, White. Dissenting: Holmes, McKenna.*

MR. JUSTICE LURTON delivered the opinion of the Court.

. . . The only question for review by us is whether the provision of the enabling act was a valid limitation upon the power of the State after its admission, which overrides any subsequent state legislation repugnant thereto.

The power to locate its own seat of government and to determine when and how it shall be changed from one place to another, and to appropriate its own public funds for that purpose, are essentially and peculiarly state powers. That one of the original thirteen States could now be shorn of such powers by an act of Congress would not be for a moment entertained. The question then comes to this: Can a State be placed upon a plane of inequality with its sister States in the Union if the Congress chooses to impose conditions which so operate, at the time of its admission? The argument is, that while Congress may not deprive a State of any power which it possesses, it may, as a condition to the admission of a new State, constitutionally restrict its authority, to the extent at least, of suspending its powers for a definite time in respect to the location of its seat of government. . . .

The power of Congress in respect to the admission of new States is found in the third section of the fourth Article of the Constitution. That provision is that, "new States may be admitted by the Congress into this Union." . . .

. . . "This Union" was and is a union of States, equal in power, dignity and authority, each competent to exert that residuum of sovereignty not delegated to the United States by the Constitution itself. To maintain otherwise would be to say that the Union, through the power of Congress to admit new States, might come to be a union of States unequal in power, as including States whose powers were restricted only by the Constitution, with others whose powers had been further restricted by an act of Congress accepted as a condition of admission. Thus it would result, first, that the powers of Congress would not be defined by the Constitution alone, but in respect to new States, enlarged or restricted by the conditions imposed upon new States by its own legislation admitting them into the Union; and, second, that such new States might not exercise all of the powers which had not been delegated by the Constitution, but only such as had not been further bargained away as conditions of admission. . . .

. . . When a new State is admitted into the Union, it is so admitted with all of the powers of sovereignty and jurisdiction which pertain to the original States, and . . . such powers may not be constitutionally diminished, impaired or shorn away by any conditions, compacts or stipulations embraced in the act under which the new State came into the Union, which would not be valid and effectual if the subject of congressional legislation after admission. . . .

It may well happen that Congress should embrace in an enactment introducing a new State into the Union legislation intended as a regulation of commerce among the States, or with Indian tribes situated within the limits of such new State, or regulations touching the sole care and disposition of the public lands or reservations therein which might be upheld as legislation within the sphere of the plain power of Congress. But in every such case such legislation would derive its force not from any agreement or compact with the proposed new State, nor by reason of its acceptance of such enactment as a term of admission, but solely because the power of Congress extended to the subject, and therefore, would not operate to restrict the State's legislative power in respect of any matter which was not plainly within the regulating power of Congress. . . .

No such question is presented here. The legislation in the Oklahoma enabling act relating to the location of the capital of the State, if construed as forbidding a removal by the State after its admission as a State, is referable to no power granted to Congress over the subject, and if it is to be upheld at all, it must be implied from the power to admit new States. If power to impose such a restriction upon the general and undelegated power of a State be conceded as implied from the power to admit a new State, where is the line to be drawn against restrictions imposed upon new States? . . .

In *Texas* v. *White* [1869], Chief Justice Chase said in strong and memorable language that, "the Constitution, in all of its provisions looks to an indestructible Union, composed of indestructible States."

In *Lane County* v. *Oregon* [1869], . . . he said: "The people of the United States constitute one nation, under one government, and this government, within the scope of the powers with which it is invested, is supreme. On the other hand, the people of each State compose a State, having its own government, and endowed with all the functions essential to separate and independent existence. The States disunited might continue to exist. Without the States in union there could be no such political body as the United States."

To this we may add that the constitutional equality of the States is essential to the harmonious operation of the scheme upon which the Republic was organized. When that equality disappears we may remain a free people, but the Union will not be the Union of the Constitution.

*Judgment affirmed.*

## *Younger* v. *Harris*

**401 U.S. 37; 91 S. Ct. 746; 27 L. Ed. 2d 669 (1971)**

John Harris, a socialist, was indicted in California state court for violating California's Criminal Syndicalism Act, which prohibited "advocating, teaching or aiding and abetting the commission of crime, sabotage, . . . or unlawful acts of force and violence or unlawful methods of terrorism as a means of accomplishing a change in industrial ownership or control, or effecting any political change." After upholding the California statute in *Whitney* v. *California* (1927), the Supreme Court had subsequently overruled *Whitney* in *Brandenburg* v. *Ohio* (1969). Harris, alleging that the very existence of the statute had a "chilling effect" on his First Amendment rights, filed suit in federal district court seeking to enjoin Los Angeles County District Attorney Evelle Younger from prosecuting him under its provisions. A three-judge panel held the act void because of vagueness and overbreadth and enjoined Harris' prosecution. The state thereupon appealed to the Supreme Court. *Opinion of the Court: Black, Blackmun, Burger, Harlan, Stewart. Concurring opinion: Stewart, Harlan. Concurring in the result: Brennan, Marshall, White. Dissenting opinion: Douglas.*

MR. JUSTICE BLACK delivered the opinion of the Court. . . .

A federal lawsuit to stop a prosecution in a state court is a serious matter.

Since the beginning of this country's history Congress has, subject to few exceptions, manifested a desire to permit state courts to try state cases free from interference by federal courts. . . .

The precise reasons for this longstanding public policy against federal court interference with state court proceedings have never been specifically identified but the primary sources of the policy are plain. One is the basic doctrine of equity jurisprudence that courts of equity should not act, and particularly should not act to restrain a criminal prosecution, when the moving party has an adequate remedy at law and will not suffer irreparable injury if denied equitable relief. The doctrine . . . is . . . important under our Constitution, in order to prevent erosion of the role of the jury and avoid a duplication of legal proceedings and legal sanctions where a single suit would be adequate to protect the rights asserted. This underlying reason for restraining courts of equity from interfering with criminal prosecutions is reinforced by an even more vital consideration, the notion of "comity," that is, a proper respect for state functions, a recognition of the fact that the entire country is made up of a Union of separate state governments, and a continuance of the belief that the National Government will fare best if the States and their institutions are left free to perform their separate functions in their separate ways. This, perhaps for lack of a better and clearer way to describe it, is referred to by many as "Our Federalism," and one familiar with the profound debates that ushered our Federal Constitution into existence is bound to respect those who remain loyal to the ideals and dreams of "Our Federalism." The concept does not mean blind deference to "States' Rights" any more than it means centralization of control over every important issue in our National Government and its courts. The Framers rejected both these courses. What the concept does represent is a system in which there is sensitivity to the legitimate interests of both State and National Governments, and in which the National Government, anxious though it may be to vindicate and protect federal rights and federal interests, always endeavors to do so in ways that will not unduly interfere with the legitimate activities of the States. It should never be forgotten that this slogan, "Our Federalism," born in the early struggling days of our Union of States, occupies a highly important place in our Nation's history and its future. . . .

This is where the law stood when the Court decided *Dombrowski* v. *Pfister*. . . . (1965), and held that an injunction against the enforcement of certain state criminal statutes could properly issue under the circumstances presented in that case. In Dombrowski, unlike many of the earlier cases denying injunctions, the complaint made substantial allegations that: "the threats to enforce the statutes against appellants are not made with any expectation of securing valid convictions, but rather are part of a plan to employ arrests, seizures, and threats of prosecution under color of the statutes to harass appellants and discourage them and their supporters from asserting and attempting to vindicate the constitutional rights of Negro citizens of Louisiana." . . .

. . . These circumstances, as viewed by the Court sufficiently establish the kind of irreparable injury, above and beyond that associated with the defense of a single prosecution brought in good faith, that had always been considered sufficient to justify federal intervention.

The District Court, however, thought that the *Dombrowski* decision substantially broadened the availability of injunctions against state criminal prosecutions and that under that decision the federal courts may give equitable relief, without regard to any showing of bad faith or harassment, whenever a state statute is found "on its face" to be vague or overly broad, in violation of the First Amendment. We recognize that there are some statements in the *Dombrowski* opinion that would seem to support this argument. But, as we have already seen, such statements were unnecessary to the decision of that case, because the Court found that the plaintiffs had alleged a basis for equitable relief under the long-established standards. In addition, we do not regard the reasons adduced to support this position as sufficient to justify such a substantial departure from the established doctrines regarding the availability of injunctive relief. It is undoubtedly true, as the Court stated in *Dombrowski* that "[a] criminal prosecution under a statute regulating expression usually involves imponderables and contingencies that themselves may inhibit the full exercise of First Amendment Freedoms."

But this sort of "chilling effect," as the Court called it, should not itself justify federal intervention. . . .

Beyond all this is another, more basic consideration. Procedures for testing the constitutionality of a statute "on its face" in the manner apparently contemplated by *Dombrowski,* and for then enjoining all action to enforce the statute until the State can obtain court approval for a modified version, are fundamentally at odds with the function of the federal courts in our constitutional plan. The power and duty of the judiciary to declare laws unconstitutional is in the final analysis derived from its responsibility for resolving concrete disputes brought before the courts for decision; a statute apparently governing a dispute cannot be applied by judges, consistently with their obligations under the Supremacy Clause, when such an application of the statute would conflict with the Constitution. . . . But this vital responsibility, broad as it is, does not amount to an unlimited power to survey the statute books and pass judgment on laws before the courts are called upon to enforce them. Ever since the Constitutional Convention rejected a proposal for having members of the Supreme Court render advice concerning pending legislation it has been clear that, even when suits of this kind involve a "case or controversy" sufficient to satisfy the requirements of Article III of the Constitution, the task of analyzing a proposed statute, pinpointing its deficiencies, and requiring correction of these deficiencies before the statute is put into effect, is rarely if ever an appropriate task for the judiciary. . . . In light of this fundamental conception of the Framers as to the proper place of the federal courts in the governmental processes of passing and enforcing laws, it can seldom be appropriate for these courts to exercise any such power of prior approval or veto over the legislative process.

For these reasons, fundamental not only to our federal system but also to the basic functions of the Judicial Branch of the National Government under our Constitution, we hold that the *Dombrowski* decision should not be regarded as having upset the settled doctrines that have always confined very narrowly the availability of injunctive relief against state criminal prosecutions. We do not think that opinion stands for the proposition that a federal court can properly enjoin enforcement of a statute solely on the basis of a showing that the statute "on its face" abridges First Amendment rights. . . .

The judgment of the District Court is reversed, and the case is remanded for further proceedings not inconsistent with this opinion.

*Reversed.*

## *Baldwin* v. *Montana Fish and Game Commission*

**436 U. S. 371; 98 S. Ct. 1852; 56 L. Ed. 2d 354 (1978)**

Under Montana's elk-hunting license system, nonresidents were charged substantially higher fees than residents and were required to purchase a combination hunting and fishing license in order to be able to hunt elk. In 1976, for example, a Montana resident could purchase a license solely for elk for $9, whereas a nonresident had to pay $225 for a combination license. Lester Baldwin, a Montana hunting guide, and four nonresident elk hunters brought suit in federal court seeking declaratory and injunctive relief and reimbursement of fees already paid. They contended that Montana's elk-hunting licensing scheme violated the Privileges and Immunities Clause of Article IV, Section 2. A divided three-judge district court denied all relief to the appellants, who appealed to the Supreme Court. *Opinion of the Court: Blackmun, Burger, Powell, Rehnquist, Stevens, Stewart. Concurring opinion: Burger. Dissenting opinion: Brennan, Marshall, White.*

MR. JUSTICE BLACKMUN delivered the opinion of the Court.

. . . Appellants strongly urge here that the Montana licensing scheme for the hunting of elk violates the Privileges and Immunities Clause of Art. IV, § 2, of our Constitution. That Clause is not one the contours of which have been precisely shaped by the process and wear of constant litigation and judicial interpretation over the years since 1789. . . . We are, nevertheless, not without some pronouncements by this Court as to the Clause's significance and reach. . . .

When the Privileges and Immunities Clause has been applied to specific cases, it has been interpreted to prevent a State from imposing unreasonable burdens on citizens of other States in their pursuit of common callings within the State, . . . in the ownership and disposition of privately held property within the State, . . . and in access to the courts of the State. . . .

It has not been suggested, however, that state citizenship or residency may never be used by a State to distinguish among persons. Suffrage, for example, always has been understood to be tied to an individual's identification with a particular State. . . . No one would suggest that the Privileges and Immunities Clause requires a State to open its polls to a person who declines to assert that the State is the only one where he claims a right to vote. The same is true as to qualification for an elective office of the State. . . . Nor must a State always apply all its laws or all its services equally to anyone, resident or nonresident, who may request it so to do. . . . Some distinctions between residents and nonresidents merely reflect the fact that this is a Nation composed of individual States, and are permitted; other distinctions are prohibited because they hinder the formation, the purpose, or the development of a single Union of those States. Only with respect to those "privileges" and "immunities" bearing upon the vitality of the Nation as a single entity must the State treat all citizens, resident and nonresident, equally. Here we must decide into which category falls a distinction with respect to access to recreational big-game hunting.

Many of the early cases embrace the concept that the States had complete ownership over wildlife within their boundaries, and, as well, the power to preserve this bounty for their citizens alone. It was enough to say "that in regulating the use of the common property of the citizens of [a] state, the legislature is [not] bound to extend to the citizens of all the other states the same advantages as are secured to their own citizens." *Corfield* v. *Coryell*, . . . (1825). It appears to have been generally accepted that although the States were obligated to treat all those within their territory equally in most respects, they were not obliged to share those things they held in trust for their own people. In *Corfield*, . . . Mr. Justice Washington, sitting as Circuit Justice, although recognizing that the States may not interfere with the "right of a citizen of one state to pass through, or to reside in any other state, for purposes of trade, agriculture, professional pursuits, or otherwise; to claim the benefit of the writ of habeas corpus; to institute and maintain actions of any kind in the courts of the state; to take, hold and dispose of property, either real or personal," . . . nonetheless concluded that access to oyster beds determined to be owned by New Jersey could be limited to New Jersey residents. This holding, and the conception of state sovereignty upon which it relied, formed the basis for similar decisions during later years of the 19th century. . . .

In more recent years, however, the Court has recognized that the States' interest in regulating and controlling those things they claim to "own," including wildlife, is by no means absolute. States may not compel the confinement of the benefits of their resources, even their wildlife, to their own people whenever such hoarding and confinement impedes interstate commerce. . . . And a State's interest in its wildlife and other resources must yield when, without reason, it interferes with a nonresident's right to pursue a livelihood in a State other than his own, a right that is protected by the Privileges and Immunities Clause. . . .

Appellants contend that the doctrine on which *Corfield*, . . . relied has no remaining vitality. We do not agree. . . . The fact that the State's control over wildlife is not exclusive and absolute in the face of federal regulation and certain federally protected interests does not compel the conclusion that it is meaningless in their absence. . . .

Appellants have demonstrated nothing to convince us that we should completely reject the Court's earlier decisions. In his opinion in *Coryell*, Mr. Justice Washington, although he seemingly relied on notions of "natural rights" when he considered the reach of the Privileges and Immunities Clause, included in his list of situations, in which he believed the States would be obligated to treat each other's residents equally, only those where a nonresident sought to engage in an essential activity or exercise a basic right. He himself used the term "fundamental," . . . in the modern as well as the "natural right" sense. . . . With respect to such basic and essential activities, interference with which would frustrate the purposes of the formation of the Union, the States must treat residents and nonresidents without unnecessary distinctions.

Does the distinction made by Montana between residents and nonresidents in establishing access to elk hunting threaten a basic right in a way that offends the Privileges and Immunities Clause? Merely to ask the question seems to provide the answer. . . . Elk hunting by nonresidents in Montana is a recreation and a sport. In itself—wholly apart from license fees—it is costly and obviously available only to the wealthy nonresident or to the one so taken with the sport that he sacrifices other values in order to indulge in it and to enjoy what it offers. It is not a means to the nonresident's livelihood. The mastery of the animal and the trophy are the ends that are sought; appellants are not totally excluded from these. The elk supply, which has been entrusted to the care of the State by the people of Montana, is finite and must be carefully tended in order to be preserved.

Appellants' interest in sharing this limited resource on more equal terms with Montana residents simply does not fall within the purview of the Privileges and Immunities Clause. Equality in access to Montana elk is not basic to the maintenance or well-being of the Union. . . . We do not decide the full range of activities that are sufficiently basic to the livelihood of the Nation that the States may not interfere with a nonresident's participation therein without similarly interfering with a resident's participation. Whatever rights or activities may be "fundamental" under the Privileges and Immunities Clause, we are persuaded, and hold, that elk hunting by nonresidents in Montana is not one of them. . . .

MR. JUSTICE BRENNAN, with whom MR. JUSTICE WHITE and MR. JUSTICE MARSHALL join, dissenting.

Far more troublesome than the Court's narrow holding—elk hunting in Montana is not a privilege or immunity entitled to protection under Art. IV, § 2, cl. 1, of the Constitution—is the rationale of the holding that Montana's elk-hunting licensing scheme passes constitutional muster. The Court concludes that because elk hunting is not a "basic and essential activit[y], interference with which would frustrate [the] purposes of the formation of the Union," . . . the Privileges and Immunities Clause of Art. IV, § 2 . . . does not prevent Montana from irrationally, wantonly, and even invidiously discriminating against nonresidents seeking to enjoy natural treasures it alone among the 50 States possesses. I cannot agree that the Privileges and Immunities Clause is so impotent a guarantee that such discrimination remains wholly beyond the purview of that provision.

I think the time has come to confirm explicitly that which has been implicit in our modern privileges and immunities decisions, namely that an inquiry into whether a given right is "fundamental" has no place in our analysis of whether a State's discrimination against nonresidents—who "are not represented in the [discriminating] State's legislative halls," . . .—violates the Clause. Rather, our primary concern is the State's justification for its discrimination. . . . A State's discrimination against nonresidents is permissible where (1) the presence or activity of nonresidents is the source or cause of the problem or effect with which the State seeks to deal, and (2) the discrimination practiced against nonresidents bears a substantial relation to the problem they present. . . .

It is clear that under a proper privileges and immunities analysis Montana's discriminatory treatment of nonresident big-game hunters in this case must fall. . . . There are three possible justifications for charging nonresident elk hunters an amount at least 7.5 times the fee imposed on resident big-game hunters.* The first is conservation. . . . There is nothing in the record to indicate that the influx of nonresident hunters created a special danger to Montana's elk or to any of its other wildlife species. . . . Moreover, . . .

*This is the cost ratio of the 1976 nonresident combination license fee ($225) to the 1976 resident combination license fee ($30). Since a Montana resident wishing to hunt only elk could purchase an elk-hunting license for only $9, a nonresident who wanted to hunt only elk had to pay a fee 25 times as great as that charged a similarly situated resident of Montana.

if Montana's discriminatorily high big-game license fee is an outgrowth of general conservation policy to discourage elk hunting, this too fails as a basis for the licensing scheme. Montana makes no effort similarly to inhibit its own residents. . . .

The second possible justification for the fee differential. . . . is a cost justification. . . . The licensing scheme, appellants contend, is simply an attempt by Montana to shift the costs of its conservation efforts, however commendable they may be, onto the shoulders of nonresidents who are powerless to help themselves at the ballot box. . . . The District Court agreed, finding that "[o]n a consideration of [the] evidence . . . and with due regard to the presumption of constitutionality . . . the ratio of 7.5 to 1 cannot be justified on any basis of cost allocation." . . . Montana's attempt to cost-justify its discriminatory licensing practices thus fails under the second prong of a correct privileges and immunities analysis—that which requires the discrimination a State visits upon nonresidents to bear a substantial relation to the problem or burden they pose.

The third possible justification for Montana's licensing scheme, . . . is actually no justification at all, but simply an assertion that a State "owns" the wildlife within its borders in trust for its citizens and may therefore do with it what it pleases.

In unjustifiably discriminating against nonresident elk hunters, Montana has not "exercised its police power in conformity with the . . . Constitution." The State's police power interest in its wildlife cannot override the appellants' constitutionally protected privileges and immunities right. I respectfully dissent and would reverse.

## *Garcia* v. *San Antonio Metropolitan Transit Authority*

**469 U.S. 528, 105 S. Ct. 1005, 83 L. Ed. 2d 1016 (1985)**

San Antonio Metropolitan Transit Authority (SAMTA), a public mass-transit authority, is the major provider of public transportation in San Antonio, Texas. In 1979, the Wage and Hour Administration of the U.S. Department of Labor issued an opinion that SAMTA's operations were not immune from the minimum-wages and overtime provisions of the Fair Labor Standards Act (FLSA) under *National League of Cities* v. *Usery* (1976), in which it was held that the Commerce Clause does not empower Congress to enforce such requirements against the States in "areas of traditional governmental functions." SAMTA then brought action in the U.S. District Court for the Western District of Texas seeking declaratory judgment that municipal ownership and operation of a mass-transit system is a traditional governmental function and, under *National League of Cities,* exempt from the obligations imposed by the FLSA. The Department of Labor counterclaimed for enforcement of the overtime and record-keeping requirements of the FLSA, and Joe G. Garcia and several other SAMTA employees intervened, seeking overtime pay under the FLSA. The District Court granted SAMTA's motion for summary judgment, and the Department of Labor and the SAMTA employees appealed directly to the U.S. Supreme Court. *Opinion of the Court: Blackmun, Brennan, Marshall, Stevens, White. Dissenting opinions: Powell, Burger, O'Connor, Rehnquist; O'Connor, Powell, Rehnquist; Rehnquist.*

JUSTICE BLACKMUN delivered the opinion of the Court.

We revisit in these cases an issue raised in *National League of Cities* v. *Usery* . . . (1976). In that litigation, this Court, by a sharply divided vote, ruled that the Commerce Clause does not empower Congress to enforce the minimum-wage and overtime provisions of the Fair Labor Standards Act (FLSA) against the States "in areas of traditional governmental functions." . . . Although *National League of Cities* supplied some examples of "traditional governmental functions," it did not offer a general explanation of how a "traditional" function is to be distinguished from a "nontraditional" one. Since then, federal and state courts have struggled with the task, thus imposed, of identifying a traditional function for purposes of state immunity under the Commerce Clause.

In the present cases, a Federal District Court concluded that municipal ownership and operation of a mass-transit system is a traditional governmental function and thus, under *National League of Cities,* is exempt from the obligations imposed by the FLSA. Faced with the identical question, three Federal Courts of Appeals and one state appellate court have reached the opposite conclusion.

Our examination of this "function" standard applied in these and other cases over the last eight years now persuades us that the attempt to draw the boundaries of state regulatory immunity in terms of "traditional governmental function" is not only unworkable but is inconsistent with established principles of federalism and, indeed, with those very federalism principles on which *National League of Cities* purported to rest. That case, accordingly, is overruled. . . .

The controversy in the present case has focused on the third . . . requirement—that the challenged federal statute trench on "traditional governmental functions." The District Court voiced a common concern: "Despite the abundance of adjectives, identifying which particular state functions are immune remains difficult." . . . . Just how troublesome the task has been is revealed by the results reached in other federal cases. Thus courts have held that regulating ambulance services, . . . licensing automobile drivers, . . . operating a municipal airport, . . . performing solid waste disposal, . . . and operating a highway authority . . . are functions *protected* under *National League of Cities.* At the same time, courts have held that issuance of industrial development bonds, . . . regulation of intrastate natural gas sales, . . . regulation of traffic on public roads, . . . regulation of air transportation, . . . operation of a telephone system, . . . leasing and sale of natural gas, . . . operation of a mental health facility, . . . and provision of in-house domestic services for the aged and handicapped . . . are *not* entitled to immunity. We find it difficult, if not impossible, to identify an organizing principle that places each of the cases in the first group on one side of a line and each of the cases in the second group on the other side. The constitutional distinction between licensing drivers and regulating traffic, for example, or between operating a highway authority and operating a mental health facility, is elusive at best. . . .

We believe, however, that there is a more fundamental problem at work here. The problem is that no distinction that purports to separate out important governmental functions can be faithful to the role of federalism in a democratic society. The essence of our federal system is that within the realm of authority left open to them under the Constitution, the States must be equally free to engage in any activity that their citizens choose for the common weal, no matter how unorthodox or unnecessary anyone else—including the judiciary—deems state involvement to be. Any rule of state immunity that looks to the "traditional," "integral," or "necessary" nature of governmental functions inevitably invites an unelected federal judiciary to make decisions about which state policies it favors and which ones it dislikes. . . .

The central theme of *National League of Cities* was that the States occupy a special position in our constitutional system and that the scope of Congress' authority under the Commerce Clause must reflect that position. . . .

What has proved problematic is not the perception that the Constitution's federal structure imposes limitations on the Commerce Clause, but rather the nature and content of those limitations. . . .

We doubt that courts ultimately can identify principled constitutional limitations on the scope of Congress' Commerce Clause powers over the States merely by relying on *a priori* definitions of state sovereignty. In part, this is because of the elusiveness of objective criteria for "fundamental" elements of state sovereignty, a problem we have witnessed in the search for "traditional governmental functions." There is, however, a more fundamental reason: the sovereignty of the States is limited by the Constitution itself. A variety of sovereign powers, for example, are withdrawn from the States by Article I, § 10. Section 8 of the same Article works an equally sharp contraction of state sovereignty by authorizing Congress to exercise a wide range of legislative powers and (in conjunction with the Supremacy Clause of Article VI) to displace contrary state legislation. . . . By providing for final review of questions of federal law in this Court, Article III curtails the sovereign power of the States' judiciaries to make authoritative determinations of law. . . . Finally, the developed application, through the Fourteenth Amendment, of the greater part of the Bill of Rights to the States limits the sovereign authority that States otherwise would possess to legislate with respect to their citizens and to conduct their own affairs.

The States unquestionably do "retai[n] significant measure of sovereign authority." . . . They do so, however, only to the extent that the Constitution has not divested them of their original powers and transferred those powers to the Federal Government. In the words of James Madison to the Members of the First Congress: "Interference with the power of the States was no constitutional criterion of the power of Congress. If the power was not given, Congress could not exercise it; if given, they might exercise it, although it should interfere with the laws, or even the Constitution of the States."

As a result, to say that the Constitution assumes the continued role of the States is to say little about the nature of that role. . . . The fact that the States remain sovereign as to all powers not vested in Congress or denied them by the Constitution offers no guidance about where the frontier between state and federal power lies. In short, we have no license to employ freestanding conceptions of state sovereignty when measuring congressional authority under the Commerce Clause.

When we look for the States' "residuary and inviolable sovereignty," *The Federalist* No. 39, . . . in the shape of the constitutional scheme rather than in predetermined notions of sovereign power, a different measure of state sovereignty emerges. Apart from the limitation on federal authority inherent in the delegated nature of Congress' Article I powers, the principal means chosen by the Framers to ensure the role of the States in the federal system lies in the structure of the Federal Government itself. It is no novelty to observe that the composition of the Federal Government was designed in large part to protect the States from overreaching by Congress. The Framers thus gave the States a role in the selection both of the Executive and the Legislative Branches of the Federal Government. The States were vested with indirect influence over the House of Representatives and the Presidency by their control of electoral qualifications and their role in presidential elections. U.S. Const., Art. I, § 2, and Art. II, § 1. They were given more direct influence in the Senate, where each State received equal representation and each Senator was to be selected by the legislature of his State. Art. I, § 3. The significance attached to the States' equal representation in the Senate is underscored by the prohibition of any constitutional amendment divesting a State of equal representation without the State's consent. Art. V.

The extent to which the structure of the Federal Government itself was relied on to insulate the interests of the States is evident in the views of the Framers. James Madison explained that the Federal Government "will partake sufficiently of the spirit [of the States], to be disinclined to invade the rights of the individual States, or the prerogatives of their governments." *The Federalist* No. 46. . . The Framers chose to rely on a federal system in which special restraints on federal power over the States inhered principally in the workings of the National Government itself, rather than in discrete limitations on the objects of federal authority. State sovereign interests, then, are more properly protected by procedural safeguards inherent in the structure of the federal system than by judicially created limitations on federal power. . . .

We realize that changes in the structure of the Federal Government have taken place since 1789, not the least of which has been the substitution of popular election of Senators by the adoption of the Seventeenth Amendment in 1913, and that these changes may work to alter the influence of the States in the federal political process. Nonetheless, against this background, we are convinced that the fundamental limitation that the constitutional scheme imposes on the Commerce Clause to protect the "States as States" is one of process rather than one of result. Any substantive restraint on the exercise of Commerce Clause powers must find its justification in the procedural nature of this basic limitation, and it must be tailored to compensate for possible failings in the national political process rather than to dictate a "sacred province of state autonomy." . . .

Insofar as the present cases are concerned, then, we need go no further than to state that we perceive nothing in the overtime and minimum-wage requirements of the FLSA, as applied to SAMTA, that is destructive of state sovereignty or violative of any constitutional provision. SAMTA faces nothing more than the same minimum-wage and overtime obligations that hundreds of thousands of other employers, public as well as private, have to meet.

In these cases, the status of public mass transit simply underscores the extent to which the structural protections of the Constitution insulate the States from federally imposed burdens. When Congress first subjected state mass-transit systems to FLSA obligations in 1966, and when it expanded those obligations in 1974, it simultaneously provided extensive funding for state and local mass transit. . . . In the two decades since it . . . has provided over $22 billion in mass transit aid to States and localities. . . . SAMTA and its immediate predecessor have received a substantial amount of . . . funding, including over $12 million during SAMTA's first two fiscal years alone. In short, Congress has not simply placed a financial burden on the shoulders of States and localities that operate mass-transit systems, but has provided substantial countervailing financial assistance as well, assistance that may leave individual mass-transit systems better off than they would have been had Congress never intervened at all in the area. Congress' treatment of public mass transit reinforces our conviction that the national political process systematically protects States from the risk of having their functions in that area handicapped by Commerce Clause regulation.

This analysis makes clear that Congress' action in affording SAMTA employees the protections of the wage and hour provisions of the FLSA contravened no affirmative limit on Congress' power under the Commerce Clause. The judgment of the District Court therefore must be reversed.

JUSTICE POWELL, with whom THE CHIEF JUSTICE, JUSTICE REHNQUIST, and JUSTICE O'CONNOR join, dissenting.

The Court today, in its 5–4 decision, overrules *National League of Cities* v. *Usery*, . . . (1976), a case in which we held that Congress lacked authority to impose the requirements of the Fair Labor Standards Act on state and local governments. Because I believe this decision substantially alters the federal system embodied in the Constitution, I dissent.

Whatever effect the Court's decision may have in weakening the application of *stare decisis*, it is likely to be less important than what the Court has done to the Constitution itself. A unique feature of the United States is the *federal* system of government guaranteed by the Constitution and implicit in the very name of our country. Despite some genuflecting in the Court's opinion to the concept of federalism, today's decision effectively reduces the Tenth Amendment to meaningless rhetoric when Congress acts pursuant to the Commerce Clause. . . .

To leave no doubt about its intention, the Court renounces its decision in *National League of Cities* because it "inevitably invites an unelected federal judiciary to make decisions about which state policies it favors and which ones it dislikes." . . . In other words, the extent to which the States may exercise their authority, when Congress purports to act under the Commerce Clause, henceforth is to be determined from time to time by political decisions made by members of the federal government, decisions the Court says will not be subject to judicial review. I note that it does not seem to have occurred to the Court that *it*—an unelected majority of five Justices—today rejects almost 200 years of the understanding of the constitutional status of federalism. In doing so, there is only a single passing reference to the Tenth Amendment. Nor is so much as a dictum of any court cited in support of the view that the role of the States in the federal system may depend upon the grace of elected federal officials, rather than on the Constitution as interpreted by this Court. . . .

Today's opinion does not explain how the States' role in the electoral process guarantees that particular exercises of the Commerce

Clause power will not infringe on residual State sovereignty. Members of Congress are elected from the various States, but once in office they are members of the federal government. Although the States participate in the Electoral College, this is hardly a reason to view the President as a representative of the States' interest against federal encroachment. We noted recently "the hydraulic pressure inherent within each of the separate Branches to exceed the outer limits of its power. . . ." *Immigration and Naturalization Service* v. *Chadha,* . . . (1983). The Court offers no reason to think that this pressure will not operate when Congress seeks to invoke its powers under the Commerce Clause, notwithstanding the electoral role of the States.

The Court apparently thinks that the State's success at obtaining federal funds for various projects and exemptions from the obligations of some federal statutes is indicative of the "effectiveness of the federal political process in preserving the States' interests. . . ." . . . But such political success is not relevant to the question whether the political *processes* are the proper means of enforcing constitutional limitations. The fact that Congress generally does not transgress constitutional limits on its power to reach State activities does not make judicial review any less necessary to rectify the cases in which it does do so. The States' role in our system of government is a matter of constitutional law, not of legislative grace. "The powers not delegated to the United States by the Constitution, nor prohibited by it to the States, are reserved to the States, respectively, or to the people." U.S. Const., Amend. 10.

More troubling than the logical infirmities in the Court's reasoning is the result of its holding, i.e., that federal political officials, invoking the Commerce Clause, are the sole judges of the limits of their own power. This result is inconsistent with the fundamental principles of our constitutional system. . . . At least since *Marbury* v. *Madison* it has been the settled province of the federal judiciary "to say what the law is" with respect to the constitutionality of acts of Congress. . . . In rejecting the role of the judiciary in protecting the States from federal overreaching, the Court's opinion offers no explanation for ignoring the teaching of the most famous case in our history.

In our federal system, the States have a major role that cannot be preempted by the national government. As contemporaneous writings and the debates at the ratifying conventions make clear, the States' ratification of the Constitution was predicated on this understanding of federalism. Indeed, the Tenth Amendment was adopted specifically to ensure that the important role promised the States by the proponents of the Constitution was realized. . . .

The Framers had definite ideas about the nature of the Constitution's division of authority between the federal and state governments. . . .

The Framers believed that the separate sphere of sovereignty reserved to the States would ensure that the States would serve as an effective "counterpoise" to the power of the federal government. The States would serve this essential role because they would attract and retain the loyalty of their citizens. The roots of such loyalty, the Founders thought, were found in the objects peculiar to state government. For example, Hamilton argued that the States "regulat[e] all those personal interests and familiar concerns to which the sensibility of individuals is more immediately awake. . . ." *The Federalist* No. 17. . . . Thus, he maintained that the people would perceive the States as "the immediate and most visible guardian of life and property," a fact which "contributes more than any other circumstance to impressing upon the minds of the people affection, esteem and reverence towards the government." . . . Madison took the same position, explaining that "the people will be more familiarly and minutely conversant" with the business of state governments, and "with the members of these, will a greater proportion of the people have the ties of personal acquaintance and friendship, and of family and party attachments. . . ." *The Federalist* No. 46. . . . Like Hamilton, Madison saw the States' involvement in the everyday concerns of the people as the source of their citizens' loyalty. . . .

Thus, the harm to the States that results from federal overreaching under the Commerce Clause is not simply a matter of dollars and cents. . . . Nor is it a matter of the wisdom or folly of certain policy choices. . . . Rather, by usurping functions traditionally performed by the States, federal overreaching under the Commerce Clause undermines the constitutionally mandated balance of power between the States and the federal government, a balance designed to protect our fundamental liberties.

In *National League of Cities,* we spoke of fire prevention, police protection, sanitation, and public health as "typical of [the services] performed by state and local governments in discharging their dual functions of administering the public law and furnishing public services." . . . Not only are these activities remote from any normal concept of interstate commerce, they are also activities that epitomize the concerns of local, democratic self-government. . . . In emphasizing the need to protect traditional governmental functions, we identified the kinds of activities engaged in by state and local governments that affect the everyday lives of citizens. These are services that people are in a position to understand and evaluate, and in a democracy, have the right to oversee. We recognized that "it is functions such as these which governments are created to provide . . . " and that the states and local governments are better able than the national government to perform them. . .

The Court maintains that the standard approved in *National League of Cities* "disserves principles of democratic self government." . . . In reaching this conclusion, the Court looks myopically only to persons elected to positions in the federal government. It disregards entirely the far more effective role of democratic self-government at the state and local levels. One must compare realistically the operation of the state and local governments with that of the federal government. Federal legislation is drafted primarily by the staffs of the congressional committees. In view of the hundreds of bills introduced at each session of Congress and the complexity of many of them, it is virtually impossible for even the most conscientious legislators to be truly familiar with many of the statutes enacted. Federal departments and agencies customarily are authorized to write regulations. Often these are more important than the text of the statutes. As is true of the original legislation, these are drafted largely by staff personnel. The administration and enforcement of federal laws and regulations necessarily are largely in the hands of staff and civil service employees. These employees may have little or no knowledge of the States and localities that will be affected by the statutes and regulations for which they are responsible. In any case, they hardly are as accessible and responsive as those who occupy analogous positions in State and local governments.

In drawing this contrast, I imply no criticism of these federal employees or the officials who are ultimately in charge. The great majority are conscientious and faithful to their duties. My point is simply that members of the immense federal bureaucracy are not elected, know less about the services traditionally rendered by States and localities, and are inevitably less responsive to recipients of such services, than are state legislatures, city councils, boards of supervisors, and state and local commissions, boards, and agencies. It is at these state and local levels—not in Washington as the Court so mistakenly thinks—that "democratic self-government" is best exemplified.

The Court emphasizes that municipal operation of an intracity mass-transit system is relatively new in the life of our country. It nevertheless is a classic example of the type of service traditionally provided by local government. It is *local* by definition. State and local officials of course must be intimately familiar with these services and sensitive to their quality as well as cost. Such officials also know that their constituents and the press respond to the adequacy, fair distribution, and cost of these services. It is this kind of state and local control and accountability that the Framers understood would insure the vitality and preservation of the federal system that the Constitution explicitly requires. . . .

JUSTICE O'CONNOR, with whom JUSTICE POWELL and JUSTICE REHNQUIST join, dissenting.

The Court today surveys the battle scene of federalism and sounds a retreat. Like Justice Powell, I would prefer to hold the field and, at the very least, render a little aid to the wounded. I join Justice Powell's opinion. I also write separately to note my fundamental disagreement with the majority's views of federalism and the duty of this Court. . . .

The true "essence" of federalism is that the States *as States* have legitimate interest which the National Government is bound to respect even though its laws are supreme. . . . If federalism so conceived and so carefully cultivated by the Framers of our Constitution is to remain meaningful, this Court cannot abdicate its constitutional responsibility to oversee the Federal Government's compliance with its duty to respect the legitimate interests of the States.

Due to the emergence of an integrated and industrialized national economy, this Court has been required to examine and review a breathtaking expansion of the powers of Congress. In doing so the Court correctly perceived that the Framers of our Constitution intended Congress to have sufficient power to address national problems. But the Framers were not single-minded. The Constitution is animated by an array of intentions. . . . Just as surely as the Framers envisioned a National Government capable of solving national problems, they also envisioned a republic whose vitality was assured by the diffusion of power not only among the branches of the Federal Government, but also between the Federal Government and the States. . . . In the 18th century these intentions did not conflict because technology had not yet converted every local problem into a national one. A conflict has now emerged, and the Court today retreats rather than reconciles the Constitution's dual concerns for federalism and an effective commerce power.

. . . The Framers perceived the interstate commerce power to be important but limited, and expected that it would be used primarily if not exclusively to remove interstate tariffs and to regulate maritime affairs and large-scale mercantile enterprise. . . . This perception of a narrow commerce power is important not because it suggests that the commerce power should be as narrowly construed today. Rather, it explains why the Framers could believe the Constitution assured significant state authority even as it bestowed a range of powers, including the commerce power, on the Congress. In an era when interstate commerce represented a tiny fraction of economic activity and most goods and services were produced and consumed close to home, the interstate commerce power left a broad range of activities beyond the reach of Congress.

In the decades since ratification of the Constitution, interstate economic activity has steadily expanded. Industrialization, coupled with advances in transportation and communications, has created a national economy in which virtually every activity occurring within the borders of a State plays a part.

Incidental to this expansion of the commerce power, Congress has been given an ability it lacked prior to the emergence of an integrated national economy. Because virtually every *state* activity, like virtually every activity of a private individual, arguably "affects" interstate commerce, Congress can now supplant the States from the significant sphere of activities envisioned for them by the Framers. It is in this context that recent changes in the workings of Congress, such as the direct election of Senators and the expanded influence of national interest groups . . . become relevant. These changes may well have lessened the weight Congress gives to the legitimate interests of States as States. As a result, there is now a real risk that Congress will gradually erase the diffusion of power between state and nation on which the Framers based their faith in the efficiency and vitality of our Republic.

It is worth recalling the . . . passage in *McCulloch* v. *Maryland*, . . . that lies at the source of the recent expansion of the commerce power. "Let the end be legitimate, let it be within the scope of the constitution," Chief Justice Marshall said, "and all means which are appropriate, which are plainly adapted to that end, which are not prohibited, but consist with the letter *and spirit* of the constitution, are constitutional." (emphasis added). The *spirit* of the Tenth Amendment, of course, is that the States will retain their integrity in a system in which the laws of the United States are nevertheless supreme. . . .

It is not enough that the "end be legitimate"; the means to that end chosen by Congress must not contravene the spirit of the Constitution. Thus many of this Court's decisions acknowledge that the means by which national power is exercised must take into account concerns for state autonomy. . . .

. . . For example, Congress might rationally conclude that the location a State chooses for its capital may affect interstate commerce, but the Court has suggested that Congress would nevertheless be barred from dictating that location because such an exercise of a delegated power would undermine the state sovereignty inherent in the Tenth Amendment. *Coyle* v. *Oklahoma* . . . (1911).

The problems of federalism in an integrated national economy are capable of more responsible resolution than holding that the States as States retain no status apart from that which Congress chooses to let them retain. The proper resolution, I suggest, lies in weighing state autonomy as a factor in the balance when interpreting the means by which Congress can exercise its authority on the States as States. It is insufficient, in assessing the validity of congressional regulation of a State pursuant to the commerce power, to ask only whether the same regulation would be valid if enforced against a private party. That reasoning, embodied in the majority opinion, is inconsistent with the spirit of our Constitution. It remains relevant that a *State* is being regulated. . . . As far as the Constitution is concerned, a State should not be equated with any private litigant. . . . Instead, the autonomy of a State is an essential component of federalism. If state autonomy is ignored in assessing the means by which Congress regulates matters affecting commerce, then federalism becomes irrelevant simply because the set of activities remaining beyond the reach of such a commerce power "may well be negligible." . . .

It has been difficult for this Court to craft bright lines defining the scope of the state autonomy protected by *National League of Cities*. Such difficulty is to be expected whenever constitutional concerns as important as federalism and the effectiveness of the commerce power come into conflict. Regardless of the difficulty, it is and will remain the duty of this Court to reconcile these concerns in the final instance. That the Court shuns the task today by appealing to the "essence of federalism" can provide scant comfort to those who believe our federal system requires something more than a unitary, centralized government. I would not shirk the duty acknowledged by *National League of Cities* and its progeny.

I respectfully dissent.

*With the decision in* Garcia, *state and local governments across the United States were confronted with the prospect of having to pay up to $3 billion annually in overtime. Senator Pete Wilson of California predicted that his state, with over 89,000 state employees, would "be out some $300 million, with the city of Los Angeles accounting for perhaps $50 million." Worried about huge overtime bills and the likelihood of tax hikes to cover these costs, state and local governmental officials lobbied Congress for relief, and in November of 1985, President Reagan signed into law a bill that allowed state and local governments to continue offering compensatory time off in lieu of overtime pay.*

## *New York* v. *United States*

**505 U.S. 144, 112 S.Ct. 2408, 120 L.Ed.2d 120 (1992)**

Confronting a dire shortage of disposal sites in 31 states for low-level radioactive waste generated by the federal government, hospitals, research institutions, and various industries, Congress enacted the Low-level Radioactive Waste Policy Amendments Act of 1985. This act, based largely on a proposal submitted by the National Governors' Association, embodied a compromise between sited and unsited states, in which the sited states agreed to extend for seven years the period in which they would accept low-level radioactive waste from other states and, in exchange, the unsited states agreed to end their reliance on the sited states by 1992. To ensure that these agreements were honored, the act imposed on the states, either alone or in "regional compacts" with other states, the obligation to provide for the disposal of waste generated within their borders, and contained three provisions setting forth "incentives" to states to comply with that obligation. The first set of incentives was monetary; states with disposal sites were authorized to impose a surcharge on radioactive waste received from other states. The second set of incentives was access incentives; states and regional compacts with disposal sites were authorized to increase gradually the cost of access to their sites and eventually to deny access altogether. The third incentive was a "take title" provision, which specified that a state or regional compact that failed to provide for the disposal of all internally generated waste by a particular date must, upon the request of the waste's generator or owner, take title to and possession of the waste and become liable for all damages suffered by the generator or owner as a result of the state's failure to take prompt possession. New York State filed suit against the United States in United States District Court for the Northern District of New York, seeking a declaratory judgment that the three incentives' provisions were inconsistent with the Tenth Amendment. The District Court dismissed the complaint, and the Second Circuit Court of Appeals affirmed. The U.S. Supreme Court granted certiorari. *Opinion of the Court: O'Connor, Kennedy, Rehnquist, Scalia, Souter, Thomas. Concurring in part and dissenting in part: White, Blackmun, Stevens; Stevens.*

MS. JUSTICE O'CONNOR delivered the opinion of the Court.

This case implicates one of our Nation's newest problems of public policy and perhaps our oldest question of constitutional law. The public policy issue involves the disposal of radioactive waste: In this case, we address the constitutionality of three provisions of the Low-level Radioactive Waste Policy Amendments Act of 1985. The constitutional question is as old as the Constitution: It consists of discerning the proper division of authority between the Federal Government and the States. We conclude that while Congress has substantial power under the Constitution to encourage the States to provide for the disposal of the radioactive waste generated within their borders, the Constitution does not confer upon Congress the ability simply to compel the States to do so. We therefore find that only two of the Act's three provisions at issue are consistent with the Constitution's allocation of power to the Federal Government.

In 1788, in the course of explaining to the citizens of New York why the recently drafted Constitution provided for federal courts, Alexander Hamilton observed: "The erection of a new government, whatever care or wisdom may distinguish the work, cannot fail to originate questions of intricacy and nicety; and these may, in a particular manner, be expected to flow from the establishment of a constitution founded upon the total or partial incorporation of a number of distinct sovereignties." *The Federalist,* No. 82. Hamilton's prediction has proved quite accurate. While no one disputes the proposition that "[t]he Constitution created a Federal Government of limited powers," and while the Tenth Amendment makes explicit that "[t]he powers not delegated to the United States by the Constitution, nor prohibited by it to the States, are reserved to the States respectively, or to the people"; the task of ascertaining the constitutional line between federal and state power has given rise to many of the Court's most difficult and celebrated cases. At least as far back as *Martin* v. *Hunter's Lessee,* the Court has resolved questions "of great importance and delicacy" in determining whether particular sovereign powers have been granted by the Constitution to the Federal Government or have been retained by the States.

These questions can be viewed in either of two ways. In some cases the Court has inquired whether an Act of Congress is authorized by one of the powers delegated to Congress in Article I of the Constitution. In other cases the Court has sought to determine whether an Act of Congress invades the province of state sovereignty reserved by the Tenth Amendment. In a case like this one, involving the division of authority between federal and state governments, the two inquiries are mirror images of each other. If a power is delegated to Congress in the Constitution, the Tenth Amendment expressly disclaims any reservation of that power to the States; if a power is an attribute of state sovereignty reserved by the Tenth Amendment, it is necessarily a power the Constitution has not conferred on Congress.

It is in this sense that the Tenth Amendment "states but a truism that all is retained which has not been surrendered." *United States* v. *Darby* (1941). As Justice Story put it, "[t]he amendment is a mere affirmation of what, upon any just reasoning, is a necessary rule of interpreting the constitution. Being an instrument of limited and enumerated powers, it follows irresistibly, that what is not conferred, is withheld, and belongs to the state authorities." 3 J. Story, Commentaries on the Constitution of the United States 752 (1833). This has been the Court's consistent understanding: "The States unquestionably do retai[n] a significant measure of sovereign authority . . . to the extent that the Constitution has not divested them of their original powers and transferred those powers to the Federal Government." *Garcia* v. *San Antonio Metropolitan Transit Authority* (1985).

Congress exercises its conferred powers subject to the limitations contained in the Constitution. Thus, for example, under the Commerce Clause Congress may regulate publishers engaged in interstate commerce, but Congress is constrained in the exercise of that power by the First Amendment. The Tenth Amendment likewise restrains the power of Congress, but this limit is not derived from the text of the Tenth Amendment itself, which, as we have discussed, is essentially a tautology. Instead, the Tenth Amendment confirms that the power of the Federal Government is subject to limits that may, in a given instance, reserve power to the States. The Tenth Amendement thus directs us to determine, as in this case, whether an incident of state sovereignty is protected by a limitation on an Article I power.

The actual scope of the Federal Government's authority with respect to the States has changed over the years, but the constitutional structure underlying and limiting that authority has not. In the end, just as a cup may be half empty or half full, it makes no difference whether one views the question at issue in this case as one of ascertaining the limits of the power delegated to the Federal Government under the affirmative provisions of the Constitution or one of discerning the core of sovereignty retained by the States under the Tenth Amendment. Either way, we must determine whether any of the three challenged provisions of the Low-level Radioactive Waste Policy Amendments of 1985 oversteps the boundary between federal and state authority.

Petitioners do not contend that Congress lacks the power to regulate the disposal of low-level radioactive waste. Space in radioactive waste disposal sites is frequently sold by residents of one State to residents of another. Regulation of the resulting interstate market in waste disposal is therefore well within Congress's authority under the Commerce Clause. Petitioners likewise do not dispute that under the Supremacy Clause Congress could, if it wished, pre-empt state radioactive waste regulation. Petitioners contend only that the Tenth Amendment limits the power of Congress to regulate in the way it has chosen. Rather than addressing the problem of waste disposal by directly regulating the generators and disposers of waste, petitioners argue, Congress has impermissibly directed the States to regulate in this field.

Most of our recent cases interpreting the Tenth Amendment have concerned the authority of Congress to subject state governments to generally applicable laws.

This case presents no occasion to apply or revisit the holdings of any of these cases, as this is not a case in which Congress has subjected a State to the same legislation applicable to private parties.

This case instead concerns the circumstances under which Congress may use the States as implements of regulation; that is, whether Congress may direct or otherwise motivate the States to regulate in a particular field or a particular way. Our cases have established a few principles that guide our resolution of the issue.

As an initial matter, Congress may not simply "commandee[r] the legislative processes of the States by directly compelling them to enact and enforce a federal regulatory program."

While Congress has substantial powers to govern the Nation directly, including in areas of intimate concern to the States, the Constitution has never been understood to confer upon Congress the ability to require the States to govern according to Congress' instructions.

The question whether the Constitution should permit Congress to employ state governments as regulatory agencies was a topic of lively debate among the Framers.

The Convention generated a great number of proposals for the structure of the new Government, but two quickly took center stage. Under the Virginia Plan, as first introduced by Edmund Randolph, Congress would exercise legislative authority directly upon individuals, without employing the States as intermediaries. Under the

New Jersey Plan, as first introduced by William Paterson, Congress would continue to require the approval of the States before legislating, as it had under the Articles of Confederation. These two plans underwent various revisions as the Convention progressed, but they remained the two primary options discussed by the delegates. One frequently expressed objection to the New Jersey Plan was that it might require the Federal Government to coerce the States into implementing legislation.

In the end, the Convention opted for a Constitution in which Congress would exercise its legislative authority directly over individuals rather than over States; for a variety of reasons, it rejected the New Jersey Plan in favor of the Virginia Plan. This choice was made clear to the subsequent state ratifying conventions. Oliver Ellsworth, a member of the Connecticut delegation in Philadelphia, explained the distinction to his State's convention: "This Constitution does not attempt to coerce sovereign bodies, states, in their political capacity. . . . But this legal coercion singles out the . . . individual."

Rufus King, one of Massachusetts' delegates, returned home to support ratification by recalling the Commonwealth's unhappy experience under the Articles of Confederation and arguing: "Laws, to be effective, therefore, must not be laid on states, but upon individuals." At New York's convention, Hamilton (another delegate in Philadelphia) exclaimed: "But can we believe that one state will ever suffer itself to be used as an instrument of coercion? The thing is a dream; it is impossible. Then we are brought to this dilemma—either a federal standing army is to enforce the requisitions, or the federal treasury is left without supplies and the government without support. What, sir, is the cure for this great evil? Nothing, but to enable the national laws to operate on individuals, in the same manner as those of the states do."

In providing for a stronger central government, therefore, the Framers explicitly chose a Constitution that confers upon Congress the power to regulate individuals, not States. As we have seen, the Court has consistently respected this choice. We have always understood that even where Congress has the authority under the Constitution to pass laws requiring or prohibiting certain acts, it lacks the power directly to compel the States to require or prohibit those acts.

This is not to say that Congress lacks the ability to encourage a State to regulate in a particular way, or that Congress may not hold out incentives to the States as a method of influencing a State's policy choices. Our cases have identified a variety of methods, short of outright coercion, by which Congress may urge a State to adopt a legislative program consistent with federal interests. Two of these methods are of particular relevance here.

First, under Congress' spending power, "Congress may attach conditions on the receipt of federal funds." *South Dakota* v. *Dole* (1987) was one such case: The Court found no constitutional flaw in a federal statute directing the Secretary of Transportation to withhold federal highway funds from States failing to adopt Congress' choice of a minimum drinking age.

Second, where Congress has the authority to regulate private activity under the Commerce Clause, we have recognized Congress' power to offer States the choice of regulating that activity according to federal standards or having state law pre-empted by federal regulation. This arrangement, which has been termed "a program of cooperative federalism," is replicated in numerous federal statutory schemes. These include the Clean Water Act, the Occupational Safety and Health Act of 1970, the Resource Conservation and Recovery Act of 1976, and the Alaska National Interest Lands Conservation Act.

By either of these two methods, as by any other permissible method of encouraging a State to conform to federal policy choices, the residents of the State retain the ultimate decision as to whether or not the State will comply. If a State's citizens view federal policy as sufficiently contrary to local interests, they may elect to decline a federal grant. If state residents would prefer their government to devote its attention and resources to problems other than those deemed important by Congress, they may choose to have the Federal Government rather than the State bear the expense of a federally mandated regulatory program, and they may continue to supplement that program to the extent state law is not pre-empted. Where Congress encourages state regulation rather than compelling it, state governments remain responsive to the local electorate's preferences; state officials remain accountable to the people.

By contrast, where the Federal Government compels States to regulate, the accountability of both state and federal officials is diminished. If the citizens of New York, for example, do not consider that making provision for the disposal of radioactive waste is in their best interest, they may elect state officials who share their view. That view can always be pre-empted under the Supremacy Clause if it is contrary to the national view, but in such a case it is the Federal Government that makes the decision in full view of the public, and it will be federal officials that suffer the consequences if the decision turns out to be detrimental or unpopular. But where the Federal Government directs the States to regulate, it may be state officials who will bear the brunt of public disapproval, while the federal officials who devised the regulatory program may remain insulated from the electoral ramifications of their decision. Accountability is thus diminished when, due to federal coercion, elected state officials cannot regulate in accordance with the views of the local electorate in matters not preempted by federal regulation.

With these principles in mind, we turn to the three challenged provisions of the Low-level Radioactive Waste Policy Amendments Act of 1985.

The Act's first set of incentives, in which Congress has conditioned grants to the States upon the States' attainment of a series of milestones, is thus well within the authority of Congress under the Commerce and Spending Clauses. Because the first set of incentives is supported by affirmative constitutional grants of power to Congress, it is not inconsistent with the Tenth Amendment.

In the second set of incentives, Congress has authorized States and regional compacts with disposal sites gradually to increase the cost of access to the sites, and then to deny access altogether, to radioactive waste generated in States that do not meet federal deadlines. As a simple regulation, this provision would be within the power of Congress to authorize the States to discriminate against interstate commerce. Where federal regulation of private activity is within the scope of the Commerce Clause, we have recognized the ability of Congress to offer states the choice of regulating that activity according to federal standards or having state law pre-empted by federal regulation.

This is the choice presented to nonsited States by the Act's second set of incentives: States may either regulate the disposal of radioactive waste according to federal standards by attaining local or regional self-sufficiency, or their residents who produce radioactive waste will be subject to federal regulation authorizing sited States and regions to deny access to their disposal sites. The affected States are not compelled by Congress to regulate, because any burden caused by a State's refusal to regulate will fall on those who generate waste and find no outlet for its disposal, rather than on the State as a sovereign. A State whose citizens do not wish it to attain the Act's milestones may devote its attention and its resources to issues its citizens deem more worthy; the choice remains at all times with the residents of the State, not with Congress. The State need not expend any funds, or participate in any federal program, if local residents do not view such expenditures or participation as worthwhile. Nor must the State abandon the field if it does not accede to federal direction; the State may continue to regulate the generation and disposal of radioactive waste in any manner its citizens see fit.

The Act's second set of incentives thus represents a conditional exercise of Congress' commerce power, along the lines of those we have held to be within Congress' authority. As a result, the second set of incentives does not intrude on the sovereignty reserved to the States by the Tenth Amendment.

The take title provision is of a different character. This third so-called "incentive" offers States, as an alternative to regulating pursuant to Congress' direction, the option of taking title to and possession of the low-level radioactive waste generated within their borders and becoming liable for all damages waste generators suffer as a result of the States' failure to do so promptly. In this provision, Congress has crossed the line distinguishing encouragement from coercion.

Because an instruction to state governments to take title to waste, standing alone, would be beyond the authority of Congress, and because a direct order to regulate, standing alone, would also be beyond the authority of Congress, it follows the Congress lacks the power to offer the States a choice between the two. Unlike the first two sets of incentives, the take title incentive does not represent the conditional exercise of any congressional power enumerated in the Constitution. In this provision, Congress has not held out the threat of exercising its spending power or its commerce power; it has instead held out the threat, should the States not regulate according to one federal instruction, of simply forcing the States to submit to another federal instruction. A choice between two unconstitutionally coercive regulatory techniques is no choice at all. Either way, "the Act commandeers the legislative processes of the States by directly compelling them to enact and enforce a federal regulatory program," an outcome that has never been understood to lie within the authority conferred upon Congress by the Constitution.

The take title provision appears to be unique. No other federal statute has been cited which offers a state government no option other than that of implementing legislation enacted by Congress. Whether one views the take title provision as lying outside Congress' enumerated powers, or as infringing upon the core of state sovereignty reserved by the Tenth Amendment, the provision is inconsistent with the federal structure of our Government established by the Constitution.

Respondents raise a number of objections to this understanding of the limits of Congress' power. [They] . . . focus their attention on the process by which the Act was formulated. They correctly observe that public officials representing the State of New York lent their support to the Act's enactment. A Deputy Commissioner of the State's Energy Office testified in favor of the Act. Senator Moynihan of New York spoke in support of the Act on the floor of the Senate. Respondents note that the Act embodies a bargain among the sited and unsited States, a compromise to which New York was a willing participant and from which New York has reaped much benefit. Respondents then pose what appears at first to be a troubling question: How can a federal statute be found an unconstitutional infringement of State sovereignty when state officials consented to the statute's enactment?

The answer follows from an understanding of the fundamental purpose served by our Government's federal structure. The Constitution does not protect the sovereignty of States for the benefit of the States or state governments as abstract political entities, or even for the benefit of the public officials governing the States. To the contrary, the Constitution divides authority between federal and state governments for the protection of individuals. State sovereignty is not just an end in itself: "Rather, federalism secures to citizens the liberties that derive from the diffusion of sovereign power."

Where Congress exceeds its authority relative to the States, therefore, the departure from the constitutional plan cannot be ratified by the "consent" of state officials. An analogy to the separation of powers among the Branches of the Federal Government clarifies this point. The Constitution's division of power among the three Branches is violated where one Branch invades the territory of another, whether or not the encroached-upon Branch approves the encroachment. In *INS v. Chadha* (1983), we held that the legislative veto violated the constitutional requirement that legislation be presented to the President, despite Presidents' approval of hundreds of statutes containing a legislative veto provision. The constitutional authority of Congress cannot be expanded by the "consent" of the governmental unit whose domain is thereby narrowed, whether that unit is the Executive Branch or the States.

States are not mere political subdivisions of the United States. State governments are neither regional offices nor administrative agencies of the Federal Government. The positions occupied by state officials appear nowhere on the Federal Government's most detailed organizational chart. The Constitution instead "leaves to the several States a residuary and inviolable sovereignty," *The Federalist*, No. 39, reserved explicitly to the States by the Tenth Amendment.

Whatever the outer limits of that sovereignty may be, one thing is clear: The Federal Government may not compel the States to enact or administer a federal regulatory program. The Constitution permits both the Federal Government and the States to enact legislation regarding the disposal of low level radioactive waste. The Constitution enables the Federal Government to preempt state regulation contrary to federal interests, and it permits the Federal Government to hold out incentives to the States as a means of encouraging them to adopt suggested regulatory schemes. It does not, however, authorize Congress simply to direct the States to provide for the disposal of the radioactive waste generated within their borders. While there may be many constitutional methods of achieving regional self-sufficiency in radioactive waste disposal, the method Congress has chosen is not one of them. The judgment of the Court of Appeals is accordingly

*Affirmed in part and reversed in part.*

JUSTICE WHITE, with JUSTICE BLACKMUN and JUSTICE STEVENS, concurring in part and dissenting in part.

In *Garcia*, we stated the proper inquiry: "[W]e are convinced that the fundamental limitation that the constitutional scheme imposes on the Commerce Clause to protect the 'States as States' is one of process rather than one of result. Any substantive restraint on the exercise of Commerce Clause powers must find its justification in the procedural nature of this basic limitation, and it must be tailored to compensate for possible failings in the national political process rather than to dictate a "sacred province of state autonomy.' " Where it addresses this aspect of respondents' argument, the Court tacitly concedes that a failing of the political process cannot be shown in this case because it refuses to rebut the unassailable arguments that the States were well able to look after themselves in the legislative process that culminated in the 1985 Act's passage. Indeed, New York acknowledges that its "congressional delegation participated in the drafting and enactment of both the 1980 and the 1985 Acts." The Court rejects this process-based argument by resorting to generalities and platitudes about the purpose of federalism being to protect individual rights.

Ultimately, I suppose, the entire structure of our federal constitutional government can be traced to an interest in establishing checks and balances to prevent the exercise of tyranny against individuals. But these fears seem extremely far distant to me in a situation such as this. We face a crisis of national proportions in the disposal of low-level radioactive waste, and Congress has acceded to the wishes of the States by permitting local decisionmaking rather than imposing a solution from Washington. New York itself participated and supported passage of this legislation at both the gubernatorial and federal representative levels, and then enacted state laws specifically to comply with the deadlines and timetables agreed upon by the States in the 1985 Act. For me, the Court's civics lecture has a decidedly hollow ring at a time when action, rather than rhetoric, is needed to solve a national problem.*

*With selective quotations from the era in which the Constitution was adopted, the majority attempts to bolster its holding that the take title provision is tantamount to federal "commandeering" of the States. In view of the many Tenth Amendment cases decided over the past two decades in which resort to the kind of historical analysis generated in the majority opinion was not deemed necessary, I do not read the majority's many invocations of history to be anything other than elaborate window-dressing. Certainly nowhere does the majority announce that its rule is compelled by an understanding of what the Framers may have thought about statutes of the type at issue here. Moreover, I would observe that, while its quotations add a certain flavor to the opinion, the majority's historical analysis has a distinctly wooden quality. One would not know from reading the majority's account, for instance, that the nature of federal-state relations changed fundamentally after the Civil War. That conflict produced in its wake a tremendous expansion in the scope of the Federal Government's law-making authority, so much so that the persons who helped to found the Republic would scarcely have recognized the many added roles the National Government assumed for itself. Moreover, the majority fails to mention the New Deal era, in which the Court recognized the enormous growth in Congress' power under the Commerce Clause.

While I believe we should not be blind to history, neither should we read it so selectively as to restrict the proper scope of Congress' powers under Article I, especially when the history not mentioned by the majority fully supports a more expansive understanding of the legislature's authority than may have existed in the late 18th-century.

Given the scanty textual support for the majority's position, it would be far more sensible to defer to a coordinate branch of government in its decision to devise a solution to a national problem of this kind.

## *Printz* v. *United States*

### 117 S. Ct. 2365, 138 L. Ed. 2d 914 (1997)

In 1993, Congress enacted the Brady Handgun Violence Prevention Act, which, *inter alia,* required the Attorney General to establish a national system for instantly checking prospective handgun purchasers' backgrounds and commanded the "chief law enforcement officer" (CLEO) of each local jurisdiction to conduct such checks and perform related tasks on an interim basis until the national system became operative. Jay Printz, the Sheriff of Ravalli County, Montana, and Richard Mack, the Sheriff of Graham County, Arizona, filed actions in separate U.S. District Courts challenging the interim provisions' constitutionality. In each case, the District Court held that the background-check provision was unconstitutional; they concluded, however, that it was severable from the remainder of the Act and effectively left a voluntary background-check system in place. The Ninth Circuit reversed, finding none of the interim provisions unconstitutional. The U.S. Supreme Court granted certiorari. *Opinion of the Court: Scalia, Kennedy, O'Connor, Rehnquist, Thomas. Concurring opinions: O'Connor; Thomas. Dissenting opinions: Breyer, Stevens; Souter; Stevens, Breyer, Ginsburg, Souter.*

JUSTICE SCALIA delivered the opinion of the Court.

The question presented in these cases is whether certain interim provisions of the Brady Handgun Violence Prevention Act, commanding state and local law enforcement officers to conduct background checks on prospective handgun purchasers and to perform certain related tasks, violate the Constitution. . . .

The petitioners here object to being pressed into federal service, and contend that congressional action compelling state officers to execute federal laws is unconstitutional. Because there is no constitutional text speaking to this precise question, the answer to the CLEOs' challenge must be sought in historical understanding and practice, in the structure of the Constitution, and in the jurisprudence of this Court. We treat those three sources, in that order. . . .

Petitioners contend that compelled enlistment of state executive officers for the administration of federal programs is, until very recent years at least, unprecedented. The Government contends, to the contrary, that "the earliest Congresses enacted statutes that required the participation of state officials in the implementation of federal laws." The Government's contention demands our careful consideration, since early congressional enactments "provid[e] 'contemporaneous and weighty evidence' of the Constitution's meaning." . . .

These early laws establish, at most, that the Constitution was originally understood to permit imposition of an obligation on state *judges* to enforce federal prescriptions, insofar as those prescriptions related to matters appropriate for the judicial power. That assumption was perhaps implicit in one of the provisions of the Constitution, and was explicit in another. In accord with the so-called Madisonian Compromise, Article III, § 1, established only a Supreme Court, and made the creation of lower federal courts optional with the Congress—even though it was obvious that the Supreme Court alone could not hear all federal cases throughout the United States. And the Supremacy Clause announced that "the Laws of the United States . . . shall be the supreme Law of the Land; and the Judges in every State shall be bound thereby." It is understandable why courts should have been viewed distinctively in this regard; unlike legislatures and executives, they applied the law of other sovereigns all the time. . . .

For these reasons, we do not think the early statutes imposing obligations on state courts imply a power of Congress to impress the state executive into its service. Indeed, it can be argued that the numerousness of these statutes, contrasted with the utter lack of statutes imposing obligations on the States' executive (notwithstanding the attractiveness of that course to Congress), suggests an assumed *absence* of such power. The only early federal law the Government has brought to our attention that imposed duties on state executive officers is the Extradition Act of 1793, which required the "executive authority" of a State to cause the arrest and delivery of a fugitive from justice upon the request of the executive authority of the State from which the fugitive had fled. That was in direct implementation, however, of the Extradition Clause of the Constitution itself, see Art, IV, §2.

Not only do the enactments of the early Congresses, as far as we are aware, contain no evidence of an assumption that the Federal Government may command the States' executive power in the absence of a particularized constitutional authorization, they contain some indication of precisely the opposite assumption. On September 23, 1789—the day before its proposal of the Bill of Rights—the First Congress enacted a law aimed at obtaining state assistance of the most rudimentary and necessary sort for the enforcement of the new Government's laws: the holding of federal prisoners in state jails at federal expense. Significantly, the law issued not a command to the States' executive, but a recommendation to their legislatures. Congress "recommended to the legislatures of the several States to pass laws, making it expressly the duty of the keepers of their gaols, to receive and safe keep therein all prisoners committed under the authority of the United States," and offered to pay 50 cents per month for each prisoner. Act of Sept. 23, 1789. Moreover, when Georgia refused to comply with the request. Congress's only reaction was a law authorizing the marshal in any State that failed to comply with the Recommendation of September 23, 1789, to rent a temporary jail until provision for a permanent one could be made. . . .

The constitutional practice we have examined above tends to negate the existence of the congressional power asserted here, but is not conclusive. We turn next to consideration of the structure of the Constitution, to see if we can discern among its "essential postulate[s]" a principle that controls the present cases.

It is incontestible that the Constitution established a system of "dual sovereignty." Although the States surrendered many of their powers to the new Federal Government, they retained "a residuary and inviolable sovereignty," *The Federalist* No. 39. This is reflected throughout the Constitution's text, including (to mention only a few examples) the prohibition on any involuntary reduction or combination of a State's territory, Art. IV, §3; the Judicial Power Clause, Art III, §2, and the Privileges and Immunities Clause, Act. IV §2, which speak of the "Citizens" of the States; the amendment provision, Article V, which requires the votes of three-fourths of the States to amend the Constitution; and the Guarantee Clause, Art. IV, §4, which "presupposes the continued existence of the states and . . . those means and instrumentalities which are the creation of their sovereign and reserved rights." Residual state sovereignty was also implicit, of course, in the Constitution's conferral upon Congress of not all governmental powers, but only discrete, enumerated ones, Art. I, §8, which implication was rendered express by the Tenth Amendment's assertion that "[t]he powers not delegated to the United States by the Constitution, nor prohibited by it to the States, are reserved to the States respectively, or to the people." . . .

This separation of the two spheres is one of the Constitution's structural protections of liberty. "Just as the separation and independence of the coordinate branches of the Federal Government serve to prevent the accumulation of excessive power in any one branch, a healthy balance of power between the States and the Federal Government will reduce the risk of tyranny and abuse from either front." To quote Madison:

> "In the compound republic of America, the power surrendered by the people is first divided between two distinct governments, and then the portion allotted to each subdivided among distinct and separate departments. Hence a double security arises to the rights of the people. The different governments will control each other, at the same time that each will be controlled by itself." *The Federalist* No. 51.

The power of the Federal Government would be augmented immeasurably if it were able to impress into its service—and at no cost to itself—the police officers of the 50 States.

We have thus far discussed the effect that federal control of state officers would have upon the first element of the "double security" alluded to by Madison: the division of power between State and Federal Governments. It would also have an effect upon the second element: the separation and equilibration of powers between the three branches of the Federal Government itself. The Constitution does not leave to speculation who is to administer the laws enacted by Congress; the President, it says, "shall take Care that the Laws be faithfully executed," personally and through officers whom he appoints (save for such inferior officers as Congress may authorize to be appointed by the "Courts of Law" or by "the Heads of Departments" who are themselves presidential appointees). The Brady Act effectively transfers this responsibility to thousands of CLEOs in the 50 States, who are left to implement the program without meaningful Presidential control (if indeed meaningful Presidential control is possible without the power to appoint and remove). The insistence of the Framers upon unity in the Federal Executive—to insure both vigor and accountability—is well known. That unity would be shattered, and the power of the President would be subject to reduction, if Congress could act as effectively without the President as with him, by simply requiring state officers to execute its laws.

The dissent of course resorts to the last, best hope of those who defend *ultra vires* congressional action, the Necessary and Proper Clause. It reasons that the power to regulate the sale of handguns under the Commerce Clause, coupled with the power to "make all Laws which shall be necessary and proper for carrying into Execution the foregoing Powers," conclusively establishes the Brady Act's constitutional validity, because the Tenth Amendment imposes no limitations on the exercise of *delegated* powers but merely prohibits the exercise of powers "*not* delegated to the United States." What destroys the dissent's Necessary and Proper Clause argument, however, is not the Tenth Amendment but the Necessary and Proper Clause itself. When a "La[w] . . . for carrying into Execution" the Commerce Clause violates the principle of state sovereignty reflected in the various constitutional provisions we mentioned earlier, it is not a "La[w] . . . *proper* for carrying into Execution the Commerce Clause," and is thus, in the words of *The Federalist,* "merely [an] ac[t] of usurpation" which "deserve[s] to be treated as such." *The Federalist* No. 33. . . .

Finally, and most conclusively in the present litigation, we turn to the prior jurisprudence of this Court. Federal commandeering of state governments is such a novel phenomenon that this Court's first experience with it did not occur until the 1970's . . . When we were at last confronted squarely with a federal statute that unambiguously required the States to enact or administer a federal regulatory program, our decision should have come as no surprise. At issue in *New York* v. *United States,* 505 U.S. 144 (1992), were the so-called "take title" provisions of the Low-Level Radioactive Waste Policy Amendments Act of 1985, which required States either to enact legislation providing for the disposal of radioactive waste generated within their borders, or to take title to, and possession of the waste—effectively requiring the States either to legislate pursuant to Congress's directions, or to implement an administrative solution. We concluded that Congress could constitutionally require the States to do neither. "The Federal Government," we held, "may not compel the States to enact or administer a federal regulatory program."

The Government contends that *New York* is distinguishable on the following ground: unlike the "take title" provisions invalidated there, the background-check provision of the Brady Act does not require state legislature or executive officials to make policy, but instead issues a final directive to state CLEOs. It is permissible, the Government asserts, for Congress to command state or local officials to assist in the implementation of federal law so long as "Congress itself devises a clear legislative solution that regulates private conduct" and requires state or local officers to provide only "limited, non-policymaking help in enforcing that law." . . . Even assuming . . . that the Brady Act leaves no "policymaking" discretion with the States, we fail to see how that improves rather than worsens the intrusion upon state sovereignty. . . . It is an essential attribute of the States' retained sovereignty that they remain independent and autonomous within their proper sphere of authority. It is no more compatible with this independence and autonomy that their officers be "dragooned" (as Judge Fernandez put it in his dissent [from the Ninth Circuit decision]) into administering federal law, than it would be compatible with the independence and autonomy of the United States that its officers be impressed into service for the execution of state laws. . . .

The dissent makes no attempt to defend the Government's basis for distinguishing *New York,* but instead advances what seems to us an even more implausible theory. The Brady Act, the dissent asserts, is different from the "take title" provisions invalidated in *New York* because the former is addressed to individuals—namely CLEOs—while the latter were directed to the State itself. That is certainly a difference, but it cannot be a constitutionally significant one. While the Brady Act is directed to "individuals," it is directed to them in their official capacities as state officers; it controls their actions, not as private citizens, but as the agents of the State. The distinction between judicial writs and other government action directed against individuals in their personal capacity, on the one hand, and in their official capacity, on the other hand, is an ancient one, principally because it is dictated by common sense. We have observed that "a suit against a state official in his or her official capacity is not a suit against the official but rather is a suit against the official's office. . . . As such, it is no different from a suit against the State itself." *Will* v. *Michigan Dept. of State Police,* 491 U.S. 58, 71 (1989). And the same must be said of a directive to an official in his or her official capacity. To say that the Federal Government cannot control the State, but can control all of its officers, is to say nothing of significance. Indeed, it merits the description "empty formalistic reasoning of the highest order." By resorting to this, the dissent not so much distinguishes *New York* as disembowels it. . . .

We held in *New York* that Congress cannot compel the States to enact or enforce a federal regulatory program. Today we hold that Congress cannot circumvent that prohibition by conscripting the State officers directly. The Federal Government may neither issue directives requiring the State to address particular problems, nor command the States' officers, or those of their political subdivisions, to administer or enforce a federal regulatory program. It matters not whether policymaking is involved, and no case-by-case weighing of the burdens or benefits is necessary; such commands are fundamentally incompatible with our constitutional system of dual sovereignty. Accordingly, the judgment of the Court of Appeals for the Ninth Circuit is reversed.

JUSTICE THOMAS, concurring.

Although I join the Court's opinion in full, I write separately to emphasize that the Tenth Amendment affirms the undeniable notion that under our Constitution, the Federal Government is one of enumerated, hence limited, powers. . . . In my "revisionist" view, the Federal Government's authority under the Commerce Clause, which merely allocates to Congress the power "to regulate Commerce . . . among the several states," does not extend to the regulation of wholly *intra*state, point-of-sale transactions. See *United States* v. *Lopez,* 514 U.S. 549, 584 (1995) (concurring opinion). Absent the underlying authority to regulate the intrastate transfer of firearms, Congress surely lacks the corollary powers to impress state law enforcement officers into administering and enforcing such regulations. Although this Court has long interpreted the Constitution as ceding Congress extensive authority to regulate commerce (interstate or otherwise), I continue to believe that we must "temper our Commerce Clause jurisprudence" and return to an interpretation better rooted in the Clause's original understanding. Even if we construe Congress's authority to regulate interstate commerce to encompass those intrastate transactions that "substantially affect" interstate commerce, I question whether Congress can regulate the particular transactions at issue here. The Constitution, in addition to delegating certain enumerated powers to Congress, places whole areas outside the reach of Congress' regulatory authority. The First Amendment, for example, is fittingly celebrated for preventing Congress from "prohibiting the free exercise" of religion or "abridging the freedom of speech." The Second Amendment similarly appears to contain an express limitation on the government's authority. That Amendment provides: "[a] well regulated Militia, being necessary to the security of a free State, the right of the people to keep and bear arms, shall not be infringed." This Court has not had recent occasion to consider the nature of the substantive right safeguard by the Second Amendment. If, however, the Second Amendment is read to confer a *personal* right to "keep and bear arms," a colorable argument exists that the Federal Government's regulatory scheme, at least as it pertains to the purely intrastate sale or possession of firearms, runs afoul of that Amendment's protections. As the parties did not raise this argument, however, we need not consider it here. Perhaps, at some future date, this Court will have the opportunity to determine whether Justice Story was correct when he wrote that the right to bear arms "has justly been considered, as the palladium of the liberties of a republic." 3 J. Story, Commentaries §1890, p. 746 (1833). In the meantime, I join the Court's opinion striking down the challenged provisions of the Brady Act as inconsistent with the Tenth Amendment.

JUSTICE STEVENS, with whom JUSTICE SOUTER, JUSTICE GINSBURG, and JUSTICE BREYER join, dissenting.

When Congress exercises the powers delegated to it by the Constitution, it may impose affirmative obligations on executive and judicial officers of state and local governments as well as ordinary citizens. This conclusion is firmly supported by the text of the Constitution, the early history of the Nation, decisions of this Court, and a correct understanding of the basic structure of the Federal Government. . . .

[S]ince the ultimate issue is one of power, we must consider its implications in times of national emergency. Matters such as the enlistment of air raid wardens, the administration of a military draft, the mass inoculation of children to forestall an epidemic, or perhaps the threat of an international terrorist, may require a national response before federal personnel can be made available to respond. If the Constitution empowers Congress and the President to make an appropriate response, is there anything in the Tenth Amendment, "in historical understanding and practice, in the structure of the Constitution, [or] in the jurisprudence of this Court," that forbids the enlistment of state officers to make that response effective? More narrowly, what basis is there in any of those sources for concluding that it is the Members of this Court, rather than the elected representatives of the people, who should determine whether the Constitution contains the unwritten rule that the Court announces today?

Perhaps today's majority would suggest that no such emergency is presented by the facts of these cases. But such a suggestion is itself an expression of a policy judgment. And Congress' view of the matter is quite different from that implied by the Court today. . . .

The text of the Constitution provides a sufficient basis for a correct disposition of this case. Article I, §8, grants the Congress the power to regulate commerce among the States. Putting to one side the revisionist views expressed by Justice Thomas in his concurring opinion in *United States* v. *Lopez,* 514 U.S. 549, 584 (1995), there can be no question that that provision adequately supports the regulation of commerce in handguns effected by the Brady Act. Moreover, the additional grant of authority in that section of the Constitution "[t]o make all Laws which shall be necessary and proper for carrying into Execution the foregoing Powers" is surely adequate to support the temporary enlistment of local police officers in the process of identifying persons who should not be entrusted with the possession of handguns. In short, the affirmative delegation of power in Article I provides ample authority for the congressional enactment. . . .

There is not a clause, sentence, or paragraph in the entire text of the Constitution of the United States that supports the proposition that a local police officer can ignore a command contained in a statute enacted by Congress pursuant to an express delegation of power enumerated in Article I. . . .

[T]he historical materials strongly suggest that the Founders intended to enhance the capacity of the federal government by empowering it—as a part of the new authority to make demands directly on individual citizens—to act through local officials. . . . During the debates concerning the ratification of the Constitution, it was assumed that state agents would act as tax collectors for the federal government. Opponents of the Constitution had repeatedly expressed fears that the new federal government's ability to impose taxes directly on the citizenry would result in an overbearing presence of federal tax collectors in the States. Federalists rejoined that this problem would not arise because, as Hamilton explained, "the United States . . . will make use of the State officers and State regulations for collecting" certain taxes. Similarly, Madison made clear that the new central government's power to raise taxes directly from the citizenry would "not be resorted to, except for supplemental purposes of revenue . . . and that the eventual collection, under the immediate authority of the Union, will generally be made by the officers . . . appointed by the several States."

The Court's response to this powerful historical evidence is weak. The majority suggests that "none of these statements necessarily implies . . . Congress could impose these responsibilities without the consent of the States." No fair reading of these materials can justify such an interpretation. . . . Bereft of support in the history of the founding, the Court rests its conclusion on the claim that there is little evidence the National Government actually exercised such a power in the early years of the Republic. This reasoning is misguided in principle and in fact. . . . [T]he fact that Congress did elect to rely on state judges and the clerks of state courts to perform a variety of executive functions is surely evidence of a contemporary understanding that their status as state officials did not immunize them from federal service. The majority's description of these early statutes is both incomplete and at times misleading. . . .

[Concerning t]he Court's "structural" arguments . . . , [t]he fact that the Framers intended to preserve the sovereignty of the several States simply does not speak to the question whether individual state employees may be required to perform federal obligations. . . .

As we explained in *Garcia* v. *San Antonio Metropolitan Transit Authority,* 469 U.S. 528 (1985): "[T]he principal means chosen by the Framers to ensure the role of the States in the federal system lies in the structure of the Federal Government itself. It is no novelty to observe that the composition of the Federal Government was designed in large part to protect the States from overreaching by Congress." Given the fact that the Members of Congress are elected by the people of the several States, with each State receiving an equivalent number of Senators in order to ensure that even the smallest States have a powerful voice in the legislature, it is quite unrealistic to assume that they will ignore the sovereignty concerns of their constituents. It is far more reasonable to presume that their decisions to impose modest burdens on state officials from time to time reflect a considered judgment that the people in each of the States will benefit therefrom.

Indeed, the presumption of validity that supports all congressional enactments has added force with respect to policy judgments concerning the impact of a federal statute upon the respective States. The majority points to nothing suggesting that the political safeguards of federalism identified in *Garcia* need be supplemented by a rule, grounded in neither constitutional history nor text, flatly prohibiting the National Government from enlisting state and local officials in the implementation of federal law.

Recent developments demonstrate that the political safeguards protecting Our Federalism are effective. The majority expresses special concern that were its rule not adopted the Federal Government would be able to avail itself of the services of state government officials "at no cost to itself." But this specific problem of federal actions that have the effect of imposing so-called "unfunded mandates" on the States has been identified and meaningfully addressed by Congress in recent legislation. See Unfunded Mandates Reform Act of 1995, Pub. L. 104–4, 109 Stat. 48.

The statute was designed "to end the imposition, in the absence of full consideration by Congress, of Federal mandates on State . . . governments without adequate Federal funding, in a manner that may displace other essential State . . . governmental priorities." . . . Whatever the ultimate impact of the new legislation, its passage demonstrates that unelected judges are better off leaving the protection of federalism to the political process in all but the most extraordinary circumstances.

Perversely, the majority's rule seems more likely to damage than to preserve the safeguards against tyranny provided by the existence of vital state governments. By limiting the ability of the Federal Government to enlist state officials in the implementation of its programs, the Court creates incentives for the National Government to aggrandize itself. In the name of States' rights, the majority would have the Federal Government create vast national bureaucracies to implement its policies. This is exactly the sort of thing that the early Federalists promised would not occur, in part as a result of the National Government's ability to rely on the magistracy of the states. . . .

In response to this dissent, the majority asserts that the difference between a federal command addressed to individuals and one addressed to the State itself "cannot be a constitutionally significant one." But as I have already noted, there is abundant authority in our Eleventh Amendment jurisprudence recognizing a constitutional distinction between local government officials, such as the CLEO's who brought this action, and State entities that are entitled to sovereign immunity. To my knowledge, no one has previously thought that the distinction "disembowels" the Eleventh Amendment. . . .

The provision of the Brady Act that crosses the Court's newly defined constitutional threshold is more comparable to a statute requiring local police officers to report the identity of missing children to the Crime Control Center of the Department of Justice than to an offensive federal command to a sovereign state. If Congress believes that such a statute will benefit the people of the Nation, and serve the interests of cooperative federalism better than an enlarged federal bureaucracy, we should respect both its policy judgment and its appraisal of its constitutional power.

Accordingly, I respectfully dissent.

JUSTICE SOUTER, dissenting.

I join Justice Steven's dissenting opinion, but subject to the following qualifications. While I do not find anything dispositive in the paucity of early examples of federal employment of state officers for executive purposes, for the reason given by Justice Stevens, neither would I find myself in dissent with no more to go on than those few early instances in the administration of naturalization laws, for example, or such later instances as state support for federal emergency action. These illustrations of state action implementing congressional statutes are consistent with the Government's positions, but they do not speak to me with much force.

## *The Civil Rights Cases*

**109 U.S. 3; S. Ct. 18; 27 L. Ed. 835 (1883)**

The Civil Rights Act of 1875 prohibited any person from denying a citizen "the full and equal enjoyment of the accommodations, advantages, facilities, and privileges of inns, public conveyences on land or water, theatres, and other places of public amusement." In the five cases that were heard together as the *Civil Rights Cases,* persons were indicted for violating the act by denying accommodations to blacks in a hotel, a theatre, an opera house, and a ladies' car on a train. Two of the five cases went to the Supreme Court on writs of error sued out by the plaintiffs in federal circuit courts. The other three were certified to the Supreme Court because the lower-court judges disagreed on the constitutionality of the act. *Opinion of the Court: Bradley, Blatchford, Field, Gray, Matthews, Miller, Waite, Woods. Dissenting opinion: Harlan.*

MR. JUSTICE BRADLEY delivered the opinion of the Court. . . .

It is obvious that the primary and important question in all the cases is the constitutionality of the law: for if the law is unconstitutional none of the prosecutions can stand. . . .

The essence of the law is, not to declare broadly that all persons shall be entitled to the full and equal enjoyment of the accommodations, advantages, facilities, and privileges of inns, public conveyances, and theatres; but that such enjoyment shall not be subject to any conditions applicable only to citizens of a particular race or color, or who had been in a previous condition of servitude. In other words, it is the purpose of the law to declare that, in the enjoyment of the accommodations and privileges of inns, public conveyances, theaters, and other places of public amusement, no distinction shall be made between citizens of different race or color, or between those who have, and those who have not, been slaves. . . .

Has Congress constitutional power to make such a law? Of course, no one will contend that the power to pass it was contained in the Constitution before the adoption of the last three amendments. The power is sought, first, in the Fourteenth Amendment, and the views and arguments of distinguished Senators, advanced whilst the law was under consideration, claiming authority to pass it by virtue of that amendment, are the principal arguments adduced in favor of the power. . .

The first section of the Fourteenth Amendment (which is the one relied on), after declaring who shall be citizens of the United States, and of the several States, is prohibitory in its character, and prohibitory upon the States. It declares that:

"No State shall make or enforce any law which shall abridge the privileges or immunities of citizens of the United States; nor shall any State deprive any person of life, liberty, or property without due process of law; nor deny to any person within its jurisdiction the equal protection of the laws."

It is State action of a particular character that is prohibited. Individual invasion of individual rights is not the subject matter of the amendment. It has a deeper and broader scope. It nullifies and makes void all State legislation, and State action of every kind, which impairs the privileges and immunities of citizens of the United States, or which injures them in life, liberty or property without due process of law, or which denies to any of them the equal protection of the laws. It not only does this, but, in order that the national will, thus declared, may not be a mere *brutum fulmen,* the last section of the amendment invests Congress with power to enforce it by appropriate legislation. To enforce what? To enforce the prohibition. To adopt appropriate legislation for correcting the effects of such prohibited State laws and State acts, and thus to render them effectually null, void, and innocuous. This is the legislative power conferred upon Congress, and this is the whole of it. It does not invest Congress with power to legislate upon subjects which are within the domain of State legislation; but to provide modes of relief against State legislation, or State action, of the kind referred to. It does not authorize Congress to create a code of municipal law for the regulation of private rights; but to provide modes of redress against the operation of State laws, and the action of State officers executive or judicial, when these are subversive of the fundamental rights specified in the amendment. Positive rights and privileges are undoubtedly secured by the Fourteenth Amendment; but they are secured by way of prohibition against State laws and State proceedings affecting those rights and privileges, and by power given to Congress to legislate for the purpose of carrying such prohibition into effect. . . .

An inspection of the law shows that it makes no reference whatever to any supposed or apprehended violation of the Fourteenth Amendment on the part of the States. It is not predicated on any such view. It proceeds *ex directo* to declare that certain acts committed by individuals shall be deemed offences, and shall be prosecuted and punished by proceedings in the courts of the United States. It does not profess to be corrective of any constitutional wrong committed by the States; it does not make its operation to depend upon any such wrong committed. It applies equally to cases arising in States which have the justest laws respecting the personal rights of citizens, and whose authorities are ever ready to enforce such laws, as to those which arise in States that may have violated the prohibition of the amendment. In other words, it steps into the domain of local jurisprudence, and lays down rules for the conduct of individuals in society towards each other, and imposes sanctions for the enforcement of those rules, without referring in any manner to any supposed action of the State or its authorities.

If this legislation is appropriate for enforcing the prohibitions of the amendment, it is difficult to see where it is to stop. Why may not Congress with equal show of authority enact a code of laws for the enforcement and vindication of all rights of life, liberty, and property? If it is supposable that the States may deprive persons of life, liberty, and property without due process of law (and the amendment itself does suppose this), why should not Congress proceed at once to prescribe due process of law for the protection of every one of these fundamental rights, in every possible case, as well as to prescribe equal privileges in inns, public conveyances, and theatres? The truth is, that the implication of a power to legislate in this manner is based upon the assumption that if the States are forbidden to legislate or act in a particular way on a particular subject, and power is conferred upon Congress to enforce the prohibition, this gives Congress power to legislate generally upon that subject, and not merely power to provide modes of redress against such State legislation or action. The assumption is certainly unsound. It is repugnant to the Tenth Amendment of the Constitution, which declares that powers not delegated to the United States by the Constitution, nor prohibited by it to the States, are reserved to the States respectively or to the people. . . .

In this connection it is proper to state that civil rights, such as are guaranteed by the Constitution against State aggression, cannot be impaired by the wrongful acts of individuals, unsupported by State authority in the shape of laws, customs, or judicial or executive proceedings. The wrongful act of an individual, unsupported by any such authority, is simply a private wrong, or a crime of that individual; an invasion of the rights of the injured party, it is true, whether they affect his person, his property, or his reputation; but if not sanctioned in some way by the State, or not done under State authority, his rights remain in full force, and may presumably be vindicated by resort to the laws of the

State for redress. An individual cannot deprive a man of his right to vote, to hold property, to buy and sell, to sue in the courts, or to be a witness or a juror; he may, by force or fraud, interfere with the enjoyment of the right in a particular case; he may commit an assault against the person, or commit murder, or use ruffian violence at the polls, or slander the good name of a fellow citizen; but, unless protected in these wrongful acts by some shield of State law or State authority, he cannot destroy or injure the right; he will only render himself amenable to satisfaction or punishment; and amenable therefore to the laws of the State where the wrongful acts are committed. Hence, in all those cases where the Constitution seeks to protect the rights of the citizen against discriminative and unjust laws of the State by prohibiting such laws, it is not individual offences, but abrogation and denial of rights, which it denounces, and for which it clothes the Congress with power to provide a remedy. This abrogation and denial of rights, for which the States alone were or could be responsible, was the great seminal and fundamental wrong which was intended to be remedied. And the remedy to be provided must necessarily be predicated upon that wrong. It must assume that in the cases provided for, the evil or wrong actually committed rests upon some State law or State authority for its excuse and perpetration.

Of course, these remarks do not apply to those cases in which Congress is clothed with direct and plenary powers of legislation over the whole subject, accompanied with an express or implied denial of such power to the States, as in the regulation of commerce with foreign nations, among the several States, and with the Indian tribes, the coining of money, the establishment of post offices and post roads, the declaring of war, etc. In these cases Congress has power to pass laws for regulating the subjects specified in every detail, and the conduct and transactions of individuals in respect thereof. But where a subject is not submitted to the general legislative power of Congress, but is only submitted thereto for the purpose of rendering effective some prohibition against particular State legislation or State action in reference to that subject, the power given is limited by its object, and any legislation by Congress in the matter must necessarily be corrective in its character, adapted to counteract and redress the operation of such prohibited State laws or proceedings of State officers. . .

. . . The power of Congress to adopt direct and primary, as distinguished from corrective legislation, on the subject in hand, is sought . . . from the Thirteenth Amendment, which abolishes slavery. . . .

. . . It is assumed, that the power vested in Congress to enforce the article by appropriate legislation, clothes Congress with power to pass all laws necessary and proper for abolishing all badges and incidents of slavery in the United States: and upon this assumption it is claimed, that this is sufficient authority for declaring by law that all persons shall have equal accommodations and privileges in all inns, public conveyances, and places of amusement; the argument being, that the denial of such equal accommodations and privileges is, in itself, a subjection to a species of servitude within the meaning of the amendment. Conceding the major proposition to be true, that Congress has a right to enact all necessary and proper laws for the obliteration and prevention of slavery with all its badges and incidents, is the minor proposition also true, that the denial to any person of admission to the accommodations and privileges of an inn, a public conveyance, or a theatre, does subject that person to any form of servitude, or tend to fasten upon him any badge of slavery? If it does not, then power to pass the law is not found in the Thirteenth Amendment. . . .

It would be running the slavery argument into the ground to make it apply to every act of discrimination which a person may see fit to make as to the guests he will entertain, or as to the people he will take into his coach or cab or car, or admit to his concert or theatre, or deal with in other matters of intercourse or business. . . .

When a man has emerged from slavery, and by the aid of beneficent legislation has shaken off the inseparable concomitants of that state, there must be some stage in the progress of his elevation when he takes the rank of a mere citizen, and ceases to be the special favorite of the laws, and when his rights as a citizen, or a man, are to be protected in the ordinary modes by which other men's rights are protected. . . .

On the whole we are of opinion, that no countenance of authority for the passage of the law in question can be found in either the Thirteenth or Fourteenth Amendment of the Constitution; and no other ground of authority for its passage being suggested, it must necessarily be declared void at least so far as its operation in the several States is concerned. . . .

MR. JUSTICE HARLAN, dissenting.

The opinion in these cases proceeds, it seems to me, upon grounds entirely too narrow and artificial. I cannot resist the conclusion that the substance and spirit of the recent amendments of the Constitution have been sacrificed by a subtle and ingenious verbal criticism. . . .

There seems to be no substantial difference between my brethren and myself as to the purpose of Congress; for, they say that the essence of the law is, not to declare broadly that all persons shall be entitled to the full and equal enjoyment of the accommodations, advantages, facilities, and privileges of inns, public conveyances, and theatres; but that such enjoyment shall not be subject to conditions applicable only to citizens of a particular race or color, or who had been in a previous condition of servitude.

The court adjudges, I think erroneously, that Congress is without power, under either the Thirteenth or Fourteenth Amendment, to establish such regulations, and that the first and second sections of the statute are, in all their parts, unconstitutional and void. . . .

The Thirteenth Amendment, it is conceded, did something more than to prohibit slavery as an *institution,* resting upon distinctions of race, and upheld by positive law. My brethren admit that it established and decreed universal *civil freedom* throughout the United States. . .

That there are burdens and disabilities which constitute badges of slavery and servitude, and that the power to enforce by appropriate legislation the Thirteenth Amendment may be exerted by legislation of a direct and primary character, for the eradication, not simply of the institution, but of its badges and incidents, are propositions which ought to be deemed indisputable. They lie at the foundation of the Civil Rights Act of 1866. Whether that act was authorized by the Thirteenth Amendment alone, without the support which it subsequently received from the Fourteenth Amendment, after the adoption of which it was re-enacted with some additions, my brethren do not consider it necessary to inquire. But I submit, with all respect to them, that its constitutionality is conclusively shown by their opinion. They admit, as I have said, that the Thirteenth Amendment established freedom; that there are burdens and disabilities, the necessary incidents of slavery, which constitute its substance and visible form; that Congress, by the act of 1866, passed in view of the Thirteenth Amendment, before the Fourteenth was adopted, undertook to remove certain burdens and disabilities, the necessary incidents of slavery, and to secure to all citizens of every race and color, and without regard to previous servitude, those fundamental rights which are the essence of civil freedom, namely, the same right to make and enforce contracts, to sue, be parties, give evidence, and to inherit, purchase, lease, sell, and convey, property as is enjoyed by white citizens; that under the Thirteenth Amendment, Congress has to do with slavery and its incidents; and that legislation, so far as necessary or proper to eradicate all forms and incidents of slavery and involuntary servitude, may be direct and primary, operating upon the acts of individuals, whether sanctioned by State legislation or not. These propositions being conceded, it is impossible, as it seems to me, to question the constitutional validity of the Civil Rights Act of 1866. I do not contend that the Thirteenth Amendment invests Congress with authority, by legislation, to define and regulate the entire body of the civil rights which citizens enjoy, or may enjoy, in the several States. But I hold that since slavery, . . . was the moving or principal cause of the adoption of that amendment, and since that institution rested wholly upon the inferiority, as a race, of those held in bondage, their freedom necessarily involved immunity from, and protection against, all discrimination against them, because of their race, in respect of such civil rights as belong to freemen of other races. Congress, therefore, under its express power to enforce that amendment, by appropriate legislation, may enact laws to protect that people against the deprivation, *because of their race,* of any civil rights granted to other freemen in the same State; and such legislation may be of a direct and primary character, operating upon States, their officers and agents, and, also, upon, at least, such individuals and corporations as exercise public functions and wield power and authority under the State. . .

Congress has not, in these matters, entered the domain of State control and supervision. It does not, . . . assume to prescribe the general conditions and limitations under which inns, public conveyances, and places of public amusement, shall be conducted or managed. It simply declares, in effect, that since the nation has established universal freedom in this country, for all time, there shall be no discrimination, based merely upon race or color, in respect of the accommodations and advantages of public conveyances, inns, and places of public amusement.

I am of the opinion that such discrimination practised by corporations and individuals in the exercise of their public or quasi-public functions is a badge of servitude the imposition of which Congress may prevent under its power, by appropriate legislation, to enforce the Thirteenth Amendment; and, consequently, without reference to its enlarged power under the Fourteenth Amendment, the act of March 1, 1875, is not, in my judgment, repugnant to the Constitution.

It remains now to consider these cases with reference to the power Congress has possessed since the adoption of the Fourteenth Amendment. Much that has been said as to the power of Congress under the Thirteenth Amendment is applicable to this branch of the discussion, and will not be repeated. . . .

The assumption that the Fourteenth Amendment consists wholly of prohibitions upon State laws and State proceedings in hostility to its provisions, is unauthorized by its language. The first clause of the first section—"All persons born or naturalized in the United States, and subject to the jurisdiction thereof, are citizens of the United States, and of the State wherein they reside"—is of a distinctly affirmative character. In its application to the colored race, previously liberated, it created and granted, as well citizenship of the United States, as citizenship of the State in which they respectively resided. It introduced all of that race, whose ancestors had been imported and sold as slaves, at once, into the political community known as the "People of the United States." They became, instantly, citizens of the United States, *and* of their respective States.

The citizenship thus acquired, by that race, in virtue of an affirmative grant from the nation, may be protected, not alone by the judicial branch of the government, but by congressional legislation of a primary direct character; this, because the power of Congress is not restricted to the enforcement of prohibitions upon State laws or State action. It is, in terms distinct and positive, to enforce "the *provisions of this article*" of amendment; not simply those of a prohibitive character, but the provisions—*all* of the provisions—affirmative and prohibitive, of the amendment. It is, therefore, a grave misconception to suppose that the fifth section of the amendment has reference exclusively to express prohibitions upon State laws or State action. If any right was created by that amendment, the grant of power, through appropriate legislation, to enforce its provisions, authorizes Congress, by means of legislation, operating throughout the entire Union, to guard, secure, and protect that right. . . .

This construction does not in any degree intrench upon the just rights of the States in the control of their domestic affairs. It simply recognizes the enlarged powers conferred by the recent amendments upon the general government. In the view which I take of those amendments, the States possess the same authority which they have always had to define and regulate the civil rights which their own people, in virtue of State citizenship, may enjoy within their respective limits; except that its exercise is now subject to the expressly granted power of Congress, by legislation, to enforce the provisions of such amendments—a power which necessarily carries with it authority, by national legislation, to protect and secure the privileges and immunities which are created by or are derived from those amendments. That exemption of citizens from discrimination based on race or color, in respect to civil rights, is one of those privileges or immunities, can no longer be deemed an open question in this court. . . .

. . . Government has nothing to do with social, as distinguished from technically legal, rights of individuals. No government ever has brought, or ever can bring, its people into social intercourse against their wishes. Whether one person will permit or maintain social relations with another is a matter with which government has no concern. . . . The rights which Congress, by the act of 1875, endeavored to secure and protect are legal, not social rights. The right, for instance, of a colored citizen to use the accommodations of a public highway, upon the same terms as are permitted to white citizens, is no more a social right than his right, under the law, to use the public streets of a city or a town, or a turnpike road, or a public market, or a post office, or his right to sit.

My brethren say, that when a man has emerged from slavery, and by the aid of beneficent legislation has shaken off the inseparable concomitants of that state, there must be some state in the progress of his elevation when he takes the rank of a mere citizen, and ceases to be the special favorite of the laws, and when his rights as a citizen, or a man, are to be protected in the ordinary modes by which other men's rights are protected. It is, I submit, scarcely just to say that the colored race has been the special favorite of the laws. The statute of 1875, now adjudged to be unconstitutional, is for the benefit of citizens of every race and color. What the nation, through Congress, has sought to accomplish in reference to that race, is—what had already been done in every State of the Union for the white race—to secure and protect rights belonging to them as freemen and citizens; nothing more. . . . The supreme law of the land has decreed that no authority shall be exercised in this country upon the basis of discrimination, in respect of civil rights, against freemen and citizens because of their race, color, or previous condition of servitude. To that decree—for the due enforcement of which, by appropriate legislation, Congress has been invested with express power—every one must bow, whatever may have been, or whatever now are, his individual views as to the wisdom or policy, either of the recent changes in the fundamental law, or of the legislation which has been enacted to give them effect.

For the reasons stated I feel constrained to withhold my assent to the opinion of the court.

## *Jones* v. *Alfred H. Mayer Company*

**392 U. S. 409; 88 S. Ct. 2186; 20 L. Ed. 2d 1189 (1968)**

Petitioners Joseph Lee Jones and his wife, alleging that the respondents had refused to sell them a home for the sole reason that he was black, filed a complaint in federal district court, seeking injunctive and other relief. They relied in part upon 42 U.S.C. Section 1982, which provides that "all citizens of the United States shall have the same right, in every State and Territory, as is enjoyed by white citizens thereof to inherit, purchase, lease, sell, hold, and convey real and personal property." The district court dismissed the complaint, and the Court of Appeals for the Eighth Circuit affirmed, concluding that Section 1982 applies only to state action and does not reach private refusals to sell. The Supreme Court granted certiorari. *Opinion of the Court: Stewart, Black, Brennan, Fortas, Marshall, Warren. Concurring opinion: Douglas. Dissenting opinion: Harlan, White.*

MR. JUSTICE STEWART delivered the opinion of the Court.

In this case we are called upon to determine the scope and the constitutionality of an Act of Congress, 42 U. S. C. § 1982. . . .

For the reasons that follow, we reverse the judgment of the Court of Appeals. We hold that § 1982 bars *all* racial discrimination, private as well as public, in the sale or rental of property, and that the statute, thus construed, is a valid exercise of the power of Congress to enforce the Thirteenth Amendment. . . .

We begin with the language of the statute itself. In plain and unambiguous terms, § 1982 grants to *all* citizens, without regard to race or color, "the same right" to purchase and lease property "as is enjoyed by white citizens." As the Court of Appeals in this case evidently recognized, that right can be impaired as effectively by "those who place property on the market" as by the State itself. For, even if the State and its agents lend no support to those who wish to exclude persons from their communities on racial grounds, the fact remains that, whenever property "is placed on the market for whites only, whites have a right denied to Negroes." . . .

On its face, therefore, § 1982 appears to prohibit *all* discrimination against Negroes in the sale or rental of property—discrimination by private owners as well as discrimination by public authorities. Indeed, even the respondents seem to concede that, if § 1982 "means what it says"—

to use the words of the respondents' brief—then it must encompass every racially motivated refusal to sell or rent and cannot be confined to officially sanctioned segregation in housing. Stressing what they consider to be the revolutionary implications of so literal a reading of § 1982, the respondents argue that Congress cannot possibly have intended any such result. Our examination of the relevant history, however, persuades us that Congress meant exactly what it said. . . .

In its original form, 42 U. S. C. § 1982 was part of § 1 of the Civil Rights Act of 1866. . . . The crucial language (of that section) was that which guaranteed all citizens "the same right, in every State and Territory in the United States, . . . to inherit, purchase, lease, sell, hold, and convey real and personal property . . . as is enjoyed by white citizens. . . ." To the Congress that passed the Civil Rights Act of 1866, it was clear that the right to do these things might be infringed not only by "State or local law" but also by "custom, or prejudice." Thus, when Congress provided in § 1 of the Civil Rights Act that the right to purchase and lease property was to be enjoyed equally throughout the United States by Negro and white citizens alike, it plainly meant to secure that right against interference from any source whatever, whether governmental or private. . . .

In attempting to demonstrate the contrary, the respondents rely heavily upon the fact that the Congress which approved the 1866 statute wished to eradicate the recently enacted Black Codes—laws which had saddled Negroes with "onerous disabilities and burdens, and curtailed their rights . . . to such an extent that their freedom was of little value. . . ." . . . The respondents suggest that the only evil Congress sought to eliminate was that of racially discriminatory laws in the former Confederate States. But the Civil Rights Act was drafted to apply throughout the country, and its language was far broader than would have been necessary to strike down discriminatory statutes.

That broad language, we are asked to believe, was a mere slip of the legislative pen. We disagree. For the same Congress that wanted to do away with the Black Codes *also* had before it an imposing body of evidence pointing to the mistreatment of Negroes by private individuals and unofficial groups, mistreatment unrelated to any hostile state legislation. . . .

Indeed, one of the most comprehensive studies then before Congress stressed the prevalence of private hostility toward Negroes and the need to protect them from the resulting persecution and discrimination. . . .

In this setting, it would have been strange indeed if Congress had viewed its task as encompassing merely the nullification of racist laws in the former rebel States. . . .

The remaining question is whether Congress has power under the Constitution to do what § 1982 purports to do: to prohibit all racial discrimination, private and public, in the sale and rental of property. Our starting point is the Thirteenth Amendment, for it was pursuant to that constitutional provision that Congress originally enacted what is now § 1982. . . .

. . . It has never been doubted . . . "that the power vested in Congress to enforce the article by appropriate legislation," . . . includes the power to enact laws "direct and primary, operating upon the acts of individuals, whether sanctioned by State legislation or not." . . .

. . . The constitutional question in this case, therefore, comes to this: Does the authority of Congress to enforce the Thirteenth Amendment "by appropriate legislation" include the power to eliminate all racial barriers to the acquisition of real and personal property? We think the answer to that question is plainly yes. . . .

. . . Surely Congress has the power under the Thirteenth Amendment rationally to determine what are the badges and the incidents of slavery, and the authority to translate that determination into effective legislation. Nor can we say that the determination Congress has made is an irrational one. For this Court recognized long ago that, whatever else they may have encompassed, the badges and incidents of slavery—its "burdens and disabilities"—included restraints upon "those fundamental rights which are that essence of civil freedom, namely, the same right . . . to inherit, purchase, lease, sell and convey property, as is enjoyed by white citizens." *Civil Rights Cases,* 109 U.S. 3, 22. Just as the Black Codes, enacted after the Civil War to restrict the free exercise of those rights, were substitutes for the slave system, so the exclusion of Negroes from white communities became a substitute for the Black Codes. And when racial discrimination herds men into ghettos and makes their ability to buy property turn on the color of their skin, then it too is a relic of slavery. . . . At the very least, the freedom that Congress is empowered to secure under the Thirteenth Amendment includes the freedom to buy whatever a white man can buy, the right to live wherever a white man can live. If Congress cannot say that being a free man means at least this much, then the Thirteenth Amendment made a promise the Nation cannot keep. . . .

MR. JUSTICE HARLAN, whom MR. JUSTICE WHITE joins, dissenting.

The decision in this case appears to me to be most ill-considered and ill-advised. . . .

The petitioners argue that the respondents' racially motivated refusal to sell them a house entitles them to judicial relief on two separate grounds. First, they claim that the respondents acted in violation of 42 U.S.C. § 1982; second, they assert that the respondents' conduct amounted in the circumstances to "state action" and was therefore forbidden by the Fourteenth Amendment even in the absence of any statute.

For reasons which follow, I believe that the Court's construction of § 1982 as applying to purely private action is almost surely wrong, and at the least is open to serious doubt. The issues of the constitutionality of § 1982, as construed by the Court, and of liability under the Fourteenth Amendment alone, also present formidable difficulties. Moreover, the political processes of our own era have, since the date of oral argument in this case, given birth to [the Civil Rights Act of 1968] embodying "fair housing" provisions which would at the end of this year make available . . . the type of relief which the petitioners now seek. It seems to me that this latter factor so diminishes the public importance of this case that by far the wisest course would be for this Court to refrain from decision and to dismiss the writ as improvidently granted. . . .

Like the Court, I begin analysis of § 1982 by examining its language. . . .

The Court finds it "plain and unambiguous," . . . that this language forbids purely private as well as state-authorized discrimination. With all respect, I do not find it so. For me, there is an inherent ambiguity in the term "right," as used in § 1982. The "right" referred to may either be a right to equal status under the law, in which case the statute operates only against state-sanctioned discrimination, or it may be an "absolute" right enforceable against private individuals. To me, the words of the statute, taken alone, suggest the former interpretation, not the latter. . . .

The Court rests its opinion chiefly upon the legislative history of the Civil Rights Act of 1866. . . . Those debates do not, as the Court would have it, overwhelmingly support the result reached by the Court, . . . in fact, a contrary conclusion may equally well be drawn.

[*Justice Harlan then engages in a lengthy review of the Act's legislative history.*]

The foregoing, I think, amply demonstrates that the Court has chosen to resolve this case by according to a loosely worded statute a meaning which is open to the strongest challenge in light of the statute's legislative history. In holding that the Thirteenth Amendment is sufficient constitutional authority for § 1982 as interpreted, the Court also decides a question of great importance. Even contemporary supporters of the aims of the 1866 Civil Rights Act doubted that those goals could constitutionally be achieved under the Thirteenth Amendment, and this Court has twice expressed similar doubts. . . . Thus, it is plain that the course of decision followed by the Court today entails the resolution of important and difficult issues. . . .

## *Patterson* v. *McLean Credit Union*

**491 U. S. 164, 109 S. Ct. 2363, 105 L. Ed. 2d 132 (1989)**

Brenda Patterson, a black woman, was employed by the McLean Credit Union as a teller and file coordinator for 10 years until she was laid off in 1982. Thereafter, she brought suit in U.S. District Court under 42 U.S.C Section 1981, relying on *Runyon* v. *McCrary,* 427 U.S. 160 (1976) and alleging that the credit union had harassed her, failed to promote her to accounting clerk, and then discharged her, all because of her race. The District Court determined that a claim for racial harassment is not actionable under Section 1981 and declined to submit that part of the case to the jury. The court instructed the jury that in order to prevail in her promotion-discrimination claim Patterson had to prove that she was better qualified than the white employee who received the promotion. The jury found for the credit union on this claim, as well as on Patterson's discriminatory-discharge claim. The Court of Appeals for the Fourth Circuit affirmed the District Court's judgment, and the Supreme Court granted certiorari. *Opinion of the Court: Kennedy, O'Connor, Rehnquist, Scalia, White. Concurring in the judgment and dissenting in part: Brennan, Blackmun, Marshall, Stevens; Stevens.*

JUSTICE KENNEDY delivered the opinion of the Court.

In this case, we consider important issues respecting the meaning and coverage of one of our oldest civil rights statutes, 42 U. S. C. § 1981. . . .

We granted certiorari to decide whether petitioner's claim of racial harassment in her employment is actionable under § 1981, and whether the jury instruction given by the District Court on petitioner's § 1981 promotion claim was error. 484 U.S. 814 (1987). After oral argument on these issues, we requested the parties to brief and argue an additional question:

> Whether or not the interpretation of 42 U. S. C. § 1981 adopted by this Court in *Runyon* v. *McCrary* . . . (1976), should be reconsidered.

We now decline to overrule our decision in *Runyon* v. *McCrary*. . . . We hold . . . that racial harassment relating to the conditions of employment is not actionable under § 1981 because that provision does not apply to conduct which occurs after the formation of a contract and which does not interfere with the right to enforce established contract obligations. Finally, we hold that the District Court erred in instructing the jury regarding petitioner's burden in proving her discriminatory promotion claim. . . .

In *Runyon*, the Court considered whether § 1981 prohibits private schools from excluding children who are qualified for admission, solely on the basis of race. We held that § 1981 did prohibit such conduct, noting that it was already well established in prior decisions that § 1981 "prohibits racial discrimination in the making and enforcement of private contracts." . . . The arguments about whether *Runyon* was decided correctly in light of the language and history of the statute were examined and discussed with great care in our decision. It was recognized at the time that a strong case could be made for the view that the statute does not reach private conduct, . . . but that view did not prevail. Some Members of this Court believe that *Runyon* was decided incorrectly, and others consider it correct on its own footing, but the question before us is whether it ought now to be overturned. We conclude after reargument that *Runyon* should not be overruled, and we now reaffirm that § 1981 prohibits racial discrimination in the making and enforcement of private contracts. . . .

Our precedents are not sacrosanct, for we have overruled prior decisions where the necessity and propriety of doing so has been established. . . . Nonetheless, we have held that "any departure from the doctrine of *stare decisis* demands special justification." . . . We have said also that the burden borne by the party advocating the abandonment of an established precedent is greater where the Court is asked to overrule a point of statutory construction. Considerations of *stare decisis* have special force in the area of statutory interpretation, for here, unlike in the context of constitutional interpretation, the legislative power is implicated, and Congress remains free to alter what we have done. . . .

Our conclusion that we should adhere to our decision in *Runyon* that § 1981 applies to private conduct is not enough to decide this case. We must decide also whether the conduct of which petitioner complains falls within one of the enumerated rights protected by § 1981. . . .

Section 1981 reads as follows:

> All persons within the jurisdiction of the United States shall have the same right in every State and Territory to make and enforce contracts, to sue, be parties, give evidence, and to the full and equal benefit of all laws and proceedings for the security of per-

> sons and property as is enjoyed by white citizens, and shall be subject to like punishment, pains, penalties, taxes, licenses, and exactions of every kind, and to no other. Rev. Stat. § 1977.

The most obvious feature of the provision is the restriction of its scope to forbidding discrimination in the "mak[ing] and enforce[ment]" of contracts alone. Where an alleged act of discrimination does not involve the impairment of one of these specific rights, § 1981 provides no relief. Section 1981 cannot be construed as a general proscription of racial discrimination in all aspects of contract relations, for it expressly prohibits discrimination only in the making and enforcement of contracts. . . .

By its plain terms, the relevant provision in § 1981 protects two rights: "the same right . . . to make . . . contracts" and "the same right . . . to . . . enforce contracts." The first of these protections extends only to the formation of a contract, but not to problems that may arise later from the conditions of continuing employment. The statute prohibits, when based on race, the refusal to enter into a contract with someone, as well as the offer to make a contract only on discriminatory terms. But the right to make contracts does not extend, as a matter of either logic or semantics, to conduct by the employer after the contract relation has been established, including breach of the terms of the contract or imposition of discriminatory working conditions. Such postformation conduct does not involve the right to make a contract, but rather implicates the performance of established contract obligations and the conditions of continuing employment, matters more naturally governed by state contract law and Title VII. . . .

The second of these guarantees, "the same right . . . to . . . enforce contracts . . . as is enjoyed by white citizens," embraces protection of a legal process, and of a right of access to legal process, that will address and resolve contract-law claims without regard to race. In this respect, it prohibits discrimination that infects the legal process in ways that prevent one from enforcing contract rights, by reason of his or her race, and this is so whether this discrimination is attributed to a statute or simply to existing practices. It also covers wholly *private* efforts to impede access to the courts or obstruct nonjudicial methods of adjudicating disputes about the force of binding obligations, as well as discrimination by private entities, such as labor unions, in enforcing the terms of a contract. . . . The right to enforce contracts does not, however, extend beyond conduct by an employer which impairs an employee's ability to enforce through legal process his or her established contract rights. . . .

Applying these principles to the case before us, we agree with the Court of Appeals that petitioner's racial harassment claim is not actionable under § 1981. Petitioner has alleged that during her employment with respondent, she was subjected to various forms of racial harassment from her supervisor. As summarized by the Court of Appeals, petitioner testified that

> [her supervisor] periodically stared at her for several minutes at a time; that he gave her too many tasks, causing her to complain that she was under too much pressure; that among the tasks given her were sweeping and dusting, jobs not given to white employees. On one occasion, she testified, [her supervisor] told [her] that blacks are known to work slower than whites. According to [petitioner, her supervisor] also criticized her in staff meetings while not similarly criticizing white employees. . . .

Petitioner also alleges that she was passed over for promotion, not offered training for higher level jobs, and denied wage increases, all because of her race. . . .

This type of conduct, reprehensible though it be if true, is not actionable under § 1981, which covers only conduct at the initial formation of the contract and conduct which impairs the right to enforce contract obligations through legal process. Rather, such conduct is actionable under the more expansive reach of Title VII of the Civil Rights Act of 1964. The latter statute makes it unlawful for an employer to "discriminate against any individual with respect to his compensation, terms, conditions, or privileges of employment." . . . Racial harassment in the course of employment is actionable under Title VII's prohibition against discrimination in the "terms, conditions, or privileges of employment." . . .

Interpreting § 1981 to cover postformation conduct unrelated to an employee's right to enforce her contract, such as incidents relating to the conditions of employment, is not only inconsistent with that statute's limitation to the making and enforcement of contracts, but would also undermine the detailed and well-crafted procedures for conciliation and resolution of Title VII claims. In Title VII, Congress set up an elaborate administrative procedure, implemented through the EEOC [Equal Employment Opportunity Commission], that is designed to assist in the investigation of claims of racial discrimination in the workplace and to work towards the resolution of these claims through conciliation rather than litigation. . . . Only after these procedures have been exhausted, and the plaintiff has obtained a "right to sue" letter from the EEOC, may she bring a Title VII action in court. . . . Section 1981, by contrast, provides no administrative review or opportunity for conciliation.

Where conduct is covered by both § 1981 and Title VII, the detailed procedures of Title VII are rendered a dead letter, as the plaintiff is free to pursue a claim by bringing suit under § 1981 without resort to those statutory prerequisites. . . . We should be reluctant, however, to read an earlier statute broadly where the result is to circumvent the detailed remedial scheme constructed in a later statute. . . .

By reading § 1981 not as a general proscription of racial discrimination in all aspects of contract relations, but as limited to the enumerated rights within its express protection, specifically the right to make and enforce contracts, we may preserve the integrity of Title VII's procedures without sacrificing any significant coverage of the civil rights laws. . . .

Petitioner's claim that respondent violated § 1981 by failing to promote her, because of race, to a position as an intermediate accounting clerk is a different matter. As a preliminary point, we note that the Court of Appeals distinguished between petitioner's claims of racial harassment and discriminatory promotion, stating that although the former did not give rise to a discrete § 1981 claim, "[c]laims of racially discriminatory . . . promotion go to the very existence and nature of the employment contract and thus fall easily within § 1981's protection." . . . We think that somewhat overstates the case. Consistent with what we have said, . . . the question whether a promotion claim is actionable under § 1981 depends upon whether the nature of the change in position was such that it involved the opportunity to enter into a new contract with the employer. If so, then the employer's refusal to enter the new contract is actionable under § 1981. In making this determination, a lower court should give a fair and natural reading to the statutory phrase "the same right . . . to make . . . contracts," and should not strain in an undue manner the language of § 1981. Only where the promotion rises to the level of an opportunity for a new and distinct relation between the employee and the employer is such a claim actionable under § 1981. . . . Because respondent has not argued at any stage that petitioner's promotion claim is not cognizable under § 1981, we need not address the issue further here.

This brings us to the question of the District Court's jury instructions on petitioner's promotion claim. We think the District Court erred when it instructed the jury that petitioner had to prove that she was better qualified than the white employee who allegedly received the promotion. In order to prevail under § 1981, a plaintiff must prove purposeful discrimination. . . . Under our well-established framework, the plaintiff has the initial burden of proving, by the preponderance of the evidence, a prima facie case of discrimination. . . . The burden is not onerous. . . . Here, petitioner need only prove by a preponderance of the evidence that she applied for and was qualified for an available position, that she was rejected, and that after she was rejected respondent either continued to seek applicants for the position, or, as is alleged here, filled the position with a white employee.

Once the plaintiff establishes a prima facie case, an inference of discrimination arises. . . . In order to rebut this inference, the employer must present evidence that the plaintiff was rejected, or the other applicant was chosen, for a legitimate nondiscriminatory reason. . . . Here, respondent presented evidence that it gave the job to the white applicant because she was better qualified for the position, and therefore rebutted any presumption of discrimination that petitioner may have established. At this point, as our prior cases make clear, petitioner retains the final burden of persuading the jury of intentional discrimination.

Although petitioner retains the ultimate burden of persuasion, our cases make clear that she must also have the opportunity to demonstrate that respondent's proffered reasons for its decision were not its true reasons. . . . In doing so, petitioner is not limited to presenting evidence of a certain type. This is where the District Court erred. The evidence which petitioner can present in an attempt to establish that respondent's stated reasons are pretextual may take a variety of forms. . . . Indeed, she might seek to demonstrate that respondent's claim to have promoted a better-qualified applicant was pretextual by showing that she was in fact better qualified than the person chosen for the position. The District Court erred, however, in instructing the jury that in order to succeed petitioner was *required* to make such a showing. There are certainly other ways in which petitioner could seek to prove that respondent's reasons were pretextual. Thus, for example, petitioner could seek to persuade the jury that respondent had not offered the true reason for its promotion decision by presenting evidence of respondent's past treatment of petitioner, including the instances of the racial harassment which she alleges and respondent's failure to train her for an accounting position. . . . While we do not intend to say this evidence necessarily would be sufficient to carry the day, it cannot be denied that it is one of the various ways in which petitioner might seek to prove intentional discrimination on the part of respondent. She may not be forced to pursue any particular means of demonstrating that respondent's stated reasons are pretextual. It was, therefore, error for the District Court to instruct the jury that petitioner could carry her burden of persuasion only by showing that she was in fact better qualified than the white applicant who got the job. . . . The judgment of the Court of Appeals is therefore vacated insofar as it relates to petitioner's discriminatory promotion claim, and the case is remanded for further proceedings consistent with this opinion.

JUSTICE BRENNAN, with whom JUSTICE MARSHALL and JUSTICE BLACKMUN and JUSTICE STEVENS join, concurring in the judgment in part and dissenting in part.

What the Court declines to snatch away with one hand, it takes with the other. Though the Court today reaffirms § 1981's applicability to private conduct, it simultaneously gives this landmark civil rights statute a needlessly cramped interpretation. The Court has to strain hard to justify this choice to confine § 1981 within the narrowest possible scope, selecting the most pinched reading of the phrase "same right to make a contract," ignoring powerful historical evidence about the Reconstruction Congress' concerns, and bolstering its parsimonious rendering by reference to a statute enacted nearly a century after § 1981, and plainly not intended to affect its reach. When it comes to deciding whether a civil rights statute should be construed to further our Nation's commitment to the eradication of racial discrimination, the Court adopts a formalistic method of interpretation antithetical to Congress' vision of a society in which contractual opportunities are equal. I dissent from the Court's holding that § 1981 does not encompass Patterson's racial harassment claim. . . .

I turn now to the two issues on which certiorari was originally requested and granted in this case. The first of these is whether a plaintiff may state a cause of action under § 1981 based upon allegations that her employer harassed her because of her race. In my view, she may. . . .

The Court holds that § 1981, insofar as it gives an equal right to make a contract, "covers only conduct at the initial formation of the contract." . . . This narrow interpretation is not, as the Court would have us believe, . . . the inevitable result of the statutory grant of an equal right "to make contracts." On the contrary, the language of § 1981 is quite naturally read as extending to cover postformation conduct that demonstrates that the contract was not really made on equal terms at all.

. . . In my view, harassment is properly actionable under the language of § 1981 mandating that all persons "shall have the same right . . . to make . . . contracts . . . as is enjoyed by white citizens" if it demonstrates that the employer has in fact imposed discriminatory terms and hence has not allowed blacks to make a contract on an equal basis.

The question in a case in which an employee makes a § 1981 claim alleging racial harassment should be whether the acts constituting harassment were sufficiently severe or pervasive as effectively to belie any claim that the contract was entered into in a racially neutral manner. Where a black employee demonstrates that she has worked in conditions substantially different from those enjoyed by similarly situated white employees, and can show the necessary racial animus, a jury may infer that the black employee has not been afforded the same right to make an employment contract as white employees. . . .

Having reached its decision based upon a supposedly literal reading of § 1981, the Court goes on to suggest that its grudging interpretation of this civil rights statute has the benefit of not undermining Title VII. . . .

The Court's use of Title VII is . . . misleading. Section 1981 is a statute of general application, extending not just to employment contracts, but to *all* contracts. Thus we have held that it prohibits a private school from applying a racially discriminatory admissions policy . . . and a community recreational facility from denying membership based on race. . . . The Court, however, demonstrates no awareness at all that § 1981 is so much broader in scope than Title VII, instead focusing exclusively upon the claim that its cramped construction of § 1981 "preserve[s] the integrity of Title VII's procedures," . . . Rights as between an employer and employee simply are not involved in many § 1981 cases, and the Court's restrictive interpretation of § 1981, minimizing the overlap with Title VII, may also have the effect of restricting the availability of § 1981 as a remedy for discrimination in a host of contractual situations to which Title VII does not extend.

Applying the standards set forth above, I believe the evidence in this case brings petitioner's harassment claim firmly within the scope of § 1981.

★

THE COMMERCE POWER

*Gibbons* v. *Ogden* (1824)
*United States* v. *E. C. Knight Company* (1895)
*Hammer* v. *Dagenhart* (1918)
*National Labor Relations Board* v. *Jones & Laughlin Steel Corporation* (1937)
*Wickard* v. *Filburn* (1942)
*Heart of Atlanta Motel* v. *United States* (1964)
*United States* v. *Lopez* (1995)

THE TAXING POWER

*United States* v. *Butler* (1936)
*United States* v. *Kahriger* (1953)

THE SPENDING POWER

*South Dakota* v. *Dole* (1987)

LIMITATIONS ON NATIONAL POWER

NOTES

SELECTED READING

CASES

★

# 8
# THE EXERCISE OF NATIONAL POWER

The defects of the Articles of Confederation convinced the Framers that the United States needed a substantially stronger national government.[1] Under the Articles the national government could not regulate domestic commerce or levy taxes, and its powers were limited to those expressly enumerated. In the absence of a national commerce power, states taxed goods that were in transit for sale in other states and devised regulations to protect local producers from out-of-state competition, thereby impeding the flow of commerce and producing a stagnant national economy. The national government, meanwhile, was forced to rely on state contributions for its revenues—and because the states were notoriously unresponsive to requests for funds, forceful national action was impossible. Without implied powers, moreover, the national government lacked the flexibility necessary for effective responses to changing situations. To correct these problems, the Framers considerably augmented the powers of the national government. Article I, Section 8, of the new Constitution gives Congress the power "to regulate Commerce with foreign Nations, and among the several States, and with the Indian Tribes," the power to tax and to spend its revenues "to provide for the common Defense and the general Welfare of the United States," and all powers necessary and proper for carrying out its enumerated powers.

During the twentieth century, Congress has used these provisions to justify legislation affecting virtually every aspect of American life. On the basis of the commerce power, it has regulated interstate and intrastate economic activities of all sorts, to the extent that in 1970 it authorized the president to freeze all wages and prices throughout the

United States.[2] It has also relied on the commerce power in dealing with noneconomic concerns as diverse as civil rights, kidnapping, and pollution control. And relying on the spending power, Congress dispenses tax revenues through grant programs that at times have accounted for over 20 percent of the budgets of state and local governments. As a result, according to one expert, "There is hardly an activity that does not involve the federal, state, and some local government in important responsibilities."[3] Is such an expansion of national concerns compatible with the constitutional division of powers between the national and state governments? Or does it threaten the federal system established by the Constitution? To answer these questions, we must trace the emergence of the contemporary interpretation of national power and analyze the constitutional arguments for and against the broad scope of that power.

## THE COMMERCE POWER

Although Congress's power to regulate foreign trade has seldom been seriously challenged, its attempts to regulate commerce "among the several States" have aroused fierce resistance. The range of congressional control over commerce is crucial to American federalism because in large measure it determines the distribution of power between the national and state governments. Debate over the interpretation of the Commerce Clause generally has focused on three questions: (1) What activities constitute "commerce"? (2) If the power to regulate commercial activities is divided between the national and state governments, what portion of these activities can Congress regulate? (3) For what purposes may Congress regulate these activities? Different historical periods have supplied very different answers to these questions.

### Marshall's Interpretation

Chief Justice John Marshall's opinion in *Gibbons* v. *Ogden* (1824) provides the starting point for all subsequent interpretations of the Commerce Clause. Although the case eventually was decided on the basis of a conflict between federal and state law, Marshall used the occasion *Gibbons* provided to develop a broad interpretation of national power. First of all, Marshall observed, constitutional grants of power must be construed in terms of the ends for which they were conferred, for the Framers must have intended that those powers be sufficient to achieve their objectives. Because the Framers established a national commerce power to eliminate the economic chaos of the Confederation period, the Commerce Clause at a minimum must provide Congress with power adequate to accomplish this purpose. This premise supports an expansive definition of commerce. Because commerce "describes the commercial intercourse between nations, and parts of nations, in all its branches," the commerce power cannot be limited to the regulation of buying and selling but instead must encompass all aspects of economic activity. Elastic as well as broad, this power could be used to regulate new forms of commercial intercourse fostered by inventions and changes in business organization, including those unknown to the Framers. (In *Pensacola Telegraph Company* v. *Western Union Telegraph Company* (1878), for example, the Supreme Court recognized the authority of Congress to regulate telegraph companies.) With advances in transportation and communications, congressional authority has expanded accordingly.

In Marshall's view, the aims of the Commerce Clause also dictated a wide scope for congressional regulation. Since the commerce power was designed to promote the free flow of commerce among the states, he contended, Congress can deal with all obstacles to that flow, no matter how local they may be. Thus, congressional power necessarily extends to "that commerce which concerns more states than one"—a formulation that includes but is not limited to interstate commerce. Insofar as intrastate activities affect commerce "among the several states," they too are subject to congressional regulation. As the expansion of business enterprises has produced a more interdependent national economy, the range of economic activities subject to congressional regulation has increased accordingly.

Because the Marshall Court never confronted a constitutional use of the commerce power for noncommercial purposes, it never directly considered whether such a use was permissible. On the one hand, Marshall's opinion in *Gibbons* seems to suggest that Congress can regulate commerce for whatever purposes it wishes. The power to regulate, he noted, is "the power to prescribe the rules by which commerce is to be governed. This power, like all others vested in Congress, is complete in itself, may be exercised to its utmost extent, and acknowledges no limitations, other than are prescribed in the Constitution. . . ." On the other hand, Marshall in *Gibbons* specifically refers to the "immense mass of legislation" left to the states, embracing "inspection laws, quarantine laws, health laws of every description"—in short, laws which regulate commercial activity for noncommercial ends. Moreover, in *McCulloch* v. *Maryland* and other cases, Marshall emphasized that the Constitution conveyed powers to the national government to achieve certain broad ends. From this it follows that the use of these powers for other ends is improper. In sum, the best interpretation is probably that Marshall did not believe that Congress could use its commerce power to pursue noncommercial ends.

Whatever the conclusion on this point, the *Gibbons* opinion did recognize that the Framers vested Congress with broad authority to regulate commerce. Within its sphere Congress was supreme, and that sphere included all economic transactions, of any nature, that affected more states than one. Although Congress did not immediately accept Marshall's implicit invitation to expand its use of the commerce power, his analysis supplied the justification that would be used in upholding vigorous congressional action during the twentieth century.

### Contraction of the Commerce Power: 1888–1936

For almost a century after the Founding, the national commerce power was not a major issue, as Congress enacted little commercial legislation. The passage of the Interstate Commerce Act (1887), however, heralded a more active national role, and conflict over the scope of congressional power soon reached the Supreme Court. Starting from premises that differed from those that had guided Marshall's analysis, the Court in the late nineteenth and early twentieth centuries developed a more restrictive conception of the commerce power and invalidated important congressional legislation. Underlying the Court's interpretation of the Commerce Clause during this period was the doctrine of dual federalism (see Chapter 7), which suggests that in dividing governmental functions between the national and state governments, the Framers reserved important powers—including the police power—to the states.[4] In exercising their powers, therefore, neither the national nor the state governments may invade the other's sphere—and in particular, the national government may not use the pretext of its delegated powers to usurp the powers reserved to the states. The Court, accordingly, must interpret the Commerce Clause—along with other constitutional grants of power—so that the Framers' dual aims of adequate national power and a federal balance are both achieved. The restrictive interpretation of the Commerce Power required by this doctrine was justified in *United States* v. *E. C. Knight Company* (1895) by noting the dire effects that would presumably flow from a broad interpretation of that provision: "If the national power extends to all contracts and combinations in manufacture, agriculture, mining, and other productive industries, whose ultimate result may affect external commerce, comparatively little of business operations and affairs would be left for state control."

Under the influence of dual federalism, the Court attempted to safeguard state power by defining commerce narrowly, restricting the range of commercial activities under congressional control, and limiting the purposes for which the commerce power could be exercised. In *Knight,* which provided the authoritative interpretation of the Sherman Antitrust Act, the Court first announced its definition of commerce. At issue here were the activities of the American Sugar Refining Company, which controlled over 98 percent of the nation's sugar refining business. In holding that the antitrust act did not apply to the company's actions, the Court contended that congressional power extends only to commerce, and "commerce succeeds to manufacture, and is not a part of it." The implications of this distinction between commerce and production were enormous: At a stroke the justices had immunized from congressional regulation major elements of the national economy, including manufacturing, oil production, agriculture, and mining.

This distinction between production and commerce might not have precluded congressional regulation if the Court had accepted Marshall's interpretation of the scope of congressional power: "that commerce which concerns more states than one." For production, even if not a part of commerce, unquestionably affects it and thus would fall within congressional control. The Court adopted a more exacting standard, however. Congress was permitted to regulate the flow of goods in interstate commerce, as well as those local transactions incidental to the transportation of goods in interstate commerce. In *Swift & Company* v. *United States* (1905), for example, the justices ruled that the national government could prosecute stockyard firms that had conspired to monopolize the sale and distribution of fresh beef, because the purchase of cattle was merely an element in the "current of commerce" among the states. But congressional regulation of intrastate activities, was limited to those activities that had a "direct effect," not merely an "indirect effect," on interstate commerce.

This distinction between "direct" and "indirect" effects, which in effect insulated some intrastate activities from congressional regulation, eventually proved unworkable. A vague criterion, it offered little guidance in the analysis of specific cases and contributed greatly to the inconsistency that marked the Court's decisions during the early twentieth century. Judicial efforts to clarify the distinction between direct and indirect effects met with little success. When Justice George Sutherland undertook to do so in *Carter* v. *Carter Coal Company* (1936), which invalidated congressional regulation of labor relations throughout the mining industry, his explanation revealed the problems with this approach:

> The extent of the effect bears no logical relation to its character. The distinction between a direct and indirect effect turns, not upon the magnitude of either the cause or the effect, but entirely upon the manner in which the effect has been brought about. If the production by one man of a single ton of coal intended for interstate sale and shipment, and actually so sold and shipped, affects interstate commerce indirectly, the effect does not become direct by multiplying the tonnage, or increasing the number of men employed, or adding to the expense or complexities of the business, or by all combined.[5]

Following this line of logic, the Court in *Carter Coal* held that the distinction between direct and indirect effects turned on the proximity of the effect to interstate commerce, rather than on the extent of the effect. No matter how severe the effect on interstate commerce of intrastate activity, if the effect was indirect the remedy lay solely with the states. So Congress could not prevent such major interferences with the flow of commerce as nationwide strikes, because they affected commerce only "indirectly."

Even within Congress's recognized sphere of interstate commerce, the Court eventually discovered a further implicit limitation on legislative action, ruling that Congress could not use this power for noncommercial purposes. Initially, no such restriction was apparent to the Court. In *Champion* v. *Ames* (1903) the justices sustained legislation prohibiting the interstate transportation of lottery tickets, even though the law served police-power ends. Following *Champion,* Congress enacted extensive regulatory legislation—the Pure Food Act, the Narcotics Acts, and the White Slave Act, to name but a few—that also was upheld. In *Hammer* v. *Dagenhart* (1918), however, the Court reversed its position in striking down a ban on interstate shipment of goods produced by child labor. Noting that the regulations in previous cases involved inherently harmful items, the majority in *Hammer* pointed out that items produced by child labor were indistinguishable from other goods except in terms of the workers involved, and that therefore the only congressional interest in banning their shipment was to prevent the employment of child labor. Because control over such matters was vested in the states, the justices concluded, Congress could not interfere in this matter. In reaching this decision, the Court followed the dictates of dual federalism, according to which grants of power to the national government were conditioned by the reserved powers of the states.

So long as Congress exercised the commerce power sparingly, collisions between Court and Congress were intermittent.[6] With the advent of the Great Depression, however, more active governmental intervention in the economy made confrontation almost inevitable. In 1935–1936 the Court struck down such important New Deal measures as the National Industrial Recovery Act, the Agricultural Adjustment Act, and the Bituminous Coal Conservation Act.[7] The bases for the Court's rulings presaged the invalidation of further New Deal measures. In 1937, following his landslide reelection, President Franklin Roosevelt proposed a plan to expand the membership of the Supreme Court.[8] Although the measure was defended as necessary to help the Court with its workload, in fact the expansion of the Court was intended to give the president a chance to appoint justices more sympathetic to New Deal legislation. While the court-packing bill was before Congress (where it ultimately died), the Court upheld the National Labor Relations Act, signaling a new approach to the interpretation of the Commerce Clause. The retirement of Justices Willis Van Devanter in 1937 and George Sutherland in 1938 and their replacement by Roosevelt appointees solidified support for a broad view of the national commerce power.

### The Contemporary Era

In *National Labor Relations Board* v. *Jones & Laughlin Steel Corporation* (1937), the Supreme Court adopted a considerably broader view of the congressional commerce power. At least one commentator, Bruce Ackerman, has argued that the decision reflected a recognition by the justices that the electorate's overwhelming endorsement of Roosevelt's economic program in the presidential election of 1936 had produced a basic change in the Constitution, accomplished outside the normal channels for constitutional amendment.[9] Many commentators, however, have concluded that the Court merely adopted Marshall's interpretation of the commerce power and applied it to twentieth-century economic conditions. Whichever interpretation is correct, the Court's shift was dramatic. Gone were the production/commerce dichotomy and the artificial distinction between direct and indirect effects. Asserting that judgments concerning interstate commerce must take into account "actual experience," the Court in *Jones & Laughlin* recognized that labor-management strife in nationwide industries threatens interstate commerce and so can be regulated by Congress. Other decisions indicated that the scope of congressional power turned on the *existence* of an effect on interstate commerce, not on the *extent* of the effect.[10] If Congress indicated that a class of activities had an effect on interstate commerce, then the Court would defer to that legislative judgment. The broad scope of this power was strikingly confirmed in *Wickard* v. *Filburn* (1942), in which the Court unanimously upheld congressional legislation governing the growing of wheat for domestic consumption.

Another series of decisions removed restrictions on the purposes for which Congress can employ the commerce power. In *United States* v. *Darby* (1941), the Court expressly overruled *Hammer*, holding that Congress could prohibit the interstate shipment of goods produced by workers receiving substandard wages. Justice Harlan Stone's opinion acknowledged that the *Darby* decision gave Congress wide leeway: "The motive and purpose of a regulation of interstate commerce are matters for the legislative judgment upon the exercise of which the Constitution places no restriction and over which the courts are given no control."[11]

Subsequently, Congress has relied on the commerce power in pursuing such noncommercial ends as the protection of civil rights and the suppression of crime. Relying on the Commerce Clause, Congress in 1964 banned racial discrimination in public accommodations (restaurants, theatres, hotels, etc.) throughout the nation. The Court in *Heart of Atlanta Motel* v. *United States* (1964) upheld this ban as a valid exercise of the commerce power, and in later cases, citing *Wickard* v. *Filburn*, sustained its application to small enterprises whose individual effect on interstate commerce was minimal.[12] In the matter of crime control, the justices ruled in *Perez* v. *United States* (1971) that the Commerce Clause provided Congress with broad authority to deal with crime. Previous Court decisions had endorsed congressional efforts to prevent misuse of the channels of interstate commerce, such as the transportation of stolen goods or kidnapped persons, and to protect the instrumentalities of interstate commerce against theft or destruction.[13] In *Perez*, however, the Court for the first time upheld congressional regulation of local criminal activity (loan sharking) that could supply funds for organized crime and thereby affect interstate commerce, even though the activities of the defendant in this particular case were purely intrastate, were unconnected to organized crime, and had no measurable effect on interstate commerce. Justice William Douglas, writing for the Court, noted that "where the *class of activities* is regulated and that *class* is within the reach of federal power, the courts have no power 'to excise as trivial, individual instances' of the class."[14] In solitary dissent, Justice Potter Stewart complained that the Court's opinion offered no basis for distinguishing those crimes subject to congressional regulation from those traditionally dealt with by the states. And in recent years, Congress has enacted legislation making crimes that had previously been state concerns, such as carjacking and various firearms offenses, violations of federal law.[15]

### A New Direction?

From 1937 to 1995, the Supreme Court endorsed an expansive interpretation of the national commerce power. Only once during this period, in *National League of Cities* v. *Usery* (1976), did the justices rule that an enactment exceeded Congress's power under the commerce power; and the Court expressly overruled that 5 to 4 decision nine years later in *Garcia* v. *San Antonio Metropolitan Transit Authority* (1985). Since 1995, however, the Court has twice sought to rein in the national commerce power. In *United States* v. *Lopez* (1995), it struck down a federal enactment creating gun-free zones near schools; and two years later, in *Printz* v. *United States* (1997), it invalidated a provision of a federal statute that required local law enforcement officials to check the backgrounds of prospective handgun purchasers. In each case, the dissenters insisted that the challenged enactments were consistent with the Court's prior rulings interpreting the national commerce power, such as *Wickard* v. *Filburn* and *Perez* v. *United States.* According to the Court majority, however, Congress had exceeded its authority. Speaking for a five-member majority in *Lopez,* Chief Justice Rehnquist argued that the connection between gun ownership in school zones and interstate commerce was tenuous at best. To accept the government's rationale for upholding the statue, he complained, would in effect remove all limits on congressional regulatory authority. Because this would transform the constitutional system from a federal to a unitary system, such an interpretation could not be right. Justice Clarence Thomas, concurring in both cases, proposed going even further. Fidelity to the original understanding of the Commerce Clause, he argued, would require the Court to reexamine its conclusion that the national commerce power extends to purely intrastate activities as long as they bear a "substantial relationship" to interstate commerce. Whether *Lopez* and *Printz* signal a major change in the Court's interpretation or whether, like *National League of Cities* v. *Usery,* they will have little long-term effect remains to be seen.

## THE TAXING POWER

The Framers gave Congress the power to tax so that the national government could raise the revenue necessary to finance its operations. The Constitution imposes only three express limitations on this power. Congress may not tax exports, must apportion direct taxes among the states in relation to their populations, and must impose taxes uniformly throughout the nation.[16] Only the limitation on "direct taxes"—a vague phrase neither discussed in the Constitutional Convention nor defined in the Constitution—has provoked much litigation. In *Hylton* v. *United States* (1796), the Supreme Court rejected a claim that a tax on carriages was a direct tax, noting that the term applied to head taxes and land taxes. And in *Springer* v. *United States* (1881), it concluded that the Civil War income tax was not a direct tax. But in *Pollock* v. *Farmer's Loan & Trust Company* (1895), it abandoned this position, holding that since taxes on real estate were direct taxes, so were taxes on the income from real estate. This decision, which in effect prevented the imposition of any type of federal income tax, was reversed by the ratification of the Sixteenth Amendment (1913).

A more serious constitutional issue stems from the uses Congress may make of its taxing power. All taxes, in addition to raising revenues, make goods more expensive, and thereby discourage their purchase. Obviously, this side effect of taxation can serve regulatory purposes. But does the mere fact that the Constitution places few restrictions on the goods and activities Congress can tax mean that the taxing power can be used for regulatory—as opposed to revenue-raising—purposes?

During the nineteenth century, debate over this question centered on protective tariffs, which both raise revenues and shield American industries from foreign competition. In pursuing the latter objective, Congress was using its taxing power for a regulatory purpose. Because the Constitution grants Congress regulatory authority over commerce with foreign nations, however, protective tariffs involve activities that Congress could regulate by other means, if it so chose. Thus the constitutionality of this use of the taxing power was generally recognized long before the Supreme Court upheld a protective tariff in *J. W. Hampton, Jr. & Company* v. *United States* (1928).

With the resolution of the controversy over protective tariffs, debate shifted to congressional use of the taxing power to reach activities it could not otherwise regulate. In *McCrary* v. *United States* (1904), the Court endorsed one such use of the taxing power, upholding a heavy excise tax on margarine that had been colored yellow to resemble butter. Although the tax was designed to discourage purchase of the colored margarine, the Court insisted that it could not question the motives underlying the exercise of constitutionally granted powers. Yet it did exactly that in *Bailey* v. *Drexel Furniture Company* (1922), in striking down a law that imposed a 10 percent tax on the profits of businesses employing children. Writing for the Court, Chief Justice Howard Taft acknowledged that all taxes have regulatory effects but noted that "there comes a time in the extension of the penalizing features of the so-called tax when it loses its character as such and becomes a mere penalty, with the characteristics of regulation and punishment."[17] And if Congress cannot regulate an activity—and the Court in *Hammer* v. *Dagenhart* had ruled that it could not regulate child labor—then it cannot regulate indirectly through the subterfuge of a "so-called tax." Interestingly, although the Court was closely divided in *Hammer*, only one justice dissented in *Bailey*.

In *United States* v. *Butler* (1936), the Court employed the *Bailey* rationale in striking down a major piece of New Deal legislation, the Agricultural Adjustment Act of 1933. Since 1937, however, the Court has refused to monitor the motives underlying congressional tax laws. In *Mulford* v. *Smith* (1939), it upheld an act virtually identical to the one it had invalidated in *Butler* only three years previously, and in *United States* v. *Kahriger* (1953), it ruled that an occupational tax on gamblers was constitutional, even though the tax's primary aim was to suppress gambling. Although the justices eventually struck down the tax on gamblers on self-incrimination grounds in *Marchetti* v. *United States* (1968), in doing so they reasserted that only explicit constitutional prohibitions—not the reserved powers of the states—justified invalidation of congressional tax statutes. Thus the power to tax, like the power to regulate commerce among the several states, is plenary.

## THE SPENDING POWER

Article I, Section 8 authorizes Congress "to pay the debts and provide for the common defense and general welfare of the United States." During the ratification debates, this broad grant of power worried critics of the Constitution, who asserted that it would transform the national government into a government of indefinite, rather than enumerated, powers. James Madison rejected this interpretation, maintaining in *The Federalist,* No. 41, that the enumeration of congressional powers that followed the general authorization served to "explain and qualify" it. To Madison, then, the spending power was subordinate to, rather than independent of, the Constitution's grants of legislative power. In his famous *Report on Manufactures,* however, Alexander Hamilton challenged Madison's view that the enumeration of powers served to limit the spending power and proposed a more expansive interpretation:

> The phrase is as comprehensive as any that could have been used, because it was not fit that the constitutional authority of the Union to appropriate its revenues should have been restricted within narrower limits than the "general welfare" and because this necessarily embraces a vast variety of particulars which are susceptible neither of specification nor of definition. It is therefore of necessity left to the discretion of the National Legislature to pronounce upon the objects which concern the general welfare, and for which, under the description, an appropriation of money is requisite and proper.[18]

Throughout most of the nation's history, Congressional practice has been guided by the Hamiltonian position, which the Supreme Court explicitly endorsed in *Butler.* Justice Owen Roberts did maintain in *Butler* that the spending power was limited by the reserved powers of the states, but the Court repudiated this position in *Steward Machine Company* v. *Davis* (1937) and *Helvering* v. *Davis* (1937).

Congress's power to spend is not completely unrestricted, however. All congressional expenditures must provide for the "common defense" or the "general welfare." In practice, this requirement is easily met: As the Court has recognized, Congress has primary responsibility for determining whether expenditures promote the general welfare, and courts may challenge only those determinations that are "clearly wrong, a display of arbitrary power, not an exercise of judgment."[19] Expenditures, like all other congressional actions, also are subject to express constitutional limitations, such as the Bill of Rights. The requirement of standing to sue (see Chapter 3), however, has limited judicial enforcement of these restrictions. In *Frothingham* v. *Mellon* (1923), the Court, rejecting a challenge to congressional appropriations in aid of expectant mothers, held that ordinary taxpayers generally lacked standing to contest Federal expenditures. This stricture was eased somewhat by the holding in *Flast* v. *Cohen* (1968) that taxpayers could sue when the "challenged enactment exceeds specific constitutional limitations imposed upon the exercise of the congressional taxing and spending power."[20] But later decisions—most notably *United States* v. *Richardson* (1974)—cast considerable doubt on the Court's willingness to entertain taxpayer challenges to appropriations.

## LIMITATIONS ON NATIONAL POWER

Responding to the deficiencies of the Articles of Confederation, the Framers vested Congress with broad powers to tax, to spend, and to regulate commerce. Yet although these grants of power were broad, they were not unlimited, and controversy has arisen periodically about the scope of these powers. In the aftermath of the New Deal conflict between Franklin Roosevelt and the Supreme Court, the justices interpreted these powers so expansively that commentators questioned whether any constitutional limitations remained on the exercise of national power. Since 1995, however, the Supreme Court has attempted to reimpose some limits, striking down two federal statutes as beyond the scope of the national commerce power. Equally important as a check on national power are the limitations found in the Bill of Rights. It is no coincidence that as the scope of national activity has expanded, the Court has found increasing occasion to invalidate congressional legislation violating these protections.

Nevertheless, the primary limitation on the exercise of national power is political, not constitutional, in character. As Chief Justice Marshall observed in *Gibbons* v. *Ogden,* "The wisdom and the discretion of Congress, their identity with the people, and the influence which their constituents possess at election, are . . . the restraints on which the people must often rely solely, in all representative governments."

## NOTES

1 Alexander Hamilton opens *The Federalist,* No. 1, by noting the "unequivocal experience of the inefficacy of the subsisting federal government," and many of the early papers are devoted to elaborating the defects of the Articles of Confederation.

2 The Economic Stabilization Act of 1970 was upheld against constitutional challenge in *Amalgamated Meat Cutters & Butcher Workmen* v. *Connally,* 337 F. Supp. 737 (D.D.C. 1971).
3 Morton Grodzins, *The American System; A New View of Government in the United States,* ed. Daniel J. Elazar (Chicago: Rand McNally, 1966), p. 4.
4 For a penetrating discussion of dual federalism, see Edward S. Corwin, "The Passing of Dual Federalism," in Robert G. McCloskey, ed., *Essays in Constitutional Law* (New York: Alfred A. Knopf, 1957).
5 *Carter* v. *Carter Coal Co.,* 298 U.S. 238, 308 (1936).
6 From 1888 to 1933, the Supreme Court struck down forty federal laws; from 1934 to 1936, it struck down thirteen. For a listing of these cases, see Henry J. Abraham, *The Judicial Process,* 6th ed. (New York: Oxford University Press, 1993), Table 9, pp. 274–279.
7 *Schecter Poultry Corp.* v. *United States* (1935), *United States* v. *Butler* (1936), and *Carter* v. *Carter Coal Co.* (1936).
8 This plan is discussed in Robert H. Jackson, *The Struggle for Judicial Supremacy* (New York: A. A. Knopf, 1941) and William E. Lenchtenberg, *The Supreme Court Reborn: The Constitutional Revolution in the Age of Roosevelt* (New York: Oxford University Press, 1995).
9 Bruce Ackerman, *We the People* (Cambridge, Mass.: Belknap Press, 1991).
10 This is illustrated in a series of cases, including *NLRB* v. *Friedman-Harry Marks Clothing Co.* (1937), *NLRB* v. *Fainblatt* (1939), and *Santa Cruz* v. *NLRB* (1938).
11 *United States* v. *Darby,* 312 U.S. 100, 115 (1941).
12 In *Katzenbach* v. *McClung* (1964), the Court upheld application of the Civil Rights Act of 1964 to Ollie's Barbecue, a family-owned restaurant that did not cater to interstate travelers; and in *Daniel* v. *Paul* (1969), the act was held to apply to a rural amusement park in Arkansas.
13 On interstate transportation of stolen automobiles, see *Brooks* v. *United States* (1925); on interstate transportation of kidnapped persons, see *Gooch* v. *United States* (1936).
14 *Perez* v. *United States,* 402 U.S. 146, 154 (1971).
15 See "The Federal Role in Criminal Law." *Annals of the American Academy of Political and Social Science* 543 (1995): 9–166.
16 These restrictions on the federal taxing power are found in Article I, Section 8, Paragraph 1, and Article I, Section 9, Paragraphs 4 and 5.
17 *Bailey* v. *Drexel Furniture Co.,* 259 U.S. 20, 38 (1922).
18 Alexander Hamilton, *The Works of Alexander Hamilton,* ed. Henry Cabot Lodge (New York: Federal Edition, 1904), 4:151.
19 *Helvering* v. *Davis,* 301 U.S. 619, 640 (1937).
20 *Flast* v. *Cohen,* 392 U.S. 83, 102–103 (1968).

## SELECTED READING

*The Federalist,* Nos. 30–36, 41–42, 56.

*Bailey* v. *Drexel Furniture Company,* 259 U. S. 20 (1992).
*Carter* v. *Carter Coal Company,* 298 U. S. 238 (1936).
*Garcia* v. *San Antonio Metropolitan Transit Authority,* Chapter 7 (1985).

*Perez* v. *United States,* 402 U. S. 146 (1971).
*United States* v. *Darby,* 312 U. S. 100 (1941).

Ackerman, Bruce A. *We the People* (Cambridge, Mass.: Belknap Press, 1991).

Baker, Leonard. *Back to Back: The Duel between FDR and the Supreme Court* (New York: Macmillan, 1967).

Barber, Sotirios A. *On What the Constitution Means* (Baltimore: Johns Hopkins University Press, 1984), Chapter 4.

Berger, Raoul. *Federalism: The Founders' Design* (Norman: University of Oklahoma Press, 1987), Chapters 4–6.

Choper, Jesse H. *Judicial Review and the National Political Process: A Functional Reconsideration of the Role of the Supreme Court* (Chicago: University of Chicago Press, 1990).

Corwin, Edward S. "The Passing of Dual Federalism." In Robert G. McCloskey, ed. *Essays in Constitutional Law* (New York: Vintage, 1957).

Epstein, Richard A. "The Proper Scope of the Commerce Power." *Virginia Law Review* 73 (1987): 1387–1455.

Frankfurter, Felix. *The Commerce Clause Under Marshall, Taney, and Waite* (Chapel Hill: University of North Carolina Press, 1937).

McCoy, Thomas R. and Barry Friedman. "Conditional Spending: Federalism's Trojan Horse." In Philip B. Kurland, Gerhard Casper, and Dennis J. Hutchinson, eds. *The Supreme Court Review 1988* (Chicago: University of Chicago Press, 1989).

Sunstein, Cass. *After the Rights Revolution: Reconceiving the Regulatory State* (Cambridge, Mass.: Harvard University Press, 1990).

Swisher, Carl Brent. *The Growth of Constitutional Power in the United States,* 2nd ed. (Chicago: University of Chicago Press, 1963).

## *Gibbons* v. *Ogden*

**9 Wheat 1, 6 L. Ed. 23 (1824)**

Robert Fulton and Robert Livingston, having obtained from the state of New York an exclusive right to operate steamboats in its waters, licensed Aaron Ogden to operate steamboats between New Jersey and New York. But Thomas Gibbons, armed with a federal license under the Coasting Act of 1793 (in which Congress provided for the licensing of "vessels employed in the coasting trade"), challenged the state-granted monopoly by running two steamboats between Elizabethtown, New Jersey, and New York City. When the New York Court of Chancery enjoined Gibbons from continuing to operate his boats, he appealed the decision to the United States Supreme Court. *Opinion of the Court: Marshall, Todd, Duval, Story, Thompson. Concurring opinion: Johnson.*

MR. CHIEF JUSTICE MARSHALL delivered the opinion of the Court.

As preliminary to the very able discussions of the constitution, which we have heard from the bar, and as having some influence on its construction, reference has been made to the political situation of these states, anterior to its formation. It has been said, that they were sovereign, were completely independent, and were connected with each other only by a league. This is true. But when these allied sovereigns converted their league into a government, when they converted their congress of ambassadors, deputed to deliberate on their common concerns, and to recommend measures of general utility into a legislature, empowered to enact laws on the most interesting subjects, the whole character in which the states appear, underwent a change, the extent of which must be determined by a fair consideration of the instrument by which that change was effected.

This instrument contains an enumeration of powers expressly granted by the people to their government. It has been said, that these powers ought to be construed strictly. But why ought they to be so construed? Is there one sentence in the constitution which gives countenance to this rule? In the last of the enumerated powers, that which grants, expressly, the means for carrying all others into execution, congress is authorized "to make all laws which shall be necessary and proper" for the purposes. But this limitation on the means which may be used, is not extended to the powers which are conferred; nor is there one sentence in the constitution which has been pointed out by the gentlemen of the bar, or which we have been able to discern, that prescribes this rule. We do not, therefore, think ourselves justified in adopting it. What do gentlemen mean, by a strict construction? If they contend only against that enlarged construction, which would extend words beyond their natural and obvious import, we might question the application of the term, but should not controvert the principle. If they contend for that narrow construction which, in support of some theory not to be found in the constitution, would deny to the government those powers which the words of the grant, as usually understood, import, and which are consistent with the general views and objects of the instrument—for that narrow construction, which would cripple the government, and render it unequal to the objects for which it is declared to be instituted, and to which the powers given, as fairly understood, render it competent—then we cannot perceive the propriety of this strict construction, nor adopt it as the rule by which the constitution is to be expounded. . . .

The words are, "congress shall have power to regulate commerce with foreign nations, and among the several states, and with the Indian tribes." The subject to be regulated is commerce; and our constitution being, as was aptly said at the bar, *one of enumeration, and not of definition,* to ascertain the extent of the power, it becomes necessary to settle the meaning of the word. The counsel for the appellee would limit it to traffic, to buying and selling, or the interchange of commodities, and do not admit that it comprehends navigation. This would restrict a general term, applicable to many objects, to one of its significations. Commerce, undoubtedly, is traffic, but it something more—it is intercourse. It describes the commercial intercourse between nations, and parts of nations, in all its branches, and is regulated by prescribing rules for carrying on that intercourse. The mind can scarcely conceive a system for regulating commerce between nations, which shall exclude all laws concerning navigation, which shall be silent on the admission of the vessels of the one nation into the parts of the other, and be confined to prescribing rules for the conduct of individuals, in the actual employment of buying and selling, or of barter. If commerce does not include navigation, the government of the Union has no direct power over that subject, and can make no law prescribing what shall constitute American vessels or requiring that they shall be navigated by American seamen. Yet this power has been exercised from the commencement of the government, has been exercised with the consent of all, and has been understood by all to be a commercial regulation. All America understands, and has uniformly understood, the word "commerce," to comprehend navigation. It was so understood, and must have been so understood, when the constitution was framed. The power over commerce, including navigation, was one of the primary objects for which the people of America adopted their government, and must have been contemplated in forming it. The convention must have used the word in that sense, because all have understood it in that sense; and the attempt to restrict it comes too late.

The word used in the constitution, then, comprehends, and has been always understood to comprehend, navigation within its meaning; and a power to regulate navigation, is as expressly granted, as if that term had been added to the word "commerce." To what commerce does this power extend? The constitution informs us, to commerce "with foreign nations, and among the several states, and with the Indian tribes." It has, we believe, been universally admitted, that these words comprehend every species of commercial intercourse between the United States and foreign nations. . . .

If this be the admitted meaning of the word, in its application to foreign nations, it must carry the same meaning throughout the sentence, and remain a unit, unless there be some plain intelligible cause which alters it. The subject to which the power is next applied, is to commerce, "among the several states." The word "among" means intermingled with. A thing which is among others, is intermingled with them. Commerce among the states, cannot stop at the external boundary line of each state, but may be introduced into the interior. It is not intended to say, that these words comprehend that commerce, which is completely internal, which is carried on between man and man in a state, or between different parts of the same state, and which does extend to or affect other states. Such a power would be inconvenient, and is certainly unnecessary. Comprehensive as the word "among" is, it may very properly be restricted to that commerce which concerns more states than one. . . . The genius and character of the whole government seem to be, that its action is to be applied to all the external concerns of the nation, and to those internal concerns which affect the states generally; but not to those which are completely within a particular state, which do not affect other states, and with which it is not necessary to interfere, for the purpose of executing some of the general powers of the government. The completely internal commerce of a state, then, may be considered as reserved for the state itself.

But in regulating commerce with foreign nations, the power of congress does not stop at the jurisdictional lines of the several states. . . . If congress has the power to regulate it, that power must be exercised whenever the subject exists. If it exists within the states, if a foreign voyage may commence or terminate at a port within a state, then the power of congress may be exercised within a state.

This principle is, if possible, still more clear, when applied to commerce "among the several states." They either join each other, in which case they are separated by a mathematical line, or they are remote from each other, in which case other states lie between them. What is commerce "among" them; and how is it to be conducted? Can a trading expedition between two adjoining states, commence and terminate outside of each? And if the trading intercourse be between two states remote from each other, must it not commence in one, terminate in the other, and probably pass through a third? . . . The power of congress, then, whatever it may be, must be exercised within the territorial jurisdiction of the several states. . . .

We are now arrived at the inquiry—what is the power? It is the power to regulate; that is, to prescribe the rule by which commerce is to be governed. This power, like all others vested in congress, is complete in itself, may be exercised to its utmost extent, and acknowledges no limitations, other than are prescribed in the constitution. If, as has always been understood, the sovereignty of congress, though limited to specified objects, is plenary as to those objects, the power over commerce with foreign nations, and among the several states, is vested in congress as absolutely as it would be in a single government, having in its constitution the same restrictions on the exercise of the power as are found in the constitution of the United States. The wisdom and the discretion of congress, their identity with the people, and the influence which their constituents possess at elections, are, in this, as in many other instances, as that, for example, of declaring war, the sole restraints on which they have relied, to secure them from its abuse. They are the restraints on which the people must often rely solely, in all representative governments.

But it has been urged, with great earnestness, that although the power of congress to regulate commerce with foreign nations, and among the several states, be co-extensive with the subject itself, and have no other limits than are prescribed in the constitution, yet the states may severally exercise the same power, within their respective jurisdictions.

The grant of the power to lay and collect taxes is, like the power to regulate commerce, made in general terms, and has never been understood to interfere with the exercise of the same power by the states; and hence has been drawn an argument which has been applied to the question under consideration. But the two grants are not, it is conceived, similar in their terms or their nature. Although many of the powers formerly exercised by the states, are transferred to the government of the Union, yet the state governments remain, and constitute a most important part of our system. The power of taxation is indispensable to their existence, and is a power which, in its own nature, is capable of residing in, and being exercised by, different authorities, at the same time. We are accustomed to see it placed, for different purposes, in different hands. Taxation is the simple operation of taking small portions from a perpetually accumulating mass, susceptible of almost infinite division; and a power in one to take what is necessary for certain purposes, is not, in its nature, incompatible with a power in another to take what is necessary for other purposes. Congress is authorized to lay and collect taxes, &c., to pay the debts, and provide for the common defense and general welfare of the United States. This does not interfere with the power of the states to tax for the support of their own governments; nor is the exercise of that power by the states, an exercise of any portion of the power that is granted to the United States. In imposing taxes for state purposes, they are not doing what congress is empowered to do. Congress is not empowered to tax for those purposes which are within the exclusive province of the states. When, then, each government exercises the power of taxation, neither is exercising the power of the other. But when a state proceeds to regulate commerce with foreign nations, or among the several states, it is exercising the very power that is granted to congress, and is doing the very thing which congress is authorized to do. There is no analogy, then, between the power of taxation and the power of regulating commerce.

In discussing the question, whether this power is still in the states, in the case under consideration, we may dismiss from it the inquiry, whether it is surrendered by the mere grant to congress, or is retained until congress shall exercise the power. We may dismiss that inquiry, because it has been exercised, and the regulations which congress deemed it proper to make, are now in full operation. The sole question is, can a state regulate commerce with foreign nations and among the states, while congress is regulating it?

. . . The inspection laws are said to be regulations of commerce and are certainly recognised in the constitution, as being passed in the exercise of a power remaining with the states. That inspection laws may have a remote and considerable influence on commerce, will not be denied: but that a power to regulate commerce is the source from which the right to pass them is derived cannot be admitted. The object of inspection laws, is to improve the quality of articles produced by the labor of a country: to do them for exportation; or, it may be, for domestic use. They act upon the subject, before it becomes an article of foreign commerce, or of commerce among the states, and prepare it for that purpose. They form a portion of that immense mass of legislation, which embraces everything within the territory of a state, not surrendered to the general government; all which can be most advantageously exercised by the states themselves. Inspection laws, quarantine laws, health laws of every description, as well as laws for regulating the internal commerce of a state, and those which respect turnpike-roads, ferries, &c., are component parts of this mass.

No direct general power over these objects is granted to congress; and, consequently, they remain subject to state legislation. If the legislative power of the Union can reach them, it must be for national purposes; it must be, where the power is expressly given for a special purpose, or is clearly incidental to some power which is expressly given. It is obvious, that the government of the Union, in the exercise of its express powers, that, for example, of regulating commerce with foreign nations and among the states, may use means that may also be employed by a state, in the exercise of its acknowledged powers; that, for example, of regulating commerce within the state. . . .

In our complex system, presenting the rare and difficult scheme of one general government, whose action extends over the whole, but which possesses only certain enumerated powers; and of numerous state governments, which retain and exercise all powers not delegated to the Union, contests respecting power must arise. Were it even otherwise, the measures taken by the respective governments to execute their acknowledged powers, would often be of the same description, and might, sometimes, interfere. This, however, does not prove that the one is exercising, or has a right to exercise, the powers of the other. . . .

Since, however, in exercising the power of regulating their own purely internal affairs, whether of trading or police, the states may sometimes enact laws, the validity of which depends on their interfering with, and being contrary to, an act of congress passed in pursuance of the constitution, the court will enter upon the inquiry, whether the laws of New York, as expounded by the highest tribunal of that state, have in their application to this case, come into collision with an act of congress and deprived a citizen of a right to which that act entitles him. Should this collision exist, it will be immaterial, whether those laws were passed in virtue of a concurrent power "to regulate commerce with foreign nations and among the several states" or in virtue of a power to regulate their domestic trade and police. In one case and the other, the acts of New York must yield to the law of congress; and the decision sustaining the privilege they confer, against a right given by a law of the Union, must be erroneous. This opinion has been frequently expressed in this court, and is founded, as well on the nature of the government, as on the words of the constitution. In argument, however, it has been contended, that if a law passed by a state, in the exercise of its acknowledged sovereignty, comes into conflict with a law passed by congress in pursuance of the constitution, they affect the subject, and each other, like equal opposing powers. But the framers of our constitution foresaw this state of things, and provided for it, by developing the supremacy not only of itself, but of the laws made in pursuance of it. The nullity of any act, inconsistent with the constitution is produced by the declaration, that the constitution is the supreme law. The appropriate application of that part of the clause which confers the same supremacy on laws and treaties, is to such acts of the state legislatures do not transcend their powers, by though enacted in the execution of acknowledged state powers, interfere with, or are contrary to the laws of congress, made in pursuance of the constitution, or some treaty made under the authority of the United

States. In every such case the acts of congress, or the treaty, is supreme; and the law of the state, though enacted in the exercise of powers not controverted, must yield to it. . . .

But all inquiry into this subject seems to the court to be put completely at rest, by the act already mentioned, entitled, "an act for the enrolling and licensing of steamboats." This act authorizes a steam boat employed, or intended to be employed, only in a river or bay of the United States, owned wholly or in part by an alien, resident within the United States, to be enrolled and licensed as if the same belonged to a citizen of the United States. This act demonstrates the opinion of congress, that steamboats may be enrolled and licensed, in common with vessels using sails. They are, of course, entitled to the same privileges, and can no more be restrained from navigating waters, and entering ports which are free to such vessels, than if they were wafted on their voyage by the winds, instead of being propelled by the agency of fire. The one element may be as legitimately used as the other, for every commercial purpose authorized by the laws of the Union; and the act of a state inhibiting the use of either, to any vessel having a license under the act of congress, comes, we think, in direct collision with that act.

MR. JUSTICE JOHNSON, concurring.

The judgment entered by the court in this cause, has my entire approbation; but having adopted my conclusions on views of the subject materially different from those of my brethren, I feel it incumbent on me to exhibit those views. . . .

In attempts to construe the constitution, I have never found much benefit resulting from the inquiry, whether the whole; or any part of it, is to be construed strictly or liberally. The simple, classical, precise, yet comprehensive language in which it is couched, leaves, at most, but very little latitude for construction; and when its intent and meaning are discovered, nothing remains but to execute the will of those who made it, in the best manner to effect the purposes intended. The great and paramount purpose was, to unite this mass of wealth and power, for the protection of the humblest individual; his rights, civil and political, his interests and prosperity, are the sole end; the rest are nothing but the means. . . .

The history of the times will . . . sustain the opinion, that the grant of power over commerce, if intended to be commensurate with the evils existing, and the purpose of remedying those evils, could be only commensurate with the power of the states over the subject. . . .

. . . But what was that power? The states were, unquestionably, supreme; and each possessed that power over commerce, which is acknowledged to reside in every sovereign state. . . . The power of a sovereign state over commerce, therefore, amounts to nothing more than a power to limit and restrain it at pleasure. And since the power to prescribe the limits to its freedom, necessarily implies the power to determine what shall remain unrestrained, it follows, that the power must be exclusive: it can reside but in one potentate; and hence, the grant of this power carries with it the whole subject, leaving nothing for the state to act upon.

## *United States* v. *E. C. Knight Company*

### 156 U.S. 1, 15 S. Ct. 249, 39 L. Ed. 325 (1895)

By purchasing the stock of four Philadelphia sugar refineries with shares of its own stock, the American Sugar Refining Company acquired control of over 98 percent of the nation's sugar refining business. The federal government charged that this action constituted a violation of the Sherman Antitrust Act, passed by Congress in 1890, which made it illegal to monopolize or restrain—or seek to monopolize or restrain—interstate or foreign commerce through any contact, combination, or conspiracy. The basic issue in this case was thus the interpretation of the statute: Does the acquisition of control over the sugar refining business constitute a monopoly in interstate commerce? But in interpreting the statute, the Court sought to construe it so as to render it constitutional. Thus the Court's construction of the statute depended upon its understanding of the scope of national regulatory authority under the Commerce Clause. *Opinion of the Court: Fuller, Field, Gray, Brewer, Brown, Shiras, White, Peckham. Dissenting opinion: Harlan.*

MR. CHIEF JUSTICE FULLER . . . delivered the opinion of the Court.

The fundamental question is, whether conceding that the existence of a monopoly in manufacture is established by the evidence, that monopoly can be directly suppressed under the act of Congress in the mode attempted by this bill.

It cannot be denied that the power of a State to protect the lives, health, and property of its citizens, and to preserve good order and the public morals, "the power to govern men and things within the limits of its dominion," is a power originally and always belonging to the States, not surrendered by them to the general government, nor directly restrained by the Constitution of the United States, and essentially exclusive. . . . On the other hand, the power of Congress to regulate commerce among the several States is also exclusive. . . . That which belongs to commerce is within the jurisdiction of the United States, but that which does not belong to commerce is within the jurisdiction of the police power of the State. . . .

The argument is that the power to control the manufacture of refined sugar is a monopoly over a necessary of life, to the enjoyment of which by a large part of the population of the United States interstate commerce is indispensable, and that, therefore, the general government in the exercise of the power to regulate commerce may repress such monopoly directly and set aside the instruments which have created it. But this argument cannot be confined to necessaries of life merely, and must include all articles of general consumption. Doubtless the power to control the manufacture of a given thing involves in a certain sense the control of its disposition, but this is a secondary and not the primary sense; and although the exercise of that power may result in bringing the operation of commerce into play, it does not control it, and affects it only incidentally and indirectly. Commerce succeeds to manufacture, and is not a part of it. The power to regulate commerce is the power to prescribe the rule by which commerce shall be governed, and is a power independent of the power to suppress monopoly. But it may operate in repression of monopoly whenever that comes within the rules by which commerce is governed or whenever the transaction is itself a monopoly of commerce.

It is vital that the independence of the commercial power and of the police power, and the delimitation between them, however sometimes perplexing, should always be recognized and observed, for while the one furnishes the strongest bond of union, the other is essential to the preservation of the autonomy of the States as required by our dual form of government; and acknowledged evils, however grave and urgent they may appear to be, had better be borne, than the risk be run, in the effort to suppress them, of more serious consequences by resort to expedients of even doubtful constitutionality.

It will be perceived how far-reaching the proposition is that the power of dealing with a monopoly directly may be exercised by the general government whenever interstate or international commerce may be ultimately affected. The regulation of commerce applies to the subjects of commerce and not to matters of internal police. Contracts to buy, sell, or exchange goods to be transported among the several States, the transportation and its instrumentalities, and articles bought, sold, or exchanged for the purposes of such transit among the States, or put in the way of transit, may be regulated, but this is because they form part of interstate trade or commerce. The fact that an article is manufactured for export to another State does not of itself make it an article of interstate commerce, and the intent of the manufacturer does not determine the time when the article or product passes from the control of the State and belongs to commerce. . . .

Contracts, combinations, or conspiracies to control domestic enterprise in manufacture, agriculture, mining, production in all its forms, or to raise or lower prices or wages, might unquestionably tend to restrain external as well as domestic trade, but the restraint would be an indirect result, however inevitable and whatever its extent, and such result would not necessarily determine the object of the contract, combination, or conspiracy.

. . . Slight reflection will show that if the national power extends to all contracts and combinations in manufacture, agriculture, mining, and other productive industries, whose ultimate result may affect external commerce, comparatively little of business operations and affairs would be left for state control.

It was in the light of well-settled principles that the act of July 2, 1890, was framed. Congress did not attempt thereby to assert the power to deal with monopoly directly as such. . . . What the law struck at was combinations, contracts, and conspiracies to monopolize trade and commerce among the several States or with foreign nations; but the contracts and acts of the defendants related exclusively to the acquisition of the Philadelphia refineries and the business of sugar refining in Pennsylvania, and bore no direct relation to commerce between the States or with foreign nations. The object was manifestly private gain in the manufacture of the commodity, but not through the control of interstate or foreign commerce. It is true that the bill alleged that the products of these refineries were sold and distributed among the several States, and that all the companies were engaged in trade or commerce with the several States and with foreign nations; but this was no more than to say that trade and commerce served manufacture to fulfill its function. . . . It does not follow that an attempt to monopolize, or the actual monopoly of, the manufacture was an attempt, whether executory or consummated, to monopolize commerce, even though, in order to dispose of the product, the instrumentality of commerce was necessarily invoked. There was nothing in the proofs to indicate any intention to put a restraint upon trade or commerce, and the fact, was we have seen, that trade or commerce might be indirectly affected was not enough to entitle complainants to a decree. . . .

*Decree affirmed.*

## *Hammer* v. *Dagenhart*

**247 U.S. 251, 38 S. Ct. 529, 62 L. Ed. 1101 (1918)**

The Federal Child Labor Act of 1916, which was designed to discourage the employment of child labor, prohibited the shipment in interstate commerce of goods produced in factories that employed children under the age of fourteen or permitted children under age sixteen to work either at night or for more than eight hours a day. Dagenhart, whose sons worked in his cotton mill, challenged the act in federal district court. When the district court invalidated the act, the case was appealed to the Supreme Court. *Opinion of the Court: Day, White, Van Devanter, Pitney, McReynolds. Dissenting opinion: Holmes, McKenna, Brandeis, Clarke.*

MR. JUSTICE DAY delivered the opinion of the Court. . . .

The controlling question for decision is: Is it within the authority of Congress in regulating commerce among the States to prohibit the transportation in interstate commerce of manufactured goods, the product of a factory in which, within thirty days prior to their removal therefrom, children under the age of fourteen have been employed or permitted to work, or children between the ages of fourteen and sixteen years have been employed or permitted to work more than eight hours in any day, or more than six days in any week, or after the hour of seven o'clock P.M. or before the hour of 6 o'clock A.M.? . . .

*[Mr. Justice Day then reviewed the Court's previous decisions regarding the use of the Commerce Clause for noncommercial purposes.]*

In each of these instances the use of interstate transportation was necessary to the accomplishment of harmful results. In other words, although the power over interstate transportation was to regulate, that could only be accomplished by prohibiting the use of facilities of interstate commerce to effect the evil intended.

This element is wanting in the present case. The thing intended to be accomplished by this statute is the denial of the facilities of interstate commerce to those manufacturers in the States who employ children within the prohibited ages. The act in its effect does not regulate transportation among the States, but aims to standardize the ages at which children may be employed in mining and manufacturing within the States. The goods shipped are of themselves harmless. The act permits them to be freely shipped after thirty days from the time of their removal from the factory. When offered for shipment, and before transportation begins, the labor of their production is over, and the mere fact that they were intended for interstate commerce transportation does not make their production subject to federal control under the commerce power. . . .

It is further contended that the authority of Congress may be exerted to control interstate commerce in the shipment of child-made goods because of the effects of the circulation of such goods in other States where the evil of this class of labor has been recognized by local legislation, and the right to thus employ child labor has been more rigorously restrained than in the State of production. In other words, that the unfair competition, thus engendered, may be controlled by closing the channels of interstate commerce to manufacturers in those States where the local laws do not meet what Congress deems to be the more just standard of other States.

There is no power vested in Congress to require the States to exercise their police power so as to prevent possible unfair competition. Many causes may cooperate to give one State, by reason of local laws or conditions, an economic advantage over others. The Commerce Clause was not intended to give to Congress a general authority to equalize such conditions. . . .

A statute must be judged by its natural and reasonable effect. . . . The control by Congress over interstate commerce cannot authorize the exercise of authority not entrusted to it by the Constitution. . . . The maintenance of the authority of the States over matters purely local is as essential to the preservation of our institutions as is the conservation of the supremacy of the federal power in all matters entrusted to the Nation by the Federal Constitution. . . .

. . . To sustain this statute would not be in our judgment a recognition of the lawful exertion of congressional authority over interstate commerce, but would sanction an invasion by the federal power of the control of a matter purely local in its character, and over which no authority has been delegated to Congress in conferring the power to regulate commerce among the States.

In our view the necessary effect of this act is, by means of a prohibition against the movement in interstate commerce of ordinary commercial commodities, to regulate the hours of labor of children in factories and mines within the States, a purely state authority. Thus the act in a twofold sense is repugnant to the Constitution. It not only transcends the authority delegated to Congress over commerce but also exerts a power as to a purely local matter to which the federal authority does not extend. The far reaching result of upholding the act cannot be more plainly indicated than by pointing out that if Congress can thus regulate matters entrusted to local authority by prohibition of the movement of commodities in interstate commerce, all freedom of commerce will be at an end, and the power of the States over local matters may be eliminated, and thus our system of government be practically destroyed.

*Affirmed.*

MR. JUSTICE HOLMES, dissenting.

The first step in my argument is to make plain what no one is likely to dispute—that the statute in question is within the power expressly given to Congress if considered only as to its immediate effects and that if invalid it is so only upon some collateral ground. The statute confines itself to prohibiting the carriage of certain goods in interstate or foreign commerce. Congress is given power to regulate such commerce in unqualified terms. . . .

The question then is narrowed to whether the exercise of its otherwise constitutional power by Congress can be pronounced unconstitutional because of its possible reaction upon the conduct of the States in a matter upon which I have admitted that they are free from direct control. I should have thought that that matter had been disposed of so fully as to leave no room for doubt. I should have thought that the most conspicuous decisions of this Court had made it clear that the power to regulate commerce and other constitutional powers could not be cut down or qualified by the fact that it might interfere with the carrying out of the domestic policy of any State. . . .

The notion that prohibition is any less prohibition when applied to things now thought evil I do not understand. But if there is any matter upon which civilized countries have agreed—far more unanimously than they have with regard to intoxicants and some other matters over which this country is now emotionally aroused—it is the evil of premature and excessive child labor. I should have thought that if we were to introduce our own moral conceptions where in my opinion they do not belong, this was preeminently a case for upholding the exercise of all its powers by the United States.

But I had thought that the propriety of the exercise of a power admitted to exist in some cases was for the consideration of Congress alone and that this Court always had disavowed the right to intrude its judgment upon questions of policy or morals. . . .

The act does not meddle with anything belonging to the States. They may regulate their internal affairs and their domestic commerce as they like. But when they seek to send their products across the state line they are no longer within their rights. If there were no Constitution and no Congress their power to cross the line would depend upon their neighbors. Under the Constitution such commerce belongs not to the States but to Congress to regulate. It may carry out its views of public policy whatever indirect effect they may have upon the activities of the States. . . . The national welfare as understood by Congress may require a different attitude within its sphere from that of some self-seeking State. It seems to me entirely constitutional for Congress to enforce its understanding by all the means at its command.

## *National Labor Relations Board* v. *Jones & Laughlin Steel Corporation*

**301 U.S. 1; 57 S. Ct. 615; 81 L. Ed. 893 (1937)**

The National Labor Relations Act (also called the Wagner Act) was designed to protect the rights of workers to form unions and to bargain collectively. The act prohibited a variety of unfair labor practices and authorized the National Labor Relations Board to issue cease-and-desist orders to employers who engaged in such practices. Jones & Laughlin, one of the nation's largest steel producers, violated the act by firing ten workers for engaging in union activities. The company then refused to comply with an NLRB order to reinstate the workers. After a court of appeals declined to enforce the board's order, the Supreme Court granted certiorari.

This decision—the so-called switch in time that saved nine—was announced amid intense controversy over the Supreme Court's rulings. Following his landslide reelection in 1936, President Franklin Roosevelt, frustrated by adverse Supreme Court rulings and sure that the nation supported his program of economic reform, sent to Congress a proposal to expand the number of Supreme Court justices. By upholding the Wagner Act, the Court largely defused the controversy and ensured the defeat of the so-called court-packing scheme. Shortly thereafter, President Roosevelt had the opportunity to name his first justice to the Court, and his appointment of eight justices by 1941 produced unanimous support for the conception of national power over the economy enunciated in this case. *Opinion of the Court: Hughes, Brandeis, Stone, Roberts, Cardozo. Dissenting opinion: McReynolds, Van Devanter, Sutherland, Butler.*

MR. CHIEF JUSTICE HUGHES delivered the opinion of the Court. . . .

*First. The scope of the Act.*—The Act is challenged in its entirety as an attempt to regulate all industry, thus invading the reserved powers of the States over their local concerns. It is asserted that the references in the Act to interstate and foreign commerce are colorable at best; that the Act is not a true regulation of such commerce or of matters which directly affect it but on the contrary has the fundamental object of placing under the compulsory supervision of the federal government all industrial labor relations within the nation. . . .

. . . The grant of authority to the Board does not purport to extend to the relationship between all industrial employees and employers. Its terms do not impose collective bargaining upon all industry regardless of effects upon interstate or foreign commerce. It purports to reach only what may be deemed to burden or obstruct that commerce and, thus qualified, it must be construed as contemplating the exercise of control within constitutional bounds. It is a familiar principle that acts which directly burden or obstruct interstate or foreign commerce, or its free flow, are within the reach of the congressional power. Acts having that effect are not rendered immune because they grow out of labor disputes. . . . It is the effect upon commerce, not the source of the injury, which is the criterion. . . . Whether or not particular action does affect commerce in such a close and intimate fashion as to be subject to federal control, and hence to lie within the authority conferred upon the Board, is left by the statute to be determined as individual cases arise. . . .

*Second. The unfair practices in question.* . . . In its present application, the statute goes no further than to safeguard the right of employees to self-organization and to select representatives of their own choosing for collective bargaining or other mutual protection without restraint or coercion by their employer.

That is a fundamental right. Employees have as clear a right to organize and select their representatives for lawful purposes as the respondent has to organize its business and select its own officers and agents. Discrimination and coercion to prevent the free exercise of the right of employees to self-organization and representation is a proper subject for condemnation by competent legislative authority. . . . Hence the prohibition by Congress of interference with the selection of representatives for the purpose of negotiation and conference between employers and employees, "instead of being an invasion of the constitutional right of either was based on the recognition of the rights of both." *Texas & N.O.R.C.* v. *Railway Clerks* [1930]. . . .

*Third. The application of the Act to employees engaged in production.—The principle involved.*—Respondent says that whatever may be said of employees engaged in interstate commerce, the industrial relations and activities in the manufacturing department of respondent's enterprise are not subject to federal regulation. The argument rests upon the proposition that manufacturing in itself is not commerce. . . .

. . . The congressional authority to protect interstate commerce from burdens and obstructions is not limited to transactions which can be deemed to be an essential part of a "flow" of interstate or foreign commerce. Although activities may be intrastate in character when separately considered if they have such a close and substantial relation to interstate commerce that their control is essential or appropriate to protect that commerce from burdens and obstructions, Congress cannot be denied the power to exercise that control. . . . Undoubtedly the scope of this power must be considered in the light of our dual system of government and may not be extended so as to embrace effects upon interstate commerce so indirect and remote that to embrace them, in view of our complex society, would effectually obliterate the distinction between what is national and what is local and create a completely centralized government. . . . The question is necessarily one of degree. . . .

It is thus apparent that the fact that the employees here concerned were engaged in production is not determinative. The question remains as to the effect upon interstate commerce of the labor practice involved. . . .

*Fourth. Effects of the unfair labor practice in respondent's enterprise.*—Giving full weight to respondent's contention with respect to a break in the complete continuity of the "stream of commerce" by reason of respondent's manufacturing operations, the fact remains that the stoppage of those operations by industrial strife would have a most serious effect upon interstate commerce. In view of respondent's far-flung activities, it is idle to say that the effect would be indirect or remote. It is obvious that it would be immediate and might be catastrophic. We are asked to shut our eyes to the plainest facts of our national life and to deal with the question of direct and indirect effects in an intellectual vacuum. Because there may be but indirect and remote effects upon interstate commerce in connection with a host of local enterprises throughout the country, it does not follow that other industrial activities do not have such a close and intimate relation to interstate commerce as to make the presence of industrial strife a matter of the most urgent national concern. When industries organize themselves on a national scale, making their relation to interstate commerce the dominant factor in their activities, how can it be maintained that their industrial labor relations constitute a forbidden field into which Congress may not enter when it is necessary to protect interstate commerce from the paralyzing consequences of industrial war? We have often said that interstate commerce itself is a practical conception. It is equally true that interferences with that commerce must be appraised by a judgment that does not ignore actual experience.

Experience has abundantly demonstrated that the recognition of the right of employees to self-organization and to have representatives of their own choosing for the purpose of collective bargaining is often an essential condition of industrial peace. Refusal to confer and negotiate has been one of the most prolific causes of strife. This is such an outstanding fact in the history of labor disturbances that it is a proper subject of judicial notice and requires no citation of instances. . . .

Our conclusion is that the order of the Board was within it competency and that the Act is valid as here applied. The judgment of the Circuit Court of Appeals is reversed and the cause is remanded for further proceedings in conformity with this opinion.

*Reversed.*

MR. JUSTICE MCREYNOLDS, dissenting.

The Court, as we think, departs from well-established principles followed in *Schechter Corp.* v. *United States* [1935] and *Carter* v. *Carter Coal Co* [1936]. Six district courts, on the authority of *Schechter*'s and *Carter*'s cases, have held that the Board has no authority to regulate relations between employers and employees engaged in local production. No decision or judicial opinion to the contrary has been cited, and we find none. Every consideration brought forward to uphold the Act before us was applicable to support the acts held unconstitutional in causes decided within two years. . . .

An effect on interstate commerce by the discharge of employees shown here, would be indirect and remote in the highest degree as consideration of the facts will show. [*In Jones & Laughlin*] ten men out of ten thousand were discharged: in the other cases only a few. The immediate effect in the factory may be to create discontent among all those employed and a strike may follow, which, in turn, may result in reducing production, which ultimately may reduce the volume of goods moving in interstate commerce. By this chain of indirect and progressively remote events we finally reach the evil with which it is said the legislation under consideration undertakes to deal. A more remote and indirect interference with interstate commerce or a more definite invasion of the powers reserved to the states is difficult, if not impossible, to imagine.

## *Wickard* v. *Filburn*

**317 U.S. 111, 63 S. Ct. 82, 87 L. Ed. 122 (1942)**

The Agricultural Adjustment Act of 1938 imposed limitations on the acreage individual farmers could devote to wheat production. In setting such limits, Congress sought to control the volume of wheat moving in interstate and foreign commerce, in order to avoid surpluses and shortages and thereby prevent abnormally low or high wheat prices. Filburn, who owned a small farm in Ohio, exceeded his allotment of 11.1 acres for the 1941 wheat crop. He produced 23 acres of wheat, intending to keep the excess for use on his own farm. Penalized $117.11 for growing the excess wheat, he refused to pay and brought action to prevent collection. When the district court granted an injunction on nonconstitutional grounds, the government appealed. *Opinion of the Court: Jackson, Stone, Roberts, Black, Reed, Frankfurter, Douglas, Murphy, Byrnes.*

MR. JUSTICE JACKSON delivered the opinion of the Court.

It is urged that under the Commerce Clause of the Constitution, Article I, § 8, clause 3, Congress does not possess the power it has in this instance sought to exercise. The question would merit little consideration since our decision in *United States* v. *Darby* [1941] sustaining the federal power to regulate production of goods for commerce, except for the fact that this Act extends federal regulation to production not intended in any part for commerce but wholly for consumption on the farm. . . .

Appellee says that this is a regulation of production and consumption of wheat. Such activities are, he urges, beyond the reach of Congressional power under the Commerce Clause, since they are local in character, and their effects upon interstate commerce are at most "indirect." In answer the Government argues that the statute regulates neither production nor consumption, but only marketing; and, in the alternative, that if the Act does go beyond the regulation of marketing it is sustainable as a "necessary and proper" implementation of the power of Congress over interstate commerce. . . .

Whether the subject of the regulation in question was "production," "consumption," or "marketing" is . . . not material for purposes for deciding the question of federal power before us. That an activity is of local character may help in a doubtful case to determine whether Congress intended to reach it. . . . But even if appellee's activity be local and though it may not be regarded as commerce, it may still, whatever its nature, be reached by Congress if it exerts a substantial economic effect on interstate commerce, and this irrespective of whether such effect is what might at some earlier time have been defined as "direct" or "indirect."

The effect of consumption of home-grown wheat on interstate commerce is due to the fact that it constitutes the most variable factor in the disappearance of the wheat crop. Consumption on the farm where grown appears to vary in an amount greater than 20 percent of average production. The total amount of wheat consumed as food varies but relatively little, and use as seed is relatively constant.

The maintenance by government regulation of a price for wheat undoubtedly can be accomplished as effectively by sustaining or increasing the demand as by limiting the supply. The effect of the statute before us is to restrict the amount which may be produced for market and the extent as well to which one may forestall resort to the market by producing to meet his own needs. That appellee's own contribution to the demand for wheat may be trivial by itself is not enough to remove him from the scope of federal regulation where, as here, his contribution, taken together with that of many others similarly situated, is far from trivial. . . .

It is well established by decisions of this Court that the power to regulate commerce includes the power to regulate the prices at which commodities in that commerce are dealt in and practices affecting such prices. One of the primary purposes of the Act in question was to increase the market price of wheat, and to that end to limit the volume thereof that could affect the market. It can hardly be denied that a factor of such volume and variability as home-consumed wheat would have a substantial influence on price and market conditions. . . . This record leaves us in no doubt that Congress may properly have considered that wheat consumed on the farm where grown, if wholly outside the scheme of regulation, would have a substantial effect in defeating and obstructing its purpose to stimulate trade therein at increased prices.

It is said, however, that this Act, forcing some farmers into the market to buy what they could provide for themselves, is an unfair promotion of the markets and prices of specializing wheat growers. It is of the essence of regulation that it lays a restraining hand on the self-interest of the regulated and that advantages from the regulation commonly fall to others. The conflicts of economic interest between the regulated and those who advantage by it are wisely left under our system to resolution by the Congress under its more flexible and responsible legislative process. Such conflicts rarely lend themselves to judicial determination. And with the wisdom, workability, or fairness, of the plan of regulation we have nothing to do. . . .

*Reversed.*

## *Heart of Atlanta Motel* v. *United States*

**379 U.S. 241, 85 S. Ct. 348, 13 L. Ed. 2d 258 (1964)**

The Heart of Atlanta Motel, located near major highways and interstates, sought patronage from outside Georgia through national advertising campaigns; and approximately 75 percent of its patrons were from out of state. Prior to passage of the Civil Rights Act of 1964, which outlawed discrimination in public accommodations, the motel refused to rent rooms to blacks. It indicated that it intended to continue this policy and sought a declaratory judgment attacking the validity of Title II (the public accommodations section). A three-judge district court sustained the challenged legislation, and the case was appealed to the Supreme Court. In a companion case argued at the same time—*Katzenbach* v. *McClung* (379 U.S. 294)—the Court upheld application of the act to a family-owned restaurant serving a primarily local clientele. *Opinion of the Court: Clark, Warren, Black, Douglas, Harlan, Brennan, Stewart, White, Goldberg. Concurring opinions: Black; Douglas.*

MR. JUSTICE CLARK delivered the opinion of the Court. . . .

It is admitted that the operation of the motel brings it within the provisions of § 201 (a) of the Act and that appellant refused to provide lodging for transient Negroes because of their race or color and that it intends to continue that policy unless restrained.

The sole question posed is, therefore, the constitutionality of the Civil Rights Act of 1964 as applied to these facts. The legislative history of the Act indicates that Congress based the Act on § 5 and the Equal Protection Clause of the Fourteenth Amendment as well as its power to regulate interstate commerce under Art. I. § 8, cl. 3, of the Constitution. . . .

While the act as adopted carried no congressional findings the records of its passage through each house is replete with evidence of the burdens that discrimination by race or color places upon interstate commerce. . . . This testimony included the fact that our people have become increasingly mobile with millions of people of all races traveling from State to State; that Negroes in particular have been the subject of discrimination in transient accommodations, having to travel great distances to secure the same; that often they have been unable to obtain accommodations and have had to call upon friends to put them up overnight. . . ; and that these conditions had become so acute as to require the listing of available lodging for Negroes in a special guidebook. . . . This testimony indicated a qualitative as well as quantitative effect on interstate travel by Negroes. The former was the obvious impairment of the Negro traveler's pleasure and convenience that resulted when he continually was uncertain of finding lodging. As for the latter, there was evidence that this uncertainty stemming from racial discrimination had the effect of discouraging travel on the part of a substantial portion of the Negro community. . . . The voluminous testimony presents overwhelming evidence that discrimination by hotels and motels impedes interstate travel.

*[Mr. Justice Clark then reviewed the Court's earlier decisions regarding the use of the Commerce Clause for noncommercial purposes.]*

That Congress was legislating against moral wrongs in many of these areas rendered its enactments no less valid. In framing Title II of this Act Congress was also dealing with what it considered a moral problem. But that fact does not detract from the overwhelming evidence of the disruptive effect that racial discrimination has had on commercial intercourse. It was this burden which empowered Congress to enact appropriate legislation and, given this basis for the exercise of its power, Congress was not restricted by the fact that the particular obstruction to interstate commerce with which it was dealing was also deemed a moral and social wrong.

It is said that the operation of the motel here is of a purely local character. But, assuming this to be true, "if it is interstate commerce that feels the pinch, it does not matter how local the operation which applies the squeeze." *United States* v. *Women's Sportswear Mfrs* [1949]. . . .

Thus the power of Congress to promote interstate commerce also includes the power to regulate the local incidents thereof, including local activities in both the States of origin and destination, which might have a substantial and harmful effect upon that commerce. One need only examine the evidence which we have discussed above to see that Congress may—as it has—prohibit racial discrimination by motels serving travelers, however "local" their operations may appear. . . .

*Affirmed.*

MR. JUSTICE DOUGLAS, concurring. . . .

Though I join the Court's opinion, I am somewhat reluctant here . . . to rest solely on the Commerce Clause. My reluctance is not due to any conviction that Congress lacks power to regulate commerce in the interests of human rights. It is rather my belief that the right of people to be free of state action that discriminates against them because of race, like the "right of persons to move freely from State to State" (*Edwards* v. *California* [1941]) "occupies a more protected position in our constitutional system than does the movement of cattle, fruit, steel and coal across state lines." *Ibid.* . . .

Hence I would prefer to rest on the assertation of legislative power contained in § 5 of the Fourteenth Amendment which states: "The Congress shall have power to enforce, by appropriate legislation, the provisions of this article"—a power which the Court concedes was exercised at least in part in this Act.

A decision based on the Fourteenth Amendment would have a more settling effect, making unnecessary litigation over whether a particular restaurant or inn is within the commerce definitions of the Act or whether a particular customer is an interstate traveler. Under my construction, the Act would apply to all customers in all the enumerated places of public accommodation. And that construction would put an end to all obstructionist strategies and finally close one door on a bitter chapter in American history.

# *United States* v. *Lopez*

**511 U.S. 1029, 131 L. Ed. 2d 626, 115 S. Ct. 1624 (1995)**

In 1990 Congress enacted the Gun-Free School Zones Act. This Act, referred to in the justices' opinions as section 922(q), made it a federal offense "for any individual knowingly to possess a firearm at a place that the individual knows, or has reasonable cause to believe, is a school zone." Alfonso Lopez, then a senior at Edison High School in San Antonio, Texas, was arrested and charged under the Act when he brought to school a concealed .38 caliber handgun and five bullets. He was convicted in Federal District Court, after the Court denied his claim that the statute under which he was charged exceeded Congress's authority under the Commerce Clause. On appeal, the Court of Appeals reversed, holding that section 922(q) was invalid in the absence of congressional findings and legislative history demonstrating the connection between commerce and the evil addressed by the statue. The Supreme Court then granted certiorari. *Opinion of the Court: Rehnquist, O'Connor, Scalia, Kennedy, Thomas. Concurring opinions: Kennedy, O'Connor; Thomas. Dissenting opinions: Stevens; Souter; Breyer, Stevens, Souter, Ginsburg.*

Chief Justice Rehnquist delivered the opinion of the Court.

We start with first principles. The Constitution creates a Federal Government of enumerated powers. See U.S. Const., Art. I, § 8. As James Madison wrote, "[t]he powers delegated by the proposed Constitution to the federal government are few and defined. Those which are to remain in the State governments are numerous and indefinite." *The Federalist* No. 45.

The Constitution delegates to Congress the power "[t]o regulate Commerce with foreign Nations, and among the several States, and with the Indian Tribes." The Court, through Chief Justice Marshall, first defined the nature of Congress's commerce power in *Gibbons* v. *Ogden* (1824). The *Gibbons* Court acknowledged that limitations on the commerce power are inherent in the very language of the Commerce Clause.

> It is not intended to say that these words comprehend that commerce, which is completely internal, which is carried on between man and man in a State, or between different parts of the same State, and which does not extend to or affect other States. Such a power would be inconvenient, and is certainly unnecessary.
>
> Comprehensive as the word "among" is it may very properly be restricted to that commerce which concerns more States than one. . . . The enumeration presupposes something not enumerated; and that something, if we regard the language or the subject of the sentence, must be the exclusively internal commerce of a State.

*[Chief Justice Rehnquist then reviewed the development of the Supreme Court's interpretation of the Commerce Clause, particularly the Court's shift in interpretation in* National Labor Relations Board *v.* Jones & Loughlin Steel *(1937),* United States *v.* Darby *(1941), and* Wickard *v.* Filburn *(1942).]*

*Jones & Laughlin Steel, Darby,* and *Wickard* ushered in an era of Commerce Clause jurisprudence that greatly expanded the previously defined authority of Congress under that Clause. In part, this was a recognition of the great changes that had occurred in the way business was carried on in this country. Enterprises that had once been local or at most regional in nature had become national in scope. But the doctrinal change also reflected a view that earlier Commerce Clause cases artificially had constrained the authority of Congress to regulate interstate commerce.

But even these modern-era precedents which have expanded congressional power under the Commerce Clause confirm that this power is subject to outer limits. In *Jones & Laughlin Steel,* the Court warned that the scope of the interstate commerce power "must be considered in the light of our dual system of government and may not be extended so as to embrace effects upon interstate commerce so indirect and remote that to embrace them, in view of our complex society, would effectually obliterate the distinction between what is national and what is local and create a completely centralized government." See also *Darby* (Congress may regulate intrastate activity that has a "substantial effect" on interstate commerce); *Wickard* (Congress may regulate activity that "exerts a substantial economic effect on interstate commerce"). Since that time, the Court has heeded that warning and undertaken to decide whether a rational basis existed for concluding that a regulated activity sufficiently affected interstate commerce.

Consistent with this structure, we have identified three broad categories of activity that Congress may regulate under its commerce power. First, Congress may regulate the use of the channels of interstate commerce. Second, Congress is empowered to regulate and protect the instrumentalities of interstate commerce, or persons or things in interstate commerce, even though the threat may come only from intrastate activities.

Finally, Congress's commerce authority includes the power to regulate those activities having a substantial relation to interstate commerce, those activities that substantially affect interstate commerce.

We now turn to consider the power of Congress, in the light of this framework, to enact § 922(q). The first two categories of authority may be quickly disposed of: § 922(q) is not a regulation of the use of the channels of interstate commerce, nor is it an attempt to prohibit the interstate transportation of a commodity through the channels of commerce; nor can § 922(q) be justified as a regulation by which Congress has sought to protect an instrumentality of interstate commerce or a thing in interstate commerce. Thus, if § 922(q) is to be sustained, it must be under the third category as a regulation of an activity that substantially affects interstate commerce.

First, we have upheld a wide variety of Congressional Acts regulating intrastate economic activity where we have concluded that the activity substantially affected interstate commerce. Examples include the regulation of intrastate coal mining, intrastate extortionate credit transactions, restaurants utilizing substantial interstate supplies, inns and hotels catering to interstate guests, and production and consumption of home-grown wheat. These examples are by no means exhaustive, but the pattern is clear. Where economic activity substantially affects interstate commerce, legislation regulating that activity will be sustained. . . .

Section 922(q) is a criminal statute that by its terms has nothing to do with "commerce" or any sort of economic enterprise, however broadly one might define those terms. Section 922(q) is not an essential part of a larger regulation of economic activity, in which the regulatory scheme could be undercut unless the intrastate activity were regulated. It cannot, therefore, be sustained under our cases upholding regulations of activities that arise out of or are connected with a commercial transaction, which viewed in the aggregate, substantially affects interstate commerce.

The Government's essential contention, *in fine,* is that we may determine here that § 922(q) is valid because possession of a firearm in a local school zone does indeed substantially affect interstate commerce. The Government argues that possession of a firearm in a school zone may result in violent crime and that violent crime can be expected to affect the functioning of the national economy in two ways. First, the costs of violent crime are substantial, and, through the mechanism of insurance, those costs are spread throughout the population. Second, violent crime reduces the willingness of individuals to travel to areas within the country that are perceived to be unsafe. The Government also argues that the presence of guns in schools poses a substantial threat to the educational process by threatening the learning environment. A handicapped educational process, in turn, will result in a less productive citizenry. That, in turn, will result in a less productive citizenry. That, in turn, would have an adverse effect on the Nation's economic well-being. As a result, the Government argues that Congress could rationally have concluded that § 922(q) substantially affects interstate commerce.

We pause to consider the implications of the Government's arguments. The Government admits, under its "costs of crime" reasoning, that Congress could regulate not only all violent crime, but all activities that might lead to violent crime, regardless of how tenuously they relate to interstate commerce. Similarly, under the Government's "national productivity" reasoning, Congress could regulate any activity that it found was related to the economic productivity of individual citizens: family law (including marriage, divorce, and child custody), for example. Under the theories that the Government presents in support of § 922(q), it is difficult to perceive any limitation on federal power, even in areas such as criminal law enforcement or education where States historically have been sovereign. Thus, if we were to accept the Government's arguments, we are hard-pressed to posit any activity by an individual that Congress is without power to regulate. . . .

JUSTICE BREYER rejects our reading of precedent and argues that "Congress . . . could rationally conclude that schools fall on the commercial side of the line." Again JUSTICE BREYER'S rationale lacks any real limits because, depending on the level of generality, any activity can be looked upon as commercial. Under the dissent's rationale, Congress could just as easily look at child rearing as "fall[ing] on the commercial side of the line" because it provides a "valuable service—namely, to equip [children] with the skills they need to survive in life and, more specifically, in the workplace." We do not doubt that Congress has authority under the Commerce Clause to regulate numerous commercial activities that substantially affect interstate commerce and also affect the educational process. That authority, though broad, does not include the authority to regulate each and every aspect of local schools. . . .

To uphold the Government's contentions here, we would have to pile inference upon inference in a manner what would bid fair to convert congressional authority under the Commerce Clause to a general police power of the sort retained by the States. Admittedly, some of our prior cases have taken long steps down that road, giving great deference to congressional action. The broad language in these opinions has suggested the possibility of additional expansion, but we decline here to proceed any further. To do so would require us to conclude that the Constitution's enumeration of powers does not presuppose something not enumerated, cf. *Gibbons* v. *Ogden,* and that there never will be a distinction between what is truly national and what is truly local, cf. *Jones & Laughlin Steel.* This we are unwilling to do. For the foregoing reasons the judgment of the Court of Appeals is *Affirmed.*

JUSTICE THOMAS, concurring.

The Court today properly concludes that the Commerce Clause does not grant Congress the authority to prohibit gun possession within 1,000 feet of a school, as it attempted to do in the Gun-Free School Zones Act of 1990. Although I join the majority, I write separately to observe that our case law has drifted far from the original understanding of the Commerce Clause. In a future case, we ought to temper our Commerce Clause jurisprudence in a manner that both makes sense of our more recent case law and is more faithful to the original understanding of that Clause.

We have said that Congress may regulate not only "Commerce . . . among the several states," but also anything that has a "substantial effect" on such commerce. This test, if taken to its logical extreme, would give Congress a "police power" over all aspects of American life. Unfortunately, we have never come to grips with this implication of our substantial effects formula. Although we have supposedly applied the substantial effects test for the past 60 years, we *always* have rejected readings of the Commerce Clause and the scope of federal power that would permit Congress to exercise a police power; our cases are quite clear that there are real limits to federal power.

While the principal dissent concedes that there are limits to federal power, the sweeping nature of our current test enables the dissent to argue that Congress can regulate gun possession.

But it seems to me that the power to regulate "commerce" can by no means encompass authority over mere gun possession, any more than it empowers the Federal Government to regulate marriage, littering, or cruelty to animals, throughout the 50 States. Our Constitution quite properly leaves such matters to the individual States, notwithstanding these activities' effects on interstate commerce. Any interpretation of the Commerce Clause that even suggests that Congress could regulate such matters is in need of reexamination.

In an appropriate case, I believe that we must further reconsider our "substantial effects" test with an eye toward constructing a standard that reflects the text and history of the Commerce Clause without totally rejecting our more recent Commerce Clause jurisprudence.

JUSTICE BREYER, with whom JUSTICE STEVENS, JUSTICE SOUTER, and JUSTICE GINSBURG join, dissenting.

The issue in this case is whether the Commerce Clause authorizes Congress to enact a statute that makes it a crime to possess a gun in, or near, a school. In my view, the statute falls well within the scope of the commerce power as this Court has understood that power over the last half-century.

## I

In reaching this conclusion, I apply three basic principles of Commerce Clause interpretation. First, the power to "regulate Commerce . . . among the several States," encompasses the power to regulate local activities insofar as they significantly affect interstate commerce. See, e.g., *Gibbons* v. *Ogden* (1824), *Wickard* v. *Filburn* (1942). Second, in determining whether a local activity will likely have a significant effect upon interstate commerce, a court must consider, not the effect of an individual act (a single instance of gun possession), but rather the cumulative effect of all similar instances (i.e., the effect of all guns possessed in or near schools). Third, the Constitution requires us to judge the connection between a regulated activity and interstate commerce, not directly, but at one remove. Courts must give Congress a degree of leeway in determining the existence of a significant factual connection between the regulated activity and interstate commerce—both because the Constitution delegates the commerce power directly to Congress and because the determination requires an empirical judgment of a kind that a legislature is more likely than a court to make with accuracy. The traditional words "rational basis" capture this leeway. Thus, the specific question before us, as the Court recognizes, is not whether the "regulated activity sufficiently affected interstate commerce," but, rather, whether Congress could have had *"a rational basis"* for so concluding.

## II

Applying these principles to the case at hand, we must ask whether Congress could have had a *rational basis* for finding a significant (or substantial) connection between gun-related school violence and interstate commerce. . . . [T]he answer to this question must be yes. Numerous reports and studies—generated both inside and outside government—make clear that Congress could reasonably have found the empirical connection that its law, implicitly, or explicitly, asserts. And, they report that this widespread violence in schools throughout the Nation significantly interferes with the quality of education in those schools. Based on reports such as these, Congress obviously could have thought that guns and learning are mutually exclusive.

And, Congress could therefore have found a substantial educational problem—teachers unable to teach, students unable to learn—and concluded that guns near schools contribute substantially to the size and scope of that problem.

Having found that guns in schools significantly undermine the quality of education in our Nation's classrooms, Congress could also have found, given the effect of education upon interstate and foreign commerce, that gun-related violence in and around schools is a commercial, as well as a human, problem. . . .

The economic links I have just sketched seem fairly obvious. Why then is it not equally obvious, in light of those links, that a widespread, serious, and substantial physical threat to teaching and learning *also* substantially threatens the commerce to which that teaching and learning is inextricably tied? That is to say, guns in the hands of six percent of inner-city high school students and gun-related violence throughout a city's schools must threaten the trade and commerce that those schools support. The only question, then, is whether the latter threat is (to use the majority's terminology) "substantial." And, the evidence of (1) the *extent* of the gun-related violence problem, (2) the *extent* of the resulting negative effect on classroom learning, and (3) the *extent* of the consequent negative commercial effects, when taken together, indicate a threat to trade and commerce that is "substantial." At the very least, Congress could rationally have concluded that the links are "substantial." . . .

In sum, a holding that the particular statute before us falls within the commerce power would not expand the scope of the Clause. Rather, it simply would apply pre-existing law to changing economic circumstances. It would recognize that, in today's economic world, gun-related violence near the classroom makes a significant difference to our economic, as well as our social, well-being. In accordance with well-accepted precedent, such a holding would permit Congress "to act in terms of economic . . . realities," would interpret the commerce power as "an affirmative power commensurate with the national needs," and would acknowledge that the "commerce clause does not operate so as to render the nation powerless to defend itself against economic forces that Congress decrees inimical or destructive of the national economy." *North American Co.* v. *SEC* (1946).

## *United States* v. *Butler*

**297 U.S. 1; 56 S. Ct. 312; 80 L. Ed. 477 (1936)**

The Agricultural Adjustment Act of 1933, in seeking to curtail excess farm production, provided that farmers who reduced their production be compensated. This compensation came from a tax, levied by the Act, on the processing of agricultural commodities. Butler, the receiver for a cotton processing firm, refused to pay the tax. The district court ordered Butler to pay the tax, the court of appeals reversed, and the government appealed. *Opinion of the Court: Roberts, Hughes, Van Devanter, McReynolds, Sutherland, Butler. Dissenting opinion: Stone, Brandeis, Cardozo.*

MR. JUSTICE ROBERTS delivered the opinion of the Court.

. . . The Government asserts that even if the respondents may question the propriety of the appropriation embodied in the statute their attack must fail because Article I, § 8 of the Constitution authorizes the contemplated expenditure of the funds raised by the tax. This contention presents the great and the controlling question in the case. We approach its decision with a sense of our grave responsibility to render judgment in accordance with the principles established for the governance of all three branches of the Government.

There should be no misunderstanding as to the function of this court in such a case. It is sometimes said that the court assumes a power to overrule or control the action of the people's representatives. This is a misconception. The Constitution is the supreme law of the land ordained and established by the people. All legislation must conform to the principles it lays down. When an act of Congress is appropriately challenged in the courts as not conforming to the constitutional mandate the judicial branch of the Government has only one duty—to lay the article of the Constitution which is invoked beside the statute which is challenged and to decide whether the latter squares with the former. All the court does, or can do, is to announce its considered judgment upon the question. The only power it has, if such it may be called, is the power of judgment. This court neither approves nor condemns any legislative policy. Its delicate and difficult office is to ascertain and declare whether the legislation is in accordance with, or in contravention of, the provisions of the Constitution; and, having done that, its duty ends.

The question is not what power the Federal Government ought to have but what powers in fact have been given by the people. It hardly seems necessary to reiterate that ours is a dual form of government; that in every state there are two governments,—the state and the United States. Each State has all governmental powers save such as the people, by their Constitution, have conferred upon the United States, denied to the States, or reserved to themselves. The federal union is a government of delegated powers. It has only such as are expressly conferred upon it and such as are reasonably to be implied from those granted. In this respect we differ radically from nations where all legislative power, without restriction or limitation, is vested in a parliament or other legislative body subject to no restrictions except the discretion of its members.

Article I, § 8, of the Constitution vests sundry powers in the Congress. But two of its clauses have any bearing upon the validity of the statute under review.

The clause thought to authorize the legislation,—the first,—confers upon the Congress power "to lay and collect Taxes, Duties, Imports and Excises, to pay the Debts and provide for the common Defence and general Welfare of the United States. . . ." It is not contended that this provision grants power to regulate agricultural production upon the theory that such legislation would promote the general welfare. The Government concedes that the phrase "to provide for the general welfare" qualifies the power "to lay and collect taxes." The view that the clause grants power to provide for the general welfare, independently of the taxing power, has never been authoritatively accepted. Mr. Justice Story points out that if it were adopted "it is obvious that under color of the generality of the words, to 'provide for the common defence and general welfare,' the government of the United States is, in reality, a government of general and unlimited powers, notwithstanding the subsequent enumeration of specific powers." The true construction undoubtedly is that the only thing granted is the power to tax for the purpose of providing funds for payment of the nation's debt and making provision for the general welfare.

Nevertheless the Government asserts that warrant is found in this clause for the adoption of the Agricultural Adjustment Act. The argument is that Congress may appropriate and authorize the spending of moneys for the "general welfare"; that the phrase should be liberally construed to cover anything conducive to national welfare; that decision as to what will promote such welfare rests with Congress alone, and the courts may not review its determination; and finally that the appropriation under attack was in fact for the general welfare of the United States.

The Congress is expressly empowered to lay taxes to provide for the general welfare. Funds in the Treasury as a result of taxation may be expended only through appropriation. (Art. I, § 9, cl. 7.) They can never accomplish the objects for which they were collected unless the power to appropriate is as broad as the power to tax. The necessary implication from the terms of the grant is that the public funds may be appropriated "to provide for the general welfare of the United States." These words cannot be meaningless, else they would not have been used. The conclusion must be that they were intended to limit and define the granted power to raise and to expend money. How shall they be construed to effectuate the intent of the instrument?

Since the foundation of the Nation sharp differences of opinion have persisted as to the true interpretation of the phrase. Madison asserted it amounted to no more than a reference to the other powers enumerated in the subsequent clauses of the same section; that, as the United States is a government of limited and enumerated powers, the grant of power to tax and spend for the general national welfare must be confined to the enumerated legislative fields committed to the Congress. In this view the phrase is mere tautology, for taxation and appropriation are or may be necessary incidents of the exercise of any of the enumerated legislative powers. Hamilton, on the other hand, maintained the clause confers a power separate and distinct from those later enumerated, is not restricted in meaning by the grant of them, and Congress consequently has a substantive power to tax and to appropriate, limited only by the requirement that it shall be exercised to provide for the general welfare of the United States. Each contention has had the support of those whose views are entitled to weight. This court has noticed the question, but has never found it necessary to decide which is the true construction. Mr. Justice Story, in his Commentaries, espouses the Hamiltonian position. We shall not review the writings of public men and commentators or discuss the legislative practice. Study of all these leads us to conclude that the reading advocated by Mr. Justice Story is the correct one. While, therefore, the power to tax is not unlimited, its confines are set in the clause which confers it, and not in those of § 8 which bestow and define the legislative powers of the Congress. It results that the power of Congress to authorize expenditure of public moneys for public purposes is not limited by the direct grants of legislative power found in the Constitution.

But the adoption of the broader construction leaves the power to spend subject to limitations. Story says that if the tax be not proposed for the common defence or general welfare, but for other objects wholly extraneous, it would be wholly indefensible upon constitutional principles. And he makes it clear that the powers of taxation and appropriation extend only to matters of national, as distinguished from local welfare.

We are not now required to ascertain the scope of the phrase "general welfare of the United States" or to determine whether an appropriation in aid of agriculture falls within it. Wholly apart from that question, another principle embedded in our Constitution prohibits the enforcement of the Agricultural Adjustment Act. The act invades the reserved rights of states. It is a statutory plan to regulate and control agricultural production, a matter beyond the powers delegated to the federal government. The tax, the appropriation of the funds raised, and the direction for their disbursement, are but parts of the plan. They are but means to an unconstitutional end.

From the accepted doctrine that the United States is a government of delegated powers, it follows that those not expressly granted, or reasonably to be implied from such as are conferred are reserved to the states or to the people. To forestall any suggestion to the contrary, the Tenth Amendment was adopted. The same proposition, otherwise stated, is that powers not granted are prohibited. None to regulate agricultural production is given, and therefore legislation by Congress for that purpose is forbidden.

It is an established principle that the attainment of a prohibited end may not be accomplished under the pretext of the exertion of powers which are granted. . . .

. . . If the taxing power may not be used as the instrument to enforce a regulation of matters of state concern with respect to which the Congress has no authority to interfere, may it, as in the present case, be employed to raise the money necessary to purchase a compliance which the Congress is powerless to command? The Government asserts that whatever might be said against the validity of the plan if compulsory, it is constitutionally sound because the end is accomplished by voluntary cooperation. The regulation is not in fact voluntary. The farmer, of course, may refuse to comply, but the price of such refusal is the loss of benefits. The amount offered is intended to be sufficient to exert pressure on him to agree to the proposed regulation. The power to confer or withhold unlimited benefits is the power to coerce or destroy.

But if the plan were one for purely voluntary co-operation it would stand no better so far as federal power is concerned. At best it is a scheme for purchasing with federal funds submission to federal regulation of a subject reserved to the states.

Congress has no power to enforce its commands on the farmer to the ends sought by the Agricultural Adjustment Act. It must follow that it may not indirectly accomplish those ends by taxing and spending to purchase compliance. The Constitution and the entire plan of our government negative any such use of the power to tax and to spend as the act undertakes to authorize. It does not help declare that local conditions throughout the nation have created a situation of national concern; for this is but to say that whenever there is a widespread similarity of local conditions, Congress may ignore constitutional limitations upon its own powers and usurp those reserved to the states. If, in lieu of compulsory regulation of subjects within the states' reserved jurisdiction, which is prohibited, the Congress could invoke the taxing and spending power as a means to accomplish the same end, clause 1 of § 8 of Article I would become the instrument for total subversion of the governmental powers reserved to the individual states.

If the act before us is a proper exercise of the federal taxing power, evidently the regulation of all industry throughout the United States may be accomplished by similar exercises of the same power. It would be possible to exact money from one branch of an industry and pay it to another branch in every field of activity which lies within the province of the states. The mere threat of such a procedure might well induce the surrender of rights and the compliance with federal regulation as the price of continuance in business. . . .

The judgment is

*Affirmed.*

MR. JUSTICE STONE, dissenting.

1. The power of courts to declare a statute unconstitutional is subject to two guiding principles of decision which ought never to be absent from judicial consciousness. One is that courts are concerned only with the power to enact statutes, not with their wisdom. The other is that while unconstitutional exercise of power by the executive and legislative branches of the government is subject to judicial restraint, the only check upon our own exercise of power is our own sense of self-restraint. For the removal of unwise laws from the statute books appeal lies not to the courts but to the ballot and to the processes of democratic government.

2. The constitutional power of Congress to levy an excise tax upon the processing of agricultural products is not questioned. The present levy is held invalid, not for any want of power in Congress to lay such a tax to defray public expenditures, including those for the general welfare, but because the use to which its proceeds are put is disapproved.

3. As the present depressed state of agriculture is nation wide in its extent and effects, there is no basis for saying that the expenditure of public money in aid of farmers is not within the specifically granted power of Congress to levy taxes to "provide for the . . . general welfare." The opinion of the Court does not declare otherwise. . . .

It is with these preliminary and hardly controverted matters in mind that we should direct our attention to the pivot on which the decision of the Court is made to turn. It is that a levy unquestionably within the taxing power of Congress may be treated as invalid because it is a step in a plan to regulate agricultural production and is thus a forbidden infringement of state power. The levy is not any the less an exercise of taxing power because it is intended to defray an expenditure for the general welfare rather than for some other support of government. Nor is the levy and collection of the tax pointed to as effecting the regulation. While all federal taxes inevitably have some influence on the internal economy of the states, it is not contended that the levy of a processing tax upon manufacturers using agricultural products as raw material has any perceptible regulatory effect upon either their production or manufacture. . . . Here regulation, if any there be, is accomplished not by the tax but by the method by which its proceeds are expended, and would equally be accomplished by any like use of public funds, regardless of their source. . . .

It is upon the contention that state power is infringed by purchased regulation of agricultural production that chief reliance is placed. It is insisted that, while the Constitution gives to Congress, in specific and unambiguous terms, the power to tax and spend, the power is subject to limitations which do not find their origin in any express provision of the Constitution and to which other expressly delegated powers are not subject.

Such a limitation is contradictory and destructive of the power to appropriate for the public welfare, and is incapable of practical application. The spending power of Congress is in addition to the legislative power and not subordinate to it. This independent grant of the power of the purse, and its very nature, involving in its exercise the duty to insure expenditure within the granted power, presuppose freedom of selection among divers ends and aims, and the capacity to impose such conditions as will render the choice effective. It is a contradiction in terms to say that there is power to spend for the national welfare while rejecting any power to impose conditions reasonably adapted to the attainment of the end which alone would justify the expenditure.

A tortured construction of the Constitution is not to be justified by recourse to extreme examples of reckless congressional spending which might occur if courts could not prevent—expenditures which even if they could be thought to effect any national purpose, would be possible only by action of a legislature lost to all sense of public responsibility. Such suppositions are addressed to the mind accustomed to belief that it is the business of courts to sit in judgment on the wisdom of legislative action. Courts are not the only agency of government that must be assumed to have capacity to govern. Congress and the courts both unhappily may falter or be mistaken in the performance of their constitutional duty. But interpretation of our great charter of government which proceeds on any assumption that the responsibility for the preservation of our institutions is the exclusive concern of any one of the three branches of government, or that it alone can save them from destruction is far more likely, in the long run, "to obliterate the constituent members" of "an indestructible union of indestructible states" than the frank recognition that language, even of a constitution, may mean what it says: that the power to tax and spend includes the power to relieve a nationwide economic maladjustment by conditional gifts of money.

## *United States* v. *Kahriger*

**345 U.S. 22; 73 S. Ct. 510; 97 L. Ed. 754 (1953)**

Congress enacted a law levying an annual tax of $50 on persons in the business of taking bets. Persons paying the tax were required to register with the Federal Collector of Internal Revenue their names, addresses, and places of business. Kahriger was indicted for running a gambling business without paying the tax, but the district court dismissed the charge, ruling the law unconstitutional. The government then appealed the case to the Supreme Court. *Opinion of the Court: Reed, Warren, Jackson, Burton, Clark, Minton. Concurring opinion: Jackson. Dissenting opinions: Frankfurter, Douglas (in part); Black, Douglas.*

Mr. Justice Reed delivered the opinion of the Court.

The issue raised by this appeal is the constitutionality of the occupational tax provisions of the Revenue Act of 1951, which levy a tax on persons engaged in the business of accepting wagers, and require such persons to register with the Collector of Internal Revenue. The unconstitutionality of the tax is asserted on two grounds. First, it is said that Congress, under the pretense of exercising its power to tax has attempted to penalize illegal intrastate gambling through the regulatory features of the Act. . . . and has thus infringed the police power which is reserved to the states. Secondly, it is urged that the registration provisions of the tax violate the privilege against self-incrimination and are arbitrary and vague, contrary to the guarantees of the Fifth Amendment. . . .

It is conceded that a federal excise tax does not cease to be valid merely because it discourages or deters the activities taxed. Nor is the tax invalid because the revenue obtained is negligible. Appellee, however, argues that the sole purpose of the statute is to penalize only illegal gambling in the states through the guise of a tax measure. . . . The instant tax has a regulatory effect. But regardless of its regulatory effect, the wagering tax produces revenue. As such it surpasses both the narcotics and firearms taxes which we have found valid.

. . . It is hard to understand why the power to tax should raise more doubts because of indirect effects than other federal powers. . . .

Appellee's second assertion is that the wagering tax is unconstitutional because it is a denial of the privilege against self-incrimination as guaranteed by the Fifth Amendment.

Since appellee failed to register for the wagering tax, it is difficult to see how he can now claim the privilege even assuming that the disclosure of violations of law is called for. . . .

Assuming that respondent can raise the self-incrimination issue, that privilege has relation only to past acts, not to future acts that may or may not be committed. . . . If respondent wishes to take wagers subject to excise taxes under § 3285, . . . he must pay an occupational tax and register. Under the registration provisions of the wagering tax, appellee is not compelled to confess to acts already committed, he is merely informed by the statute that in order to engage in the business of wagering in the future he must fulfill certain conditions.

MR. JUSTICE BLACK, with whom MR. JUSTICE DOUGLAS concurs, dissenting.

. . . The Act . . . creates a squeezing device contrived to put a man in federal prison if he refuses to confess himself into a state prison as a violator of state gambling laws. The coercion of confessions is a common but justly criticized practice of many countries that do not have or live up to a Bill of Rights. But we have a Bill of Rights that condemns coerced confessions, however refined or legalistic may be the technique of extortion. I would hold that this Act violates the Fifth Amendment. . . .

MR. JUSTICE FRANKFURTER, dissenting.

. . . Constitutional issues are likely to arise whenever Congress draws on the taxing power not to raise revenue but to regulate conduct. This is so, of course, because of the distribution of legislative power as between the Congress and the State Legislatures in the regulation of conduct. . . .

. . . When oblique use is made of the taxing power as to matters which substantively are not within the powers delegated to Congress, the Court cannot shut its eyes to what is obviously, because designedly, an attempt to control conduct which the Constitution left to the responsibility of the States, merely because Congress wrapped the legislation in the verbal cellophane of a revenue measure. . . .

. . . Congress, which cannot constitutionally grapple directly with gambling in the States, may not compel self-incriminating disclosures for the enforcement of State gambling laws, merely because it does so under the guise of a revenue measure obviously passed not for revenue purposes. The motive of congressional legislation is not for our scrutiny, provided only that the ulterior purpose is not expressed in ways which negative what the revenue words on their face express and which do not seek enforcement of the formal revenue purpose through means that offend those standards of decency in our civilization against which due process is a barrier.

I would affirm this judgment.

## *South Dakota* v. *Dole*

**483 U.S. 203, 107 S. Ct. 2793, 97 L. Ed. 2d 171 (1987)**

In 1984 Congress enacted legislation directing the secretary of transportation to withhold 5 percent of federal highway funds from states that permitted purchase or public possession of alcoholic beverages by persons less than 21 years of age. South Dakota, which permitted persons 19 years of age or older to purchase 3.2 percent beer, sought a declaratory judgment that the law exceeded the constitutional limitations on the congressional spending power and violated the Twenty-First Amendment, which it viewed as granting the states exclusive authority to regulate the sale of alcohol within their borders. In support of this latter contention, South Dakota pointed to Section 2 of the amendment, which provides: "The transportation or importation into any State, Territory, or possession of the United States for delivery or use therein of intoxicating liquors, in violation of the laws thereof, is hereby prohibited." After its claims were rejected in federal district court and in the court of appeals, South Dakota appealed the case to the Supreme Court. *Opinion of the Court: Rehnquist, White, Marshall, Blackmun, Powell, Stevens, Scalia. Dissenting opinions: Brennan, O'Connor.*

CHIEF JUSTICE REHNQUIST delivered the opinion of the Court.

[W]e need not decide in this case whether [the Twenty-First] Amendment would prohibit an attempt by Congress to legislate directly a national minimum drinking age. Here, Congress has acted indirectly under its spending power to encourage uniformity in the States' drinking ages. As we explain below, we find this legislative effort within constitutional bounds even if Congress may not regulate drinking ages directly.

. . . The Constitution empowers Congress to "lay and collect Taxes, Duties, Imports, and Excises, to pay the Debts and provide for the common Defence and general Welfare of the United States." Art. I, § 8, cl. 1. Incident to this power, Congress may attach conditions on the receipt of federal funds, and has repeatedly employed the power "to further broad policy objectives by conditioning receipt of federal moneys upon compliance by the recipient with federal statutory and administrative directives." *Fullilove* v. *Klutznick* . . . The breadth of this power was made clear in *United States* v. *Butler* . . . (1936), where the Court, resolving a longstanding debate over the scope of the Spending Clause, determined that "the power of Congress to authorize expenditure of public moneys for public purposes is not limited by the direct grants of legislative power found in the Constitution." Thus, objectives not thought to be within Article I's "enumerated legislative fields" . . . may nevertheless be attained through the use of the spending power and the conditional grant of federal funds. . . . We can readily conclude that the provision is designed to serve the general welfare, especially in light of the fact that "the concept of welfare or the opposite is shaped by Congress. . . ." *Helvering* v. *Davis* [1937] . . . Congress found that the differing drinking ages in the States created particular incentives for young persons to combine their desire to drink with their ability to drive, and that this interstate problem required a national solution. The means it chose to address this dangerous situation were reasonably calculated to advance the general welfare. The conditions upon which States receive the funds, moreover, could not be more clearly stated by Congress. . . . And the State itself, rather than challenging the germaneness of the condition to federal purposes, admits that it "has never contended that the congressional action was . . . unrelated to a national concern in the absence of the Twenty-first Amendment." . . . Indeed, the condition imposed by Congress is directly related to one of the main purposes for which highway funds are expended—safe interstate travel. . . .

The . . . basic point of disagreement between the parties—is whether the Twenty-first Amendment constitutes an "independent constitutional bar" to the conditional grant of federal funds. . . . Petitioner, relying on its view that the Twenty-first Amendment prohibits *direct* regulation of drinking ages by Congress, asserts that "Congress may not use the spending power to regulate that which it is prohibited from regulating directly under the Twenty-first Amendment." . . . But our cases show that this "independent constitutional bar" limitation on the spending power is not of the kind petitioner suggests. . . .

Our decisions have recognized that in some circumstances the financial inducement offered by Congress might be so coercive as to pass the point at which "pressure turns into compulsion." *Steward Machine Co.* v. *Davis* [1937]. . . .

Here Congress has offered relatively mild encouragement to the States to enact higher minimum drinking ages than they would otherwise choose. But the enactment of such laws remains the prerogative of the States not merely in theory but in fact. Even if Congress might lack the power to impose a national minimum drinking age directly, we conclude that encouragement to state action found in § 158 is a valid use of the spending power. Accordingly, the judgment of the Court of Appeals is

*Affirmed.*

JUSTICE O'CONNOR, dissenting.

My disagreement with the Court is relatively narrow on the Spending Power issue: it is a disagreement about the application of a principle rather than a disagreement on the principle itself. I agree with the Court that Congress may attach conditions on the receipt of federal funds to further "the federal interest in particular national projects or programs." *Massachusetts* v. *United States,* . . . (1978). . . . In my view, establishment of a minimum drinking age of 21 is not sufficiently related to interstate highway construction to justify so conditioning funds appropriated for that purpose.

. . . The Court reasons that Congress wishes that the roads it builds may be used safely, that drunk drivers threaten highway safety, and that young people are more likely to drive while under the influence of alcohol under existing law than would be the case if there were a uniform national drinking age of 21. It hardly needs saying, however, that if the purpose of [this law] is to deter drunken driving, it is far too over- and under-inclusive. It is over-inclusive because it stops teenagers from drinking even when they are not about to drive on interstate highways. It is under-inclusive because teenagers pose only a small part of the drunken driving problem in this Nation. . . .

When Congress appropriates money to build a highway, it is entitled to insist that the highway be a safe one. But it is not entitled to insist as a condition of the use of highway funds that the State impose or change regulations in other areas of the State's social and economic life because of an attenuated or tangential relationship to highway use or safety. Indeed, if the rule were otherwise, the Congress could effectively regulate almost any area of a State's social, political, or economic life on the theory that use of the interstate transportation system is somehow enhanced. . . .

There is a clear place at which the Court can draw the line between permissible and impermissible conditions on federal grants. It is the line identified in the Brief for the National Conference of State Legislatures et al. as *Amici Curiae:*

> Congress has the power to *spend* for the general welfare, it has the power to *legislate* only for delegated purposes. . . . The appropriate inquiry, then, is whether the spending requirement or prohibition is a condition on a grant or whether it is regulation. The difference turns on whether the requirement specifies in some way how the money should be spent, so that Congress' intent in making the grant will be effectuated. Congress has no power under the Spending Clause to impose requirements on a grant that go beyond specifying how the money should be spent. A requirement that is not such a specification is not a condition, but a regulation, which is valid only if it falls within one of Congress' delegated regulatory powers.

This approach harks back to *United States* v. *Butler* . . . (1936), the last case in which this Court struck down an Act of Congress as beyond the authority granted by the Spending Clause. . . .

While *Butler's* authority is questionable insofar as it assumes that Congress has no regulatory power over farm production, its discussion of the Spending Power and its description of both the power's breadth and its limitations remains sound. The Court's decision in *Butler* also properly recognizes the gravity of the task of appropriately limiting the Spending Power. If the Spending Power is to be limited only by Congress' notion of the general welfare, the reality, given the vast financial resources of the Federal Government, is that the Spending Clause gives "power to the Congress to tear down the barriers, to invade the states' jurisdiction, and to become a parliament of the whole people, subject to no restrictions save such as are self-imposed." *United States* v. *Butler*. . . . This, of course, as *Butler* held, was not the Framers' plan and it is not the meaning of the Spending Clause.

★

## CONSTITUTIONAL PRINCIPLES

## PREEMPTION

*Pacific Gas & Electric Company* v. *State Energy Resources Conservation & Development Commission* (1983)

## NEGATIVE IMPLICATIONS OF THE COMMERCE CLAUSE

*Cooley* v. *Board of Wardens* (1852)
*Dean Milk Company* v. *City of Madison* (1951)

## STATE REGULATION AND THE MODERN COURT

*Southern Pacific Company* v. *Arizona* (1945)
*Camps Newfound/Owatonna, Inc.* v. *Town of Harrison* (1997)

## THE ROLE OF THE COURT

## NOTES

## SELECTED READING

## CASES

★

# 9
# THE EXERCISE OF STATE POWER

The paramount development in American constitutional history has been the expansion of the power of the national government. This process has been aided by the Supreme Court's broad interpretation of the powers granted to Congress and by constitutional amendments—especially the 14th and 16th—that have conferred important additional powers on the legislative branch. So although the Tenth Amendment provides that the states retain those powers not delegated to the national government, the areas of exclusive state control have progressively narrowed. And as the national government has come to regulate areas traditionally dominated by the states, collisions between state and federal claims of authority have increased.

## CONSTITUTIONAL PRINCIPLES

Alexander Hamilton observed in *The Federalist,* No. 32, that "the State governments would clearly retain all the rights of sovereignty which they before had, and which were not, by the ratification of the Constitution *exclusively* delegated to the United States." This statement suggests that the powers delegated to the national government can be divided into three categories: exclusive powers, which cannot be exercised by the states; concurrent powers, whose delegation to the national government does not restrict state power; and powers that are neither altogether exclusive nor altogether concurrent, whose delegation to the national government limits but does not completely preclude their exercise by the states.

The Constitution grants exclusive authority to the national government in various ways. Some exclusive powers, such as jurisdiction over the seat of government (Article I, Section 8), are granted expressly. Others are both granted to the national government and denied to the states: For example, the Constitution both authorizes the president to make treaties, with the advice and consent of the Senate (Article II, Section 2), and forbids the states to make them (Article I, Section 10). Finally, some powers granted to the national government, such as the power to declare war (Article I, Section 8), are by their very nature exclusive and thus cannot be exercised by the states.

In granting yet other powers to the national government, the Constitution neither expressly nor implicitly precludes state legislation. A prime example of these concurrent powers is the power to tax. Under the Supremacy Clause (Article VI), enactments made by the states under their concurrent powers may still be unconstitutional, if they conflict with federal legislation. In this way, the vigorous exercise of national power can diminish state power. In the absence of conflicting federal legislation, however, the states remain free to exercise their concurrent powers.

Finally, some constitutional grants of power are neither wholly exclusive nor wholly concurrent. If the states exercised these powers to the fullest possible extent, the national government would be prevented from achieving the ends for which the powers were granted to it. Elimination of all state authority, on the other hand, would imperil legitimate state objectives. By far the most important of the powers that fall into this category is the commerce power. In the words of Thomas Reed Powell, "Congress may regulate interstate commerce. The states may also regulate interstate commerce, but not too much."[1] The responsibility for deciding what constitutes "too much" has fallen largely to the Supreme Court, which has heard hundreds of cases involving the validity of state regulations affecting interstate commerce.

## PREEMPTION

Since the early 1930s, the national government has entered a variety of policy areas—for example, pollution control, race relations, and consumer protection—that previously had been predominantly state concerns. This expansion of national power has not invariably produced conflict, because national and state policies often have been complementary. When national and state policies are incompatible, however, the Supremacy Clause mandates that national policy prevail. The process by which national policies supersede inconsistent state policies is referred to as preemption.

Federal preemption of state and local powers has reached unprecedented levels over the past thirty years. Of the 439 congressional enactments from 1789–1991 that expressly indicated an intention to preempt state laws, 233 were enacted since 1969.[2] Yet congressional statutes can affect state power even without an explicit reference to preemption. For in such circumstances the Court may review congressional hearings and floor debates to determine Congress's intention. But if Congress did not consider the effect of its action on state laws, such a search is fruitless, and the Court then must consider "whether the state action stands as an obstacle to the accomplishment and execution of the full purposes and objectives of Congress."[3] In doing so the Court examines: (1) whether the state regulations conflict with federal requirements; (2) whether the pervasiveness of federal regulation signals an intention to "occupy the field" and exclude state regulation; and (3) whether the state regulations, although not directly in conflict with federal law, nevertheless may frustrate the purposes of that law.

Although these criteria may guide its decisions, the Court must analyze preemption claims on a case-by-case basis. From 1940, when it ruled in *Hines* v. *Davidowitz* that congressional legislation precluded state registration of aliens, through the late 1960s, the Court tended to assume the incompatibility of state law with federal initiatives. In recent years, however, the Court has been more reluctant to infer preemption in the absence of clear direction from Congress. In *Pacific Gas & Electric Company* v. *State Energy Resources and Development Commission* (1983), for example, the Court ruled that although the national government under the Federal Atomic Energy Act had occupied the field of nuclear safety, California's moratorium on the construction of new nuclear power plants could be upheld as an economic regulation. A year later in *Silkwood* v. *Kerr-McGee Corporation,* however, it also upheld a state-authorized award of punitive damages for conduct which created nuclear hazards, because Congress had not intended to preclude states from providing remedies for those suffering injuries from radiation in a nuclear plant. Altogether, from 1970–1991 states won 51 percent of preemption cases before the Supreme Court, up from 41 percent during the 1930–1969 period.[4]

The Court's current approach to preemption appears designed to protect the legitimate concerns of both the state and national governments. Its reluctance to infer preemption of state laws maximizes the exercise of state power. Yet national concerns are protected, because Congress can override Court rulings by clarifying its preemptive intent. Thus Congress, rather than the Court, is accorded the final responsibility for maintaining the federal balance.

## NEGATIVE IMPLICATIONS OF THE COMMERCE CLAUSE

Where preemption is not an issue, state laws can violate the Constitution by invading the powers granted to the national government. In this respect, the Commerce Clause is particularly important. The Framers gave Congress the power to regulate commerce in order to promote economic prosperity throughout the nation, and, as Justice Robert Jackson observed in *H. P. Hood & Sons* v. *DuMond* (1949), accomplishment of this aim demands some exclusivity of regulation:

> Our system, fostered by the Commerce Clause, is that every farmer and every craftsman shall be encouraged by the certainty that he will

> have free access to every market in the Nation, that no home embargoes will withhold his exports, and no foreign state will by customs duties or regulations exclude them. Likewise, every consumer may look to the free competition from every producing area in the Nation to protect him from exploitation by any.[5]

On the other hand, the states traditionally have exercised considerable power over commerce, not only by regulating commerce for commercial purposes but also by taxing interstate commerce to raise revenue and by enacting "police power" regulations to protect the health, safety, welfare, and morals of the state population. If the Commerce Clause foreclosed all such regulation, the states would be deprived of much of their governing authority.

Not surprisingly, then, the Supreme Court in the first century of the Republic was called upon to render several important decisions relating to how the national commerce power affected state authority to regulate commerce, tax commercial activities, and enforce police-power regulations. Two questions were of particular concern: Was the grant of power to Congress an exclusive mandate that precluded all state regulation? And if not, what standards should govern the exercise of state power over commerce?

## The Exclusivity Issue

The case for exclusivity is presented in the dormant-power theory, which suggests that by granting Congress the power to regulate commerce among the several states, the Constitution implicitly prohibited state regulation of that commerce. The scope of state power over commerce, accordingly, could be defined by subtraction: The states may regulate only those commercial transactions that Congress cannot regulate. With the expansion of national regulatory power during the twentieth century, this theory would virtually eliminate state power over commerce.

The most persuasive argument for this theory was offered by Justice William Johnson in his concurring opinion in *Gibbons* v. *Ogden* (1824). According to Johnson, economic warfare among the states during the Confederation period was one of the primary concerns of the Framers, who attempted to eliminate state barriers to the flow of commerce by vesting exclusive regulatory authority in Congress. If a state enactment conflicts with a congressional regulation, the congressional policy necessarily prevails. But even in failing to regulate, Johnson maintained, Congress makes a policy choice, for it indicates thereby that commerce should not be regulated. To allow state regulation when Congress fails to act, therefore, would frustrate national policy as surely as would permitting state regulations that are inconsistent with congressional action.

Chief Justice John Marshall acknowledged in *Gibbons* that "there is great force in the argument, and the Court is not satisfied that it has been refuted." But adoption of the dormant-power theory, when joined with Marshall's expansive definition of the commerce power, would have stripped the states of much of their traditional regulatory authority. Perhaps for this reason, Marshall twice sidestepped the issue: in *Gibbons,* by concluding that the New York law involved was preempted by congressional legislation; and in *Willson* v. *Black Bird Creek Marsh Company* (1829), by asserting that the Delaware law authorizing a dam across a navigable stream was an exercise of the police power rather than a regulation of commerce. Some members of the Court majority in the *License Cases* (1847) did endorse the dormant-power theory, and the Court employed it in invalidating a state tax in the *Passenger Cases* (1849). In *Cooley* v. *Board of Wardens* (1852), however, the Court decisively rejected the dormant-power concept.

The Court's rejection of the dormant-power theory left important questions unanswered. If the national commerce power does not foreclose all state regulation, does it foreclose any? And if it does, how does one determine the validity of state enactments? To understand how the Court answered these questions, we must return to *Gibbons.*

## The Search for a Standard

In arguing for the validity of New York's regulation of ferry service in *Gibbons,* the counsel for Ogden maintained that national and state powers over commerce were altogether concurrent: That is, in conferring the commerce power on Congress, the Constitution did not thereby withdraw any field of endeavor from state regulation. In this respect the commerce power was analogous to the taxing power: Just as the grant to Congress of the power to tax did not interfere with the states' taxing power, the power granted in the Commerce Clause did not limit the states' regulatory authority. Thus, state laws would be invalid only if they conflicted with congressional legislation.

Chief Justice Marshall persuasively disposed of the concurrent power theory in his opinion in *Gibbons.* The commerce power is not analogous to the taxing power, he noted, since it is not "in its own nature . . . capable of residing in, and being exercised by, different authorities at the same time." For in regulating commerce, a state "is exercising the very power that is granted to Congress, and is doing the very thing which Congress is authorized to do." Accordingly, Marshall concluded, the constitutional grant of power to Congress, by its own force and in the absence of congressional legislation, precludes some state regulations.

Another interpretation of state regulatory authority was provided by the mutual-exclusiveness theory, which was championed by Thomas Jefferson and other proponents of state power. According to this theory, the Constitution, although conferring the commerce power on Congress, left the states free to exercise the police power—the power to protect the health, safety, welfare, and morals of their citizens. In doing so, it established separate spheres for state and federal activity, and neither government could trespass on the other's domain. These spheres were distinguished not by what was regulated—state and federal laws might touch the same activities—but by the ends served by regulation. Because the police power resided in the states, then, the validity of a state regulation affecting commerce depended upon whether or not the regulatory act served legitimate police-power ends. In his opinions in *Gibbons* and *Black Bird,* Marshall neither endorsed nor rejected the mutual-exclusiveness theory. On the one hand, he recognized that the states had not surrendered all power to enact legislation that affected commerce. He acknowledged in *Gibbons* that the states could enact "[i]nspection laws, quarantine laws, health laws of every description, as well as laws for regulating the internal commerce of the state, and those which respect turnpike-roads, ferries, etc." And in *Black Bird* he ruled that a state law authorizing the damming of a navigable stream constituted a valid exercise of the police power rather than a regulation of commerce. On the other hand, Marshall also recognized that even state legislation which served valid state ends, might be "repugnant to the power to regulate commerce in its dormant state, or . . . in conflict with a law passed on the subject."[6] So although states in the exercise of their police power could enact laws that affected commerce, state laws could be struck down if they infringed on the field of regulation that the Commerce Clause reserved to the national government.

The search for an appropriate standard governing state regulation of commerce ended in the *Cooley* case, in which the Court adopted the selective-exclusiveness theory. Speaking for the Court, Justice Benjamin Curtis noted that since the Constitution does not expressly bar state regulation of commerce, such regulations are valid unless "the nature of the power, thus granted to Congress, requires a similar authority should not exist in the states." Whether or not such a requirement exists can only be determined by examining the nature of the subjects to be regulated. According to Curtis, previous theories upholding or denying state regulatory power had proved inadequate because no simple standard could take into account the diversity of the subjects that might be regulated. Having thus disposed of the dormant power and concurrent power theories, he proposed a different approach:

> Now the power to regulate commerce, embraces a vast field, containing not only many, but exceedingly various subjects, quite unlike in their nature; some imperatively demanding a single uniform rule, operating equally on the commerce of the United States in every port; and some like the subject now in question, as imperatively demanding that diversity which alone can meet the local necessities of navigation.

By directing attention to the particular factual situation in each case rather than to the nature of national and state power, the *Cooley* standard marked a major advance in Commerce Clause analysis. Exactly how the standard should be applied, however, is not always clear. For one thing, most subjects, rather than demanding national or state regulation, could "admit of" either. In addition, states might regulate a subject for either legitimate or illegitimate purposes. In *Dean Milk Company* v. *City of Madison* (1951), for example, the Court observed that a state could regulate milk sold in the state to protect the health of residents but not to protect its dairy industry from competition. In cases involving state regulations, therefore, the Court has undertaken to balance the national interest in uniformity against the interests served by state regulation.

## STATE REGULATION AND THE MODERN COURT

In determining the validity of state regulations that affect interstate commerce, the contemporary Supreme Court's approach in many ways resembles the selective-exclusiveness standard announced in *Cooley.* State regulations that serve no valid purpose or unduly impede interstate commerce are struck down. But those that serve important state interests and impose a minimal burden on commerce are upheld. In determining whether the benefits of state regulation outweigh the burdens on interstate commerce, the court employs a balancing test.

### Discrimination against Interstate Commerce

The Supreme Court consistently has struck down state laws designed to shield local businesses from interstate competition. Such discrimination defeats the very purpose of the Commerce Clause—the creation of "a federal free trade unit"—and encourages retaliatory legislation reminiscent of the Confederation period. In *Foster-Fountain Packing Company* v. *Haydel* (1928), for example, the Court invalidated a Louisiana law forbidding the exportation of shrimp from which the heads and tails had not been removed—a measure designed to aid the state's processing and canning industries. In *Edwards* v. *California* (1941), it struck down a California law prohibiting any person from knowingly bringing nonresident indigents into the state, ruling that the measure had been designed in part to limit competition for jobs.[7] And, in *Crutcher* v. *Kentucky* (1891), it ruled that Kentucky could not require corporations to obtain permits in order to conduct interstate business within the state.

A more difficult problem is posed by state statutes that discriminate against interstate commerce but also (at least arguably) serve legitimate state interests. Examples have been plentiful. In *City of Philadelphia* v. *New Jersey* (1978), the New Jersey statute prohibited the importation of out-of-state wastes, largely for environmental and health reasons. In *Dean Milk Company* v. *City of Madison,* the municipal ordinance purportedly safeguarded local health by limiting the sale of milk unless it was processed and bottled in an approved plant within five miles of the city's central square. And in *Camps Newfound/Owatonna* v. *Town of Harrison* (1997), Maine limited its tax exemption to charitable institutions serving state residents, in order to compensate or subsidize those organizations dispensing public benefits the state might otherwise provide. In each of these cases, the Court struck down the challenged legislation, ruling that a legitimate state objective is not enough. When a state law impedes the flow of interstate commerce, the Court has indicated, it will be upheld only when it serves a particularly important state end that cannot be achieved by nondiscriminatory legislation. Few state enactments can survive such exacting scrutiny.

## Burdens on Commerce

Even nondiscriminatory state regulations may impose diverse requirements that tend to make interstate commerce less convenient and more expensive. The Supreme Court nonetheless has upheld such regulations unless they unduly interfere with interstate commerce. Each case has required the Court to examine the operation of the state law and to balance the benefits it produces against the burden it imposes on interstate commerce.

The Court's case-by-case approach to this issue is reflected in several decisions involving interstate transportation. Whereas in *Missouri Pacific Company* v. *Norwood* (1931), the Court upheld state legislation requiring "full-crews" on trains, in *Southern Pacific Company* v. *Arizona* (1945), it struck down a law restricting the length of trains traveling through Arizona. These divergent rulings reflected the differing operation of the statutes. The train-length law produced negligible safety gains but posed a major obstacle to the flow of interstate train traffic. The "full-crew" laws, on the other hand, had demonstrable safety benefits and did not significantly interfere with interstate transportation.

Similar considerations have governed the Court's treatment of state laws dealing with highway safety. Although such laws burden interstate commerce, particularly when adjoining states impose different requirements, the Court has upheld state regulations that effectively promote highway safety and do not place interstate commerce at a competitive disadvantage. In *South Carolina Highway Department* v. *Barnwell Brothers, Inc.* (1938), for example, it upheld a South Carolina law that imposed weight and width limitations on trucks operating on state roads. When the safety benefits are negligible, however, the Court has struck down the state legislation. In *Raymond Motor Transportation, Inc.* v. *Rice* (1978), for example, it invalidated a Wisconsin law that imposed a fifty-five-foot length limitation on trucks and prohibited double-trailer trucks. The aim of the law was valid, the Court acknowledged, but it imposed a substantial burden on interstate commerce, and Wisconsin had offered no evidence supporting the safety benefits of the limitations. Similarly, in *Kassel* v. *Consolidated Freightways Corporation* (1981), the justices struck down an Iowa truck-length law, endorsing the trial court's conclusion that the state's safety evidence was unpersuasive.

## THE ROLE OF THE COURT

The Supreme Court's balancing of national and state interests in Commerce Clause cases has been questioned by several justices, among them Justice Hugo Black and, more recently, Justices Antonin Scalia and Clarence Thomas. These justices have argued that such balancing involves the Court in making policy judgments that Congress and state legislatures are more qualified to make. They thus propose a much narrower role for the Court. As long as a state does not discriminate against interstate commerce in order to advantage in-state economic interests, it should be allowed to determine how heavily commerce should be regulated and whether particular regulations effectively promote health and safety. If the regulations impose too heavy a burden on interstate commerce, Congress can always intervene to remedy the situation.[8]

Other justices—most eloquently, Justice Robert Jackson—have defended the Court's current approach. The question, they have insisted, is not one of competence but of responsibility. More specifically, the Court's responsibility to enforce the Constitution includes enforcement of the negative implications of the Commerce Clause. Furthermore, they point out, Congress lacks the time to oversee the multitude of state regulations that, although of limited importance individually, collectively can pose a serious barrier to interstate commerce and threaten the national common market the Framers sought to create. As Justice Oliver Wendell Holmes argued:

> I do not think the United States would come to an end if we lost our power to declare an Act of Congress void. I do think the Union would be imperiled if we could not make that declaration as to the laws of the several States. For one in my place sees how often a local policy prevails with those who are not trained to national views and how often action is taken that embodies what the Commerce Clause was meant to end.[9]

Although the Court has accepted this viewpoint, the more basic concern raised by Black and others remains valid. By dividing governing authority between nation and state, the Constitution created a potential for conflict between the levels of government. When state enactments are challenged as inconsistent with the Constitution or federal law, the Court must consider both the aims of union and the legitimate regulatory concerns of the states. The sensitivity of the Court in balancing these valid but competing claims can affect substantially the role that the states play in governing.

## NOTES

1 Thomas Reed Powell, *Vagaries and Varieties in Constitutional Interpretation* (New York: Columbia University Press, 1956), p. ix.

2 U.S. Advisory Commission on Intergovernmental Relations, *Federal Statutory Preemption of State and Local Authority* (Washington, D.C.: ACIR, 1992).

3 *Hines* v. *Davidowitz,* 312 U. S. 52, 67.

4 David M. O'Brien, "The Rehnquist Court and Federal Preemption: In Search of a Theory," *Publius: The Journal of Federalism* 23 (Fall 1993): 15–31.

5 336 U.S. 525, 539 (1949).

6 *Willson* v. *Black Bird Creek Marsh Co.,* 2 Pet. 245, 252 (1829).

7 Four justices would have struck down the law as a violation of the Privileges and Immunities Clause of the Fourteenth Amendment. In 1978, the Court in *Hicklin* v. *Orbeck* struck down an "Alaska Hire" law on that basis.

8 Even if the Court declares a state law unconstitutional, Congress can override the Court's ruling and legitimize the regulation. This paradoxical situation is a natural consequence of the congressional power over commerce. Because Congress can prescribe the rules by which commerce is to be governed, it has the power to subject commerce to relevant state regulations. For an example of such congressional action, see *Prudential Insurance Co.* v. *Benjamin* (1946).

9 *Collected Legal Papers* (New York: Harcourt, Brace, 1921), pp. 295–296.

## SELECTED READING

*The Federalist,* Nos. 31–34, 44–46.

*Brown* v. *Maryland,* 12 Wheat. 419 (1827).
*CTS Corp.* v. *Dynamics Corp.,* 481 U.S. 69 (1987).
*Edwards* v. *California,* 314 U.S. 160 (1941).
*Gibbons* v. *Ogden,* Volume I, Chapter 8.
*Hood* v. *DuMond,* 336 U.S. 525 (1949).
*Hughes* v. *Oklahoma,* 441 U.S. 322 (1979).

Benson, Paul R. T*he Supreme Court and the Commerce Power, 1937–1970* (New York: Dunellen, 1970).

Elazar, Daniel J. *American Federalism: A View from the States,* 3rd ed. (New York: Harper & Row, 1984).

Kincaid, John. "From Cooperative to Coercive Federalism." *Annals of the American Academy of Political and Social Science* 509 (1990): 139–152.

Maltz, Earl M. "The Impact of the Constitutional Revolution of 1937 on the Dormant Commerce Clause—A Case Study in the Decline of State Autonomy." *Harvard Journal of Law and Public Policy* 19 (1995): 121–145.

Powell, Thomas Reed. *Vagaries and Varieties in Constitutional Interpretation* (New York: Columbia University Press, 1956).

Tarr, G. Alan and Mary Cornelia Aldis Porter. *State Supreme Courts in State and Nation* (New Haven, Conn.: Yale University Press, 1988).

Tushnet, Mark. "Rethinking the Dormant Commerce Clause." *Wisconsin Law Review* (1979): 125–165.

U.S. Advisory Commission on Intergovernmental Relations. *Federal Statutory Preemption of State and Local Authority* (Washington, D.C.: ACIR, 1992).

Zimmerman, Joseph F. *Federal Preemption: The Silent Revolution* (Ames: Iowa State University Press, 1991).

## *Pacific Gas & Electric Company* v. *State Energy Resources Conservation & Development Commission*

**461 U.S. 190, 103 S. Ct. 1713, 75 L. Ed. 2d 752 (1983)**

The Federal Government has long regulated the development of nuclear energy under the Atomic Energy Act of 1954 and subsequent legislation. Growing opposition to nuclear power, however, has led some states to impose their own restrictions on its development. The present case involves a California law providing that before additional nuclear power plants could be built, the state energy commission had to determine on a case-by-case basis that there would be adequate capacity for storage of the plant's spent fuel rods. The statute also imposed a moratorium on the certification of new nuclear plants until the energy commission determined that an adequate technology had been developed for the disposal of high-level nuclear waste. Two electric utility companies challenged these provisions, claiming that they had been preempted by the Atomic Energy Act.

A federal district court ruled in favor of the utility companies. However, a federal court of appeals ruled that the moratorium on certification of new nuclear power plants was not preempted and that the provision dealing with capacity for storing spent fuel rods was not ripe for review. (For a discussion of ripeness, see Chapter 3.) The excerpts from the U.S. Supreme Court's decision presented below focus on whether federal legislation had preempted the state moratorium on certification of new plants. *Opinion of the Court: White, Burger, Brennan, Marshall, Powell, Rehnquist, O'Connor. Concurring opinion (in part): Blackmun, Stevens.*

JUSTICE WHITE delivered the opinion of the Court.

It is well-established that within Constitutional limits Congress may preempt state authority by so stating in express terms. Absent explicit preemptive language, Congress' intent to supercede state law altogether may be found from a "scheme of federal regulation so pervasive as to make reasonable the inference that Congress left no room to supplement it," "because the Act of Congress may touch a field in which the federal interest is so dominant that the federal system will be assumed to preclude enforcement of state laws on the same subject," or because "the object sought to be obtained by the federal law and the character of obligations imposed by it may reveal the same purpose." Even where Congress has not entirely displaced state regulation in a specific area, state law is preempted to the extent that it actually conflicts with federal law. Such a conflict arises when "compliance with both federal and state regulations is a physical impossibility," or where state law "stands as an obstacle to the accomplishment and execution of the full purposes and objectives of Congress."

Petitioners, the United States, and supporting *amici*, present three major lines of argument as to why § 25524.2 is preempted. First, they submit that the statute—because it regulates construction of nuclear plants and because it is allegedly predicated on safety concerns—ignores the division between federal and state authority created by the Atomic Energy Act, and falls within the field that the federal government has preserved for its own exclusive control. Second, the statute, and the judgments that underlie it, conflict with decisions concerning the nuclear waste disposal issue made by Congress and the Nuclear Regulatory Commission. Third, the California statute frustrates the federal goal of developing nuclear technology as a source of energy. We consider each of these contentions in turn.

. . . From the passage of the Atomic Energy Act in 1954, through several revisions, and to the present day, Congress has preserved the dual regulation of nuclear-powered electricity generation: the federal government maintains complete control of the safety and "nuclear" aspects of energy generation; the states exercise their traditional authority over the need for additional generating capacity, the type of generating facilities to be licensed, land use, ratemaking, and the like.

The above is not particularly controversial. But deciding how § 25524.2 is to be construed and classified is a more difficult proposition. At the outset, we emphasize that the statute does not seek to regulate the construction or operation of a nuclear powerplant. It would clearly be impermissible for California to attempt to do so, for such regulation, even if enacted out of nonsafety concerns, would nevertheless directly conflict with the NRC's exclusive authority over plant construction and operation. Respondents appear to concede as much. Respondents do broadly argue, however, that although safety regulation of nuclear plants by states is forbidden, a state may completely prohibit new construction until its safety concerns are satisfied by the federal government. We reject this line of reasoning. State safety regulation is not preempted only when it conflicts with federal law. Rather, the federal government has occupied the entire field of nuclear safety concerns, except the limited powers expressly ceded to the states. When the federal government completely occupies a given field or an identifiable portion of it, as it has done here, the test of preemption is whether "the matter on which the state asserts the right to act is in any way regulated by the federal government." A state moratorium on nuclear construction grounded in safety concerns falls squarely within the prohibited field. . . .

That being the case, it is necessary to determine whether there is a non-safety rationale for § 25524.2. . . .

Although [several] indicia of California's intent in enacting § 25524.2 are subject to varying interpretation, there are two reasons why we should not become embroiled in attempting to ascertain California's true motive. First, inquiry into legislative motive is often an unsatisfactory venture. What motivates one legislator to vote for a statute is not necessarily what motivates scores of others to enact it. Second, it would be particularly pointless for us to engage in such inquiry here when it is clear that the states have been allowed to retain authority over the need for electrical generating facilities easily sufficient to permit a state so inclined to halt the construction of new nuclear plants by refusing on economic grounds to issue certificates of public convenience in individual proceedings. In these circumstances, it should be up to Congress to determine whether a state has misused the authority left in its hands.

Therefore, we accept California's avowed economic purpose as the rationale for enacting § 25524.2. Accordingly, the statute lies outside the occupied field of nuclear safety regulation.

Petitioners' second major argument concerns federal regulation aimed at the nuclear waste disposal problem itself. It is contended that § 25524.2 conflicts with federal regulation of nuclear waste disposal, with the NRC's decision that it is permissible to continue to license reactors, notwithstanding uncertainty surrounding the waste disposal problem, and with Congress' recent passage of legislation directed at that problem. . . .

The NRC's imprimatur, however, indicates only that it is safe to proceed with such plants, not that it is economically wise to do so. Because the NRC order does not and could not compel a utility to develop a nuclear plant, compliance with both it and § 25524.2 are possible. Moreover, because the NRC's regulations are aimed at insuring that plants are safe, not necessarily that they are economical, § 25524.2 does not interfere with the objective of the federal regulation.

Nor has California sought through § 25524.2 to impose its own standards on nuclear waste disposal. The statute accepts that it is the federal responsibility to develop and license such technology. As there is no attempt on California's part to enter this field, one which is occupied by the federal government, we do not find § 25524.2 preempted any more by the NRC's obligations in the waste disposal field than by its licensing power over the plants themselves. . . .

Finally, it is strongly contended that § 25524.2 frustrates the Atomic Energy Act's purpose to develop the commercial use of nuclear power. . . .

There is little doubt that a primary purpose of the Atomic Energy Act was, and continues to be, the promotion of nuclear power. The Act itself states that it is a program "to encourage widespread participation in the development and utilization of atomic energy for peaceful purposes to the maximum extent consistent with the common defense and security and with the health and safety of the public." The House and Senate Reports confirmed that it was "a major policy goal of the United States" that the involvement of private industry would "speed the further development of the peaceful uses of atomic energy." The same purpose is manifest in the passage of the Price-Anderson Act, which limits private liability from a nuclear accident. The Act was passed "in order to protect the public and to encourage the development of the atomic energy industry. . . ."

The Court of Appeals' suggestion that legislation since 1974 has indicated a "change in congressional outlook" is unconvincing. . . . The Court of Appeals is right, however, that the promotion of nuclear power is not to be accomplished "at all costs." The elaborate licensing and safety provisions and the continued preservation of state regulation in traditional areas belie that. Moreover, Congress has allowed the States to determine—as a matter of economics—whether a nuclear plant vis-a-vis a fossil fuel plant should be built. The decision of California to exercise that authority does not, in itself, constitute a basis for preemption. Therefore, while the argument of petitioners and the United States has considerable force, the legal reality remains that Congress has left sufficient authority in the states to allow the development of nuclear power to be slowed or even stopped for economic reasons. Given this statutory scheme, it is for Congress to rethink the division of regulatory authority in light of its possible exercise by the states to undercut a federal objective. The courts should not assume the role which our system assigns to Congress.

The judgment of the Court of Appeals is

*Affirmed.*

JUSTICE BLACKMUN, with whom JUSTICE STEVENS joins, concurring in part and concurring in the judgment.

I join the Court's opinion, except to the extent it suggests that a State may not prohibit the construction of nuclear power plants if the State is motivated by concerns about the safety of such plants. . . .

Congress has not required States to "go nuclear," in whole or in part. The Atomic Energy Act's twin goals were to promote the development of a technology and to ensure the safety of that technology. Although that Act reserves to the NRC decisions about how to build and operate nuclear plants, the Court reads too much into the Act in suggesting that it also limits the States' traditional power to decide what types of electric power to utilize. Congress simply has made the nuclear option available, and a State may decline that option for any reason. Rather than rest on the elusive test of legislative motive, therefore, I would conclude that the decision whether to build nuclear plants remains with the States. In my view, a ban on construction of nuclear power plants would be valid even if its authors were motivated by fear of a core meltdown or other nuclear catastrophe.

## *Cooley* v. *Board of Wardens*

**53 U.S. (12 How.) 299, 13 L. Ed. 996 (1852)**

In 1803, Pennsylvania passed a law requiring all ships entering or leaving the port of Philadelphia to engage a local pilot or to pay a fine amounting to half the pilotage fee for the "use of the society for the relief of distressed and decayed pilots" and their families. A 1789 Act of Congress had provided that "all pilots in the bays, inlets, rivers, harbors, and ports of the United States shall continue to be regulated in conformity with the existing laws of the states, respectively, wherein such pilots may be, or with such laws as the states may respectively hereafter enact for the purpose, until further legislative provision shall be made by Congress." After being fined for failure to engage a pilot, Aaron Cooley challenged the Pennsylvania law as an impermissible regulation of interstate commerce. *Opinion of the Court: Curtis, Taney, Catron, McKinley, Nelson, Grier. Concurring opinion: Daniel. Dissenting opinion: McLean, Wayne.*

MR. JUSTICE CURTIS delivered the opinion of the Court. . . .

That the power to regulate commerce includes the regulation of navigation, we consider settled. And when we look to the nature of the service performed by pilots, to the relations which that service and its compensations bear to navigation between the several states, and between the ports of the United States and foreign countries, we are brought to the conclusion, that the regulation of the qualifications of pilots, of the modes and times of offering and rendering their services, of the responsibilities which shall rest upon them, of the powers they shall possess, of the compensation they may demand, and of the penalties by which their rights and duties may be enforced, do constitute regulations of navigation, and consequently of commerce, within the just meaning of this clause of the Constitution. . . .

It becomes necessary, therefore, to consider whether this law of Pennsylvania, being a regulation of commerce, is valid. . . .

. . . We are brought directly and unavoidably to the consideration of the question, whether the grant of the commercial power to Congress, did *per se* deprive the states of all power to regulate pilots. This question has never been decided by this court, nor, in our judgment, has any case depending upon all the considerations which must govern this one, come before this court. The grant of commercial power to Congress does not contain any terms which expressly exclude the states from exercising an authority over its subject-matter. If they are excluded it must be because the nature of the power, thus granted to Congress, requires that a similar authority should not exist in the states. If it were conceded on the one side, that the nature of this power, like that to legislate for the District of Columbia, is absolutely and totally repugnant to the existence of similar power in the states, probably no one would deny that the grant of the power to Congress, as effectually and perfectly excludes the states from all future legislation on the subject, as if express words had been used to exclude them. And on the other hand, if it were admitted that the existence of this power in Congress, like the power of taxation, is compatible with the existence of a similar power in the states, then it would be in conformity with the contemporary exposition of the Constitution (Federalist, No. 32), and with the judicial construction, given from time to time by this court, after the most deliberate consideration, to hold that the mere grant of such a power to Congress, did not imply a prohibition on the states to exercise the same power; that it is not the mere existence of such a power, but its exercise by Congress, which may be incompatible with the exercise of the same power by the states, and that the states may legislate in the absence of congressional regulations. . . .

The diversities of opinion, therefore, which have existed on this subject, have arisen from the different views taken of the nature of this power. But when the nature of a power like this is spoken of, when it is said that the nature of the power requires that it should be exercised exclusively by Congress, it must be intended to refer to the subjects of that power, and to say they are of such a nature as to require exclusive legislation by Congress. Now the power to regulate commerce, embraces a vast field, containing not only many, but exceedingly various subjects, quite unlike in their nature; some imperatively demanding a single uniform rule, operating equally on the commerce of the United States in every port; and some, like the subject now in question, as imperatively demanding that diversity, which alone can meet the local necessities of navigation.

Either absolutely to affirm, or deny that the nature of this power requires exclusive legislation by Congress, is to lose sight of the nature of the subjects of this power, and to assert concerning all of them, what is really applicable but to a part. Whatever subjects of this power are in their nature national, or admit only of one uniform system, or plan of regulation, may justly be said to be of such a nature as to require exclusive legislation by Congress. That this cannot be affirmed of laws for the regulation of pilots and pilotage is plain. The act of 1789 contains a clear and authoritative declaration by the first Congress, that the nature of this subject is such, that until Congress should find it necessary to exert its power, it should be left to the legislation of the states; that it is local and not national; that it is likely to be the best provided for, not by one system, or plan of regulations, but by as many as the legislative discretion of the several states should deem applicable to the local peculiarities of the ports within their limits.

Viewed in this light, so much of this act of 1789 as declares that pilots shall continue to be regulated "by such laws as the states may respectively hereafter enact for that purpose," instead of being held to be inoperative, as an attempt to confer on the states a power to legislate, of which the Constitution had deprived them, is allowed an appropriate and important signification. It manifests the understanding of Congress, at the outset of the government, that the nature of this subject is not such as to require its exclusive legislation. The practice of the states, and of the national government, has been in conformity with this declaration, from the origin of the national government to this time; and the nature of the subject when examined, is such as to leave no doubt of the superior fitness and propriety, not to say the absolute necessity, of different systems of regulation, drawn from local knowledge and experience, and conformed to local wants. How then can we say that by the mere grant of power to regulate commerce, the states are deprived of all the power to legislate on this subject, because from the nature of the power the legislation of Congress must be exclusive. This would be to affirm that the nature of the power is in any case, something different from the nature of the subject to which, in such case, the power extends, and that the nature of the power necessarily demands, in all cases, exclusive legislation by Congress, while the nature of one of the subjects of that power, not only does not require such exclusive legislation, but may be best provided for by many different systems enacted by the states, in conformity with the circumstances of the ports within their limits. In construing an instrument designed for the formation of a government, and in determining the extent of one of its important grants of power to legislate, we can make no such distinction between the nature of the power and the nature of the subject on which that power was intended practically to operate, nor consider the grant more extensive by affirming of the power, what is not true of its subject now in question.

It is the opinion of a majority of the court that the mere grant to Congress of the power to regulate commerce, did not deprive the states of power to regulate pilots, and that although Congress has legislated on this subject, its legislation manifests an intention, with a single exception, not to regulate this subject, but to leave its regulation to the several states. . . .

We are of opinion that this state law was enacted by virtue of a power, residing in the state to legislate; that it is not in conflict with any law of Congress; that it does not interfere with any system which Congress has established by making regulations, or by intentionally leaving individuals to their own unrestricted action; that this law is therefore valid, and the judgment of the Supreme Court of Pennsylvania in each case must be affirmed.

## *Dean Milk Company* v. *City of Madison*

**340 U.S. 349; 71 S. Ct. 295; 95 L. Ed. 329 (1951)**

A Madison, Wisconsin, ordinance prohibited the sale of milk in the city unless it came from a farm less than twenty-five miles from or was pasteurized and bottled at approved plants within five miles of the center of the city. Dean Milk was denied a license to sell milk because it pasteurized its milk at its plant in Illinois, beyond the five-mile limit. Both a county court and the Wisconsin Supreme Court upheld the ordinance, and the company appealed to the Supreme Court. *Opinion of the Court: Clark, Vinson, Reed, Frankfurter, Jackson, Burton. Dissenting opinion: Black, Douglas, Minton.*

MR. JUSTICE CLARK delivered the opinion of the Court. . . .

. . . [W]e agree with appellant that the ordinance imposes an undue burden on interstate commerce. This is not an instance in which an enactment falls because of federal legislation which, as a proper exercise of paramount national power over commerce, excludes measures which might otherwise be within the police power of the states. . . . There is no pertinent national regulation by the Congress, and statutes enacted for the District of Columbia indicate that Congress has recognized the appropriateness of local regulation of the sale of fluid milk. . . .

Nor can there be objection to the avowed purpose of this enactment. We assume that difficulties in sanitary regulation of milk and milk products originating in remote areas may present a situation in which "upon a consideration of all the relevant facts and circumstances it appears that the matter is one which may appropriately be regulated in the interest of the safety, health and well-being of local communities. . . ." . . . We also assume that since Congress has not spoken to the contrary, the subject matter of the ordinance lies within the sphere of state regulation even though interstate commerce may be affected. . . .

But this regulation . . . in practical effect excludes from distribution in Madison wholesome milk produced and pasteurized in Illinois. . . . In thus erecting an economic barrier protecting a major local industry against competition from without the State, Madison plainly discriminates against interstate commerce. This it cannot do, even in the exercise of its unquestioned power to protect the health and safety of its people, if reasonable nondiscriminatory alternatives, adequate to conserve legitimate local interests, are available. . . . A different view, that the ordinance is valid simply because it professes to be a health measure, would mean that the Commerce Clause of itself imposes no limitations on state action other than those laid down by the Due Process Clause, save for the rare instance where a state artlessly discloses an avowed purpose to discriminate against interstate goods. . . . Our issue then is whether the discrimination inherent in the Madison ordinance can be justified in view of the character of the local interests and the available methods of protecting them. . . .

It appears that reasonable and adequate alternatives are available. If the City of Madison prefers to rely upon its own officials for inspection of distant milk sources, such inspection is readily open to it without hardship for it could charge the actual and reasonable cost of such inspection to the importing producers and processors. . . . Moreover, appellee Health Commissioner of Madison testified that as proponent of the local milk ordinance he had submitted the provisions here in controversy and an alternative proposal based on § 11 of the Model Milk Ordinance recommended by the United States Public Health Service. The model provision imposes no geographical limitation on location of milk sources and processing plants but excludes from the municipality milk not produced and pasteurized conformably to standards as high as those enforced by the receiving city. In implementing such an ordinance, the importing city obtains milk ratings based on uniform standards and established by health authorities in the jurisdiction where production and processing occur. The receiving city may determine the extent of enforcement of sanitary standards in the exporting area by verifying the accuracy of safety ratings of specific plants or of the milkshed in the distant jurisdiction through the United States Public Health Service, which routinely and on request spot checks the local ratings. The Commissioner testified that Madison consumers "would be safeguarded adequately" under either proposal and that he had expressed no preference. . . .

To permit Madison to adopt a regulation not essential for the protection of local health interests and placing a discriminatory burden on interstate commerce would invite a multiplication of preferential trade areas destructive of the very purpose of the Commerce Clause. Under the circumstances here presented, the regulation must yield to the principle that "one state in its dealings with another may not place itself in a position of economic isolation." . . . *Baldwin* v. *G.A.F. Seelig, Inc.* [1935].

For these reasons we conclude that the judgment below sustaining the five-mile provision as to pasteurization must be reversed.

MR. JUSTICE BLACK, with whom MR. JUSTICE DOUGLAS and MR. JUSTICE MINTON concur, dissenting.

Today's holding invalidates § 7.21 of the Madison, Wisconsin, ordinance on the following reasoning: (1) the section excludes wholesome milk coming from Illinois; (2) this imposes a discriminatory burden on interstate commerce; (3) such a burden cannot be imposed where, as here, there are reasonable, nondiscriminatory and adequate alternatives available. I disagree with the Court's premises, reasoning, and judgment.

1. This ordinance does not exclude wholesome milk coming from Illinois or anywhere else. It does require that all milk sold in Madison must be pasteurized within five miles of the center of the city. But there was no finding in the state courts, nor evidence to justify a finding there or here, that appellant, Dean Milk Company, is unable to have its milk pasteurized within the defined geographical area. As a practical matter, so far as the record shows, Dean can easily comply with the ordinance whenever it wants to. Therefore, Dean's personal preference to pasteurize in Illinois, not the ordinance, keeps Dean's milk out of Madison.

2. Characterization of § 7.21 as a "discriminatory burden" on interstate commerce is merely a statement of the Court's result, which I think incorrect. The section does prohibit the sale of milk in Madison by interstate and intrastate producers who prefer to pasteurize over five miles distant from the city. But both state courts below found that § 7.21 represents a good-faith attempt to safeguard public health by making adequate sanitation inspections possible. While we are not bound by these findings, I do not understand the Court to overturn them. Therefore, the fact that § 7.21, like all health regulations, imposes some burden on trade, does not mean that it "discriminates" against interstate commerce.

3. This health regulation should not be invalidated merely because the Court believes that alternative milk-inspection methods might insure the cleanliness and healthfulness of Dean's Illinois milk. I find it difficult to explain why the Court uses the "reasonable alternative" concept to protect trade when today it refuses to apply the same principle to protect freedom of speech. . . .

If, however, the principle announced today is to be followed, the Court should not strike down local health regulations unless satisfied beyond a reasonable doubt that the substitutes it proposes would not lower health standards. I do not think that the Court can so satisfy itself on the basis of its judicial knowledge. And the evidence in the record leads me to the conclusion that the substitute health measures suggested by the Court do not insure milk as safe as the Madison ordinance requires.

One of the Court's proposals is that Madison require milk processors to pay reasonable inspection fees at the milk supply "sources." Experience shows, however, that the fee method gives rise to prolonged litigation over the calculation and collection of the charges. . . . To throw local milk regulation into such a quagmire of uncertainty jeopardizes the admirable milk-inspection systems in force in many municipalities. . . .

The Court's second proposal is that Madison adopt § 11 of the "Model Milk Ordinance." . . . The evidence indicates to me that enforcement of the Madison law would assure a more healthful quality of milk than that which is entitled to use the label of "Grade A" under the Model Ordinance. Indeed, the United States Board of Public Health, which drafted the Model Ordinance, suggests that the provisions are "minimum" standards only. The Model Ordinance does not provide for continuous investigation of all pasteurization plants as does § 7.21 of the Madison ordinance. Under § 11, moreover, Madison would be required to depend on the Chicago inspection system since Dean's plants, and the farms supplying them with raw milk, are located in the Chicago milkshed. But there is direct and positive evidence in the record that milk produced under Chicago standards did not meet the Madison requirements.

Furthermore, the Model Ordinance would force the Madison health authorities to rely on "spot checks" by the United States Public Health Service to determine whether Chicago enforced its milk regulations. The evidence shows that these "spot checks" are based on random inspection of farms and pasteurization plants: the United States Public Health Service rates the ten thousand or more dairy farms in the Chicago milkshed by a sampling of no more than two hundred farms. The same sampling technique is employed to inspect pasteurization plants. There was evidence that neither the farms supplying Dean with milk nor Dean's pasteurization plants were necessarily inspected in the last "spot check" of the Chicago milkshed made two years before the present case was tried.

From what this record shows, and from what it fails to show, I do not think that either of the alternatives suggested by the Court would assure the people of Madison as pure a supply of milk as they receive under their own ordinance. On this record I would uphold the Madison law. . . .

## *Southern Pacific Company* v. *Arizona*

**325 U.S. 761, 65 S. Ct. 1515, 89 L. Ed. 1915 (1945)**

The Arizona Train Limit Law prohibited passenger trains of more than fourteen cars and freight trains of more than seventy cars from operating in the state. When the Southern Pacific Railroad violated these safety restrictions by operating longer trains on interstate routes through the state, Arizona brought action in state court. The trial court ruled in favor of the company, the Arizona Supreme Court reversed, and Southern Pacific appealed to the Supreme Court. *Opinion of the Court: Stone, Reed, Frankfurter, Murphy, Jackson, Burton. Concurring in result: Rutledge. Dissenting opinions: Black, Douglas.*

MR. CHIEF JUSTICE STONE delivered the opinion of the Court. . . .

Although the commerce clause conferred on the national government power to regulate commerce, its possession of the power does not exclude all state power of regulation. . . . In the absence of conflicting legislation by Congress, there is a residuum of power in the state to make laws governing matters of local concern which nevertheless in some measure affect interstate commerce or even, to some extent, regulate it. . . . Thus the states may regulate matters which, because of their number and diversity, may never be adequately dealt with by Congress. . . . When the regulation of matters of local concern is local in character and effect, and its impact on the national commerce does not seriously interfere with its operation, and the consequent incentive to deal with them nationally is slight, such regulation has been generally held to be within state authority. . . .

But ever since *Gibbons* v. *Ogden* . . . the states have not been deemed to have authority to impede substantially the free flow of commerce from state to state, or to regulate those phases of the national commerce which, because of the need of national uniformity, demand that their regulation, if any, be prescribed by a single authority. . . .

In the application of these principles some enactments may be found to be plainly within and others plainly without state power. But between these extremes lies the infinite variety of cases, in which regulation of local matters may also operate as a regulation of commerce, in which reconciliation of the conflicting claims of state and national power is to be attained only by some appraisal and accommodation of the competing demands of the state and national interests involved. . . .

Hence the matters for ultimate determination here are the nature and extent of the burden which the state regulation of interstate trains, adopted as a safety measure, imposes on interstate commerce, and whether the relative weights of the state and national interests involved are such as to make inapplicable the rule, generally observed, that the free flow of interstate commerce and its freedom from local restraints in matters requiring uniformity of regulation are interests safeguarded by the commerce clause from state interference. . . .

The findings show that the operation of long trains, that is trains of more than fourteen passenger and more than seventy freight cars, is standard practice over the main lines of the railroads of the United States, and that, if the length of trains is to be regulated at all, national uniformity in the regulation adopted, such as only Congress can prescribe, is practically indispensable to the operation of an efficient and economical national railway system. On many railroads passenger trains of more than fourteen cars and freight trains of more than seventy cars are operated, and on some systems freight trains are run ranging from one hundred and twenty-five to one hundred and sixty cars in length. Outside of Arizona, where the length of trains is not restricted, appellant runs a substantial proportion of long trains. In 1939 on its comparable route for through traffic through Utah and Nevada from 66 to 85% of its freight trains were seventy cars in length and over 43% of its passenger trains included more than fourteen passenger cars.

In Arizona, approximately 93% of the freight traffic and 95% of the passenger traffic is interstate. Because of the Train Limit Law appellant is required to haul over 30% more trains in Arizona than would otherwise have been necessary. The record shows a definite relationship between operating costs and the length of trains, the increase in length resulting in a reduction of operating costs per car. The additional cost of operation of trains complying with the Train Limit Law in Arizona amounts for the two railroads traversing that state to about $1,000,000 a year. The reduction in train lengths also impedes efficient operation. More locomotives and more manpower are required; the necessary conversion and reconversion of train lengths at terminals and the delay caused by breaking up and remaking long trains upon entering and leaving the state in order to comply with the law, delays the traffic and diminishes its volume moved in a given time, especially when traffic is heavy. . . .

The unchallenged findings leave no doubt that the Arizona Train Limit Law imposes a serious burden on the interstate commerce conducted by appellant. . . . Compliance with a state statute limiting train lengths requires interstate trains of a length lawful in other states to be broken up and reconstituted as they enter each state according as it may impose varying limitations upon train lengths. The alternative is for the carrier to conform to the lowest train limit restriction of any of the states through which its trains pass, whose laws thus control the carriers' operations both within and without the regulating state. . . .

The trial court found that the Arizona law had no reasonable relation to safety, and made train operation more dangerous. . . .

The principal source of danger of accident from increased length of trains is the resulting increase of "slack action" of the train. . . . The length of the train increases the slack since the slack action of a train is the total of the free movement between its several cars. The amount of slack action has some effect on the severity of the shock of train movements, and on freight trains sometimes results in injuries to operatives, which most frequently occur to occupants of the caboose. The amount and severity of slack action, however, are not wholly dependent upon the length of train, as they may be affected by the mode and conditions of operation as to grades, speed, and load. . . .

On comparison of the number of slack action accidents in Arizona with those in Nevada, where the length of trains is now unregulated, the trial court found that with substantially the same amount of traffic in each state the number of accidents was relatively the same in long as in short train operations . . . reduction of the length of trains tends to increase the number of accidents because of the increase in the number of trains. . . . The accident rate in Arizona is much higher than on comparable lines elsewhere, where there is no regulation of length of trains. The record lends support to the trial court's conclusion that the train length limitation increased rather than diminished the number of accidents.

. . . [Arizona's] regulation of train lengths, admittedly obstructive to interstate train operation, and having a seriously adverse effect on transportation efficiency and economy, passes beyond what is plainly essential for safety since it does not appear that it will lessen rather than increase the danger of accident. . . . Examination of all the relevant factors makes it plain that the state interest is outweighed by the interest of the nation in an adequate, economical and efficient railway transportation service, which must prevail.

*Reversed.*

MR. JUSTICE BLACK, dissenting.

. . . I . . . think that the "findings" of the state court do not authorize today's decision. That court did not find that there is no unusual danger from slack movements in long trains. It did decide on disputed evidence that the long train "slack movement" dangers were more than offset by prospective dangers as a result of running a larger number of short trains, since many people might be hurt at grade crossing. There was undoubtedly some evidence before the state court from which it could have reached such a conclusion. There was undoubtedly as much evidence before it which would have justified a different conclusion.

Under those circumstances, the determination of whether it is in the interest of society for the length of trains to be governmentally regulated is a matter of public policy. Someone must fix that policy—either the Congress, or the state, or the courts. A century and a half of constitutional history and government admonishes this Court to leave that choice to the elected legislative representatives of the people themselves, where it properly belongs both on democratic principles and the requirements of efficient government. . . .

When we finally get down to the gist of what the Court today actually decides, it is this: Even though more railroad employees will be injured by "slack action" movements on long trains than on short trains, there must be no regulation of this danger in the absence of "uniform regulations." . . .

We are not left in doubt as to why, as against the potential peril of injuries to employees, the Court tips the scales on the side of "uniformity." For the evil it finds in a lack of uniformity is that it (1) delays interstate commerce, (2) increases its cost and (3) impairs its efficiency. All three of these boil down to the same thing, and that is that running shorter trains would increase the cost of railroad operations. . . .

. . . Thus the conclusion that a requirement for long trains will "burden interstate commerce" is a mere euphemism for the statement that a requirement for long trains will increase the cost of railroad operations. . . .

. . . I would affirm the judgment of the Supreme Court of Arizona.

## *Camps Newfound/Owatonna, Inc.* v. *Town of Harrison*

**516 U.S. 1157; 134 L. Ed. 2d 187, 117 S. Ct. 1590 (1997)**

Under the Maine statute at issue in this case, "benevolent and charitable institutions" incorporated in the State received a general exemption from real estate and personal property taxes if conducted principally for the benefit of residents of the state. However, institutions "conducted or operated principally for the benefit of persons who are not residents of Maine" received a reduced exemption and that only if the weekly charge for services provided did not exceed $30 per person.

Camps Newfound/Owatonna, a Maine nonprofit corporation, operated a church camp for children of the Christian Science faith, 95 percent of whom were not residents of Maine. The camp was financed through camper tuition and other revenues. From 1989 to 1991, the camp paid over $20,000 per year in real estate and personal property taxes. When the camp's request for a refund of taxes paid from 1989 through 1991 and for a continuing exemption from future property taxes was denied, the camp filed suit in the Superior Court against the Town and its tax assessors and collectors, claiming that the tax exemption statute violated the Commerce Clause. The Superior Court ruled for Camps Newfound/Owatonna, but the Maine Supreme Judicial Court reversed. The U. S. Supreme Court then granted certiorari. *Opinion of the Court: Stevens, O'Connor, Kennedy, Souter, Breyer. Dissenting opinions: Scalia, Rehnquist, Thomas, Ginsburg; Thomas, Scalia, Rehnquist (in part).*

JUSTICE STEVENS delivered the opinion of the Court.

The question presented is whether an otherwise generally applicable state property tax violates the Commerce Clause of the United States Constitution, because its exemption for property owned by charitable institutions excludes organizations operated principally for the benefit of nonresidents.

During the first years of our history as an independent confederation, the National Government lacked the power to regulate commerce among the States. Because each State was free to adopt measures fostering its own local interests without regard to possible prejudice to nonresidents, what JUSTICE JOHNSON characterized as a "conflict of commercial regulations, destructive to the harmony of the States" ensued. See *Gibbons* v. *Ogden* (1824) (opinion concurring in judgment). We have subsequently endorsed JUSTICE JOHNSON'S appraisal of the central importance of federal control over interstate and foreign commerce and, more narrowly, his conclusion that the Commerce Clause had not only granted Congress express authority to override restrictive and conflicting commercial regulations adopted by the States, but that it also had immediately effected a curtailment of state power. In short, the Commerce Clause even without implementing legislation by Congress is a limitation upon the power of the States.

This case involves an issue that we have not previously addressed—the disparate real estate tax treatment of a nonprofit service provider based on the residence of the consumers that it serves. The Town argues that our dormant Commerce Clause jurisprudence is wholly inapplicable to this case, because interstate commerce is not implicated here and Congress has no power to enact a tax on real estate.

We are unpersuaded by the Town's argument that the dormant Commerce Clause is inapplicable here, either because campers are not "articles of commerce," or more generally because the camp's "product is delivered and 'consumed' entirely within Maine." Even though petitioner's camp does not make a profit, it is unquestionably engaged in commerce, not only as a purchaser, see *Katzenbach* v. *McClung* (1964); *United States* v. *Lopez* (1995), but also as a provider of goods and services. It markets those services, together with an opportunity to enjoy the natural beauty of an inland lake in Maine, to campers who are attracted to its facility from all parts of the Nation. The record reflects that petitioner "advertises for campers in [out-of-state] periodicals . . . and sends its Executive Director annually on camper recruiting trips across the country." Petitioner's efforts are quite successful; 95 percent of its campers come from out of State. The attendance of these campers necessarily generates the transportation of persons across state lines that has long been recognized as a form of "commerce."

Summer camps are comparable to hotels that offer their guests goods and services that are consumed locally. In *Heart of Atlanta Motel, Inc.* v. *United States* (1964), we recognized that interstate commerce is substantially affected by the activities of a hotel that "solicits patronage from outside the State of Georgia through various national advertising media, including magazines of national circulation." In that case, we held that commerce was substantially affected by private race discrimination that limited access to the hotel and thereby impeded interstate commerce in the form of travel. Official discrimination that limits the access of nonresidents to summer camps creates a similar impediment. Even when business activities are purely local, if " 'it is interstate commerce that feels the pinch, it does not matter how local the operation which applies the squeeze.' " *Heart of Atlanta* (quoting *United States* v. *Women's Sportswear Mfrs. Assn.* [1949]).

The Town's arguments that the dormant Commerce Clause is inapplicable to petitioner because the campers are not "articles of commerce," or more generally that interstate commerce is not at issue here, are therefore unpersuasive. The services that petitioner provides to its principally out-of-state campers clearly have a substantial effect on commerce, as do state restrictions on making those services available to nonresidents.

The Town also argues that the dormant Commerce Clause is inapplicable because a real estate tax is at issue. We disagree. A tax on real estate, like any other tax, may impermissibly burden interstate commerce. A State's "power to lay and collect taxes, comprehensive and necessary as that power is, cannot be exerted in a way which involves a discrimination against [interstate] commerce." *Pennsylvania* v. *West Virginia* (1923). To allow a State to avoid the strictures of the dormant Commerce Clause by the simple device of labeling its discriminatory tax a levy on real estate would destroy the barrier against protectionism that the Constitution provides. We therefore turn to the question whether our prior cases preclude a State from imposing a higher tax on a camp that serves principally nonresidents than on one that limits its services primarily to residents.

There is no question that were this statute targeted at profit-making entities, it would violate the dormant Commerce Clause. It is not necessary to look beyond the text of this statute to determine that it discriminates against interstate commerce. The Maine law expressly distinguishes between entities that serve a principally interstate clientele and those that primarily serve an intrastate market, singling out camps that serve mostly in-staters for beneficial tax treatment, and penalizing those camps that do a principally interstate business. As a practical matter, the statute encourages affected entities to limit their out-of-state clientele, and penalizes the principally nonresident customers of business catering to a primarily interstate market.

If such a policy were implemented by a statutory prohibition against providing camp services to nonresidents, the statute would almost certainly be invalid. We have "consistently . . . held that the Commerce Clause . . . precludes a state from mandating that its residents be given a preferred right of access, over out-of-state consumers, to natural resources located within its borders or to the products derived therefrom." *New England Power Co.* v. *New Hampshire* (1982). Petitioner's "product" is in part the natural beauty of Maine itself, and in addition the special services that the camp provides. In this way, the Maine statute is like a law that burdens out-of-state access to domestically generated hydroelectric power, *New England Power,* or to local landfills, *Philadelphia* v. *New Jersey* (1978).

Of course, this case does not involve a total prohibition. Rather, the statute provides a strong incentive for affected entities not to do business with nonresidents if they are able to so avoid the discriminatory tax. That the tax discrimination comes in the form of a deprivation of a generally available tax benefit, rather than a specific penalty on the activity itself, is of no moment. Given the fact that the burden of Maine's facially discriminatory tax scheme falls by design in a predictably disproportionate way on out-of-staters, the pernicious effect on interstate commerce is the same as in our cases involving taxes targeting out-of-staters alone.

[W]e recognize that here the discriminatory burden is imposed on the out-of-state customer indirectly by means of a tax on the entity transacting business with the non-Maine customer. This distinction makes no analytic difference. The record demonstrates that the economic incidence of the tax falls at least in part on the campers, the Town has not contested the point, and the courts below based their decision on this presumption. [T]he Maine statute therefore functionally serves as an export tariff that targets out-of-state consumers by taxing the businesses that principally serve them. This sort of discrimination is at the very core of activities forbidden by the dormant Commerce Clause.

The unresolved question presented by this case is whether a different rule should apply to tax exemptions for charitable and benevolent institutions. Though we have never had cause to address the issue directly . . . , [w]e see no reason why the nonprofit character of an enterprise should exclude it from the coverage of either the affirmative or the negative aspect of the Commerce. Nothing intrinsic to the nature of nonprofit entities prevents them from engaging in interstate commerce. Summer camps may be operated as for-profit or nonprofit entities; nonprofits may depend—as here—in substantial part on fees charged for their services. Whether operated on a for-profit or nonprofit basis, they purchase goods and services in competitive markets, offer their facilities to a variety of patrons, and derive revenues from a variety of sources, some of which are local and some out of State. For purposes of Commerce Clause analysis, any categorical distinction between the activities of profit-making enterprises and not-for-profit entities is therefore wholly illusory. Entities in both categories are major participants in interstate markets. And, although the summer camp involved in this case may have a relatively insignificant impact on the commerce of the entire Nation, the interstate commercial activities of nonprofit entities as a class are unquestionably significant. See *Wickard* v. *Filburn* (1942); *Lopez.*

Rather than urging us to create a categorical exception for nonprofit entities, the Town argues that Maine's exemption statute should be viewed as an expenditure of government money designed to lessen its social service burden and to foster the societal benefits provided by charitable organizations. So characterized, the Town submits that its tax exemption scheme is either a legitimate discriminatory subsidy of only those charities that choose to focus their activities on local concerns, or alternatively a governmental "purchase" of charitable services falling within the narrow exception to the dormant Commerce Clause for States in their role as "market participants," see, e.g., *Hughes* v. *Alexandria Scrap Corp.* (1976); *Reeves, Inc.* v. *Stake* (1980).

The Town argues that its discriminatory tax exemption is, in economic reality, no different from a discriminatory subsidy of those charities that cater principally to local needs. Noting our statement in *West Lynn Creamery* that "[a] pure subsidy funded out of general revenue ordinarily imposes no burden on interstate commerce, but merely assists local business," the Town submits that since a discriminatory subsidy may be permissible, a discriminatory exemption must be too. Assuming, *arguendo,* that the Town is correct that a direct subsidy benefiting only those nonprofits serving principally Maine residents would be permissible, our cases do not sanction a tax exemption serving similar ends.

In *Walz* v. *Tax Comm'n of City of New York* (1970), notwithstanding our assumption that a direct subsidy of religious activity would be invalid, we held that New York's tax exemption for church property did not violate the Establishment Clause of the First Amendment. That holding rested, in part, on the premise that there is a constitutionally significant difference between subsidies and tax exemptions. We have expressly recognized that this distinction is also applicable to claims that certain state action designed to give residents an advantage in the market place is prohibited by the Commerce Clause. In *New Energy Co. of Ind.* v. *Limbach* (1988), we found unconstitutional under the Commerce Clause an Ohio tax scheme that provided a sales tax credit for ethanol produced in State, or manufactured in another State to the extent that State gave similar tax advantages to ethanol produced in Ohio. We recognized that the party challenging the Ohio scheme was "eligible to receive a cash subsidy" from its home State, and was therefore "the potential beneficiary of a scheme no less discriminatory than the one that it attacks, and no less effective in conferring a commercial advantage over out-of-state competitors." That was of no importance. We noted: "The Commerce Clause does not prohibit all state action designed to give its residents an advantage in the marketplace, but only action of that description *in connection with the State's regulation of interstate commerce.* Direct subsidization of domestic industry does not ordinarily run afoul of that prohibition; discriminatory taxation . . . does." The town's claim that its discriminatory tax scheme should be viewed as a permissible subsidy is therefore unpersuasive.

Finally, the Town argues that its discriminatory tax exemption scheme falls within the "market participant" exception. As we explained in *New Energy Co.*: "That doctrine differentiates between a State's acting in its distinctive governmental capacity, and a State's acting in the more general capacity of a market participant; only the former is subject to the limitations of the negative Commerce Clause." Maine's tax exemption statute cannot be characterized as a proprietary activity falling within the market-participant exception. A tax exemption is not the sort of direct state involvement in the market that falls within the market-participation doctrine. Even if we were prepared to expand the exception in the manner suggested by the Town, the Maine tax statute at issue here would be a poor candidate. Like the tax exemption upheld in *Walz*—which applied to libraries, art galleries, and hospitals as well as churches—the exemption that has been denied to petitioner is available to a broad category of charitable and benevolent institutions. For that reason, nothing short of a dramatic expansion of the "market participant" exception would support its application to this case. Maine's tax exemption—which sweeps to cover broad swatches of the nonprofit sector—must be viewed as action taken in the State's sovereign capacity rather than a proprietary decision to make an entry into all of the markets in which the exempted charities function. The Town's version of the "market participant" exception would swallow the rule against discriminatory tax schemes.

The Judgment of the Maine Supreme Judicial Court is reversed.

*It is so ordered.*

JUSTICE SCALIA, with whom THE CHIEF JUSTICE, JUSTICE THOMAS, and JUSTICE GINSBURG join, dissenting.

The Court's negative-commerce-clause jurisprudence has drifted far from its moorings. Originally designed to create a national market for commercial activity, it is today invoked to prevent a State from giving a tax break to charities that benefit the State's inhabitants. In my view, Maine's tax exemption, which excuses from taxation only that property used to relieve the State of its burden of caring for its residents, survives even our most demanding commerce-clause scrutiny.

We have often said that the purpose of our negative-commerce-clause jurisprudence is to create a national market. In our zeal to advance this policy, however, we must take care not to overstep our mandate, for the Commerce Clause was not intended "to cut the States off from legislating on all subjects relating to the health, life, and safety of their citizens, though the legislation might indirectly affect the commerce of the country." *Huron Portland Cement Co.* v. *Detroit* (1960).

Our cases have struggled (to put it nicely) to develop a set of rules by which we may preserve a national market without needlessly intruding upon the States' police powers, each exercise of which no doubt has some effect on the commerce of the Nation. The rules that we currently use can be simply stated, if not simply applied: Where a State law facially discriminates against interstate commerce, we observe what has sometimes been referred to as a "virtually *per se* rule of invalidity;" where, on the other hand, a state law is nondiscriminatory, but nonetheless adversely affects interstate commerce, we employ a deferential "balancing test," under which the law will be sustained unless "the burden imposed on [interstate] commerce is clearly excessive in relation to the putative local benefits," *Pike* v. *Bruce Church, Inc.* (1970). While the "virtually *per se* rule of invalidity" entails application of the "strictest scrutiny," *Hughes* v. *Oklahoma* (1979), it does not necessarily result in the invalidation of facially discriminatory State legislation, for "what may appear to be a 'discriminatory' provision in the constitutionally prohibited sense—that is, a protectionist enactment—may on closer analysis not be so," *New Energy Co. of Ind.* v. *Limbach* (1988). Thus, even a statute that erects an absolute barrier to the movement of goods across state lines will be upheld if "the discrimination is demonstrably justified by a valid factor unrelated to economic protectionism," or to put a finer point on it, if the State law "advances a legitimate local purpose that cannot be adequately served by reasonable nondiscriminatory alternatives."

In addition to laws that employ suspect means as a necessary expedient to the advancement of legitimate State ends, we have also preserved from judicial invalidation laws that confer advantages upon the State's residents but do so without *regulating* interstate commerce. We have therefore excepted the State from scrutiny when it participates in markets rather than regulates them. Likewise, we have said that direct subsidies to domestic industry do not run afoul of the Commerce Clause. In sum, we have declared that "[t]he Commerce Clause does not prohibit all state action designed to give its residents an advantage in the marketplace, but only action of that description *in connection with the State's regulation of interstate commerce.*"

In applying the foregoing principles to the case before us, it is of course important to understand the precise scope of the exemption created by [the Maine law]. The Court's analysis suffers from the misapprehension that [the law] "sweeps to cover broad swathes of the nonprofit sector," including nonprofit corporations engaged in quintessentially commercial activities. That is not so. A review of Maine law demonstrates that the provision at issue here is a narrow tax exemption, designed merely to compensate or subsidize those organizations that contribute to the public fisc by dispensing public benefits the State might otherwise provide.

I turn next to the validity of this focused tax exemption—applicable only to property used solely for charitable purposes by organizations devoted exclusively to charity—under the negative-commerce-clause principles discussed earlier. The Court readily concludes that, by limiting the class of eligible property to that which is used "principally for the benefit of persons who are Maine residents," the statute "facially discriminates" against interstate commerce. That seems to me not necessarily true. Disparate treatment constitutes discrimination only if the objects of the disparate treatment are, for the relevant purposes, similarly situated. And for purposes of entitlement to a tax subsidy from the State, it is certainly reasonable to think that property gratuitously devoted to relieving the State of some of its welfare burden is not similarly situated to property used "principally for the benefit of persons who are not residents of [the State]." As we have seen, the theory underlying the exemption is that it is a *quid pro quo* for uncompensated expenditures that lessen the State's burden of providing assistance to its residents.

The Court seeks to establish "facial discrimination" by showing that the effect of treating disparate property disparately is to produce higher costs for those users of the property who come from out of State. But that could be regarded as an *indirect* effect upon interstate commerce produced by a tax scheme that is *not* facially discriminatory, which means that the proper mode of analysis would be the more lenient "balancing" standard discussed above. Even if, however, the Maine statute displays "facial discrimination" against interstate commerce, that is not the end of the analysis. The most remarkable thing about today's judgment is that it is rendered without inquiry into whether the purposes of the tax exemption *justify* its favoritism. If the Court were to proceed with that further analysis it would have to conclude, in my view, that this is one of those cases in which the "virtually *per se* rule of invalidity" does not apply. Facially discriminatory or not, the exemption is no more an artifice of economic protectionism than any state law which dispenses public assistance only to the State's residents. Our cases have always recognized the legitimacy of limiting state-provided welfare benefits to bona fide residents. If the negative Commerce Clause requires the invalidation of a law like [this one], as a logical matter it also requires invalidation of the laws involved in [our earlier] cases. After all, the Court today relies not on any discrimination against out-of-state nonprofits, but on the supposed discrimination against nonresident would-be *recipients* of charity (the nonprofits' "customers"); surely those individuals are similarly discriminated against in the direct distribution of state benefits. The problem, of course, is not limited to municipal employment and free public schooling, but extends also to libraries, orphanages, homeless shelters and refuges for battered women. One could hardly explain the constitutionality of a State's limiting its provision of these to its own residents on the theory that the State is a "market participant." These are traditional governmental functions, far removed from commercial activity and utterly unconnected to any genuine private market.

If, however, a State that provides social services directly *may* limit its largesse to its own residents, I see no reason why a State that chooses to provide some of its social services indirectly—by compensating or subsidizing private charitable providers—cannot be similarly restrictive.

I respectfully dissent.

JUSTICE THOMAS, with whom JUSTICE SCALIA joins, and with whom CHIEF JUSTICE REHNQUIST joins [in part], dissenting.

I write separately because I believe that the improper expansion undertaken today is possible only because our negative Commerce Clause jurisprudence, developed primarily to invalidate discriminatory state taxation of interstate commerce, was already both overbroad and unnecessary. It was overbroad because, unmoored from any constitutional text, it brought within the supervisory authority of the federal courts state action far afield from the discriminatory taxes it was primarily designed to check. It was unnecessary because the Constitution would seem to provide an *express* check on the States' power to levy certain discriminatory taxes on the commerce of other States—not in the judicially created negative Commerce Clause, but in the Article I, § 10 Import-Export Clause. That the expansion effected by today's decision finds some support in the morass of our negative Commerce Clause caselaw only serves to highlight the need to abandon that failed jurisprudence and to consider restoring the original Import-Export Clause check on discriminatory state taxation to what appears to be its proper role.

To cover its exercise of judicial power in an area for which there is no textual basis, the Court has historically offered two different theories in support of its negative Commerce Clause jurisprudence. The first theory posited was that the Commerce Clause itself constituted an *exclusive* grant of power to Congress. The "exclusivity" rationale was likely wrong from the outset, however. See, *e.g.,* The Federalist No. 32. It was seriously questioned even in early cases. And, in any event, the Court has long since "repudiated" the notion that the Commerce Clause operates as an exclusive grant of power to Congress, and thereby forecloses state action respecting interstate commerce. [A]s this Court's definition of the scope of congressional authority under the positive Commerce Clause has expanded, the exclusivity rationale has moved from untenable to absurd.

The second theory offered to justify creation of a negative Commerce Clause is that Congress, by its silence, pre-empts state legislation. To the extent that the "preemption-by-silence" rationale ever made sense, it too has long since been rejected by this Court in virtually every analogous area of the law. Similarly, even where Congress *has* legislated in an area subject to its authority, our preemption jurisprudence explicitly rejects the notion that mere congressional silence on a particular issue may be read as preempting state law. To be sure, we have overcome our reluctance to pre-empt state law in two types of situations: (1) where a state law directly conflicts with a federal law; and (2) where Congress, through extensive legislation, can be said to have pre-empted the field. But those two forms of preemption provide little aid to defenders of the negative Commerce Clause. Conflict preemption only applies when there is a direct clash between an Act of Congress and a state statute, but the very premise of the negative Commerce Clause is the *absence* of congressional action. Field preemption likewise is of little use in areas where Congress has failed to enter the field, and certainly does not support the general proposition of "preemption-by-silence" that is used to provide a veneer of legitimacy to our negative Commerce Clause forays. In sum, neither of the Court's proffered theoretical justifications—exclusivity or preemption-by-silence—currently supports our negative Commerce Clause jurisprudence, if either ever did. Despite the collapse of its theoretical foundation, I suspect we have nonetheless adhered to the negative Commerce Clause because we believed it necessary to check state measures contrary to the perceived *spirit,* if not the actual letter, of the Constitution.

Moreover, our negative Commerce Clause jurisprudence has taken us well beyond the invalidation of obviously discriminatory taxes on interstate commerce. We have used the Clause to make policy-laden judgments that we are ill-equipped and arguably unauthorized to make. In so doing, we have developed multifactor tests in order to assess the perceived "effect" any particular state tax or regulation has on interstate commerce. And in an unabashedly legislative manner, we have balanced that "effect" against the perceived interests of the taxing or regulating State. Any test that requires us to assess (1) whether a particular statute serves a "legitimate" local public interest; (2) whether the effects of the statute on interstate commerce are merely "incidental" or "clearly excessive in relation to the putative benefits"; (3) the "nature" of the local interest; and (4) whether there are alternative means of furthering the local interest that have a "lesser impact" on interstate commerce, and even then makes the question "one of degree," surely invites us, if not compels us, to function more as legislators than as judges. In my view, none of this policy-laden decisionmaking is proper. Rather, the Court should confine itself to interpreting the text of the Constitution, which itself seems to prohibit in plain terms certain of the more egregious state taxes on interstate commerce described above, and leaves to Congress the policy choices necessary for any further regulation of interstate commerce.

★

MARSHALL'S EXPANSION OF THE CONTRACT CLAUSE

*Fletcher* v. *Peck* (1810)
*Dartmouth College* v. *Woodward* (1819)

THE DECLINE OF THE CONTRACT CLAUSE

*Charles River Bridge Company* v. *Warren Bridge Company* (1837)
*Home Building and Loan Association* v. *Blaisdell* (1934)

A CONTINUED RELEVANCE?

*United States Trust Company* v. *New Jersey* (1977)

NOTES

SELECTED READING

CASES

★

# 10
# THE CONTRACT CLAUSE

Article I, Section 10 of the Constitution declares that no state shall pass any "Law impairing the Obligations of Contracts." This language was included in order to protect "vested rights"—those so fundamental to an individual that they must remain beyond governmental control. Among the most important of these rights is the individual's right to security in the acquisition and possession of private property. The doctrine of vested rights thus precludes not only expropriation of an individual's property but also damaging interferences with future property interests, such as obligations embodied in contractual arrangements.[1]

James Madison's *Essay on Property,* first published in 1792 in *The National Gazette,* shows just how important property rights were for the Framers. He wrote:

> [Property] in its particular application means "that dominion which one man claims and exercises over the external things of the world, in exclusion of every other individual." In its larger and juster meaning, it embraces everything to which a man may attach a value and have a right; and which leaves to every one else the like advantage. In the former sense, a man's land, or merchandize, or money is called his property. In the latter sense, a man has property in his opinions and the free communication of them. He has a property of peculiar value in his religious opinions, and in the profession and practice dictated by them. He has property very dear to him in the safety and liberty of his person. He has an equal property in the free use of his faculties and free choice of the objects on which to employ them. In a word, as a man is said to have a right to property, he may be said to have a property in his rights.[2]

As noted in Chapter One, a principal aim of the Constitution was to secure private rights (and especially property rights) from the dangers of an overbearing majority while at the same time preserving the spirit and form of popular government. This goal was underscored in an exchange between Roger Sherman and James Madison early in the Constitutional Convention. Sherman suggested that the objects of the union include no more than defense against foreign danger and internal disputes and the establishment of a central authority to make treaties with foreign nations and to regulate foreign commerce. In rejoinder, Madison argued that another such object should be more effective provision "for the security of private rights, and the steady dispensation of justice." Interferences with these rights by state legislatures, Madison insisted, had been a principal force behind the calling of the convention.[3] And interferences there were. In Rhode Island, contemptuously referred to by many at the time as Rogues' Island, the legislature had passed a bill that allowed for the payment of debts with a worthless paper currency and that made it a criminal offense, punishable by death by hanging without benefit of clergy, for a creditor to refuse to accept such payment.[4] Such acts of oppression by the majority were not confined to the smaller, less important states: in Massachusetts, impoverished back-country farmers led by Daniel Shays had taken up arms against the government, demanding cheap paper money and a suspension of mortgage foreclosures.

The Framers adopted two principal defenses against the violation of property rights. At the national level, they relied upon the multiplicity of interests present in the extended republic they were creating. At the state level, where territorial and population restrictions precluded formation of a multiplicity of interests, the Framers trusted in the language of Article I, Section 10, whose prohibition of state laws that impair obligations of contracts helped to create a "constitutional bulwark in favor of personal security and private rights."

## MARSHALL'S EXPANSION OF THE CONTRACT CLAUSE

In the hands of John Marshall, the Contract Clause became a powerful instrument for the protection of private property. The Marshall Court not only resisted any state encroachments on private contracts (i.e., contracts between individuals), but also expanded the scope of the term *contract* to include public contracts such as public grants and corporate charters.

Marshall's opinion for the Court in *Sturges* v. *Crowninshield* (1819) and his dissent in *Ogden* v. *Saunders* (1827) indicate how he sought to preserve private contractual relations against state interference. In *Sturges,* the Court invalidated a New York bankruptcy act as it applied to a debt incurred before the law was passed. Although the Constitution had given Congress the power to establish uniform nationwide bankruptcy laws, Marshall recognized that until Congress exercised its power in such a way as to exclude state legislation on the subject, the states were free to regulate "such cases as the laws of the Union may not reach." But, he continued, New York's law violated the Contract Clause by relieving debtors of preexisting financial obligations. Marshall went even further in *Ogden,* insisting that the Contract Clause prevented legislative impairments not only of contracts already in force but also of contracts entered into after the passage of the legislation in question. A bankruptcy law already in force before a contract was made, he declared, should be unconstitutional. In this case, however, Marshall was unable to persuade a majority of the Court to accept his point of view, and for the only time in his thirty-four years as Chief Justice, he was forced to dissent on a constitutional issue.[5] The general position taken by the Court majority was that a statute in effect at the time a contract is formed is "the law of the contract," and "a part of the contract," and therefore cannot be held to impair its obligation. In the words of Justice William Johnson, the Contract Clause is "a general provision against arbitrary and tyrannical legislation over existing rights, whether personal or property." Bankruptcy legislation, accordingly, is no more constitutionally infirm than laws regulating usurious contracts or the collection of gaming debts. Since *Ogden,* this view of insolvency laws has been maintained consistently by the Court.

Of even greater importance for the protection of the vested rights of private property was Marshall's expansion of the constitutional definition of contract. In *Fletcher* v. *Peck* (1810), he extended the purview of the Contract Clause to public as well as private contracts, thereby making it applicable to transactions to which the state itself was a party. *Fletcher,* the first case in which a state statute was held void under the United States Constitution, originated in an action of the Georgia legislature, which in 1795 was induced by bribery to grant public lands, comprising much of what is now the states of Alabama and Mississippi, to four groups of purchasers known collectively as the Yazoo Land Companies.[6] Popular indignation forced the legislature in 1796 to rescind the grant, on the ground that it had been secured by fraud. By that time, however, some of the land had been purchased by innocent third parties in New England and other parts of the country. These buyers contested the validity of the rescinding act, contending that the original grant could not be repealed without violating the Contract Clause. Marshall, speaking for a unanimous Court, agreed: "Is a clause to be considered as inhibiting the State from impairing the obligation of contracts between two individuals, but as excluding from that inhibition contracts made with itself? The words themselves contain no such distinction. They are general, and are applicable to contracts of every description." Declaring that a public grant qualified as a contractual obligation and could not be abrogated without fair compensation, he therefore held that the rescinding act was an unconstitutional impairment of the obligations of contract.

Marshall further broadened the Contract Clause's coverage of public contracts in *Dartmouth College* v. *Woodward* (1819), in which a corporate charter was held to be a contract protected from infringement by state legislatures. Although this case concerned a college, it fostered the economic development of the nation by assuring business corporations that they would be protected from political interference. As Marshall's biographer, Albert J. Beveridge, has noted, *Dartmouth College* was announced at the very time that corporations were coming into their own, "springing up in response to the necessity for larger and more constant business units and because of the convenience and profit of such organizations. Marshall's opinion was a tremendous stimulant to this natural economic tendency. It reassured investors in corporate securities and gave confidence and steadiness to the business world."[7]

## THE DECLINE OF THE CONTRACT CLAUSE

Marshall's efforts to transform the Contract Clause into a powerful guarantor of vested property rights profoundly affected constitutional law for the remainder of the nineteenth century. In a definitive study of the Contract Clause, Benjamin F. Wright noted that up to 1889, it figured in about 40 percent of all Supreme Court cases involving the validity of state legislation. During that time, moreover, it provided the constitutional justification for seventy-five invalidations of state legislation on constitutional grounds—on almost half of all cases in which such legislation was held invalid by the Court.[8]

Over time, however, the Contract Clause has come to lose much of the potency that Marshall gave it. One of the principal reasons for the decline in the importance of the Contract Clause was the increased use of reservation clauses. As Justice Joseph Story pointed out in his *Dartmouth College* concurrence, states could insert as a condition in a corporate charter the power to "amend, alter, and repeal" the charter. Because such a reservation would be a part of the charter, legislative interference would not constitute an impairment of obligations of contract. Several states, taking Story's argument one step further, passed general legislation incorporating the reservation in all subsequently granted charters. Reservation clauses soon became quite common, and by 1865, fourteen states had written general reservation clauses into their constitutions.[9]

The Contract Clause's ability to protect vested rights also was diminished by the Court's strict construction of public contracts or grants after Chief Justice Roger Taney's famous opinion in *Charles River Bridge Company* v. *Warren Bridge Company* (1837). Taney insisted that any ambiguity in the terms of a grant "must operate against the adventurers [i.e., grantees] and in favor of the public" and that the grantees can claim only what is clearly given to them. Nothing could pass to the grantees by implication. "While the rights of private property are sacredly guarded," Taney observed, "we must not forget that the community also have rights, and that the happiness and well being of every citizen depends on their faithful preservation."[10]

Yet a third contributor to the weakening of the Contract Clause was the rise of the doctrine of inalienable police power. Beginning with *Fertilizing Company* v. *Hyde Park* (1878), the Court has held that the states may not contract away certain police powers. At issue in *Fertilizing Company* was a municipal ordinance that rendered valueless a franchise to operate a fertilizer factory, by prohibiting the transportation of offal through the streets and forbidding the operation of such a factory within a certain distance of the town limits. In upholding the ordinance, Justice Noah Swayne emphasized the principle that all grants are to be construed in favor of the state and argued that because the franchise grant contained no expressed exemption from the power to abate a nuisance, it had been made subject to the police power of the state. Two years later, in *Stone* v. *Mississippi,* the Court held that the grant of a twenty-five-year charter to operate a lottery was subject to later application of the police power and did not bar a subsequent statute prohibiting lotteries. The statute in question had been passed to implement a recently ratified provision of Mississippi's new constitution. Insisting that the power of governing is a trust committed by the people to the government, no part of which can be granted away, the Court found in the charter an implied agreement that the privilege granted by the state was subject to the exercise of police power: "Anyone who accepts a lottery charter does so with the implied understanding that the people may resume it at any time when the public good shall require. . . . He has in legal effect nothing more than a license to enjoy the privilege on the terms named for the specified time, unless it be sooner abrogated by the sovereign power of the State."[11] Since these two decisions, the Court consistently has upheld the supremacy of the state's police power against claims deriving from previously existing business franchises and public grants.

The doctrine of inalienable police power, like strict construction of public contracts and the use of reservation clauses, was aimed at ensuring that governments would retain the ability to govern. In reaction, those business interests that traditionally had relied on the Contract Clause for protection turned increasingly to the Due Process Clause of the Fourteenth Amendment, which in time became an even more important vehicle for the protection of vested property rights. This trend confirmed the decline of the once-potent Contract Clause. According to Professor Wright, "The displacement of the contract clause by due process of law is but an incident in the continuous development of an idea. The former clause had become too circumscribed by judicially created or permitted limitations, and its place was gradually taken by another clause where the absence of restrictive precedent allowed freer play to judicial discretion."[12]

The demise of the Contract Clause is perhaps nowhere more apparent than in *Home Building and Loan Association* v. *Blaisdell* (1934). At issue here was a Depression-inspired Minnesota act providing for a moratorium on mortgage payments. In upholding the act, the Court declared that states have a reserved power to protect the interests of their citizens in times of emergency. Writing for the majority, Chief Justice Hughes argued that "state power exists to give temporary relief from the enforcement of contracts in the presence of disasters due to physical causes such as fire, flood or earthquake," and that the same power must exist "when the urgent public need demanding such relief is produced by other and economic causes." In the end, Hughes declared, "The question is no longer merely that of one party to a contract as against another, but of the use of reasonable means to safeguard the economic structure upon which the good of all depends. . . . The principle of this development is . . . that the reservation of the reasonable exercise of the protective power of the State is read into all contracts."

The majority opinion in *Blaisdell* seems directly to contradict the principle embodied in the contract clause, and in a lengthy dissent Justice George Sutherland severely criticized it on these grounds. After describing the economic conditions that prevailed when the Constitution was adopted, Sutherland pointed out that the Contract Clause was specifically intended to prevent the states from mitigating the effects of financial emergency. He charged that in asserting that the Depression legitimated remedial actions by the state, the *Blaisdell* majority violated the intentions of those who wrote the Constitution. "With due regard for the processes of logical thinking," he wrote, "it legitimately cannot be urged that conditions which produced the rule may now be invoked to destroy it."

Many defenders of *Blaisdell* accept Justice Sutherland's analysis of the intent of the Framers but contend that the Court must adapt the Constitution "to the various crises of human affairs."[13] Not every defender of *Blaisdell* accepts Sutherland's analysis, however. Professor Gary Jacobsohn, for example, argues that Chief Justice Hughes's majority opinion reveals a deeper and more profound appreciation for the Framers' enterprise than does Sutherland's dissent. Admitting that Sutherland was correct in asserting that the Contract Clause was intended to protect creditors from their debtors (even in times of emergencies), Jacobsohn insists that "beyond this, there was a deeper intent, which was to promote the conditions of economic stability."[14] The emergency conditions created by the Depression threatened the stability necessary for sound financial arrangements in a commercial economy. "An appropriate response to this problem required a recognition of the radical changes that had occurred in the nation's economy since the time of the founding fathers. Its new complexity, a consequence of modern industrialization, commerce, and technology, meant that the interests of the society were intimately intertwined with the interests of the parties joined in a private contract."[15] According to Jacobsohn, Hughes, unlike Sutherland, recognized that in some circumstances a temporary restraint of enforcement may be "consistent with the spirit and purpose of the constitutional provision and thus be found to be within the range of the reserved power of the State to protect the vital interests of the community." Hughes thus permitted the impairment of the obligations of a specific contract in order to preserve the principle embodied in the Contract Clause itself.

Although instructive, Jacobsohn's analysis of the "deeper intent" of the Framers raises a troubling question for defenders of *Blaisdell:* If the economic stability of the nation required the passage of a mortgage moratorium law, why was it appropriate that this law be passed by a particular state legislature rather than by the national legislature? Had Congress been persuaded that the economic stability of the nation required a mortgage moratorium law, it could have passed a law virtually identical to the Minnesota act, declaring therein that its provisions would go into effect in any state in which the mortgage foreclosure rate exceeded a predetermined level. A national problem then would have had a national solution, and no controversy would have arisen over the meaning of the Contract Clause, whose provisions are limited solely to the states.

Professor Wright has pointed out that Minnesota's mortgage moratorium law was a carefully drafted statute that attempted to protect the interests of the creditor and debtor alike.[16] Nonetheless, it could not possibly protect the interests of society as a whole as fully as could a national moratorium act. Only the multiplicity of interests present at the national level is sufficient to contribute to protection of "the public good and private rights." Specifically, not every creditor affected by Minnesota's law resided in that state; many were spread across the country and had no effective voice in the Minnesota legislature. To the extent that their interests were to be protected, they had to be protected at the national level. This point of view is in keeping with one of the principal means by which the ends of the Constitution are to be secured.

## A CONTINUED RELEVANCE?

Many scholars of the Court believe that *Blaisdell* effectively ended the relevance of the Contract Clause. For them, the clause has become "a tail to the due process kite . . . , a fifth wheel to the Constitutional Law coach."[17] Decisions at the state and federal levels lend credence to this point of view.[18] The remarks by Judge Howard Baer of the New York Supreme Court for New York County in *Flushing National Bank* v. *Municipal Assistance Corporation* (1977) are illustrative. When the Emergency Moratorium Act of 1975, passed by the New York State Legislature to help New York City avoid bankruptcy, was challenged in his court for violating the contract clause (because it imposed a three-year moratorium on the repayment of $4.7 billion in outstanding short-term city debt), Judge Baer rejected this challenge, noting that both state and federal courts "have given priority to the public interest over strict compliance with the contract clause." He continued: "Numerous decisions . . . long ago repudiated the notion which plaintiff here espouses that the contract clause presents a rigid bar to the protection of vital public interests, recognizing instead the power, and indeed, the duty of states to prevent the literal enforcement of contractual terms in order to protect the health, safety, or welfare of their citizens."

*United States Trust Company* v. *New Jersey* (1977) indicated, however, that the contract clause has not become a dead letter—at least not in cases involving unilateral legislative impairment of government contracts. In *United States Trust,* the states were warned that they could not impair their obligations under contracts with private individuals in which the states receive direct, bargained-for benefits and are subject, in turn, to financial obligations that benefit the private parties to the contract. The reason is clear enough: In such instances, the states cannot be trusted to behave as referees, impartially acting in the best interests of the public. As Justice Blackmun noted for the Court majority in *United States Trust,* "Complete deference to a legislative assessment of reasonableness and necessity is not appropriate because the State's self-interest is at stake. A governmental entity can always find a use for extra money, especially when taxes do not have to be raised."[19] While *United States Trust* reflects that the Contract Clause remains a defense against self-interested governments that attempt to impair their financial obligations, it would be a mistake to read too much into the case and conclude that it represents the beginning of the clause's revitalization. As Douglas W. Kmiec has observed, the Contract Clause is "routinely subordinated to the modern Court's substantial deference to state legislative judgment in matters of economics."[20] Justice Stevens's words in *Keystone Bituminous Coal Association* v. *DeBenedictis* (1987) capture well the current desuetude into which it has fallen: "Unlike other provisions in [Article I, Section 10], it is well settled that the prohibition against impairing the obligation of contracts is not to be read literally."[21]

## NOTES

1 See Edward S. Corwin, "The Basic Doctrine of American Constitutional Law," *Michigan Law Review* 12 (February 1914): 255.

2 James Madison, "Essay on Property," in *The Writings of James Madison,* ed. Gaillard Hunt, 9 vols. (New York: G. P. Putnam's Sons, 1906), vol. 6: 101. For a contemporary reaffirmation of this view, see Justice Stewart's opinion for the Court in *Lynch* v. *Household Finance Corporation* (1972).

3 Max Farrand, ed., *The Records of the Federal Convention of 1787,* 4 vols. (New Haven, Conn.: Yale University Press, 1937), vol. 1: 133–134.

4 See Andrew C. McLaughlin, *The Confederation and the Constitution: 1787–1789* (New York: Collier, 1962), pp. 107–109.

5 Benjamin F. Wright, *The Contract Clause of the Constitution* (Cambridge, Mass.: Harvard University Press, 1938), p. 50.

6 For the details of this episode, see C. Peter Magrath, *Yazoo: Land and Politics in the New Republic* (Providence, R.I.: Brown University Press, 1966).

7 Albert J. Beveridge, *The Life of John Marshall,* 4 vols. (Boston: Houghton Mifflin, 1919), vol. 4: 276.

8 Wright, *The Contract Clause,* p. 95. Curiously, under the Taney Court, the Contract Clause also became a limitation on "judicial impairments" and not simply on "legislative enactments" as its language suggests (the Clause, after all, refers to the "pass[ing]" of "Laws." See Barton H. Thompson, Jr., "The History of the Judicial Impairment 'Doctrine' and Its Lessons for the Contract Clause," *Stanford Law Review* 44 (July 1992): 1388–1418.

9 See *Ibid.*, p. 84.

10 It must be emphasized that Chief Justice Taney's opinion in *Charles River Bridge Company* did not break with the Marshall tradition. Taney shared Marshall's view that "the rights of private property are sacredly guarded" and accepted without question Marshall's application of the Contract Clause to public as well as private contracts. See Wright, *The Contract Clause,* pp. 62–63, 245–246.

11 101 U. S. at 821. The police power prevails over private contracts with even greater force than over public contracts. As the Court observed in *Manigault* v. *Springs* (1905), "Parties by entering into contracts may not stop the legislature from enacting laws intended for the public good."

12 Wright, *The Contract Clause,* p. 258.

13 See Chapter 1 and its discussion of the adaptive approach to constitutional interpretation. See also Samuel R. Olken, who argues that Chief Justice Hughes "inherently perceived the Minnesota mortgage moratorium as presenting the Court with a classic problem in federalism over the limitations of state government" and therefore "crafted an opinion imbued with progressive notions of governmental authority and constitutional interpretation that essentially balanced the interests of individuals with the paramount objectives of the state in maintaining its economic structure." Olken, "Charles Evans Hughes and the *Blaisdell* Decision: A Historical Study of Contract Clause Jurisprudence," *Oregon Law Review* 72 (Fall 1993): 603.

14 Gary J. Jacobsohn, *Pragmatism, Statesmanship, and the Supreme Court* (Ithaca, N.Y.: Cornell University Press, 1977), p. 188.

15 *Ibid.*, p. 192.

16 Wright, *The Contract Clause,* p. 110.

17 Edward S. Corwin, *The Constitution of the United States of America: Analysis and Interpretation* (Washington, D.C.: Government Printing Office, 1953), p. 362.

18 At the federal level, see *Faitoute Iron & Steel Company* v. *City of Asbury Park* (1942); *East New York Savings Bank* v. *Hahn* (1945); and *El Paso* v. *Simmons* (1965).

19 Henry N. Butler and Larry E. Ribstein advance another possible use of the Contract Clause: to challenge the constitutionality of state statutes that regulate corporate takeovers. Operating from the premises of the "modern contractual theory of the corporation," they understand the "corporation as a set of contracts among shareholders, managers, creditors, and others" rather than "as a concession or franchise granted by the state" and therefore contend that the Contract Clause restrains the ability of states to alter the corporate con-

tract. See Butler and Ribstein, "Regulating Corporate Takeovers: State Anti-Takeovers Statutes and the Contract Clause," *University of Cincinnati Law Review* 57 (1988): 611–656.

20 Douglas W. Kmiec. "Contracts Clause," in *The Oxford Companion to the Supreme Court of the United States,* ed. Kermit L. Hall (New York: Oxford University Press, 1992), p. 196.

21 480 U.S. 470, 502 (1987).

## SELECTED READING

*The Federalist,* No. 44.

*Allied Structural Steel Company* v. *Spannaus,* 438 U.S. 234 (1978).
*East New York Savings Bank* v. *Hahn,* 326 U.S. 230 (1945).
*El Paso* v. *Simmons,* 379 U.S. 497 (1965).
*Faitoute Iron & Steel Company* v. *City of Asbury Park,* 316 U.S. 502 (1942).
*Sturges* v. *Crowninshield,* 4 Wheaton 122 (1819).

Butler, Henry N. and Larry E. Ribstein. "Regulating Corporate Takeovers: State Anti-Takeovers Statutes and the Contract Clause," *University of Cincinnati Law Review* 57 (1988): 611–656.

Ely, James W., Jr. *The Contract Clause in American History* (New York: Garland, 1997).

Epstein, Richard A. "Toward a Revitalization of the Contract Clause," *University of Chicago Law Review* 51 (Summer 1984): 703–751.

Kmiec, Douglas W. and John O McGinnis. "The Contract Clause: A Return to the Original Understanding," *Hastings Constitutional Law Quarterly* (1987): 525–544.

Magrath, C. Peter. *Yazoo: Law and Politics in the New Republic: The Case of Fletcher* v. *Peck* (Providence, R.I.: Brown University Press, 1966).

Nedelsky, Jennifer. *Private Property and the Limits of American Constitutionalism: The Madisonian Framework and Its Legacy* (Chicago: University of Chicago Press, 1990).

Olken, Samuel R. "Charles Evans Hughes and the *Blaisdell* Decision: A Historical Study of Contract Clause Jurisprudence," *Oregon Law Review* 72 (Fall 1993): 513–603.

Story, Joseph. *Commentaries on the Constitution of the United States.* Vol. 3. (Boston: Hilliard, Gray, 1833), pp. 240—269.

Thompson, Barton H., Jr. "The History of the Judicial Impairment 'Doctrine' and Its Lessons for the Contract Clause," *Stanford Law Review* 44, (July 1992): 1373–1466.

Wright, Benjamin F. *The Contract Clause of the Constitution* (Cambridge, Mass.: Harvard University Press, 1938).

## *Fletcher* v. *Peck*

**6 Cranch 87 (1810)**

In 1795, the Georgia legislature was bribed into authorizing the sale of over 35 million acres of land in what was known as the Yazoo tracts (located in the present states of Alabama and Mississippi) to four land companies for $500,000, or about 1.5 cents an acre, in return for a share of lands amounting to approximately $1,000 per legislator. An outraged Georgia electorate voted the bribed legislators out at the next election, and in 1796, the new legislature repealed the year-old land grant and voided all property rights created by it. It declared that since the 1795 law "was made without constitutional authority, and fraudulently obtained, it is hereby declared of no binding force or effect on this state, or the people thereof. . . ." Between the 1795 and 1796 acts, however, the four land companies sold off many parcels of the Yazoo tracts to purchasers who were unaware of the fraud behind the original land grants. Among the purchasers were John Peck and Robert Fletcher, who were shareholders in a New England land company. To test the validity of their land titles, Peck, a Massachusetts resident, sold 15,000 acres of his Yazoo land to Fletcher, a citizen of New Hampshire, for $3,000. Fletcher then sued Peck in federal court for breach of contract, claiming that Peck could not convey clear title of the land to him. The Circuit Court for the District of Massachusetts found the 1795 act valid and the rescinding act of 1796 invalid and held that Peck had acquired clear title, which he conveyed to Fletcher. Fletcher appealed to the United States Supreme Court. *Opinion of the Court: Marshall, Johnson, Livingston, Todd, Washington. Concurring opinion: Johnson. Not participating: Chase, Cushing.*

Chief Justice Marshall delivered the opinion of the Court.

The lands in controversy vested absolutely in the original grantees by the conveyance of the governor, made in pursuance of an act of assembly to which the legislature was fully competent. Being thus in full possession of the legal estate, they, for a valuable consideration, conveyed portions of the land to those who were willing to purchase. If the original transaction was infected with fraud, these purchasers did not participate in it, and had no notice of it. They were innocent. Yet the legislature of Georgia has involved them in the fate of the first parties to the transaction, and, if the act be valid, has annihilated their rights also.

The legislature of Georgia was a party to this transaction; and for a party to pronounce its own deed invalid, whatever cause may be assigned for its invalidity, must be considered as a mere act of power which must find its vindication in a train of reasoning not often heard in courts of justice. . . .

If a suit be brought to set aside a conveyance obtained by fraud, and the fraud be clearly proved, the conveyance will be set aside, as between the parties; but the parties of third persons, who are purchasers without notice, for a valuable consideration, cannot be disregarded. Titles which, according to every legal test, are perfect, are acquired with that confidence which is inspired by the opinion that the purchaser is safe. If there be any concealed defect, arising from the conduct of those who had held the property long before he acquired it, of which he had no notice, that concealed defect cannot be set up against him. He has paid his money for a title good at law, he is innocent, whatever may be the guilt of others, and equity will not subject him to the penalties attached to that guilt. All titles would be insecure, and the intercourse between man and man would be very seriously obstructed, if this principle be overturned. . . .

In this case the legislature may have had ample proof that the original grant was obtained by practices which can never be too much reprobated, and which would have justified its abrogation so far as respected those to whom crime was imputable. But the grant, when issued, conveyed an estate in fee-simple to the grantee, clothed with all the solemnities which law can bestow. This estate was transferable; and those who purchased parts of it were not stained by that guilt which infected the original transaction. Their case is not distinguishable from the ordinary case of purchasers of a legal estate without knowledge of any secret fraud which might have led to the emanation of the original grant. According to the well known course of equity, their rights could not be affected by such fraud. Their situation was the same, their title was the same, with that of every other member of the community who holds land by regular conveyances from the original patentee.

Is the power of the legislature competent to the annihilation of such title, and to a resumption of the property thus held?

The principle asserted is, that one legislature is competent to repeal any act which a former legislature was competent to pass; and that one legislature cannot abridge the powers of a succeeding legislature.

The correctness of this principle, so far as respects general legislation, can never be controverted. But, if an act be done under a law, a succeeding legislature cannot undo it. The past cannot be recalled by the most absolute power. Conveyances have been made; those conveyances have vested legal estates, and, if those estates may be seized by the sovereign authority, still, that they originally vested is a fact, and cannot cease to be a fact.

When, then, a law is in its nature a contract, when absolute rights have vested under that contract; a repeal of the law cannot devest those rights; and the act of annulling them, if legitimate, is rendered so by a power applicable to the case of every individual in the community. . . .

The constitution of the United States declares that no state shall pass any bill of attainder, ex post facto law or law impairing the obligation of contracts.

Does the case now under consideration come within this prohibitory section of the constitution?

In considering this very interesting question, we immediately ask ourselves what is a contract? Is a grant a contract?

A contract is a compact between two or more parties, and is either executory or executed. An executory contract is one in which a party binds himself to do, or not to do, a particular thing; such was the law under which the conveyance was made by the [Georgia] governor. A contract executed is one in which the object of contract is performed; and this, says Blackstone, differs in nothing from a grant. The contract between Georgia and the purchasers was executed by the grant. A contract executed, as well as one which is executory, contains obligations binding on the parties. A grant, in its own nature, amounts to an extinguishment of the right of the grantor, and implies a contract not to re-assert that right. A party is, therefore, always estopped by his own grant.

Since, then, in fact, a grant is a contract executed, the obligation of which still continues, and since the constitution uses the general term contract, without distinguishing between those which are executory and those which are executed, it must be construed to comprehend the latter as well as the former. A law annulling conveyances between individuals, and declaring that the grantors should stand seised of their former estates, notwithstanding those grants, would be as repugnant to the constitution as a law discharging the vendors of property from the obligation of executing their contracts by conveyances. It would be strange if a contract to convey was secured by the constitution, while an absolute conveyance remained unprotected.

If, under a fair construction of the constitution, grants are comprehended under the term contracts, is a grant from the state excluded from the operation of the provision? Is the clause to be considered as inhibiting the state from impairing the obligation of contracts between two individuals, but as excluding from that inhibition contracts made with itself?

The words themselves contain no such distinction. They are general, and are applicable to contracts of every description. If contracts made with the state are to be exempted from their operation, the exception must arise from the character of the contracting party, not from the words which are employed.

Whatever respect might have been felt for the state sovereignties, it is not to be disguised that the framers of the constitution viewed, with some apprehension, the violent acts which might grow out of the feelings of the moment; and that the people of the United States, in adopting that instrument, have manifested a determination to shield themselves and their property from the effects of those sudden and strong passions to which men are exposed. The restructions on the legislative power of the states are obviously founded in this sentiment; and the constitution of the United States contains what may be deemed a bill of rights for the people of each state. . . .

It is, then, the unanimous opinion of the court, that, in this case, the estate having passed into the hands of a purchaser for a valuable consideration, without notice, the state of Georgia was restrained, either by general principles which are common to our free institutions, or by the particular provisions of the constitution of the United States, from passing a law whereby the estate of the plaintiff in the premises so purchased could be constitutionally and legally impaired and rendered null and void. . . .

Judgment affirmed with costs.

## *Dartmouth College* v. *Woodward*

**17 U.S. (4 Wheaton) 518; 4 L. Ed. 629 (1819)**

In 1769 the British Crown granted a corporate charter to the trustees of Dartmouth College, conveying to them "forever" the right to govern the institution and to appoint their own successors. After remaining unchallenged through the revolutionary era, the charter was dramatically altered in 1816. The Republican governor and legislature of New Hampshire, having concluded that the old charter was based on principles more congenial to monarchy than to free government, sought to bring the college under public control by enacting three laws that took control of the college from the hands of the Federalist-dominated trustees and placed it under a board of overseers appointed by the governor. The trustees turned for relief to the state's judiciary. Contending that the 1816 laws impaired the obligation of contract contained in the original charter of 1769, they brought an action against William Woodward, the secretary and treasurer of the college, to recover the college's records, corporate seal, and other corporate property temporarily entrusted to him by one of the 1816 acts. The New Hampshire Supreme Court upheld the legislature's acts, chiefly on the grounds that the college was essentially a public corporation whose powers were exercised for public purposes and that it was therefore subject to public control. The trustees of the college then appealed the case upon a writ of error to the United States Supreme Court. *Opinion of the Court: Marshall, Johnson, Livingston, Story, Washington. Concurring opinions: Story, Livingston; Washington, Livingston. Dissent: Duvall.*

MR. CHIEF JUSTICE MARSHALL delivered the opinion of the Court. . . .

It can require no argument to prove, that the circumstances of this case constitute a contract. An application is made to the crown for a charter to incorporate a religious and literary institution. In the application, it is stated, that large contributions have been made for the object, which will be conferred on the corporation, as soon as it shall be created. The charter is granted, and on its faith the property is conveyed. Surely, in this transaction every ingredient of a complete and legitimate contract is to be found. The points for consideration are, 1. Is this contract protected by the constitution of the United States? 2. Is it impaired by the acts under which the defendant holds?

1. On the first point, it has been argued, that the word "contract," in its broadest sense, would comprehend the political relations between the government and its citizens, would extend to offices held within a state, for state purposes, and to many of those laws concerning civil institutions, which must change with circumstances, and be modified by ordinary legislation; which deeply concern the public, and which, to preserve good government, the public judgment must control. That even marriage is a contract, and its obligations are affected by the laws respecting divorces. That the clause in the constitution, if construed in its greatest latitude, would prohibit these laws. Taken in its broad, unlimited sense, the clause would be an unprofitable and vexatious interference with the internal concerns of a state, would unnecessarily and unwisely embarrass its legislation, and render immutable those civil institutions, which are established for purposes of internal government, and which, to subserve those purposes, ought to vary with varying circumstances. That as the framers of the constitution could never have intended to insert in that instrument, a provision so unnecessary, so mischievous, and so repugnant to its general spirit, the term "contract" must be understood in a more limited sense. That it must be understood as intended to guard against a power, of at least doubtful utility, the abuse of which had been extensively felt; and to restrain the legislature in future from violating the right to property. That, anterior to the formation of the constitution, a course of legislation had prevailed in many, if not in all, of the states, which weakened the confidence of man in man, and embarrassed all transactions between individuals, by dispensing with a faithful performance of engagements. To correct this mischief, by restraining the power which produced it, the state legislatures were forbidden "to pass any law impairing the obligation of contracts," that is, of contracts respecting property, under which some individual could claim a right to something beneficial to himself; and that, since the clause in the constitution must in construction receive some limitation, it may be confined, and ought to be confined, to cases of this description; to cases within the mischief it was intended to remedy. . . .

The parties in this case differ less on general principles, less on the true construction of the constitution in the abstract, than on the application of those principles to this case, and on the true construction of the charter of 1769. This is the point on which the cause essentially depends. If the act of incorporation be a grant of political power, if it create a civil institution, to be employed in the administration of the government, or if the funds of the college be public property, or if the state of New Hampshire, as a government, be alone interested in its transactions, the subject is one in which the legislature of the state may act according to its own judgment, unrestrained by any limitation of its power imposed by the constitution of the United States.

But if this be a private eleemosynary institution, endowed with a capacity to take property, for objects unconnected with government, whose funds are bestowed by individuals, on the faith of the charter; if the donors have stipulated for the future disposition and management of those funds, in the manner prescribed by themselves; there may be more difficulty in the case. . . . It becomes then the duty of the court, most seriously to examine this charter, and to ascertain its true character. . . .

A corporation is an artificial being, invisible, intangible, and existing only in contemplation of law. Being the mere creature of law, it possesses only those properties which the charter of its creation confers upon it, either expressly, or as incidental to its very existence. These are such as are supposed best calculated to effect the object for which it was created. Among the most important are immortality, and, if the expression may be allowed, individuality; properties, by which a perpetual succession of many persons are considered as the same, and may act as a single individual. They enable a corporation to manage its own affairs, and to hold property, without the perplexing intricacies, the hazardous and endless necessity, of perpetual conveyances for the purpose of transmitting it from hand to hand. It is chiefly for the purpose of clothing bodies of men, in succession, with these qualities and capacities, that corporations were invented, and are in use. By these means, a perpetual succession of individuals are capable of acting for the promotion of the particular object, like one immortal being. But this being does not share in the civil government of the country, unless that be the purpose for which it was created. . . .

From the fact, then, that a charter of incorporation has been granted, nothing can be inferred, which changes the character of the institution, or transfers to the government any new power over it. The character of civil institutions does not grow out of their incorporation, but out of the manner in which they are formed, and the objects for which they are created. The right to change them is not founded on their being incorporated, but on their being the instruments of government, created for its purposes. The same institutions, created for the same objects, though not incorporated, would be public institutions, and, of course, be controllable by the legislature. The incorporating act neither gives nor prevents this control. Neither, in reason, can the incorporating act change the character of a private eleemosynary institution. . . .

. . . It appears, that Dartmouth College is an eleemosynary institution, incorporated for the purpose of perpetuating the application of the bounty of the donors, to the specified objects of that bounty; that its trustees or governors were originally named by the founder, and invested with the power of perpetuating themselves; that they are not public officers, nor is it a civil institution, participating in the administration of government; but a charity-school, or a seminary of education, incorporated for the preservation of its property, and the perpetual application of that property to the objects of its creation. . . .

This is plainly a contract to which the donors, the trustees and the crown (to whose rights and obligations New Hampshire succeeds) were the original parties. It is a contract made on a valuable consideration. It is a contract for the security and disposition of property. It is a contract, on the faith of which, real and personal estate has been conveyed to the corporation. It is, then, a contract within the letter of the constitution, and within its spirit also, unless the fact, that the property is invested by the donors in trustees, for the promotion of religion and education, for the benefit of persons who are perpetually changing, though the objects remain the same, shall create a particular exception, taking this case out of the prohibition created in the constitution.

It is more than possible, that the preservation of rights of this description was not particularly in the view of the framers of the constitution, when the clause under consideration was introduced into that instrument. It is probable, that interferences of more frequent occurrence, to which the temptation was stronger, and of which the mischief was more extensive, constituted the great motive for imposing this restriction on the state legislatures. But although a particular and a rare case may not, in itself, be of sufficient magnitude to induce a rule, yet it must be governed by the rule, when established, unless some plain and strong reason for excluding it can be given. It is not enough to say, that this particular case was not in the mind of the convention, when the article was framed, nor of the American people, when it was adopted. It is necessary to go further, and to say that, had this particular case been suggested, the language would have been so varied, as to exclude it, or it would have been made a special exception. The case being within the words of the rule, must be within its operation likewise, unless there be something in the literal construction, so obviously absurd or mischievous, or repugnant to the general spirit of the instrument, as to justify those who expound the constitution in making it an exception.

On what safe and intelligible ground, can this exception stand? There is no expression in the constitution, no sentiment delivered by its contemporaneous expounders, which would justify us in making it.

The opinion of the court, after mature deliberation, is, that this is a contract, the obligation of which cannot be impaired, without violating the constitution of the United States.

2. We next proceed to the inquiry, whether its obligation has been impaired by those acts of the legislature of New Hampshire, to which the special verdict refers?

From the review of this charter, which has been taken, it appears that the whole power of governing the college, of appointing and removing tutors, of fixing their salaries, of directing the course of study to be pursued by the students, and of filling up vacancies created in their own body, was vested in the trustees. On the part of the crown, it was expressly stipulated, that this corporation, thus constituted, should continue for ever. . . . By this contract, the crown was bound, and could have made no violent alteration in its essential terms, without impairing its obligation.

By the revolution, the duties, as well as the powers, of government devolved on the people of New Hampshire. It is admitted, that among the latter was comprehended the transcendent power of parliament, as well as that of the executive department. It is too clear, to require the support of argument, that all contracts and rights respecting property, remained unchanged by the revolution. The obligations, then, which were created by the charter to Dartmouth College, were the same in the new, that they had been in the old government. The power of the government was also the same. A repeal of this charter, at any time prior to the adoption of the present constitution of the United States, would have been an extraordinary and unprecedented act of power, but one which could have been contested only by the restrictions upon the legislature, to be found in the constitution of the state. But the constitution of the United States has imposed this additional limitation, that the legislature of a state shall pass no act "impairing the obligation of contracts." . . .

On the effect of this law . . . the whole power of governing the college is transferred from trustees, appointed according to the will of the founder, expressed in the charter, to the executive of New Hampshire. The management and application of the funds of this eleemosynary institution, which are placed by the donors in the hands of trustees named in the charter, and empowered to perpetuate themselves, are placed by this act under the control of the government of the state. The will of the state is substituted for the will of the donors, in every essential operation of the college. This may be for the advantage of this college in particular, and may be for the advantage of literature in general; but it is not according to the will of the donors, and is subversive of that contract, on the faith of which their property was given. . . .

It results from this opinion, that the acts of the legislature of New Hampshire, which are stated in the special verdict found in this cause, are repugnant to the constitution of the United States; and that the judgment on this special verdict ought to have been for the plaintiffs. The judgment of the state court must, therefore, be reversed.

## *Charles River Bridge Company* v. *Warren Bridge Company*

**36 U.S. (11 Peters) 420; 9 L. Ed. 773 (1837)**

In 1785 the Massachusetts legislature granted a charter to the Charles River Bridge Company, authorizing it to construct a bridge between Charlestown and Boston and to collect tolls for forty years. (In 1792, the charter was extended to seventy years.) This franchise replaced an exclusive ferry right granted to Harvard College in 1650, and provision was made for compensating Harvard for the impairment of its ferry franchise. In 1828, however, the legislature incorporated the Warren Bridge Company and authorized it to construct another bridge, only 264 feet away from the Charles River Bridge on the Charlestown side and 825 feet away on the Boston side. No tolls were to be charged on the Warren Bridge after its construction costs were recovered or after a maximum period of six years. The Charles River Bridge Company entered state court and sought an injunction to prevent the erection of the Warren Bridge; then, after the bridge was constructed, they sought general relief, contending that the legislature, in authorizing the new bridge, had violated the contract clause. The Massachusetts Supreme Judicial Court dismissed the complaint, and the case went to the U.S. Supreme Court on a writ of error. *Opinion of the Court: Taney, Baldwin, Barbour, McLean, Wayne. Concurring opinion: McLean. Dissenting opinion: Story, Thompson.*

MR. CHIEF JUSTICE TANEY delivered the opinion of the Court. . . .

The plaintiffs in error insist that the acts of the legislature of Massachusetts of 1785, and 1792, by their true construction, necessarily implied that the legislature would not authorize another bridge, and especially a free one, by the side of this, and placed in the same line of travel, whereby the franchise granted to the "proprietors of the Charles River Bridge" should be rendered of no value; and the plaintiffs in error contend, that the grant of the charter to the proprietors of the bridge is a contract on the part of the state; and that the law authorizing the erection of the Warren Bridge in 1828, impairs the obligation of this contract. . . .

This brings us to the act of the legislature of Massachusetts, of 1785, by which the plaintiffs were incorporated by the name of "The Proprietors of the Charles River Bridge;" and it is here, and in the law of 1792, prolonging their charter, that we must look for the extent and nature of the franchise conferred upon the plaintiffs.

Much has been said in the argument of the principles of construction by which this law is to be expounded, and what undertakings, on the part of the state, may be implied. The Court think there can be no serious difficulty on that head. It is the grant of certain franchises by the public to a private corporation, and in a matter where the public interest is concerned. The rule of construction in such cases is well settled, both in England, and by the decisions of our own tribunals. . . . The rule of construction in all such cases, is now fully established to be this; that any ambiguity in the terms of the contract, must operate against the adventurers, and in favour of the public, and the plaintiffs can claim nothing that is not clearly given them by the act." . . .

. . . The object and end of all government is to promote the happiness and prosperity of the community by which it is established; and it can never be assumed, that the government intended to diminish its power of accomplishing the end for which it was created. And in a country like ours, free, active, and enterprising, continually advancing in numbers and wealth; new channels of communication are daily found necessary, both for travel and trade; and are essential to the comfort, convenience, and prosperity of the people. A state ought never to be presumed to surrender this power, because, like the taxing power, the whole community have an interest in preserving it undiminished. And when a corporation alleges, that a state has surrendered for seventy years, its power of improvement and public accommodation, in a great and important line of travel, along which a vast number of its citizens must daily pass; the community have a right to insist . . . "that its abandonment ought not be presumed, in a case, in which the deliberate purpose of the state to abandon it does not appear." The continued existence of a government would be of no great value, if by implications and presumptions, it was disarmed of the powers necessary to accomplish the ends of its creation; and the functions it was designed to perform, transferred to the hands of privileged corporations. . . . No one will question that the interests of the great body of the people of the state, would, in this instance, be affected by the surrender of this great line of travel to a single corporation, with the right to exact toll, and exclude competition for seventy years. While the rights of private property are sacredly guarded, we must not forget that the community also have rights, and that the happiness and well being of every citizen depends on their faithful preservation.

Adopting the rule of construction above stated as the settled one, we proceed to apply it to the charter of 1785, to the proprietors of the Charles River Bridge. This act of incorporation is in the usual form, and the privileges such as are commonly given to corporations of that kind. It confers on them the ordinary faculties of a corporation, for the purpose of building the bridge; and establishes certain rates of toll, which the company are authorized to take. This is the whole grant. There is no exclusive privilege given to them over the waters of Charles river, above or below their bridge. No right to erect another bridge themselves, nor to prevent other persons from erecting one. No engagement from the state, that another shall not be erected; and no undertaking not to sanction competition, nor to make improvements that may diminish the amount of its income. Upon all these subjects the charter is silent; and nothing is said in it about a line of travel, so much insisted on in the argument, in which they are to have exclusive privileges. No words are used, from which an intention to grant any of these rights can be inferred. If the plaintiff is entitled to them, it must be implied, simply, from the nature of the grant; and cannot be inferred from the words by which the grant is made.

The relative position of the Warren Bridge has already been described. It does not interrupt the passage over the Charles River Bridge, nor make the way to it or from it less convenient. None of the faculties or franchises granted to that corporation, have been revoked by the legislature; and its right to take the tolls granted by the charter remains unaltered. In short, all the franchises and rights of property enumerated in the charter, and there mentioned to have been granted to it, remain unimpaired. But its income is destroyed by the Warren Bridge; which, being free, draws off the passengers and property which would have gone over it, and renders their franchise of no value. This is the gist of the complaint. For it is not pretended, that the erection of the Warren Bridge would have done them any injury, or in any degree affected their right of property; if it had not diminished the amount of their tolls. In order then to entitle themselves to relief, it is necessary to show, that the legislature contracted not to do the act of which they complain; and that they impaired, or in other words, violated the contract by the erection of the Warren Bridge.

The inquiry then is, does the charter contain such a contract on the part of the state? Is there any such stipulation to be found in that instrument? It must be admitted on all hands, that there is none—no words that even relate to another bridge, or to the diminution of their tolls, or to the line of travel. If a contract on that subject can be gathered from the charter, it must be by implication; and cannot be found in the words used. Can such an agreement be implied? The rule of construction before stated is an answer to the question. In charters of this description, no rights are taken from the public, or given to the corporation, beyond those which the words of the charter, by their natural and proper construction, purport to convey. There are no words which import such a contract as the plaintiffs in error contend for, and none can be implied. . . .

Indeed, the practice and usage of almost every state in the Union, old enough to have commenced the work of internal improvement, is opposed to the doctrine contended for on the part of the plaintiffs in error. Turnpike roads have been made in succession, on the same line of travel; the later ones interfering materially with the profits of the first. These corporations have, in some instances, been utterly ruined by the introduction of newer and better modes of transportation, and travelling. In some cases, rail roads have rendered the turnpike roads on the same line of travel so entirely useless, that the franchise of the turnpike corporation is not worth preserving. Yet in none of these cases have the corporations supposed that their privileges were invaded, or any contract violated on the part of the state. The absence of any such controversy, when there must have been so many occasions to give rise to it, proves that neither states, nor individuals, nor corporations, ever imagined that such a contract could be implied from such characters. It shows that the men who voted these laws, never imagined that they were forming such a contract; and if we maintain that they have made it, we must create it by a legal fiction, in opposition to the truth of the fact, and the obvious intention of the party. We cannot deal thus with the rights reserved to the states; and by legal intendments and mere technical reasoning, take away from them any portion of that power over their own internal police and improvement, which is so necessary to their well being and prosperity. . . .

The judgment of the supreme judicial court of the commonwealth of Massachusetts, dismissing the plaintiffs' bill, must, therefore, be affirmed, with costs.

MR. JUSTICE STORY, dissenting. I maintain that upon the principle of common reason and legal interpretation, the present grant carries with it a necessary implication that the legislature shall do no act to destroy or essentially to impair the franchise; that (as one of the learned judges of the state court expressed it), there is an implied agreement of the state to grant the undisturbed use of the bridge and its tolls, so far as respects any acts of its own, or of any persons acting under its authority. In other words, the state, impliedly, contracts not to resume its grants, or to do any act to the prejudice or destruction of its grant. I maintain, that there is no authority or principle established in relation to the construction of crown grants, or legislative grants; which does not concede and justify this doctrine. Where the thing is given, the incidents, without which it cannot be enjoyed, are also given. . . . I maintain that a different doctrine is utterly repugnant to all the principles of the common law, applicable to all franchises of a like nature; and that we must overturn some of the best securities of the rights of property, before it can be established. . . . I maintain, that under the principles of the common law, there exists no more right in the legislature of Massachusetts, to erect the Warren bridge, to the ruin of the franchise of the Charles River bridge, than exists to transfer the latter to the former, or authorize the former to demolish the latter. If the legislature does not mean in its grant to give any exclusive rights, let it say so, expressly; directly; and in terms admitting of no misconstruction. . . .

My judgment is formed upon the terms of the grant, its nature and objects, its design and duties; and, in its interpretation, I seek for no new principles, but I apply such as are as old as the very rudiments of the common law. . . .

Upon the whole, my judgment is, that the act of the legislature of Massachusetts granting the charter of Warren bridge, is an act impairing the obligation of the prior contract and grant to the proprietors of Charles River bridge; and, by the constitution of the United States, it is therefore utterly void. I am for reversing the decree of the state court (dismissing the bill); and for remanding the cause to the state court for further proceedings, as to law and justice shall appertain.

## *Home Building and Loan Association* v. *Blaisdell*

**290 U.S. 398; 54 S. Ct. 231; 78 L. Ed. 413 (1934)**

In 1933, at the depth of the Depression, Minnesota passed a mortgage moratorium act designed to prevent the loss of mortgaged property by individuals temporarily unable to meet their financial obligations. The act authorized the state courts, upon application of the mortgagor, to extend the period of redemption from foreclosure sales for such a period as the courts might deem equitable, but not beyond May 1, 1935. The act was to remain in effect "only during the continuance of the emergency and in no event beyond May 1, 1935." During the emergency period, the mortgagor was required to apply the income or reasonable rental value, as fixed by the courts, to the payment of taxes, interest, insurance, and the mortgage indebtedness. It was a carefully drafted statute that attempted to protect the interest of the creditor as well as that of the debtor. Despite the care that went into its drafting, the moratorium act did alter the arrangement of existing contracts and thus raised a question of whether or not the act was an unconstitutional impairment of the obligations of contract. This question ultimately was brought before the Supreme Court when John Blaisdell and his wife, owners of a lot that was mortgaged to the Home Building and Loan Association, applied to the District Court of Hennepin County for an extension of time so that they could retain ownership of their home. The District Court extended the redemption period, and the Supreme Court of Minnesota affirmed the judgment. The loan company appealed. *Opinion of the Court: Hughes, Brandeis, Cardozo, Roberts, Stone. Dissenting opinion: Sutherland, Butler, McReynolds, Van Devanter.*

MR. CHIEF JUSTICE HUGHES delivered the opinion of the Court. . . .

The state court upheld the statute as an emergency measure. Although conceding that the obligations of the mortgage contract were impaired, the court decided that what it thus described as an impairment was, notwithstanding the contract clause of the Federal Constitution, within the police power of the State as that power was called into exercise by the public economic emergency which the legislature had found to exist. Attention is thus directed to the preamble and the first section of the statute, which described the existing emergency in terms that were deemed to justify the temporary relief which the statute affords. . . .

In determining whether the provision for this temporary and conditional relief exceeds the power of the State by reason of the clause in the Federal Constitution prohibiting impairment of the obligations of contracts, we must consider the relation of emergency to constitutional power, the historical setting of the contract clause, the development of the jurisprudence of this Court in the construction of that clause, and the principles of construction which we may consider to be established.

Emergency does not create power. Emergency does not increase granted power or remove or diminish the restrictions imposed upon power granted or reserved. The Constitution was adopted in a period of grave emergency. Its grants of power to the Federal Government and its limitations of the power of the States were determined in the light of emergency and they are not altered by emergency. What power was thus granted and what limitations were thus imposed are questions which have always been, and always will be, the subject of close examination under our constitutional system.

While emergency does not create power, emergency may furnish the occasion for the exercise of power. . . . The constitutional question presented in the light of an emergency is whether the power possessed embraces the particular exercise of it in response to particular conditions. Thus, the war power of the Federal Government is not created by the emergency of war, but it is a power given to meet that emergency. It is a power to wage war successfully, and thus it permits the harnessing of the entire energies of the people in a supreme cooperative effort to preserve the nation. But even the war power does not remove constitutional limitations safeguarding essential liberties. When the provisions of the Constitution, in grant or restriction are specific, so particularized as not to admit of construction, no question is presented. Thus, emergency would not permit a State to have more than two Senators in the Congress, or permit the election of President by a general popular vote without regard to the number of electors to which the States are respectively entitled, or permit the States to "coin money" or to "make anything but gold and silver coin a tender in payment of debts." But where constitutional grants and limitations of power are set forth in general clauses, which afford a broad outline, the process of construction is essential to fill in the details. That is true of the contract clause. . . .

In the construction of the contract clause, the debates in the Constitutional Covention are of little aid. But the reasons which led to the adoption of that clause, and of the other prohibitions of Section 10 of Article I, are not left in doubt and have frequently been described with eloquent emphasis. The widespread distress following the revolutionary period, and the plight of debtors, had called forth in the States an ignoble array of legislative schemes for the defeat of creditors and the invasion of contractual obligations. Legislative interferences had been so numerous and extreme that the confidence essential to prosperous trade had been undermined and the utter destruction of credit was threatened. . . .

But full recognition of the occasion and general purpose of the clause does not suffice to fix its precise scope. Nor does an examination of the details of prior legislation in the States yield criteria which can be considered controlling. To ascertain the scope of the constitutional prohibition we examine the course of judicial decisions in its application. These put it beyond question that the prohibition is not an absolute one and is not to be read with literal exactness like a mathematical formula. . . .

Not only is the constitutional provision qualified by the measure of control which the State retains over remedial processes, but the State also continues to possess authority to safeguard the vital interests of its people. It does not matter that legislation appropriate to that end "has the result of modifying or abrogating contracts already in effect." . . . Not only are existing laws read into contracts in order to fix obligations as between the parties, but the reservation of essential attributes of sovereign power is also read into contracts as a postulate of the legal order. The policy of protecting contracts against impairment presupposes the maintenance of a government by virtue of which contractual relations are worth while,—a government which retains adequate authority to secure the peace and good order of society. This principle of harmonizing the constitutional prohibition with the necessary residuum of state power has had progressive recognition in the decisions of this Court. . . .

The legislature cannot "bargain away the public health or public morals." Thus, the constitutional provision against the impairment of contracts was held not to be violated by an amendment of the state constitution which put an end to a lottery theretofore authorized by the legislature. *Stone* v. *Mississippi*, . . . (1880). . . . The lottery was a valid enterprise when established under express state authority, but the legislature in the public interest could put a stop to it. A similar rule has been applied to the control by the State of the sale of intoxicating liquors. . . . The States retain adequate power to protect the public health against the maintenance of nuisances despite insistence upon existing contracts. . . . Legislation to protect the public safety comes within the same category of reserved power. . . . This principle has had recent and noteworthy application to the regulation of the use of public highways by common carriers and "contract carriers," where the assertion of interference with existing contract rights has been without avail. . . .

The argument is pressed that in the cases we have cited the obligation of contracts was affected only incidentally. This argument proceeds upon a misconception. The question is not whether the legislative action affects contracts incidentally, or directly or indirectly, but whether the legislation is addressed to a legitimate end and the measures taken are reasonable and appropriate to that end. Another argument, which comes more closely to the point, is that the state power may be addressed directly to the prevention of the enforcement of contracts only when these are of a sort which the legislature in its discretion may denounce as being in themselves hostile to public morals, or public health, safety, or welfare, or where the prohibition is merely of injurious practices; that interference with the enforcement of other and valid contracts according to appropriate legal procedure, although the interference is temporary and for a public purpose, is not permissible. This is but to contend that in the latter case the end is not legitimate in the view that it cannot be reconciled with a fair interpretation of the constitutional provision.

Undoubtedly, whatever is reserved of state power must be consistent with the fair intent of the constitutional limitation of that power. The reserved power cannot be construed so as to destroy the limitation, nor is the limitation to be construed to destroy the reserved power in its essential aspects. They must be construed in harmony with each other. This principle precludes a construction which would permit the State to adopt as its policy the repudiation of debts or the destruction of contracts or the denial of means to enforce them. But it does not follow that conditions may not arise in which a temporary restraint of enforcement may be consistent with the spirit and purpose of the constitutional provision and thus be found to be within the range of the reserved power of the State to protect the vital interests of the community. It cannot be maintained that the constitutional prohibition should be so construed as to prevent limited and temporary interpositions with respect to the enforcement of contracts if made necessary by a great public calamity such as fire, flood, or earthquake. . . . The reservation of state power appropriate to such extraordinary conditions may be deemed to be as much a part of all contracts, as is the reservation of state power to protect the public interest in the other situations to which we have referred. And if state power exists to give temporary relief from the enforcement of contracts in the presence of disasters due to physical causes such as fire, flood or earthquake, that power cannot be said to be nonexistent when the urgent public need demanding such relief is produced by other and economic causes. . . .

It is manifest from this review of our decisions that there has been a growing appreciation of public needs and of the necessity of finding ground for a rational compromise between individual rights and public welfare. The settlement and consequent contraction of the public domain, the pressure of a constantly increasing density of population, the interrelation of the activities of our people and the complexity of our economic interests, have inevitably led to an increased use of the organization of society in order to protect the very bases of individual opportunity. Where, in earlier days, it was thought that only the concerns of individuals or of classes were involved, and that those of the State itself were touched only remotely, it has later been found that the fundamental interests of the State are directly affected; and that the question is no longer merely that of one party to a contract as against another, but of the use of reasonable means to safeguard the economic structure upon which the good of all depends. . . .

Applying the criteria established by our decisions we conclude:

1. An emergency existed in Minnesota which furnished a proper occasion for the exercise of the reserved power of the State to protect the vital interests of the community. The declarations of the existence of this emergency by the legislature and by the Supreme Court of Minnesota cannot be regarded as a subterfuge or as lacking in adequate basis. . . . The finding of the legislature and state court has support in the facts of which we take judicial notice. . . .

2. The legislation was addressed to a legitimate end, that is, the legislation was not for the mere advantage of particular individuals but for the protection of a basic interest of society.

3. In view of the nature of the contracts in question—mortgages of unquestionable validity—the relief afforded and justified by the emergency, in order not to contravene the constitutional provision, could only be of a character appropriate to that emergency and could be granted only upon reasonable conditions.

4. The conditions upon which the period of redemption is extended do not appear to be unreasonable. . . . The integrity of the mortgage indebtedness is not impaired; interest continues to run; the validity of the sale and the right of a mortgagee-purchaser to title or to obtain a deficiency judgment, if the mortgagor fails to redeem within the extended period, are maintained; and the conditions of redemption, if redemption there be, stand as they were under the prior law. . . . Also important is the fact that mortgagees, as is shown by official reports of which we may take notice, are predominantly corporations, such as insurance companies, banks, and investment and mortgage companies. These, and such individual mortgagees as are small investors, are not seeking homes or the opportunity to engage in farming. Their chief concern is the reasonable protection of their investment security. It does not matter that there are, or may be, individual cases of another aspect. The legislature was entitled to deal with the general or typical situation. The relief afforded by the statute has regard to the interest of mortgagees as well as to the interest of mortgagors. The legislation seeks to prevent the impending ruin of both by a considerate measure of relief.

5. The legislation is temporary in operation. It is limited to the exigency which called it forth. . . .

We are of the opinion that the Minnesota statute as here applied does not violate the contract clause of the Federal Constitution. Whether the legislation is wise or unwise as a matter of policy is a question with which we are not concerned.

MR. JUSTICE SUTHERLAND, dissenting.

Few questions of greater moment than that just decided have been submitted for judicial inquiry during this generation. He simply closes his eyes to the necessary implications of the decision who fails to see in it the potentiality of future gradual but ever-advancing encroachments upon the sanctity of private and public contracts. The effect of the Minnesota legislation, though serious enough in itself, is of trivial significance compared with the far more serious and dangerous inroads upon the limitations of the Constitution which are almost certain to ensue as a consequence naturally following any step beyond the boundaries fixed by that instrument. And those of us who are thus apprehensive of the effect of this decision would, in a matter so important, be neglectful of our duty should we fail to spread upon the permanent records of the court the reasons which move us to the opposite view.

A provision of the Constitution, it is hardly necessary to say, does not admit of two distinctly opposite interpretations. It does not mean one thing at one time and an entirely different thing at another time. If the contract impairment clause, when framed and adopted, meant that the terms of a contract for the payment of money could not be altered *in invitum* by a state statute enacted for the relief of hardly pressed debtors to the end and with the effect of postponing payment or enforcement during and because of an economic or financial emergency, it is but to state the obvious to say that it means the same now. This view, at once so rational in its application to the written word, and so necessary to the stability of constitutional principles, though from time to time challenged, has never, unless recently, been put within the realm of doubt by the decisions of this court. . . .

The whole aim of construction, as applied to a provision of the Constitution, is to discover the meaning, to ascertain and give effect to the intent, of its framers and the people who adopted it. . . . The necessities which gave rise to the provision, the controversies which preceded, as well as the conflicts of opinion which were settled by its adoption, are matters to be considered to enable us to arrive at a correct result. . . . The history of the times, the state of things existing when the provision was framed and adopted, should be looked to in order to ascertain the mischief and the remedy. . . . As nearly as possible we should place ourselves in the condition of those who framed and adopted it. . . . And if the meaning be at all doubtful, the doubt should be resolved, wherever reasonably possible to do so, in a way to forward the evident purpose with which the provision was adopted. . . .

An application of these principles to the question under review removes any doubt, if otherwise there would be any, that the contract impairment clause denies to the several states the power to mitigate hard consequences resulting to debtors from financial or economic exigencies by an impairment of the obligation of contracts of indebtedness. . . .

The lower court, and counsel for the appellees in their argument here, frankly admitted that the statute does constitute a material impairment of the contract, but contended that such legislation is brought within the state power by the present emergency. If I understand the opinion just delivered, this court is not wholly in accord with that view. The opinion concedes that emergency does not create power, or increase granted power, or remove or diminish restrictions upon power granted or reserved. It then proceeds to say, however, that while emergency does not create power, it may furnish the occasion for the exercise of power. I can only interpret what is said on that subject as meaning that while an emergency does not diminish a restriction upon power it furnishes an occasion for diminishing it; and this, as it seems to me, is merely to say the same thing by the use of another set of words, with the effect of affirming that which has just been denied.

It is quite true that an emergency may supply the occasion for the exercise of power, depending upon the nature of the power and the intent of the Constitution with respect thereto. But we are here dealing not with a power granted by the Federal Constitution, but with the state police power, which exists in its own right. Hence the question is not whether an emergency furnishes the occasion for the exercise of that state power, but whether an emergency furnishes an occasion for the relaxation of the restrictions upon the power imposed by the contract impairment clause; and the difficulty is that the contract impairment clause forbids state action under any circumstances, if it have the effect of impairing the obligation of contracts. That clause restricts every state power in the particular specified, no matter what may be the occasion. It does not contemplate that an emergency shall furnish an occasion for softening the restriction or making it any the less a restriction upon state action in that contingency than it is under strictly normal conditions.

The Minnesota statute either impairs the obligation of contracts or it does not. If it does not, the occasion to which it relates becomes immaterial, since then the passage of the statute is the exercise of a normal, unrestricted, state power and requires no special occasion to render it effective. If it does, the emergency no more furnishes a proper occasion for its exercise than if the emergency were non-existent. And so, while, in form, the suggested distinction seems to put us forward in a straight line, in reality it simply carries us back in a circle, like bewildered travelers lost in a wood, to the point where we parted company with the view of the state court. . . .

. . . The phrase, "obligation of a contract," in the constitutional sense imports a legal duty to perform the specified obligation of *that* contract, not to substitute and perform, against the will of one of the parties, a different, albeit equally valuable, obligation. And a state, under the contract impairment clause, has no more power to accomplish such a substitution than has one of the parties to the contract against the will of the other. It cannot do so either by acting directly upon the contract, or by bringing about the result under the guise of a statute in form acting only upon the remedy. If it could, the efficacy of the constitutional restriction would, in large measure, be made to disappear. . . .

I quite agree with the opinion of the court that whether the legislation under review is wise or unwise is a matter with which we have nothing to do. Whether it is likely to work well or work ill presents a question entirely irrelevant to the issue. The only legitimate inquiry we can make is whether it is constitutional. If it is not, its virtues, if it have any, cannot save it; if it is, its faults cannot be invoked to accomplish its destruction. If the provisions of the Constitution be not upheld when they pinch as well as when they comfort, they may as well be abandoned. Being unable to reach any other conclusion than that the Minnesota statute infringes the constitutional restriction under review, I have no choice but to say so.

## *United States Trust Company* v. *New Jersey*

**431 U.S. 1; 97 S. Ct. 1505; 52 L. Ed. 2d 92 (1977)**

A 1962 interstate compact between New York and New Jersey limited the ability of the Port Authority of New York and New Jersey to subsidize mass transit from revenues and reserves pledged as security for consolidated bonds issued by the Authority. In 1974, in the face of an emerging national energy crisis, the New Jersey and New York legislatures, acting concurrently, retroactively repealed the 1962 covenant. United States Trust Company, a trustee and bondholder of the Port Authority, brought suit in a New Jersey Superior Court, attacking New Jersey's statutory repeal as a violation of the Contract Clause and seeking declaratory relief. The trial court dismissed the complaint on the grounds that the statute repealing the covenant was a reasonable exercise of New Jersey's police power. The New Jersey Supreme Court affirmed the decision, and the case was appealed to the Supreme Court. *Opinion of the Court: Blackmun, Burger, Rehnquist, Stevens. Concurring opinion: Burger. Dissenting opinion: Brennan, Marshall, White. Powell and Stewart did not participate.*

MR. JUSTICE BLACKMUN delivered the opinion of the Court. . . .

. . . Whether or not the protection of contract rights comports with current views of wise public policy, the Contract Clause remains a part of our written Constitution. We therefore must attempt to apply that constitutional provision to the instant case with due respect for its purpose and the prior decisions of this Court. . . .

Although the Contract Clause appears literally to proscribe "any" impairment, this Court observed in *Blaisdell* that "the prohibition is not an absolute one and is not to be read with literal exactness like a mathematical formula." . . . Thus, a finding that there has been a technical impairment is merely a preliminary step in resolving the more difficult question whether that impairment is permitted under the Constitution. In the instant case, as in *Blaisdell*, we must attempt to reconcile the strictures of the Contract Clause with the "essential attributes of sovereign power ". . . necessarily reserved by the States to safeguard the welfare of their citizens. . . .

The States must possess broad power to adopt general regulatory measures without being concerned that private contracts will be impaired, or even destroyed, as a result. Otherwise, one would be able to obtain immunity from state regulation by making private contractual arrangements. . . .

Yet private contracts are not subject to unlimited modification under the police power. . . . Legislation adjusting the rights and responsibilities of contracting parties must be upon reasonable conditions and of a character appropriate to the public purpose justifying its adoption. . . . As is customary in reviewing economic and social regulation, however, courts properly defer to legislative judgment as to the necessity and reasonableness of a particular measure. . . .

When a State impairs the obligation of its own contract, . . . complete deference to a legislative assessment of reasonableness and necessity is not appropriate because the State's self-interest is at stake. A governmental entity can always find a use for extra money, especially when taxes do not have to be raised. If a State could reduce its financial obligations whenever it wanted to spend the money for what it regarded as an important public purpose, the Contract Clause would provide no protection at all.

Mass transportation, energy conservation, and environmental protection are goals that are important and of legitimate public concern. Appellees contend that these goals are so important that any harm to bondholders from repeal of the 1962 covenant is greatly outweighed by the public benefit. We do not accept this invitation to engage in a utilitarian comparison of public benefit and private loss. . . . The Court has not "balanced away" the limitation on state action imposed by the Contract Clause. Thus a State cannot refuse to meet its legitimate financial obligations simply because it would prefer to spend the money to promote the public good rather than the private welfare of its creditors. We can only sustain the repeal of the 1962 covenant if that impairment was both reasonable and necessary to serve the admittedly important purposes claimed by the State.

The more specific justification offered for the repeal of the 1962 covenant was the States' plan for encouraging users of private automobiles to shift to public transportation. The States intended to discourage private automobile use by raising bridge and tunnel tolls and to use the extra revenue from those tolls to subsidize improved commuter railroad service. Appellees contend that repeal of the 1962 covenant was necessary to implement this plan because the new mass transit facilities could not possibly be self-supporting and the covenant's "permitted deficits" level had already been exceeded. We reject this justification because the repeal was neither necessary to achievement of the plan nor reasonable in light of the circumstances.

The determination of necessity can be considered on two levels. First, it cannot be said that total repeal of the covenant was essential; a less drastic modification would have permitted the contemplated plan without entirely removing the covenant's limitations on the use of Port Authority revenues and reserves to subsidize commuter railroads. Second, without modifying the covenant at all, the States could have adopted alternative means of achieving their twin goals of discouraging automobile use and improving mass transit. Appellees contend, however, that choosing among these alternatives is a matter for legislative discretion. But a State is not completely free to consider impairing the obligations of its own contracts on a par with other policy alternatives. Similarly, a State is not free to impose a drastic impairment when an evident and more moderate course would serve its purposes equally well. . . .

We also cannot conclude that repeal of the covenant was reasonable in light of the surrounding circumstances. . . .

. . . In the instant case the need for mass transportation in the New York metropolitan area was not a new development, and the likelihood that publicly owned commuter railroads would produce substantial deficits was well known. As early as 1922, over a half century ago, there were pressures to involve the Port Authority in mass transit. It was with full knowledge of these concerns that the 1962 covenant was adopted. Indeed, the covenant was specifically intended to protect the pledged revenues and reserves against the possibility that such concerns would lead the Port Authority into greater involvement in deficit mass transit. . . .

. . . We cannot conclude that the repeal was reasonable in the light of changed circumstances.

We therefore hold that the Contract Clause of the United States Constitution prohibits the retroactive repeal of the 1962 covenant. The judgment of the Supreme Court of New Jersey is reversed.

MR. JUSTICE BRENNAN, with whom MR. JUSTICE WHITE and MR. JUSTICE MARSHALL join, dissenting.

Decisions of this Court for at least a century have construed the Contract Clause largely to be powerless in binding a State to contracts limiting the authority of successor legislatures to enact laws in furtherance of the health, safety, and similar collective interests of the polity. In short, those decisions established the principle that lawful exercises of a State's police powers stand paramount to private rights held under contract. Today's decision, in invalidating the New Jersey Legislature's 1974 repeal of its predecessor's 1962 covenant, rejects this previous understanding and remolds the Contract Clause into a potent instrument for overseeing important policy determinations of the state legislature. At the same time, by creating a constitutional safe haven for property rights embodied in a contract, the decision substantially distorts modern constitutional jurisprudence governing regulation of private economic interests. I might understand, though I could not accept, this revival of the Contract Clause were it in accordance with some coherent and constructive view of public policy. But elevation of the Clause to the status of regulator of the municipal bond market at the heavy price of frustration of sound legislative policy-making is as demonstrably unwise as it is unnecessary. The justification for today's decision, therefore, remains a mystery to me, and I respectfully dissent. . . .

One of the fundamental premises of our popular democracy is that each generation of representatives can and will remain responsive to the needs and desires of those whom they represent. Crucial to this end is the assurance that new legislators will not automatically be bound by the policies and undertakings of earlier days. In accordance with this philosophy, the Framers of our Constitution conceived of the Contract Clause primarily as protection for economic transactions entered into by purely private parties, rather than obligations involving the State itself. . . . The Framers fully recognized that nothing would so jeopardize the legitimacy of a system of government that relies upon the ebbs and flows of politics to "clean out the rascals" than the possibility that those same rascals might perpetuate their policies simply by locking them into binding contracts.

I would not want to be read as suggesting that the States should blithely proceed down the path of repudiating their obligations, financial or otherwise. Their credibility in the credit market obviously is highly dependent on exercising their vast lawmaking powers with self-restraint and discipline, and I, for one, have little doubt that few, if any, jurisdictions would choose to use their authority "so foolishly as to kill a goose that lays golden eggs for them," . . . But in the final analysis, there is no reason to doubt that appellant's financial welfare is being adequately policed by the political processes and the bond marketplace itself. The role to be played by the Constitution is at most a limited one. . . . For this Court should have learned long ago that the Constitution—be it through the Contract or Due Process Clause—can actively intrude into such economic and policy matters only if my Brethren are prepared to bear enormous institutional and social costs. Because I consider the potential dangers of such judicial interference to be intolerable, I dissent.

★

RIGHTS AND THE FOUNDING

*Barron* v. *Baltimore* (1833)

THE FOURTEENTH AMENDMENT

DUE PROCESS AND THE BILL OF RIGHTS

*Palko* v. *Connecticut* (1937)
*Adamson* v. *California* (1947)
*Duncan* v. *Louisiana* (1968)

NOTES

SELECTED READING

CASES

★

# 11
# RIGHTS UNDER THE CONSTITUTION

The constitutional guarantees for Americans' most fundamental rights—freedom of speech, the free exercise of religion, freedom from unreasonable searches and seizures, and the like—did not appear in the original Constitution. Only with the ratification of the Bill of Rights, amendments added three years after the adoption of the Constitution, were these rights given express constitutional protection. Moreover, the Bill of Rights originally provided protection only against violations of rights by the national government, leaving state governments largely free to deal with rights as they saw fit.[1] Not until the ratification of the Fourteenth Amendment in 1868 did the Constitution include substantial restrictions on state invasions of rights. And not until the second half of the twentieth century did the Supreme Court interpret that amendment as imposing on the states most of the same requirements that had previously been imposed on the national government.

This chapter analyzes these dramatic changes in the protection of rights under the Constitution. Initially, it considers why the original Constitution did not contain express guarantees of rights and how those guarantees became part of the Constitution. Next, it examines the adoption of the Fourteenth Amendment and its effects on the division of responsibility between the national and state governments for the protection of rights. Finally, it traces the U.S. Supreme Court's changing perspectives on extending constitutional protection against state violations of rights.

## RIGHTS AND THE FOUNDING

### The Creation and Ratification of the Constitution

The Constitution originally did not include a bill of rights because few delegates at the Constitutional Convention believed that one was needed. In fact, neither the Virginia Plan nor the New Jersey Plan, the two major plans of government introduced at the convention, contained a bill of rights. During the latter stages of the convention, the delegates added various rights guarantees to the Constitution on a piecemeal basis. Among these were restrictions on suspending the privilege of the writ of *habeas corpus* (protecting against illegal imprisonment) and bans on *ex post facto* laws (criminalizing conduct after it has already taken place) and on religious tests for federal office. But when George Mason of Virginia proposed, a week before adjournment, that a bill of rights be added to the Constitution, arguing that "[i]t would give great quiet to the people," no state supported his proposal.

This refusal to include a bill of rights in the Constitution did not stem from a hostility to rights. But having witnessed the failure of state declarations of rights to prevent violations of rights, most delegates were skeptical about the efficacy of parchment barriers." Real security for rights, they believed, came not from constitutional prohibitions, but from a well-constructed government that lacked the propensity to violate rights. The creation of such a government was the delegates' primary concern throughout the convention. Thus they believed that the Constitution already protected rights against invasion by the national government by: (1) enumerating and limiting national powers, (2) making governmental officials accountable to the people, (3) promoting the establishment of an extended republic" (see Chapter 1), in which majority factions were unlikely to form, and (4) establishing a system of separation of powers and checks and balances. These features led Alexander Hamilton to conclude in *The Federalist,* No. 84, that "the Constitution is itself, in every rational sense, and to every useful purpose, a bill of rights."[2]

Hamilton argued that the inclusion of a bill of rights was unnecessary: Because the Constitution granted only a limited legislative power to the national government, Congress did not have the power to invade rights. In fact, he suggested, inclusion of a bill of rights could be dangerous. To prohibit Congress from invading the freedom of the press or violating other rights would seem to imply that in the absence of the prohibition, Congress could do just that. So instead of limiting national power, a bill of rights would in effect expand it. In addition, Hamilton noted that no bill of rights could hope to be comprehensive. However, the failure to include a right in the bill of rights would seem to imply that Congress was not prohibited from invading that right. Thus, the inclusion of some rights would in practice make other rights less secure.

Whatever the merits of Hamilton's arguments, they did not persuade the Anti-Federalists, who opposed the ratification of the Constitution. Some Anti-Federalists argued that the Constitution itself undermined

Hamilton's argument: If a non-comprehensive list of rights was dangerous, why did the Constitution already include some rights guarantees? More generally, they emphasized the need to rein in what they viewed as a dangerously powerful national government. "Universal experience," they insisted, demonstrated "that the most express declarations and reservations are necessary to protect the just rights and liberty of mankind from the silent, powerful and ever active conspiracy of those who govern."[3] This argument proved extremely effective.[4] At the Massachusetts ratifying convention, the Federalists were forced to agree to introduce amendments as the price of ratification. Several subsequent ratifying conventions likewise submitted suggestions for amendments along with their instruments of ratification. At least some Anti-Federalists hoped through this process of amendment to undermine the powers of the national government.

## The Creation of the Bill of Rights

As a member of the House of Representatives from Virginia, James Madison played the leading role in the creation of the Bill of Rights.[5] Madison prepared an initial list of amendments, largely culled from the proposals submitted by the various states, and pushed vigorously for their consideration in the face of general disinterest on the part of his fellow representatives. Madison's persistence did not stem from a conviction that the absence of a bill of rights was a major defect in the Constitution. Rather, by introducing the amendments, he sought both to quell the fears of citizens sincerely concerned about abuses of governmental power and to forestall the introduction of amendments by opponents of the Constitution that would subvert the new government. As he put it: "it is possible the abuse of the powers of the General Government may be guarded against in a more secure manner than is now done, while no one advantage arising from the exercise of that power shall be damaged or endangered by it."[6]

Madison's strategy succeeded brilliantly. Congress for the most part accepted his amendments and rejected proposals that would have crippled the national government. The states quickly ratified ten of the twelve amendments sent to them, rejecting an amendment affecting representation in the House and belatedly ratifying one regulating congressional pay increases in 1992. Ratification of the ten amendments, the Bill of Rights, reassured the populace that their rights were secure and effectively ended Anti-Federalist efforts to tamper with the Constitution.

Two aspects of the Bill of Rights are particularly noteworthy. First, Madison consciously designed the amendments to avoid the problems raised by Hamilton in *The Federalist,* No. 84. The Ninth Amendment responded to Hamilton's concern that no listing of rights could be comprehensive by noting that "[t]he enumeration in the Constitution, of certain rights, shall not be construed to deny or disparage others retained by the people." The Tenth Amendment responded to the concern that the national government might derive additional powers from the listing of rights by emphasizing that "[t]he powers not delegated to the United States by the Constitution, nor prohibited by it to the States, are reserved to the States respectively, or to the people."

Second, the Bill of Rights only placed restrictions on the national government. Concerned about abuses by factional majorities in the states, Madison had proposed an amendment securing freedom of conscience, freedom of the press, and trial by jury in criminal cases against state violation. The Senate, however, rejected his proposal. In part, the limited reach of the amendments reflected the perceived source of threats to rights—after all, the impetus for the amendments was the creation of a substantially stronger national government. It is also possible that Congress recognized that state declarations of rights already forbade state violations of rights.

When the question of applying the Bill of Rights to the states first arose in *Barron* v. *Baltimore* (1833), the U.S. Supreme Court unanimously confirmed that the Bill of Rights placed restrictions only on the national government. In reaching this conclusion, Chief Justice John Marshall looked to the constitutional text, observing that the First Amendment begins with the phrase "Congress shall make no law" and that no subsequent provision of the Bill of Rights indicates any limitation upon state action. In addition, he reasoned:

> had the framers of these amendments intended them to be limitations on the powers of the state governments, they would have imitated the framers of the original Constitution, and have expressed that intention. Had Congress engaged in the extraordinary occupation of improving the constitutions of the several states by affording the people additional protections from the exercise of power by their own governments in matters which concerned themselves alone, they would have declared this purpose in plain and intelligible language.

The adoption of the Fourteenth Amendment in 1868, however, required a reconsideration of the Court's position in *Barron.* Did that amendment impose on the states the same restrictions that the Bill of Rights had imposed on the national government? If not, what was its effect on the division of responsibility between nation and state for defining and protecting rights? It is to these questions that we now turn.

## THE FOURTEENTH AMENDMENT

Constitutional historians disagree vehemently over the meaning of the Fourteenth Amendment. Some scholars argue that the amendment applies the Bill of Rights to the states, guarantees other rights against state infringement as well, and gives the national government broad authority to protect those rights.[7] Reviewing the same evidence, other scholars emphasize the attachment to federalism of the amendment's authors, depict the amendment's aims as specific rather than open-ended, and deny that these aims encompassed the application of the Bill of Rights to the states.[8] Still other scholars take a position between these two extremes.[9] Although we cannot resolve this important scholarly debate, an examination of the history and language of the Fourteenth Amendment is vital to understanding its effects on the protection of rights.

## The Creation of the Fourteenth Amendment

The Fourteenth Amendment was the second of three amendments adopted after the Civil War during Reconstruction. Although the Thirteenth Amendment (adopted in 1865) had outlawed slavery, the Southern states sought to perpetuate the economic and social subordination of African Americans through the adoption of the infamous Black Codes. These Black Codes deprived African Americans of basic rights, such as the right to contract and to testify in court, subjected them to heavier penalties for violations of the law, and bound them to employers through harsh vagrancy and apprenticeship provisions. Congress responded to this Southern intransigence with the Civil Rights Act of 1866 and the Fourteenth Amendment. The Civil Rights Act guaranteed to blacks the rights "to make and enforce contracts, to inherit, purchase, lease, sell, hold, and convey real and personal property" and to enjoy the "full and equal benefit of all laws and proceedings for the security of person and property, as is enjoyed by white citizens." The constitutional basis for this enactment, however, remained questionable. Few members of Congress believed that Congress had such power to protect rights against state violation prior to the Civil War. Some concluded that the Thirteenth Amendment, which authorized Congress to enact "appropriate legislation" to enforce its provisions, provided the constitutional basis for the law. They reasoned that the amendment was designed not only to eliminate slavery but also to secure to the emancipated slaves the rights associated with their new status as free men. Others in Congress, however, doubted that the amendment conferred such broad authority, and even after Congress had repassed the law over President Andrew Johnson's veto, doubts lingered about the law's constitutionality.

The Fourteenth Amendment removed those doubts by expanding congressional authority to secure rights against state violation. An initial version of the amendment assigned Congress primary responsibility for protecting rights against state infringement. But in response to objections that such a grant of authority invaded the reserved powers of the states, Section 1 of the amendment was redrafted to ensure that initial responsibility for the protection of rights remained with the states. However, Section 1 also made clear what that responsibility entailed. States were (1) prohibited from abridging the privileges and immunities of citizens of the United States, (2) required to observe due process of law in depriving any person of life, liberty, or property, and (3) prohibited from denying equal protection of the laws to any person. If the states failed to meet their obligations under the amendment, those whose rights had been violated could sue to vindicate their rights. More importantly, Congress, under Section 5 of the amendment, could enforce the provisions of the amendment "'by appropriate legislation."

The Fourteenth Amendment was obviously designed to constitutionalize the Civil Rights Act of 1866. However, the language of the Fourteenth Amendment is considerably broader than the list of rights found in the Civil Rights Act. Did this choice of broader language mean that the amendment's framers intended to do more than merely constitutionalize the Civil Rights Act? If so, what are the privileges and immunities against state abridgement, and what constituted due process of law? Scholars and Supreme Court justices have offered a variety of answers to these questions.

## Privileges and Immunities

The Framers of the Fourteenth Amendment expected that its Privileges and Immunities Clause would furnish the primary vehicle for protecting against state infringements on rights. The Privileges and Immunities Clause found in the original Constitution (Article IV, Section 2) forbids discrimination against out-of-staters. More specifically, it prohibits states from distinguishing between their citizens and those of other states in safeguarding "all Privileges and Immunities of Citizens in the several States." The Fourteenth Amendment's Privileges and Immunities Clause extends this protection by prohibiting states from distinguishing among their own citizens with regard to the privileges and immunities of citizens of the United States.

Neither the original Constitution nor the Fourteenth Amendment defines what the privileges and immunities of citizens of the United States are. Some scholars argue that they involve the rights guaranteed to all citizens, including those found in the first ten amendments.[10] In support of this conclusion, they observe first of all that both Representative John Bingham of Ohio, who proposed the amendment, and Senator Jacob Howard of Michigan, who presented the proposal to the Senate, expressly stated that the Fourteenth Amendment made the Bill of Rights applicable to the states. In addition, they note that in *Corfield* v. *Coryell* (1823), a decision quoted approvingly by several congressional proponents of the Fourteenth Amendment, Justice Bushrod Washington offered a broad interpretation of privileges and immunities as including those protections which "belong, of right, to the citizens of all free governments." Finally, they point out that members of Congress frequently complained that the slave states had denied opponents of slavery freedom of speech and other basic rights, and the Framers of the amendment referred directly to such concerns during the debates over the amendment.

Other scholars deny that the Privileges and Immunities Clause made the Bill of Rights applicable to the states.[11] They dismiss Bingham as inconsistent and confused and Howard as unrepresentative of congressional views. Instead, they point to statements by several members of Congress that the clause constitutionalized the Civil Rights Act of 1866. More generally, they stress that the amendment's proponents were strongly committed to federalism and would not have adopted a provision which would have compromised state sovereignty.

In *The Slaughterhouse Cases* (1873), the Supreme Court's first opportunity to interpret the Fourteenth Amendment, the justices gave a very narrow reading to "privileges and immunities," limiting them to such rights as access to the nation's seaports and the privilege of the writ of habeas corpus. This ruling, never overturned, in effect read the Fourteenth Amendment's Privileges and Immunities Clause out of the Constitution. In subsequent cases, therefore, debate shifted from the Privileges and Immunities Clause to the Due Process Clause and its effect on the protection of rights against state violation.

## DUE PROCESS AND THE BILL OF RIGHTS

Three separate and distinct views of the the appropriate relationship between the Due Process Clause and the Bill of Rights have been advanced: the "fundamental rights" interpretation, total incorporation, and selective incorporation.

### "Fundamental Rights" Interpretation

Advocates of the "fundamental rights" interpretation find no necessary relationship between the Fourteenth Amendment and the guarantees of the Bill of Rights. Rather, they understand the Fourteenth Amendment as protecting "traditional notions" of due process, which were described variously by Justice Henry Brown in *Holden* v. *Hardy* (1898) as those "certain immutable principles of justice which inhere in the very idea of free government which no member of the Union may disregard" and by Justice Benjamin Cardozo in *Palko* v. *Connecticut* (1937) as those principles "implicit in the concept of ordered liberty." As applied to criminal procedure, this interpretation requires that a state grant the defendant "that fundamental fairness essential to the very concept of justice." The Bill of Rights is regarded as a likely, but not necessarily conclusive, indicator of "fundamental fairness." As Justice John Harlan observed in *Griswold* v. *Connecticut* (1965), "The Due Process Clause of the Fourteenth Amendment stands in my opinion on its own bottom." Just as this view of due process does not impose upon the states all the requirements of the Bill of Rights, neither does it restrict the reach of the Fourteenth Amendment to only those rights enumerated in the first eight amendments. Fundamental fairness, not mere compliance with the Bill of Rights, is its touchstone. Consequently, under the "fundamental rights" interpretation a state procedure may violate due process even though its operation is not contrary to any specific guarantee in the first eight amendments.

To its critics, the "fundamental rights" interpretation fosters subjective considerations based on some murky notion of natural justice, and thereby helps to promote an *ad hoc,* personal application of the Fourteenth Amendment. In reply, supporters of this interpretation contend that its application rests on a societal consensus that can be determined quite independently of the justice's personal views, and that various "objective" factors are available to the Court as it determines whether a particular procedural right traditionally has been recognized as an essential ingredient of fairness. Justice Benjamin Curtis cited two such factors in *Murray's Lessee* v. *Hoboken Land and Improvement Company* (1856): the significance attached to the right by the Framers of the Constitution, and the importance of the right as recognized by "those settled usages and modes of proceedings existing in the common and statute law of England, before the immigration of our ancestors, and which are shown not to have been unsuited to their civil and political conditions by having been acted on by them after the settlement of this country." Other often-cited "objective" factors include the subsequent treatment of the right in state courts and legislatures and the significance attached to the right in countries with similar jurisprudential traditions. Although these factors do not provide "a mathematical calculus" for application of the Fourteenth Amendment, the argument continues, they go as far as is possible. After all, as Justice Felix Frankfurter observed,

> "Due Process", unlike some legal rules, is not a technical conception with a fixed content unrelated to time, place, and circumstances. Expressing as it does in its ultimate analysis respect enforced by law for the feeling of just treatment which has been evolved through centuries of Anglo-American constitutional history and civilization, "due process" cannot be imprisoned within the treacherous limits of any formula. Representing a profound attitude of fairness between man and man, and more particularly between the individual and the government, due process is compounded of history, reason, the past course of decisions, and stout confidence in the strength of the democratic faith which we profess. Due process is not a mechanical instrument. It is not a yardstick. It is a process.[12]

To Frankfurter and other proponents of the "fundamental rights" interpretation, judgment as to what due process requires must be made on a case-by-case basis. This interpretation, they continue, should prevail because it is the only interpretation of the Fourteenth Amendment that requires judges to engage in judgment—that activity that uniquely defines the behavior of a judge.

### Total Incorporation

According to the total incorporation interpretation, the Fourteenth Amendment was intended simply and exclusively "to extend to all the people of the nation the complete protection of the Bill of Rights." Advocates of total incorporation insist that the legislative history and language of the amendment support total incorporation and that judges are bound by that clear intention of the Founders. In addition, they make the pragmatic argument that, by restricting judges to the specific language of the Bill of Rights, total incorporation avoids much of the subjectivity inherent in a "fundamental rights" approach.

Critics of total incorporation challenge these contentions. They argue that neither the legislative history nor the language of the amendment supports this view. Thus, they point out that the Due Process Clause of the Fourteenth Amendment merely restates a single provision of the Fifth Amendment of the Bill of Rights. Reflecting on this fact in *Hurtado v. California,* an 1884 decision in which the Court concluded that the Fourteenth Amendment's Due Process Clause did not require indictment by grand jury in state prosecutions, Justice Stanley Matthews observed:

> According to a recognized canon of interpretation, especially applicable to formal and solemn instruments of constitutional law, we are forbidden to assume, without clear reason to the contrary, that any part of . . . [the Fifth] Amendment is superfluous. The natural and obvious inference is, that in the sense of the Constitution, "due process of law" was not meant or intended to include . . . the institution and procedure of a grand jury in any case. The conclusion is equally irresistable, that when the same phrase was employed in the Fourteenth Amendment to restrain the action of the States, it was used in the same sense and with no greater extent; and that if in the adoption of that amendment it had been part of its purpose to perpetuate the institution of the grand jury in all the States, it would have embodied, as to the Fifth Amendment, express declaration to that effect.

Of course, this argument derives much of its force from the fact that proponents of total incorporation have been forced to base their arguments on the Fourteenth Amendment's Due Process Clause, given the Supreme Court's gutting of the amendment's Privileges and Immunities Clause in *The Slaughterhouse Cases.*

Opponents of total incorporation also reject the notion that it avoids subjectivity. They criticize Justice Black—total incorporation's leading judicial exponent—for merely shifting the focus of judicial inquiry from the flexible concept of fundamental fairness to equally flexible terms in the specific amendments. Such terms as "probable cause," "speedy and public trial," and "cruel and unusual punishments," they observe, are hardly self-defining and must be interpreted in light of the same contemporary notions of fairness considered in applying a "fundamental rights" standard. As Justice Harlan chided Justice Black in *Griswold,* "'Specific' provisions of the Constitution, no less than 'due process' lend themselves readily to 'personal' interpretations by judges whose constitutional outlook is simply to keep the Constitution in supposed 'tune with the times.'" Finally, critics contend that total incorporation imposes an undue burden on the states and deprives them of any opportunity to act as social and legal laboratories—to experiment with reforms designed to enhance the protections and freedom of the people.

## Selective Incorporation

Selective incorporation, the third view of the appropriate relationship between the Fourteenth Amendment and the Bill of Rights, combines aspects of both the "fundamental rights" and the total incorporation interpretations. Along with the "fundamental rights" interpretation, it holds that the Fourteenth Amendment encompasses all rights, substantive and procedural, that are "of the very essence of a scheme of ordered liberty." It recognizes that not all rights enumerated in the Bill of Rights are fundamental, and that some rights may be fundamental even if not specifically guaranteed in the Bill of Rights. But in determining whether an enumerated right is fundamental, this interpretation, like the total incorporation view, focuses on the *total* right guaranteed by the individual amendment, not merely on the element of that right before the Court or the application of that right in a particular case. In other words, by deciding that a particular guarantee within the first eight amendments is fundamental, the Supreme Court incorporates that guarantee into the Fourteenth Amendment "whole and intact" and enforces it against the states in every case, according to the same standards applied to the federal government. *Duncan* v. *Louisiana* (1968), which incorporated the right to a jury trial, expressed this understanding: "Because . . . trial by jury in criminal cases is fundamental to the American scheme of justice, we hold that the Fourteenth Amendment guarantees a right of jury trial in all criminal cases which—were they to be tried in a Federal court—would come within the Sixth Amendment's guarantee."

Proponents of selective incorporation maintain that it represents an improvement over both other interpretations. They argue that a fundamental right should not be denied merely because the "totality of circumstances" in a particular case does not disclose "a denial of fundamental fairness," pointing out that judicial evaluation of the factual circumstances surrounding any particular case often is extremely subjective and discretionary. On the other hand, they continue, selective incorporation avoids the rigidity and extremism of total incorporation, under which, for example, the Seventh Amendment right of trial by jury in all suits at common law in excess of twenty dollars logically should be incorporated.

In the view of its detractors, however, selective incorporation is an unacceptable compromise that is inconsistent with the logic and historical support of either of the doctrines it attempts to combine. Those who embrace total incorporation charge that it is merely another example of "natural law due process philosophy." Proponents of "fundamental rights," on the other hand, contend that selective incorporation fails to appreciate the special burdens it imposes on the administration of criminal justice at the state level. They fear that the imposition of a single standard regulating both state and federal practice would either place an unrealistic "constitutional straight-jacket" on the states or result in a relaxing of standards as applied to both state and federal officials, in order to meet the special problems of the states.

Despite these criticisms, selective incorporation during the 1960s replaced the "fundamental rights" interpretation as the dominant view on the Court. Justice William Brennan advanced the doctrine for the first time in his dissent in *Cohen* v. *Hurley* (1961), and just two years later it had the support of at least four justices. It also was accepted by Justice Black, who, although remaining committed to total incorporation, accepted selective incorporation as a lesser evil than the "mysterious and uncertain law concepts" of the "fundamental rights" interpretation.

As Table 11.1 indicates, the Court's endorsement of selective incorporation led to the incorporation of several constitutional guarantees, including eleven dealing with criminal procedure. By 1972, only two criminal procedure guarantees—the Eighth Amendment prohibition of excessive fines and the Fifth Amendment requirement of prosecutions by grand jury indictment—had not been held to apply to the states.

Table 11.1 also reveals that even before the selective-incorporation era, the justices had begun the process of incorporation. Through this process, the Court has in piecemeal fashion achieved almost the same result as if it had endorsed the total incorporation interpretation.

### State Constitutional Guarantees

Although the extension of federal protection against states' violations of rights is a relatively recent phenomenon, this does not mean that previously Americans had no protection against state infringements on rights. Rather, as proponents of the "fundamental rights" approach recognized, our federal system rested on the assumption of a rough division of labor in protecting rights. State laws and state constitutions were to serve as the primary guarantees against oppressive state governments, with the federal Constitution securing fundamental rights against state violation only when state judicial processes afforded no redress. Beginning in the mid-twentieth century, however, this balance began to shift. Defendants in state courts began looking primarily to the federal Constitution and federal judicial precedent for vindication of their rights, assuming that state constitutional guarantees either duplicated federal protections or were altogether irrelevant.

During the last 25 years, however, lawyers and scholars have rediscovered state constitutions. Motivated both by rulings of the Burger Court that narrowed rights protections and by its encouragement of reliance on state constitutional guarantees, they have begun to study state

**TABLE 11.1 Incorporation of Provisions of the Bill of Rights**

| Right | Case and Year |
|---|---|
| *First Amendment* | |
| Freedom of speech | *Gitlow* v. *New York* (1925) |
| Freedom of the press | *Near* v. *Minnesota* (1931) |
| Freedom of assembly | *De Jonge* v. *Oregon* (1937) |
| Free exercise of religion | *Cantwell* v. *Connecticut* (1940) |
| Establishment clause | *Everson* v. *Board of Education* (1947) |
| *Second Amendment* | |
| Right to bear arms | Not incorporated |
| *Third Amendment* | |
| Freedom from quartering of troops in peacetime | Not incorporated |
| *Fourth Amendment* | |
| Unreasonable search and seizure | *Wolf* v. *Colorado* (1949) |
| Exclusionary rule | *Mapp* v. *Ohio* (1961) |
| *Fifth Amendment* | |
| Grand jury clause | Not incorporated |
| Self-incrimination clause | *Malley* v. *Hogan* (1964) |
| Double jeopardy clause | *Benton* v. *Maryland* (1969) |
| *Sixth Amendment* | |
| Right to a public trial | *In re Oliver* (1948) |
| Notice clause | *Cole* v. *Arkansas* (1948) |
| Right to counsel | *Gideon* v. *Wainright* (1963)/ *Argersinger* v. *Hamlin* (1972) |
| Confrontation clause | *Pointer* v. *Texas* (1965) |
| Right to impartial jury | *Parker* v. *Gladden* (1966) |
| Right to a speedy trial | *Klopfer* v. *North Carolina* (1967) |
| Compulsory process clause | *Washington* v. *Texas* (1967) |
| Right to jury trial (criminal cases) | *Duncan* v. *Louisiana* (1968) |
| *Seventh Amendment* | |
| Right to jury trial (civil cases) | Not incorporated |
| *Eighth Amendment* | |
| Ban on cruel and unusual punishments | *Robinson* v. *California* (1962) |
| Ban on excessive bail | *Schilb* v. *Kuebel* (1971) |
| Ban on excessive fines | Not incorporated |
| *Other* | |
| Right to privacy | *Griswold* v. *Connecticut* (1965) |

*Source:* The United States Department of Justice, 1998.

constitutions more closely and to fashion legal arguments based on the distinctive text and history of those state charters. Although it is unlikely that state constitutions will again become the primary guarantors of rights, this new attention to state constitutions represents a positive step toward reconciling federalism and the protection of rights.

## NOTES

1 The original Constitution did impose some restrictions on state violations of rights. For example, Article IV, Section 2 mandates that "[t]he Citizens of each State shall be entitled to all Privileges and Immunities of Citizens in the several States," and Article IV, Section 4 authorizes Congress to "guarantee to every State in this Union a Republican Form of Government." In addition, it should be noted that most state constitutions contained declarations of rights, which also secured rights against state governments.

2 Some modern constitutional authorities have echoed Hamilton. In a speech in 1964, Justice John Marshall Harlan declared: "We are accustomed to speak of the Bill of Rights and the Fourteenth Amendment as the principle guarantees of personal liberty. Yet it would surely be shallow not to recognize that the structure of our political system accounts no less for the free society we have." The Framers, Justice Harlan argued, "staked their faith that liberty would prosper in the new nation not primarily upon declaration of individual rights but upon the kind of government the Union was to have." John M. Harlan, "The Bill of Rights and the Constitution," address at the dedication of the Bill of Rights Room, U.S. Subtreasury Building, New York City, August 9, 1964.

3 Richard Henry Lee to Governor Edmund Randolph, October 16, 1787.

4 Even some proponents of the Constitution—among them, Thomas Jefferson and John Adams—favored the addition of a bill of rights. As Jefferson put it, "a bill of rights is what the people are entitled to against every government on earth, general or particular, and what no government should refuse, or rest on inference." Thomas Jefferson to James Madison, December 20, 1787. Thomas Jefferson, *The Papers of Thomas Jefferson,* Julian P. Boyd, ed. (Princeton, N.J.: Princeton University Press, 1950– ), vol. 12, p. 440.

5 Our analysis follows that of Herbert J. Storing, "The Constitution and the Bill of Rights," in Robert A. Goldwin and William A. Schambra, eds., *How Does the Constitution Secure Rights?* (Washington, D.C.: American Enterprise Institute, 1985).

6 *The Debates and Proceedings of the Congress of the United States* (Washington, D.C.: 1834), I, 432.

7 Scholars adopting this expansive interpretation of the Fourteenth Amendment include: Jacobus tenBroek, *The Anti-Slavery Origins of the Fourteenth Amendment* (Berkeley: University of California Press, 1951); Judith A. Baer, *Equality Under the Constitution: Reclaiming the Fourteenth Amendment* (Ithaca, N.Y.: Cornell University Press, 1983); and Michael Kent Curtis, *No State Shall Abridge: The Fourteenth Amendment and the Bill of Rights* (Durham, N.C.: Duke University Press, 1986).

8 This narrower view of the scope of the Fourteenth Amendment is presented in Charles Fairman, "Does the Fourteenth Amendment Incorporate the Bill of

Rights? The Original Understanding," *Stanford Law Review* 2 (1949): 5–138; Raoul Berger, *Government by Judiciary: The Transformation of the Fourteenth Amendment* (Cambridge, Mass.: Harvard University Press, 1977); Berger, *The Fourteenth Amendment and the Bill of Rights* (Norman: University of Oklahoma Press, 1989); and Earl M. Maltz, *Civil Rights, the Constitution, and Congress, 1863–1869* (Lawrence: University Press of Kansas, 1990).

9 See, for example, William E. Nelson, *The Fourteenth Amendment: From Political Principle to Judicial Doctrine* (Cambridge, Mass.: Harvard University Press, 1988); and Michael P. Zuckert, "Completing the Constitution: The Fourteenth Amendment and Constitutional Rights," *Publius: The Journal of Federalism* 22 (1992): 69–91.

10 See, for example, Curtis, *No State Shall Abridge;* and Baer, *Equality Under the Constitution.*

11 See, for example, Berger, *The Fourteenth Amendment and the Bill of Rights;* and Fairman, "Does the Fourteenth Amendment Incorporate the Bill of Rights?"

12 *Joint Anti-Fascist Refugee Committee* v. *McGrath* (1951).

## SELECTED READING

*The Federalist,* No. 84.

*Hurtado* v. *California,* 110 U.S. 516 (1884).
*Rochin* v. *California,* 342 U.S. 165 (1952).
*The Slaughterhouse Cases,* Volume I, Chapter 12.
*Williams* v. *Florida,* 399 U.S. 78 (1970).

Amar, Akhil Reed. "The Bill of Rights as a Constitution." *Yale Law Journal* 100 (1991): 1131–1210.

Anastaplo, George, *The Amendments to the Constitution: A Commentary* (Baltimore: Johns Hopkins Press, 1995).

Baer, Judith A. *Equality Under the Constitution: Reclaiming the Fourteenth Amendment* (Ithaca, N.Y.: Cornell University Press, 1983).

Barnett, Randy E., ed. *History and Meaning of the Ninth Amendment* (Fairfax, Va.: George Mason University Press, 1989).

Berger, Raoul. *The Fourteenth Amendment and the Bill of Rights* (Norman: University of Oklahoma Press, 1989).

Curtis, Michael Kent. *No State Shall Abridge: The Fourteenth Amendment and the Bill of Rights* (Durham, N.C.: Duke University Press, 1986).

Goldwin, Robert A. *From Parchment to Power: How James Madison Used the Bill of Rights to Save the Constitution* (Washington, D.C.: American Enterprise Institute, 1997).

Goldwin, Robert A. and William A. Schambra, eds. *How Does the Constitution Secure Rights?* (Washington, D.C.: American Enterprise Institute, 1985).

Hickok, Eugene, ed. T*he Bill of Rights: Original Meaning and Current Understanding* (Charlottesville: University Press of Virginia, 1991).

Katz, Ellis and G. Alan Tarr, eds. *Federalism and Rights* (Lanham, Md.: Rowman & Littlefield, 1996).

Lutz, Donald S. "The State Constitutional Pedigree of the U.S. Bill of Rights." *Publius: The Journal of Federalism* 22 (1992): 19–45.

Maltz, Earl M. *Civil Rights, the Constitution, and Congress: 1863–1869* (Lawrence: University Press of Kansas, 1990).

Nelson, William E. *The Fourteenth Amendment: From Political Principle to Judicial Doctrine* (Cambridge, Mass.: Harvard University Press, 1988).

Rossum, Ralph A. "*The Federalist's* Understanding of the Constitution as a Bill of Rights," in *Saving the Revolution: The Federalists Papers and the American Founding,* ed. Charles R. Kesler (New York: Free Press, 1987): 219–233.

Schwartz, Bernard. *The Great Rights of Mankind: A History of the American Bill of Rights* (expanded ed.) (Madison, Wisc.: Madison House, 1992).

Veit, Helen E., Kenneth R. Bowling, and Charles Bangs Bickford. *Creating the Bill of Rights: The Documentary Record from the First Federal Congress* (Baltimore: Johns Hopkins University Press, 1991).

Zuckert, Michael P. "Completing the Constitution: The Fourteenth Amendment and Constitutional Rights." *Publius: The Journal of Federalism 22* (1992): 69–91.

## *Barron v. Baltimore*

**32 U.S. (7 Peters) 243; 8 L. Ed. 672 (1833)**

In grading and paving its streets, the city of Baltimore redirected the course of several streams flowing into its harbor. As a result, deposits of sand and gravel built up near John Barron's wharf, which was rendered inaccessible to ships. This seriously diminished the wharf's commercial value, and Barron brought suit in county court against the city, alleging a violation of the Fifth Amendment clause that forbids taking private property for public use without just compensation. The county court awarded Barron $4,500 in damages, but the Maryland Court of Appeals for the Western Shore reversed that decision. Barron appealed, and the case was brought before the United States Supreme Court on a writ of error. *Opinion of the Court: Marshall, Baldwin, Duvall, Johnson, McLean, Story, Thompson.*

MR. CHIEF JUSTICE MARSHALL delivered the opinion of the Court. . . .

The question thus presented is, we think, of great importance, but not of much difficulty.

The constitution was ordained and established by the people of the United States for themselves, for their own government, and not for the government of the individual states. Each state established a constitution for itself, and, in that constitution, provided such limitations and restrictions on the powers of its particular government as its judgment dictated. The people of the United States framed such a government for the United States as they supposed best adapted to their situation, and best calculated to promote their interests. The powers they conferred on this government were to be exercised by itself; and the limitations on power, if expressed in general terms, are naturally, and, we think, necessarily applicable to the government created by the instrument. They are limitations of power granted in the instrument itself; not of distinct governments, framed by different persons and for different purposes.

If these propositions be correct, the fifth amendment must be understood as restraining the power of the general government, not as applicable to the states. In their several constitutions they have imposed such restrictions on their respective governments as their own wisdom suggested; such as they deemed most proper for themselves. It is a subject on which they judge exclusively, and with which others interfere no farther than they are supposed to have a common interest.

Had the people of the several states, or any of them, required changes in their constitutions; had they required additional safeguards to liberty from the apprehended encroachments of their particular governments: the remedy was in their own hands, and would have been applied by themselves. A convention would have been assembled by the discontented state, and the required improvements would have been made by itself. The unwieldly and cumbrous machinery of procuring a recommendation from two-thirds of congress, and the assent of three-fourths of their sister states, could never have occurred to any human being as a mode of doing that which might be effected by the state itself. Had the framers of these amendments intended them to be limitations on the powers of the state governments, they would have imitated the framers of the original constitution, and have expressed that intention. Had congress engaged in the extraordinary occupation of improving the constitutions of the several states by affording the people additional protection from the exercise of power by their own governments in matters which concerned themselves alone, they would have declared this purpose in plain and intelligible language.

But it is universally understood, it is a part of the history of the day, that the great revolution which established the constitution of the United States, was not effected without immense opposition. Serious fears were extensively entertained that those powers which the patriot statesmen, who then watched over the interests of our country, deemed essential to union, and to the attainment of those invaluable objects for which union was sought, might be exercised in a manner dangerous to liberty. In almost every convention by which the constitution was adopted, amendments to guard against the abuse of power were recommended. These amendments demanded security against the apprehended encroachments of the general government—not against those of the local governments.

In compliance with a sentiment thus generally expressed to quiet fears thus extensively entertained, amendments were proposed by the required majority in congress, and adopted by the states. These amendments contain no expression indicating an intention to apply them to the state governments. This court cannot so apply them.

We are of the opinion that the provision in the fifth amendment to the constitution, declaring that private property shall not be taken for public use without just compensation, is intended solely as a limitation on the exercise of power by the government of the United States, and is not applicable to the legislation of the states. . . .

## *Palko v. Connecticut*

**302 U.S. 319; 58 S. Ct. 149; 82 L. Ed. 288 (1937)**

Frank Palko was indicted for the crime of first-degree murder. A jury found him guilty of second-degree murder, and he was sentenced to life imprisonment. Thereafter, the state of Connecticut, with the permission of the trial judge, appealed to the Connecticut Supreme Court of Errors under a statute that permitted appeals from the rulings and decisions of the trial court "upon all questions of law arising on the trial of criminal cases . . . in the same manner and to the same effect as if made by the accused." The Supreme Court of Errors set aside the trial court's judgment and ordered a new trial, at which Palko was found guilty of first-degree murder and sentenced to death. The conviction was affirmed by the Supreme Court of Errors, and the case was appealed to the United States Supreme Court. Palko contended that the Connecticut statute was unconstitutional in that the Due Process Clause of the Fourteenth Amendment protected individuals from being tried twice for the same offense. *Opinion of the Court: Cardozo, Black, Brandeis, Hughes, McReynolds, Roberts, Stone, Sutherland. Dissent: Butler.*

MR. JUSTICE CARDOZO delivered the opinion of the Court. . . .

The argument for appellant is that whatever is forbidden by the Fifth Amendment is forbidden by the Fourteenth also. The Fifth Amendment, which is not directed to the states, but solely to the federal government, creates immunity from double jeopardy. No person shall be "subject for the same offense to be twice put in jeopardy of life or limb." The Fourteenth Amendment ordains, "nor shall any State deprive any person of life, liberty, or property, without due process of law." To retry a defendant, though under one indictment and only one, subjects him, it is said, to double jeopardy in violation of the Fifth Amendment, if the prosecution is one on behalf of the United States. From this the consequence is said to follow that there is a denial of life or liberty without due process of law, if the prosecution is one on behalf of the People of a State. . . .

We have said that in appellant's view the Fourteenth Amendment is to be taken as embodying the prohibitions of the Fifth. His thesis is even broader. Whatever would be a violation of the original bill of rights (Amendments I to VIII) if done by the federal government is now equally unlawful by force of the Fourteenth Amendment if done by a state. There is no such general rule.

The Fifth Amendment provides, among other things, that no person shall be held to answer for a capital or otherwise infamous crime unless on presentment or indictment of a grand jury. This court has held that, in prosecutions by a state, presentment or indictment by a grand jury may give way to informations at the instance of a public officer. . . . The Fifth Amendment provides also that no person shall be compelled in any criminal case to be a witness against himself. This court has said that, in prosecutions by a state the exemption will fail if the state elects to end it. . . . The Sixth Amendment calls for a jury trial in criminal cases and the Seventh for a jury trial in civil cases at common law where the value in controversy shall exceed twenty dollars. This court has ruled that consistently with those amendments trial by jury may be modified by a state or abolished altogether. . . .

On the other hand, the due process clause of the Fourteenth Amendment may make it unlawful for a state to abridge by its statutes the freedom of speech which the First Amendment safeguards against encroachment by the Congress, . . . or the like freedom of the press, . . . or the free exercise of religion, . . . or the right of peaceable assembly without which speech would be unduly trammeled, . . . or the right of one accused of crime to the benefit of counsel. . . . In these and other situations immunities that are valid as against the federal government by force of the specific pledges of particular amendments have been found to be implicit in the concept of ordered liberty, and thus, through the Fourteenth Amendment, become valid as against the states.

The line of division may seem to be wavering and broken if there is a hasty catalogue of the cases on the one side and the other. Reflection and analysis will induce a different view. There emerges the perception of a rationalizing principle which gives to discrete instances a proper order and coherence. The right to trial by jury and the immunity from prosecution except as the result of an indictment may have value and importance. Even so, they are not of the very essence of a scheme of ordered liberty. To abolish them is not to violate "a principle of justice so rooted in the traditions and conscience of our people as to be ranked as fundamental." . . . Few would be so narrow or provincial as to maintain that a fair and enlightened system of justice would be impossible without them. What is true of jury trials and indictments is true also, as the cases show, of the immunity from compulsory self-incrimination . . . . This too might be lost, and justice still be done. Indeed, today as in the past there are students of our penal system who look upon the immunity as a mischief rather than a benefit, and who would limit its scope, or destroy it altogether. No doubt there would remain the need to give protection against torture, physical or mental. . . . Justice, however, would not perish if the accused were subject to a duty to respond to orderly inquiry. The exclusion of these immunities and privileges from the privileges and immunities protected against the action of the states has not been arbitrary or casual. It has been dictated by a study and appreciation of the meaning, the essential implications, of liberty itself.

We reach a different plane of social and moral values when we pass to the privileges and immunities that have been taken over from the earlier articles of the federal bill of rights and brought within the Fourteenth Amendment by a process of absorption. These in their origin were effective against the federal government alone. If the Fourteenth Amendment has absorbed them, the process of absorption has had its source in the belief that neither liberty nor justice would exist if they were sacrificed. . . . This is true, for illustration, of freedom of thought, and speech. Of that freedom one may say that it is the matrix, the indispensable condition, of nearly every other form of freedom. With rare aberrations a pervasive recognition of that truth can be traced in our history, political and legal. So it has come about that the domain of liberty, withdrawn by the Fourteenth Amendment from encroachment by the states, has been enlarged by latter-day judgments to include liberty of the mind as well as liberty of action. The extension became, indeed, a logical imperative when once it was recognized, as long ago it was, that liberty is something more than exemption from physical restraint, and that even in the field of substantive rights and duties the legislative judgment, if oppressive and arbitrary, may be overridden by the courts. . . . Fundamental too in the concept of due process, and so in that of liberty, is the thought that condemnation shall be rendered only after trial. . . . The hearing, moreover, must be a real one, not a sham or a pretense. . . . For that reason, ignorant defendants in a capital case were held to have been condemned unlawfully when in truth, though not in form, they were refused the aid of counsel. . . . The decision did not turn upon the fact that the benefit of counsel would have been guaranteed to the defendants by the provisions of the Sixth Amendment if they had been prosecuted in a federal court. The decision turned upon the fact that in the particular situation laid before us in the evidence the benefit of counsel was essential to the substance of a hearing.

. . . On which side of the line the case made out by the appellant has appropriate location must be the next inquiry and the final one. Is that kind of double jeopardy to which the statute has subjected him a hardship so acute and shocking that our polity will not endure it? Does it violate those "fundamental principles of liberty and justice which lie at the base of all our civil and political institutions"? . . . The answer surely must be "no." What the answer would have to be if the state were permitted after a trial free from error to try the accused over again or to bring another case against him, we have no occasion to consider. We deal with the statute before us and no other. The state is not attempting to wear the accused out by a multitude of cases with accumulated trials. It asks no more than this, that the case against him shall go on until there shall be a trial free from the corrosion of substantial legal error. . . . This is not cruelty at all, nor even vexation in any immoderate degree. If the trial had been infected with error adverse to the accused, there might have been review at his instance, and as often as necessary to purge the vicious taint. A reciprocal privilege, subject at all times to the discretion of the presiding judge, . . . has now been granted to the state. There is here no seismic innovation. The edifice of justice stands, its symmetry, to many, greater than before. . . .

## *Adamson* v. *California*

**332 U.S. 46; 67 S. Ct. 1672; 91 L. Ed. 1903 (1947)**

The Constitution and penal code of California permitted the trial judge and prosecuting attorneys to comment adversely upon, and juries to consider as evidence of guilt, a defendant's failure to testify on his own behalf. Admiral Dewey Adamson had declined to testify at his trial for first-degree murder. In the presentation of the case to the jury, the prosecuting attorneys argued that Adamson's refusal to testify was an indication of his guilt. He was convicted and sentenced to death. His conviction was affirmed by the state supreme court and appealed to the United States Supreme Court. *Opinion of the Court: Reed, Burton, Frankfurter, Jackson, Vinson. Concurring opinion: Frankfurter. Dissenting opinions: Black, Douglas; Murphy, Rutledge.*

MR. JUSTICE REED delivered the opinion of the Court.

. . . Appellant urges that the provision of the Fifth Amendment that no person "shall be compelled in any criminal case to be a witness against himself" is a fundamental national privilege or immunity protected against state abridgment by the Fourteenth Amendment or a privilege or immunity secured, through the Fourteenth Amendment, against deprivation by state action because it is a personal right, enumerated in the federal Bill of Rights. . . .

It is settled law that the clause of the Fifth Amendment, protecting a person against being compelled to be a witness against himself, is not made effective by the Fourteenth Amendment as a protection against state action on the ground that freedom from testimonial compulsion is a right of national citizenship, or because it is a personal privilege or immunity secured by the Federal Constitution as one of the rights of man that are listed in the Bill of Rights.

The reasoning that leads to those conclusions starts with the unquestioned premise that the Bill of Rights, when adopted, was for the protection of the individual against the federal government and its provisions were inapplicable to similar actions done by the states. . . . With the adoption of the Fourteenth Amendment, it was suggested that the dual citizenship recognized by its first sentence secured for citizens federal protection for their elemental privileges and immunities of state citizenship. The *Slaughter-House Cases* decided, contrary to the suggestion, that these rights, as privileges and immunities of state citizenship, remained under the sole protection of the state governments. This Court, without the expression of a contrary view upon that phase of the issues before the Court, has approved this determination. . . . This leaves a state free to abridge, within the limits of the due process clause, the privileges and immunities flowing from state citizenship. This reading of the Federal Constitution has heretofore found favor with the majority of this Court as a natural and logical interpretation. It accords with the constitutional doctrine of federalism by leaving to the states the responsibility of dealing with the privileges and immunities of their citizens except those inherent in national citizenship. It is the construction placed upon the amendment by justices whose own experience had given them contemporaneous knowledge of the purposes that led to the adoption of the Fourteenth Amendment. This construction has become embedded in our federal system as a functioning element in preserving the balance between national and state power. We reaffirm the conclusion . . . that protection against self-incrimination is not a privilege or immunity of national citizenship. . . .

MR. JUSTICE FRANKFURTER, concurring. . . .

The short answer to the suggestion that the provision of the Fourteenth Amendment, which ordains "nor shall any State deprive any person of life, liberty, or property, without due process of law," was a way of saying that every State must thereafter initiate prosecutions through indictment by a grand jury, must have trial by such a jury of twelve in criminal cases, and must have trial by such a jury in common law suits where the amount in controversy exceeds twenty dollars, is that it is a strange way of saying it. It would be extraordinarily strange for a Constitution to convey such specific commands in such a roundabout and inexplicit way. . . . Those reading the English language with the meaning which it ordinarily conveys, those conversant with the political and legal history of the concept of due process, those sensitive to the relations of the States to the central government as well as the relation of some of the provisions of the Bill of Rights to the process of justice, would hardly recognize the Fourteenth Amendment as a cover for the various explicit provisions of the first eight Amendments. Some of these are enduring reflections of experience with human nature, while some express the restricted views of Eighteenth-Century England regarding the best methods for the ascertainment of facts. . . .

It may not be amiss to restate the pervasive function of the Fourteenth Amendment in exacting from the States observance of basic liberties. . . . The Amendment neither comprehends the specific provisions by which the founders deemed it appropriate to restrict the Federal Government nor is it confined to them. The Due Process Clause of the Fourteenth Amendment has an independent potency, precisely as does the Due Process Clause of the Fifth Amendment in relation to the Federal Government. It ought not to require argument to reject the notion that due process of law meant one thing in the Fifth Amendment and another in the Fourteenth. The Fifth Amendment specifically prohibits prosecution of an "infamous crime" except upon indictment; it forbids double jeopardy; it bars compelling a person to be a witness against himself in any criminal case; it precludes deprivation of "life, liberty, or property, without due process of law. . . ." Are Madison and his contemporaries in the framing of the Bill of Rights to be charged with writing into it a meaningless clause? To consider "due process of law" as merely a shorthand statement of other specific clauses in the same amendment is to attribute to the authors and proponents of this Amendment ignorance of, or indifference to, a historic conception which was one of the great instruments in the arsenal of constitutional freedom which the Bill of Rights was to protect and strengthen. . . .

. . . The relevant question is whether the criminal proceedings which resulted in conviction deprived the accused of the due process of law to which the United States Constitution entitled him. Judicial review of that guaranty of the Fourteenth Amendment inescapably imposes upon this Court an exercise of judgment upon the whole course of the proceedings in order to ascertain whether they offend those canons of decency and fairness which express the notions of justice of English-speaking peoples even toward those charged with the most heinous offenses. These standards of justice are not authoritatively formulated anywhere as though as they were prescriptions in a pharmacopoeia. But neither does the application of the Due Process Clause imply that judges are wholly at large. The judicial judgment in applying the Due Process Clause must move within the limits of accepted notions of justice and is not to be based upon the idiosyncrasies of a merely personal judgment. The fact that judges among themselves may differ whether in a particular case a trial offends accepted notions of justice is not disproof that general rather than idiosyncratic standards are applied. An important safeguard against such merely individual judgment is an alert deference to the judgment of the State court under review.

MR. JUSTICE BLACK, dissenting. . . .

This decision reasserts a constitutional theory spelled out in *Twining* v. *New Jersey* [1908], that this Court is endowed by the Constitution with boundless power under "natural law" periodically to expand and contract constitutional standards to conform to the Court's conception of what at a particular time constitutes "civilized decency" and "fundamental liberty and justice." Invoking this *Twining* rule, the Court concludes that although comment upon testimony in a federal court would violate the Fifth Amendment, identical comment in a state court does not violate today's fashion in civilized decency and fundamentals and is therefore not prohibited by the Federal Constitution as amended. . . .

. . . I would not reaffirm the *Twining* decision. I think that decision and the "natural law" theory of the Constitution upon which it relies degrade the constitutional safeguards of the Bill of Rights and simultaneously appropriate for this Court a broad power which we are not authorized by the Constitution to exercise. . . . My reasons for believing that the *Twining* decision should not be revitalized can best be understood by reference to the constitutional, judicial, and general history that preceded and followed the case. That reference must be abbreviated far more than is justified but for the necessary limitations of opinion-writing. . . .

My study of the historical events that culminated in the Fourteenth Amendment, and the expressions of those who sponsored and favored, as well as those who opposed its submission and passage, persuades me that one of the chief objects that the provisions of the Amendment's first section, separately, and as a whole, were intended to accomplish was to make the Bill of Rights, applicable to the states.

. . . I am attaching to this dissent an appendix which contains a résumé, by no means complete, of the Amendment's history. In my judgment that history conclusively demonstrates that the language of the first section of the Fourteenth Amendment, taken as a whole, was thought by those responsible for its submission to the people, and by those who opposed its submission, sufficiently explicit to guarantee that thereafter no state could deprive its citizens of the privileges and protections of the Bill of Rights. . . .

. . . I further contend that the "natural law" formula which the Court uses to reach its conclusion in this case should be abandoned as an incongruous excrescence on our Constitution. I believe that formula to be itself a violation of our Constitution, in that it subtly conveys to courts, at the expense of legislatures, ultimate power over public policies in fields where no specific provision of the Constitution limits legislative power. . . .

It is an illusory apprehension that literal application of some or of all the provisions of the Bill of Rights to the States would unwisely increase the sum total of the powers of this Court to invalidate state legislation. The Federal Government has not been harmfully burdened by the requirement that enforcement of federal laws affecting civil liberty conform literally to the Bill of Rights. Who would advocate its repeal? It must be conceded, of course, that the natural-law-due-process formula, which the Court today reaffirms, has been interpreted to limit substantially this Court's power to prevent state violations of the individual civil liberties guaranteed by the Bill of Rights. But this formula also has been used in the past, and can be used in the future, to license this Court, in considering regulatory legislation, to roam at large in the broad expanses of policy and morals and to trespass, all too freely, on the legislative domain of the states as well as the Federal Government. . . .

MR. JUSTICE MURPHY, with whom MR. JUSTICE RUTLEDGE concurs, dissenting.

While in substantial agreement with the views of MR. JUSTICE BLACK, I have one reservation and one addition to make. . . .

I agree that the specific guarantees of the Bill of Rights should be carried over intact into the first section of the Fourteenth Amendment. But I am not prepared to say that the latter is entirely and necessarily limited by the Bill of Rights. Occasions may arise where a proceeding falls so far short of conforming to fundamental standards of procedure as to warrant constitutional condemnation in terms of a lack of due process despite the absence of a specific provision in the Bill of Rights. . . .

## *Duncan* v. *Louisiana*

**391 U.S. 145; 88 S. Ct. 1444; 20 L. Ed. 2d 491 (1968)**

Gary Duncan, a black, was convicted in a Louisiana court of simple battery for slapping a white person on the elbow. Under state law, the maximum sentence for this misdemeanor was two years imprisonment and a $300 fine. During his court proceedings, Duncan requested a jury trial, but the judge denied his request, noting that the state constitution permitted jury trials only in instances in which hard labor or capital punishment might be imposed. Sentenced to sixty days in prison and a fine of $150, Duncan unsuccessfully petitioned the Louisiana Supreme Court for review, and then he appealed to the United States Supreme Court. He contended that the Sixth and Fourteenth amendments guaranteed the right to a jury trial in state prosecutions for crimes punishable by two years imprisonment or more. *Opinion of the Court: White, Black, Brennan, Douglas, Fortas, White, Marshall. Concurring opinions: Black, Douglas; Fortas. Dissenting opinion: Harlan, Stewart.*

MR. JUSTICE WHITE delivered the opinion of the Court. . . .

The test for determining whether a right extended by the Fifth and Sixth Amendments with respect to federal criminal proceedings is also protected against state action by the Fourteenth Amendment has been phrased in a variety of ways in the opinions of this Court. The question has been asked whether a right is among those "'fundamental principles of liberty and justice which lie at the base of all our civil and political institutions,'" . . . whether it is "basic in our system of jurisprudence," . . . and whether it is "a fundamental right, essential to a fair trial." . . . The claim before us is that the right to trial by jury guaranteed by the Sixth Amendment meets these tests. The position of Louisiana, on the other hand, is that the Constitution imposes upon the States no duty to give a jury trial in any criminal case, regardless of the seriousness of the crime or the size of the punishment which may be imposed. Because we believe that trial by jury in criminal cases is fundamental to the American scheme of justice, we hold that the Fourteenth Amendment guarantees a right of jury trial in all criminal cases which—were they to be tried in a federal court—would come within the Sixth Amendment's guarantee. Since we consider the appeal before us to be such a case, we hold that the Constitution was violated when appellant's demand for jury trial was refused. . . .

The guarantees of jury trial in the Federal and State Constitutions reflect a profound judgment about the way in which law should be enforced and justice administered. A right to jury trial is granted to criminal defendants in order to prevent oppression by the Government. Those who wrote our constitutions knew from history and experience that it was necessary to protect against unfounded criminal charges brought to eliminate enemies and against judges too responsive to the voice of higher authority. The framers of the constitutions strove to create an independent judiciary but insisted upon further protection against arbitrary action. Providing an accused with the right to be tried by a jury of his peers gave him an inestimable safeguard against the corrupt or overzealous prosecutor and against the compliant, biased, or eccentric judge. If the defendant preferred the common-sense judgment of a jury to the more tutored but perhaps less sympathetic reaction of the single judge, he was to have it. Beyond this, the jury trial provisions in the Federal and State Constitutions reflect a fundamental decision about the exercise of official power—a reluctance to entrust plenary powers over the life and liberty of the citizen to one judge or to a group of judges. Fear of unchecked power, so typical of our State and Federal Governments in other respects, found expression in the criminal law in this insistence upon community participation in the determination of guilt or innocence. The deep commitment of the Nation to the right of jury trial in serious criminal cases as a defense against arbitrary law enforcement qualifies for protection under the Due Process Clause of the Fourteenth Amendment, and must therefore be respected by the States.

Louisiana's final contention is that even if it must grant jury trials in serious criminal cases, the conviction before us is valid and constitutional because here the petitioner was tried for simple battery and was sentenced to only 60 days in the parish prison. We are not persuaded. It is doubtless true that there is a category of petty crimes or offenses which is not subject to the Sixth Amendment jury trial provision and should not be subject to the Fourteenth Amendment jury trial requirement here applied to the States. Crimes carrying possible penalties up to six months do not require a jury trial if they otherwise qualify as petty offenses. . . . But the penalty authorized for a particular crime is of major relevance in determining whether it is serious or not and may in itself, if severe enough, subject the trial to the mandates of the Sixth Amendment. . . . The penalty authorized by the law of the locality may be taken "as a gauge of its social and ethical judgments" . . . of the crime in question. . . . In the case before us the Legislature of Louisiana has made simple battery a criminal offense punishable by imprisonment for up to two years and a fine. The question, then, is whether a crime carrying such a penalty is an offense which Louisiana may insist on trying without a jury.

We think not. . . . Of course the boundaries of the petty offense category have always been ill-defined, if not ambulatory. In the absence of an explicit constitutional provision, the definitional task necessarily falls on the courts, which must either pass upon the validity of legislative attempts to identify those petty offenses which are exempt from jury trial or, where the legislature has not addressed itself to the problem, themselves face the question in the first instance. In either case it is necessary to draw a line in the spectrum of crime, separating petty from serious infractions. This process, although essential, cannot be wholly satisfactory, for it requires attaching different consequences to events which, when they lie near the line, actually differ very little.

. . . In the federal system, petty offenses are defined as those punishable by no more than six months in prison and a $500 fine. In 49 of the 50 States crimes subject to trial without a jury, which occasionally include simple battery, are punishable by not more than one year in jail. Moreover, in the late 18th century in America crimes triable without a jury were for the most part punishable by no more than a six-month prison term, although there appear to have been exceptions to this rule. We need not, however, settle in this case the exact location of the line between petty offenses and serious crimes. It is sufficient for our purposes to hold that a crime punishable by two years in prison is, based on past and contemporary standards in this country, a serious crime and not a petty offense. Consequently, appellant was entitled to a jury trial and it was error to deny it.

MR. JUSTICE BLACK, with whom MR. JUSTICE DOUGLAS joins, concurring. . . .

In closing I want to emphasize that I believe as strongly as ever that the Fourteenth Amendment was intended to make the Bill of Rights applicable to the States. I have been willing to support the selective incorporation doctrine, however, as an alternative, although perhaps less historically supportable than complete incorporation. The selective incorporation process, if used properly, does limit the Supreme Court in the Fourteenth Amendment field to specific Bill of Rights' protections only and keeps judges from roaming at will in their own notions of what policies outside the Bill of Rights are desirable and what are not. And, most importantly for me, the selective incorporation process has the virtue of having already worked to make most of the Bill of Rights' protections applicable to the States.

MR. JUSTICE HARLAN, whom MR. JUSTICE STEWART joins, dissenting.

Every American jurisdiction provides for trial by jury in criminal cases. The question before us is not whether jury trial is an ancient institution, which it is; nor whether it plays a significant role in the administration of criminal justice, which it does; nor whether it will endure, which it shall. The question in this case is whether the State of Louisiana, which provides trial by jury for all felonies, is prohibited by the Constitution from trying charges of simple battery to the court alone. In my view, the answer to that question, mandated alike by our constitutional history and by the longer history of trial by jury, is clearly "no.". . .

The Court's approach to this case is an uneasy and illogical compromise among the views of various Justices on how the Due Process Clause should be interpreted. The Court does not say that those who framed the Fourteenth Amendment intended to make the Sixth Amendment applicable to the States. And the Court concedes that it finds nothing unfair about the procedure by which the present appellant was tried. Nevertheless, the Court reverses his conviction: it holds, for some reason not apparent to me, that the Due Process Clause incorporates the particular clause of the Sixth Amendment that requires trial by jury in federal criminal cases—including, as I read its opinion, the sometimes trivial accompanying baggage of judicial interpretation in federal contexts. . . .

A few members of the Court have taken the position that the intention of those who drafted the first section of the Fourteenth Amendment was simply, and exclusively, to make the provisions of the first eight Amendments applicable to state action. . . . Neither history, nor sense, supports using the Fourteenth Amendment to put the States in a constitutional straitjacket with respect to their own development in the administration of criminal or civil law.

Although I therefore fundamentally disagree with the total incorporation view of the Fourteenth Amendment, it seems to me that such a position does at least have the virtue, lacking in the Court's selective incorporation approach, of internal consistency: we look to the Bill of Rights, word for word, clause for clause, precedent for precedent because, it is said, the men who wrote the Amendment wanted it that way. . . .

Apart from the approach taken by the absolute incorporationists, I can see only one method of analysis that has any internal logic. That is to start with the words "liberty" and "due process of law" and attempt to define them in a way that accords with American traditions and our system of government. This approach, involving a much more discriminating process of adjudication than does "incorporation," is, albeit difficult, the one that was followed throughout the 19th and most of the present century. It entails a "gradual process of judicial inclusion and exclusion," seeking, with due recognition of constitutional tolerance for state experimentation and disparity, to ascertain those "immutable principles . . . of free government which no member of the Union may disregard." . . .

The relationship of the Bill of Rights to this "gradual process" seems to me to be twofold. In the first place it has long been clear that the Due Process Clause imposes some restrictions on state action that parallel Bill of Rights restrictions on federal action. Second, and more important than this accidental overlap, is the fact that the Bill of Rights is evidence, at various points, of the content Americans find in the term "liberty" and of American standards of fundamental fairness. . . .

Today's Court still remains unwilling to accept the total incorporationists' view of the history of the Fourteenth Amendment. This, if accepted, would afford a cogent reason for applying the Sixth Amendment to the States. The Court is also, apparently, unwilling to face the task of determining whether denial of trial by jury in the situation before us, or in other situations, is fundamentally unfair. Consequently, the Court has compromised on the case of the incorporationist position, without its internal logic. It has simply assumed that the question before us is whether the Jury Trial Clause of the Sixth Amendment should be incorporated into the Fourteenth, jot-for-jot and case-for-case, or ignored. Then the Court merely declares that the clause in question is "in" rather than "out." . . .

Since, as I see it, the Court has not even come to grips with the issues in this case, it is necessary to start from the beginning. When a criminal defendant contends that his state conviction lacked "due process of law," the question before this Court, in my view, is whether he was denied any element of fundamental procedural fairness. . . .

The argument that jury trial is not a requisite of due process is quite simple. The central proposition . . . is that "due process of law" requires only that criminal trials be fundamentally fair. As stated above, apart from the theory that it was historically intended as a mere shorthand for the Bill of Rights, I do not see what else "due process of law" can intelligibly be thought to mean. If due process of law requires only fundamental fairness, then the inquiry in each case must be whether a state trial process was a fair one. The Court has held, properly I think, that in an adversary process it is a requisite of fairness, for which there is no adequate substitute, that a criminal defendant be afforded a right to counsel and to cross-examine opposing witnesses. But it simply has not been demonstrated, nor, I think, can it be demonstrated, that trial by jury is the only fair means of resolving issues of fact. . . .

. . . There is a wide range of views on the desirability of trial by jury, and on the ways to make it most effective when it is used; there is also considerable variation from State to State in local conditions such as the size of the criminal caseload, the ease or difficulty of summoning jurors, and other trial conditions bearing on fairness. We have before us, therefore, an almost perfect example of a situation in which the celebrated dictum of Mr. Justice Brandeis should be invoked. It is, he said, "one of the happy incidents of the federal system that a single courageous State may, if its citizens choose, serve as a laboratory. . . ." [*New State Ice Co.* v. *Liebmann* . . . (dissenting opinion)]. This Court, other courts, and the political process are available to correct any experiments in criminal procedure that prove fundamentally unfair to defendants. That is not what is being done today: instead, and quite without reason, the Court has chosen to impose upon every State one means of trying criminal cases; it is a good means, but it is not the only fair means, and it is not demonstrably better than the alternatives States might devise.

★

## THE FOURTEENTH AMENDMENT

### THE EVISCERATION OF THE PRIVILEGES OR IMMUNITIES CLAUSE

*The Slaughterhouse Cases* (1873)

### ECONOMIC REGULATION AND THE RISE OF SUBSTANTIVE DUE PROCESS

*Munn* v. *Illinois* (1877)
*Lochner* v. *New York* (1905)

### THE REPUDIATION OF SUBSTANTIVE DUE PROCESS

*West Coast Hotel Company* v. *Parrish* (1937)
*Williamson* v. *Lee Optical Company* (1955)
*BMW of North America, Inc.* v. *Gore* (1996)
*United States* v. *Carolene Products Company* (1938)

### THE TAKINGS CLAUSE

*Hawaii Housing Authority* v. *Midkiff* (1984)
*Nollan* v. *California Coastal Commission* (1987)
*Lucas* v. *South Carolina Coastal Council* (1992)
*Dolan* v. *City of Tigard* (1994)

### NOTES

### SELECTED READING

### CASES

★

# 12
# ECONOMIC DUE PROCESS AND THE TAKINGS CLAUSE

Prior to the Civil War, the only constitutional restrictions on the power of the states to regulate economic activity were those found in Article I, Section 10, which prohibits the states from emitting bills of credit, making anything but gold or silver a tender in payment of debts, and passing ex post facto laws or laws impairing obligations of contracts. With the adoption of the Fourteenth Amendment in 1868, this situation changed. As pointed out in Chapter 10, this amendment, especially through its Due Process Clause, supplied the Supreme Court with a potent weapon for invalidating state efforts at economic regulation and for protecting vested property rights. In the early part of the twentieth century, the Due Process Clause was wielded by the Court to strike down state laws that, in its estimation, arbitrarily, unreasonably, and capriciously interfered with the rights of life, liberty, and property.[1] During this period, various justices used the clause to justify substantive reviews of governmental actions, scrutinizing not only how the government acted, but also what the government did.

As with the Contract Clause before it, substantive due process gradually lost its potency, until by the late 1930s it no longer represented a major obstacle to economic regulation by the states. Such obstacles as remain are found in the Takings Clause of the Fifth Amendment as incorporated to apply to the states, in the Court's expanding interpretations of congressional power to regulate commerce among the several states, or in the state constitutions themselves. It was wholly within the realm of civil liberties that substantive due process retained its potency and continued to serve as a constitutional limitation not only on legislative and executive procedure, but also on legislative and executive power to act at all. This chapter traces the rise and decline of substantive due process in the economic realm, as well as its subsequent revival as a strong check on the substance of legislation infringing upon civil liberties. It also explores the emerging significance of the Takings Clause as a check on state regulation of property rights.

## THE FOURTEENTH AMENDMENT

The Fourteenth Amendment commands that "no state shall make or enforce any law which shall abridge the privileges or immunities of citizens of the United States; nor shall any State deprive any person of life, liberty, or property, without due process of law; nor deny to any person within its jurisdiction the equal protection of the laws." Out of an acrimonious debate over the specific intentions of the members of the Thirty-ninth Congress who framed this amendment[2] has emerged general agreement as to the overall ends that the amendment was intended to advance and as to how its three major provisions were to serve as means for the advancement of these ends. As a group, the Privileges or Immunities, Due Process, and Equal Protection clauses were intended to place economic and civil liberties on the safe and secure foundation of federal protection. To that end, the Privileges or Immunities Clause was to protect substantive rights (e.g., freedom of speech, religious freedom, the right to engage in lawful occupations, freedom from improper police violence) and the Equal Protection and Due Process clauses were to protect procedural rights, with the former barring legislative discrimination with respect to substantive rights and the latter guaranteeing procedural safeguards and judicial regularity in the enforcement of those rights.

The Fourteenth Amendment can be visualized as a platform erected above the surface of state action for the protection of economic and civil liberties. In this metaphor, the Privileges or Immunities, Due Process, and Equal Protection clauses represent the platform's three legs: Each performs different functions, yet collectively they render the platform stable and secure. The amendment's framers believed that all three legs were essential, but that the Privileges or Immunities Clause would be the most important of the three, because it was designed to be the major load-bearing leg. This design is reflected clearly in Section 5 of the amendment, which provides that "Congress shall have power to enforce, by appropriate legislation, the provisions of this article." Looking at these provisions from the point of view of Congress, the Privileges or Immunities Clause provides the simplest framework for such enforcement legislation. Under that clause, Congress can set out, through a single act or a series of acts, a comprehensive list of the vast number of substantive rights that flow from United States citizenship and make it unlawful for any state, or its agents, to abridge such substantive rights.[3] In contrast, the Due Process and Equal Protection clauses, with their procedural emphases, represent far more elusive reference points for enforcement legislation, because of the formidable technical difficulties involved in avoiding unconstitutional vagueness while framing statutes that protect persons from state deprivation of their lives, liberty, or property "without due process of law" or that guarantee "equal protection of the laws" without interference with essential classificatory schemes.

Just five years after the Fourteenth Amendment was ratified, however, the Supreme Court in *The Slaughterhouse Cases* (1873) effectively kicked out the critical privileges-or-immunities leg and left the protective platform precariously supported by its two spindly procedural legs—due process and equal protection. To keep the platform of protections from collapsing altogether, subsequent Courts have found it imperative to increase substantially the size and strength of these procedural legs. Through judicial interpretation, the justices have added layer upon layer of meaning and coverage to these legs, in an effort to render secure those substantive economic and civil rights that originally were to have been protected by the Privileges or Immunities Clause.

## THE EVISCERATION OF THE PRIVILEGES OR IMMUNITIES CLAUSE

In *Butcher's Benevolent Association* v. *Crescent City Livestock Landing and Slaughterhouse Company,* more commonly known as *The Slaughterhouse Cases,* the Court upheld an act of the Louisiana legislature that had conferred upon one firm what was in effect a monopoly of the slaughterhouse business in New Orleans. The plaintiffs had asserted, among other things, that the law in question was in violation of the Fourteenth Amendment. In a 5–4 decision, the Court rejected this claim, principally on the ground of an especially narrow construction of the Privileges or Immunities Clause. Speaking for the majority, Justice Samuel F. Miller drew a distinction between state citizenship and national citizenship and, hence, between those privileges or immunities that accrued to an individual by virtue of state citizenship and those that stemmed from national citizenship. Only the latter, he insisted, were protected by the Fourteenth Amendment.

In distinguishing the privileges or immunities of state citizenship from those of national citizenship, Justice Miller quoted earlier decisions in an effort to demonstrate that the whole body of commonly accepted civil and economic rights—including the right to pursue a lawful employment in a lawful manner, which lay at the heart of *The Slaughterhouse Cases*—fell within the privileges or immunities of state citizenship. Such rights included "protection by the government, with the right to acquire and possess property of every kind, and to pursue and obtain happiness and safety, subject, nevertheless, to such restraints as the [state] government may prescribe for the general good of the whole." Miller contended that the Framers of the Fourteenth Amendment had not intended to transfer this whole body of rights to the protection of the federal government. To interpret the amendment otherwise, he argued, would be to accept consequences "so serious, so far-reaching and pervading" that they would alter radically "the whole theory of the relations of the state and Federal governments to each other." This the Court refused to do, "in the absence of language which expresses such a purpose too clearly to admit of doubt."

Miller and the majority did not argue that national citizenship conferred no privileges or immunities. Although declining to define them precisely, they did suggest that such privileges or immunities included the right of a citizen "to come to the seat of the government to assert any claim he may have upon that government"; the "right of free access to its seaports"; and the right "to demand the care and protection of the Federal government over his life, liberty, and property when on the high seas, or within the jurisdiction of a foreign government." This list left the whole body of traditional economic and civil rights solely under the protection of the states. As far as the federal Constitution was concerned, therefore, the privileges or immunities of the citizens of the separate states remained exactly as they had been before the Fourteenth Amendment was adopted. Justice Miller's argument prompted Justice Stephen B. Field to complain in frustration in his dissent that if that was all the Privileges or Immunities Clause meant, "it was a vain and idle enactment, which accomplished nothing, and most unnecessarily excited Congress and the people on its passage." For Justice Field, the clause was intended to have a "profound significance and consequence." He argued that what the Privileges and Immunities Clause of Article IV, Section 2 "did for the protection of the citizens of one State against hostile and discriminating legislation of other States, the Fourteenth Amendment does for the protection of every citizen of the United States against hostile and discriminating legislation against him in favor of others, whether they reside in the same or in different states."

The *Slaughterhouse* decision knocked out the only substantive (and therefore, the most important) leg supporting the platform of economic and civil liberties erected by the Fourteenth Amendment. It was, in the words of Michael Kent Curtis, "one of the signal disasters of American judicial history."[4] This leg has not been resurrected—with respect to the Privileges and Immunities Clause, the Court's decision in *The Slaughterhouse Cases* is still good law. The Court did announce in *Colgate* v. *Harvey* (1935) that the right of a U.S. citizen to do business and place a loan in a state other than that in which he resided was a privilege of national citizenship, but it expressly overruled that decision and returned to the old interpretation only five years later, holding in *Madden* v. *Kentucky* (1940) that "the right to carry out an incident to a trade, business or calling such as the deposit of money in banks is not a privilege of national citizenship." The *Slaughterhouse* interpretation also was affirmed in *Snowden* v. *Hughes* (1944), in which the Court held that the right to become a candidate for and be elected to a state office was an attribute of state citizenship, not a privilege of national citizenship. Those who had been denied this right, the Court declared, must look to their own state constitutions and laws for redress.[5]

## ECONOMIC REGULATION AND THE RISE OF SUBSTANTIVE DUE PROCESS

The permanent emasculation of the Privileges or Immunities Clause left the substantive economic and civil liberties guaranteed by the Fourteenth Amendment wholly dependent for support upon the Due Process and Equal Protection clauses. The *Slaughterhouse* majority, however, also construed these clauses in a narrow, restrictive fashion.[6] In response to the plaintiffs' assertion that the Louisiana statute in question deprived them of their property without due process of law, the Court observed that "under no construction of that provision that we have ever seen, or that we deem admissible, can the restraint imposed by the State of Louisiana . . . be held to be a deprivation of property within the meaning of that provision."[7] And to a plea that the act deprived them of equal protection of the laws, the Court responded that the Equal Protection Clause had been aimed only at laws in the States where the newly emancipated Negroes resided, "which discriminated with gross injustice and hardship against them as a class."

Over time, these narrow interpretations—these spindly legs—have been expanded and enlarged, until today the Due Process and Equal Protection clauses solidly support the protection of a vast array of substantive rights. This chapter and Chapters 5 through 7 of Volume II explore the growth of the Due Process Clause, initially as a means of protecting economic rights and subsequently as a means of protecting civil liberties. Chapters 8 through 10 in Volume II then explore the somewhat later growth of the Equal Protection Clause and the way that this procedural leg, too, has come to protect substantive civil liberties.

The narrow procedural interpretation given the Due Process Clause in *The Slaughterhouse Cases* gave way only gradually to a broader, more substantive understanding. In the significant case of *Munn* v. *Illinois* (1877), the Court reaffirmed the restrictive *Slaughterhouse* interpretation and refused to hold that Illinois legislation setting maximum rates for grain elevators denied the elevator operators use of their property without due process of law. Chief Justice Morrison Waite argued that since the days of the common law, grain elevators and warehouses had been recognized as businesses "clothed with a public interest," and as such were subject to public regulation by the legislature. Although he conceded that this regulatory power might be abused, the Chief Justice insisted that abuse "is no argument against the [law's] existence. For protection against abuses by legislatures the people must resort to the polls, not to the courts." In dissent, Justice Stephen J. Field argued that there was nothing in the character of the grain-elevator business that justified state regulation, and hence Illinois' legislation was "nothing less than a bold assertion of absolute power by the State to control at its discretion the property and business of the citizen, and fix the compensation he shall receive." To Field, this "unrestrained license" to regulate was incompatible with due process of law.

Field's broader conception of due process was articulated further by Justice Joseph Bradley in his concurring opinion in *Davidson* v. *New Orleans* (1878). Justice Miller, writing for the majority in *Davidson*, rejected a New Orleans landowner's claim that he had been deprived of his property without due process of law by being forced to pay a special assessment whose purpose (the draining of swamp lands) allegedly would not benefit him. After confessing that "the Constitutional meaning or value of the phrase 'due process of law' remains today without that satisfactory precision of definition which judicial decisions have given to nearly all the other guarantees of personal rights found in the constitutions of the several States and of the United States," Justice Miller went on to declare that the phrase's meaning, however unclear, must be understood in a procedural sense only:

> It is not possible to hold that a party has, without due process of law, been deprived of his property, when, as regards the issues affecting it, he has, by the laws of the State, a fair trial in a court of justice, according to the modes of proceedings applicable to such a case. . . . This proposition covers the present case. Before the assessment could be collected, or become effective, the statute required that the tableau of assessments should be filed in the proper District Court of the State; that personal service of notice, with reasonable time to object, should be served on all owners who were known and within reach of process, and due advertisement made as to those who were unknown, or could not be found. This was complied with; and the party complaining here appeared, and had a full and fair hearing in the court of first instance, and afterwards in the Supreme Court. If this be not due process of law, then the words can have no definite meaning as used in the Constitution.

Justice Bradley, although agreeing with the decision, insisted that the Due Process Clause had a substantive dimension as well. Making explicit what was implicit in Justice Field's dissent in *Munn*, he argued,

> I think . . . we are entitled under the fourteenth amendment, not only to see that there is some process of law, but "due process of law," provided by the State law when a citizen is deprived of his property; and that, in judging what is "due process of law," respect must be had to the cause and object of the taking, whether under the taxing power, the power of eminent domain, or the power of assessment for local improvements, or none of these: and if found to be suitable or admissible in the special case, it will be adjudged to be "due process of law;" but if found to be arbitrary, oppressive, and unjust, it may be declared to be not "due process of law."

According to this view, the Due Process Clause requires courts to review not only how, procedurally, the government acts (procedural due process)—but also what, substantively, the government does (substantive due process). If the Court discerns that a law is unreasonable—that is, "arbitrary, oppressive, and unjust"—then it is justified in declaring the law to be a denial of due process and, hence, constitutionally infirm.

These substantive due process arguments did not originate with Justices Field and Bradley. As far back as 1856, in *Wynehamer* v. *New York*, the New York Court of Appeals (the state's highest court) had invalidated a Prohibition law on the grounds that such an exercise of the police power infringed on the economic liberty of tavern proprietors to practice their livelihood and therefore denied them due process of law.[8] Justices Field and Bradley, however, were the first to give expression to these sentiments at the level of the United States Supreme Court, and the arguments that they introduced in *Munn* and *Davidson* were to gain ascendency in *Mugler* v. *Kansas* (1887) and *Allgeyer* v. *Louisiana* (1897), and to receive their clearest constitutional expression in *Lochner* v. *New York* (1905).

In *Mugler*, the Court upheld Kansas's Prohibition law but warned that it would begin examining the reasonableness of legislation. Justice John Marshall Harlan stressed that if "a statute purporting to have been enacted to protect the public health, the public morals, or the public safety has no real or substantial relation to those objects, or is a palpable invasion of rights secured by the fundamental law, it is the duty of the Courts to so adjudge." Then, in *Allgeyer*, the Court for the first time relied on substantive due process to invalidate state legislation. Louisiana had enacted legislation designed to regulate out-of-state insurance companies doing business in the state. Justice Rufus Peckham, writing for the majority, argued that the statute in question "is not due process of law, because it prohibits an act which under the federal constitution the defendant has a right to perform." The state's legitimate exercise of its police power, he contended, did not extend to "prohibiting a citizen from making contracts of the nature involved in this case outside of the limits of the jurisdiction of the state, and which are also to be performed outside of such jurisdiction." In the course of his opinion, Justice Peckham forthrightly announced the principle that the right to make contracts was a part of the liberty guaranteed by the Due Process Clause:

> The liberty mentioned in the [Fourteenth] Amendment means not only the right of the citizen to be free from the mere physical restraint of his person, as by incarceration, but the term is deemed to embrace the right of the citizen to be free in the enjoyment of all his faculties; to be free to use them in all lawful ways; to live and work where he will; to earn his livelihood by any lawful calling; to pursue any livelihood or avocation, and for that purpose to enter into all contracts which may be proper, necessary and essential to his carrying out to a successful conclusion the purposes above mentioned.

These substantive due process arguments received their clearest expression in *Lochner* v. *New York,* in which Justice Peckham declared that New York had unreasonably and arbitrarily interfered with the "freedom of master and employee to contract with each other in relation to their employment" by passing a law limiting the number of hours a baker could work in a bakery. Finding no valid health or safety reasons that could justify such a law, Peckham ruled that it amounted to an unreasonable deprivation of liberty (i.e., the liberty to contract) and violated the Due Process Clause. Justices Harlan and Holmes each wrote separate dissents. Justice Harlan charged the majority with "enlarging the scope of the Amendment far beyond its original purpose" and with "bringing under the supervision of this court matters which have been supposed to belong exclusively to the legislative departments of the several States." Justice Holmes penned one of his most memorable passages: "The Fourteenth Amendment does not enact Mr. Spencer's Social Statics. . . . A constitution . . . is made for people of fundamentally differing views."

By embracing the notion of substantive due process, the *Lochner* Court assumed the very role that Justice Miller had warned against in *The Slaughterhouse Cases:* It became a "perpetual censor," reviewing the reasonableness of state efforts at economic regulation. It continued to play this role at least through *Adkins* v. *Children's Hospital* (1923), in which the District of Columbia's minimum wage law for women and children was branded "the product of a naked arbitrary exercise of power" and thus a violation of the Fifth Amendment's Due Process Clause. Prior to *Adkins,* the Court had appeared to moderate its position toward economic legislation. In *Muller* v. *Oregon* (1908) and *Bunting* v. *Oregon* (1917), for example, the justices upheld the constitutionality of state legislation that, respectively, limited the workday for women to ten hours and extended the same maximum-hours limitation to all mill and factory workers. Of decisive importance in both of these decisions, however, was the Court's belief that the regulations in question were a reasonable exercise of the state's police powers—not its subsequent conviction that any judicial inquiry into the substance or reasonableness of economic legislation was inappropriate.

## THE REPUDIATION OF SUBSTANTIVE DUE PROCESS

As the Court's subsequent decision in *Adkins* makes apparent, *Muller* and *Bunting* did not represent a repudiation of substantive due process—in these cases the Court merely judged that the economic regulations in question were reasonable; it did not conclude that it was inappropriate for the Court to make such judgments in the first place. The disavowal of substantive due process began somewhat later in *Nebbia* v. *New York* (1934), in which the Court, by a 5–4 vote, upheld the validity of a Depression-era law regulating the price of milk. The New York legislature had sought to prevent ruinous price cutting by establishing a milk control board with power to fix minimum and maximum retail prices, and the appellant claimed that enforcement of the milk price regulations denied him due process of law by preventing him from selling his product at whatever price he desired. In rejecting this claim, Justice Owen Roberts, speaking for the majority, declared,

> So far as the requirement of due process is concerned, and in the absence of other constitutional restrictions, a state is free to adopt whatever economic policy may reasonably be deemed to promote public welfare, and to enforce that policy by legislation adapted to its purpose. The courts are without authority either to declare such policy, or, when it is declared by the legislature, to override it.

What was begun in *Nebbia* was completed in *West Coast Hotel Company* v. *Parrish* (1937). This case arose under a Washington state minimum-wage law that had been passed in 1913 and enforced continuously thereafter, quite irrespective of *Adkins*. In the midst of the intense political controversy generated by President Roosevelt's Court-packing plan, the Court upheld the law. Chief Justice Hughes insisted that the state legislature had the right to use its minimum-wage requirements to help implement its policy of protecting women from exploitive employers. He noted that "the adoption of similar requirements by many States evidences a deepseated conviction both as to the presence of the evil and as to the means adopted to check it. Legislative response to that conviction cannot be regarded as arbitrary or capricious, and that is all we have to decide." The Chief Justice then went even further: "Even if the wisdom of the policy is regarded as debatable and its effects uncertain, still the legislature is entitled to its judgment."

The Court's refusal in *Parrish* to contradict the judgment of the legislature on economic matters and its outright repudiation of substantive due process in the economic realm through the explicit overruling of *Adkins* remain controlling precedents. Subsequent decisions, in fact, suggest a reluctance to subject economic legislation to any constitutional test at all.[9] *Day-Brite Lighting* v. *Missouri* (1952) provides a clear example of this trend. In reviewing a state law that provided that employees could absent themselves from their jobs for four hours on election days and forbade employers from deducting wages for their absence, the Court admitted that the social policy embodied in the law was debatable but pointed out that "our recent decisions make plain that we do not sit as a superlegislature to weigh the wisdom of legislation nor to decide whether the policy it expresses offends the public welfare." This argument was repeated in *Williamson* v. *Lee Optical Company* (1955), which involved a statute that forbade any person but an ophthalmologist or an optometrist from fitting lenses to the face or duplicating or replacing lenses into frames, except on the prescription of an ophthalmologist or optometrist. After acknowledging that the law was "a needless, wasteful requirement in many cases," the Court went on to insist that "the day is gone" when it would strike down "state laws regulatory of business and industrial conditions, because they may be unwise, improvident, or out of harmony with a particular school of thought." Eight years later, in *Ferguson* v. *Skrupa* (1963), the Court applied the same reasoning in upholding a Kansas statute prohibiting anyone except lawyers from engaging in the business of debt adjustment, with Justice Black noting in his majority opinion that "it is up to legislatures, not Courts, to decide on the wisdom and utility of legislation." The *Ferguson* opinion elicited some judicial protests, however. Despite his abiding commitment to judicial self-restraint, Justice John Marshall Harlan felt compelled to protest against what he perceived to be judicial abdication. In his concurrence, he insisted that even economic legislation must bear "a rational relation to a constitutionally permissible objective"—a relationship that he found to exist in the instant case.

Justice Black's words in *Ferguson,* echoing as they do Chief Justice Waite's opinion in *Munn* v. *Illinois,* highlight the full circle traveled by the Court in its consideration of the Due Process Clause and economic rights. The spindly due-process leg in *Munn,* which by *Lochner* had grown enormously in size and strength, had lost its potency by *Parrish* and atrophied to the spindly reed it once again became by *Williamson.* So it has remained, at least until *BMW* v. *Gore* (1996), which raises the interesting question of whether the Court is not once again embracing substantive due process, if not to limit what legislatures can do, at least to limit the size of punitive damage awards that civil juries can impose. In this Alabama case, the Supreme Court held the Due Process Clause of the Fourteenth Amendment prohibits a State from imposing punitive damage awards that are "grossly excessive"—in this instance, a punitive damages award that was 500 times compensatory damages. Justice Stevens for the majority identified three "guideposts" that led the Court to the conclusion that the Alabama courts had entered "the zone of arbitrariness" and deprived the defendant of "elementary notions of fairness": the degree of reprehensibility of the defendant's conduct, the ratio between the punitive award and the plaintiff's actual harm, and the difference between the courts' sanction and legislative sanctions authorized for comparable misconduct. In his dissent, Justice Scalia complained that these guideposts "mark a road to nowhere; they provide no real guidance at all." Justice Ginsburg, in her dissent, likewise objected to the way in which the majority "leads us into territory traditionally within the States' domain" with "only a vague concept of substantive due process, a 'raised eyebrow' test, as its ultimate guide."

It is too early to determine whether *BMW* v. *Gore* is the beginning of a renewed judicial infatuation with substantive due process in the economic realm or whether it will prove to be an isolated, if provocative, exception. What can be said with certainty, however, is that the Court, for whatever reason, has never before embraced substantive due process simultaneously in both the economic and civil liberties realms. When substantive due process was at its height in the economic realm in the early part of the twentieth century, it was nonexistent in the realm of civil liberties, as *Buck* v. *Bell* (1927) makes abundantly clear. In *Buck*, the Court denied a substantive due process objection to a 1924 Virginia statute that, on the grounds of the "health of the patient and the welfare of society," provided for the sexual sterilization of inmates of institutions supported by the State who were found to be afflicted with hereditary forms of insanity or imbecility. The preamble of the Virginia statute declared that the Commonwealth was supporting in various institutions many "defective persons" who, if discharged, would become a menace, but who, if rendered incapable of procreating, might be discharged with safety and become self-supporting, with benefits both to themselves and society; it also declared that experience had shown that "heredity plays an important part in the transmission of insanity, imbecility, etc." Justice Holmes upheld the sterilization of Carrie Buck, whom he described as a "feeble minded white woman," "the daughter of a feeble minded mother," and herself "the mother of an illegitimate feeble minded child." He argued first that the statute met all the requirements of procedural due process: "There can be no doubt that, so far as procedure is concerned, the rights of the patient are most carefully considered, and, as every step in this case was taken in scrupulous compliance with the statute and after months of observation, there is no doubt that, in that respect, the plaintiff in error has had due process of law." But, he noted, Carrie Buck also objected on substantive due process grounds: "The attack is [also] upon the substantive law. It seems to be contended that in no circumstances could such an order be justified." The Court, however, was unpersuaded, and so, just four years after it had found in *Adkins* that a minimum wage law for women and children was "the product of a naked arbitrary exercise of power," it held that Virginia's eugenics-inspired statute passed constitutional muster. Justice Holmes wrote for an eight-member majority (Justice Butler dissented but did not write an opinion) when he declared:

> We have seen more than once that the public welfare may call upon the best citizens for their lives. It would be strange if it could not call upon those who already sap the strength of the State for these lesser sacrifices, often not felt to be such by those concerned, in order to prevent our being swamped with incompetence. It is better for all the world if, instead of waiting to execute degenerate offspring for crime or to let them starve for their imbecility, society can prevent those who are manifestly unfit from continuing their kind. The principle that sustains compulsory vaccination is broad enough to cover cutting the Fallopian tubes. Three generations of imbeciles are enough.[10]

At about the time that the Court was abandoning the protection of economic rights by substantive due process, it was beginning to embrace the concept to protect civil rights. The contemptuous disregard for the civil rights of Carrie Buck was soon replaced by a particular judicial solicitude for the rights of "discrete and insular minorities." In footnote four of the Court's opinion in *United States* v. *Carolene Products Company* (1938), decided just one year after its repudiation of substantive due process in *West Coast Hotel* v. *Parrish,* Justice Harlan Fiske Stone outlined a justification for "more exacting judicial scrutiny" where infringements of civil liberties were involved. The Court's subsequent embrace of substantive due process in the realm of civil liberties will be an underlying concern in Volume II.

## THE TAKINGS CLAUSE

Just as the Due Process Clause supplanted the Contract Clause as a means of protecting property rights,. so, too, the Takings Clause of the Fifth Amendment as incorporated to apply to the states by the Fourteenth Amendment appears to have supplanted due process. It states that private property shall not "be taken for public use, without just compensation," and is variously referred to as the Takings Clause, the Public Use Clause, or the Just Compensation Clause.

Both the federal and state governments have the power of eminent domain, the power to condemn or expropriate private property for public purposes upon just compensation of the owner. The decision to invoke the power of eminent domain is a legislative one, and the Court has been reluctant to question whether the compensation offered is "just" or whether the confiscated property has been taken for a "public use." In *Hawaii Housing Authority* v. *Midkiff* (1984), for example, the Supreme Court unanimously upheld Hawaii's use of its power of eminent domain to acquire property from large landowners and transfer it to lessees living on single-family residential lots on the land. The purpose of this land condemnation scheme was to reduce the concentration of land ownership, and Justice O'Connor, equating public purpose with public use, declared that "our cases make clear that empirical debates over the wisdom of takings—no less than debates over the wisdom of other kinds of socioeconomic legislation—are not to be carried out in the federal courts."

While the Court has been hesitant to challenge legislative judgments concerning just compensation and public use, it has become increasingly assertive in concluding that various governmental regulations that restrict, diminish, or destroy the value of property can be as much a taking as eminent domain. In *First English Evangelical Lutheran Church* v. *Los Angeles County* (1987), the Court held in a 6–3 decision that a county decision to prohibit a church from constructing buildings on a campground it owned after there had been extensive damage from a flood constituted a taking for which the county must pay compensation. Moreover, the Court continued, once a taking has been determined, the government must compensate the owner for the period during which the taking was in effect. The mere fact that the taking was temporary—either because subsequently invalidated by the courts or repealed by a successor ordinance—does not eliminate the need for compensation. As Chief Justice

Rehnquist noted: "[T]he Los Angeles County ordinances have denied appellant all use of its property for a considerable period of years, and we hold that invalidation of the ordinance without payment of fair value for the use of the property during this period of time would be a constitutionally insufficient remedy."

*Nollan* v. *California Coastal Commission* (1987) shows the Court's new assertiveness even more clearly. The coastal commission granted a permit to the Nollans to replace a small bungalow on their beachfront lot with a larger house. As a condition, however, the commission insisted that the Nollans grant an easement to the public across their land to the beach. The Nollans claimed that this requirement constituted a taking, and the Supreme Court, with Justice Scalia writing the majority opinion, agreed.

Among the justices on the Court, Justice Scalia appears the most willing to treat the Takings Clause as a successor to the Due Process Clause and use it to strike down governmental regulation of private property. In *Pennell* v. *City of San Jose* (1988), a case involving a rent control ordinance that allowed administrative reductions on rent in case of "tenant hardship," Justice Scalia dissented from Chief Justice Rehnquist's majority decision that the case was not ripe for judicial resolution, reached the merits on the hardship provision, and expanded on the themes he advanced in *Nollan*. He denied the landlords were the cause of the problem at which the hardship provision was aimed. Rather, he insisted that the provision was drafted "to meet a quite different social problem: the existence of some renters who are too poor to afford even reasonably priced housing. But that problem is no more caused or exploited by landlords than it is by the grocers who sell needy renters their food, or the department stores that sell them their clothes, or the employers who pay them their wages, or the citizens of San Jose holding the higher-paying jobs from which they are excluded." Moreover, Scalia continued, "even if the neediness of renters could be regarded as a problem distinctively attributable to landlords in general, it is not remotely attributable to the particular landlords that the ordinance singles out—namely, those who happen to have a 'hardship' tenant at the present time, or who may happen to rent to a 'hardship' tenant in the future, or whose current or future affluent tenants may happen to decline into the 'hardship' category." He then drove home his primary point: "The fact that government acts through the landlord-tenant relationship does not magically transform general public welfare, which must be supported by all the public, into mere 'economic regulation,' which can disproportionately burden particular individuals."

Justice Scalia's insistence in *Pennell* that the government (and hence taxpayer) pay for public welfare and not transfer these costs to particular discrete individuals takes on added significance today, with a public whose appetite for governmental services is greater than its willingness to pay for them, and with his majority opinion for the Court in *Lucas* v. *South Carolina Coastal Council* (1992). In this case, a landowner was deprived of all "economically viable use" of his $1 million property when the state enacted a coastal zone act, designed to prevent beach erosion, that prevented him from building a beachfront home on his property. Justice Scalia held that regulatory takings that deprive land of all economically beneficial use require compensation, regardless of the importance of the public interests served, unless an "inquiry into the nature of the owner's estate shows that the proscribed use interests were not part of his title to begin with."

The Court's takings cases, no less than its substantive due process cases, pose the question of the proper role of the Court. To what extent should the Court be a check on the wishes of the popular branches? To what extent should it protect the few from the wishes of the majority? To what extent should it protect the rights of property with the same dedication it displays for other rights?[11] The 1994 case of *Dolan* v. *City of Tigard* squarely frames these questions. Chief Justice Rehnquist held that "We see no reason why the Takings Clause of the Fifth Amendment, as much a part of the Bill of Rights as the First Amendment or Fourth Amendment, should be relegated to the status of a poor relation" and held that the City of Tigard, Oregon, violated the constitutional rights of Florence Dolan when it held that it would approve her application to expand her plumbing and electric supply store only if she dedicated ten percent of her land to the city.

## NOTES

1 For an especially useful essay on this matter, see Edward S. Corwin, "The Supreme Court and the Fourteenth Amendment," *Michigan Law Review* 7 (June 1909): 643.

2 See Raoul Berger, *Government by Judiciary: The Transformation of the Fourteenth Amendment* (Cambridge, Mass.: Harvard University Press, 1977); Jacobus Tenbroek, *Equal under Law* (New York: Macmillan, 1965); Alexander M. Bickel, "The Original Understanding and the Segregation Decision," *Harvard Law Review* 69, no. 1 (November 1955); Charles Fairman, "Does the Fourteenth Amendment Incorporate the Bill of Rights?", *Stanford Law Review* 2, no. 1 (1949); and William W. Van Alstyne, "The Fourteenth Amendment, the 'Right to Vote,' and the Understanding of the Thirty-Ninth Congress," in *Supreme Court Review,* ed. Philip Kurland (Chicago: University of Chicago Press, 1966); and Alford H. Kelly, "Clio and the Court: An Illicit Love Affair," 1965 *Supreme Court Review.*

3 See Corwin, "The Supreme Court and the Fourteenth Amendment"; Tenbroek, *Equal under Law,* pp. 236–238; M. Glenn Abernathy, *Civil Liberties under the Constitution,* 3d ed. (New York: Harper and Row, 1977), pp. 32–33; and Berger, *Government by Judiciary*, pp. 18–19.

4 Michael Kent Curtis, "Resurrecting the Privileges and Immunities Clause and Revising the *Slaughterhouse Cases* without Exhuming *Lochner:* Individual Rights and the Fourteenth Amendment," *Boston College Law Review* 38 (December 1966): 105.

5 Unsuccessful attempts to broaden the scope of privileges and immunities include *Hague* v. *Committee for Industrial Organization* (1939); *Edwards* v. *California* (1941); and *Oyama* v. *California* (1948).

6 It could be said that with respect to the Due Process and Equal Protection clauses, the Court correctly identified the intentions of the Thirty-ninth Con-

gress in drafting these clauses and acted accordingly. But given its concurrent construction of the Privileges or Immunities Clause, the Court's fidelity to the intentions of the Thirty-ninth Congress simply served to exacerbate matters and led directly to the development of substantive due process (discussed below). For an excellent treatment of the development of substantive due process, see Chapter 4: "Doing Justice in the Name of the Law: The Transformation of Due Process of Law," in Eugene W. Hickok and Gary L. McDowell, *Law vs. Justice: Courts and Politics in American Society* (New York: Free Press, 1993), pp. 80–121.

7 The Court accepted without debate the procedural interpretation of due process. For differing views of what due process could have meant, however, see *Scott* v. *Sandford* (1857); *Hepburn* v. *Griswold* (1870); and Edward S. Corwin, "Due Process of Law before the Civil War," *Harvard Law Review* 24 (March 1911): 366*ff*. and (April 1911): 460*ff*.

8 As Justice Comstock put the question: "Do the prohibitions and penalties of the act for the prevention of intemperance, pauperism, and crime pass the utmost boundaries of mere regulation and police, and by their own force, assuming them to be valid and faithfully obeyed and executed, work the essential loss or destruction of the property at which they are aimed? . . . In my judgment, they do plainly work this result."

9 Guy Miller Struve, "The Less-Restrictive-Alternative Principle and Economic Due Process," *Harvard Law Review* 80 (1967): 1463–1488.

10 Carrie Buck also objected on equal protection grounds. Justice Holmes was equally unpersuaded here: "But, it is said . . . this reasoning . . . fails when it is confined to the small number who are in the institutions named and is not applied to the multitudes outside. It is the usual last resort of constitutional arguments to point out shortcomings of this sort. But the answer is that the law does all that is needed when it does all that it can, indicates a policy, applies it to all within the lines, and seeks to bring within the lines all similarly situated so far and so fast as its means allow. Of course, so far as the operations enable whose who otherwise must be kept confined to be returned to the world, and thus open the asylum to others, the equality aimed at will be more nearly reached."

11 See Roger Clegg, "Reclaiming the Takings Clause," *South Carolina Law Review* 46 (Summer 1995): 532–533, 576, who argues that the Court has reduced the Takings Clause to an "ad hoc balancing test" that has "degenerate[d] into a mere mask for judicial predilections." This balancing of (1) the economic impact of the regulation on the claimant, (2) the extent to which the regulation has interfered with the claimant's investment-backed expectations, and (3) the character of the governmental action "results, unsurprisingly, in each justice voting his or her own policy preferences. Clegg concludes: "This balancing has no textual justification, and its lawless result if flatly inconsistent with [the] Constitution's letter and spirit."

## SELECTED READING

*Adair* v. *United States*, 208 U.S. 161 (1908).

*Concrete Pipe & Products* v. *Construction Laborers Pension Trust*, 508 U.S. 602 (1993).

*Coppage* v. *Kansas*, 236 U.S. 1 (1915).

*Dean* v. *Gadsden Times Publishing Company,* 412 U.S. 543 (1973).
*Ferguson* v. *Skrupa,* 372 U.S. 726 (1963).
*First English Evangelical Lutheran Church of Glendale* v. *Los Angeles County,* 482 U.S. 304 (1987).
*Morehead* v. *New York ex rel. Tipaldo,* 298 U.S. 587 (1936).
*Pacific Mutual Life Insurance* v. *Haslip,* 499 U.S. 1 (1991).
*Pennell* v. *City of San Jose,* 485 U.S. 1 (1988).

Berger, Raoul. *Government by Judiciary: The Transformation of the Fourteenth Amendment* (Cambridge, Mass.: Harvard University Press, 1977).

Clegg, Roger. "Reclaiming the Takings Clause." *South Carolina Law Review* 46 (Summer 1995): 531–578.

Curtis, Michael Kent. "Resurrecting the Privileges and Immunities Clause and Revising the *Slaughterhouse Cases* without Exhuming *Lochner:* Individual Rights and the Fourteenth Amendment." *Boston College Law Review* 38 (December 1996): 1–106.

Dorn, James A. and Henry G. Manne, eds. *Economic Liberties and the Judiciary* (Fairfax, Va.: George Mason University Press, 1987).

Easterbrook, Frank H. "Substance and Due Process." *1982 Supreme Court Review,* edited by Philip B. Kurland, Gerhard Casper, and Dennis Hutchinson (Chicago: University of Chicago Press, 1983).

Epstein, Richard A. *Takings: Property and the Power of Eminent Domain* (Cambridge, Mass.: Harvard University Press, 1985).

Galie, Peter J. "State Courts and Economic Rights." *Annals* 496 (1988): 76–87.

Kitch, Edmund W. and Clara Ann Bowler. "The Facts of *Munn* v. *Illinois.*" *1978 Supreme Court Review,* edited by Philip B. Kurland and Gerhard Casper (Chicago: University of Chicago Press, 1979).

McCloskey, Robert. "Economic Due Process and the Supreme Court: An Exhumation and Reburial." *1962 Supreme Court Review,* edited by Philip B. Kurland (Chicago: University of Chicago Press, 1962).

Nelson, William E. *The Fourteenth Amendment: From Political Principle to Judicial Doctrine* (Cambridge, Mass.: Harvard University Press, 1988).

Porter, Mary Cornelia. "That Commerce Shall Be Free: A New Look at the Old Laissez-Faire Court." *1976 Supreme Court Review,* edited by Philip B. Kurland (Chicago: University of Chicago Press, 1977).

Sallet, Jonathan D. "Regulatory 'Takings' and Just Compensation: The Supreme Court's Search for a Solution Continues." *Urban Lawyer* 18 (1986): 635.

Shapiro, Martin. "The Constitution and Economic Rights." In *Essays on the Constitution of the United States,* edited by M. Judd Harmon (Port Washington, N.Y.: Kennikat Press, 1978).

Siegan, Bernard H. *Economic Liberties and the Constitution* (Chicago: University of Chicago Press, 1981).

Treanor, William Michael. "The Origins and Original Significance of the Just Compensation Clause of the Fifth Amendment." *Yale Law Journal* 94 (1985): 694–717.

Tushnet, Mark. "The Newer Property: Suggestion for the Revival of Substantive Due Process." *1975 Supreme Court Review,* edited by Philip B. Kurland (Chicago: University of Chicago Press, 1976).

Zuckert, Michael P. "Congressional Power Under the Fourteenth Amendment—The Original Understanding of Section Five." *Constitutional Commentary* 3 (1986): 123–147.

# *The Slaughterhouse Cases*

**83 U.S. (16 Wallace) 36; 21 L. Ed. 394 (1873)**

In 1869, the Louisiana legislature passed an act designed to "protect the health of the City of New Orleans" by granting to the Crescent City Livestock Landing and Slaughterhouse Co. a twenty-five-year monopoly on the sheltering and slaughtering of animals in the city and surrounding parishes. The law required that all other butchers in the New Orleans area come to that company and pay for the use of its abattoir. Although the law was in response to a cholera epidemic and represented an attempt to end contamination of the city's water supply caused by the dumping of refuse into the Mississippi River by small independent slaughterhouses, the state legislature at the time was dominated by carpetbag elements, and charges of corruption were rampant. The Butcher's Benevolent Association, a group of small independent slaughterers who had been deprived of their livelihood by the legislation, challenged the act on the grounds that it violated the Thirteenth Amendment and the Privileges and Immunities, Due Process, and Equal Protection clauses of the Fourteenth Amendment. A state district court and the Louisiana Supreme Court upheld the legislation, at which point this case, along with two others involving the same controversy, was brought to the United States Supreme Court on a writ of error. These three cases have come to be known simply as *The Slaughterhouse Cases. Opinion of the Court: Miller, Clifford, Davis, Hunt, Strong. Dissenting opinions: Bradley; Field, Bradley, Chase, Swayne; Swayne.*

MR. JUSTICE MILLER delivered the opinion of the Court. . . .

The plaintiffs in error . . . allege that the statute is a violation of the Constitution of the United States in these several particulars:

That it creates an involuntary servitude forbidden by the thirteenth article of amendment;

That it abridges the privileges and immunities of citizens of the United States;

That it denies to the plaintiffs the equal protection of the laws; and,

That it deprives them of their property without due process of law; contrary to the provisions of the first section of the fourteenth article of amendment.

This court is thus called upon for the first time to give construction to these articles.

. . . In the light of . . . recent . . . history, . . . and on the most casual examination of the language of these amendments, no one can fail to be impressed with the one pervading purpose found in them all, lying at the foundation of each, and without which none of them would have been even suggested; we mean the freedom of the slave race, the security and firm establishment of that freedom, and the protection of the newly-made freeman and citizen from the oppressions of those who had formerly exercised unlimited dominion over him. . . .

We do not say that no one else but the negro can share in this protection. . . . But what we do say, and what we wish to be understood is, that in any fair and just construction of any section or phrase of these amendments, it is necessary to look to the purpose which we have said was the pervading spirit of them all, the evil which they were designed to remedy, and the process of continued addition to the Constitution, until that purpose was supposed to be accomplished, as far as constitutional law can accomplish it.

The first section of the fourteenth article, to which our attention is more specially invited, opens with a definition of citizenship—not only citizenship of the United States, but citizenship of the States. . . .

"All persons born or naturalized in the United States, and subject to the jurisdiction thereof, are citizens of the United States and of the State wherein they reside." . . .

It declares that persons may be citizens of the United States without regard to their citizenship of a particular State, and it overturns the Dred Scott decision by making *all persons* born within the United States and subject to its jurisdiction citizens of the United States. . . . Not only may a man be a citizen of the United States without being a citizen of a State, but an important element is necessary to convert the former into the latter. He must reside within the State to make him a citizen of it, but it is only necessary that he should be born or naturalized in the United States to be a citizen of the Union.

It is quite clear, then, that there is a citizenship of the United States, and a citizenship of a State, which are distinct from each other, and which depend upon different characteristics or circumstances in the individual.

We think this distinction and its explicit recognition in this amendment of great weight in this argument, because the next paragraph of this same section, which is the one mainly relied on by the plaintiffs in error, speaks only of privileges and immunities of citizens of the United States, and does not speak of those of citizens of the several States. The argument, however, in favor of the plaintiffs rests wholly on the assumption that the citizenship is the same, and the privileges and immunities guaranteed by the clause are the same.

The language is, "No State shall make or enforce any law which shall abridge the privileges or immunities of citizens of the United States." It is a little remarkable, if this clause was intended as a protection to the citizen of a State against the legislative power of his own State, that the word citizen of the State should be left out when it is so carefully used, and used in contradistinction to citizens of the United States, in the very sentence which precedes it. It is too clear for argument that the change in phraseology was adopted understandingly and with a purpose.

Of the privileges and immunities of the citizen of the United States, and of the privileges and immunities of the citizen of the State, and what they respectively are, we will presently consider; but we wish to state here that it is only the former which are placed by this clause under the protection of the Federal Constitution, and that the latter, whatever they may be, are not intended to have any additional protection by this paragraph of the amendment.

If, then, there is a difference between the privileges and immunities belonging to a citizen of the United States as such, and those belonging to the citizen of the State as such, the latter must rest for their security and protection where they have heretofore rested; for they are not embraced by this paragraph of the amendment.

The first occurrence of the words "privileges and immunities" in our constitutional history, is to be found in the fourth of the articles of the old Confederation.

It declares "that . . . the free inhabitants of each of these States . . . shall be entitled to all the privileges and immunities of free citizens in the several States." . . .

In the Constitution of the United States, which superseded the Articles of Confederation, the corresponding provision is found in section two of the fourth article, in the following words: "The citizens of each State shall be entitled to all the privileges and immunities of citizens of the several States." . . .

That constitutional provision . . . did not create those rights, which it called privileges and immunities of citizens of the States. It threw around them in that clause no security for the citizen of the State in which they were claimed or exercised. Nor did it profess to control the power of the State governments over the rights of its own citizens.

Its sole purpose was to declare to the several States, that whatever those rights, as you grant or establish them to your own citizens, or as you limit or qualify, or impose restrictions on their exercise, the same, neither more nor less, shall be the measure of the rights of citizens of other States within your jurisdiction.

It would be the vainest show of learning to attempt to prove by citations of authority, that up to the adoption of the recent amendments, no claim or pretence was set up that those rights depended on the Federal government for their existence or protection, beyond the very few express limitations which the Federal Constitution imposed upon the States—such, for instance, as the prohibition against ex post facto laws, bills of attainder, and laws impairing the obligation of contracts. But with the exception of these and a few other restrictions, the entire domain of the privileges and immunities of citizens of the States, as above defined, lay within the constitutional and legislative power of the States, and without that of the Federal government. Was it the purpose of the fourteenth amendment, by the simple declaration that no State should make or enforce any law which shall abridge the privileges and immunities of *citizens of the United States,* to transfer the security and protection of all the civil rights which we have mentioned, from the States to the Federal government? And where it is declared that Congress shall have the power to enforce that article, was it intended to bring within the power of Congress the entire domain of civil rights heretofore belonging exclusively to the States?

All this and more must follow, if the proposition of the plaintiffs in error be sound. For not only are these rights subject to the control of Congress whenever in its discretion, any of them are supposed to be abridged by State legislation, but that body may also pass laws in advance, limiting and restricting the exercise of legislative power by the States, in their most ordinary and usual functions, as in its judgment it may think proper on all such subjects. And still further, such a construction followed by the reversal of the judgments of the Supreme Court of Louisiana in these cases, would constitute this court a perpetual censor upon all legislation of the States, on the civil rights of their own citizens, with authority to nullify such as it did not approve as consistent with those rights, as they existed at the time of the adoption of this amendment. The argument we admit is not always the most conclusive which is drawn from the consequences urged against the adoption of a particular construction of an instrument. But when, as in the case before us, these consequences are so serious, so far-reaching and pervading, so great a departure from the structure and spirit of our institutions; when the effect is to fetter and degrade the State governments by subjecting them to the control of Congress, in the exercise of powers heretofore universally conceded to them of the most ordinary and fundamental character; when in fact it radically changes the whole theory of the relations of the State and Federal governments to each other and of both these governments to the people; the argument has a force that is irresistible, in the absence of language which expresses such a purpose too clearly to admit of doubt.

We are convinced that no such results were intended by the Congress which proposed these amendments, nor by the legislatures of the States which ratified them.

Having shown that the privileges and immunities relied on in the argument are those which belong to citizens of the States as such, and that they are left to the State governments for security and protection, and not by this article placed under the special care of the Federal government, we may hold ourselves excused from defining the privileges and immunities of citizens of the United States which no State can abridge, until some case involving those privileges may make it necessary to do so.

But lest it should be said that no such privileges and immunities are to be found if those we have been considering are excluded, we venture to suggest some which owe their existence to the Federal government, its National character, its Constitution, or its laws.

One of these is well described in the case of *Crandall* v. *Nevada.* It is said to be the right of the citizen of this great country, protected by implied guarantees of its Constitution, "to come to the seat of government to assert any claim he may have upon that government, to transact any business he may have with it, to seek its protection, to share its offices, to engage in administering its functions. He has the right of free access to its seaports, through which all operations of foreign commerce are conducted, to the subtreasuries, land offices, and courts of justice in the several States." . . .

Another privilege of a citizen of the United States is to demand the care and protection of the Federal government over his life, liberty, and property when on the high seas or within the jurisdiction of a foreign government. Of this there can be no doubt, nor that the right depends upon his character as a citizen of the United States. The right to peaceably assemble and petition for redress of grievances, the privilege of the writ of *habeas corpus*, are rights of the citizen guaranteed by the Federal Constitution. The right to use the navigable waters of the United States, however they may penetrate the territory of the several States, all rights secured to our citizens by treaties with foreign nations, are dependent upon citizenship of the United States, and not citizenship of a State. One of these privileges is conferred by the very article under consideration. It is that a citizen of the United States can, of his own volition, become a citizen of any State of the Union by a *bonâ fide* residence therein, with the same rights as other citizens of that State. To these may be added the rights secured by the thirteenth and fifteenth articles of amendment, and by the other clause of the fourteenth, next to be considered.

But it is useless to pursue this branch of the inquiry, since we are of opinion that the rights claimed by these plaintiffs in error, if they have any existence, are not privileges and immunities of citizens of the United States within the meaning of the clause of the fourteenth amendment under consideration. . . .

The argument has not been much pressed in these cases that the defendant's charter deprives the plaintiffs of their property without due process of law. . . .

We are not without judicial interpretation, . . . both State and National, of the meaning of this clause. And it is sufficient to say that under no construction of that provision that we have ever seen, or any that we deem admissible, can the restraint imposed by the State of Louisiana upon the exercise of their trade by the butchers of New Orleans be held to be a deprivation of property within the meaning of that provision.

"Nor shall any State deny to any person within its jurisdiction the equal protection of the laws."

In the light of the history of these amendments, and the pervading purpose of them, which we have already discussed, it is not difficult to give a meaning to this clause. The existence of laws in the States where the newly emancipated negroes resided, which discriminated with gross injustice and hardship against them as a class, was the evil to be remedied by this clause, and by it such laws are forbidden. . . .

The judgments of the Supreme Court of Louisiana in these cases are

*Affirmed.*

MR. JUSTICE FIELD, dissenting. . . .

The question presented is . . . . one of the gravest importance, not merely to the parties here, but to the whole country. It is nothing less than the question whether the recent amendments to the Federal Constitution protect the citizens of the United States against the deprivation of their common rights by State legislation. In my judgment the fourteenth amendment does afford such protection, and was so intended by the Congress which framed and the States which adopted it.

The counsel for the plaintiffs in error have contended, with great force, that the act in question is also inhibited by the thirteenth amendment. . . .

. . . I have been so accustomed to regard it as intended to meet that form of slavery which had previously prevailed in this country, and to which the recent civil war owed its existence, that I was not prepared, nor am I yet, to give to it the extent and force ascribed by counsel. Still it is evident that the language of the amendment is not used in a restrictive sense. It is not confined to African slavery alone. It is general and universal in its application. . . .

It is not necessary, however, . . . to rest my objections to the act in question upon the terms and meaning of the thirteenth amendment. The provisions of the fourteenth amendment, which is properly a supplement to the thirteenth, cover, in my judgment, the case before us, and inhibit any legislation which confers special and exclusive privileges like these under consideration. . . It first declares that "all persons born or naturalized in the United States, and subject to the jurisdiction thereof, are citizens of the United States and of the State wherein they reside." . . .

. . . It recognizes in express terms, if it does not create, citizens of the United States, and it makes their citizenship dependent upon the place of their birth, or the fact of their adoption, and not upon the constitution or laws of any State or the condition of their ancestry. A citizen of a State is now only a citizen of the United States residing in that State. The fundamental rights, privileges, and immunities which belong to him as a free man and a free citizen, now belong to him as a citizen of the United States, and are not dependent upon his citizenship of any State. . . .

The amendment does not attempt to confer any new privileges or immunities upon citizens, or to enumerate or define those already existing. It assumes that there are such privileges and immunities which belong of right to citizens as such, and ordains that they shall not be abridged by State legislation. If this inhibition has no reference to privileges and immunities of this character, but only refers, as held by the majority of the court in their opinion, to such privileges and immunities as were before its adoption specially designated in the Constitution or necessarily implied as belonging to citizens of the United States, it was a vain and idle enactment, which accomplished nothing, and most unnecessarily excited Congress and the people on its passage. With privileges and immunities thus designated or implied no State could ever have interfered by its laws, and no new constitutional provision was required to inhibit such interference. The supremacy of the Constitution and the laws of the United States always controlled any State legislation of that character. But if the amendment refers to the natural and inalienable rights which belong to all citizens, the inhibition has a profound significance and consequence.

What, then, are the privileges and immunities which are secured against abridgment by State legislation? . . .

The terms, privileges and immunities, are not new in the amendment; they were in the Constitution before the amendment was adopted. They are found in the second section of the fourth article, which declares that "the citizens of each State shall be entitled to all privileges and immunities of citizens in the several States," and they have been the subject of frequent consideration in judicial decisions. In *Corfield* v. *Coryell*, Mr. Justice Washington said he had "no hesitation in confining these expressions to those privileges and immunities which were, in their nature, fundamental; which belong of right to citizens of all free governments, and which have at all times been enjoyed by the citizens of the several States which compose the Union, from the time of their becoming free, independent, and sovereign;" and, in considering what those fundamental privileges were, he said that perhaps it would be more tedious than difficult to enumerate them, but that they might be "all comprehended under the following general heads: protection by the government; the enjoyment of life and liberty, with the right to acquire and possess property of every kind, and to pursue and obtain happiness and safety, subject, nevertheless, to such restraints as the government may justly prescribe for the general good of the whole." This appears to me to be a sound construction of the clause in question. The privileges and immunities designated are those *which of right belong to the citizens of all free governments.* Clearly among these must be placed the right to pursue a lawful employment in a lawful manner, without other restraint than such as equally affects all persons. . . .

What the clause in question did for the protection of the citizens of one State against hostile and discriminating legislation of other States, the fourteenth amendment does for the protection of every citizen of the United States against hostile and discriminating legislation against him in favor of others, whether they reside in the same or in different States. If under the fourth article of the Constitution equality of privileges and immunities is secured between citizens of different States, under the fourteenth amendment the same equality is secured between citizens of the United States. . . .

This equality of right, with exemption from all disparaging and partial enactments, in the lawful pursuits of life, throughout the whole country, is the distinguishing privilege of citizens of the United States. To them, everywhere, all pursuits, all professions, all avocations are open without other restrictions than such as are imposed equally upon all others of the same age, sex, and condition. The State may prescribe such regulations for every pursuit and calling of life as will promote the public health, secure the good order and advance the general prosperity of society, but when once prescribed, the pursuit or calling must be free to be followed by every citizen who is within the conditions designated, and will conform to the regulations. This is the fundamental idea upon which our institutions rest, and unless adhered to in the legislation of the country our government will be a republic only in name. The fourteenth amendment, in my judgment, makes it essential to the validity of the legislation of every State that this equality of right should be respected. . . .

MR. JUSTICE BRADLEY, dissenting. . . .

In my view, a law which prohibits a large class of citizens from adopting a lawful employment, or from following a lawful employment previously adopted, does deprive them of liberty as well as property, without due process of law. Their right of choice is a portion of their liberty; their occupation is their property. Such a law also deprives those citizens of the equal protection of the laws, contrary to the last clause of the section.

It is futile to argue that none but persons of the African race are intended to be benefited by this amendment. They may have been the primary cause of the amendment, but its language is general, embracing all citizens, and I think it was purposely so expressed.

# *Munn* v. *Illinois*

**94 U.S. 113; 24 L. Ed. 77 (1877)**

Pursuant to Article XIII of the Illinois Constitution of 1870, which empowered the state legislature to regulate the storage of grain, the Illinois General Assembly enacted a statute in 1871 that required grain warehouses and elevators to obtain operating licenses and that established the maximum rates they could charge for the handling and storage of grain. Ira Y. Munn was convicted in county court of operating a grain warehouse without a license and of charging higher rates than those allowed by the law, and was fined $100. The Illinois Supreme Court affirmed his conviction, and Munn brought the case to the United States Supreme Court on a writ of error. *Opinion of the Court: Waite, Bradley, Clifford, Davis, Hunt, Miller, Swayne. Dissenting opinion: Field, Strong.*

MR. CHIEF JUSTICE WAITE delivered the opinion of the Court.

The question to be determined in this case is whether the general assembly of Illinois can, under the limitations upon the legislative power of the States imposed by the Constitution of the United States, fix by law the maximum of charges for the storage of grain in warehouses at Chicago and other places in the State. . . .

It is claimed that such a law is repugnant—To that part of amendment 14 which ordains that no State shall "deprive any person of life, liberty, or property, without due process of law." . . .

The Constitution contains no definition of the word "deprive," as used in the Fourteenth Amendment. To determine its signification, therefore, it is necessary to ascertain the effect which usage has given it, when employed in the same or a like connection.

While this provision of the amendment is new in the Constitution of the United States, as a limitation upon the powers of the States, it is old as a principle of civilized government. It is found in Magna Charta, and, in substance if not in form, in nearly or quite all the constitutions that have been from time to time adopted by the several States of the Union. By the Fifth Amendment, it was introduced into the Constitution of the United States as a limitation upon the powers of the national government, and by the Fourteenth, as a guaranty against any encroachment upon an acknowledged right of citizenship by the legislatures of the States. . . .

When one becomes a member of society, he necessarily parts with some rights or privileges which, as an individual not affected by his relations to others, he might retain. . . . This does not confer power upon the whole people to control rights which are purely and exclusively private, . . . but it does authorize the establishment of laws requiring each citizen to so conduct himself, and so use his own property, as not unnecessarily to injure another. . . . From this source come the police powers. . . . Under these powers the government regulates the conduct of its citizens one towards another, and the manner in which each shall use his own property, when such regulation becomes necessary for the public good. In their exercise it has been customary in England from time immemorial, and in this country from its first colonization, to regulate ferries, common carriers, hackmen, bakers, millers, wharfingers, innkeepers, &c., and in so doing to fix a maximum of charge to be made for services rendered, accommodations furnished, and articles sold. To this day, statutes are to be found in many of the States upon some or all these subjects; and we think it has never yet been successfully contended that such legislation came within any of the constitutional prohibitions against interference with private property. . . .

This brings us to inquire as to the principles upon which this power of regulation rests, in order that we may determine what is within and what without its operative effect. Looking, then, to the common law, from whence came the right which the Constitution protects, we find that when private property is "affected with a public interest, it ceases to be *juris privati* only." This was said by Lord Chief Justice Hale more than two hundred years ago, in his treatise *De Portibus Maris*, . . . and has been accepted without objection as an essential element in the law of property ever since. Property does become clothed with a public interest when used in a manner to make it of public consequence, and affect the community at large. When, therefore, one devotes his property to a use in which the public has an interest, he, in effect, grants to the public an interest in that use, and must submit to be controlled by the public for the common good, to the extent of the interest he has thus created. He may withdraw his grant by discontinuing the use; but, so long as he maintains the use, he must submit to the control. . . .

. . . When private property is devoted to a public use, it is subject to public regulation. It remains only to ascertain whether the warehouses of these plaintiffs in error, and the business which is carried on there, come within the operation of this principle.

. . . It is difficult to see why, if the common carrier, or the miller, or the ferryman, or the innkeeper, or the wharfinger, or the baker, or the cartman, or the hackney-coachman, pursues a public employment and exercises "a sort of public office," these plaintiffs in error do not. They stand . . . in the very "gateway of commerce," and take toll from all who pass. Their business most certainly "tends to a common charge, and is become a thing of public interest and use." Every bushel of grain for its passage "pays a toll, which is a common charge," and, therefore, according to Lord Hale, every such warehouseman "ought to be under public regulation, viz., that he . . . take but reasonable toll." Certainly, if any business can be clothed "with a public interest, and cease to be *juris privati* only," this has been. . . .

. . . For our purposes we must assume that, if a state of facts could exist that would justify such legislation, it actually did exist when the statute now under consideration was passed. For us the question is one of power, not of expediency. If no state of circumstances could exist to justify such a statute, then we may declare this one void, because in excess of the legislative power of the State. But if it could, we must presume it did. Of the propriety of legislative interference within the scope of legislative power, the legislature is the exclusive judge. . . .

We know that this is a power which may be abused; but that is no argument against its existence. For protection against abuses by legislatures the people must resort to the polls, not to the courts. . . .

We conclude, therefore, that the statute in question is not repugnant to the Constitution of the United States, and that there is no error in the judgment. . . .

*Judgment affirmed.*

MR. JUSTICE FIELD, with whom MR. JUSTICE STRONG concurs, dissenting. . . .

. . . I am compelled to dissent from the decision of the court in this case, and from the reasons upon which that decision is founded. The principle upon which the opinion of the majority proceeds is, in my judgment, subversive of the rights of private property, heretofore believed to be protected by constitutional guaranties against legislative interference. . . .

The question presented . . . is one of the greatest importance,—whether it is within the competency of a State to fix the compensation which an individual may receive for the use of his own property in his private business, and for his services in connection with it. . . .

. . . The court holds that property loses something of its private character when employed in such a way as to be generally useful. The doctrine declared is that property "becomes clothed with a public interest when used in a manner to make it of public consequence, and affect the community at large;" and from such clothing the right of the legislature is deduced to control the use of the property, and to determine the compensation which the owner may receive for it.

When Sir Matthew Hale, and the sages of the law in his day, spoke of property as affected by a public interest, and ceasing from that cause to be *juris privati* solely, that is, ceasing to be held merely in private right, they referred to property dedicated by the owner to public uses, or to property the use of which was granted by the government, or in connection with which special privileges were conferred. Unless the property was thus dedicated, or some right bestowed by the government was held with the property, either by specific grant or by prescription of so long a time as to imply a grant originally, the property was not affected by any public interest so as to be taken out of the category of property held in private right. But it is not in any such sense that the terms "clothing property with a public interest" are used in this case. From the nature of the business under consideration—the storage of grain—which, in any sense in which the words can be used, is a private business, in which the public are interested only as they are interested in the storage of other products of the soil, or in articles of manufacture, it is clear that the court intended to declare that, whenever one devotes his property to a business which is useful to the public,—"affects the community at large,"—the legislature can regulate the compensation which the owner may receive for its use, and for his own services in connection with it.

If this be sound law, if there be no protection, either in the principles upon which our republican government is founded, or in the prohibitions of the Constitution against such invasion of private rights, all property and all business in the State are held at the mercy of a majority of its legislature. . . .

. . . It is only where some right or privilege is conferred by the government or municipality upon the owner, which he can use in connection with his property, or by means of which the use of his property is rendered more valuable to him, or he thereby enjoys an advantage over others, that the compensation to be received by him becomes a legitimate matter of regulation. Submission to the regulation of compensation in such cases is an implied condition of the grant, and the State, in exercising its power of prescribing the compensation, only determines the conditions upon which its concession shall be enjoyed. When the privilege ends, the power of regulation ceases.

There is nothing in the character of the business of the defendants as warehousemen which called for the interference complained of in this case. Their buildings are not nuisances; their occupation of receiving and storing grain infringes upon no rights of others, disturbs no neighborhood, infects not the air, and in no respect prevents others from using and enjoying their property as to them may seem best. The legislation in question is nothing less than a bold assertion of absolute power by the State to control at its discretion the property and business of the citizen, and fix the compensation he shall receive. The will of the legislature is made the condition upon which the owner shall receive the fruits of his property and the just reward of his labor, industry, and enterprise. . . . The decision of the court in this case gives unrestrained license to legislative will. . . .

I am of opinion that the judgment of the Supreme Court of Illinois should be reversed.

## *Lochner* v. *New York*

**198 U.S. 45; 25 S. Ct. 539; 49 L. Ed. 937 (1905)**

Joseph Lochner, a Utica, New York, bakery proprietor, was found guilty and fined $50 for violating an 1897 New York law that limited the hours of employment in bakeries and confectionery establishments to ten hours a day and sixty hours a week. When his conviction was sustained by the New York appellate courts, Lochner brought the case to the Supreme Court on a writ of error. *Opinion of the Court: Peckham, Brewer, Brown, Fuller, McKenna. Dissenting opinions: Harlan, Day, White; Holmes.*

MR. JUSTICE PECKHAM delivered the opinion of the Court. . . .

The statute necessarily interferes with the right of contract between the employer and employés, concerning the number of hours in which the latter may labor in the bakery of the employer. The general right to make a contract in relation to his business is part of the liberty of the individual protected by the Fourteenth Amendment of the Federal Constitution. . . . Under that provision no State can deprive any person of life, liberty or property without due process of law. The right to purchase or to sell labor is part of the liberty protected by this amendment, unless there are circumstances which exclude the right. There are, however, certain powers, existing in the sovereignty of each State in the Union, somewhat vaguely termed police powers, the exact description and limitation of which have not been attempted by the courts. Those powers, broadly stated, . . . relate to the safety, health, morals and general welfare of the public. Both property and liberty are held on such reasonable conditions as may be imposed by the governing power of the State in the exercise of those powers, and with such conditions the Fourteenth Amendment was not designed to interfere. . . .

It must, of course, be conceded that there is a limit to the valid exercise of the police power by the State. There is no dispute concerning this general proposition. Otherwise the Fourteenth Amendment would have no efficacy and the legislatures of the States would have unbounded power, and it would be enough to say that any piece of legislation was enacted to conserve the morals, the health or the safety of the people; such legislation would be valid, no matter how absolutely without foundation the claim might be. The claim of the police power would be a mere pretext—become another and delusive name for the supreme sovereignty of the State to be exercised free from constitutional restraint. This is not contended for. In every case that comes before this court, therefore, where legislation of this character is concerned and where the protection of the Federal Constitution is sought, the question necessarily arises: Is this a fair, reasonable and appropriate exercise of the police power of the State, or is it an unreasonable, unnecessary and arbitrary interference with the right of the individual to his personal liberty or to enter into those contracts in relation to labor which may seem to him appropriate or necessary for the support of himself and his family? Of course the liberty of contract relating to labor includes both parties to it. The one has as much right to purchase as the other to sell labor.

This is not a question of substituting the judgment of the court for that of the legislature. If the act be within the power of the State it is valid, although the judgment of the court might be totally opposed to the enactment of such a law. But the question would still remain: Is it within the police power of the State? and that question must be answered by the court.

The question whether this act is valid as a labor law, pure and simple, may be dismissed in a few words. There is no reasonable ground for interfering with the liberty of person or the right of free contract, by determining the hours of labor, in the occupation of a baker. There is no contention that bakers as a class are not equal in intelligence and capacity to men in other trades or manual occupations, or that they are not able to assert their rights and care for themselves without the protecting arm of the State, interfering with their independence of judgment and of action. They are in no sense wards of the State. Viewed in the light of a purely labor law, with no reference whatever to the question of health, we think that a law like the one before us involves neither the safety, the morals nor the welfare of the public, and that the interest of the public is not in the slightest degree affected by such an act. The law must be upheld, if at all, as a law pertaining to the health of the individual engaged in the occupation of a baker. It does not affect any other portion of the public than those who are engaged in that occupation. Clean and wholesome bread does not depend upon whether the baker works but ten hours per day or only sixty hours a week. . . .

We think the limit of the police power has been reached and passed in this case. There is, in our judgment, no reasonable foundation for holding this to be necessary or appropriate as a health law to safeguard the public health or the health of the individuals who are following the trade of a baker. . . .

We think that there can be no fair doubt that the trade of a baker, in and of itself, is not an unhealthy one to that degree which would authorize the legislature to interfere with the right to labor, and with the right of free contract on the part of the individual, either as employer or employé. In looking through statistics regarding all trades and occupations, it may be true that the trade of a baker does not appear to be as healthy as some other trades, and is also vastly more healthy than still others. . . .

. . . The act is not, within any fair meaning of the term, a health law, but is an illegal interference with the rights of individuals, both employers and employés, to make contracts regarding labor upon such terms as they may think best, or which they may agree upon with the other parties to such contracts. Statutes of the nature of that under review, limiting the hours in which grown and intelligent men may labor to earn their living, are mere meddlesome interferences with the rights of the individual, and they are not saved from condemnation by the claim that they are passed in the exercise of the police power and upon the subject of the health of the individual whose rights are interfered with, unless there be some fair ground, reasonable in and of itself, to say that there is material danger to the public health or to the health of the employés, if the hours of labor are not curtailed. . . .

It was further urged on the argument that restricting the hours of labor in the case of bakers was valid because it tended to cleanliness on the part of the workers, as a man was more apt to be cleanly when not overworked, and if cleanly then his "output" was also more likely to be so. . . . The connection, if any exists, is too shadowy and thin to build any argument for the interference of the legislature. If the man works ten hours a day it is all right, but if ten and a half or eleven his health is in danger and his bread may be unhealthful, and, therefore, he shall not be permitted to do it. This, we think, is unreasonable and entirely arbitrary. . . .

It is manifest to us that the limitation of the hours of labor as provided for in this section of the statute . . . has no such direct relation to and no such substantial effect upon the health of the employé, as to justify us in regarding the section as really a health law. It seems to us that the real object and purpose were simply to regulate the hours of labor between the master and his employés . . . in a private business, not dangerous in any degree to morals or in any real and substantial degree, to the health of the employés. Under such circumstances the freedom of master and employé to contract with each other in relation to their employment, and in defining the same, cannot be prohibited or interfered with, without violating the Federal Constitution. . . .

*Reversed.*

MR. JUSTICE HARLAN, with whom MR. JUSTICE WHITE and MR. JUSTICE DAY concur, dissenting. . . .

I take it to be firmly established that what is called the liberty of contract may, within certain limits, be subjected to regulations designed and calculated to promote the general welfare or to guard the public health, the public morals or the public safety. . . .

Granting . . . that there is a liberty of contract which cannot be violated even under the sanction of direct legislative enactment, but assuming, as according to settled law we may assume, that such liberty of contract is subject to such regulations as the State may reasonably prescribe for the common good and the well-being of society, what are the conditions under which the judiciary may declare such regulations to be in excess of legislative authority and void? Upon this point there is no room for dispute; for, the rule is universal that a legislative enactment, Federal or state, is never to be disregarded or held invalid unless it be, beyond question, plainly and palpably in excess of legislative power. . . . If there be doubt as to the validity of the statute, that doubt must therefore be resolved in favor of its validity, and the courts must keep their hands off, leaving the legislature to meet the responsibility for unwise legislation. If the end which the legislature seeks to accomplish be one to which its power extends, and if the means employed to that end, although not the wisest or best, are yet not plainly and palpably unauthorized by law, then the court cannot interfere. In other words, when the validity of a statute is questioned, the burden of proof, so to speak, is upon those who assert it to be unconstitutional. . . .

Let these principles be applied to the present case. . . .

It is plain that this statute was enacted in order to protect the physical well-being of those who work in bakery and confectionery establishments. . . . I find it impossible, in view of common experience, to say that there is here no real or substantial relation between the means employed by the State and the end sought to be accomplished by its legislation. . . . Nor can I say that the statute has no appropriate or direct connection with that protection to health which each State owes to her citizens, . . . or that it is not promotive of the health of the employés in question, . . . or that the regulation prescribed by the State is utterly unreasonable and extravagant or wholly arbitrary. . . . Still less can I say that the statute is, beyond question, a plain, palpable invasion of rights secured by the fundamental law. . . . Therefore I submit that this court will transcend its functions if it assumes to annul the statute of New York. It must be remembered that this statute does not apply to all kinds of business. It applies only to work in bakery and confectionery establishments, in which, as all know, the air constantly breathed by workmen is not as pure and healthful as that to be found in some other establishments or out of doors. . . .

. . . There are many reasons of a weighty, substantial character, based upon the experience of mankind, in support of the theory that, all things considered, more than ten hours' steady work each day, from week to week, in a bakery or confectionery establishment, may endanger the health, and shorten the lives of the workmen, thereby diminishing their physical and mental capacity to serve the State, and to provide for those dependent upon them.

If such reasons exist that ought to be the end of this case, for the State is not amenable to the judiciary, in respect of its legislative enactments, unless such enactments are plainly, palpably, beyond all question, inconsistent with the Constitution of the United States. We are not to presume that the state of New York has acted in bad faith. Nor can we assume that its legislature acted without due deliberation, or that it did not determine this question upon the fullest attainable information, and for the common good. We cannot say that the State has acted without reason nor ought we to proceed upon the theory that its action is a mere sham. Our duty, I submit, is to sustain the statute as not being in conflict with the Federal Constitution, for the reason—and such is an all-sufficient reason—it is not shown to be plainly and palpably inconsistent with that instrument. . . .

I take leave to say that the New York statute, in the particulars here involved, cannot be held to be in conflict with the Fourteenth Amendment, without enlarging the scope of the Amendment far beyond its original purpose and without bringing under the supervision of this court matters which have been supposed to belong exclusively to the legislative departments of the several States when exerting their conceded power to guard the health and safety of their citizens by such regulations as they in their wisdom deem best. . . .

MR. JUSTICE HOLMES, dissenting. . . .

This case is decided upon an economic theory which a large part of the country does not entertain. If it were a question whether I agreed with that theory, I should desire to study it further and long before making up my mind. But I do not conceive that to be my duty, because I strongly believe that my agreement or disagreement has nothing to do with the right of a majority to embody their opinions in law. It is settled by various decisions of this court that state constitutions and state laws may regulate life in many ways which we as legislators might think as injudicious or if you like as tyrannical as this, and which equally with this interfere with the liberty to contract. Sunday laws and usury laws are ancient examples. A more modern one is the prohibition of lotteries. . . . The Fourteenth Amendment does not enact Mr. Herbert Spencer's Social Statics. . . . A constitution is not intended to embody a particular economic theory, whether of paternalism and the organic relation of the citizen to the State or of *laissez faire*. It is made for people of fundamentally differing views, and the accident of our finding certain opinions natural and familiar or novel and even shocking ought not to conclude our judgment upon the question whether statutes embodying them conflict with the Constitution of the United States.

. . . I think that the word liberty in the Fourteenth Amendment is perverted when it is held to prevent the natural outcome of a dominant opinion, unless it can be said that a rational and fair man necessarily would admit that the statute proposed would infringe fundamental principles as they have been understood by the traditions of our people and our law. It does not need research to show that no such sweeping condemnation can be passed upon the statute before us. A reasonable man might think it a proper measure on the score of health. Men whom I certainly could not pronounce unreasonable would uphold it as a first instalment of a general regulation of the hours of work. . . .

## *West Coast Hotel Company* v. *Parrish*

**300 U.S. 379; 57 S. Ct. 578; 81 L. Ed. 703 (1937)**

In 1913 the state legislature of Washington enacted a minimum wage law covering women and minors. The law provided for the establishment of an Individual Welfare Commission, which was authorized "to establish such standards of wages and conditions of labor for women and minors employed within the State of Washington as shall be held hereunder to be reasonable and not detrimental to health and morals, and which shall be sufficient for the decent maintenance of women." Elsie Parrish, employed as a chambermaid by the West Coast Hotel Company, together with her husband brought suit to recover the difference between the wages paid her and the minimum wage fixed pursuant to the state law. The minimum wage for her job was $14.50 for a forty-eight hour week. The trial court decided against Parrish and declared the law to be repugnant to the Due Process Clause of the Fourteenth Amendment. The Washington Supreme Court reversed the trial court and sustained the statute. The hotel company brought the case to the U.S. Supreme Court on appeal. *Opinion of the Court: Hughes, Brandeis, Cardozo, Roberts, Stone. Dissenting opinion: Sutherland, Butler, McReynolds, Van Devanter.*

MR. CHIEF JUSTICE HUGHES delivered the opinion of the Court.

This case presents the question of the constitutional validity of the minimum wage law of the State of Washington. . . .

The appellant relies upon the decision of this Court in *Adkins* v. *Children's Hospital* . . . , which held invalid the District of Columbia Minimum Wage Act, which was attacked under the due process clause of the Fifth Amendment. . . . The state court has refused to regard the decision in the *Adkins* case as determinative and has pointed to our decisions both before and since that case as justifying its position. We are of the opinion that this ruling of the state court demands on our part a reëxamination of the *Adkins* case. The importance of the question, in which many States having similar laws are concerned, the close division by which the decision in the *Adkins* case was reached, and the economic conditions which have supervened, and in the light of which the reasonableness of the exercise of the protective power of the State must be considered, make it not only appropriate, but we think imperative, that in deciding the present case the subject should receive fresh consideration. . . .

. . . The violation alleged by those attacking minimum wage regulation for women is deprivation of freedom of contract. What is this freedom? The Constitution does not speak of freedom of contract. It speaks of liberty and prohibits the deprivation of liberty without due process of law. In prohibiting that deprivation the Constitution does not recognize an absolute and uncontrollable liberty. Liberty in each of its phases has its history and connotation. But the liberty safeguarded is liberty in a social organization which requires the protection of law against the evils which menace the health, safety, morals and welfare of the people. Liberty under the Constitution is thus necessarily subject to the restraints of due process, and regulation which is reasonable in relation to its subject and is adopted in the interests of the community is due process.

. . . What can be closer to the public interest than the health of women and their protection from unscrupulous and overreaching employers? And if the protection of women is a legitimate end of the exercise of state power, how can it be said that the requirement of the payment of a minimum wage fairly fixed in order to meet the very necessities of existence is not an admissible means to that end? The legislature of the State was clearly entitled to consider the situation of women in employment, the fact that they are in the class receiving the least pay, that their bargaining power is relatively weak, and that they are the ready victims of those who would take advantage of their necessitous circumstances. The legislature was entitled to adopt measures to reduce the evils of the "sweating system," the exploiting of workers at wages so low as to be insufficient to meet the bare cost of living, thus making their very helplessness the occasion of a most injurious competition. The legislature had the right to consider that its minimum wage requirements would be an important aid in carrying out its policy of protection. The adoption of similar requirements by many States evidences a deepseated conviction both as to the presence of the evil and as to the means adapted to check it. Legislative response to that conviction cannot be regarded as arbitrary or capricious, and that is all we have to decide. Even if the wisdom of the policy be regarded as debatable and its effects uncertain, still the legislature is entitled to its judgment.

There is an additional and compelling consideration which recent economic experience has brought into a strong light. The exploitation of a class of workers who are in an unequal position with respect to bargaining power and are thus relatively defenceless against the denial of a living wage is not only detrimental to their health and well being but casts a direct burden for their support upon the community. What these workers lose in wages the taxpayers are called upon to pay. The bare cost of living must be met. . . . The community is not bound to provide what is in effect a subsidy for unconscionable employers. The community may direct its law-making power to correct the abuse which springs from their selfish disregard of the public interest. . . .

Our conclusion is that the case of *Adkins* v. *Children's Hospital* . . . should be, and it is, overruled. The judgment of the Supreme Court of the State of Washington is

*Affirmed.*

MR. JUSTICE SUTHERLAND, dissenting.

It is urged that the question involved should now receive fresh consideration, among other reasons, because of "the economic conditions which have supervened"; but the meaning of the Constitution does not change with the ebb and flow of economic events. We frequently are told in more general words that the Constitution must be construed in the light of the present. If by that it is meant that the Constitution is made up of living words that apply to every new condition which they include, the statement is quite true. But to say, if that be intended, that the words of the Constitution mean today what they did not mean when written—that is, that they do not apply to a situation now to which they would have applied then—is to rob that instrument of the essential element which continues it in force as the people have made it until they, and not their official agents, have made it otherwise. . . .

The judicial function is that of interpretation; it does not include the power of amendment under the guise of interpretation. To miss the point of difference between the two is to miss all that the phrase "supreme law of the land" stands for and to convert what was intended as inescapable and enduring mandates into mere moral reflections. . . .

Coming, then, to a consideration of the Washington statute, it first is to be observed that it is in every substantial respect identical with the statute involved in the *Adkins* case. Such vices as existed in the latter are present in the former. And if the *Adkins* case was properly decided, as we who join in this opinion think it was, it necessarily follows that the Washington statute is invalid. . . .

Neither the statute involved in the *Adkins* case nor the Washington statute, so far as it is involved here, has the slightest relation to the capacity or earning power of the employee, to the number of hours which constitute the day's work, the character of the place where the work is to be done, or the circumstances or surroundings of the employment. The sole basis upon which the question of validity rests is the assumption that the employee is entitled to receive a sum of money sufficient to provide a living for her, keep her in health and preserve her morals. . . .

What we said further, in that case . . . is equally applicable here . . . : "A statute which prescribes payment without regard to any of these things and solely with relation to circumstances apart from the contract of employment, the business affected by it and the work done under it, is so clearly the product of a naked, arbitrary exercise of power that it cannot be allowed to stand under the Constitution of the United States." . . .

## *Williamson* v. *Lee Optical Company*

**348 U.S. 483; 75 S. Ct. 461; 99 L. Ed. 563 (1955)**

In 1953 the Oklahoma legislature passed a law that made it unlawful for any person other than a licensed ophthalmologist or optometrist to fit lenses to the face or to duplicate or replace lenses, except upon written prescriptive authority of a licensed ophthalmologist or optometrist. Lee Optical challenged the constitutionality of this law before a federal district court of three judges, alleging in part that it violated the Due Process Clause of the Fourteenth Amendment. The district court agreed, holding portions of the act unconstitutional, and the state of Oklahoma appealed to the Supreme Court. *Opinion of the Court: Douglas, Black, Burton, Clark, Frankfurter, Minton, Reed, Warren. Harlan did not participate.*

MR. JUSTICE DOUGLAS delivered the opinion of the Court. . . .

An ophthalmologist is a duly licensed physician who specializes in the care of the eyes. An optometrist examines eyes for refractive error, recognizes (but does not treat) diseases of the eye, and fills prescriptions for eyeglasses. The optician is an artisan qualified to grind lenses, fill prescriptions, and fit frames.

The effect of § 2 is to forbid the optician from fitting or duplicating lenses without a prescription from an ophthalmologist or optometrist. In practical effect, it means that no optician can fit old glasses into new frames or supply a lens, whether it be a new lens or one to duplicate a lost or broken lens, without a prescription. The District Court . . . rebelled at the notion that a State could require a prescription from an optometrist or ophthalmologist "to take old lenses and place them in new frames and then fit the completed spectacles to the *face* of the eyeglass wearer." . . . It held that such a requirement was not "reasonably and rationally related to the health and welfare of the people." . . . It was, accordingly, the opinion of the court that this provision of the law violated the Due Process Clause by arbitrarily interfering with the optician's right to do business.

The Oklahoma law may exact a needless, wasteful requirement in many cases. But it is for the legislature, not the courts, to balance the advantages and disadvantages of the new requirement. It appears that in many cases the optician can easily supply the new frames or new lenses without reference to the old written prescription. It also appears that many written prescriptions contain no directive data in regard to fitting spectacles to the face. But in some cases the directions contained in the prescription are essential, if the glasses are to be fitted so as to correct the particular defects of vision or alleviate the eye condition. The legislature might have concluded that the frequency of occasions when a prescription is necessary was sufficient to justify this regulation of the fitting of eyeglasses. Likewise, when it is necessary to duplicate a lens, a written prescription may or may not be necessary. But the legislature might have concluded that one was needed often enough to require one in every case. Or the legislature may have concluded that eye examinations were so critical, not only for correction of vision but also for detection of latent ailments or diseases, that every change in frames and every duplication of a lens should be accompanied by a prescription from a medical expert. To be sure, the present law does not require a new examination of the eyes every time the frames are changed or the lenses duplicated. For if the old prescription is on file with the optician, he can go ahead and make the new fitting or duplicate the lenses. But the law need not be in every respect logically consistent with its aims to be constitutional. It is enough that there is an evil at hand for correction, and that it might be thought that the particular legislative measure was a rational way to correct it.

The day is gone when this Court uses the Due Process Clause of the Fourteenth Amendment to strike down state laws, regulatory of business and industrial conditions, because they may be unwise, improvident, or out of harmony with a particular school of thought. . . . We emphasize again what Chief Justice Waite said in *Munn* v. *Illinois*, . . . "For protection against abuses by legislatures the people must resort to the polls, not to the courts." . . .

## *BMW of North America, Inc.* v. *Gore*

**517 U.S. 559, 116 S. Ct. 1589, 134 L. Ed. 2d 809 (1996)**

Nine months after Dr. Ira Gore purchased a new black BMW sport sedan for approximately $41,000 from an authorized Alabama dealer, he brought his car to an automobile detailer, who detected evidence that portions of the car had been repainted. Dr. Gore subsequently brought suit in Alabama court for $500,000 in compensatory and punitive damages against the American distributor of BMWs, alleging that the failure to disclose the repainting constituted fraud under Alabama law. At trial, BMW acknowledged that it followed a nationwide policy of not advising its dealer, and hence their customers, of predelivery damage to new cars when the cost of repair did not exceed 3 percent of the car's suggested retail price. The cost of repainting Dr. Gore's vehicle was $601.37 (or about 1.5 percent of its suggested retail price) and therefore fell into that category. The jury returned a verdict finding BMW liable for compensatory damages of $4,000 (its judgment of how much less Dr. Gore's car was worth because it had been repainted) and assessing $4 million in punitive damages (its judgment of the appropriate punishment for BMW for selling approximately 1,000 repainted cars nationally for approximately $4,000 more than each was worth). The trial judge denied BMW's post-trial motion to set aside the punitive damages award, holding, among other things, that the award was not "grossly excessive" and thus did not violate the Due Process Clause of the Fourteenth Amendment as interpreted in two earlier damages cases: *Pacific Mutual Insurance Co.* v. *Haslip,* 499 U.S. 1 (1991), and *TXO Production Corp.* v. *Alliance Resources Corp.,* 509 U.S. 443 (1993). The Alabama Supreme Court agreed, but reduced the award to $2 million on the ground that, in computing the amount, the jury had improperly multiplied Dr. Gore's compensatory damages by the number of similar sales in all States, not just those in Alabama. BMW petitioned the Supreme Court for a writ of certiorari. *Opinion of the Court: Stevens, Breyer, Kennedy, O'Connor, Souter. Concurring opinion: Breyer, O'Connor, Souter. Dissenting opinions: Scalia, Thomas; Ginsburg, Rehnquist.*

JUSTICE STEVENS delivered the opinion of the Court.

The Due Process Clause of the Fourteenth Amendment prohibits a State from imposing a "grossly excessive" punishment on a tortfeasor. The wrongdoing involved in this case was the decision by a national distributor of automobiles not to advise its dealers, and hence their customers, of predelivery damage to new cars when the cost of repair amounted to less than 3 percent of the car's suggested retail price. The question presented is whether a $2 million punitive damages award to the purchaser of one of these cars exceeds the constitutional limit. . . .

Punitive damages may properly be imposed to further a State's legitimate interests in punishing unlawful conduct and deterring its repetition. In our federal system, States necessarily have considerable flexibility in determining the level of punitive damages that they will allow in different classes of cases and in any particular case. Most States that authorize exemplary damages afford the jury similar latitude, requiring only that the damages awarded be reasonably necessary to vindicate the State's legitimate interests in punishment and deterrence. Only when an award can fairly be categorized as "grossly excessive" in relation to these interests does it enter the zone of arbitrariness that violates the Due Process Clause of the Fourteenth Amendment. . . .

Elementary notions of fairness enshrined in our constitutional jurisprudence dictate that a person receive fair notice not only of the conduct that will subject him to punishment, but also of the severity of the penalty that a State may impose. Three guideposts, each of which indicates that BMW did not receive adequate notice of the magnitude of the sanction that Alabama might impose for adhering to the nondisclosure policy adopted in 1983, lead us to the conclusion that the $2 million award against BMW is grossly excessive: the degree of reprehensibility of the nondisclosure; the disparity between the harm or potential harm suffered by Dr. Gore and his punitive damages award; and the difference between this remedy and the civil penalties authorized or imposed in comparable cases. We discuss these considerations in turn.

## DEGREE OF REPREHENSIBILITY

Perhaps the most important indicium of the reasonableness of a punitive damages award is the degree of reprehensibility of the defendant's conduct. As the Court stated nearly 150 years ago, exemplary damages imposed on a defendant should reflect "the enormity of his offense." *Day v. Woodworth,* 13 How. 363, 371 (1852). This principle reflects the accepted view that some wrongs are more blameworthy than others. Thus, we have said that "nonviolent crimes are less serious than crimes marked by violence or the threat of violence." Similarly, "trickery and deceit" are more reprehensible than negligence.

In this case, none of the aggravating factors associated with particularly reprehensible conduct is present. The harm BMW inflicted on Dr. Gore was purely economic in nature. The presale refinishing of the car had no effect on its performance or safety features, or even its appearance for at least nine months after his purchase. BMW's conduct evinced no indifference to or reckless disregard for the health and safety of others. To be sure, infliction of economic injury, especially when done intentionally through affirmative acts of misconduct, or when the target is financially vulnerable, can warrant a substantial penalty. But this observation does not convert all acts that cause economic harm into torts that are sufficiently reprehensible to justify a significant sanction in addition to compensatory damages. . . .

[T]he record in this case discloses no deliberate false statements, acts of affirmative misconduct, or concealment of evidence of improper motive. We accept, of course, the jury's finding that BMW suppressed a material fact which Alabama law obligated it to communicate to prospective purchasers of repainted cars in that State. But the omission of a material fact may be less reprehensible than a deliberate false statement, particularly when there is a good-faith basis for believing that no duty to disclose exists. That conduct is sufficiently reprehensible to give rise to tort liability, and even a modest award of exemplary damages, does not establish the high degree of culpability that warrants a substantial punitive damages award. Because this case exhibits none of the circumstances ordinarily associated with egregiously improper conduct, we are persuaded that BMW's conduct was not sufficiently reprehensible to warrant imposition of a $2 million exemplary damages award.

**RATIO**

The second and perhaps most commonly cited indicium of an unreasonable or excessive punitive damages award is its ratio to the actual harm inflicted on the plaintiff. The principle that exemplary damages must bear a "reasonable relationship" to compensatory damages has a long pedigree. Scholars have identified a number of early English statutes authorizing the award of multiple damages for particular wrongs. Some 65 different enactments during the period between 1275 and 1753 provided for double, treble, or quadruple damages. . . .

The $2 million in punitive damages awarded to Dr. Gore by the Alabama Supreme Court is 500 times the amount of his actual harm as determined by the jury. Moreover, there is no suggestion that Dr. Gore or any other BMW purchaser was threatened with any additional potential harm by BMW's nondisclosure policy. . . .

Of course, we have consistently rejected the notion that the constitutional line is marked by a simple mathematical formula, even one that compares actual and potential damages to the punitive award. Indeed, low awards of compensatory damages may properly support a higher ratio than high compensatory awards, if, for example, a particularly egregious act has resulted in only a small amount of economic damages. A higher ratio may also be justified in cases in which the jury is hard to detect or the monetary value of noneconomic harm might have been difficult to determine. It is appropriate, therefore, to reiterate our rejection of a categorical approach. . . . "We need not, and indeed we cannot, draw a mathematical bright line between the constitutionally acceptable and the constitutionally unacceptable that would fit every case. We can say, however, that [a] general concer[n] of reasonableness . . . properly enter[s] into the constitutional calculus." [*Pacific Mutual Life Insurance Co.* v.] *Haslip,* 499 U. S. 1, 18 (1991). In most cases, the ratio will be within a constitutionally acceptable range, and remittitur will not be justified on this basis. When the ratio is a breathtaking 500 to 1, however, the award must surely "raise a suspicious judicial eyebrow."

**SANCTIONS FOR COMPARABLE MISCONDUCT**

Comparing the punitive damages award and the civil or criminal penalties that could be imposed for comparable misconduct provides a third indicium of excessiveness. . . . In this case the $2 million economic sanction imposed on BMW is substantially greater than the statutory fines available in Alabama and elsewhere for similar malfeasance.

The maximum civil penalty authorized by the Alabama Legislature for a violation of its Deceptive Trade Practices Act is $2,000; other States authorize more severe sanctions, with the maxima ranging from $5,000 to $10,000. Significantly, some statutes draw a distinction between first offenders and recidivists; thus, in New York the penalty is $50 for a first offense and $250 for subsequent offenses. None of these statutes would provide an out-of-state distributor with fair notice that the first violation . . . of its provisions might subject an offender to a multimillion dollar penalty. . . .

[W]e of course accept the Alabama courts' view that the state interest in protecting its citizens from deceptive trade practices justifies a sanction in addition to the recovery of compensatory damages. We cannot, however, accept the conclusion of the Alabama Supreme Court that BMW's conduct was sufficiently egregious to justify a punitive sanction that is tantamount to a severe criminal penalty. . . .

The Judgment is reversed, and the case is remanded for further proceedings not inconsistent with this opinion.

JUSTICE BREYER, with whom JUSTICE O'CONNOR and JUSTICE SOUTER join, concurring.

. . . Members of this Court have generally thought . . . that if "fair procedures were followed, a judgment that is a product of that process is entitled to a strong presumption of validity." And the Court also has found that punitive damages procedures very similar to those followed here were not, by themselves, fundamentally unfair. Thus, I believe it important to explain why this presumption of validity is overcome in this instance.

The reason flows from the Court's emphasis upon the constitutional importance of legal standards that provide "reasonable constraints" within which "discretion is exercised." . . .

This constitutional concern, itself harkening back to the Magna Carta, arises out of the basic unfairness of depriving citizens of life, liberty, or property, through the application, not of law and legal processes, but of arbitrary coercion. Requiring the application of law, rather than a decisionmaker's caprice, does more than simply provide citizens notice of what actions may subject them to punishment; it also helps to assure the uniform general treatment of similarly situated persons that is the essence of law itself. . . .

Legal standards need not be precise in order to satisfy this constitutional concern. But they must offer some kind of constraint upon a jury or court's discretion, and thus protection against purely arbitrary behavior. The standards the Alabama courts applied here are vague and open-ended to the point where they risk arbitrary results. In my view, although the vagueness of those standards does not, by itself, violate due process, it does invite the kind of scrutiny the Court has given the particular verdict before us.

First, the Alabama statute that permits damages does not itself contain a standard that readily distinguishes between conduct warranting very small, and conduct warranting very large, punitive damages awards. . . .

Second, the Alabama courts, in this case, have applied the "factors" intended to constrain punitive damages awards, in a way that belies that purpose. . . . [A]s the Alabama courts have authoritatively interpreted them, and as their application in this case illustrates, they impose little actual constraint. . . .

Third, the state courts neither referred to, nor made any effort to find, nor enunciated any other standard, that either directly, or indirectly as background, might have supplied the constraining legal force that the statute and [Alabama court] standards lack. . . .

The record before us . . . contains nothing suggesting that the Alabama Supreme Court, when determining the allowable award, applied any "economic" theory that might explain the $2 million recovery. . . . [C]ourts properly tend to judge the rationality of judicial actions in terms of the reasons that were given, and the facts that were before the court, not those that might have been given on the basis of some conceivable set of facts. . . . Therefore, reference to a constraining "economic" theory, which might have counseled more deferential review by this Court, is lacking in this case.

Fourth, I cannot find any community understanding or historic practice that this award might exemplify and which, therefore, would provide background standards constraining arbitrary behavior and excessive awards. . . .

Fifth, there are no other legislative enactments here that classify awards and impose quantitative limits that would significantly cabin the fairly unbounded discretion created by the absence of constraining legal standards. . . .

The upshot is that the rules that purport to channel discretion in this kind of case, here did not do so in fact. That means that the award in this case was both (a) the product of a system of standards that did not significantly constrain a court's, and hence a jury's, discretion in making that award; and (b) was grossly excessive in light of the State's legitimate punitive damages objectives.

The first of these reasons has special importance where courts review a jury-determined punitive damages award. That is because one cannot expect to direct jurors like legislators through the ballot box; nor can one expect those jurors to interpret law like judges, who work within a discipline and hierarchical organization that normally promotes roughly uniform interpretation and application of the law. Yet here Alabama expects jurors to act, at least a little, like legislators or judges, for it permits them, to a certain extent, to create public policy and to apply that policy, not to compensate a victim, but to achieve a policy-related objective outside the confines of the particular case.

To the extent that neither clear legal principles, nor fairly obvious historical or community-based standards (defining, say, especially egregious behavior) significantly constrain punitive damages awards, is there not a substantial risk of outcomes so arbitrary that they become difficult to square with the Constitution's assurance, to every citizen, of the law's protection? The standards here, as authoritatively interpreted, in my view, make this threat real and not theoretical. And, in these unusual circumstances, where legal standards offer virtually no constraint, I believe that this lack of constraining standards warrants this Court's detailed examination of the award.

The second reason—the severe disproportionality between the award and the legitimate punitive damages objectives—reflects a judgment about a matter of degree. I recognize that it is often difficult to determine just when a punitive award exceeds an amount reasonably related to a State's legitimate interests, or when that excess is so great as to amount to a matter of constitutional concern. Yet whatever the difficulties of drawing a precise line, once we examine the award in this case, it is not difficult to say that this award lies on the line's far side. The severe lack of proportionality between the size of the award and the underlying punitive damages objectives shows that the award falls into the category of "gross excessiveness" set forth in this Court's prior cases.

These two reasons taken together overcome what would otherwise amount to a "strong presumption of validity." And, for those two reasons, I conclude that the award in this unusual case violates the basic guarantee of nonarbitrary governmental behavior that the Due Process Clause provides.

JUSTICE SCALIA, with whom JUSTICE THOMAS joins, dissenting.

Today we see that latest manifestation of this Court's recent and increasingly insistent "concern about punitive damages that 'run wild.'" Since the Constitution does not make that concern any of our business, the Court's activities in this area are an unjustified incursion into the province of state governments.

In earlier cases that were the prelude to this decision, I set forth my view that a state trial procedure that commits the decision whether to impose punitive damages, and the amount, to the discretion of the jury, subject to some judicial review for "reasonableness," furnishes a defendant with all the process that is "due." I do not regard the Fourteenth Amendment's Due Process Clause as a secret repository of substantive guarantees against "unfairness"—neither the unfairness of an excessive civil compensatory award, nor the unfairness of an "unreasonable" punitive award. What the Fourteenth Amendment's procedural guarantee assures is an opportunity to contest the reasonableness of a damages judgment in state court; but there is no federal guarantee a damage award actually be reasonable.

This view, which adheres to the text of the Due Process Clause, has not prevailed in our punitive-damages cases. When, however, a constitutional doctrine adopted by the Court is not only mistaken but also insusceptible of principled application, I do not feel bound to give it stare decisis effect—indeed, I do not feel justified in doing so. Our punitive-damages jurisprudence compels such a response. The Constitution provides no warrant for federalizing yet another aspect of our Nation's legal culture (no matter how much in need of correction it may be), and the application of the Court's new rule of constitutional law is constrained by no principle other than the Justices' subjective assessment of the "reasonableness" of the award in relation to the conduct for which it was assessed.

Because today's judgment represents the first instance of this Court's invalidation of a state-court punitive assessment as simply unreasonably large, I think it a proper occasion to discuss these points at some length.

The most significant aspects of today's decision—the identification of a "substantive due process" right against a "grossly excessive" award, and the concomitant assumption of ultimate authority to decide anew a matter of "reasonableness" resolved in lower court proceedings—are of course not new. *Haslip* and *TXO* revived the notion, moribund since its appearance in the first years of this century, that the measure of civil punishment poses a question of constitutional dimension to be answered by this Court. Neither of those cases, however, nor any of the precedents upon which they relied, actually took the step of declaring a punitive award unconstitutional simply because it was "too big."

At the time of adoption of the Fourteenth Amendment, it was well understood that punitive damages represent the assessment by the jury, as the voice of the community, of the measure of punishment the defendant deserved. Today's decision, though dressed up as a legal opinion, is really no more than a disagreement with the community's sense of indignation or outrage expressed in the punitive award of the Alabama jury, as reduced by the State Supreme Court. It reflects not merely, as the concurrence candidly acknowledges, "a judgment about a matter of degree," but a judgment about the appropriate degree of indignation or outrage, which is hardly an analytical determination. . . .

One might understand the Court's eagerness to enter this field, rather than leave it with the state legislatures, if it had something useful to say. In fact, however, its opinion provides virtually no guidance to legislatures, and to state and federal courts, as to what a "constitutionally proper" level of punitive damages might be. . . .

In . . . its opinion, the Court identifies "[t]hree guideposts" that lead it to the conclusion that the award in this case is excessive: degree of reprehensibility, ratio between punitive award and plaintiff's actual harm, and legislative sanctions provided for comparable misconduct. The legal significance of these "guideposts" is nowhere explored, but their necessary effect is to establish federal standards governing the hitherto exclusively state law of damages. Apparently (though it is by no means clear) all three federal "guideposts" can be overridden if "necessary to deter future misconduct,"—a loophole that will encourage state reviewing courts to uphold awards as necessary for the "adequat[e] protect[ion] of state consumers. By effectively requiring state reviewing courts to concoct rationalizations—whether within the "guideposts" or through the loophole—to justify the intuitive punitive reactions of state juries, the Court accords neither category of institution the respect it deserves.

Of course it will not be easy for the States to comply with this new federal law of damages, no matter how willing they are to do so. In truth, the "guideposts" mark a road to nowhere; they provide no real guidance at all. As to "degree of reprehensibility" of the defendant's conduct, we learn that "nonviolent crimes are less serious than crimes marked by violence or the threat of violence," and that "trickery and deceit" are "more reprehensible than negligence." As to the ratio of punitive to compensatory damages, we are told that a "general concer[n] of reasonableness . . . enter[s] into the constitutional calculus,"—though even "a breathtaking 500 to 1" will not necessarily do anything more than "raise a suspicious judicial eyebrow." And as to legislative sanctions provided for comparable misconduct, they should be accorded "substantial deference." One expects the Court to conclude "To thine own self be true."

These criss-crossing platitudes yield no real answers in no real cases. And it must be noted that the Court nowhere says that these three "guideposts" are the only guideposts; indeed, it makes very clear that they are not—explaining away the earlier opinions that do not really follow these "guideposts" on the basis of additional factors, thereby "reiterat[ing] our rejection of a categorical approach." In other words, even these utter platitudes, if they should ever happen to produce an answer, may be overridden by other unnamed considerations. The Court has constructed a framework that does not genuinely constrain, that does not inform state legislatures and lower courts—that does nothing at all except confer an artificial air of doctrinal analysis upon its essentially ad hoc determination that this particular award of punitive damages was not "fair." . . .

The elevation of "fairness" in punishment to a principle of "substantive due process" means that every punitive award unreasonably imposed is unconstitutional; such an award is by definition excessive, since it attaches a penalty to conduct undeserving of punishment. Indeed, if the Court is correct, it must be that every claim that a state jury's award of compensatory damages is "unreasonable" (because not supported by the evidence) amounts to an assertion of constitutional injury. And the same would be true for determinations of liability. By today's logic, every dispute as to evidentiary sufficiency in a state civil suit poses a question of constitutional moment, subject to review in this Court. That is a stupefying proposition.

For the foregoing reasons, I respectfully dissent.

Justice Ginsburg, with whom The Chief Justice joins, dissenting.

The Court, I am convinced, unnecessarily and unwisely ventures into territory traditionally within the States' domain, and does so in the face of reform measures recently adopted or currently under consideration in legislative arenas.

The Alabama Supreme Court, in this case, endeavored to follow this Court's prior instructions; and, more recently, Alabama's highest court has installed further controls on awards of punitive damages. I would therefore leave the state court's judgment undisturbed, and resist unnecessary intrusion into an area dominantly of state concern. . . .

The Court finds Alabama's $2 million award not simply excessive, but grossly so, and therefore unconstitutional. The decision leads us further into territory traditionally within the States' domain, and commits the Court, now and again, to correct "misapplication of a properly stated rule of law." The Court is not well equipped for this mission. Tellingly, the Court repeats that it brings to the task no "mathematical formula," no "categorical approach," no "bright line." It has only a vague concept of substantive due process, a "raised eyebrow" test, as its ultimate guide.

In contrast to habeas corpus review under 28 U. S. C. 2254, the Court will work at this business alone. It will not be aided by the federal district courts and courts of appeals. It will be the only federal court policing the area. The Court's readiness to superintend state court punitive damages awards is all the more puzzling in view of the Court's longstanding reluctance to countenance review, even by courts of appeals, of the size of verdicts returned by juries in federal district court proceedings. And the reexamination prominent in state courts and in legislative arenas serves to underscore why the Court's enterprise is undue.

For the reasons stated, I dissent from this Court's disturbance of the judgment the Alabama Supreme Court has made.

## *United States* v. *Carolene Products Company*

**304 U.S. 144; 58 S. Ct. 778; 82 L. Ed. 1234 (1938)**

In what has become a famous footnote in an otherwise unimportant case, Justice Stone developed the justification for "more exact judicial scrutiny" where infringements of civil liberties (as opposed to economic rights) are involved. *Opinion of the Court: Stone, Brandeis, Hughes, Roberts. Concurring opinions: Black; Butler. Dissenting opinion: McReynolds. Cardozo and Reed did not participate.*

MR. JUSTICE STONE delivered the opinion of the Court. . . .

Regulatory legislation affecting ordinary commercial transactions is not to be pronounced unconstitutional unless in the light of the facts made known or generally assumed it is of such a character as to preclude the assumption that it rests upon some rational basis within the knowledge and experience of the legislators.[4]

[4]There may be narrower scope for operation of the presumption of constitutionality when legislation appears on its face to be within a specific prohibition of the Constitution, such as those of the first ten amendments, which are deemed equally specific when held to be embraced within the Fourteenth.

It is unnecessary to consider now whether legislation which restricts those political processes which can ordinarily be expected to bring about repeal of undesirable legislation, is to be subjected to more exacting judicial scrutiny under the general prohibitions of the Fourteenth Amendment than are most other types of legislation. . . .

Nor need we enquire whether similar considerations enter into the review of statutes directed at particular religious . . . or national . . . or racial minorities . . . whether prejudice against discrete and insular minorities may be a special condition, which tends seriously to curtail the operation of those political processes ordinarily to be relied upon to protect minorities, and which may call for a correspondingly more searching judicial inquiry.

## *Hawaii Housing Authority* v. *Midkiff*

**467 U.S. 229, 104 S. Ct. 2321 81, L. Ed. 2d 186 (1984)**

As a result of the feudal land tenure system of the early high chiefs of the Hawaiian Islands, land in Hawaii was concentrated in the hands of a few large landowners. In the mid-1960s, after extensive hearings, the Hawaii Legislature discovered that while the Federal and State Governments owned almost 49 percent of the State's land, another 47 percent was in the hands of only 72 private landowners. To reduce the perceived social and economic problems that resulted from this land concentration, the Hawaii Legislature enacted the Land Reform Act of 1967, which created a land condemnation scheme whereby title in real property could be taken from lessors and transferred to lessees. Under the Act, lessees living on single-family residential lots within tracts at least five acres in size can ask the Hawaii Housing Authority (HHA) to condemn the property on which they live. If the HHA determines that a "public purpose" will be served, it is authorized to designate some or all of the lots in the tract for acquisition. Once it has acquired the "right, title, and interest" in the land, at prices set by a condemnation trial or by negotiation between lessors and lessees, it can sell the land titles to the applicant lessees. After the HHA had held a public hearing on the proposed acquisition of Frank E. Midkiff's lands, he and other trustees of landholding estates filed suit in U.S. District Court for the District of Hawaii, asking that the Act be declared unconstitutional and that its enforcement be enjoined. The District Court held the Act constitutional under the Public Use Clause of the Fifth Amendment, made applicable to the State under the Fourteenth Amendment. The Court of Appeals for the Ninth Circuit reversed, holding that the Act violated the "public use" requirement of the Fifth Amendment, and the HHA appealed to the U.S. Supreme Court. *Unanimous Opinion of the Court: O'Connor, Burger, Blackmun, Brennan, Powell, Rehnquist, Steven, White. Marshall did not participate.*

JUSTICE O'CONNOR delivered the opinion of the Court.

The Fifth Amendment of the United States Constitution provides, in pertinent part, that "private property [shall not] be taken for public use, without just compensation." These cases present the question whether the Public Use Clause of that Amendment, made applicable to the States through the Fourteenth Amendment, prohibits the State of Hawaii from taking, with just compensation, title in real property from lessors and transferring it to lessees in order to reduce the concentration of ownership of fees simple in the State. We conclude that it does not. . . .

The starting point for our analysis of the Act's constitutionality is the Court's decision in *Berman* v. *Parker* . . . (1954). In *Berman*, the Court held constitutional the District of Columbia Redevelopment Act of 1945. That Act provided both for the comprehensive use of the eminent domain power to redevelop slum areas and for the possible sale or lease of the condemned lands to private interests. In discussing whether the takings authorized by that Act were for a "public use," . . . the Court stated:

"We deal, in other words, with what traditionally has been known as the police power. An attempt to define its reach or trace its outer limits is fruitless, for each case must turn on its own facts. The definition is essentially the product of legislative determinations addressed to the purposes of government, purposes neither abstractly nor historically capable of complete definition. Subject to specific constitutional limitations, when the legislature has spoken, the public interest has been declared in terms well-nigh conclusive. In such cases the legislature, not the judiciary, is the main guardian of the public needs to be served by social legislation, whether it be Congress legislating concerning the District of Columbia . . . or the States legislating concerning local affairs. . . . This principle admits of no exception merely because the power of eminent domain is involved." . . .

There is, of course, a role for courts to play in reviewing a legislature's judgment of what constitutes a public use, even when the eminent domain power is equated with the police power. But . . . the Court has made clear that it will not substitute its judgment for a legislature's judgment as to what constitutes a public use "unless the use be palpably without reasonable foundation.". . .

To be sure, the Court's cases have repeatedly stated that "one person's property may not be taken for the benefit of another private person without a justifying public purpose, even though compensation be paid." . . . But where the exercise of the eminent domain power is rationally related to a conceivable public purpose, the Court has never held a compensated taking to be proscribed by the Public Use Clause. . . .

On this basis, we have no trouble concluding that the Hawaii Act is constitutional. The people of Hawaii have attempted, much as the settlers of the original 13 Colonies did, to reduce the perceived social and economic evils of a land oligopoly traceable to their monarchs. The land oligopoly has, according to the Hawaii Legislature, created artificial deterrents to the normal functioning of the State's residential land market and forced thousands of individual homeowners to lease, rather than buy, the land underneath their homes. Regulating oligopoly and the evils associated with it is a classic exercise of a State's police powers. . . . We cannot disapprove of Hawaii's exercise of this power.

Nor can we condemn as irrational the Act's approach to correcting the land oligopoly problem. The Act presumes that when a sufficiently large number of persons declare that they are willing but unable to buy lots at fair prices the land market is malfunctioning. When such a malfunction is signalled, the Act authorizes HHA to condemn lots in the relevant tract. The Act limits the number of lots any one tenant can purchase and authorizes HHA to use public funds to ensure that the market dilution goals will be achieved. This is a comprehensive and rational approach to identifying and correcting market failure.

Of course, this Act, like any other, may not be successful in achieving its intended goals. But "whether *in fact* the provision will accomplish its objectives is not the question: the [constitutional requirement] is satisfied if . . . the . . . [state] Legislature *rationally could have believed* that the [Act] would promote its objective." . . . When the legislature's purpose is legitimate and its means are not irrational, our cases make clear that empirical debates over the wisdom of takings—no less than debates over the wisdom of other kinds of socioeconomic legislation—are not to be carried out in the federal courts. Redistribution of fees simple to correct deficiencies in the market determined by the state legislature to be attributable to land oligopoly is a rational exercise of the eminent domain power.

The mere fact that property taken outright by eminent domain is transferred in the first instance to private beneficiaries does not condemn that taking as having only a private purpose. The Court long ago rejected any literal requirement that condemned property be put into use for the general public. . . . As the unique way titles were held in Hawaii skewed the land market, exercise of the power of eminent domain was justified. The Act advances its purposes without the State taking actual possession of the land. In such cases, government does not itself have to use property to legitimate the taking; it is only the taking's purpose, and not its mechanics, that must pass scrutiny under the Public Use Clause.

Similarly, the fact that a state legislature, and not the Congress, made the public use determination does not mean that judicial deference is less appropriate. Judicial deference is required because, in our system of government, legislatures are better able to assess what public purposes should be advanced by an exercise of the taking power. State legislatures are as capable as Congress of making such determinations within their respective spheres of authority. . . . Thus, if a legislature, state or federal, determines there are substantial reasons for an exercise of the taking power, courts must defer to its determination that the taking will serve a public use.

The State of Hawaii has never denied that the Constitution forbids even a compensated taking of property when executed for no reason other than to confer a private benefit on a particular private party. A purely private taking could not withstand the scrutiny of the public use requirement; it would serve no legitimate purpose of government and would thus be void. But no purely private taking is involved in this case. The Hawaii Legislature enacted its Land Reform Act not to benefit a particular class of identifiable individuals but to attack certain perceived evils of concentrated property ownership in Hawaii—a legitimate public purpose. Use of the condemnation power to achieve this purpose is not irrational. Since we assume for purposes of this appeal that the weighty demand of just compensation has been met, the requirements of the Fifth and Fourteenth Amendments have been satisfied. Accordingly, we reverse the judgment of the Court of Appeals, and remand these cases for further proceedings in conformity with this opinion.

## *Nollan* v. *California Coastal Commission*

**483 U.S. 825, 107 S. Ct. 3141, 97 L. Ed. 2d 677 (1987)**

The California Coastal Commission granted a permit to James and Marilyn Nollan to replace a small bungalow on their beachfront lot with a larger house upon the condition that they allow the public an easement to pass across their beach, which was located between two public beaches. The Nollans filed a petition for writ of administrative mandamus asking the Ventura County Superior Court to invalidate the access condition. They argued that the condition could not be imposed absent evidence that their proposed development would have a direct adverse impact on public access to the beach. The Court agreed and remanded the case to the Commission for a full evidentiary hearing on that issue. On remand, the Commission held a public hearing and made further factual findings; it reaffirmed its imposition of the condition, finding that the new house would increase blockage of the view of the ocean, thus contributing to the development of "a 'wall' of residential structures" that would prevent the public "psychologically . . . from realizing a stretch of coastline exists nearby that they have every right to visit." The Nollans filed a supplemental petition for a writ of administrative mandamus with the Superior Court, arguing that imposition of the access condition violated the Takings Clause of the Fifth Amendment, as incorporated against the states by the Fourteenth Amendment. The Superior Court avoided the constitutional question but ruled in their favor on statutory grounds. In its view, the administrative record did not provide an adequate factual basis for concluding that replacement of the bungalow with the house would create a direct or cumulative burden on public access to the sea. The Commission appealed to the California Court of Appeal, which reversed, holding that the access condition violated neither California statutes nor the Takings Clause of the U.S. Constitution. The Nollans appealed to the U.S. Supreme Court. *Opinion of the Court: Scalia, Rehnquist, O'Connor, Powell, White. Dissenting opinions: Brennan, Marshall; Blackmun; Stevens, Blackmun.*

JUSTICE SCALIA delivered the opinion of the Court. . . .

Had California simply required the Nollans to make an easement across their beachfront available to the public on a permanent basis in order to increase public access to the beach, rather than conditioning their permit to rebuild their house on their agreeing to do so, we have no doubt there would have been a taking. To say that the appropriation of a public easement across a landowner's premises does not constitute the taking of a property interest but rather (as Justice Brennan contends) "a mere restriction on its use," is to use words in a manner that deprives them of all their ordinary meaning. Indeed, one of the principal uses of the eminent domain power is to assure that the government be able to require conveyance of just such interests, so long as it pays for them. . . . Perhaps because the point is so obvious, we have never been confronted with a controversy that required us to rule upon it, but our cases' analysis of the effect of other governmental action leads to the same conclusion. We have repeatedly held that, as to property reserved by its owner for private use, "the right to exclude [others is] 'one of the most essential sticks in the bundle of rights that are commonly characterized as property.'" . . .

Given, then, that requiring uncompensated conveyance of the easement outright would violate the Fourteenth Amendment, the question becomes whether requiring it to be conveyed as a condition for issuing a land-use permit alters the outcome. We have long recognized that land-use regulation does not effect a taking if it "substantially advance[s] legitimate state interests" and does not "den[y] an owner economically viable use of his land," *Agins* v. *Tiburon*, 447 U. S. 255, 260 (1980). See also *Penn Central Transportation Co.* v. *New York City*, 438 U. S. 104, 127 (1978) ("[A] use restriction may constitute a 'taking' if not reasonably necessary to the effectuation of a substantial government purpose"). Our cases have not elaborated on the standards for determining what constitutes a "legitimate state interest" or what type of connection between the regulation and the state interest satisfies the requirement that the former "substantially advance" the latter. They have made clear, however, that a broad range of governmental purposes and regulations satisfies these requirements. . . . The Commission argues that among these permissible purposes are protecting the public's ability to see the beach, assisting the public in overcoming the "psychological barrier" to using the beach created by a developed shorefront, and preventing congestion on the public beaches. We assume, without deciding, that this is so—in which case the Commission unquestionably would be able to deny the Nollans their permit outright if their new house (alone, or by reason of the cumulative impact produced in conjunction with other construction,*) would substantially impede these purposes, unless the denial would interfere so drastically with the Nollans' use of their property as to constitute a taking. . . .

The Commission argues that a permit condition that serves the same legitimate police-power purpose as a refusal to issue the permit should not be found to be a taking if the refusal to issue the permit would not constitute a taking. We agree. Thus, if the Commission attached to the permit some condition that would have protected the public's ability to see the beach notwithstanding construction of the new house—for example, a height limitation, a width restriction, or a ban on fences—so long as the Commission could have exercised its police power (as we have assumed it could) to forbid construction of the house altogether, imposition of the condition would also be constitutional. Moreover (and here we come closer to the facts of the present case), the condition would be constitutional even if it consisted of the requirement that the Nollans provide a viewing spot on their property for passersby with whose sighting of the ocean their new house would interfere. Although such a requirement, constituting a permanent grant of continuous access to the property, would have to be considered a taking if it were not attached to a development permit, the Commission's assumed power to forbid construction of the house in order to protect the public's view of

*If the Nollans were being singled out to bear the burden of California's attempt to remedy these problems, although they had not contributed to it more than other coastal landowners, the State's action, even if otherwise valid, might violate either the incorporated Takings Clause or the Equal Protection Clause.

the beach must surely include the power to condition construction upon some concession by the owner, even a concession of property rights, that serves the same end. If a prohibition designed to accomplish that purpose would be a legitimate exercise of the police power rather than a taking, it would be strange to conclude that providing the owner an alternative to that prohibition which accomplishes the same purpose is not.

The evident constitutional propriety disappears, however, if the condition substituted for the prohibition utterly fails to further the end advanced as the justification for the prohibition. When that essential nexus is eliminated, the situation becomes the same as if California law forbade shouting fire in a crowded theater, but granted dispensations to those willing to contribute $100 to the state treasury. While a ban on shouting fire can be a core exercise of the State's police power to protect the public safety, and can thus meet even our stringent standards for regulation of speech, adding the unrelated condition alters the purpose to one which, while it may be legitimate, is inadequate to sustain the ban. Therefore, even though, in a sense, requiring a $100 tax contribution in order to shout fire is a lesser restriction on speech than an outright ban, it would not pass constitutional muster. Similarly here, the lack of nexus between the condition and the original purpose of the building restriction converts that purpose to something other than what it was. The purpose then becomes, quite simply, the obtaining of an easement to serve some valid governmental purpose, but without payment of compensation. Whatever may be the outer limits of "legitimate state interests" in the takings and land-use context, this is not one of them. In short, unless the permit condition serves the same governmental purpose as the development ban, the building restriction is not a valid regulation of land use but "an out-and-out plan of extortion.". . .

The Commission claims that it concedes as much, and that we may sustain the condition at issue here by finding that it is reasonably related to the public need or burden that the Nollans' new house creates or to which it contributes. We can accept, for purposes of discussion, the Commission's proposed test as to how close a "fit" between the condition and the burden is required, because we find that this case does not meet even the most untailored standards. The Commission's principal contention to the contrary essentially turns on a play on the word "access." The Nollans' new house, the Commission found, will interfere with "visual access" to the beach. That in turn (along with other shorefront development) will interfere with the desire of people who drive past the Nollans' house to use the beach, thus creating a "psychological barrier" to "access." The Nollans' new house will also, by a process not altogether clear from the Commission's opinion but presumably potent enough to more than offset the effects of the psychological barrier, increase the use of the public beaches, thus creating the need for more "access." These burdens on "access" would be alleviated by a requirement that the Nollans provide "lateral access" to the beach.

Rewriting the argument to eliminate the play on words makes clear that there is nothing to it. It is quite impossible to understand how a requirement that people already on the public beaches be able to walk across the Nollans' property reduces any obstacles to viewing the beach created by the new house. It is also impossible to understand how it lowers any "psychological barrier" to using the public beaches, or how it helps to remedy any additional congestion on them caused by construction of the Nollans' new house. We therefore find that the Commission's imposition of the permit condition cannot be treated as an exercise of its land-use power for any of these purposes. Our conclusion on this point is consistent with the approach taken by every other court that has considered the question, with the exception of the California state courts.

Justice Brennan argues that imposition of the access requirement is not irrational. In his version of the Commission's argument, the reason for the requirement is that in its absence, a person looking toward the beach from the road will see a street of residential structures including the Nollans' new home and conclude that there is no public beach nearby. If, however, that person sees people passing and repassing along the dry sand behind the Nollans' home, he will realize that there is a public beach somewhere in the vicinity. . . . The Commission's action, however, was based on the opposite factual finding that the wall of houses completely blocked the view of the beach and that a person looking from the road would not be able to see it at all.

Even if the Commission had made the finding that Justice Brennan proposes, however, it is not certain that it would suffice. We do not share Justice Brennan's confidence that the Commission "should have little difficulty in the future in utilizing its expertise to demonstrate a specific connection between provisions for access and burdens on access," . . . that will avoid the effect of today's decision. We view the Fifth Amendment's Property Clause to be more than a pleading requirement, and compliance with it to be more than an exercise in cleverness and imagination. As indicated earlier, our cases describe the condition for abridgment of property rights through the police power as a "*substantial* advanc[ing]" of a legitimate state interest. We are inclined to be particularly careful about the adjective where the actual conveyance of property is made a condition to the lifting of a land-use restriction, since in that context there is heightened risk that the purpose is avoidance of the compensation requirement, rather than the stated police power objective.

We are left, then, with the Commission's justification for the access requirement unrelated to land-use regulation:

> Finally, the Commission notes that there are several existing provisions of pass and repass lateral access benefits already given by past Faria Beach Tract applicants as a result of prior coastal permit decisions. The access required as a condition of this permit is part of a comprehensive program to provide continuous public access along Faria Beach as the lots undergo development or redevelopment. . . .

That is simply an expression of the Commission's belief that the public interest will be served by a continuous strip of publicly accessible beach along the coast. The Commission may well be right that it is a good idea, but that does not establish that the Nollans (and other coastal residents) alone can be compelled to contribute to its realization. Rather, California is free to advance its "comprehensive program," if it wishes, by using its power of eminent domain for this "public purpose," but if it wants an easement across the Nollans' property, it must pay for it.

*Reserved.*

JUSTICE BRENNAN, with whom JUSTICE MARSHALL joins, dissenting.

Appellants in this case sought to construct a new dwelling on their beach lot that would both diminish visual access to the beach and move private development closer to the public tidelands. The Commission reasonably concluded that such "buildout," both individually and cumulatively, threatens public access to the shore. It sought to offset this encroachment by obtaining assurance that the public may walk along the shoreline in order to gain access to the ocean. The Court finds this an illegitimate exercise of the police power, because it maintains that there is no reasonable relationship between the effect of the development and the condition imposed.

The first problem with this conclusion is that the Court imposes a standard of precision for the exercise of a State's police power that has been discredited for the better part of this century. Furthermore, even under the Court's cramped standard, the permit condition imposed in this case directly responds to the specific type of burden on access created by appellants' development. Finally, a review of those factors deemed most significant in takings analysis makes clear that the Commission's action implicates none of the concerns underlying the Takings Clause.

Even if we accept the Court's unusual demand for a precise match between the condition imposed and the specific type of burden on access created by the appellants, the State's action easily satisfies this requirement. First, the lateral access condition serves to dissipate the impression that the beach that lies behind the wall of homes along the shore is for private use only. It requires no exceptional imaginative powers to find plausible the Commission's point that the average person passing along the road in front of a phalanx of imposing permanent residences, including the appellants' new home, is likely to conclude that this particular portion of the shore is not open to the public. If, however, that person can see that numerous people are passing and repassing along the dry sand, this conveys the message that the beach is in fact open for use by the public. Furthermore, those persons who go down to the public beach a quarter-mile away will be able to look down the coastline and see that persons have continuous access to the tidelands, and will observe signs that proclaim the public's right of access over the dry sand. The burden produced by the diminution in visual access—the impression that the beach is not open to the public—is thus directly alleviated by the provision for public access over the dry sand. The Court therefore has an unrealistically limited conception of what measures could reasonably be chosen to mitigate the burden produced by a diminution of visual access. . . .

The fact that the Commission's action is a legitimate exercise of the police power does not, of course, insulate it from a takings challenge, for when "regulation goes too far it will be recognized as a taking." *Pennsylvania Coal Co.* v. *Mahon.* Conventional takings analysis underscores the implausibility of the Court's holding, for it demonstrates that this exercise of California's police power implicates none of the concerns that underlie our takings jurisprudence. . . .

. . . The character of the regulation in this case is not unilateral government action, but a condition on approval of a development request submitted by appellants. The state has not sought to interfere with any pre-existing property interest, but has responded to appellants' proposal to intensify development on the coast. Appellants themselves chose to submit a new development application, and could claim no property interest in its approval. They were aware that approval of such development would be conditioned on preservation of adequate public access to the ocean. The State has initiated no action against appellants' property; had the Nollans' not proposed more intensive development in the coastal zone, they would never have been subject to the provision that they challenge.

Examination of the economic impact of the Commission's action reinforces the conclusion that no taking has occurred. Allowing appellants to intensify development along the coast in exchange for ensuring public access to the ocean is a classic instance of government action that produces a "reciprocity of advantage." . . . Appellants have been allowed to replace a one-story 521-square-foot beach home with a two-story 1,674-square-foot residence and an attached two-car garage, resulting in development covering 2,464 square feet of the lot. Such development obviously significantly increases the value of appellants' property; appellants make no contention that this increase is offset by any diminution in value resulting from the deed restriction, much less that the restriction made the property less valuable than it would have been without the new construction. Furthermore, appellants gain an additional benefit from the Commission's permit condition program. They are able to walk along the beach beyond the confines of their own property only because the Commission has required deed restrictions as a condition of approving other new beach developments. Thus appellants benefit both as private landowners and as members of the public from the fact that new development permit requests are conditioned on preservation of public access. . . .

. . . State agencies therefore require considerable flexibility in responding to private desires for development in a way that guarantees the preservation of public access to the coast. They should be encouraged to regulate development in the context of the overall balance of competing uses of the shoreline. The Court today does precisely the opposite, overruling an eminently reasonable exercise of an expert state agency's judgment, substituting its own narrow view of how this balance should be struck. Its reasoning is hardly suited to the complex reality of natural resource protection in the 20th century. I can only hope that today's decision is an aberration, and that a broader vision ultimately prevails.

I dissent.

# *Lucas* v. *South Carolina Coastal Council*

**112 S. Ct. 2886, 120 L. Ed. 2d 798 (1992)**

In 1986, David Lucas paid $975,000 for two residential lots on the Isle of Palms, a barrier island situated to the east of Charleston, South Carolina. He intended to build single-family houses on them, such as were found on the immediately adjacent lots. At the time, Lucas's lots were not subject to South Carolina's coastal zone building permit requirements. In 1988, however, the South Carolina Legislature enacted the Beachfront Management Act, which had the direct effect of prohibiting Lucas from erecting any permanent habitable structures on his land. He filed suit against the newly created Coastal Council in the South Carolina Court of Common Pleas, contending that the Beachfront Management Act's ban on construction effected a taking of his property under the Fifth and Fourteenth Amendments and therefore required the payment of just compensation. He did not deny the validity of the act as a lawful exercise of South Carolina's police power; he simply contended that the act deprived him of all "economically viable use" of his property and that he was entitled to compensation, regardless of whether the legislature had acted in furtherance of a legitimate police power objective. The state trial court agreed, finding that the ban had rendered Lucas's parcels "valueless," and ordered the Coastal Council to pay Lucas "just compensation" in the amount of $1,232,387.50. The Supreme Court of South Carolina reversed. Since Lucas had not attacked the validity of the statute as such, it found itself bound to accept the uncontested findings of the South Carolina legislature that new construction in the coastal zone of the sort that Lucas intended threatened South Carolina's beaches. It concluded on the basis of *Muglar* v. *Kansas* (1887) and a long line of cases that followed it that when regulation is necessary to prevent "harmful or noxious uses" of property akin to public nuisances, no compensation is owed under the Takings Clause, regardless of the regulation's effect on the property's value. The U.S. Supreme Court granted certiorari. *Opinion of the Court: Scalia, O'Connor, Rehnquist, Thomas, White. Concurring in the judgment: Kennedy. Dissenting opinions: Blackmun; Stevens. Separate statement voting to dismiss the writ of certiorari: Souter.*

JUSTICE SCALIA delivered the opinion of the Court.

Prior to Justice Holmes' exposition in *Pennsylvania Coal Co.* v. *Mahon* (1922), it was generally thought that the Takings Clause reached only a "direct appropriation" of property. *Legal Tender Cases* (1871), or the functional equivalent of a "practical ouster of [the owner's] possession." *Transportation Co.* v. *Chicago* (1879). Justice Holmes recognized in *Mahon*, however, that if the protection against physical appropriations of private property was to be meaningfully enforced, the government's power to redefine the range of interests included in the ownership of property was necessarily constrained by constitutional limits. If, instead, the uses of private property were subject to unbridled, uncompensated qualification under the police power, "the natural tendency of human nature [would be] to extend the qualification more and more until at last private property disappear[ed]." These considerations gave birth in that case to the oft-cited maxim that, "while property may be regulated to a certain extent, if regulation goes too far it will be recognized as a taking." Nevertheless, our decision in *Mahon* offered little insight into when, and under what circumstances, a given regulation would be seen as going "too far" for purposes of the Fifth Amendment. In 70-odd years of succeeding "regulatory takings" jurisprudence, we have generally eschewed any "set formula" for determining how far is too far, preferring to "engag[e] in . . . essentially *ad hoc*, factual inquiries," *Penn Central Transportation Co.* v. *New York City* (1978). We have, however, described at least two discrete categories of regulatory action as compensable without case-specific inquiry into the public interest advanced in support of the restraint. The first encompasses regulations that compel the property owner to suffer a physical "invasion" of his property. In general (at least with regard to permanent invasions), no matter how minute the intrusion, and no matter how weighty the public purpose behind it, we have required compensation. For example, in *Loretto* v. *Teleprompter Manhattan CATV Corp.* (1982), we determined that New York's law requiring landlords to allow television cable companies to emplace cable facilities in their apartment buildings constituted a taking, even though the facilities occupied at most only 1½ cubic feet of the landlords' property.

The second situation in which we have found categorical treatment appropriate is where regulation denies all economically beneficial or productive use of land. As we have said on numerous occasions, the Fifth Amendment is violated when land-use regulation "does not substantially advance legitimate state interests or denies an owner economically viable use of his land."

We have never set forth the justification for this rule. Perhaps it is simply, as Justice Brennan suggested, that total deprivation of beneficial use is, from the landowner's point of view, the equivalent of a physical appropriation.

. . . On the other side of the balance, affirmatively supporting a compensation requirement, is the fact that regulations that leave the owner of land without economically beneficial or productive options for its use—typically, as here, by requiring land to be left substantially in its natural state—carry with them a heightened risk that private property is being pressed into some form of public service under the guise of mitigating serious public harm. We think, in short, that there are good reasons for our frequently expressed belief that when the owner of real property has been called upon to sacrifice all economically beneficial uses in the name of the common good, that is, to leave his property economically idle, he has suffered a taking.

The trial court found Lucas's two beachfront lots to have been rendered valueless by respondent's enforcement of the coastal-zone construction ban. Under Lucas's theory of the case, which rested upon our "no economically viable use" statements, that finding entitled him to compensation. Lucas believed it unnecessary to take issue with either the purposes behind the Beachfront Management Act, or the means chosen by the South Carolina Legislature to effectuate those purposes. The South Carolina Supreme Court, however, thought otherwise. In its view, the Beachfront Management Act was no ordinary enactment, but involved an exercise of South Carolina's "police powers" to mitigate the harm to the public interest that petitioner's use of his land might occasion. By neglecting to dispute the findings enumerated in the Act or otherwise to challenge the legislature's purposes, petitioner "concede[d] that the beach/dune area of South Carolina's shores is an extremely valuable public resource; that the erection of new construction, inter alia, contributes to the erosion and destruction of this public resource; and that discouraging new construction in close proximity to the beach/dune area is necessary to prevent a great public harm." In the court's view, these concessions brought petitioner's challenge within a long line of this Court's cases sustaining against Due Process and Takings Clause challenges the State's use of its "policy powers" to enjoin a property owner from activities akin to public nuisances.

It is correct that many of our prior opinions have suggested that "harmful or noxious uses" of property may be proscribed by government regulation without the requirement of compensation. However, we think the South Carolina Supreme Court was too quick to conclude that that principle decides the present case. . . .

*A fortiori* the legislature's recitation of a noxious-use justification cannot be the basis for departing from our categorical rule that total regulatory takings must be compensated. If it were, departure would virtually always be allowed. The South Carolina Supreme Court's approach would essentially nullify *Mahon*'s affirmation of limits to the noncompensable exercise of the police power. . . .

Where the State seeks to sustain regulation that deprives land of all economically beneficial use, we think it may resist compensation only if the logically antecedent inquiry into the nature of the owner's estate shows that the proscribed use interests were not part of his title to begin with. This accords, we think, with our "takings" jurisprudence, which has traditionally been guided by the understandings of our citizens regarding the content of, and the State's power over, the "bundle of rights" that they acquire when they obtain title to property. Confiscatory regulations, i.e., regulations that prohibit all economically beneficial use of land, cannot be newly legislated or decreed (without compensation), but must inhere in the title itself, in the restrictions that background principles of the State's law of property and nuisance already place upon land ownership. . . .

On this analysis, the owner of a lake bed, for example, would not be entitled to compensation when he is denied the requisite permit to engage in a landfilling operation that would have the effect of flooding others' land. Nor the corporate owner of a nuclear generating plant, when it is directed to remove all improvements from its land upon discovery that the plant sits astride an earthquake fault. Such regulatory action may well have the effect of eliminating the land's only economically productive use, but it does not proscribe a productive use that was previously permissible under relevant property and nuisance principles. The use of these properties for what are now expressly prohibited purposes was always unlawful, and (subject to other constitutional limitations) it was open to the State at any point to make the implication of those background principles of nuisance and property law explicit. When, however, a regulation that declares "off-limits" all economically productive or beneficial uses of land goes beyond what the relevant background principles would dictate, compensation must be paid to sustain it. The "total taking" inquiry we require today will ordinarily entail (as the application of state nuisance law ordinarily entails) analysis of, among other things, the degree of harm to public lands and resources, or adjacent private property, posed by the claimant's proposed activities, the social value of the claimant's activities and their suitability to the locality in question, and the relative ease with which the alleged harm can be avoided through measures taken by the claimant and the government (or adjacent private landowners) alike. The fact that a particular use has long been engaged in by similarly situated owners ordinarily imports a lack of any common-law prohibition. So also does the fact that other landowners, similarly situated, are permitted to continue the use denied to the claimant.

We emphasize that to win its case South Carolina must do more than proffer the legislature's declaration that the uses Lucas desires are inconsistent with the public interest. As we have said, a "State, by ipse dixit, may not transform private property into public property without compensation. . . ." Instead, as it would be required to do if it sought to restrain Lucas in a common-law action for public nuisance, South Carolina must identify background principles of nuisance and property law that prohibit the uses he now intends in the circumstances in which the property is presently found. Only on this showing can the State fairly claim that, in proscribing all such beneficial uses, the Beachfront Management Act is taking nothing. . . .

The judgment is reversed and the cause remanded for proceedings not inconsistent with this opinion.

JUSTICE BLACKMUN, dissenting.

. . . This Court repeatedly has recognized the ability of government, in certain circumstances, to regulate property without compensation no matter how adverse the financial effect on the owner may be. More than a century ago, the Court explicitly upheld the right of States to prohibit uses of property injurious to public health, safety, or welfare without paying compensation: "A prohibition simply upon the use of property for purposes that are declared, by valid legislation, to be injurious to the health, morals, or safety of the community, cannot, in any just sense, be deemed a taking or an appropriation of property." *Mugler* v. *Kansas* (1887). On this basis, the Court upheld an ordinance effectively prohibiting operation of a previously lawful brewery, although the "establishments will become of no value as property."

*Mugler* was only the beginning in a long line of cases. In none of the cases did the Court suggest that the right of a State to prohibit certain activities without paying compensation turned on the availability of some residual valuable use. Instead, the cases depended on whether the government interest was sufficient to prohibit the activity, given the significant private cost.

## *Dolan* v. *City of Tigard*

**512 U.S. 374, 114 S. Ct. 2309, 129 L. Ed. 2d 304 (1994)**

Florence Dolan sought a city permit to expand her plumbing and electric supply store from 9,700 square feet to 17,600 square feet and to pave her 39-space parking lot. The City Planning Commission of Tigard, Oregon, approved her permit application on the condition that she dedicate approximately 10 percent of her 1.67 acre parcel of land to the city for a public greenway along an adjacent creek (to minimize flooding that would be exacerbated by the increases in impervious surfaces associated with her development) and for a pedestrian/bicycle pathway (intended to relieve traffic congestion in the central business district caused by the additional customers visiting her enlarged store). Dolan appealed the Commission's denial of her request for a waiver of this condition to the Land Use Board of Appeals, alleging that the land dedication requirements were unrelated to the proposed development and thus constituted an uncompensated taking of her property in violation of the Fifth Amendment. The Land Use Board of Appeals rejected her appeal, and the State Court of Appeals and the Oregon State Supreme Court both affirmed its decision. The United States Supreme Court granted certiorari. *Opinion of the Court: Rehnquist, Kennedy, O'Connor, Scalia, Thomas. Dissenting opinions: Stevens, Blackmun, Ginsburg; Souter.*

CHIEF JUSTICE REHNQUIST delivered the opinion of the Court.

Petitioner challenges the decision of the Oregon Supreme Court which held that the city of Tigard could condition the approval of her building permit on the dedication of a portion of her property for flood control and traffic improvements. We granted certiorari to resolve a question left open by our decision in *Nollan* v. *California Coastal Commn'n*, 483 U.S. 825 (1987), of what is the required degree of connection between the exactions imposed by the city and the projected impacts of the proposed development. . . .

The Takings Clause of the Fifth Amendment of the United States Constitution, made applicable to the States through the Fourteenth Amendment, *Chicago B. & Q. R. Co.* v. *Chicago*, 166 U.S. 226, 239 (1897), provides: "[N]or shall private property be taken for public use, without just compensation." One of the principal purposes of the Takings Clause is "to bar Government from forcing some people alone to bear public burdens which, in all fairness and justice, should be borne by the public as a whole." *Armstrong* v. *United States*, 364 U.S. 40, 49 (1960). Without question, had the city simply required petitioner to dedicate a strip of land along Fanno

Creek for public use, rather than conditioning the grant of her permit to redevelop her property on such a dedication, a taking would have occurred. Such public access would deprive petitioner of the right to exclude others, "one of the most essential sticks in the bundle of rights that are commonly characterized as property." *Kaiser Aetna* v. *United States,* 444 U.S. 164, 176 (1979).

On the other side of the ledger, the authority of state and local governments to engage in land use planning has been sustained against constitutional challenge as long ago as our decision in *Euclid* v. *Ambler Realty Co.,* 272 U.S. 365 (1926). "Government hardly could go on if to some extent values incident to property could not be diminished without paying for every such change in the general law." *Pennsylvania Coal Co.* v. *Mahon,* 260 U.S. 393, 413 (1922). A land use regulation does not effect a taking if it "substantially advance[s] legitimate state interests" and does not "den[y] an owner economically viable use of his land." *Agins* v. *Tiburon,* 447 U.S. 255, 260 (1980).

The sort of land use regulations discussed in the cases just cited, however, differ in two relevant particulars from the present case. First, they involved essentially legislative determinations classifying entire areas of the city, whereas here the city made an adjudicative decision to condition petitioner's application for a building permit on an individual parcel. Second, the conditions imposed were not simply a limitation on the use petitioner might make of her own parcel, but a requirement that she deed portions of the property to the city. In *Nollan,* we held that governmental authority to exact such a condition was circumscribed by the Fifth and Fourteenth Amendments. Under the well-settled doctrine of "unconstitutional conditions," the government may not require a person to give up a constitutional right—here the right to receive just compensation when property is taken for a public use—in exchange for a discretionary benefit conferred by the government where the property sought has little or no relationship to the benefit.

Petitioner contends that the city has forced her to choose between the building permit and her right under the Fifth Amendment to just compensation for the public easements. Petitioner does not quarrel with the city's authority to exact some forms of dedication as a condition for the granting of a building permit, but challenges the showing made by the city to justify these exactions. She argues that the city has identified "no special benefits" conferred on her, and has not identified any "special quantifiable burdens" created by her new store that would justify the particular dedications required from her which are not required from the public at large.

In evaluating petitioner's claim, we must first determine whether the "essential nexus" exists between the "legitimate state interest" and the permit condition exacted by the city. *Nollan,* 483 U.S., at 837. If we find that a nexus exists, we must then decide the required degree of connection between the exactions and the projected impact of the proposed development. We were not required to reach this question in Nollan, because we concluded that the connection did not meet even the loosest standard. Here, however, we must decide this question. . . .

It seems obvious that a nexus exists between preventing flooding along Fanno Creek and limiting development within the creek's 100-year floodplain. Petitioner proposes to double the size of her retail store and to pave her now-gravel parking lot, thereby expanding the impervious surface on the property and increasing the amount of stormwater runoff into Fanno Creek.

The same may be said for the city's attempt to reduce traffic congestion by providing for alternative means of transportation. . . .

The second part of our analysis requires us to determine whether the degree of the exactions demanded by the city's permit conditions bear the required relationship to the projected impact of petitioner's proposed development. . . .

We think a term such as "rough proportionality" best encapsulates what we hold to be the requirment of the Fifth Amendment. No precise mathematical calculation is required, but the city must make some sort of individualized determination that the required dedication is related both in nature and extent to the impact of the proposed development.

JUSTICE STEVENS' dissent relies upon the proposition that the city's conditional demands for part of petitioner's property are "a species of business regulation that heretofore warranted a strong presumption of constitutional validity." But simply denominating a governmental measure as a "business regulation" does not immunize it from constitutional challenge on the grounds that it violates a provision of the Bill of Rights. In *Marshall* v. *Barlow's, Inc.*, 436 U.S. 307 (1978), we held that a statute authorizing a warrantless search of business premises in order to detect OSHA violations violated the Fourth Amendment. And in *Central Hudson Gas & Electric Corp.* v. *Public Service Comm'n. of N.Y.*, 447 U.S. 557 (1980), we held that an order of the New York Public Service Commission, designed to cut down the use of electricity because of a fuel shortage, violated the First Amendment insofar as it prohibited advertising by a utility company to promote the use of electricity. We see no reason why the Takings Clause of the Fifth Amendment, as much a part of the Bill of Rights as the First Amendment or Fourth Amendment, should be relegated to the status of a poor relation in these comparable circumstances. We turn now to analysis of whether the findings relied upon by the city here, first with respect to the floodplain easement, and second with respect to the pedestrian/bicycle path, satisfied these requirements.

It is axiomatic that increasing the amount of impervious surface will increase the quantity and rate of stormwater flow from petitioner's property. Therefore, keeping the floodplain open and free from development would likely confine the pressures on Fanno Creek created by petitioner's development. In fact, because petitioner's property lies within the Central Business District, the Community Development Code already required that petitioner leave 15% of it as open space and the undeveloped floodplain would have nearly satisfied that requirement. But the city demanded more—it not only wanted petitioner not to build in the floodplain, but it also wanted petitioner's property along Fanno Creek for its Greenway system. The city has never said why a public greenway, as opposed to a private one, was required in the interest of flood control.

The difference to petitioner, of course, is the loss of her ability to exclude others. As we have noted, this right to exclude others is "one of the most essential sticks in the bundle of rights that are commonly characterized as property." It is difficult to see why recreational visitors tramping along petitioner's floodplain easement are sufficiently related to the city's legitimate interest in reducing flooding problems along Fanno Creek, and the city has not attempted to make any individualized determination to support this part of its request. . . .

We conclude that the findings upon which the city relies do not show the required reasonable relationship between the floodplain easement and the petitioner's proposed new building.

With respect to the pedestrian/bicycle pathway, the city has not met its burden of demonstrating that the additional number of vehicle and bicycle trips generated by the petitioner's development reasonably relate to the city's requirement of the pedestrian/bicycle pathway easement. The city simply found that the creation of the pathway "could offset some of the traffic demand . . . and lessen the increase in traffic congestion." . . .

No precise mathematical calculation is required, but the city must make some effort to quantify its findings in support of the dedication for the pedestrian/bicycle pathway beyond the conclusory statement that it could offset some of the traffic demand generated. . . .

The judgment of the Supreme Court of Oregon is reversed, and the case is remanded for further proceedings consistent with this opinion.

JUSTICE STEVENS, with whom JUSTICE BLACKMUN and JUSTICE GINSBURG join, dissenting.

. . . The Court has made a serious error by abandoning the traditional presumption of constitutionality and imposing a novel burden of proof on a city implementing an admittedly valid comprehensive land use plan. Even more consequential than its incorrect disposition of this case, however, is the Court's resurrection of a species of substantive due process analysis that it firmly rejected decades ago. . . .

Dolan has no right to be compensated for a taking unless the city acquires the property interests that she has refused to surrender. Since no taking has yet occurred, there has not been any infringement of her constitutional right to compensation.

Even if Dolan should accept the city's conditions in exchange for the benefit that she seeks, it would not necessarily follow that she had been denied "just compensation" since it would be appropriate to consider the receipt of that benefit in any calculation of "just compensation." . . . The city's conditons are by no means immune from constitutional scrutiny. The level of scrutiny, however, does not approximate the kind of review that would apply if the city had insisted on a surrender of Dolan's First Amendment rights in exchange for a building permit. One can only hope that the Court's reliance today on First Amendment cases, and its candid disavowal of the term "rational basis" to describe its new standard of review, do not signify a reassertion of the kind of superlegislative power the Court exercised during the *Lochner* era.

# THE CONSTITUTION OF THE UNITED STATES OF AMERICA

*We the People of the United States, in Order to form a more perfect Union, establish Justice, insure domestic Tranquility, provide for the common defence, promote the general Welfare, and secure the Blessings of Liberty to ourselves and our Posterity, do ordain and establish this CONSTITUTION for the United States of America.*

## ARTICLE I

SECTION 1. All legislative Powers herein granted shall be vested in a Congress of the United States, which shall consist of a Senate and House of Representatives.

SECTION 2. [1] The House of Representatives shall be composed of Members chosen every second Year by the People of the several States, and the Electors in each State shall have the Qualifications requisite for Electors of the most numerous Branch of the State Legislature.

[2] No person shall be a Representative who shall not have attained to the Age of twenty-five Years, and been seven Years a Citizen of the United States, and who shall not, when elected, be an Inhabitant of that State in which he shall be chosen.

[3] Representatives and direct Taxes shall be apportioned among the several States which may be included within this Union, according to their respective Numbers, which shall be determined by adding to the whole Number of free Persons, including those bound to Service for a Term of Years, and excluding Indians not taxed, three fifths of all other Persons. The actual Enumeration shall be made within three Years after the first Meeting of the Congress of the United States, and within every subsequent Term of ten Years, in such Manner as they shall by Law direct. The Number of Representatives shall not exceed one for every thirty Thousand, but each State shall have at Least one Representative; and until such enumeration shall be made, the State of New Hampshire shall be entitled to chuse three, Massachusetts eight, Rhode-Island and Providence Plantations

one, Connecticut five, New York six, New Jersey four, Pennsylvania eight, Delaware one, Maryland six, Virginia ten, North Carolina five, South Carolina five, and Georgia three.

[4] When vacancies happen in the Representation from any State, the Executive Authority thereof shall issue Writs of Election to fill such Vacancies.

[5] The House of Representatives shall chuse their Speaker and other Officers; and shall have the sole Power of Impeachment.

SECTION 3. [1] The Senate of the United States shall be composed of two Senators from each State, chosen by the Legislature thereof, for six Years; and each Senator shall have one Vote.

[2] Immediately after they shall be assembled in Consequence of the first Election, they shall be divided as equally as may be into three Classes. The Seats of the Senators of the first Class shall be vacated at the Expiration of the Second Year, of the second Class at the Expiration of the fourth Year, and of the third Class at the Expiration of the sixth Year, so that one-third may be chosen every second Year; and if Vacancies happen by Resignation, or otherwise, during the Recess of the Legislature of any State, the Executive thereof may make temporary Appointments until the next Meeting of the Legislature, which shall then fill such Vacancies.

[3] No person shall be a Senator who shall not have attained to the Age of thirty Years, and been nine Years a Citizen of the United States, and who shall not, when elected, be an Inhabitant of that State for which he shall be chosen.

[4] The Vice President of the United States shall be President of the Senate, but shall have no Vote, unless they be equally divided.

[5] The Senate shall chuse their Officers, and also a President pro tempore, in the absence of the Vice President, or when he shall exercise the Office of the President of the United States.

[6] The Senate shall have the sole Power to try all Impeachments. When sitting for that Purpose, they shall be on Oath or Affirmation. When the President of the United States is tried, the Chief Justice shall preside: And no Person shall be convicted without the Concurrence of two-thirds of the Members present.

[7] Judgment in Cases of Impeachment shall not extend further than to removal from Office, and disqualification to hold and enjoy any Office of honor, Trust, or Profit under the United States: but the Party convicted shall nevertheless be liable and subject to Indictment, Trial, Judgment and Punishment, according to Law.

SECTION 4. [1] The Times, Places and Manner of holding Elections for Senators and Representatives, shall be prescribed in each State by the Legislature thereof; but the Congress may at any time by Law make or alter such Regulations, except as to the Places of chusing Senators.

[2] The Congress shall assemble at least one in every Year, and such Meeting shall be on the first Monday in December, unless they shall by Law appoint a different Day.

SECTION 5. [1] Each House shall be the Judge of the Elections, Returns, and Qualifications of its own Members, and a Majority of each shall constitute a Quorum to do Business, but a smaller Number may adjourn for day to day, and may be authorized to compel the Attendance of absent Members, in such Manner, and under such Penalties as each House may provide.

[2] Each House may determine the Rules of its Proceedings, punish its Members for disorderly Behavior, and with the Concurrence of two thirds, expel a Member.

[3] Each House shall keep a Journal of its Proceedings, and from time to time publish the same, excepting such Parts as may in their Judgment require Secrecy; and the Yeas and Nays of the Members of either House or any question shall, at the Desire of one fifth of those Present, be entered on the Journal.

[4] Neither House, during the Session of Congress, shall, without the Consent of the other, adjourn for more than three days, nor to any other Place than that in which the two Houses shall be sitting.

SECTION 6. [1] The Senators and Representatives shall receive a Compensation for their Services, to be ascertained by Law, and paid out of the treasury of the United States. They shall in all Cases, except Treason, Felony and Breach of the Peace, be privileged from Arrest during their Attendance at the Session of their respective Houses, and in going to and returning from the same; and for any Speech or Debate in either House, they shall not be questioned in any other Place.

[2] No Senator or Representative shall, during the Time for which he was elected, be appointed to any civil Office under the Authority of the United States, which shall have been created, or the Emoluments whereof shall have been encreased during such time; and no Person holding any Office under the United States, shall be a Member of either House during his Continuance in Office.

SECTION 7. [1] All Bills for raising Revenue shall originate in the House of Representatives; but the Senate may propose or concur with Amendments as on other Bills.

[2] Every Bill shall have passed the House of Representatives and the Senate, shall, before it become a Law, be presented to the President of the United States; if he approve he shall sign it, but if not he shall return it, with his Objections to that House in which it shall have originated, who shall enter the Objections at large on their Journal, and proceed to reconsider it. If after such Reconsideration two thirds of that House shall agree to pass the Bill, it shall be sent, together with the Objections, to the other House, by which it shall likewise be reconsidered, and if approved by two thirds of that House, it shall become a Law. But in all such Cases, the Votes of both Houses shall be determined by Yeas and Nays, and the Names of the Persons voting for and against the Bill shall be entered on the Journal of each House respectively. If any Bill shall not be returned by the President within ten Days (Sundays excepted) after it shall have been presented to him, the Same shall be a Law, in like Manner as if he had signed it, unless the Congress by their Adjournment prevent its Return, in which Case it shall not be a Law.

[3] Every Order, Resolution, or Vote to which the Concurrence of the Senate and House of Representatives may be necessary (except on a question of Adjournment) shall be presented to the President of the United States; and before the Same shall take Effect, shall be approved by him, or being disapproved by him, shall be repassed by two thirds of the Senate and House of Representatives, according to the Rules and Limitations prescribed in the Case of a Bill.

SECTION 8. The Congress shall have Power

[1] To lay and collect Taxes, Duties, Imposts and Excises, to pay the Debts and provide for the common Defence and general Welfare of the United States, but all Duties, Imposts and Excises shall be uniform throughout the United States;

[2] To borrow money on the credit of the United States;

[3] To regulate Commerce with foreign Nations, and among the several States, and with the Indian Tribes;

[4] To establish an uniform Rule of Naturalization, and uniform Laws on the subject of Bankruptcies throughout the United States;

[5] To coin Money, regulate the Value thereof, and of foreign Coin, and fix the Standard of Weights and Measures;

[6] To provide for the Punishment of counterfeiting the Securities and current Coin of the United States;

[7] To Establish Post Offices and post Roads;

[8] To promote the Progress of Science and useful Arts, by securing for limited Times to Authors and Inventors the exclusive Right to their respective Writings and Discoveries;

[9] To constitute Tribunals inferior to the Supreme Court;

[10] To define and punish Piracies and Felonies committed on the high Seas, and Offenses against the Law of Nations;

[11] To declare War, grant Letters of Marque and Reprisal, and make Rules concerning Captures on Land and Water;

[12] To raise and support Armies, but no Appropriation of Money to that Use shall be for a longer Term than two Years;

[13] To provide and maintain a Navy;

[14] To make Rules for the Government and Regulation of the land and naval Forces;

[15] To provide for calling forth the Militia to execute the Laws of the Union, suppress Insurrections and repel Invasions;

[16] To provide for organizing, arming, and disciplining the Militia, and for Governing such Part of them as may be employed in the Service of the United States, reserving to the States respectively, the Appointment of the Officers, and the Authority of training the Militia according to the discipline prescribed by Congress;

[17] To exercise exclusive Legislation in all Cases whatsoever, over such District (not exceeding ten Miles square) as may, by Cession of particular States, and the acceptance of Con-

gress, become the Seat of the Government of the United States, and to exercise like Authority over all Places purchased by the Consent of the Legislature of the State in which the Same shall be, for the Erection of Forts, Magazines, Arsenals, dock-Yards, and other needful Buildings;—And

[18] To make all Laws which shall be necessary and proper for carrying into Execution the foregoing Powers, and all other Powers vested by this Constitution in the Government of the United States, or in any Department or Officer thereof.

SECTION 9. [1] The Migration or Importation of Such Persons as any of the States now existing shall think proper to admit, shall not be prohibited by the Congress prior to the Year one thousand eight hundred and eight, but a tax or duty may be imposed on such Importation, not exceeding ten dollars for each Person.

[2] The privilege of the Writ of Habeas Corpus shall not be suspended, unless when in Cases of Rebellion or Invasion the public Safety may require it.

[3] No Bill of Attainder or ex post facto Law shall be passed.

[4] No capitation, or other direct, Tax shall be laid, unless in Proportion to the Census or Enumeration herein before directed to be taken.

[5] No Tax or Duty shall be laid on Articles exported from any State.

[6] No preference shall be given by any Regulation of Commerce or Revenue to the Ports of one State over those of another; nor shall Vessels bound to, or from, one State be obliged to enter, clear, or pay Duties in another.

[7] No money shall be drawn from the Treasury, but in Consequence of Appropriations made by Law; and a regular Statement and Account of the Receipts and Expenditures of all public Money shall be published from time to time.

[8] No Title of Nobility shall be granted by the United States: And no Person holding any Office of Profit or Trust under them, shall, without the Consent of the Congress, accept of any present, Emolument, Office, or Title, of any kind whatever, from any King, Prince, or foreign State.

SECTION 10. [1] No State shall enter into any Treaty, Alliance, or Confederation; grant Letters of Marque and Reprisal; coin Money; emit Bills of Credit; make any Thing but gold and silver Coin a Tender in Payment of Debts; pass any Bill of Attainder, ex post facto Law, or Law impairing the Obligation of Contracts, or grant any Title of Nobility.

[2] No State shall, without the Consent of the Congress, lay any Imposts or Duties on Imports or Exports, except what may be absolutely necessary for executing its inspection Laws: and the net Produce of all Duties and Imposts, laid by any State on Imports or Exports, shall be for the Use of the Treasury of the United States; and all such Laws shall be subject to the Revision and Control of the Congress.

[3] No State shall, without the Consent of Congress, lay any duty of Tonnage, keep Troops, or Ships of War in time of Peace, enter into any Agreement or Compact with another State, or with a foreign Power, or engage in War, unless actually invaded, or in such imminent Danger as will not admit of delay.

## ARTICLE II

SECTION 1. [1] The executive Power shall be vested in a President of the United States of America. He shall hold his Office during the Term of four Years, and together with the Vice President, chosen for the same Term, be elected, as follows:

[2] Each State shall appoint, in such Manner as the Legislature thereof may direct, a Number of Senators and Representatives to which the State may be entitled in the Congress: but no Senator or Representative, or Person holding an Office of Trust or Profit under the United States, shall be appointed an Elector.

[3] The Electors shall meet in their respective States, and vote by Ballot for two persons, of whom one at least shall not be an Inhabitant of the same State with themselves. And they shall make a List of all the Persons voted for, and of the Number of Votes for each; which List they shall sign and certify, and transmit sealed to the Seat of the Government of the United States, directed to the President of the Senate. The President of the Senate shall, in the Presence of the Senate and House of Representatives, open all the Certificates, and the Votes shall then be counted. The Person having the greatest Number of Votes shall be the President, if such Number

be a Majority of the whole Number of Electors appointed; and if there be more than one who have such Majority, and have an equal Number of Votes, then the House of Representatives shall immediately chuse by Ballot one of them for President; and if no Person have a Majority, then from the five highest on the List the said House shall in like Manner chuse the President. But in chusing the President, the Votes shall be taken by States, the Representation from each State having one Vote; A quorum for this Purpose shall consist of a Member or Members from two-thirds of the States, and a Majority of all the States shall be necessary to a Choice. In every Case, after the Choice of the President, the Person having the greatest Number of Votes of the Electors shall be the Vice President. But if there shall remain two or more who have equal Votes, the Senate shall chuse from them by Ballot the Vice President.

[4] The Congress may determine the Time of chusing the Electors, and the Day on which they shall give their Votes; which Day shall be the same throughout the United States.

[5] No person except a natural born Citizen, or a Citizen of the United States, at the time of the Adoption of this Constitution, shall be eligible to the Office of President; neither shall any Person be eligible to that Office who shall not have attained to the Age of thirty-five Years, and been fourteen Years a Resident within the United States.

[6] In case of the removal of the President from Office, or of his Death, Resignation, or Inability to discharge the Powers and Duties of the said Office, the same shall devolve on the Vice President, and the Congress may by Law provide for the Case of Removal, Death, Resignation or Inability, both of the President and Vice President, declaring what Officer shall then act as President, and such Officer shall act accordingly, until the Disability be removed, or a President shall be elected.

[7] The President shall, at stated Times, receive for his Services, a Compensation, which shall neither be encreased nor diminished during the Period for which he shall have been elected, and he shall not receive within that Period any other Emolument from the United States, or any of them.

[8] Before he enter on the Execution of his Office, he shall take the following Oath or Affirmation:—"I do solemnly swear [or affirm] that I will faithfully execute the Office of President of the United States, and will to the best of my Ability, preserve, protect and defend the Constitution of the United States."

SECTION 2. [1] The President shall be Commander in Chief of the Army and Navy of the United States, and of the Militia of the several States, when called into the actual Service of the United States; he may require the Opinion, in writing, of the Principal Officer in each of the executive Departments, upon any subject relating to the Duties of their respective Offices, and he shall have Power to grant Reprieves and pardons for Offenses against the United States, except in Cases of Impeachment.

[2] He shall have Power, by and with the Advice and Consent of the Senate, to make Treaties, provided two-thirds of the Senators present concur; and he shall nominate, and by and with the Advice and Consent of the Senate, shall appoint Ambassadors, other public Ministers and Consuls, Judges of the Supreme Court, and all other Officers of the United States, whose Appointments are not herein otherwise provided for, and shall be established by Law, but the Congress may by Law vest the Appointment of such inferior Officers, as they think proper, in the President alone, in the Courts of Law, or in the Heads of Departments.

[3] The President shall have Power to fill up all Vacancies that may happen during the Recess of the Senate, by granting Commissions which shall expire at the End of their next Session.

SECTION 3. He shall from time to time give to the Congress Information of the State of the Union, and recommend to their Consideration such Measures as he shall judge necessary and expedient; he may, on extraordinary Occasions, convene both Houses, or either of them, and in Case of Disagreement between them, with Respect to the Time of Adjournment, he may adjourn them to such Time as he shall think proper; he shall receive Ambassadors and other public Ministers; he shall take Care that the Laws be faithfully executed, and shall Commission all the Officers of the United States.

SECTION 4. The President, Vice President and all civil Officers of the United States, shall be removed from Office on Impeachment for, and Conviction of, Treason, Bribery, or other high Crimes and Misdemeanors.

## ARTICLE III

SECTION 1. The judicial Power of the United States, shall be vested in one supreme Court, and in such inferior Courts as the Congress may from time to time ordain and establish. The Judges, both of the supreme and inferior Courts, shall hold their Offices during good Behaviour, and shall, at stated Times, receive for their Services a Compensation which shall not be diminished during their Continuance in Office.

SECTION 2. [1] The judicial Power shall extend to all Cases, in Law and Equity, arising under this Constitution, the Laws of the United States, and Treaties made, or which shall be made under their Authority;—to all Cases affecting Ambassadors, other public Ministers and Consuls;—to all Cases of admiralty and maritime Jurisdiction;—to Controversies to which the United States shall be a Party;—to Controversies between two or more States;—between a State and Citizens of another State;—between Citizens of different States;—between Citizens of the same State claiming Lands under Grants of different States, and between a State, or the Citizens thereof, and foreign States, Citizens or Subjects.

[2] In all Cases affecting Ambassadors, other public Ministers and Consuls, and those in which a State shall be Party, the supreme Court shall have original Jurisdiction. In all the other Cases before mentioned, the supreme Court shall have appellate Jurisdiction, both as to Law and Fact, with such Exceptions, and under such Regulations as the Congress shall make.

[3] The trial of all Crimes, except in Case of Impeachment, shall be by Jury; and such Trial shall be held in the State where the said Crimes shall have been committed, but when not committed within any State, the Trial shall be at such Place or Places as the Congress may by Law have directed.

SECTION 3. [1] Treason against the United States, shall consist only in levying War against them, or, in adhering to their Enemies, giving them Aid and Comfort. No Person shall be convicted of Treason unless on the Testimony of two Witnesses to the same overt Act, or on Confession in open Court.

[2] The Congress shall have power to declare the Punishment of Treason, but no Attainder of Treason shall work Corruption of Blood, or Forfeiture except during the Life of the Person attained.

## ARTICLE IV

SECTION 1. Full Faith and Credit shall be given in each State to the public Acts, Records, and judicial Proceedings of every other State. And the Congress may by general Laws prescribe the Manner in which such Acts, Records and Proceedings shall be proved, and the Effect thereof.

SECTION 2. [1] The Citizens of each State shall be entitled to all Privileges and Immunities of Citizens in the several States.

[2] A Person charged in any State with Treason, Felony, or other Crime, who shall flee from Justice, and be found in another State, shall on demand of the executive Authority of the State from which he fled, be delivered up, to be removed to the State having Jurisdiction of the Crime.

[3] No Person held to Service or Labour in one State, under the Laws thereof, escaping into another, shall, in Consequence of any Law or Regulation therein, be discharged from such Service or Labour, but shall be delivered up on Claim of the Party to whom such Service or Labour may be due.

SECTION 3. [1] New States may be admitted by the Congress into this Union; but no new State shall be formed or erected within the Jurisdiction of any other State; nor any State be formed by the Junction of two or more States, or parts of States, without the Consent of the Legislature of the States concerned as well as of the Congress.

[2] The Congress shall have Power to dispose of and make all needful Rules and Regulations respecting the Territory or other Property belonging to the United States; and nothing in this Constitution shall be so construed as to Prejudice any Claims of the United States, or of any particular State.

SECTION 4. The United States shall guarantee to every State in this Union a Republican Form of Government, and shall protect each of them against Invasion; and on Application of the Legislature, or of the Executive (when the Legislature cannot be convened) against domestic Violence.

## ARTICLE V

The Congress, whenever two-thirds of both Houses shall deem it necessary, shall propose Amendments to this Constitution, or, on the Application of the Legislatures of two-thirds of the several States, shall call a Convention for proposing Amendments, which, in either Case, shall be valid to all Intents and Purposes, as part of this Constitution, when ratified by the Legislatures of three-fourths of the several States, or by Conventions in three-fourths thereof, as the one or the other Mode of Ratification may be proposed by the Congress; Provided that no Amendment which may be made prior to the Year One thousand eight hundred and eight shall in any Manner affect the first and fourth Clauses in the Ninth Section of the first Article; and that no State, without its Consent, shall be deprived of its equal Suffrage in the Senate.

## ARTICLE VI

[1] All Debts contracted and Engagements entered into, before the Adoption of this Constitution shall be valid against the United States under this Constitution, as under the Confederation.

[2] This Constitution, and the Laws of the United States which shall be made in Pursuance thereof; and all Treaties made, or which shall be made, under the Authority of the United States, shall be the supreme Law of the Land; and the Judges in every State shall be bound thereby, any Thing in the Constitution or Laws of any State to the Contrary notwithstanding.

[3] The Senators and Representatives before mentioned, and the Members of the several State Legislatures, and all executive and judicial Officers, both of the United States and of the several States, shall be bound by Oath or Affirmation, to support this Constitution; but no religious Test shall ever be required as a Qualification to any Office or public Trust under the United States.

## ARTICLE VII

The Ratification of the Conventions of nine States shall be sufficient for the Establishment of this Constitution between the States so ratifying the Same.

Done in Convention by the Unanimous Consent of the States present the Seventeenth Day of September in the Year of our Lord one thousand seven hundred and Eighty seven and of the Independence of the United States of America the Twelfth. In witness whereof We have hereunto subscribed our Names,

Go WASHINGTON—Presidt
and deputy from Virginia

| | |
|---|---|
| New Hampshire | John Langdon<br>Nicholas Gilman |
| Massachusetts | Nathaniel Gorham<br>Rufus King |
| Connecticut | Wm Saml Johnson<br>Roger Sherman |
| New York | Alexander Hamilton |
| New Jersey | Wil: Livingston<br>David Brearley<br>Wm Paterson<br>Jona: Dayton |
| Pennsylvania | B Franklin<br>Thomas Mifflin<br>Robt Morris<br>Geo. Clymer<br>Thos FitzSimons<br>Jared Ingersoll<br>James Wilson<br>Gouv Morris |
| Delaware | Geo: Read<br>Gunning Bedford jun<br>John Dickinson<br>Richard Bassett<br>Jaco: Broom |
| Maryland | James McHenry<br>Dan of St Thos Jenifer<br>Danl Carroll |
| Virginia | John Blair—<br>James Madison Jr. |

| | |
|---|---|
| North Carolina | Wm Blount<br>Richd Dobbs Spaight<br>Hu Williamson |
| South Carolina | J. Rutledge<br>Charles Cotesworth Pinckney<br>Charles Pinckney<br>Pierce Butler |
| Georgia | William Few<br>Abr Baldwin |

ARTICLES IN ADDITION TO, AND AMENDMENT OF, THE CONSTITUTION OF THE UNITED STATES OF AMERICA, PROPOSED BY CONGRESS, AND RATIFIED BY THE LEGISLATURES OF THE SEVERAL STATES, PURSUANT TO THE FIFTH ARTICLE OF THE ORIGINAL CONSTITUTION

## AMENDMENT I [1791]

Congress shall make no law respecting an establishment of religion, or prohibiting the free exercise thereof; or abridging the freedom of speech, or of the press; or the right of the people peaceably to assemble and to petition the Government for a redress of grievances.

## AMENDMENT II [1791]

A well regulated Militia, being necessary to the security of a free State, the right of the people to keep and bear Arms, shall not be infringed.

## AMENDMENT III [1791]

No Soldier shall, in time of peace be quartered in any house, without the consent of the Owner, nor in time of war, but in a manner to be prescribed by Law.

## AMENDMENT IV [1791]

The right of the people to be secure in their persons, houses, papers, and effects, against unreasonable searches nd seizures, shall not be violated, and no Warrants shall issue, but upon probable cause, supported by Oath or affirmation, and particularly describing the place to be searched, and the persons or things to be seized.

## AMENDMENT V [1791]

No person shall be held to answer for a capital, or otherwise infamous crime, unless on a presentment or indictment of a Grand Jury, except in cases arising in the land or naval forces, or in the Militia, when in actual service in time of War or public danger; nor shall any person be subject for the same offence to be twice put in jeopardy of life or limb; nor shall be compelled in any criminal case to be a witness against himself, nor be deprived of life, liberty, or property, without due process of law; nor shall private property be taken for public use, without just compensation.

## AMENDMENT VI [1791]

In all criminal prosecutions, the accused shall enjoy the right to a speedy and public trial, by an impartial jury of the State and district wherein the crime shall have been committed, which district shall have been previously ascertained by law, and to be informed of the nature and cause of the accusation; to be confronted with the witnesses against him; to have compulsory process for obtaining witnesses in his favor, and to have the Assistance of Counsel for his defence.

## AMENDMENT VII [1791]

In suits at common law, where the value in controversy shall exceed twenty dollars, the right of trial by jury shall be preserved, and no fact tried by jury, shall be otherwise reexamined in any Court of the United States, than according to the rules of the common law.

## AMENDMENT VIII [1791]

Excessive bail shall not be required, nor excessive fines imposed, nor cruel and unusual punishments inflicted.

## AMENDMENT IX [1791]

The enumeration in the Constitution, of certain rights, shall not be construed to deny or disparage others retained by the people.

### AMENDMENT X [1791]

The powers not delegated to the United States by the Constitution, nor prohibited by it to the States, are reserved to the States respectively, or to the people.

### AMENDMENT IX [1798]

The Judicial power of the United States shall not be construed to extend to any suit in law or equity, commenced or prosecuted against one of the United States by Citizens of another State, or by Citizens or Subjects of any Foreign State.

### AMENDMENT XII [1804]

The electors shall meet in their respective states and vote by ballot for President and Vice-President, one of whom, at least, shall not be an inhabitant of the same state with themselves; they shall name in their ballots the person voted for as President, and in distinct ballots the person voted for as Vice-President, and they shall make distinct lists of all persons voted for as President, and of all persons voted for as Vice-President, and of the number of votes for each, which lists they shall sign and certify, and transmit sealed to the seat of the government of the United States, directed to the President of the Senate;—The President of the Senate shall, in presence of the Senate and House of Representatives, open all the certificates and the votes shall then be counted;—The person having the greatest number of votes for President, shall be the President, if such number be a majority of the whole number of Electors appointed; and if no person have such majority, then from the persons having the highest numbers not exceeding three on the list of those voted for as President, the House of Representatives shall choose immediately, by ballot, the President. But in choosing the President, the votes shall be taken by states, the representation from each state have one vote; a quorum for this purpose shall consist of a member or members from two-thirds of the states, and a majority of all the states shall be necessary to a choice. And if the House of Representatives shall not choose a President whenever the right of choice shall devolve upon them, before the fourth day of March next following, then the Vice-President shall act as President, as in the case of the death or other constitutional disability of the President.—The person having the greatest number of votes as Vice-President, shall be the Vice-President, if such number be a majority of the whole number of Electors appointed, and if no person have a majority, then from the two highest numbers on the list, the Senate shall choose the Vice-President; a quorum for the purpose shall consist of two-thirds of the whole number of Senators, and a majority of the whole number shall be necessary to a choice. But no person constitutionally ineligible to the office of President shall be eligible to that of Vice-President of the United States.

### AMENDMENT XIII [1865]

SECTION 1. Neither slavery nor involuntary servitude, except as a punishment for crime whereof the party shall have been duly convicted, shall exist within the United States, or any place subject to their jurisdiction.

SECTION 2. Congress shall have power to enforce this article by appropriate legislation.

### AMENDMENT XIV [1868]

SECTION 1. All persons born or naturalized in the United States, and subject to the jurisdiction thereof, are citizens of the United States and of the State wherein they reside. No State shall make or enforce any law which shall abridge the privileges or immunities of citizens of the United States; nor shall any State deprive any person of life, liberty, or property, without due process of law; nor deny to any person within its jurisdiction the equal protection of the laws.

SECTION 2. Representatives shall be apportioned among the several States according to their respective numbers, counting the whole number of persons in each State, excluding Indians not taxed. But when the right to vote at any election for the choice of electors for President and Vice-President of the United States, Representatives in Congress, the Executive and Judicial officers of a State, or the members of the Legislature thereof, is denied to any of the male inhabitants of such State, being twenty-one years of age, and citizens of the United

States, or in any way abridged, except for participation in rebellion, or other crime, the basis of representation therein shall be reduced in the proportions which the number of such male citizens shall bear to the whole number of male citizens twenty-one years of age in such State.

SECTION 3. No person shall be a Senator or Representative in Congress, or elector of President and Vice-President, or hold any office, civil or military, under the United States, or under any State, who, having previously taken an oath, as a member of Congress, or as an officer of the United States, or as a member of any State legislature, or as an executive or judicial officer of any State, to support the Constitution of the United States, shall have engaged in insurrection or rebellion against the same, or given aid or comfort to the enemies thereof. But congress may by a vote of two-thirds of each House, remove such disability.

SECTION 4. The validity of the public debt of the United States, authorized by law, including debts incurred for payment of pensions and bounties for services in suppressing insurrection or rebellion, shall not be questioned. But neither the United States nor any State shall assume or pay any debt or obligation incurred in aid of insurrection or rebellion against the United States, or any claim for the loss or emancipation of any slave; but all such debts, obligations and claims shall be held illegal and void.

SECTION 5. The Congress shall have power to enforce, by appropriate legislation, the provisions of this article.

## AMENDMENT XV [1870]

SECTION 1. The right of citizens of the United States to vote shall not be denied or abridged by the United States or by any State on account of race, color, or previous condition of servitude.

SECTION 2. The Congress shall have power to enforce this article by appropriate legislation.

## AMENDMENT XVI [1913]

The Congress shall have power to lay and collect taxes on incomes, from whatever source derived, without apportionment among the several States, and without regard to any census or enumeration.

## AMENDMENT XVII [1913]

The Senate of the United States shall be composed of two Senators from each State, elected by the people thereof, for six years, and each Senator shall have one vote. The electors in each State shall have the qualifications requisite for electors of the most numerous branch of the State legislatures.

When vacancies happen in the representation of any State in the Senate, the executive authority of such State shall issue writs of election to fill such vacancies: *Provided,* That the legislature of any State may empower the executive thereof to make temporary appointments until the people fill the vacancies by election as the legislature may direct.

This amendment shall not be so construed as to affect the election or term of any Senator chosen before it becomes valid as part of the Constitution.

## AMENDMENT XVIII [1919]

SECTION 1. After one year from the ratification of this article the manufacture, sale, or transportation of intoxicating liquors within, the importation thereof into, or the exportation thereof from the United States and all territory subject to the jurisdiction thereof for beverage purposes is hereby prohibited.

SECTION 2. The Congress and the several States shall have concurrent power to enforce this article by appropriate legislation.

SECTION 3. This article shall be inoperative unless it shall have been ratified as an amendment to the Constitution by the legislatures of the several States, as provided in the Constitution, within seven years from the date of the submission hereof to the States by the Congress.

## AMENDMENT XIX [1920]

The right of citizens of the United States to vote shall not be denied or abridged by the United States or by any State on account of sex.

Congress shall have the power to enforce this article by appropriate legislation.

## AMENDMENT XX [1933]

SECTION 1. The terms of the President and Vice President shall end at noon on the 20th day of January, and the terms of Senators and Representatives at noon on the 3rd day of January, of the years in which such terms would have ended if this article had not been ratified; and the terms of their successors shall then begin.

SECTION 2. The Congress shall assemble at least once in every year, and such meeting shall begin at noon on the 3rd day of January, unless they shall by law appoint a different day.

SECTION 3. If, at the time fixed for the beginning of the term of the President, the President elect shall have died, the Vice President elect shall become President. If a President shall not have been chosen before the time fixed for the beginning of his term, or if the President elect shall have failed to qualify, then the Vice President elect shall act as President until a President shall have qualified; and the Congress may by law provide for the case wherein neither a President elect nor a Vice President elect shall have qualified, declaring who shall then act as President, or the manner in which one who is to act shall be selected, and such person shall act accordingly until a President or vice President shall have qualified.

SECTION 4. The Congress may by law provide for the case of the death of any of the persons from whom the House of Representatives may choose a President whenever the right of choice shall have devolved upon them, and for the case of the death of any of the persons from whom the Senate may choose a Vice President whenever the right of choice shall have devolved upon them.

SECTION 5. Sections 1 and 2 shall take effect on the 15th day of October following the ratification of this article.

SECTION 6. This article shall be inoperative unless it shall have been ratified as an amendment to the Constitution by the legislatures of three-fourths of the several States within seven years from the date of its submission.

## AMENDMENT XXI [1933]

SECTION 1. The eighteenth article of amendment to the Constitution of the United States is hereby repealed.

SECTION 2. The transportation or importation into any State, Territory, or possession of the United States for delivery of use therein of intoxicating liquors, in violation of the laws thereof, is hereby prohibited.

SECTION 3. This article shall be inoperative unless it shall have been ratified as an amendment to the Constitution by conventions in the several States, as provided in the Constitution, within seven years from the date of the submission hereof to the States by the Congress.

## AMENDMENT XXII [1951]

SECTION 1. No person shall be elected to the office of the President more than twice, and no person who has held the office of President, or acted as President, for more than two years of a term to which some other person was elected President shall be elected to the office of the President more than once. But this Article shall not apply to any person holding the office of President when this Article was proposed by the Congress, and shall not prevent any person who may be holding the office of President, or acting as President, during the term within which the Article becomes operative from holding the office of President or acting as President during the remainder of such term.

SECTION 2. This article shall be inoperative unless it shall have been ratified as an amendment to the Constitution by the legislatures of three-fourths of the several States within seven years from the date of its submission to the States by the Congress.

## AMENDMENT XXIII [1961]

SECTION 1. The District constituting the seat of Government of the United States shall appoint in such manner as the Congress may direct:

A number of electors of President and Vice President equal to the whole number of Senators and Representatives in Congress to which the District would be entitled if it were a State, but in no event more than the least populous State; they shall be in addition to those appointed by the States, but they shall be considered, for the purposes of the election of President and Vice President, to be electors appointed by a State; and they shall meet in the District and perform such duties as provided by the twelfth article of amendment.

SECTION 2. The Congress shall have power to enforce this article by appropriate legislation.

### AMENDMENT XXIV [1964]

SECTION 1. The right of citizens of the United States to vote in any primary or other election for President or Vice President, for electors for President or Vice President, or for Senator or Representative in Congress, shall not be denied or abridged by the United States or any State by reason of failure to pay any poll tax or other tax.

SECTION 2. The Congress shall have power to enforce this article by appropriate legislation.

### AMENDMENT XXV [1967]

SECTION 1. In case of the removal of the President from office or his death or resignation, the Vice President shall become President.

SECTION 2. Whenever there is a vacancy in the office of the Vice President, the President shall nominate a Vice President who shall take the Office upon confirmation by a majority vote of both houses of Congress.

SECTION 3. Whenever the President transmits to the President pro tempore of the Senate and the Speaker of the House of Representatives his written declaration that he is unable to discharge the powers and duties of his office, and until he transmits to them a written declaration to the contrary, such powers and duties shall be discharged by the Vice President as Acting President.

SECTION 4. Whenever the Vice President and a majority of either the principal officers of the executive departments, or of such other body as Congress may by law provide, transmit to the President pro tempore of the Senate and the Speaker of the House of Representatives their written declaration that the President is unable to discharge the powers and duties of his office, the Vice President shall immediately assume the powers and duties of the office as Acting President.

Thereafter, when the President transmits to the President pro tempore of the Senate and the Speaker of the House of Representatives his written declaration that no inability exists, he shall resume the powers and the duties of his office unless the Vice President and a majority of either the principal officers of the executive department, or of such other body as Congress may by law provide, transmit within four days to the President pro tempore of the Senate and the Speaker of the House of Representatives their written declaration that the President is unable to discharge the powers and duties of his office. Thereupon Congress shall decide the issue, assembling within 48 hours for that purpose if not in session. If the Congress, within 21 days after receipt of the latter written declaration, or, if Congress is not in session, within 21 days after Congress is required to assemble, determines by two-thirds vote of both houses that the President is unable to discharge the powers and duties of his office, the Vice President shall continue to discharge the same as Acting President; otherwise, the President shall resume the powers and duties of his office.

### AMENDMENT XXVI [1971]

SECTION 1. The right of citizens of the United States, who are eighteen years of age, or older, to vote shall not be denied or abridged by the United States or by any state on account of age.

SECTION 2. The Congress shall have the power to enforce this article by appropriate legislation.

### AMENDMENT XXVII [1992]

No law varying the compensation for the services of the Senators and Representatives shall take effect until an election of Representatives shall have intervened.*

---

*Adopted in 1992, 203 years after it was first proposed by James Madison and approved by the First Congress. Six states ratified the amendment in 1792, a seventh in 1873, an eighth in 1978, and 32 more in recent years, with Illinois becoming the thirty-eighth state to ratify it on May 12, 1992.

# JUSTICES OF THE SUPREME COURT

| | Term | Appointed by | Replaced |
|---|---|---|---|
| *John Jay** | 1789–1795 | Washington | |
| John Rutledge | 1789–1791 | Washington | |
| William Cushing | 1789–1810 | Washington | |
| James Wilson | 1789–1798 | Washington | |
| John Blair | 1789–1796 | Washington | |
| James Iredell | 1790–1799 | Washington | |
| Thomas Johnson | 1791–1793 | Washington | Rutledge |
| William Paterson | 1793–1806 | Washington | Johnson |
| *John Rutledge* | 1795 | Washington | Jay |
| Samuel Chase | 1796–1811 | Washington | Blair |
| *Oliver Ellsworth* | 1796–1800 | Washington | Rutledge |
| Bushrod Washington | 1798–1829 | J. Adams | Wilson |
| Alfred Moore | 1799–1804 | J. Adams | Iredell |
| *John Marshall* | 1801–1835 | J. Adams | Ellsworth |
| William Johnson | 1804–1834 | Jefferson | Moore |
| Brockholst Livingston | 1806–1823 | Jefferson | Paterson |
| Thomas Todd | 1807–1826 | Jefferson | (new seat) |
| Gabriel Duval | 1811–1835 | Madison | Chase |
| Joseph Story | 1811–1845 | Madison | Cushing |
| Smith Thompson | 1823–1843 | Monroe | Livingston |
| Robert Trimble | 1826–1828 | J.Q. Adams | Todd |
| John McLean | 1829–1861 | Jackson | Trimble |
| Henry Baldwin | 1830–1844 | Jackson | Washington |
| James Wayne | 1835–1867 | Jackson | Johnson |

*The names of the Chief Justices are italicized.

| | Term | Appointed by | Replaced |
|---|---|---|---|
| *Roger Taney* | 1836–1864 | Jackson | Marshall |
| Philip Barbour | 1836–1841 | Jackson | Duval |
| John Catron | 1837–1865 | Van Buren | (new seat) |
| John McKinley | 1837–1852 | Van Buren | (new seat) |
| Peter Daniel | 1841–1860 | Van Buren | Barbour |
| Samuel Nelson | 1845–1872 | Tyler | Thompson |
| Levi Woodbury | 1845–1851 | Polk | Story |
| Robert Grier | 1846–1870 | Polk | Baldwin |
| Benjamin Curtis | 1851–1857 | Fillmore | Woodbury |
| John Campbell | 1853–1861 | Pierce | McKinley |
| Nathan Clifford | 1858–1881 | Buchanan | Curtis |
| Noah Swayne | 1862–1881 | Lincoln | McLean |
| Samuel Miller | 1862–1890 | Lincoln | Daniel |
| David Davis | 1862–1877 | Lincoln | Campbell |
| Stephen Field | 1863–1897 | Lincoln | (new seat) |
| *Salmon Chase* | 1864–1873 | Lincoln | Taney |
| William Strong | 1870–1880 | Grant | Grier |
| Joseph Bradley | 1870–1892 | Grant | Wayne |
| Ward Hunt | 1872–1882 | Grant | Nelson |
| *Morrison Waite* | 1874–1888 | Grant | Chase |
| John Marshall Harlan | 1877–1911 | Hayes | Davis |
| William Woods | 1880–1887 | Hayes | Strong |
| Stanley Matthews | 1881–1889 | Garfield | Swayne |
| Horace Gray | 1881–1902 | Arthur | Clifford |
| Samuel Blatchford | 1882–1893 | Arthur | Hunt |
| Lucius Lamar | 1888–1893 | Cleveland | Woods |
| *Melville Fuller* | 1888–1910 | Cleveland | Waite |
| David Brewer | 1889–1910 | Harrison | Matthews |
| Henry Brown | 1890–1906 | Harrison | Miller |
| George Shiras | 1892–1903 | Harrison | Bradley |
| Howell Jackson | 1893–1895 | Harrison | Lamar |
| Edward White | 1894–1910 | Cleveland | Blatchford |
| Rufus Peckham | 1895–1909 | Cleveland | Jackson |
| Joseph McKenna | 1898–1925 | McKinley | Field |
| Oliver Wendell Holmes | 1902–1932 | T. Roosevelt | Gray |
| William Day | 1903–1922 | T. Roosevelt | Shiras |
| William Moody | 1906–1910 | T. Roosevelt | Brown |
| Horace Lurton | 1909–1914 | Taft | Peckham |
| Charles Evans Hughes | 1910–1916 | Taft | Brewer |
| *Edward White* | 1910–1921 | Taft | Fuller |
| Willis Van Devanter | 1910–1937 | Taft | White |
| Joseph Lamar | 1910–1916 | Taft | Moody |
| Mahlon Pitney | 1912–1922 | Taft | Harlan |
| James McReynolds | 1914–1941 | Wilson | Lurton |
| Louis Brandeis | 1916–1939 | Wilson | Lamar |
| John Clarke | 1916–1922 | Wilson | Hughes |
| *William Taft* | 1921–1930 | Harding | White |
| George Sutherland | 1922–1938 | Harding | Clarke |
| Pierce Butler | 1922–1939 | Harding | Day |
| Edward Sanford | 1923–1930 | Harding | Pitney |
| Harlan Stone | 1925–1941 | Coolidge | McKenna |
| *Charles Evans Hughes* | 1930–1941 | Hoover | Taft |
| Owen Roberts | 1932–1945 | Hoover | Sanford |
| Benjamin Cardozo | 1932–1938 | Hoover | Holmes |

| | Term | Appointed by | Replaced |
|---|---|---|---|
| Hugo Black | 1937–1971 | F. Roosevelt | Van Devanter |
| Stanley Reed | 1938–1957 | F. Roosevelt | Sutherland |
| Felix Frankfurter | 1939–1962 | F. Roosevelt | Cardozo |
| William Douglas | 1939–1975 | F. Roosevelt | Brandeis |
| Frank Murphy | 1940–1949 | F. Roosevelt | Butler |
| James Byrnes | 1941–1942 | F. Roosevelt | McReynolds |
| *Harlan Stone* | 1941–1946 | F. Roosevelt | Hughes |
| Robert Jackson | 1941–1954 | F. Roosevelt | Stone |
| Wiley Rutledge | 1943–1949 | F. Roosevelt | Byrnes |
| Harold Burton | 1945–1958 | Truman | Roberts |
| *Fred Vinson* | 1946–1953 | Truman | Stone |
| Tom Clark | 1949–1967 | Truman | Murphy |
| Sherman Minton | 1949–1956 | Truman | Rutledge |
| *Earl Warren* | 1953–1969 | Eisenhower | Vinson |
| John Harlan | 1955–1971 | Eisenhower | Jackson |
| William Brennan | 1956–1990 | Eisenhower | Minton |
| Charles Whittaker | 1957–1962 | Eisenhower | Reed |
| Potter Stewart | 1958–1981 | Eisenhower | Burton |
| Arthur Goldberg | 1962–1965 | Kennedy | Frankfurter |
| Byron White | 1962–1993 | Kennedy | Whittaker |
| Abe Fortas | 1965–1969 | Johnson | Goldberg |
| Thurgood Marshall | 1967–1991 | Johnson | Clark |
| *Warren Burger* | 1969–1986 | Nixon | Warren |
| Harry Blackmun | 1970–1994 | Nixon | Fortas |
| Lewis Powell | 1972–1987 | Nixon | Black |
| William Rehnquist | 1972–1986 | Nixon | Harlan |
| John Stevens | 1975– | Ford | Douglas |
| Sandra Day O'Connor | 1981– | Reagan | Stewart |
| *William Rehnquist* | 1986– | Reagan | Burger |
| Antonin Scalia | 1986– | Reagan | Rehnquist |
| Anthony Kennedy | 1988– | Reagan | Powell |
| David Souter | 1990– | Bush | Brennan |
| Clarence Thomas | 1991– | Bush | Marshall |
| Ruth Bader Ginsburg | 1993– | Clinton | White |
| Stephen Breyer | 1994– | Clinton | Blackmun |

*The names of the Chief Justices are italicized.

# GLOSSARY OF COMMON LEGAL TERMS

**Abstention** The doctrine under which the U.S. Supreme Court and other federal courts choose not to rule on state cases, even when empowered to do so, so as to allow the issue to be decided on the basis of state law.

**Advisory Opinion** A legal opinion rendered at the request of the government or another party indicating how the court would rule if the issue arose in an adversary context.

**Amicus Curiae** "Friend of the court." A person or group not directly involved in a particular case that volunteers or is requested by the court to supply its views on the case (usually through the submission of a brief).

**Appeal** The procedure whereby a case is brought from an inferior to a superior court. In the Supreme Court, certain cases are designated as appeals under federal law and must be heard formally by the court.

**Appellant** The party who appeals a decision from a lower to a higher court.

**Appellate Jurisdiction** The authority of a court to hear, determine, and render judgment in an action on appeal from an inferior court.

**Appellee** The party against whom an appeal to a superior court is taken and who has an interest in upholding the lower court's decision.

**Arraignment** The formal process of charging a person with a crime, reading the charge, and asking for and entering his plea.

**Bail** The security (cash or a bail bond) given as a guarantee that a released prisoner will appear at trial.

**Bill of Attainder** A legislative act declaring a person guilty of a crime and passing sentence without benefit of trial.

**Brief** A document prepared by counsel as the basis for an argument in court. It sets forth the facts of the case and the legal arguments in support of the party's position.

**Case Law** The law as defined by previously decided cases.

**Certification** A method of appeal whereby a lower court requests a higher court to rule on certain legal questions so that the lower court can make the correct decision in light of the answer given.

**Certiorari, Writ of** An order from a superior court to an inferior court to forward the entire record of a case to the superior court for review. The U.S. Supreme Court may issue such writs at its discretion.

**Civil Action** A lawsuit, usually brought by a private party, seeking redress for a noncriminal act (e.g., a suit in negligence, contract, or defamation).

**Class Action** A lawsuit brought by one person or by a group on behalf of all persons similarly situated.

**Comity** Courtesy and respect. In the legal sense, the respect federal courts give to the decisions of state courts.

**Common Law** Principles and rules of action, particularly from unwritten English law, whose authority stems from long-standing usage and custom or from judicial recognition and enforcement of those customs.

**Concurrent Powers** Powers which may be exercised by both the national government and state governments.

**Concurring Opinion** An opinion submitted by a member of a court who agrees with the result by the court in a case but either disagrees with the court's reasons for the decision or wishes to address matters not touched in the opinion of the court.

**Declaratory Judgment** A judicial pronouncement declaring the legal rights of the parties involved in an actual case or controversy but not ordering a specific action.

**De Facto** "In fact." The existence of something in fact or reality, as opposed to *de jure* (by right).

**Defendant** The person against whom a civil or criminal charge is brought.

**De Jure** "By right." Lawful, rightful, legitimate; as a result of official action.

**Dissenting Opinion** An opinion submitted by a member of a court who disagrees with the result reached by the court.

**Distinguish** To point out why a previous decision is not applicable.

**Diversity Jurisdiction** The authority of federal courts to hear cases involving citizens of different states.

**Dual Federalism** The view that national powers should be interpreted so as not to invade traditional spheres of state activity.

**Equity** The administration of justice based upon principles of fairness rather than upon strictly applied rules found in the law.

**Error, Writ of** A writ issued by a superior court directing a lower court to send it the record of a case in which the lower court has entered a final judgment, for the purpose of reviewing alleged errors made by the lower court.

**Exclusionary Rule** The rule that evidence obtained by illegal means, such as unreasonable searches and seizures, cannot be introduced by the prosecution in a criminal trial.

**Ex parte** "From (or on) one side." A hearing in the presence of only one of the parties to a case, such as a hearing to review a petition for a writ of habeas corpus.

**Ex Post Facto** "After the fact." A law which makes an action for a crime after it has already been committed.

**Ex Rel** "By (or on) the information of." The designation of suit instituted by a state but at the instigation of a private individual interested in the matter.

**Federal Question** A case that contains a major issue involving the U.S. Constitution, or U.S. laws or treaties. (The jurisdiction of the federal courts is limited to federal questions and diversity suits.)

**Habeas Corpus** "You have the body." A writ inquiring of an official who has custody of a person whether that person is imprisoned or detained lawfully.

**In Camera** "In chambers." The hearing of a case or part of a case in private (without spectators).

**Incorporation** The process by which provisions of the Bill of Rights were applied as limitations on state governments through the Due Process Clause of the Fourteenth Amendment.

**In Forma Pauperis** "In the manner of a pauper." Permission for indigents to bring legal action without payment of the required fees.

**Injunction** A writ prohibiting the person to whom it is directed from performing some specified act.

**In Re** "In the matter of; concerning." The designation of judicial proceedings in which there are no adversaries.

**Judgment of the Court** The ruling of the court (independent of the reasons for the court's ruling).

**Judicial Review** The power of a court to review legislation or other governmental action in order to determine its validity with respect to the U.S. constitution or state constitutions.

**Juris Belli** "Under the law of war." That part of the law of nations which defines the rights of belligerent and neutral nations during wartime.

**Jurisdiction** The authority of a court to hear, determine, and render final judgment in an action, and to enforce its judgments by legal process.

**Justiciability** The question of whether a matter is appropriate for judicial decision. A justiciable issue is one that appropriately can be decided by a court.

**Litigant** An active participant in a lawsuit.

**Mandamus** "We command." A court order directing an individual or organization to perform a particular act.

**Moot** Unsettled, undecided. A moot question is one in which either the result sought by the lawsuit has occurred or the conditions have so changed as to render it impossible for the court to grant the relief sought.

**Obiter Dicta** (Also called *dictum* or *dicta.*) That part of the reasoning in a judicial opinion which is not necessary to resolve the case. Dicta are not necessarily binding in future cases.

**Opinion of the Court** The opinion which announces the court's decision and is adhered to by a majority of the participating judges.

**Original Jurisdiction** The authority of a court to hear, determine, and render judgment in an action as a trial court.

**Per Curiam** "By the court." an unsigned opinion by the court, or a collectively authored opinion.

**Petitioner** The party who files a petition with a court seeking action.

**Plaintiff** The party who brings a civil action or sues to obtain a remedy for an injury to his or her rights.

**Plea Bargain** Negotiations between the prosecution and defense aimed at exchanging a plea of guilty for concessions by the prosecution.

**Police Power** The power of the states to protect the health, safety, welfare, and morals of their citizens.

**Political Question** An issue that the court believes should be decided by a nonjudicial unit of government.

**Precedent** A prior case relied upon in deciding a present dispute.

**Preemption** The doctrine under which issues previously subject to state control are brought, through congressional action, within the primary or exclusive jurisdiction of the national government.

**Prima Facie** "At first sight." Evidence that, unless contradicted, is sufficient to establish a claim without investigation or evaluation.

**Pro Bono** "For the good." Legal services rendered without charge.

**Ratio Decidendi** "Reason for the decision." The principle of the case.

**Remand** To send back. In remanding a decision, a higher court sends it, for further action, back to the court from which it came.

**Respondent** The party against whom a legal action is taken.

**Special Master** A person designated by a court to hear evidence and submit findings and recommendations based on that evidence. The Supreme Court typically uses special masters in original jurisdiction cases.

**Standing** The qualifications needed to bring or participate in a case. To have standing to sue, plaintiffs must demonstrate the existence of a controversy in which they personally have suffered or are about to suffer an injury or infringement of a legally protected right.

**Stare Decisis** "Let the decision stand." The doctrine that a point settled in a previous case is a precedent that should be followed in subsequent cases with similar facts.

**State Action** Action by the state or by a private entity closely associated with it ("under color of state law"). The basis for redress under the Due Process and Equal Protection Clauses of the Fourteenth Amendments.

**Stay** To halt or suspend further judicial proceedings.

**Subpoena** An order to present oneself and to testify before a court, grand jury, or legislative hearing.

**Subpoena Duces Tecum** An order by a court or other authorized body that specified documents or papers be produced.

**Tort** Willful or negligent injury to the person, property, or reputation of another.

**Ultra Vires** "Beyond power." An action beyond the legal authority of the person or body performing it.

**Vacate** To make void, annul, or rescind.

**Venue** The jurisdiction in which a case is to be heard.

**Vested Rights** Long established rights which government should recognize and protect and which a person cannot be deprived of without injustice.

**Writ** A written court order commanding the recipient to perform or refrain from performing acts specified in the order.

# TABLE OF CASES

Case titles in capital letters are reprinted in this volume; the bold italic page numbers indicate where the case is reprinted in this volume.